D0765412

DIRTY BUSINESS

DIRTY BUSINESS

THE CORPORATE-POLITICAL
MONEY-POWER GAME

by Ovid Demaris

HARPER'S MAGAZINE PRESS
Published in Association with Harper & Row
New York

For My Daughters
Linda and Peggy

"Harper's" is the registered trademark of Harper & Row, Publishers, Inc.

DIRTY BUSINESS. Copyright © 1974 by Ovid Demaris. All rights reserved. Printed in the United States of America. No part of this book may be used or reproduced in any manner whatsoever without written permission except in the case of brief quotations embodied in critical articles and reviews. For information address Harper & Row, Publishers, Inc., 10 East 53rd Street, New York, N.Y. 10022. Published simultaneously in Canada by Fitzhenry & Whiteside Limited, Toronto.

FIRST EDITION

Designed by Sidney Feinberg

Library of Congress Cataloging in Publication Data

Demaris, Ovid.
  Dirty business; the corporate-political money-power game.

  Includes bibliographical references.
  1. Big business—United States.   2. Industry and state—United States.
3. Business and politics—United States.   4. Commercial crimes—United States.
I. Title.
HD2795.D45   338.8   73-18652
ISBN 0-06-121950-9

CONTENTS

I reject the cynical view
that politics is inevitably
or even usually dirty business.
—Richard M. Nixon

CHAPTER 1

THE PROSPERITY GAME

The survival of democracy is inexorably fused to the prosperity of business, or so the ideological zealots of the money-power elite have been telling a compliant electorate since the outbreak of the Industrial Revolution. It is no wonder that the canons of laissez-faire economics are as sacrosanct to today's ruling class as they were to the Founding Fathers. For his first Secretary of the Treasury, George Washington chose Alexander Hamilton, the most vocal apostle of big business and the progenitor of a chain of disciples in both political parties. There is compelling evidence, as George McGovern discovered in 1972, that the Democratic and Republican Parties are merely wings of the Property Party.

The delegates to the Constitutional Convention represented the right wing of the revolutionary movement and were, as Charles A. and Mary Beard noted, "practical men of affairs—holders of state and continental bonds, money lenders, merchants, lawyers and speculators in public lands." They wanted a strong central government that would levy and collect taxes, regulate commerce, control the issue of currency, assume the financial obligations of the Confederation, and prevent the impairment of contracts. They were equally in agreement on the dangers of democracy and the necessity of preventing its flowering. The delegates, said James Madison, wanted to "secure the public good and private rights against the danger of such a faction. . . ." Just before then, in Massachusetts, where the hard-money men controlled the courts and legislature, that very "faction," made up of impoverished Patriots—it was disquieting to recall how vicious and ugly they had been as anti-Tory mobs—rose in revolt under Captain Daniel Shays, and kept the state in terror for five months before being dispersed by the militia in February 1787. "You talk of employing influence," Washington wrote to General Henry (Light-Horse Harry) Lee, "to appease the present tumults in Massachusetts. I know not where the influence is to be found, or if attainable, that it would be a proper remedy for the disorders. *Influence* is no *government*. Let us have one by which our lives, liberties and properties will be secured or let us know the worst at once."*

The people wanted paper money, considered the "root of all evil" in Federalist economics, and they wanted a Bill of Rights in the Constitution. Madison wrote that the malcontents were turning to the polls, and if they could garner sufficient votes their "wicked measures" would be sheltered under the forms of the Constitution. Noting that Governor James Bowdoin of Massachusetts had been replaced by John Hancock, first president of the Continental Congress and an eminent merchant, he pointed out that his "acknowledged merits are a little tainted by a dishonourable obsequiousness to popular follies." Madison wanted constitutional safeguards for the Property Party: "In framing a system which we hope will last for ages, we must consider the changes age will produce." An increase of population would necessarily increase the proportion of those laboring under the hardships of life and who "secretly sigh for more equal distribution of its blessings." These might eventually outnumber those who are "placed above the feelings of indigence. . . . Symptoms of a levelling spirit . . . have sufficiently appeared in a certain quarter to give notice of the future danger."[1]

Aaron Burr cut short Hamilton's career but not his broad scheme—the Jeffersonians took over his policies and passed them on to John Connally and Richard Nixon. His philosophy is a basic ingredient in American political tradition: the people are turbulent, ignorant, and poverty-stricken. With the growth of wealth, inequality and class antagonism must increase. Therefore the stability of the social order and security of person and property could be maintained only by a strong government in the hands of the wealthy and intelligent. To these affluent classes, government at all times should render financial aid for the sake of attaching them to the government by the strongest bond—interest on capital—thus increasing national wealth and maintaining the employment of the people.[2]

* "We have known the 'best' for nearly two hundred years," says Gore Vidal. "What would the 'worst' have been like?"

Obviously, the Constitution was not written solely for the benefit of the Property Party, but it must be recognized that those who shaped it always had these interests in mind and never moved very far from under the shadow of money power.

The Founding Fathers would have heartily endorsed the value-added tax, an inescapable national sales tax, proposed by President Nixon. It was their contention, in view of their vast holdings and incomes, that a sales tax was fair because the rich would buy more than the poor. Except for a couple of brief interludes, this rationale prevailed until the Sixteenth Amendment was ratified in 1913.

To offset the "frightful expenditures" of the Civil War, Lincoln pressured Congress into passing an individual income tax* in 1862, no small feat when it is remembered that the Senate was the stronghold of money power. The money power of the Confederacy, represented by a few thousand large slaveowners, drew the South into rebellion and sent the laborer and farmer to fight for their "peculiar institution." Vast fortunes were made in war profits and money speculation. Big business and capitalism came of age in the North during the Civil War as the concentration of money power shifted from the slaveholding oligarchy of the South to the plutocracy of the North.

The plutocrats, who wanted to keep the South in economic bondage, opposed Lincoln's plan to reunite the nation and bind up its wounds. Following his assassination, their man in the Cabinet, Secretary of War Edwin M. Stanton, who has even been charged with a role in the assassination, became the wedge in their attempt to impeach Andrew Johnson on trumped-up charges. A lifelong foe of monopolies, Johnson had opposed the granting of public lands to railroads, the biggest giveaway in the nation's history. One vote in the Senate saved the country from an indefensible prostitution of the constitutional safeguard of impeachment to the ends of money power.

The Fourteenth Amendment, ostensibly designed to protect the rights of newly freed slaves, actually wrote laissez faire into the Constitution. In the words of one historian, it was written to stand as "the eternal bulwark of great property rights." Section 1, which conferred citizenship upon blacks, also forbade any state to abridge the privileges or immunities of citizens or to deprive any person of life, liberty, or *property* without due process of law. This last provision, together with Section 4, which by

---

* Initially the tax rates were 3 percent on income under $10,000 and 5 percent for anything above that amount, but later they were increased.

validating the public debt incurred during the war was of enormous benefit to speculators, was the meat of the amendment as far as the plutocrats were concerned—bonds purchased with depreciated currency were repaid in solid postwar coin under the Resumption Act. "Nepotism, corruption, inefficiency, misrule, bitter partisan politics—all the political crimes in the catalog flourished," Republican Senator James W. Grimes said of his party, and he went on to label it the "most corrupt and debauched political party that ever existed."

The income tax, which was abandoned in 1872 after only 250,000 returns were filed, was resurrected in 1894, with a rate of 2 percent on incomes over $4,000. The Supreme Court killed it in 1900, ruling it invalid on the basis that the Constitution required that all direct taxes must be levied in proportion to the population. The opposition generated by money power reverberated in the councils of government. The income tax was damned as "a punishment of the rich man because he is rich." Senator John Sherman called it a perfidious venture in "socialism, communism, devilism."

Sherman, a faithful disciple of Hamilton, was Secretary of the Treasury in the Hayes Administration. If ever money power was in a position to steal a presidential election outright it was in 1876, when Samuel J. Tilden, the scourge of the Tweed Ring and Tammany Hall, won 184 electoral votes, or only one less than the needed majority. The nineteen votes of three southern states, South Carolina, Louisiana, and Florida, were in doubt. Hayes acknowledged his defeat, but the chairman of the Republican National Committee boldly claimed every disputed vote, and the New York *Times* headlined its story "Hayes, 185; Tilden, 184." The certifying boards for all three states were under Republican control, and a special Electoral Commission composed of eight Republicans and seven Democrats, voting in that ratio, awarded all nineteen votes to Hayes. The bargain, one of the most evil ever struck by money power, was the Compromise of 1877, which assured Southern whites in the three states that Federal troops, charged with protecting reconstructionists and blacks in office, would be withdrawn. Hayes called it the restoration of "home rule" and it was followed by the wholesale murder of blacks throughout the "solid South." Those who survived were condemned to injustice and racial hatred that stripped them of their dignity along with their newly won civil rights. Six years later the Supreme Court ruled that the Fourteenth Amendment could not be used to restrain individuals from conduct designed to enforce social discriminations against blacks. Within a decade of "home rule," the South had devised innumerable loopholes that made a mockery of the Fourteenth Amendment and specifically of the Fifteenth, which provided that "The right of citizens of the United States to vote shall not be denied or abridged by the United States or by any State on account of race, color, or previous condition of servitude"—unless, of course, one could not raise the money or find the secret place where poll taxes were collected, or pass a literacy test that would have sorely tested the education of Southern governors themselves.

It was as if the Southern whites and the Northern "malefactors of great wealth," to use Theodore Roosevelt's phrase, had been granted the keys to their own private Valhalla. They had the whole nation to loot. There was massive corruption at all levels of business and government. It seemed that every principle and institution was for sale. Nothing was too sacred to resist the lure of money power. There was a great flourishing of robber barons. In the top ranks of the new hierarchy were Jay Gould, William H. Vanderbilt, Leland Stanford, James J. Hill, and Edward H. Harriman in railroads; Andrew Carnegie and Henry C. Frick in steel; John D. Rockefeller, Henry H. Rogers, John D. Archbold, and Stephen V. Harkness in oil; Philip D. Armour and Gustavus F. Swift in meat packing; William A. Clark, John William Mackay, and the Guggenheims in minerals; J. Pierpont Morgan, Jay Cook, and James Stillman in banking. Over all ruled the two supreme potentates: Rockefeller and Morgan.

In his cry against the income tax of 1894, one Tammany boss put his finger on the pulse of the system: It is "a betrayal of our ancient principles . . . this treason to our faith, to our platform, to our tradition, to our heroes."

The rich are heroes to be emulated. Persuading the people that the American Dream is there for the taking has been money power's greatest stroke of genius. "What you don't understand," John Adams told his Federalist colleagues, "is that most people would rather protect against the possibility of being rich than face the reality of being poor." His political views were more aristocratic than democratic: men love equality when they look up to higher ranks, and they love distinction when they look downward. This tendency to "superiority" must be supported by a hierarchy of officers and ranks. The Americans have avoided an institutional nobility, but no well-ordered community has existed for long without one. Society will always be divided into plebeians, the "simplemen," obscure, ignorant, mean, and poor; and the patricians, the rich and well-born, the gentlemen, who always administer government. In America as elsewhere, wealth and good birth exercise dominance *de facto*. The poor are dependent on the rich for their subsistence; many of small fortunes will be in debt or under obligations to the wealthy. Still others, such as men of letters and the learned professions, will from acquaintance, "conversation," and expectation be connected with them. Finally, among the wisest people there is a degree of admiration, subtracted from all dependence, "which accompanies splendid wealth, insures . . . respect, and bestows . . . influence." A few, having all the advantages of birth and fortune, constitute the "natural aristocracy," the grand repository of virtue and abilities in a free government.[3]

Men of letters, including those in journalism, have benefited from "conversation" with the "natural aristocracy." However, on rare occasion throughout history, there have been minor revolts in the ranks, particularly by those with gumption enough to face the reality of poverty. "Teddy the Trustbuster" called them "Socialists! Sensationalists! Agitators and puzzleheads! . . . These reckless journalists, these wild preachers of reform, are the most dangerous opponents of reform." They reminded him of the man with the muckrake in John Bunyan's *Pilgrim's Progress*, ". . . who could look no way but downward, . . . who was offered a celestial crown for his muckrake, but who would neither look up nor regard the crown he was offered, but continued to rake to himself the filth of the floor."

Lincoln Steffens, Ida M. Tarbell, Upton Sinclair, Ray Stannard Baker, Charles Edward Russell, Samuel Hopkins Adams, David Graham Phillips . . . barely a handful of muckrakers and one magazine in particular, *McClure's*, raised hell with money power for a little over a decade starting at the turn of the century. "Graft ivrywhere," sighed Mr. Dooley, a fictional Irish barkeep created by Finley Peter Dunne, a Chicago newspaper columnist. " 'Graft in th' Insurance Comp'nies,' 'Graft in Congress,' 'Graft in th' Supreen Coort,' 'Graft be an Old Grafter,' 'Graft in Lithrachoor,' be Hinnery James: 'Graft in Its Relation to th' Higher Life,' be Dock Eliot [president of Harvard]. . . . An' so it goes, till I'm that blue, discouraged an' broken-hearted I cud go to th' edge iv th' wurruld an' jump off."

The muckrakers brashly exposed the collectors of "celestial crowns" as they attacked all forms of double-dealing, price fixing, and cutthroat power struggles, from corruption in executive suites right down to the political precinct. By 1905, railroad accidents were taking twenty thousand lives a year. Unsafe mines took countless thousands of lives. Thousands more died because of unsanitary food. During a federal investigation in 1899, General Nelson A. Miles charged that "embalmed meat," packaged by Armour, Swift, Wilson, and other large Chicago packers, had killed more of his troops during the Spanish-American War than had enemy bullets (Colonel Teddy Roosevelt was quoted as saying that he would rather have eaten his old hat than canned meat), but the Presidential commission dismissed the charges, concluding that since meat inspection laws were on the books, they "must have been followed." Patent medicines were equally dangerous. Lydia Pinkham's Vegetable Compound —"Only a woman can understand a woman's ills"—was 20 percent alcohol, and pacifying syrups for babies were laced with morphine and cocaine. Opium was peddled in a variety of elixirs prescribed by doctors for everything from melancholia to constipation. At the turn of the century, heroin was introduced as a new miracle drug and Bayer was the first to package it. Statistics then estimated the ratio of drug addiction as one in every hundred adults, or half a million addicts, which makes today's binge look like a passing fancy. They went after politicians, naming a whole gallery of culprits. In an article, "The Treason of the Senate," David Graham Phillips charged that "The Senators are not elected by the people; they are elected by the 'interests.' . . . Did you ever think where the millions for watchers, spellbinders, halls, processions, posters, pamphlets, that are spent in national, state and local campaigns come from? Do you imagine those who foot those huge bills are fools?"

The muckrakers tackled a multitude of injustices: race problems, child labor, prison abuses, church-owned slums, industrial accidents, monopolies, working conditions, the looting of the nation's forests and other natural resources, an impressive catalogue of white-collar crimes. Great sound and fury signifying what? "I see gr-reat changes takin' place ivry day," said Mr. Dooley, "but no change at all ivry fifty years."

That is the great secret resource of the Property Party—it endures. On the other hand, muckraking ain't what it used to be. The libel laws and high legal fees—win or lose, a lawsuit is expensive—have made crusading a costly enterprise these days—even against the Mafia, as the *Saturday Evening Post, Look*, and *Life* discovered shortly before slipping into oblivion. Yet we are blessed with the likes of Ralph Nader and John Gardner, men whose integrity and industry stand up to monumental corruption and make the truth known. The old orthodoxy survives in reporters like Jack Anderson and Richard Strout, who writes under the byline of TRB. Although the Washington *Post*, the New York *Times*, and the Los Angeles *Times* are quick to display the courage of their convictions, the list of stouthearted writers and publishers grows shorter as giant conglomerates continue to swallow up the book-publishing business, not to mention radio, television, and newspapers—Nixon received the editorial support of 753 daily newspapers in the 1972 presidential campaign, compared to 56 for McGovern; the circulation percentages were 71.4 to 5.3.[4] "Still the Nixon Administration continues to harp on the specter of media opposition, confusing the hard news coverage of its corruption and scandals with the overall editorial stance, which is overwhelmingly Republican. In a privately published tract, *The New Majority*, Patrick J. Buchanan, the most zealous of the White House right-wing zealots—for a time he served as spectral alliterateur for Spiro Agnew—charged that the nation is being undermined by a "marriage of left-winged bias and network power"; that "an incumbent elite, with an ideological slant unshared by the nation's majority, has acquired absolute control of the most powerful medium of communication known to man." "If it weren't from the White House," TRB concluded in the *New Republic*, "we'd say he was a crackpot."[5]

"The masters of the government of the United States are the combined capitalists and manufacturers of the United States," Woodrow Wilson said shortly before his inauguration as President in 1913. "It is written over every intimate page of the record of Congress, it is written all through the history of conferences at the White House, that the suggestions of economic policy have come from one source, not from many sources. . . . The government of the United States at present is a foster child of the special interests."[6]

As history sadly records, the worst crime has always been poverty and the greatest achievement wealth. Balzac believed that behind every fortune was a crime, but money power has revised his theory. The assumption is that behind every poor person is a potential criminal, and the government proves it by filling its prisons with them. In revising the federal criminal code, Nixon proposed severe new mandatory sentences, including capital punishment, and grimly demanded that they be applied "without pity." His spiritual mentor, Billy Graham, while evangelizing among white supremacists in South Africa, proposed that rapists be castrated.

Corporate criminals, wolves in conservative clothing, have managed to abrogate the legislative process at the source long before it could make their behavior unlawful. There is no corporate counterpart to the FBI crime statistics. Nobody in government dares keep that close an eye on money power. Yet corporate crimes are far more costly to the public health and welfare than street crimes. They rob and assault millions of consumers and innocent bystanders, but the offenses are so diffused, so obfuscated in the organization chart, that the public has no frame of reference in which to evaluate responsibility or damage. In fact, corporate crime is such an obscure concept that it is not even mentioned in the criminal index to the laws of the United States.

Whitney North Seymour, former United States Attorney for the Southern District of New York, which includes Manhattan, commanded what he calls the "most important district in the nation as far as white-collar crime is concerned. That is because Wall Street is here." That, he says, is "where the action is."[7] The Justice Department defines a white-collar crime as "an illegal act or series of illegal acts committed by nonphysical means and by concealment or guile to obtain property, to avoid the payment or loss of money or property, or to obtain business or personal advantage." Edwin H. Sutherland, author of *White Collar Crime*, defined it more simply. It is a crime "committed by a person of respectability and high social status in the course of his occupation."

The victim of a corporate crime is often unaware that he has been victimized. The method of operation is subtle. When a corporation mugs you, it does it with something soft. Corporate thefts and violence are disguised in a complex variety of ways. The stratagems include price fixing, shoddy products in fancy packages, hazardous designs, false weights and measurements, food adulteration, circumvention of antipollution laws, inferior and dangerous drugs,* lethal toys, secret rebates and kickbacks, usury hidden in service charges, bid rigging, illegal labor practices, unsafe working conditions, industrial and commercial espionage, monopolistic mergers, insider stock deals, fraudulent misrepresentations, sophisticated boiler-room stock promotions, bribery on government contracts, conflicts of interest in corporate deals† and in appointments to government services and vice versa, excessive campaign contributions, gifts and bribes, and, in

---

* Following its hearings in 1969, the House Select Committee on Crime reported that American pharmaceutical houses and wholesalers were selling about eight billion doses of amphetamines a year when the legitimate medical need could be measured in thousands of doses. Bates Laboratories of Chicago shipped some fifteen million doses of this drug to a pharmacy in Tijuana, Mexico, which serves as a discount halfway depot in the illegal California drug traffic. It is the victimized addict who serves time for his habit, not the corporate pusher who rakes in profits of a thousand percent and up.

† Numerous major corporations have been charged with conflicts in the past few years. To name a few: Equity Funding Corporation of America, Four Seasons Nursing Centers of America, Inc., American Airlines, Kaiser Industries, Penn Central, and Merrill Lynch.

gangster fashion, the use of aliases in the form of subsidiaries and dummy corporations. They hire supermouthpieces and loophole artists, along with advertising hucksters and suave public-relations counselors, captive bureaucrats and politicians, lobbyists—when does petitioning become graft? —and erudite Ivy League vice presidents to give class to the front office.

The most dramatic example of corporate venality in recent years was the General Electric-Westinghouse price-fixing case of the early 1960s. Forty-five executives and twenty-nine companies, controlling 95 percent of the heavy electrical industry, were involved in a conspiracy to rig prices on a scale so vast that it embraced everything from the Defense Department and the Tennessee Valley Authority to the private utilities that supply the nation's light and power. They used codes and fictitious names, destroyed communications, and met secretly in obscure motels in dozens of cities. They used an elaborate formula known as "phase of the moon" to indicate whose turn it was to submit a low bid, and at what price, on major contracts. All the companies and individuals pleaded guilty or *nolo contendere** to charges that they had conspired over a seven-year period† to fix prices and rig bids in the sale of some $7 billion worth of heavy electrical equipment. "These men," a defense attorney pleaded, "are not grasping, greedy, cutthroat competitors." Which was certainly true. The lawyer for William S. Ginn, a GE vice president, begged the court not to put his client "behind bars with common criminals who have been convicted of embezzlement and other serious crimes." Another defense attorney argued against any form of punishment: "Why punish these men? It is a way of life—everybody's doing it." In the reckoning, seven executives were sentenced to thirty days in jail, and twenty-one others were given suspended thirty-day sentences. The twenty-nine companies were fined a total of $1,787,000. No one in the top management of the companies was indicted.

On sentencing day, Chief Judge J. Cullen Ganey's outraged frustration matched that of Judge John J. Sirica in the first Watergate trial. Focusing on the prosecutors, Judge Ganey said that "the Department of Justice has acknowledged that they were unable to uncover probative evidence which would secure a conviction beyond a reasonable doubt of those in the

---

* By avoiding trials, the defendants were not only protecting the higher-ups against any unraveling of the conspiracies, but they were trying to minimize the companies' liability in damages to those defrauded by their price agreements.

† One of the eight conspiracies was a quarter of a century old; others had endured for more than a decade.

highest echelons of the corporations here involved. One would be most naïve indeed to believe that these violations of the law, so long persisted in, affecting so large a segment of the industry, and, finally, involving so many millions upon millions of dollars, were facts unknown to those responsible for the corporation and its conduct."

The analogy to Watergate is irresistible. "The key to successful conspiracy is that the higher-ups do not ask what's going on, and the lower-downs do not tell them," I. F. Stone wrote in *The New York Review*. Mitchell did not tell the President, he explained to the Watergate committee, because once Nixon knew, "there would be no alternative. He would have a choice of being involved in what you all referred to as a cover-up or he would be involved in the disclosures which would affect his reelection." "Mitchell," says Stone, "was only doing what any good corporation lawyer would do in analogous circumstances." "I have racked my brain," Nixon told H. R. Haldeman. "Were there any clues I should have seen . . . ?" Donald Segretti, also an attorney, assured a potential recruit for his dirty-tricks crew: "Nixon knows that something is being done. It's a typical deal: don't-tell-me-anything-and-I-won't-know." In August 1973, Nixon assured the nation that no one then in the White House was involved. Next he said, "There has been an effort to conceal the facts—both from the public—from you—and from me." Still later he said, "I took no part in—nor was I aware of" the cover-up.

"Mr. Nixon's need to know nothing seems to be violently at war with his need to know everything," says *Newsweek* columnist Shana Alexander. "Secretly, he bugs himself. But even bugging is not enough. He needs to know which corporations have 'problems with the government' and might therefore be disposed to make large campaign contributions. He needs to know who his public 'enemies' are, so that after the election they can be 'taken care of.' He confides to [Robert] Mardian in San Clemente that the Pentagon papers leak means that his 'very ability to govern was threatened; the peace of the world was threatened.' So he needs to know things that even the FBI and the CIA won't dig for, and he sets up his own secret spy force. It is not hard to imagine a man so at war with himself sitting alone, late at night, playing his tapes and asking himself: 'What did I know?' "

The cost to the public in the electrical conspiracy was estimated at $1.7 billion. Compare this to the FBI figures for the cost of street crimes against property over the entire nation in 1962. The total amount was $650 million, which included 85,260 robberies, 892,800 burglaries, 539,900 larcenies of $50 and over, and 356,100 auto thefts.

Thousands of lawsuits were brought against the companies for treble damages, which ultimately were settled for about $500 million. Unabashed by the exposure of their machinations, the electrical companies' top executives gained an audience with Internal Revenue Service Commissioner Mortimer M. Caplin and emerged with a ruling that was even more shocking than the conspiracy itself. All legal expenses, fines, and damages paid by the companies were to be written off as "ordinary and necessary" business expenses. With the existing corporate tax rate at 52 percent, this meant that the government, the principal victim of the conspiracy, picked up more than half of the tab. Senator Philip A. Hart questioned whether Caplin would allow an individual taxpayer to deduct a fine for a speeding ticket as an "ordinary and necessary" business expense. Better still, would the IRS permit a bank robber to deduct his legal expenses? IRS regulations countenance corporate machinations. For example, corporate bribes and kickbacks to nongovernmental officials are deductible unless the individual has been convicted of making the bribe or has entered a plea of guilty or *nolo contendere*. The IRS rule is that "deduction will not be disallowed merely because the payments are in contravention of public policy." The criterion is whether the expenditures were "ordinary and necessary." As for bribes to government officials, "the burden, as in fraud cases, rests with the government to prove that the payment was a bribe or kickback."[8]

Reflecting on the electrical conspiracy, *Life* concluded that the "crime was not nearly so heinous as what the original Goulds, Fisks, Vanderbilts and Rockefellers used to get away with before their piracies inspired the Sherman [Antitrust] Act in 1890. A later generation of business criminals —Insull, Wiggin, Hopson, et al.—whose stock-rigging fostered so much New Deal legislation, also operated on a far more brazen (and remunerative) scale than these gray-flannel turbine salesmen. What makes this crime so serious for American business is not that it was heinous but that it was so unexpected to the public. American business was widely believed to have become smarter and more honest than that."

What is the annual cost of corporate crime to the public? Senator Hart's Judiciary Subcommittee on Antitrust and Monopoly estimated, as a result of extensive investigation, that the cost was between $174 and $231 *billion*. These are astronomical figures, and yet they do not tell the full story. There is the more insidious despoliation and pollution of our great natural heritage. The greedy profit cry of the turn-of-the-century ravager still rings in boardrooms: "Posterity be damned—what has it ever done for us!"

Ida Tarbell documented every ruthless step in the shaping of John D. Rockefeller's Standard Oil trust, the most complete monopoly of its day. The Supreme Court's ruling against it, finding it guilty of attempting "to establish a virtual monopoly," stands as one of the rare exceptions in the annals of money power, but there were other pressures at work (see Chapter Four). The court fragmented the trust, in 1911, into thirty-eight "independent units," and today the profits of only one of those companies, Exxon, are several times greater than those of the entire trust.

"This is the original trust," a New York committee concluded after its investigation of Standard Oil in 1888. "Its success has been the incentive to the formation of all other trusts or combinations. It is the type of system which has spread like a disease through the commercial system of this country." "An incredible number of the necessaries and luxuries of life, from meat to tombstones," had fallen into the hands of monopolists who squeezed every nickel they could out of the public. But the evils of the trusts involved more than price fixing. Producers of raw materials were compelled to accept whatever the trust chose to pay, for there was no other buyer; labor was forced into line by the closing of troublesome plants, and by the circulation of blacklists that prevented agitators from obtaining employment; politicians were influenced by free railroad passes, by campaign contributions, and by outright bribes. Powerful lobbies became the "third house" of Congress. Employees were further removed from the big bosses who prided themselves upon their "hard-headedness." Business was business, and the economic ethos was Darwinian—except, as John Adams had pointed out, that patricians are fitter by birth than plebeians.

The courts sided with the Property Party. Since the Founding Fathers had never heard of a trust, the only power lodged in the central government to control such organizations was whatever the courts could infer from the right to control interstate commerce. The power of the states to control violations in their own jurisdictions was severely curtailed by the Fourteenth Amendment, which required that the states might not "deprive any person of life, liberty, or property, without due process of law." In 1886 the Supreme Court, reversing an earlier ruling, held that the use of the word "person" in this clause was meant to apply to corporations as well as to individuals. Thus the amendment, which was meaningless when it came to protecting the rights of blacks, became the Magna Carta of monopolies. And so the states, themselves the creators of corporations, were restrained by the federal government from any measures of taxation or regulation that the courts chose to regard as depriving the corporations of property "without due process of law."

The Sherman Antitrust Act was named after Senator John Sherman, the nemesis of the income tax—for no other reason, said Senator George F. Hoar, "except that Mr. Sherman had nothing to do with framing it whatever." The vigor of its language left nothing to be desired. It branded as illegal "every contract, combination in the form of trust or otherwise, or conspiracy in restraint of trade or commerce among the several states, or with foreign nations." It defined as a misdemeanor any "attempt to monopolize, or combine or conspire with any other person or persons to monopolize, any part of the trade or commerce among the several states or with foreign nations." Penalties for persons held guilty of violating the act were set at a fine not to exceed five thousand dollars and imprisonment not to exceed a year, one or both as the court might prescribe. Any person injured by violation of the act declared unlawful might recover in court "threefold the damages by him sustained."

It sounded like the death knell of monopolies, but enforcement was another matter. Seven of the first eight attempts to invoke its penalties went against the government. In the Knight case (1895), the Supreme Court held that the establishment of a monopoly in manufactures, however reprehensible, could be dealt with only by the individual states. "Commerce," said the court, "succeeds to manufacture, and is not a part of it." To all intent and purpose, the Sherman Act was dead; lawyers advised their clients that the Supreme Court had conceded the legality of private monopoly. In later years, Teddy the Trustbuster enjoyed mild success, notably in the prosecution of the Northern Securities Company, a $400-million holding company that controlled the stock of three competing railroads, a scheme worked out by James J. Hill and J. P. Morgan. Eventually Roosevelt became ambivalent as he tried to distinguish between "good" and "bad" trusts, prosecuting the latter and ignoring the former. "Th' trust, says he [Roosevelt]," Mr. Dooley reported, "are heejoous monsthers built up be th' enlightened intherprise iv th' men that have done so much to advance progress in our beloved country, he says. On wan hand I could stamp thim undher fut: on th' other hand not so fast." Or, as Senator Robert M. La Follette saw it, the trouble with Roosevelt was that he was ever ready to take the "half-loaf" if he could not easily get more.

Politicians down through the years, even those essaying the role of trustbuster, have trod lightly through the exclusive preserve of monopolies. There is no better evidence of this than the Sherman Act itself. The two principal sections of the law have remained unaltered to this day. They provide the government with a two-edged sword: one, the injunction of conspiracies in restraint of trade; the other, criminal punishment or a fine (raised to $50,000 in 1961), or both. Rockefeller, Hill, and Morgan could have gone to jail, but the United States waited almost three-quarters of a century to impose criminal sanctions on individuals, and even then the seven electrical conspirators sentenced to token jail terms were second-level executives.

When it became public knowledge that holding companies and interlocking directorates were making a dead letter of the Sherman Act, Congress, at the behest of President Wilson, passed the Clayton Act in 1914. This was a hodgepodge of several bills proposed for the amendment and clarification of the Sherman Act. It outlawed various practices, including any discrimination in prices that tended to produce a monopoly; the acquisition by any corporation of the whole or a part of the stock of a competing concern (horizontal merger) or of a supplier or customer (vertical); the existence of interlocking directorates among large corporations that were or had been competitors; and exclusive contracts that obligated a dealer not to handle the products of other manufacturers.

Businessmen grumbled over many details of the law, but again the language proved easier to effect than its enforcement. However, something even more ominous was hovering on the horizon. The Sixteenth Amendment was declared in force on February 25, 1913, just before President William Howard Taft left office. Its passage was an accident, a sort of runaway horse trade. Taft Republicans had agreed to the amendment in exchange for support of a high-tariff bill, never dreaming for a moment that it would be ratified by the necessary two-thirds of the states. The amendment gave Congress the power to "lay and collect taxes on incomes, from whatever source derived, without apportionment among the several States, and without regard to any census or enumeration." Soon after its ratification, the Democrats, who had since gained control of Congress, pushed through an income tax bill. The proposed rates were modest. Exemptions of $3,000 were granted to individuals and $4,000 to married couples, with rates of 1 percent on income up to $20,000 and 2 percent to $50,000. The rates graduated up to 6 percent on income of $500,000.

There were no loopholes to speak of until the rates began skyrocketing during World War I.

"After all," said Calvin Coolidge, in one of the few quotable utterances of his Administration, "the chief business of America is business." In his simple way, the President was paying tribute to the evolution of money-power democracy, expressing the sum of its philosophy, which penetrates into the marrow of the American ethos far more deeply than any Marxist dialectics on capitalism.

Andrew Mellon, "the greatest Secretary of the Treasury since Hamilton," or so the prosperity-bemused populace of the 1920s was periodically assured, articulated the money-power formulation for Presidents Harding, Coolidge, and Hoover. Mellon, who believed in the laissez-faire premise of soaking all of the people except the rich, outlined his wisdom in a book prophetically entitled *Taxation: The People's Business*. Justice Oliver Wendell Holmes, Jr., believed that "Taxes are what we pay for a civilized society," but he liked Mellon's "good little book," for Mellon's ideas "seemed right to me."

Mellon was a charter member of the ruling elite.* At the time of his appointment to the Treasury post, he relinquished nearly a hundred corporate offices or directorships. The family's interests, ranging from the Aluminum Company of America and Gulf Oil to the Overholt Distillery (no doubt frustrating to laissez-faire-minded prohibitionists) were estimated to be worth $2 billion. When he took office in 1921, the top income-tax rate was 73 percent on net incomes over $1 million and the top estate rate was 25 percent on net estates over $10 million. Four years later the top rates had been lowered to 25 percent on income and 20 percent on estates, and the corporate income-tax rate was 13 percent. It was the golden age of business incentive, lasting about a decade before the bottom dropped out.

In formulating his economic philosophy, Mellon borrowed heavily from Adam Smith's *The Wealth of Nations*, published in 1776 and treasured by the Founding Fathers. Mellon preached that "the prosperity of the middle and lower classes depends upon the good fortunes and light taxes of the rich." To tamper with the economic happiness of the rich will "gradually destroy business initiative" and impair "the country's future prosperity." The taxation of business must be kept at a minimum so as not to interfere with or discourage the profit motive, production, and the in-

* See Chapter Four, pages 166–169, for more details on his career.

centive to invest. But taxes on factory workers, agricultural laborers, and other poor people are beneficial to the economy because they discourage indolence and encourage industry—the poor are forced to work harder to improve their lot.

Mellon laid it on the line in plain, tough language that few politicians would dare use today. Richard Nixon, the greatest money-power missionary since Herbert Hoover, sells Mellonism in the cotton-wrapped euphemisms of Madison Avenue. The President preaches that America's success has grown out of the "competitive spirit" that motivates people to "live not by handout, not by dependence on others or in hostage to the whims of others, but proud and independent." In a travesty of Kennedy's inaugural address, the President assured the voters in 1972 that the key to the nation's economic progress "is not what government has done for the people, but what people have done for themselves." Yet this cornerstone upon which the great American system of "free competition" now rests is threatened by a potentially ruinous philosophy, the welfare ethic. The proponents of the welfare ethic believe that "the good life can be made available to everyone right now, and that this can be done by the government." Americans should reject the welfare ethic and return to the work ethic, which holds that "an able-bodied person should earn what he gets and keep most of what he earns." (This was after the President had deliberately added a million people to the unemployment rolls in a fruitless attempt to cool off the economy, and at a time when federal, state, and local taxes—not to mention inflation—were taking about forty-five cents of every dollar earned.)

Nixon believes in the basic assumption—shared by all money-power zealots—that the poor are congenitally ignorant, shiftless, lazy, and dishonest. The only liberal in White House residence (briefly), Daniel P. Moynihan, tried to sell Nixon the family-assistance plan, but he could never convince him that the work-requirement clause could be strictly enforced, with the result that the President's first halting step from the path of rugged individualism was quickly retracted. Still determined to demonstrate his social compassion, Nixon proposed to "streamline the economy," to "get big government off your back and out of your pocket"—all of which means, in the nitty-gritty of Nixonomics, that the government will continue to take from the poor to give to the rich. President George Meany of the AFL-CIO anticipated the drift of the President's "reordering of national priorities," which he believed would be applied "with a vengeance" and "in reverse":

Unprecedented and unhealthy tax relief to corporations would be the ultimate effect of the keystone of the President's new economic program. It would reverse progress in America. The government of compassion, which many believed had come into being, would be halted. Corporate profit-and-loss charts—not the public need—would have first priority. The poor, the cities and states, federal employees, wage and salary earners—all would foot the bill, and the sole beneficiaries would be the wealthy and the corporations.

Nixon spoke of a "renaissance of the individual spirit" or "a new pride of place for the family and the community—a new sense of responsibility in all that we do" or of the "need for a driving dream" or a "renewed sense of purpose." Simultaneously he was busily chopping away some $10 billion in social programs—low-income housing, manpower training, day-care centers, child-development programs, school aid, Head Start, community health clinics, Medicare, Medicaid dental care, vocational rehabilitation, community antipoverty agencies, legal aid to the poor, and environmental protection—from the fiscal 1974 budget, the same budget that doled out more than $50 billion in tax loopholes and subsidies to corporate interests and the rich who obviously need not "help themselves."

There are times when the right wing of the Property Party must surrender power to the left wing, and in the exchange a few stray wolves may become fair game (to a reasonable degree, of course),* for the people must have their token sacrifices. At times the two wings appear to behave like a pair of cops grilling a suspect—one plays the heavy while the other, the "nice guy," cons a confession from the grateful captive. This is not to imply that it is anything as simplistic as a conspiracy, something on the order of a crime syndicate, because nothing could be further from the reality of the system.

Money power has had great success with both wings. Social reform and corporate welfare are not mutually exclusive concepts, especially when businessmen are in on the deal. Sound left-wing politics is preferable to wild right-wing rantings against "creeping socialism." Barry Goldwater scared money power out of its collective wits in 1964, at a time when Johnson's Great Society was combining social programs with soaring profits. Money power knew its way around the Johnson White House. Richard J. Whalen, a former Nixon adviser and speechwriter, believes that busi-

---

* In 1934, one year after the inauguration of Franklin D. Roosevelt, a Pittsburgh grand jury refused to indict Mellon on charges that he falsified his 1931 tax returns— the government asked for $3,089,261 in taxes and penalties, and finally settled with his estate for $668,000.

nessmen are not interested in restoring "the ideology (still less the practice) of free and competitive enterprise":

> What is demanded [of Nixon] is soothing rhetoric and first-name clubbiness, but even more the same deal the Democrats provided. Businessmen want competent, gentlemanly socialism for themselves up to the established standard. They want the federal government to do less where their interests would be adversely affected (for example, in consumer protection) and a great deal more where their interests supposedly merge with a "public interest" requiring subsidy by the taxpayers. Capitalists and their anxious bankers are now unembarrassed to approach the government as the banker of last resort and to press for public money in support of insolvent private ventures [Lockheed, Penn Central, SST, etc.]. To be sure, such selective socialism, entailing nationalization of losses while profits remain private, involves a bit of ideological backpedaling, but businessmen have before them Nixon's exemplary declaration: "I am a Keynesian," meaning *We're all Democrats now, boys.*[9]

It is not the man who sits in the Oval Office who ultimately matters; rather it is the men around him, the Cabinet and commissions and agencies, the vast bureaucracy (no President can hope to cope with it—President Kennedy said dealing with it was like trying to nail jelly to the wall), the legislative and judicial branches, trade associations and lobbies, superlawyers and consultants, tax experts and economists, and that horde of influence peddlers who dwell in the niches of the marble labyrinths of government power, dispensing deep freezes and rugs, minks and vicuña coats—the Nathan Voloshens and Bobby Bakers*—and, finally, the $100 million like clockwork for campaign whoopee. It is this complex machinery that gives money power its checks and balances, its precious veto that has protected its vested inheritance for the nearly two centuries of this Republic's existence.

The Property Party has learned to bend with the winds of change. In fact, it has benefited from the infusion of new ideas, which have given it continuity rather than ideological fracture. The radical programs of William Jennings Bryan have all come to pass. Aggressive young liberals make fine old conservative leaders. Change is a gradual process. There is a time for progress, and a time to regress. The two wings maintain the equilibrium. The Great Society of Lyndon Johnson, along with four dec-

---

* In *The Washington Pay-off*, Robert Winter-Berger said that he was present in the office of Speaker of the House John W. McCormack when President Johnson rushed in and, assuming that the Speaker was alone, launched into a tirade against Bobby Baker: "John, that son of a bitch is going to ruin me. If that cocksucker talks, I'm gonna land in jail. . . . I will give him a million dollars if he takes the rap."

ades of painfully slow social progress, is being methodically dismantled by Richard Nixon without any serious challenge from the left wing.

Meanwhile, the people, who must pull themselves up by their bootstraps, have cooperatively fallen into a deep sleep. The great popular mandate delivered to Nixon in 1972 is illustrative of the apathy necessary in a period of regression. If not a single person had voted against Nixon, his "new majority" would total less than half of all qualified voters. The only issue that briefly roused the people from their comatose state was "busing." Charges of corruption—Watergate, ITT, secret campaign contributions, the Russian wheat deal, "all those dirty things" that terrified Martha Mitchell—hardly stirred a ripple in slumberland. A *Time* public-opinion sampler in October 1972 disclosed that 75 percent of the voters of sixteen states were "sick and tired" of the constant running down of the nation—"a plague on the messengers, never mind the facts."[10] Even the new youth vote, including college students, was almost identical to the older vote.

The campaign's most unexpected issue, in the opinion of columnist Max Lerner, was "the management of social change. Note that this has been the first presidential election since the great wave of dislocating and disruptive social changes of the 1960s. . . . The tide has been moving toward the deceleration of the social changes. Very early, McGovern lost his credibility for both parties on what we call the 'social issues,' which are really the change issues. When the voters rejected him, it was not because of any particular stand of his, or trait of his, but because they didn't believe that he was the person to preside over the future deceleration of changes."[11]

Still, the role of Prairie populist was ill suited to George McGovern. He wanted the presidency too badly to conceal his hunger. When he got a bearing on the political current, he quickly shifted course, but it was too late. The wobbling and waffling on social and economic issues was all unnecessary. Nobody was listening. The man who was going to revolutionize the tax code paid $21,000 for a full-page ad in the *Wall Street Journal* to assure its money-power readers that all he was asking for was corporate taxes comparable to those in the Eisenhower Administration.

"The two parties which divide the state, the party of Conservatism and that of Innovation," Emerson said, "are very old and have disputed the possession of the world ever since it was made."

What they have disputed is its representation, not possession, for that has remained the exclusive province of money power. Historically, the

Democratic wing, which traces its origins and philosophy to Jefferson and Jackson, has identified with the common man; the Republican wing, whose first President was Lincoln but which traces its philosophy to Hamilton, has identified with big business.

It is significant that Jefferson was converted to Hamilton's economic theories, and not vice versa. A man of extraordinary erudition, a fact evident in the Declaration of Independence, Thomas Jefferson started out as the great American radical. An agrarian democrat, he was suspicious of great wealth and "enterprise," and vigorously opposed its proponents in his early years. As Washington's first Secretary of State, he rejected Hamilton's plan for bounties to great "company enterprises" in manufactures as unconstitutional and oppressive. The government subsidies would not only inordinately enrich a few privileged individuals and press heavily on the citizenry because of the heavy taxation involved, but would also strengthen governmental power to a dangerous degree. But Jefferson, anti-Hamiltonian as a Cabinet member, became in good part Hamiltonian as President. And in his old age, Jefferson, who once had coalesced yeomen farmers, landed proprietors, and city bosses in opposition to the business elitism of Hamilton, found himself in opposition to a similar coalition behind Andrew Jackson, whom he distrusted as "one of the most unfit men I know of for such a place . . . a dangerous man." Time heals all political aberrations.

The Founding Fathers were avid believers in Adam Smith's thesis that enterprise thrives best when left free to individual initiative. Reduced to its basic formula, it was Smith's theory that a businessman's aggressive, predatory, selfish nature was neutralized in the marketplace—competition did the trick. When prices of goods were high, the urge for profit brought in more producers, and competition reduced prices. If wages were high, the ensuing well-being of the workers increased the population, and competition for jobs reduced wages. Everybody could pursue his own selfish interests without incurring any stigma for individual success, because the self-regulating market, "the hidden hand," as Smith called it, took care of arranging things. It was a neat little package, the product of the Age of Reason, with no loose strings anywhere for opponents to unravel.

His book was an immediate success. "Men long intimidated by taboos, priesthoods, fear of hell felt themselves emancipated," Leland Hazard wrote in a magazine article. "To pursue one's own selfish interest and at the same time, thanks to the market place, serve society well—this was a new idea. Americans liked it. It fitted the pattern of escape from too much rulership, too much dogma, too much ecclesiasticism. America was through with revealed truth; it was ready to accept what would work in the market place. Adam Smith never put it this way, but actually he had substituted the market place for God, in so far as God cares about social well-being. So, if the market place had become the god of social well-being, it must be sacrosanct."[12]

It is rather strange that Smith, who lived in the golden age of the British East India Company, the greatest monopoly in history, did not foresee the evolution of the trust. In fact, he had little faith in the future of the corporation because, in his opinion, such an artificial device could not generate the selfish drive so essential to the success of his system. Nor did he foresee a whole slew of innovations—from child-labor laws to minimum wages and labor unions—that would impede the market place in its benign work. None, of course, would have a more disruptive effect than the economic concentration of heavy technology.

Economists have been traditionally poor prophets. Commenting on today's breed, the New York *Times* editorial writer Leonard Silk noted that their "once exalted reputation for worldly wisdom has been tarnished of late. They generally failed to anticipate the deterioration of the environment stemming from rising production, population growth, and technological advance. Nor did they foresee the impact of rapid economic change on America's cities. They have been preoccupied with economic growth and full employment, but the worrisome lesson of the past decade is that growth and full employment are no answers to what ails the United States."[13] Richard Whalen thinks that the "President's Council of Economic Advisers [CEA], a trio of academics, stood in the same relation to the Chief Executive as did the ancient soothsayers to their king. But we find that the elaborate mathematical models of the Gross National Product [GNP], the comfortingly precise projections of consumer and capital spending, have as much bearing on the economy and its mysterious inner dynamics as so many dissected chicken livers. As for the immense Federal budget, the chief instrument for making our faith effective, we are told by Professor Paul McCracken, former chairman of President Nixon's CEA, that it is in a quite literal sense out of control. If we suspect that the wise men entrusted with maintaining American prosperity do not know quite what to do, we have good reason."[14]

In terms of social significance, Keynes once predicted that economists would one day rank about with dentists. In his latest book, *Economics and the Public Purpose*, John Kenneth Galbraith agrees partially with Keynes, who he said regarded economics as being primarily concerned with the production of goods and the prevention of depression. "In the modern industrial society these are not very difficult matters. . . . In trying to place all problems within the framework of the market and all behavior subordinate to market command, economists do, we have sufficiently seen, render great service to the planning system—to the disguise of the power that in fact it wields. But this is socially a dubious function and not one we need applaud." But Keynes was wrong, says Galbraith, in not foreseeing that "with economic development, power would pass from the consumer to the producer. And not seeing this, he did not see the increasing divergence between producer or planning purpose and the purpose of the public." The result of producer purpose has created undesirable effects, among them inflation, currency crises, pollution, product shortages, energy crises, an inequitable distribution of income, and myriad other problems. By their piecemeal approach, economists have added to this difficulty, Galbraith says, "making a living out of the infinitely clever gadgetry of disguise. They have concentrated on the abscesses and cavities instead of looking at the organism as a whole."

Hugh Carey, a member of the Joint Economic Committee, who represents a Brooklyn district in the House, once compared a panel of prominent economists testifying before him to the once hapless New York Mets. "You make me think of Casey Stengel's question," Carey said. " 'Can't anybody here play this game?' "

The mystique of classical competition, that blind faith in the old stereotype of supply and demand*—the *sine qua non* of the free-enterprise system—still beats warmly in the breast of Americans despite a wealth of empirical evidence to the contrary. "Every action I have taken tonight," Nixon told the nation on August 15, 1971, as he unfolded his game plan for price controls, "is designed to nurture and stimulate the competitive spirit." He spoke of the "challenge of competition," of "inner drive," and "economic and personal freedom." Nixon is not alone in abetting this archaic notion. Other Presidents have "nurtured" it, but Nixon may well be the only one in recent history who truly believes in it. It thrived in its purest form in the top ranks of the pre-Watergate White House staff—

* It is based on John Stuart Mill's 1848 "Law of Value": "Demand and supply, the quantity demanded and the quantity supplied, will be made equal. If unequal at any moment, competition equalizes them and the manner in which this is done is by an adjustment of the value. If the demand increases, the value rises; if the demand diminishes, the value falls; again if the supply falls off, the value rises; and falls, if the supply is increased."[15]

most were avid followers of Milton Friedman, who would like to see the federal government curtail almost all social services. Whatever the President believed, his "son of a bitch," as H. R. ("Bob") Haldeman cheerfully characterized his own role as chief of staff, believed it in spades, and whatever Haldeman believed, the rest of the White House cabal had damn well better believe. Nixon's economic czar, George P. Shultz, who doubled as Treasury Secretary and chairman of the President's Council on Economic Policy, is a doctrinaire free-market economist, which means that he believes in the law of supply and demand. His response to critics of Phase III was routine: "Some members of the financial committee seem to lack faith in economic freedom." Presidential Assistant Peter M. Flanigan, the executive director of the President's Council on International Economic Policy, has acquired a reputation as a fixer for big business, but he speaks with righteous emotion of the "spiritual values" inspired by the free-enterprise system.

In their philosophy, government-administered social programs violate the tenets of laissez faire and the benign work of competition in achieving the good (not necessarily humane) society. Every man is an island, a Rock of Gibraltar who must stand alone against all adversity. The good society does not function "by dependence on others." Our leader made it—what is wrong with you?

The "aggressive presidency" of Richard Nixon is an illusion. His economics is as passive as his compassion. His conversion to Lord John Maynard Keynes's hackneyed theories is typical of his passive conservatism. Events of the last two decades have shattered the delicate synthesis of economic theory now referred to by many economists as "post-Keynesian," and yet it is still popular in universities. Eminences like Paul Samuelson—Nobel Prize winner and millionaire—have taught two generations of potential policymakers that economic problems could largely be resolved by an expanding economy. Growth would solve even poverty. A rising GNP would bring higher material standards of living and spread its benefits to the poor. As the economist Daniel R. Fusfeld phrased it, "The rich might get richer, but the poor would get richer too. The paradigm sketched by the post-Keynesian synthesis was of a benign social order that would move mankind toward a better and more stable future."[16]

Keynesians believe in the viability of the free-enterprise system. In their model society, the antitrust laws protect the public against the evils of economic concentration; and where "natural" monopolies exist, such as in utilities or railroads, government agencies vigorously enforce the law.

While Keynes's followers have all but ignored the various forms of non-classical competition—the prevailing mode of price setting in concentrated industry—he himself recognized the existence of "administered or monopoly prices which are determined by other considerations besides marginal cost." Most college texts view administered prices as "imperfections of competition," naughty deviations from the norm like "the evils of monopoly" or "the curse of bigness" that deserve mention in passing.

Richard Nixon, the compulsive preemptor, who witnessed three Keynesian-inspired recessions in Eisenhower's Administration, went on to achieve the nightmare of simultaneous inflation and recession, an economic first in modern history. In other words, a planned recession with *rising* prices—a revolting development in anybody's economics, but particularly frustrating to nonclassical advocates who could only wring their hands as the President and his soothsayers stubbornly persisted in bucking the system instead of coping with its reality.

The reality, according to Gardiner C. Means, a seminal contributor in the literature of nonclassical competition, "is that in practically no industry is price determined by supply and demand; almost nowhere in industry is production pushed to the point where marginal cost approximates price. Even the concept of clearing the market has ceased to apply to commodities and services except in agriculture, which provides less than three percent of the gross national product, and in a few raw materials with an international market, like lead or zinc. The typical methods of marketing involve advertising rivalry and administered prices, neither of which can occur under classical competition."[17]

A typical example is the auto industry, which competes in styling and advertising, not in prices. Before General Motors introduced the annual model style change in 1923, there were eighty-eight automakers competing for that market. Twelve years later there were ten, and today there are four. Competition in concentrated industries is a gentleman's game. Everybody is allowed to compete—*vide* Madison Avenue—but no one is permitted to win.

As Means sees it, this "country backed into the twentieth century, and described its economy in terms of the mid-nineteenth-century types of enterprise, where there was a forest of enterprises in each industry, while the actual economy moved toward a high degree of economic concentration."[18] President Hoover believed in the free-enterprise premise that prices were highly flexible and that money had a direct effect on aggregate demand. The "system had a built-in 'cybernetic' mechanism that would automatically tend to bring economic recovery," which was always "just around the corner."

Franklin Roosevelt rejected the classical theory. His economists, including Means, demonstrated that "administered prices" were widespread and inflexible in the presence of changes in demand. "This relative inflexibility," said Means, "meant that when there was a general decline in demand, the primary effect in many industries was a drop in production and employment, rather than a drop in prices."[19] The inflexibility created unemployment instead of lower prices.

Advancing this thesis to today's problem, here is the way economist John M. Blair analyzes it in his monumental study, *Economic Concentration*, published in 1972:

> The action by President Nixon in freezing prices and wages on August 15, 1971, and subsequently establishing an elaborate system of price and wage controls was merely the logical response by government to the problems created by the growth in size and relative importance of the country's largest corporations. Had the economy been composed exclusively of small and medium-size enterprises, the need for the imposition of such controls when more than a quarter of the nation's plant capacity lay idle would never have arisen. It was the power of the large corporations to raise prices in the face of low and falling demand that set the stage for direct governmental intervention in the price-making process. And it was the repeated exercise of that power, whether triggered by an increase in labor (or other) costs or by an effort to widen profit margins, that forced the hand of a reluctant President.[20]

Make no mistake about it: the capitalistic system of free enterprise is dead.* It is as dead as the antitrust laws, which are as dead as Sherman and Clayton. The only difference is that nobody in the official family has had the heart to notify the sentimental Godfather in the Oval Office of its demise. Daniel Fusfeld has already written the eulogy:

> Within the theoretical and political framework of the post-Keynesian synthesis, solutions seemed to be present for all of the great economic problems of the postwar world. Liberals and reformers flocked to embrace it. Yet, underneath the surface it was the economics of the status quo, of anti-communism and the Cold War, of reform around the edges of the social and economic order.
>
> The post-Keynesian synthesis, in fact, reflected and provided justification for the concentration of power in American society in the years after

---

* Even the stock market, the prescient barometer of the economy, is far more responsive to myths and sex appeal for its irrational swings in prices than it is to the law of supply and demand.

World War II. The locus of governmental power had shifted to the federal government, and within the federal government to the Executive branch. With world power came a further concentration within the Executive branch itself, into the hands of the national security managers. This growing concentration of political power was paralleled by an increasing concentration of economic power in the business community. . . .

Big business and big government have been coming together in an increasingly symbiotic relationship. Big government needs big business because the giant corporation has become the key to effective functioning of the economy—witness the Penn Central and Lockheed rescue operations—and because big business is the source of the weaponry on which national power rests. Government, in turn, provides the environment of economic growth within which the large corporation flourishes, educates the managers and technicians that big enterprises need, maintains the framework for settlement of labor disputes, and seeks to maintain a system of world order conducive to the growth of international corporations. Concentrated economic and political power are allies.[21]

As we have seen, the role of government as sponsor, subsidizer, and protector of big business goes back to the Founding Fathers. Through the years the privileges have included roads and canals and harbors, land grants, protective tariffs and laws, and special tax benefits. It was money power that first persuaded the government to regulate against "ruinous" competition, stabilize markets, and guarantee a steady line of credit by creating the Interstate Commerce Commission, the Federal Trade Commission, the Federal Reserve System, and other agencies of liberal administrations. It was Herbert Hoover who created the Reconstruction Finance Corporation to rescue companies from bankruptcy, and Franklin Roosevelt who created the Securities and Exchange Commission to regulate the securities business. To help raise rock-bottom prices in the depths of the Great Depression, Roosevelt suspended the antitrust laws. Under NRA codes, business practices were fixed and sometimes prices too. Roosevelt castigated "chiselers" (competitors) in a fireside chat, and Frederick Lewis Allen, writing in *The Big Change*, concluded: "In short, while the New Deal did not abolish the market place as the determiner of values and rewards, it rigged the market plenty." The Supreme Court voided NRA in 1935 because it constituted an unlawful delegation of legislative power to the executive branch (a popular topic in 1973), not because it restrained competition. To establish "soft competition," the antitrust laws were amended in reverse to permit manufacturers of brand-named products to fix resale prices under so-called fair-trade laws enacted by the states.

In a *Time* essay, Donald M. Morrison wrote: "The most important incursion [on the free enterprise system] of all came when Congress passed the Employment Act of 1946, which once and for all committed the Government to take all necessary steps 'to promote maximum employment, production and purchasing power.' Using that broad political charter and the economic principles of John Maynard Keynes, every President since 1946 has wielded the powers of Government in attempts to keep the level of jobs high and prices low. Richard Nixon's controls are by far the most drastic moves toward that goal in the past quarter-century."[22]

Keynes's theory of fine-tuning the economy with deficit spending and other manipulation of fiscal and monetary levers finally came unglued in the 1960s when big business and big unions collided head-on, creating a cost-push strain of inflation—companies and unions used their market power to push up wages and prices at a time of high unemployment and low effective demand for goods. Then big government stepped in with its Phase II solution on how wages and profits were to be divided, another blurring of the presidential vision of unbridled competition.

Big government has laid a heavy hand on the throttle of Adam Smith's benign marketplace. The decisions of bureaucrats, Congress, and the White House have far more impact upon sales and profits than any competition between industries. But big business does not deserve all the blame. Big unions have been willing accessories in the death of capitalism. Their fingerprints are at the death scene of many small businesses forced into bankruptcy when they were unable to meet the wage requirements imposed on the giants.

As far back as twenty-five years ago, the House Judiciary Committee, in a report on a proposed bill to strengthen the antitrust laws, issued a prophetic warning: "The concentration of great economic power in a few corporations necessarily leads to the formation of large nation-wide labor unions. The development of the two necessarily leads to big bureaus in government to deal with them."[23]

How big is government? Measured in terms of the gross national product, the cost of government in 1929 amounted to less than 1 percent of the GNP. Today, with a $304-billion federal budget, it equals 25 percent. People living off the public sector now constitute a third of the whole economy.[24] Its size, however, has not improved its ability "to deal with them." John Blair, who spent sixteen years as chief economist for the Senate Judiciary Committee under Senators Estes Kefauver and Philip Hart, knows whereof he speaks when he says that the "law against existing monopolies has been permitted to lapse into a state of innocuous desuetude. The same is true of the law against sophisticated conspiracies and parallel pricing systems. The law against mergers, while effective against horizontal and vertical acquisitions, was virtually unused against the great wave of conglomerate mergers during the 1960's."[25]

For a sobering look into the cavernous reality of monopolistic and oligopolistic concentration, there is no better guide than the latest edition of the Census Bureau's report on concentration ratios, which is a sort of trustbuster's hunting guide—assuming that the breed is not extinct. Out of deference to money power, the Bureau protects the identity of individual companies by presenting their data in terms of the share of a market controlled by the four (anonymous) largest concerns. The report is nonetheless an impressive document when one considers that even classical economists concede that a true oligopoly exists when the Big Four in any product line control 50 percent or more of the market. The economist Edward H. Chamberlin, who introduced the Greek word "oligopoly" to economics, narrowed its meaning from the literal translation of "few to sell" to a few sellers "who in setting or changing their prices have to take into account the price reaction of competitors." In his book *The Theory of Monopolistic Competition*, Chamberlin explained the way oligopolistic pricing works:

> If each [oligopolist] seeks his maximum profit rationally and intelligently, he will realize that when there are only two or a few sellers his own move has a considerable effect upon his competitors, and this makes it idle to suppose that they will accept without retaliation the losses he forces upon them. Since the results of a cut by anyone are inevitably to decrease his own profits, no one will cut, and although the sellers are independent, the equilibrium result is the same as though there were a monopolistic agreement between them.[26]

Blair believes that "prices will tend to be more flexible under monopoly than under oligopoly. Eliminated is the communication problem faced by members of an oligopoly in reaching a consensus, either directly or indirectly, as to what a proper and appropriate price reduction would be. A monopolist is free to make a moderate price reduction without having to concern himself with the possibility that it might get out of hand, developing into a price war and a complete breakdown of the price structure. Nor need he concern himself with the question of whether a price decrease, which might be in his own best interest, would be less advantageous or even harmful to other oligopolists who have different cost-price relationships. And, being a monopolist, he is bound to be more sensitive than any oligopolist to public and governmental censure."[27]

When Donald I. Baker first saw the Census Bureau's report, he promised, "We are going to use it quite a lot." Baker was the chief of policy planning in the Justice Department's Antitrust Division. There was no question in his mind that in merger matters, especially, "concentration data are tremendously important, not only in the filed case but in our thinking process, picking which cases to bring and which to not."[28]

As the following table indicates, Baker found a wide selection to occupy his thinking process. The table presents only a partial listing of product lines where the Big Four shared 50 percent or more of the market in 1970. The percentages, along with figures on the total value of each market, are compared with similar data for 1947 or the closest available date:[29]

EXCERPT FROM THE CENSUS BUREAU'S "VALUE-OF-SHIPMENT
CONCENTRATION RATIOS"—NOVEMBER 1972

INDUSTRY	YEAR	TOTAL MARKET VALUE (million dollars)	BIG FOUR PERCENTAGE SHARE
Canned and cured seafoods	1970	660.9	53
	1963	452.5	38
Canned specialties	1970	1,634.2	66
	1963	1,169.3	67
Cereal preparations	1970	953.1	90
	1947	284.3	79
Wet corn milling	1970	830.5	64
	1947	460.0	77
Cookies and crackers	1970	1,545.6	59
	1963	1,150.1	59
Cane sugar refining	1970	1,583.8	59
	1963	1,271.2	63
Beet sugar	1970	726.6	65
	1947	263.9	68
Chocolate and cocoa products	1970	601.5	79
	1947	349.9	68
Chewing gum	1970	407.7	85
	1947	148.3	70

Industry	Year	Total Market Value (million dollars)	Big Four Percentage Share
Flavorings extracts and syrups	1970	1,318.8	61
	1947	313.6	50
Soybean oil mills	1970	2,609.9	56
	1947	585.7	44
Roasted coffee	1970	2,405.5	58
	1963	1,868.1	52
Cigarettes	1970	3,503.4	84
	1947	1,131.9	90
Cigars	1970	373.3	61
	1947	311.5	41
Tobacco stemming and redrying	1970	1,288.3	66
	1947	957.8	88
Weaving and finishing mills, wool	1970	770.4	54
	1963	1,010.7	51
Woven carpets and rugs	1970	102.1	80
	1963	120.0	67
Carpets and rugs	1970	200.6	76
	1963	29.6	32
Throwing and winding mills	1970	871.8	59
	1963	319.3	43
Thread mills	1970	300.7	64
	1947	154.3	65
Felt goods	1970	109.5	59
	1947	59.8	56
Tire cord and fabric	1970	597.1	83
	1963	375.7	79
Men's and boys' underwear	1970	160.9	54
	1947	49.8	47
Pressed and molded pulp goods	1970	160.1	73
	1947	16.2	86
Sanitary food containers	1970	1,226.4	50
	1963	905.9	52
Fiber cans, drums, & related material	1970	458.3	56
	1963	260.3	57
Greeting card publishing	1970	659.6	75
	1947	123.9	39

EXCERPT FROM THE CENSUS BUREAU'S "VALUE-OF-SHIPMENT
CONCENTRATION RATIOS"—NOVEMBER 1972

INDUSTRY	YEAR	TOTAL MARKET VALUE (million dollars)	BIG FOUR PERCENTAGE SHARE
Alkalies and chlorine	1970	660.3	71
	1947	208.6	70
Industrial gases	1970	665.0	75
	1947	93.5	83
Inorganic pigments	1970	635.2	56
	1954	371.4	67
Synthetic rubber	1970	992.1	64
	1954	361.1	53
Cellulosic man-made fibers	1967	902.8	86
	1963	731.8	82
Organic fibers, noncellulosic	1970	2,822.3	73
	1963	1,403.2	94
Medicinals and botanicals	1970	528.3	64
	1954	252.5	72
Soap and other detergents	1970	2,988.7	70
	1963	2,127.8	72
Gum and wood chemicals	1970	261.7	73
	1963	212.9	63
Explosives	1970	501.3	72
	1947	136.4	80
Petroleum and coal products	1970	119.0	82
	1954	58.5	58
Tires and inner tubes	1970	4,587.2	72
	1963	2,949.7	70
Rubber footwear	1970	515.0	58
	1947	198.7	81
Reclaimed rubber	1970	41.4	88
	1947	17.2	84
Industrial leather belting	1970	50.4	63
	1947	57.4	44
Flat glass	1970	669.6	92
	1954	370.5	90
Glass containers	1970	1,863.9	57
	1947	422.6	63

Industry	Year	Total Market Value (million dollars)	Big Four Percentage Share
Ceramic wall and floor tile	1970	154.1	56
	1963	164.7	49
Vitreous plumbing fixtures	1970	209.7	57
	1947	68.1	58
Vitreous china food utensils	1967	67.2	70
	1947	43.2	56
Fine earthenware food utensils	1970	48.7	62
	1947	72.1	38
Porcelain electrical supplies	1970	220.1	53
	1947	71.5	44
Gypsum products	1970	419.5	79
	1947	127.5	85
Asbestos products	1970	587.0	54
	1954	346.2	60
Mineral wool	1970	524.9	73
	1963	391.9	67
Electrometallurgical products	1970	515.7	77
	1947	150.9	88
Primary copper	1970	673.0	75
	1958	161.7	87
Primary zinc	1970	372.5	57
	1947	191.0	53
Primary nonferrous metals*	1970	492.3	61
	1958	96.5	62
Aluminum rolling and drawing	1970	3,454.3	57
	1963	2,196.4	68
Nonferrous forgings	1970	326.4	67
	1963	165.1	84
Metal cans	1970	3,912.7	72
	1947	678.9	78
Cutlery	1970	354.7	61
	1947	142.6	41
Collapsible tubes	1970	84.5	67
	1947	27.0	53
Steam engines and turbines	1970	1,791.0	77
	1963	616.4	93

* Not elsewhere classified.

EXCERPT FROM THE CENSUS BUREAU'S "VALUE-OF-SHIPMENT
CONCENTRATION RATIOS"—NOVEMBER 1972

INDUSTRY	YEAR	TOTAL MARKET VALUE (million dollars)	BIG FOUR PERCENTAGE SHARE
Internal combustion engines*	1970	2,673.7	51
	1963	1,473.6	49
Elevators and moving stairways	1970	467.8	61
	1947	101.8	63
Industrial trucks and tractors	1970	905.8	52
	1947	162.2	57
Ball and roller bearings	1970	1,314.6	54
	1947	365.6	62
Typewriters	1967	595.5	81
	1947	153.9	79
Electronic computing equipment	1970	2,816.9	57
	1967	1,926.4	66
Calculating and accounting machines	1970	887.9	83
	1967	707.8	83
Scales and balances	1970	157.3	62
	1963	98.5	69
Office machines*	1970	605.3	67
	1963	349.2	59
Automatic merchandising machines	1970	247.3	57
	1963	238.0	55
Commercial laundry equipment	1970	165.3	57
	1947	4.4	59
Measuring and dispensing pumps	1970	201.8	58
	1947	125.1	49
Transformers	1970	1,392.5	59
	1947	357.0	73
Switchgear and switchboard apparatus	1970	1,890.3	52
	1963	1,093.7	51
Motors and generators	1970	2,475.2	50
	1947	995.6	59
Carbon and graphite products	1970	369.6	87
	1947	68.7	87
Household cooking equipment	1970	656.5	61
	1963	473.5	51

* Not elsewhere classified.

Industry	Year	Total Market Value (million dollars)	Big Four Percentage Share
Household refrigerators and freezers	1970	2,022.1	82
	1963	1,306.5	74
Household laundry equipment	1970	1,081.0	83
	1947	442.3	40
Household vacuum cleaners	1970	346.1	79
	1963	175.4	81
Sewing machines	1970	135.9	80
	1947	97.0	77
Electric lamps	1970	891.5	92
	1947	203.2	92
Phonograph records	1970	437.5	62
	1947	110.2	79
Telephone and telegraph apparatus	1970	2,246.6	94
	1954	497.8	90
Electron tubes, receiving type	1970	252.8	95
	1963	321.1	87
Cathrode ray picture tubes	1970	519.1	88
	1963	269.1	91
Electron tubes, transmitting	1970	392.4	65
	1963	299.5	52
Storage batteries	1970	783.0	56
	1947	297.7	62
Primary batteries, dry and wet	1970	329.5	85
	1947	85.0	76
X-ray apparatus and tubes	1970	256.3	59
	1947	59.5	58
Engine electrical equipment	1970	1,569.9	66
	1947	357.8	67
Motor vehicles	1970	27,750.7	91
	1967	27,296.0	92
Motor vehicle parts and accessories	1970	13,073.2	58
	1967	11,623.8	60
Aircraft	1970	10,996.2	65
	1958	3,375.9	59
Aircraft engines and engine parts	1970	5,150.2	68
	1947	464.6	72

EXCERPT FROM THE CENSUS BUREAU'S "VALUE-OF-SHIPMENT
CONCENTRATION RATIOS"—NOVEMBER 1972

INDUSTRY	YEAR	TOTAL MARKET VALUE (million dollars)	BIG FOUR PERCENTAGE SHARE
Locomotives and parts	1967	689.6	97
	1947	355.2	91
Railroad and street cars	1970	2,159.6	52
	1947	726.2	56
Motorcycles, bicycles, and parts	1970	404.8	57
	1947	163.7	42
Automatic temperature controls	1970	642.2	56
	1963	527.4	55
Optical instruments and lenses	1970	431.5	54
	1958	89.0	46
Ophthalmic goods	1970	516.0	54
	1947	121.2	58
Photographic equipment and supplies	1970	4,372.5	75
	1947	457.5	77
Watches and clocks	1970	834.7	56
	1947	341.2	41
Watchcases	1970	54.0	70
	1947	44.5	40
Silverware and plated ware	1970	316.1	56
	1947	221.6	61
Children's vehicles, except bicycles	1970	122.1	52
	1947	85.8	30
Needles, pins, and fasteners	1970	531.4	51
	1947	147.2	39
Hard surface floor coverings	1970	232.6	92
	1947	173.3	80

One need not be an economist to appreciate the grim reality of the table above. The Census Bureau divided all manufactures into 422 individual product lines, and, as indicated above, 110 of them were under oligopolistic (or monopolistic—it is impossible to determine the share of individual companies) control by margins ranging from 50 percent to 97 percent. Another fifty-five industries fell within the range of 40 to 49 percent, and information on fifty others was "withheld to avoid disclosing figures for individual companies" or "data suppressed because some of the largest companies were approximately the same size as others not included in the sample." Megagiants like General Motors, DuPont, and ITT are represented in several categories, which means that the total number of companies involved is far smaller than the sample indicates. In fact, the growth of concentration has not only kept pace with that of gross income but surpasses it in most instances.

Without getting too involved in obscure hypotheses on oligopolistic price determination, it is worth noting that as far back as 1924, a General Motors vice president, Donaldson Brown, had already outlined the essentials of the formula in a series of articles for a business publication. Brown's method is known as "target return pricing," which is a variant of full-cost pricing—full costs plus an allowance for profit at some assumed volume of output. In Brown's words:

> An acceptable theory of pricing must be to gain over a protracted period of time a margin of profit which represents the highest attainable return commensurate with capital turnover and the enjoyment of wholesome expansion, with adequate regard to the economic consequences of fluctuating volume. *Thus the profit margin, translated into its salient characteristic rate of return on capital employed, is the logical yardstick by which to gauge the price of a commodity with regard to collateral circumstances affecting supply and demand.*[30]

The "profit margin" set by Brown was 20 percent. In 1955 the Brookings Institution concluded after a study of oligopolistic pricing methods used by large corporations that "target return on investment was probably the most commonly stressed of company pricing goals." It found that in "most cases the target return was regarded as a long-run objective . . . the average of the targets mentioned was about 10 percent to 15 percent (after taxes); only one was below 10 percent; and the highest was 20 percent."[31] Of course, on a before-tax basis, the figures would roughly be doubled. Note that the corporation tax is cleverly shifted to the consumer. GM, for example, prices its products to yield an amount generous enough to cover its corporate taxes *and* recapture the stockholders' investment in five years.

In his book *Economic Concentration*, Blair compared the target returns of five megagiants for a sixteen-year period (1953–68) with their actual profit rates in terms of rate of return (after taxes) on net worth— that is, stockholders' investment. Both General Motors and DuPont aimed at 20 percent and achieved 20.2 percent and 22.2 percent respectively;

U.S. Steel, Alcoa, and Standard Oil of New Jersey (Exxon) were respectively targeted at 8 percent, 10 percent, and 12 percent, and earned 8.4 percent, 9.5 percent, and 12.6 percent. The combined average target return for the five companies over the boom-and-bust sixteen-year period was 14.6 percent, with an actual return of 15.1 percent. This is economic power![32]

Money power grows bigger and stronger almost hourly. Thirty years ago thirteen family groups—including DuPonts, Mellons, Rockefellers, Fords, Pews, Dukes, Vanderbilts—owned more than 8 percent of the stock of the 200 largest corporations, which then controlled about half of the nation's corporate assets. Today the same economic power is lodged in the top 100 corporations, and the top 200 control about two-thirds of all corporate assets, a share equal to that held by the 1,000 largest in 1941. Between 1948 and 1968, these 200 corporations gobbled up more than 3,900 companies with combined assets in excess of $50 billion. By 1970 the 500 largest industrial corporations accounted for 65.4 of all industrial sales, 75.8 percent of all industrial profits, and 44.3 percent of all industrial employment. Statistics on growth concentration are simply overwhelming. For example, the total corporate profits of the 260 corporations with assets of over $1 billion has nearly doubled since 1959—from 28.4 percent of all corporate profits in that year to 54.6 percent in 1971. The other 1,700,000 corporations must divide up what is left.[33]

The compulsion for unlimited growth is pathological in big business. Normal growth, of course, is part of human nature. Most people naturally want to improve their lot, and many little men no doubt would like to be big men, but how many would chose to be Gargantua? For those who would, imagine what would happen if they could commensurately increase their size merely by eating other people. How long before a gang of skyscraper-sized giants would be stalking the land in gobbling competition—for survival! This is precisely what happens when a conglomerate goes on a merger binge. What might first begin as an exercise in greed soon turns into a death struggle. For in the peculiar arithmetic of conglomerate gobbling, 0 victims = 0 growth = death.

Of the many forces that have given impetus to conglomerate mergers, the incentives provided in the Federal tax system are not inconsiderable. In testimony before the Joint Economic Committee, Representative Charles Vanik, one of a handful of genuine tax reformers in Congress, lashed out at what he called this "horror story of tax avoidance." The tax code, he said, "has provided the launch-pad for the conglomerate growth of the

1960's." He estimated that the effective tax rate of the hundred largest corporations was 24.4 percent, about half of the nominal 48 percent rate. Small companies, however, paid an effective rate of 44 percent. Because of loopholes and subsidies, many giant corporations escape taxes completely. Summing up his findings, Vanik said:

> For the past twenty years our corporate powers have been driving the small manufacturers, businessmen, and shop owners out of business. We seem to have assumed that small business is obsolete and have equated bigness with efficiency and productivity. We have proceeded on a course of centralization—but we have moved beyond economics of people and into economics of monopoly.
>
> This trend has been no accident—the tax subsidies of the Internal Revenue Code have made a calculated attack on small businesses and provided incentives for large corporations to buy up small successful companies for tax and cash flow purposes. Often, even unsuccessful operations can be purchased and used to reduce the total liability of the larger purchasing company.
>
> Under certain definitions in section 368 of the tax code, large corporations purchase small operations permitting the seller to avoid any payments on capital gains from the sale. . . . As small operations find it hard to compete, the small owners find these offers hard to turn down. . . . In many, many cases, the purchase of smaller corporations by these industry giants has given them the opportunity to invest in tax shelters and in general to maximize their use of tax subsidies. . . . This is particularly true of an increasing number of the nation's largest banks and insurance companies. It is necessary for Congress to determine how some banks can enjoy a 16 percent tax rate. This indicates tremendous investments in tax-sheltered activities.[34]

It should be noted that most mergers are not the result of "efficient" giants coming to the rescue of failing midgets. Quite the contrary is true. Caspar W. Weinberger, when chairman of the Federal Trade Commission, discussed this problem before the Senate Subcommittee on Antitrust and Monopoly:

> In addition to the magnitude of the merger activity, a significant trend has developed in the quality of firms which are being acquired: the substantial proportion of the middle range of corporations are disappearing. Between 1948 and 1968 a total of over 1,200 manufacturing companies with assets of $10 million or more were acquired. Overwhelmingly these acquired companies have been well established, healthy firms making good profits. These are precisely the kinds of companies—the viable middle tier—which we would expect to grow in the normal way and thereafter present a real competitive challenge to the top corporations. The disap-

pearance of healthy, medium, middle-size firms is a matter of concern not only for competition but for social and political institutions.[35]

Nor is there any supportive evidence for the "synergism" notion of economists who theorize that any combination is better than its separate parts. Conglomerates, they argued, brought superior management to acquired companies. Yet private and government studies could find no corollary between size and efficiency. In fact, the Federal Trade Commission, normally an enthusiastic backer of big business, discovered that "recent and past experience of large, rapidly merging firms appears to warrant genuine skepticism as to the potential for management to capably operate large, far-flung diversified enterprises."[36]

The impetus behind the conglomerate frenzy of the 1960s had more to do with jazzing up stock prices and avoiding taxes than in fostering synergism. The go-go conglomerator was out to accumulate assets by whatever legal—and some not so legal—means available to him. More than one mad corporate cannibal dreamed of the day when he would be chairman of the board of Universal Everything, Inc., one vast conglomerate controlling the entire financial-manufacturing-retailing resources of the world's business. In 1969 alone, some 4,550 companies vanished into the limbo of statistics as stockholders traded their companies for packages of "funny money"—combinations of convertible preferreds, debentures, and warrants, as well as highly leveraged common stock. By 1969 the accounting techniques of conglomerators were beginning to worry the Federal Trade Commission:

> Many devices, of varying degrees of subtlety, enable merger-active companies to report substantial increases in earnings per share without improving operating efficiency. Among the most notable is the pool of interests method of accounting for business combinations. Despite two accounting studies recommending its abolition, pooling remains the most common method of accounting for merger effected by an exchange of voting stock. Under a pooling of interests, the book values of both businesses are simply added together. In this circumstance, the values prevailing at the time of acquisition need have no relation to the actual market value of the transaction. Through acquisition, an acquiring company can do what it cannot do through internal growth; that is, list the value of assets at less than real cost.[37]

Known as "dirty pooling," assets carried on the books of the acquired company at an unrealistically low value often yielded a windfall—a new wrinkle on J. P. Morgan's watered-stock strategy. Actually, it makes little difference to a conglomerator whether the gain in earnings is real or illusory as long as investors, who respond with Pavlovian devotion to the "p/e syndrome," believe it. The price-earnings ratio denotes the range between the price of a company's stock and its earnings; thus a stock earning $1 per share and selling for $20 has a p/e of 20 to 1. However, both these multiples are easily rigged by accountants, which makes the ratios more a product of imagination than of arithmetic.

The glamor stocks of Wall Street have always been those of companies with high price-earnings ratios—the wider the spread, the more attractive the bait. In recent years the mantle has fallen on companies pioneering in new technology—computers, aerospace, electronics, sophisticated defense gear—that conjure the mystique of "growth" industries in the mind of investors and consequently achieve spiraling p/e ratios. In the great numbers game of mergers, any time one of these companies plucks a target with a lower p/e it automatically improves its own ratio. The greater the differential in their ratios, the fewer shares it takes to swing the deal, and the greater is the increase in its earnings per share. What makes many mergers a dangerous numbers game is that they inflate stock prices long before they increase the economic values on which stock prices ultimately depend. This creates the false appearance of internal growth where none exists, often producing a chain-letter effect with predictable terminal states of indigestion.

A classic example is Litton Industries, Inc. It compounded its earnings per share at an average rate of 24 percent a year as it gobbled up seventy-nine companies between 1961 and 1968. Its 1967 year-end p/e was 43, while its common stock was selling at $109. The reversal began in 1968 and by mid-1969 its p/e had dropped to 18 and its market price to $33. Commenting on its bookkeeping practices, the FTC reported in 1969 that "Litton Industries suppressed $80 million in costs when it pooled with American Book and Jefferson Electric Company during its fiscal year ending July 31, 1967. These values, 'which presumably have produced or will produce revenues for Litton over the years, have not entered into such statements. As a result the corporation's earnings will be exaggerated over the years by the amount thus suppressed.' With pooling and other devices for cost suppression in widespread use, it is surprising that merger-active companies as a class do not inevitably indicate superior profitability by whatever measure used."[38]

Four years later, following a lengthy staff study of the performance of nine conglomerates* for the period 1960–68, the FTC charged that the way merged companies "effectively disappeared" from public view created a serious "information loss." Shareholders, competitors, and potential new competitors got an obscure view of performance data. The conglomerate's enticing p/e ratios, which had "led investors to develop unrealistic expectations for continued, geometric growth in earnings," might not have been as effective an inducement if the "internal workings" of the companies had not been "hidden from public view." Pointing to Litton, the report suggested that shareholders would have been "less inclined to believe" that Litton's management was "infallible" in continuously lifting earnings if they had been able to see the internal problem areas, such as Ingalls Shipbuilding, a unit in deep production troubles with Navy contracts.[39] After two hundred pages, the commission, retreating into typical bureaucratese, arrived at a routine inconclusive conclusion: "Perhaps the most valuable contribution of this study is that it points out how little is known about the operations of conglomerate firms. There is a serious 'information gap' between the information available to managers of conglomerates and that available to the public."[40] A staff report for a House antitrust subcommittee was more direct in expressing its contempt for Litton's bookkeeping techniques. It charged that the company had created an "image of technical and organizational superiority by developing flamboyant sham into an art."[41]

The two wizards behind the "flamboyant sham" at Litton were its chairman, Charles ("Tex") Thornton, and its president, Roy L. Ash, both joint founders, who learned their bookkeeping at Hughes Aircraft. Ash, who had served in the Air Force with Thornton, was working as acting comptroller under Thornton in 1952 when Noah Dietrich, Howard Hughes's roving alter ego for thirty years, discovered there had been "an overcrediting of the inventory accounts. The result was a corresponding increase in the recorded costs of a $200,000,000 government contract." Ash and Thornton disputed Dietrich's claim, and Hughes supported them with his customary procrastinating tactic until Dietrich, backed by a report

---

* In addition to Litton, the survey covered the following companies: Gulf & Western Industries, Inc.; International Telephone & Telegraph Corporation (ITT), Ling-Temco-Vought, Inc. (currently LTV Corporation); Textron, Inc.; FMC Corporation; Rapid-American Corporation; Norton Simon, Inc.; and White Consolidated Industries, Inc. As a group they acquired 348 companies that boosted their assets from $2 billion to $17 billion.

from an outside auditing firm, warned Hughes of a "ruinous scandal" unless he immediately notified the Air Force. The upshot was that Hughes was asked to refund $43 million to the government.*[42] A few months later Thornton and Ash left Hughes and bought a small firm, Electro-Dynamics Corporation, that grew into the giant defense-oriented Litton Industries. It may be significant to note that Litton executives and board members contributed $156,000 to the 1968 Republican campaign, more than any other defense, space, or nuclear contractor will admit. Was it a coincidence that Litton climbed from fourteenth-ranked defense contractor in 1968 to ninth two years later, or that a special tax bill in 1969 permitted Litton executives an extra four years to claim the benefits of tax-evading stock options? By their own admission, Ash's personal contributions to Nixon's campaigns ran into "five figures in 1968 and 1972" and Thornton donated $46,000 in 1972.[43]

In December 1972, Nixon appointed Roy Ash director of the Office of Management and Budget, which meant that this go-go artist would preside over this nation's $250-billion budget, with direct supervision over all defense spending. Stockholders would remember that a year prior to his appointment, Ash was predicting that Litton's earnings for fiscal 1972 would surpass the $50 million of the previous year. With almost identical sales of $2.5 billion, the result was a plunge of $2.5 million into the red—the indigestion was getting more severe if not yet terminal.† At this writing, Litton is nearly three years behind on its Army and Navy contracts, and it is estimated that its mismanagement may result in cost overruns as high as $3 billion, or almost 100 percent of the original contract figures. In 1972, when Litton fell two years behind schedule on eight container ships it was building for Farrell Lines and American President Lines, it had to pay the two shipping companies a total of $5.5 million to compensate for the delays.[44]

But in defense contracts, instead of being penalized for inefficiency, companies are rewarded with cost overruns. Few men have a better understanding of the inner machinations of this system than Roy Ash. On a visit

---

* See Chapter Four, page 259, for more details.

† By late 1973 the company's stock was locked in the $6 to $8 range, with a p/e of seven. Its convertible preference stock, which sold for $127 a share in 1967, and was guaranteed to be redeemed at $62.05 in 1973, had dropped to $16 a share in January 1973. This resulted in a class-action suit, charging Litton, along with Thornton and Ash as defendants, with fraud, breach of contract, and violation of the California Corporate Securities Act. If all remedies sought were granted, damages would run over $100 million.

to Washington in June 1972, to explain why Litton was two years behind schedule on its contract to build Navy landing helicopter assault ships (LHAs), a Navy memorandum notes that Ash opened the meeting with the comment that "based on consultations with his lawyers," Litton and the Navy had to choose one of eight alternatives, ranging from outright termination of the LHA contract to continuing "cost reimbursement payment basis beyond the 40-month current contract limit," which was when payments based only upon physical progress were to begin. Ash said that "if Litton were required to convert to a physical progress payment basis in September 1972," the company "would be unable to perform due to the impact on an already tenuous cash flow position." Maintaining the offensive, Ash charged "that some in the Navy have a built-in sense of self-righteousness concerning Litton's performance, and that the Navy would have to relax this view if Litton is expected to proceed with the contract." And if the Navy's action did not satisfy him, Ash would simply go "to the White House to explain the problem" to his good friend Nixon.[45] Six months later Ash was one of the most powerful men *in* the White House.

In a study requested by Senator William Proxmire, the General Accounting Office reported in November 1973 that there were indications of possible criminal activity by Litton officials at the Ingalls division. The auditors found evidence of conflict of interest, awards of contracts to other than low bidders and "preaward" activities to influence contractor selection. Summing up the report, Proxmire said it disclosed "the most appalling and improper behavior by officials and employees of Litton and by its subcontractors."

Several investigations were in progress in 1973. Ash was under SEC scrutiny for dumping $2.6 million worth of Litton stock in 1970, shortly before it became public knowledge that the firm's shipbuilding plant was in trouble, and the price of the stock dropped by half. Another probe by a federal grand jury in San Diego was digging into charges that a subsidiary, Litton Systems, Inc., was not paying full duties on computer equipment assembled at a Mexican factory. United States Attorney Harry Steward was accused of delaying the case nearly fifteen months. This was not an unusual tactic for Steward. During the ITT investigation, Attorney General Richard Kleindienst reluctantly conceded that Steward had improperly intervened in a criminal investigation of contributions to Nixon's 1968 election campaign. On October 29, 1973, the grand jury returned an indictment against Litton Systems, Inc., and four of its officers on charges of defrauding the government of $216,000 in customs duties on computer parts imported from Mexico and Singapore by using false customs entries and invoices. In still another action in November 1973, four top executives, including the general manager, of Litton's Business Telephone Systems division were indicted on charges of bribery and conspiracy in the procurement of a $500,000 contract from the San Mateo (California) Community College District.[46]

The merger frenzy, which had collapsed in the recession of 1969–70 —at a cost in billions of dollars to duped stockholders—was showing signs of rebounding in 1972. With spectacular corporate profits in 1972 and a 1,000-plus Dow-Jones average, businessmen, having regained their confidence, were once again getting very bullish about acquisitions. There were all those fat profits to be sheltered from the revenuer. Many grounded high-fliers, with huge tax-loss carry-forwards, were looking for mates with offsetting huge profits, or vice versa. The tax code, as Representative Vanik charged before the Joint Economic Committee, provides irresistible incentive for mergers. For example, in the dirty-pooling method, which accounted for about 60 percent of all mergers in 1968, the conglomerate buys with an exchange of its stock, either common or convertible preferred, and the acquired company is not obliged to pay capital-gains taxes until the securities are sold. Good will, which is not tax-deductible and must come wholly out of earnings, invariably ends up being charged to various assets or some euphemism such as "intangibles." The conglomerate simply adds up the assets and liabilities of both, with no consideration to the fact that it paid more than the book value or market price for the acquired stock—the value of the merged company's assets is understated and immediate earnings per share overstated. Dirty pooling is a two-edged sword: besides cheating the government out of its fair share of taxes, it enhances dubious earnings records into very real increases in stock prices.

Thanks to the peculiar economics of mergers, it is not even important for a raider to have cash for acquisitions. Funny money—that is, debt securities such as debentures and warrants—sweetened with plenty of good will is usually all it takes to seduce stockholders into parting with their securities. In a *Fortune* article, George C. Demas, a lawyer specializing in mergers, explained how it works: "A company takes over a company by using that company's own money. That is, the acquirer eventually pays off its I.O.U.'s [debentures and warrants] with the assets of the acquired company. In a sense, the weaker the acquiring company, the more it can offer, because dilution is no problem for it. Its important consideration is the assets of the company to be acquired."[47] The raider times his offer so that the dividends on the shares he is tendered fall to him. These dividends then become intercompany dividends, which are 85 percent tax-deductible. The interest on the debt securities that the raider offers comes out as a tax-deductible business expense. If he is clever enough, the tax-deductible dividends will more than offset the tax-deductible interest charges, and he will reap manna both ways. With the corporate tax rate at 48 percent, the raider gets the government to assume nearly half of his interest payments, whereas dividends on his own stock in a pooling exchange can only be paid out of after-tax earnings. The tax code encourages not only conglomerates but any company to escape into debt. By leveraging its capital—borrowing to buy up its own stock instead of issuing new stock—a company is able to increase earnings on equity. And by buying its own stock with debentures, a company reduces the cost of servicing its capital by substituting tax-deductible interest for nondeductible dividends. There are conglomerators that consider the "releveraging" of capital as the "real restructuring" of U.S. business. Writing in *Fortune*, Gilbert Burck summed it up this way:

> There is something to be said for increasing the proportion of debt in corporate capitalizations. The policy of confining debt to a certain prudent ratio dates back to the time when business cycles were steep and sudden, and when all too often heavy fixed charges squeezed companies into bankruptcy. But today there is the corporate income tax, which roughly halves the cost of carrying debt. Today the country is committed to a policy of "full" employment, which in practice tends to be accompanied by considerable inflation—and one lesson of inflation is that going into debt to buy assets can be a way of acquiring them cheaply. Today some of the most respectable and even conservative corporations have successfully taken on relatively heavy debt loads, and glamorized their shares in the bargain.[48]

With the 1969 recession and the fall from grace of the conglomerate, even Attorney General John N. Mitchell felt obliged to join the hounds: "The danger that super-concentration poses to our economic, political and social structure cannot be overestimated. . . . The Department of Justice may very well oppose any merger among the top 200 manufacturing firms . . . [or] by one of the top manufacturing firms of any leading producer in any concentrated industry." As further evidence of his deep concern, Mitchell had selected an attorney with the "right" slant to head the Department's Antitrust Division: Richard W. McLaren, who learned his trade (and politics) defending corporations in antitrust suits in that prairie citadel of political corruption, Chicago.

It is not clear whether McLaren misread his boss's message or whether the press misread McLaren's. At any rate, McLaren started out like a gangbuster, with lawsuits challenging several large mergers, including a couple of important clients of the Wall Street law firm of Mudge, Rose, Guthrie and Alexander, which before 1969 included two other illustrious partners: Mitchell and Nixon. McLaren's first mistake—or was it his first strategic move?—was to slap an injunction on the merger between the pharmaceutical houses of Warner-Lambert and Parke, Davis & Company. It would be strange indeed if McLaren had not been told that the octogenarian Elmer H. Bobst, chairman emeritus of Warner-Lambert, was not only a client of Mudge Rose but also an intimate friend of the President. In fact, it was Bobst who arranged for Nixon to be installed as senior partner of Mudge Rose following Nixon's traumatic defeat for governor of California in 1962. Bobst took him for a cruise on his yacht *Alisa* and ever since they have enjoyed a "father-son" relationship. Bobst, who is "Uncle Elmer" to Nixon's daughters (he set up trust funds for the girls), lost no time in repairing to the Oval Office to vent his spleen on McLaren.[49]

Twice summoned to the White House, McLaren, as one man working on the merger reported, "was professionally embarrassed." His alleged response was one of righteous anger: "If that happens again, I'm going to resign and tell everybody why."[50] Meanwhile, Mitchell, being a man of impeccable propriety, disqualified himself and invested his faithful deputy, Richard Kleindienst, with the charge. On the closing day of the merger, Kleindienst overruled McLaren, who was denied even the face-saving grace of delaying it a few days. The merger boosted the value of Bobst's stock holdings by $18 million.

For his second (strategic?) mistake, McLaren took on the International Telephone & Telegraph Corporation for a contest that would become a full-dress rehearsal for the Watergate *Götterdämmerung*. This was a wild Sunday punch for a second-rung bureaucrat already baptized under White House fire. To begin with, besides being a client of Mudge Rose, ITT was the world's largest conglomerate. In terms of old-line Eastern money power, ITT was a vulgar upstart, *nouveau riche* and power-mad, the king of the corporate cannibals. Between 1959, the date Harold S. Geneen became its go-go president,* and 1971, ITT gobbled up 250 or more domestic and foreign companies, climbing from eightieth in rank to ninth in *Fortune's* directory of the five hundred largest industrial corpora-

---

* For his aggressive services, Geneen received $812,000 a year, which made him the best-paid executive in the nation.

tions, with world sales stretching upward to $8 billion. What is even more astounding about this grandiose multiplication is that it was pulled off with funny money—highly leveraged common and convertible preferred shares —in dirty-pooling matings that created the longest-surviving chain letter in corporate history.

In its merger with Hartford Fire Insurance Company, one of three McLaren was to challenge,* ITT exchanged shares worth about $1.5 billion for shares valued at $1 billion, paying $500 million in goodwill but accepting the assets at book value, all of it with the approval of the Internal Revenue Service, which had issued a special pre-merger ruling exempting Hartford stockholders from capital-gains tax liabilities, saving them many millions of dollars. Thus ITT got the much-needed billion-dollar annual cash flow of the insurance company to finance its chain-letter gobbling of past and future mergers. Within months after its acquisition of Hartford's debt-free balance sheet, as opposed to its own high debt ratio, the bond-rating services elevated ITT up from a Baa rating to A. Through highly controversial fiscal legerdemain, Hartford's portfolio wealth was soon finding its way into ITT's net income. Hartford netted a total of $105 million in 1971, a fact ITT prominently recorded on its income statement, but the fact that $36 million of it came from capital gains was not recorded.[51] In the opinion of Raymond Dirks, the insurance analyst who was instrumental in exposing the massive swindle at Equity Funding Corporation, "ITT's whole objective was to demonstrate growth and profits not only for the shareholders but to the financial community. The firm wants to convince Wall Street that it is extremely stable, that it is growing at a stable rate and that it is demonstrating good management controls. When it is able to convince the financial community of this, it raises the price of the stock. The higher the price of the stock the cheaper the acquisitions."[52]

By the first quarter of 1973, ITT had reported *record* earnings for fifty-four successive quarters, yet its price-earnings ratio registered at a stolid 12. The typical reaction from analysts was "It looks good, but it doesn't smell good." Anthony Sampson, the author of *The Sovereign State of ITT*, analyzed the stench:

---

* The other two were Automatic Canteen, the nation's largest food vendor, and Grinnell Corporation, the nation's largest supplier of fire-prevention (sprinkler) systems. Hartford was the nation's second largest fire-insurance company. The ITT board, obviously not too worried over Mitchell's public stance against conglomeration, approved twenty-two domestic and eleven foreign acquisitions early in 1969.

But the steady increase in earnings was not as remarkable as it looked. The separate profits and losses of each industry—whether hotels, rented cars, or house-building—were no longer discernible in the consolidated balance sheet, and the breakdown of sales showed only the most generalized headings: "Defense and Space Programs" or "Consumer Services." The concoction of the corporate accounts thus became a challenge to the art of a master accountant; the profits and losses among companies and countries could be quietly set off against each other without anyone knowing. Sales of Japanese securities, of German factories, or of Sheraton hotels could all be jumbled together under the heading "Miscellaneous Income"; and by holding back income from one year, or bringing it forward from the next year, the graph of increased earnings could be kept miraculously steady. . . . Nearly all Geneen's acquisitions were made through pooling of interests. According to a report of a Congressional committee, ITT suppressed through this process $744,328,000 in costs incurred on its acquisitions through 1968. These suppressions, representing the hidden values of the merged companies, could then be surfaced by Geneen whenever they were needed, without anyone outside the inner circle becoming aware of it. It was not so surprising that he could maintain a continuous record growth.[53]

Nor is it surprising that ITT can evade paying any Federal corporate income taxes. As a conglomerate and a multinational corporation (see Chapter Two), in Sampson's words, it has been "exceptionally able to defend itself against taxation, like a nomadic millionaire. Soon after he became president, Geneen held a special conference of his top lawyers and accountants, to discuss how ITT could best make use of the tax havens outside the United States to cut down its American taxes. The experts were doubtful, but Geneen insisted that ways could be found; and ever since then, ITT has surprised other companies' accountants by the smallness of its taxes."[54]

In the clutter of accounting methods, it was easy for ITT to refute McGovern's campaign charges that SEC records showed that the company paid no federal income taxes in 1968, 1969, and 1970. What ITT reports to the SEC and to the IRS are two entirely different stories. In describing his own frustration over accounting methods to the Joint Economic Committee, Representative Vanik said:

> The confusion, complexity and secrecy which shrouds corporate tax and financial reporting is nearly indescribable. . . . Corporations, through complex reporting procedures [many in violation of SEC and IRS regulations], have made it impossible—in all too many cases—to accurately estimate, from public sources, the actual Federal income tax paid for any particular year. The annual reports are a mirage of ambiguous statements

that lead the stockholders to believe that business is better and profits are improving. The tax statements of these same companies to Internal Revenue often illustrate a completely different picture that reduces their profit figure, which in effect, reduces their total tax figure. Like the medieval European peasants, for their stockholder they wear their wedding clothes, for the tax man, they wear rags.[55]

Whenever it is questioned about its federal tax payments, ITT's routine reply that "some taxes are paid by subsidiaries" is as evasive as its tax practices. For example, in 1970 it filed a consolidated return with its domestic subsidiaries and reported a before-tax income to its shareholders of almost $430 million, but according to its annual report to the SEC no corporate tax was due on the consolidated return. The story was identical in 1971, with income of $410 million, which included Hartford Insurance Group—no tax was paid. Vanik reported that ITT sold stock to an overseas bank in 1970 and the foreign buyer almost immediately resold the shares to a fund in this country. "This fund already held some of ITT's pension money. This sale to a foreign bank, rather than directly to the fund, appears to have been motivated by the desire to increase its foreign tax credit benefits."[56]

A class-action suit filed against ITT in 1972 provides another glimpse at the ease with which ITT manipulates money and government agencies. Alleging that ITT got its favorable tax ruling by giving the IRS false information, the suit asks that the merger with Hartford be rescinded and that shareholders be awarded damages to cover potential tax liability. Early in 1973, according to the *Wall Street Journal*, the IRS was reconsidering its ruling on grounds that "IRS staff members handling the matter could have been confused by the extreme complexity of the contract with Mediobanca" of Milan, Italy. It seems that a month before it announced its plan to acquire Hartford, ITT had acquired 1.7 million Hartford shares for cash from various sources, a violation of the tax-exemption ruling which stipulated that cash could not be used. ITT agreed to sell those shares "unconditionally to an unrelated third party" before going ahead with the merger. As it developed, Mediobanca, to which ITT sold the stock, was not as "unrelated" to ITT as IRS criteria required. The Securities and Exchange Commission later discovered that ITT's investment banker, Lazard Frères & Company, "exercised a degree of control" over Mediobanca's handling and disposition of the ITT shares. Also the bank and Lazard Frères divided a $2.2-million fee that ITT paid for Lazard Frères' role in the transaction. One of the Lazard Frères partners, Felix

Rohatyn, was an ITT director and executive committee member. As required by law, the stakes of owning the Hartford stock never passed to Mediobanca but remained with ITT. "Informed sources," said the *Wall Street Journal*, "speculated ITT may have withheld certain details about the agreement that would have made it clearer. These sources believe ITT's overall motive was to keep the original Hartford block of shares out of unfriendly hands that might oppose the merger, while at the same time satisfying the IRS it was obeying the law."[57]

The law, as represented by Attorney General Mitchell in 1969, went in for more deception. Mitchell again disqualified himself, leaving the hatchet work to Kleindienst, who plunged ahead by refusing McLaren's request to enjoin ITT from merging with Automatic Canteen. Kleindienst, according to a Nader report, was responding to White House pressure following a campaign directed at "White House staff close to Nixon" by "ITT, aided by New York investment houses which would greatly profit if the merger were completed . . ." The suit was filed after the merger was consummated, said the Nader report, only because McLaren was able to convince the White House of the strength of his conviction.

Emboldened by his success, McLaren filed two more actions against ITT in August 1969 to prevent its acquisition of Grinnell and Hartford, as well as several suits against other conglomerates. His hard-nosed attitude toward conglomerates was belabored in financial journals. They pointed to the "dubious" wording of Section 7 of the Clayton Act, as amended and strengthened in 1950 by the Celler-Kefauver bill. A *Fortune* editorial, lambasting McLaren, charged that "The weird wording of the Clayton Act facilitates prosecution by prophecy. It forbids mergers where 'the effect of such acquisition may be substantially to lessen competition, or to tend to create a monopoly.' " Calling attention to the words "may be" and "tend," the editorial suggested that McLaren was equating "potential guilt" with "actual guilt."[58]

McLaren was more cautious about intruding upon the entrenched economic power of industrial megagiants. "After all, this is a very difficult and delicate situation," he conceded in an interview with the Associated Press. "If you're going to break up companies, you've got to consider the effect on the labor force, the national defense and other factors. It's just not something you rush into." He disagreed with the recommendations made by President Johnson's antitrust task force that an attack should be launched against oligopolies. As to President Nixon's own antitrust task force, which had recommended that no action be taken against conglomerate mergers, McLaren said the task force's message "has been widely misinterpreted. I don't think they meant to say we shouldn't attack conglomerate mergers that are anticompetitive." The AP said that "McLaren also was embarrassed when the Commerce Department, with Nixon's backing, endorsed a bill to give antitrust immunity to joint newspaper operations after he [McLaren] had testified against it."[59]

As was expected, McLaren lost the first rounds with ITT in the trial courts, but his prospects for success on appeal before the Supreme Court were conceded even by ITT attorney Lawrence G. Walsh—the Antitrust Division had never lost a merger case in the Supreme Court since the Celler-Kefauver amendment.* Briefs on appeal of the cases to the high court were filed and public pronouncements of their impending success were widely circulated in the press. Meanwhile, behind the scenes, as the political game reached its climax (McLaren secretly agreed to an out-of-court settlement on June 18, 1971), ITT officials began quietly unloading thousands of shares of ITT stock. As it turned out, the settlement caused a $7-a-share drop in the stock's price on August 2, the first trading day after the public announcement that ITT would keep Hartford but would have to shed six smaller companies.[60]

Three months later McLaren returned to Chicago as a federal district judge. "I thoroughly enjoyed my three years," he told *Newsweek*. "But I wanted the bench and I had to get going. I'll be fifty-four next spring." He said he had received support from the White House in his "activist" role and added, "The Attorney General was a very solid backer-upper." But *Newsweek* indicated that the White House was happy to see him go. "McLaren inflicted us with a lot of battle damage," one White House aide confided. "He didn't pick up signals well. President Nixon didn't have to nominate him to that judgeship."[61] That, in light of subsequent events, is debatable.

On February 29, 1972, long after the press had forgotten about the ITT-Hartford merger, Jack Anderson dropped a stink bomb under John Mitchell's desk that threatened to permeate the very matrix of the Republican hierarchy. Anderson simply published a confidential memorandum written by ITT lobbyist-in-chief Dita Beard to her boss, Vice President William R. Merriam, dated June 25, 1971—precisely one week after McLaren had agreed to the settlement. The subject was the "San Diego Convention":

---

* This situation has changed with the "Nixon court."

I just had a long talk with EJG [Edward J. ("Ned") Gerrity, ITT senior vice president for corporate relations, in charge of a $100-million annual budget]. I'm so sorry that we got that call from the White House. I thought you and I had agreed very thoroughly that under no circumstances would anyone in this office discuss with anyone our participating in the Convention, including me. Other than permitting John Mitchell, Ed Reinecke [lieutenant governor of California], Bob Haldeman and Nixon (besides [Bob] Wilson [Republican Representative from San Diego], of course) *no one* has known from whom that 400 thousand commitment had come. You can't imagine how many queries I've had from friends about this situation and I have in each and every case denied knowledge of any kind. It would be wise for all of us here to continue to do that, regardless of from whom any questions come, White House or whoever. John Mitchell has certainly kept it on the higher level only, we should be able to do the same.

I was afraid the discussion about the three hundred/four hundred thousand commitment would come up soon. If you remember, I suggested that we all stay out of that, other than the fact that I told you I had heard Hal [President Geneen] up the original amount.

Now I understand from Ned that both he and you are upset about the decision to make it four hundred [thousand] in services. Believe me, this is not what Hal said. Just after I talked with Ned, Wilson called me to report on his meeting with Hal. Hal at no time told Wilson that our donation would be in services ONLY. In fact, quite the contrary. There would be very little cash involved, but certainly some. I am convinced, because of several conversations with Louie [Louis B. Nunn, former governor of Kentucky] re Mitchell, that our noble commitment has gone a long way toward our negotiations on the mergers eventually coming out as Hal wants them. Certainly the President has told Mitchell to see that things are worked out fairly. It is still only McLaren's mickey-mouse we are suffering.

We all know Hal and his big mouth! But this is one time he cannot tell you and Ned one thing and Wilson (and me) another!

I hope, dear Bill, that all of this can be reconciled—between Hal and Wilson—if all of us in this office remain totally ignorant of any commitment ITT has made to anyone. If it gets too much publicity, you can believe our negotiations with Justice will wind up shot down. Mitchell is definitely helping us, but cannot let it be known. Please destroy this, huh?

For a while, as Dita Beard later recalled, "Our Washington and New York offices were Panicsville." But as anyone knows who read a newspaper in 1972, the bomb was safely defused by the Senate Judiciary Committee. Even at that moment the Beard memo involved numerous felonies and a dozen serious suspects, including the Attorney General, five high White House staff members, an ex-governor, a lieutenant governor, a

Congressman, several ITT big shots, some Republican National Committee muckamucks, and, of course, the mickey-mousing McLaren and his Justice Department helpers. The fact that the "sole official response to massive pressure from the press was a probe of Kleindienst by the Senate Judiciary Committee," said James Boyd in a *Washington Monthly* article, was "testimony to artifice of a consummate order."[62]

The explanation given was that Kleindienst, who was not mentioned in the memo and who had already been confirmed as Attorney General by the Judiciary Committee, wanted to clear away any dark cloud that might shadow the path to his new office. The big question, as Kleindienst saw it, concerned whether he had lied to Democratic National Committee Chairman Larry O'Brien when he wrote him that McLaren had "handled and negotiated exclusively" the ITT settlements. Suddenly that dark cloud hung in the balance of his use of the word "exclusively."

Culpable plotters breathed a sigh of relief as Kleindienst gallantly stepped into the breach as a stouthearted scapegoat. If he were reconfirmed, all would be vindicated; if not, the culprit would have to return to private law practice, an instant superlawyer with grateful friends in all the right places. The real stroke of genius was dropping the decision in the lap of the Judiciary Committee. As Boyd points out in his article:

> Ten of its 15 members have themselves been the victims of exposés by Jack Anderson: [James O.] Eastland for profiteering from agricultural subsidies; [John L.] McClellan for using his political clout to promote his banking interests; [Roman L.] Hruska for investments in pornographic movies and for being in bed with the drug industry; [Hiram L.] Fong for nepotism and for having as his chief aide a man who used that office to solicit a $100,000 bribe; [Hugh] Scott for aid and comfort to the influence peddler, Julius Klein; [Robert C.] Byrd for junketeering around the world at taxpayers' expense; [Edward J.] Gurney for taking contributions from neo-Nazi fronts; [Marlow W.] Cook for sabotaging campaign-spending reform; [Birch] Bayh for vacationing in Florida at the expense of special interests; [Edward M.] Kennedy for Chappaquiddick. It would be difficult to conceive of a jury with as much reason for personal hostility toward a claimant as this group had with regard to Anderson, whose professional reputation was now on the line.

It is beyond the scope of this book to go into all the posturing, weeping, whimpering, cursing, sabotage, subornation, vilification, perjury, conspiracies, faked documents, faked heart attack, faked amnesia (samples of Kleindienst's elusive memory: "I don't recall . . . it made no impression on my memory . . . I've got the haziest recollection . . . it just doesn't stand out in my memory"), threats, contradictions, backtracking (after "refreshing our memory" or "consulting our records"), double-dealing, reversals, buck-passing, document shredding, character assassination, and lies upon lies upon lies—that whole Wagnerian soap opera conducted by some of Dita Beard's "bunch of little bums," as she once publicly derided U.S. Senators. While they scraped timidly at her bedside —she lay hospitalized at death's door until the heat was off—she was disavowing her memo as a forgery, "a false and salacious document," and Roman Hruska was damning the hearings as "this smear-a-day campaign" brought on "because of a spurious document dredged up by the Louella Parsons of the political world." Hugh Scott, the Republicans' chief flannel-mouth (one not afraid to appear ridiculous for the sake of the party), blamed the Democrats, whom he described as somewhat akin to Weathermen—"militants on the Committee who are knee-deep in nitpicking." It was all "political jackassery." Even Murray Chotiner, Nixon's veteran masterminder, who would later secure Teamsters boss Jimmy Hoffa's presidential pardon, surfaced to suggest that "ITT might have been planning to make a $500,000 contribution to the Democratic Party." Robert Dole said the Democrats had failed to pay their phone bill to AT&T, forgetting that Republicans were likewise in arrears. An effort was made to link Anderson with Senator Kennedy in a plot "to discredit government officials," and of conducting "a purely political game" to inflict "cruel harassment" that was the direct cause of Dita Beard's heart condition.

The key defense was a blanket denial of any wrongdoing. Kleindienst, Mitchell, and Peter Flanigan, Nixon's liaison with Wall Street money power, assumed the public stand that they had nothing to do with anything —period. This posture had to be modified, of course, as new evidence cropped up. "Your credibility has gone from a hundred to damn near zero," Senator Bayh told Ed Reinecke at one point. And when Reinecke's aide later permitted himself a sheepish grin, Bayh exploded: "You smile, sir, but I have this feeling in my gut. And if my impression is right . . . you've committed perjury." Strong words for a congressional hearing. Usually testimony "tends to contradict sworn testimony," or there may be a "misstatement under oath," acts that in other tribunals are classified under felony.*

Kleindienst stuck to his statement that he had neither negotiated nor handled the ITT cases even when it was shown that his office had been a

---

* It is intriguing to speculate on the fate of Jack Anderson if the Judiciary Committee ever caught him in a "misstatement under oath."

beehive of ITT activity. He had conferences with John Ryan, a Washington attorney described in testimony as a "listening post" for ITT, and with Walsh, Rohatyn, Flanigan, Solicitor General Erwin Griswold, and Richard J. Ramsden, a Wall Street financial expert whose "brilliant" economic analysis finally persuaded McLaren to drop the ITT cases. It was true, Kleindienst admitted, that he had conferred, but he had not negotiated or handled. McLaren's position was that the cases had been handled strictly by the book; the Administration had in no way pressured him. He knew nothing—none of them did—about the $400,000 ITT had donated for the GOP convention.* He had no recollection of ever discussing the cases with Flanigan or anyone else at the White House. Then, says Boyd, "down around the righteous McLaren's ears came tumbling all the facts about Kleindienst's many interventions: a meeting presided over by Kleindienst where ITT officials lectured McLaren and his aides on the horrors Mc-Laren's announced course of action would cause; a delay in filing suit in the Supreme Court, arranged by Kleindienst and Griswold without a by-your-leave to McLaren; the recruitment and instruction of Ramsden, Mc-Laren's key financial consultant in the case, not by McLaren [as he first testified], but by Flanigan. McLaren readjusted to the facts. He confessed to the known ('It now appears that I requested Mr. Flanigan to secure the services of Mr. Ramsden'). Only he could know what pressures caused him to reverse his position on the ITT matter, and he wasn't admitting to any."

Flanigan said he merely served as a "conduit" in obtaining Ramsden's report because McLaren did not know how to get in touch with the analyst. He did admit, however, giving Ramsden an unlabeled ITT memo on the case to work from—and then delivering the report personally to Mc-Laren. On the basis of Ramsden's twelve-page report, prepared in two or three days for a reported fee of $242, the committee was asked to believe that McLaren withdrew cases on which the Supreme Court was ready to hear argument. In the opinion of Harlan M. Blake, a law professor at Columbia University, "The badly needed clarification of the law that its [Supreme Court] opinion probably would have provided almost certainly

---

* When the $400,000 got too hot to keep, Reinecke, one of the prime movers in arranging the contribution, decided that "You have got to play it super-clean and super-safe and just say, 'Thanks, but no thanks.'" When his boss, Governor Ronald Reagan, made it official, the San Diego convention came up some $300,000 short. With the San Diego millionaire C. Arnolt Smith already in financial trouble, the local boosters were unable to come up with enough new funds to swing it. Of course by then the Nixon forces were anxious for a new image and they quickly switched the convention to Miami.

would have embodied Richard McLaren's most important contribution in public service":

> The reasons given by McLaren to the Judiciary Committee for chang-ing his mind . . . were (1) that ITT's financial condition—its debt capacity and credit rating—would be jeopardized if it were denied access to the $1 billion annual cash flow of Hartford; (2) that the adverse effect on the stock market, and on the owners of ITT and Hartford shares, might be severe; and (3) that the effect on the international balance of payments might be adverse. None of these reasons, as McLaren presumably knew, could be taken seriously. . . . Most of [Ramsden's report] reads like the kind of research report on a company put out every day by the major brokerage houses. In addition, these are the kinds of arguments that every antitrust lawyer knows by heart and makes in desperation when his argu-ments "on the merits" are not strong enough to prevail. They are likely to be effective only with men who lack experience in the ways of the world, or who are looking for an excuse to be persuaded.[63]

As the hearings came to an end, Senator John V. Tunney exclaimed in defeat: "We're still left with the question of what turned McLaren around. As a result of these hearings, we'll never know the answer . . ." It was all so idiotically transparent, and yet it worked beautifully. Boyd explained the strategy:

> The idea is to bring the public to a point of bewilderment at which people will say, "it's all political." At that point the investigation can be ended by a party-line vote, with minimum backlash from the public. And so it was.
>
> One errs to think that the lawyer in such a case as this expects any of his tactics to achieve a clear victory, or the totality of them to *convince* the public or the tribunal. Only half-victories are sought, and the goal is not to convince, but to confuse and then to weary. The Senate majority does not want to devour Kleindienst or Flanigan or ITT; that would be cannibalism. It will do so only to assuage an angry public. To become angry, the public must be able to concentrate; it cannot focus if, for every ball it identifies in the air, two more are thrown up. It apprehends that it is being purposely confused, but it wearies anyway, and is at length diverted to other things. And so, however preposterous the stunts may look indi-vidually—the three Beard memos to confuse the real one, the opposed medical reports, the conflicting document analyses, the ATT gift to the Democrats to balance the ITT gift to the Republicans, explanations that a thousand conventions are "bought" each year all over America—when viewed collectively, they succeed. [The participants] . . . may look idiotic for a day, when their ball is shot down, but their embarrassment is tem-porary and their victory comes at length when the crowd tires of keeping track.

To add to the idiocy of the circus, the Judiciary Committee asked Kleindienst to review the transcript of the ITT hearings for possible perjury.* It is doubtful that the new Attorney General had much time to devote to this task because he was soon embroiled in another imbroglio—Watergate. Adhering to the earlier script, his department had no "credible evidence" that federal laws were violated during "alleged" acts of political sabotage against the Democrats by members of the Committee to Re-elect the President. There was no special investigation underway, he told newsmen a week before the election, adding that such an inquiry did not appear warranted. "The full matter," he said, "if there is one, has gotten such an exposure in some parts of the media—like I say, based on hearsay, rumor, speculation—that the public attention to it, if any does exist, is probably a great deterrent" to the operation of any other would-be "sabotage squad." "I do not believe that we have an investigation with respect to the alleged sabotage because as of right now, any evidence that has come to us would not indicate the violation of a federal law. That doesn't mean that we wouldn't [investigate] if that kind of evidence would be made available."[64]

Before Kleindienst was to get that evidence handed to him along with his head, more ITT memos were to appear in the form of an internal working paper prepared by the Securities and Exchange Commission from thirty-four boxes of ITT letters and memos the commission had subpoenaed during its two-year investigation of the company's insider practices.† SEC Chairman William J. Casey sat quietly on his treasure trove throughout the hearings, and when Senators Kennedy, Bayh, Hart, Burdick, and Tunney asked for the commission's files on April 19, 1972, Casey declined, saying he would not supply raw investigative files to anyone outside his agency. In late September Casey received requests from both Senator Kennedy and Representative Harley O. Staggers, chairman of the House Committee on Interstate and Foreign Commerce and of its special investigative subcommittee that oversees operation of the SEC. Two weeks later Casey notified Staggers that the Justice Department had "asked that our files on this matter be referred to them," a request he had felt obliged to honor. Casey's executive assistant, Charles Whitman, told Staggers' committee that the transfer was made on October 6—thirty-four

---

* The committee reconfirmed him by a vote of 11 to 4—Kennedy, Tunney, Bayh, and Quentin N. Burdick voted nay.

† The SEC suit against ITT and two of its top executives was filed in June 1972 and lasted two days. It was settled by consent agreement—the defendants, without conceding past violations, agreed not to violate securities laws in the future.

boxes were moved by panel truck while a "politically sensitive" folder, which included confidential letters from ITT to the White House, was hand-delivered to Kleindienst's deputy. Asked under oath if he had initiated the contact with the Justice Department, Casey replied, "No. . . . The Justice Department initiated the contact with me."[65]

But as it came out in the hearings, Casey had presented his dilemma to the President's counsel, John W. Dean III (later a key Watergate witness), who assured Casey that he could safely give his files to the Justice Department without fear of legal reprisal by Congress. Casey had then asked Justice if it wanted the documents, and within three days everything was with the Attorney General. Pinned down in the cross-examination, Casey finally revealed what had been troubling him. "There's no need to be naïve," he said. "There were press reports that Senator Kennedy was interested in getting selected documents. The commission recognized this was a particularly bad time [one month before the election] for documents to be floating around."

"The peculiar aspect of this case," Representative John E. Moss said, "is the fact that the chairman of the commission resorted to falsehood." Shortly thereafter Casey left the SEC to become Under Secretary of State for Economic Affairs. By having delivered the corpus to Justice beforehand, Casey could leave his old post secure in the knowledge that the SEC investigation of ITT had come a cropper in mid-course—it looked almost as if the chairman had stolen a page out of McLaren's Mickey Mouse book. His only oversight lay in not destroying the notes of his staff.*[66]

A piecing of a few fragments from the SEC summary of ITT documents since released by congressional committees makes it abundantly clear that ITT mounted a monumental effort to enlist Administration support in its campaign to turn McLaren around. The SEC summary, for example, begins with a paraphrase of a letter from Gerrity to Vice President Agnew, thanking him for setting up a meeting with McLaren:

> Letter dated August 7, 1970 . . . to Spiro Agnew from Ned Gerrity. The memo consists of a thank you letter concerning an attached memo

* At the time of his nomination to the SEC, which is the agency charged with upholding the nation's securities laws, Casey was involved in two civil actions alleging breach of these securities laws. Both cases were settled out of court. Just before he left the SEC to join the State Department, he was again named in a lawsuit on charges of mismanagement of corporate funds. The case involved the bankruptcy of Multiponics Inc., which sustained losses of more than $6 million while Casey was a director and his law firm represented the company. The outcome is pending at this writing, but the federal judge in charge of the case believes that one transaction was so questionable that "this may be a matter that should be referred to the Department of Justice."[67]

and a suggestion that Mitchell get the facts relating to ITT's position to MacClaren [*sic*]. . . . It also indicates there was a friendly session between Geneen and Mitchell prior to the meeting with MacClaren (Agnew).* It indicates that Mitchell told Geneen that Nixon was not opposed to the merger. He believed that mergers were good. Mitchell apparently said that ITT had not been sued because bigness is bad. . . . It also indicates that Geneen and Merriam met with [White House aide Charles] Colson and [John] Ehrlichman that same day.

Mitchell repeatedly testified before the Judiciary Committee that he never discussed antitrust matters with Nixon: "The President has never talked to me about any antitrust case that was in the department." Questioned about his meeting with Geneen, Mitchell testified, "I assented to the meeting on the express condition that the pending ITT litigation would not be discussed. Mr. Geneen agreed to this condition. The pending ITT litigation was not discussed at this meeting."

Memo dated August 24, 1970. Ryan to Merriam, relates to a meeting on August 19, 1970 with [Commerce Secretary] Maurice Stans. There is an indication that Kleindienst must "follow through" and that this "may be the break" that ITT is looking for. There is a rhetorical question asked, "how will MacClaren react, or how good a Republican is MacClaren?"

It takes little imagination to follow the script. To strengthen its position further, ITT approached Treasury Secretary John B. Connally, whose law firm had collected fees from ITT—at least before his appointment. A summary of an April 27, 1971, letter from Merriam to Connally indicates that Merriam and Geneen were certain that White House aide (later Commerce Secretary) Peter Peterson and Connally had been "instrumental in the delay"—this referred to the delay in filing the appeal in the Supreme Court arranged by Kleindienst and Griswold. The letter advised Connally of a meeting between Peterson and Geneen on April 16. Then on April 26, in a memo to Peterson, Merriam bemoaned the tough new antitrust legislation being proposed by Emanuel Celler, chairman of the House Judiciary Committee: "We've alerted Clark MacGregor [then chief White House lobbyist] to this matter and we plan to generate some speeches ridiculing the chairman's proposals."† A few days later Merriam expressed the hope to Peterson that "Paul and the two Johns can convince the department that merger policy as now practiced would be suicidal for the economy of the country." The "Paul" was McCracken, former chair-

---

* The summary does not make clear if Agnew participated in the meeting, only that he arranged it.
† Celler was defeated for renomination in 1972.

man of the President's Council of Economic Advisers, and the "Johns" were Mitchell and Ehrlichman.[68]

Even when out partying, Hal Geneen was minding the store. One ITT internal memo shows the degree of his homework. Titled "Roger's [sic] Party," it refers to an outing tentatively planned for September 1970 at the Maryland farm of Rogers C. B. Morton, then Republican national chairman and later elevated to Interior Secretary. Those invited included the Mitchells, the Agnews, the Bryce Harlows and Peter Flanigans, Congressmen Bob Wilson and Gerald Ford, Senator Peter Dominick, Postmaster General Winton Blount, and Hal and June Geneen. "Ned [Gerrity] asked that we put together a poop sheet for Mr. & Mrs. Geneen," a public relations man advises his boss in ITT's Washington office, "which will include not only brief bio's of the men but also their wives for June; facts about Morton's farm, a fairly complete bio on Mitchell and his recent accomplishments in other areas such as crime, drugs, etc.; some detail on the new Post Office plan; and the general information as to the type of clothes to wear, planned activities, etc."

The revelations from the SEC summary of ITT documents were soon corroborated by yet another confidential memorandum. The new memo was disclosed by chief counsel Samuel Dash during the first week of August 1973 when H. R. Haldeman was testifying before the Watergate committee. Dated March 30, 1972—at the height of the Judiciary Committee hearings on Kleindienst's fitness to be Attorney General—and written by former White House aide Charles W. Colson, the memo to Haldeman was a summary of documents possibly floating around that could "directly involve" the President in the ITT settlement. Pointing to the contradictions between sworn testimony and the evidence in the files, Colson described his own efforts to keep the information secret. "There is the possibility of serious additional exposure by the continuation of this controversy," he warned, and then listed some "embarrassing" memos, pinpointing the most dangerous among them. A memo dated April 1969 went from Kleindienst and McLaren to Ehrlichman in response to an Ehrlichman request "with respect to the rationale for bringing the case against ITT in the first place." An April 1970 memo told McLaren that "Ehrlichman had discussed his meeting with Geneen with the A.G. [Mitchell]" and suggested that "Mitchell could give McLaren 'more specific' guidance." A September 1970 memo from Ehrlichman to Mitchell was described by Colson as "referring to an 'understanding' with Geneen and complaining of McLaren's actions." Colson cited an internal ITT memo that he said the SEC did not have which "follows the 1970 Agnew meeting and suggests that Kleindienst is the key man to pressure McLaren, implying that the Vice President would implement this action." He added that "we believe that all copies of this have been destroyed." Further, a "Dear Ted" memo sent to Agnew by Gerrity "tends to contradict John Mitchell's testimony because it outlines Mitchell's agreement to talk to McLaren following Mitchell's meeting with Geneen in August 1970." Referring to the SEC files, Colson warned that if they were disclosed they would "undermine" testimony before the Judiciary Committee by Solicitor General Erwin Griswold that it was he who had decided against taking the ITT case to the Supreme Court. Colson said, "Correspondence to Connally and Peterson credits the delay in Justice's filing of the appeal to the Supreme Court in the Grinnell case to direct intervention by Peterson and Connally."

As to Mitchell, Colson said that he received a copy of a June 30, 1971, memo from then White House Communications Chief Herbert G. Klein to Haldeman "setting forth the $400,000 arrangement with ITT." The antitrust settlement was reached about a month later. "This memo," Colson noted, "put the A.G. on constructive notice at least of the ITT commitment at that time and before the settlement, facts which he has denied under oath." Elsewhere in his memo, Colson referred to assurances Ehrlichman gave Geneen "that the President had 'instructed' the Justice Department on policy, but in the context of these hearings, that revelation would lay this case on the President's doorstep." This fear was reinforced by a May 5, 1971, memo from Ehrlichman to Mitchell "alluding to discussions between the President and the A.G. as to the 'agreed upon ends' in the resolution of the ITT case and asking the A.G. whether Ehrlichman would work directly with McLaren or through Mitchell. There is also a memo to the President in the same time period," though Colson did not explain its precise contents, which "would once again contradict Mitchell's testimony and more importantly directly involve the President. We know we have control of all the copies of this, but we don't have control of the original Ehrlichman memo to the A.G."

Colson was trying to get "control" of all memos that could cause trouble. His strategy was to set up a system of "deniability"—witnesses were not allowed to review memos so that if asked they could truthfully say they had forgotten them. "Neither Kleindienst, Mitchell nor Mardian [Robert Mardian, then Assistant Attorney General] know of the potential danger," Colson told Haldeman. "I have deliberately not told Kleindienst or Mitchell since both may be recalled as witnesses." As to the ITT memos then held by Casey at the SEC, Colson noted, "We believe that all copies of this have been destroyed." He was particularly worried about the Klein memo: "We don't know whether we have recovered all the copies. In short, despite a search this memo could be lying around anywhere at 1701 [Pennsylvania Avenue, headquarters for the Committee to Re-elect the President]."* One intriguing aspect of Colson's memo is that it conflicts with his own testimony of June 14, 1973, before the House Commerce Investigations Subcommittee. Colson told the panel he had no knowledge of the shredding of ITT documents, while his memo refers in two places to shredded or destroyed documents. Although he testified that it was White House policy to refer any matter involving the Justice Department to the White House counsel's office, the memo details several communications between Haldeman, Ehrlichman, Mitchell, Kleindienst, and McLaren.[69]

It was only natural that the disclosures would spark a revival of congressional interest. Responding to the Colson memo, Senator John V. Tunney called on the Justice Department to reinstitute its antitrust action against ITT. "The memo suggests that the ITT settlements were nothing more than a fraud on the public," Tunney said. "It makes it clear that the fix was in." Attorney General Elliot L. Richardson, "on advice from antitrust officials," declined to reopen the case. In a letter to Tunney, Richardson said, "I do not believe that a reopening of the judgment at this time would give the government any greater relief than it obtained under the settlement," and he added that "the public interest would not be served and could well be injured by reopening these cases."[70] Since the cast of characters was almost identical,† it was left finally to Watergate special prosecutor Archibald Cox to pursue the matter in terms of election improprieties. But that possibility came to an abrupt end on October 20, 1973, on that memorable weekend of the great massacre that saw Nixon chop down Cox, Richardson, and William D. Ruckelshaus like so much deadwood. A few days later the New York *Times* reported that Nixon had

---

* In a *Washington Monthly* article, Timothy H. Ingram has suggested that the Watergate "burglars' main purpose was to find out whether Larry O'Brien had the missing ITT memoranda. If the documents were as damning as Colson feared, they might provide the issue that could allow even George McGovern to defeat Richard Nixon." This is a valid hypothesis, particularly since John Dean, who was intimately involved in the ITT settlement, did not even mention ITT in his testimony.

† Including G. Gordon Liddy, who spirited Dita Beard out of town, and CIA-wigged E. Howard Hunt, who according to Colson was dispatched to her bedside in a Denver hospital to reassure the lobbyist that "her many friends in Washington would not hold it against her that she had contrived the memo," if she would only "tell the truth" about it. Her lawyer later issued a statement claiming the memo was a fake.[71]

personally instructed Kleindienst not to appeal lower-court rulings in ITT antitrust cases. The first contact was made by John Ehrlichman, who "abruptly called and stated that the President directed me not to file the appeal" in the Canteen Corporation case, Kleindienst recalled. "I informed him that we had determined to make the appeal, and that he should so inform the President. Minutes later the President called me and, without any discussion, ordered me to drop the appeal." Nixon came down hard on the tough side, baring his imperial claws. "Listen, you son of a bitch," Kleindienst quoted him, "don't you understand the English language? Don't appeal that goddam case, and that's all there is to it." Kleindienst was not intimidated. "Immediately thereafter," he said, "I sent word to the President that if he persisted in that direction I would be compelled to submit my resignation."

This was not what Kleindienst testified to before the Senate Judiciary Committee. Then he was adamant in denying outside pressure: "In the discharge of my responsibilities as the acting attorney general in these cases, I was not interfered with by anybody at the White House, I was not importuned, I was not pressured, I was not directed, I did not have conferences with respect to what I should or should not do." When Senator Bayh asked him if he had "ever talked to anybody down at the White House," he replied, "No, sir. No, sir, to the best of my recollection. . . . So far as consulting about, reporting to, getting directions from, going into depth on these matters or any other antitrust case, *I have never had that experience*." Asked by Senator Kennedy why he had requested a delay of the appeal, Kleindienst said, "I do not recollect why that extension was asked." McLaren's recollection was equally fuzzy until Kennedy demanded, "You did not really care, then, if there was an extension of time, so who did care? . . . Could I have an answer to that? Who did care whether there was an extension . . . ?" McLaren replied weakly that he supposed that ITT's lawyers cared.

The matter of Kleindienst's perjury raises the question of why the President and his staff did not come forward when they heard his testimony. It appears that the Administration was willing to overlook perjury on the part of the man it chose as this nation's chief law enforcement officer. Writer Jimmy Breslin says that a "courthouse is a place where people lie to survive." And nobody, says Breslin, "understands this better than the Nixon outfit."

Obviously, ITT was able to recruit the Administration's top hounds to ferret out the fox. The only surprise left is that McLaren is not a Supreme Court justice.* If the ITT fiasco proves anything at all to those involved, it is that dress rehearsals, as Watergate dramatically confirms, are more effective on the stage because actors get a chance to memorize their lines before exposing their talent to the public.

Few Presidents have better understood the pervasive influence of money power over the nation's economy and politics than Woodrow Wilson. He knew where the greatest concentration of it was nesting. "The great monopoly in this country," he observed in 1911 when governor of New Jersey, "is the money monopoly." In his inaugural address twenty-two years later, F.D.R. would exult that "the money changers have fled from their high seats in the temple." Roosevelt's enthusiasm led him to naïve optimism. Money power holds the mortgage on the temple. Depressions and panics present only momentary setbacks. The original contract remains intact. Nothing ever changes it, except, of course, that the equity grows larger and the payments higher with time.

Few men are better qualified to document this fact than Wright Patman, the fiery Texas populist who has been grappling with the "evils" of the "Eastern" bank establishment for most of his forty-five years in Congress. Patman has long been convinced that the Federal Reserve Board, which claims to be independent of Congress and the President, is not independent of the banking industry that it is mandated to govern. He finds that the manipulation of the interest rate by major banks is tantamount to a conspiracy—the moment one major bank raises its rate, the others promptly fall in line. Patman once told former Fed chairman William McChesney Martin, who disagreed with his conspiracy theory, that the banks "have done that for thirty-five years and nobody that could not see at least a little conspiracy in that, I do not think could track an elephant in the snow."[73]

It was Patman who led the fight in 1932, his fourth year in the House, to impeach Andrew Mellon "for high crimes" arising from conflicts of interest. Patman presented his case before the Judiciary Committee, while across the table Mellon sat with a battery of thirteen attorneys. Instead of

---

* On the other hand, he did considerably better than one colleague who tried to stop General Motors from polluting the Hudson River. GM's special counsel, Lawrence Walsh, hand-carried a letter of complaint to Kleindienst and the prosecutor was fired. Walsh, who was also involved in the ITT cases, no doubt knows that there are different strokes for different folks.[72]

answering the charges, Mellon resigned his Treasury post; Hoover made him ambassador to the Court of St. James's, and the committee dropped the impeachment proceedings.

"There are two ways to have power in this town," Patman shrewdly observed about Washington. "One is to do favors for people and the other is to light fires under them."[74] In his positions as chairman of both the House Banking and Currency Committee and the Subcommittee on Small Business,* there is little question which stratagem Patman took in his lifelong tilting at money power, as represented in major financial institutions. But it has been a solitary effort, and the result has been more to inconvenience than to impede. There are good reasons for this. A 1971 survey by the National Committee for an Effective Congress revealed that one hundred Representatives held stock in or were officials of some financial institution—some actually doubled as bank presidents and vice presidents. An even dozen served on Patman's Banking Committee, and nine of them had at some time accepted bank loans at special reduced rates.[75]

Nonetheless, Patman has occupied a rare vantage point from which to monitor the growth and prosperity of money power. As he wrote in 1973:

> Under a massive public relations cover, large commercial banks have crept into every crevice of the American economy. They control assets of nearly one trillion dollars, more than four times the assets controlled by life insurance companies and nearly twenty times the assets controlled by mutual funds. . . .
>
> The concentration of economic resources of this magnitude would be serious enough by itself, but the problem is aggravated by the multiple functions and powers of commercial banks. Banks are quasi-monopolies. Their basic product, credit, is the lifeblood of commerce; their power to grant or withhold this commodity is a source of built-in intimidation that hangs over all areas of the economy. But credit is only part of the story. Commercial banks have developed new muscle through the accumulation of wealth in their trust departments and through the control by bank holding companies of nonbanking enterprises. These three sources of control—credit, trust departments and holding companies—are strengthened by the web of interlocking directorships between these banks and more than 6500 companies. More than 750 of these interlocks were with 286 of the 500 largest industrial companies in the United States. The same pattern of interlocking relationships was discovered between these 49 banks and each of the 50 largest merchandising, transportation, utility and life insurance companies. It is absurd to think that banks ignore the holdings of their trust departments when they face major loan decisions. It

* The subcommittee has conducted a ten-year probe of foundations. See Chapter Four.

is equally absurd to think that a bank will ignore the needs of its holding company subsidiaries.[76]

Nothing better illustrates the incestuous unions of large corporations than the handholding found in boardrooms of major financial institutions. Granted that the Clayton Act prohibits corporate incest in specific language that points up the "potential for evil" of such relationships, the practice has been flourishing for a long time. In November 1972, fifty-eight years after the enactment of the Clayton Act, the Federal Trade Commission, the agency charged with its enforcement, was finally spurred by social activists and irate stockholders into issuing a notice that it now considered it illegal for a director to serve on the boards of two competing companies, even if they appear to be selling different products—for example, copper and aluminum compete in tubing for heat and electrical conductors. But there is nothing in the FTC ruling to prevent directors of competing firms from cohabiting in the boardroom of a large bank they mutually control.

Take, for instance, the Chase Manhattan Bank,* the very cradle of money power, with roots going back to 1799 and currently the third largest commercial bank in the world. It has $28 billion in assets, $23 billion in deposits, and nearly two hundred domestic offices and more than a hundred in foreign countries.†[77] It is the Rockefeller bank, with David Rockefeller, a grandson of the old robber baron, as its board chairman. The mating that goes on in David's boardroom, the scrambling of blue-chip portfolios—none are bluer—violates the spirit if not the letter of the antitrust laws and any pretense to the myth of free enterprise as well.

On its board sit directors—in many instances chairmen—of the following companies: Standard Oil of New Jersey (Exxon), Standard Oil of Indiana, Atlantic Richfield, Allied Chemical, General Motors, Uniroyal, Chrysler, Anaconda Copper and Aluminum, American Smelting and Refining, International Smelting and Refining, International Nickel, R. J. Reynolds Industries, FMC Farm Machinery Corporation, United Aircraft, Aerospace Corporation, Pan American Airways, Whirlpool, General Electric, Hewlett-Packard Electronics, American Telephone and Telegraph, CBS, Charter Oak Life Insurance, Travelers Insurance, Metropolitan Life, Mutual Benefit Life, Jefferson Life, American Express, General Foods, Kellogg's, Macy's, Federated Department Stores, International Paper, and

---

* It is owned by its holding company, Chase Manhattan Corporation.

† Earnings growth for banks is twice as much overseas as it is at home. See Chapter Two.

Scott Paper.[78] Twenty-three of Chase's directors hold 105 other commercial directorships in major corporations and fifty-four noncommercial trusteeships, many on the board of wealthy foundations. (See Chapter Four.

Fourteen banks and eighteen of the largest oil companies have overlapping directorates, and similar ties exist between oil firms and insurance companies, investment banking firms and foundations. Links between the oil industry and financial institutions through control of stock and employee benefit funds "provide the means for cozy relationships which perpetuate oil company management in power," an economic study concluded. Sponsored by the Marine Engineers Beneficial Association, the 160-page report issued by Stanley H. Ruttenberg & Associates* focused primarily on the links between oil companies and banks, public utilities, foundations, accounting firms and the coal, gas and uranium industries, what it called "the sinews of control." Ruttenberg found that the eight biggest international oil companies are engaged in at least 154 joint ventures throughout the world. These include pipeline systems and joint bidding on offshore oil leases. In most cases, "the one basic motive is the desire to avoid competition." Directors of major oil companies sit on the boards of coal companies, public utilities, pipeline companies and similar businesses. Seven accounting firms audit the books of the twenty-nine largest U.S. oil companies and provide related services. They can be a binding force to create "a uniform climate of opinion and practice within which corporate policies are formed."

Financial institutions are directly involved in the energy crisis, a subject treated at some length in Chapter Three. When Secretary of Transportation Claude Brinegar was questioned by a Senate committee about the lack of independent data on the energy crisis, he urged the senators to turn to the Chase Manhattan Bank which publishes three financial reports on the oil business. What Brinegar forgot to mention was that the bank's principal source of information is the oil industry. It compiles statistics from about thirty petroleum companies which, according to a Chase spokesman, are "practically all" bank clients.

A Senate survey found that seven New York banks held 17 percent of the stock in Mobil Oil, the nation's sixth-largest firm; 10.8 percent of Atlantic Richfield, 11.8 percent of Continental Oil, and 2.7 percent of

---

* Ruttenberg headed the Manpower Administration under President Kennedy and was an assistant secretary of labor under President Johnson.

Ashland Oil. Those four were the only oil companies that complied with the committee's request for information.

The survey found that banks held significant amounts of stock in energy and broadcasting companies but that the true owners of the shares were hidden in special "nominee" or "street name" accounts. For example, four banks held 25 percent of the stock voted at the 1972 annual meeting of Burlington Northern, an energy-transportation conglomerate, but none of the banks was listed by the company in its reports to the Interstate Commerce Commission and the Securities and Exchange Commission. Only six of Burlington Northern's 30 largest stockholders were real companies. The other 24 were "nominees"—persons designated to represent a bank or company in name only. The committee's report concluded that "nominee accounts . . . may well put banks in position to use the voting authority provided in such accounts to influence corporate decisions and policy." The result "is a massive coverup of the extent to which holdings of stock have become concentrated in the hands of very few institutional investors, especially banks."

Is it any wonder that large corporations in competitive fields behave more like partners than rivals? The airline industry, for example, which is subsidized and protected by public revenues as a quasi-public utility, is controlled and exploited by ten financial institutions and three aircraft manufacturers: Bank of America, First National City Bank (Citibank), Chase Manhattan (the one, two, three biggest in the world), Bankers Trust, Morgan Guaranty, Prudential Insurance, Metropolitan Life, Equitable Life Assurance, Connecticut General Life, Aetna Life, Boeing, McDonnell Douglas, and General Electric.[79]

Their holdings in most cases are hidden in secret trust arrangements camouflaged under street names* on stockholder lists. In fact, Chase Manhattan is the only financial institution that publicly admits to any ownership of large blocks of airline stock. As of December 1971, it publicly held more than six million shares (directly or through nominees) in four major airlines. It held 6.5 percent of the stock in TWA, 9 percent in Eastern, 8.4 percent in National, and 7.5 percent in American. It also secretly held more than 6 percent of the stock in United, Northwest, and Western. Eleven other airlines were in debt to Chase to the tune of more than $400 million. Chase's participation included lease transactions in-

---

* Chase uses twenty-four (Wall) street names to disguise its holdings. Some of these names are Clint, Cudd, Egger, Gooss, Gunn, Kane, and Ring.

volving ninety-six jet aircraft currently operated by airlines. Excluding investment in airline stock, Chase's holdings in various airlines were equivalent to 16 percent of the assets of Allegheny, 17 percent of Seaboard World, 17 percent of Southern Airways, 10 percent of Ozark, 11 percent of Frontier, 15 percent of Texas International, and 7 percent of Eastern.[80]

Even this represents only one column of the balance sheet. Chase owns 8.7 percent of Boeing, which in turn owns 6 percent of Braniff, 7 percent of Continental, 7 percent of United, and 17 percent of Wien Consolidated Airlines. Chase owns 5 percent of Aetna Life, which in turn has invested some $250 million in airlines, including participation in lease transactions of sixty-one jet aircraft; Aetna's investments constitute 16 percent of the assets of Northeast, 11 percent of North Central, 10 percent of Ozark, 11 percent of Texas International, 5 percent of Allegheny, and 9 percent of Piedmont. Metropolitan Life, a director of Chase, has invested $639 million in airlines and jet aircraft, which constitute more than 10 percent of the assets of American, TWA, and United, and about 5 percent of Pan American. Another Chase director, General Electric, through its wholly owned subsidiary General Electric Credit Corporation, has $207 million invested in and controls 27 percent of the assets of Allegheny and 26 percent of Texas International.[81]

The Federal Aviation Act of 1958 flatly outlaws the control of two or more airlines by any person or corporation without approval of the Civil Aeronautics Board, a dispensation the board has never granted. Under the act, the holding of 10 percent of an airline's voting stock constitutes ownership,* and the CAB requires airlines to disclose stockholders with 5 percent or greater interest. But why quibble over percentages when ownership is a foregone conclusion? The plain truth is that this small cluster of owners holds the power of life and death over the entire airline industry. Their investment totals $6.5 billion, or more than half the assets of all certificated air carriers.

Since they do flout several laws, secrecy is imperative. K. G. J. Pillai, director of the Aviation Consumer Action Project, has made a study of this subject:

> The fragmentation of ownership into investments in stock, debentures, loans and aircraft has the effect of keeping the owners inconspicuous and at a safe distance from the Civil Aeronautics Board.
> Equally circuitous are the methods used to influence the management

* When the voting stock is scattered, 5 percent can mean control.

of airline companies. The thirteen banks, insurance companies and manufacturers seldom appoint their own directors and officers to airline boards; they appoint representatives drawn from intermediary corporations that they dominate. . . . Altogether, more than half the directors of the five largest airlines (United, TWA, Eastern, American and Pan American) maintain interlocking or representative relationships with the 13 banks, insurance companies and manufacturers. Not so coincidentally, most of the intermediary corporations are engaged in the production of goods and services purchased by airlines. Because of the interlocking relationships, it is difficult for airlines to transact business with these intermediaries on an arm's length basis.[82]

To protect their investment in aircraft manufacturers, banks encourage the airlines in their purchase of aircraft, even when they have a surplus. For example, American Airlines has leased sixty-five jets from banks and insurance companies while forty-six of its own jets of similar design were idle. From total operating revenues of $8.9 billion in 1971, the thirteen largest air carriers paid out more than $1.1 billion on nontrade debt, aircraft leases, and insurance premiums, a fact that helps explain the chronic unprofitability and excessive fares of the airline industry.[83]

The first order of business for any bank is to protect its capital. If a debtor fails to meet his obligation, then perhaps Congress will come to the rescue, as it did with Lockheed. "The United States became extremely nervous about the fate of the Lockheed airbus," said Patman, who opposed the $250-million loan guarantee for the L-1011 Tristar airbus:

> Behind all the rescue efforts were some of the nation's largest commercial banks, whose lobbyists swarmed over Capitol Hill on behalf of the loan guarantees. The tracks of the banks—led by Bankers Trust and Bank of America—were found at every turn. First, the banks had $400 million out in lines of credit to Lockheed. Then it was discovered that many of the same banks also had lines of credit out to subcontractors on the airbus project: $329 million to AVCO, $125 million to Sperry Rand, and $104 million to Collins Radio. As the covers were pulled back still further, we learned that the banks were also creditors to the airlines that were to purchase the airbus. Eastern Airlines, scheduled to be a major purchaser of the jet, had borrowed $55 million from Chase, $33 million from First National City Bank, $10 million from Bankers Trust and $9 million from Morgan Guaranty. TWA had Morgan Guaranty and Irving Trust as major creditors. Delta, another prospective airbus customer, had huge loans out from Citibank, Manufacturers Hanover, Bank of America and Morgan Guaranty. And behind the heavy lines of credit were substantial holdings of airline stock in the bank trust departments.
> Were the airlines' decisions to order the airbus based solely on their

needs, or were these decisions influenced by the fact that their creditors—
the major commercial banks—had poured hundreds of millions of dollars
into Lockheed? And was the government's decision to salvage the airbus
based on a need for that airplane, or the political power of commercial
banks?[84]

Secretary of the Treasury John B. Connally bulldozed the loan guarantee
through Congress. Long before the bailout legislation was introduced,
Connally had paid his persuasive respect to the ranking members of the
House and Senate Banking Committees. Connally, who ranks second to
none in his slavish support of money power, is a persuader from way back,
having started out in life as a lobbyist for Texas oil interests, to whom
he owes his financial and political success (see Chapter Three, page
193). Patman resisted his charm, but Chairman John B. Sparkman
of the Senate Banking, Housing and Urban Affairs Committee, and Texas
Senator John G. Tower, the committee's ranking Republican, have long
been avid fans of the banking industry. It was not difficult to convince
other fans of the merit of Lockheed's request. They ignored the fact that
because of the problem with the airbus, Lockheed had fallen far behind
schedule on the C-5A military transport, with cost overruns of some $2
billion on a plane that the Air Force Secretary said "was designed too
close to the margin," resulting in limitations detrimental to its flying profi-
ciency. Debugging the plane would cost hundreds of millions more, a
minor consideration in the face of Lockheed's banking connections. Besides, Lockheed really knows how to play the military-industrial complex
game. It employs more than two hundred retired generals, admirals, colo-
nels, and Navy captains—more than any other defense contractor.[85]

A Chase spokesman, expressing the usual rejoinder, denied in 1972
that his bank "controls any corporation, airlines or otherwise." Banks
cannot legally own stock, he explained, "for their own beneficial interests."
He neglected to mention that banks held more than $330 billion of the
$500 billion worth of securities held by all institutional investors. Just two
banks, Morgan Guaranty and Bankers Trust, together hold more stocks
and bonds than all the 500-odd mutual funds in the United States. This
makes banks by far the largest single block of institutional investors, and
their role is multiplying rapidly—another $150 billion of investment money
is expected to flow into the banks by 1980. Trust departments manage
about 70 percent of the assets of pension funds. *Half of all trust assets are
controlled by twenty banks.*[86]

Until Patman started asking questions, trust officers were the silent men of banking, and what they did with their customers' billions was nobody's business but their own. Now that Patman wants banks to spin off their trust departments, others, including the Securities and Exchange Commission, the Federal Trade Commission, and the Justice Department, have tentatively joined the attack. It is Patman's contention that bank trust officers make investment decisions based on inside information provided by other bank officers. The SEC wants Congress to let it regulate the clearing of securities, including the role that banks play in the clearing operation. Bank trust departments control so much wealth that they can change the very nature of the stock market, without having to disclose any of their manipulations. By concentrating their investing in a few dozen growth stocks while the rest of the stock market languishes, they are endangering the nation's capital markets, and the liquidity of its pension funds. The favored companies enjoy high price/earnings ratios, access to additional equity capital, and the ability to grant valuable stock options.[87] The recent emergence of the "two-tier" stock market system is also under heavy fire. As one witness warned a Senate subcommittee, "The situation resembles a pool operation, in which a few investor-traders have run up the price of stock." The danger is that banks are investing a large percent of their colossal pool of wealth in high-risk, high-multiple ventures. In fact, the holdings of the ten largest bank trust departments in the top ten stocks are often 25 percent or more of the outstanding shares. Or as another money manager suggested, what would happen "if one of those antitrust suits—against IBM, Xerox, or Kodak—looked like being successful?" Meanwhile, the FTC wants Congressional authority to protect the public against unfair and deceptive banking practices, and the Justice Department, which has been making small noises about its inability to nail down firm rules on bank mergers, has threatened to use the antitrust laws to block the banks' plans for a nationwide electronic fund-transfer system.[88]

Major commercial banks have been diversifying and merging as copiously as industrial corporations. Thirty-eight percent of all commercial banks in New York City vanished in the decade between 1950 and 1960, and some 2,200 bank mergers were effected nationwide between 1950 and 1965. The result is greater concentration of trust assets as well as basic lending resources—in 1966 the fifty largest commercial banks held 44 percent of all commercial deposits, and by 1971 the figure was nearly 50 percent. These same banks hold two-thirds of the stock held in trust, leaving the remaining third to be divided among thousands of banks.[89]

Their insatiable appetite for riper profits has carried banks far beyond the confines of commercial banking. The 1970 amendments to the Bank Holding Company Act have turned local institutions into multinational giants. By allowing holding companies to own more than one bank and to diversify in any business the Fed deems to be "closely related,"* the old staid bank has become a go-go conglomerate. "We now offer every service that anybody could want—fifty-seven varieties at least," says Samuel B. Stewart, senior vice chairman of the Bank of America.[90]

By 1973 there were 1,600 bank holding companies in the United States, twice as many as five years before, and they controlled 2,700 of the nation's 14,000 commercial banks, with two-thirds of all bank deposits. This concentration has been achieved despite regulations confining banks within a single town or state. When these barriers are swept away, as they will be in the near future, the prediction is that a handful—a dozen at most—of large international banks will dominate local as well as world banking. The new banking is already worldwide, with most of the larger U.S. banks now deriving 25 percent to 50 percent of their income from overseas—see Chapter Two. The pace in the direction of still fewer but bigger banks is intensifying the consolidation of banking assets. As things stand right now, there are no limits to how far it all can go.

It is the same story with insurance companies and the $235 billion in assets they control. Banking and insurance, supposed competitors in the investment market, have pooled their economic resources in a concerted effort to strengthen their position and perpetuate the unfair distribution of wealth and power. The 1969 FTC staff study revealed that the ten biggest life-insurance companies had thirty interlocks with the ten biggest commercial banks. The forty-nine major banks had 146 interlocks with twenty-nine of the fifty largest insurance companies, plus eighty-six interlocks with twenty-two of the fifty biggest utilities.†

Concentration of wealth plus interlocking directorates equals money power in its purest form. Protected by weak laws, and from strong laws by weak regulatory agencies, encouraged and pampered by tax breaks, shelters, and subsidies, the prosperity game for the rich goes on, gaining mo-

---

* Bank holding companies may own finance companies, lease equipment, sell insurance, provide data-processing and travel services, do factoring, mortgage banking, consumer financing, investment management, and numerous other things. They may soon own savings and loan associations.

† Chase Manhattan, using four street names, is among the top ten stockholders of forty-two utilities.

mentum and weight with the speed of a snowball rolling down a steep, endless hill.

Why do some banks, as Vanik pointed out, enjoy a 16 percent tax rate? Here are some of the ways banks and insurance companies reap windfalls and avoid taxes:

—One of the great bonanzas enjoyed by commercial banks involves billions of federal dollars deposited in interest-free "tax and loan" accounts—funds derived mostly from withholding of income and Social Security taxes, and the sale of federal securities. "These deposits of public funds, paid in by the average taxpayer, represent one of the largest single subsidies provided by the federal government," Patman said.[91] "In a Republican administration, most of the interest-free federal gravy goes to GOP banks," said Jack Anderson. "Until last year, [Citibank] was headed by one of Vice President Agnew's closest friends, Republican fat cat George Moore. In 1970, Moore's bank had well over $300 million in federal deposits." The beleaguered taxpayer, as Anderson noted, who has to take out a loan to pay his taxes, is in effect borrowing his own money at the highest interest rates the market will bear. The Treasury defends the practice by responding that the banks provide a valuable service. The controversy dates back to at least 1963, when a report by the General Accounting Office (GAO), Congress' auditing watchdog over Executive Branch spending, found that the Treasury's deposits "tended" to favor big banks. Data compiled in 1972 by the Federal Reserve Board at Senator William Proxmire's request showed that in 1970, the latest year for which detailed figures were available, the interest-free deposits at ten of the nation's largest banks increased 12 percent from their 1969 level to an average of $1.084 billion. The total for the other 11,000 banks declined 7 percent to an average of $4.022 billion. It doesn't take a mathematical genius to see that the Treasury "tends" to favor bigness.[92]

—The Banking Act of 1933 (amended in 1935) considerably prohibits commercial banks from paying interest on checking accounts. This means that banks have access to billions of interest-free dollars, which in turn earn interest for the banks. Early in the spring of 1973, the House in a 264 to 98 vote cleared a measure that would prohibit mutual savings banks from offering checking services on interest-paying savings accounts. The ban would nullify NOW accounts* currently offered by mutual banks in Massachusetts and New Hampshire. Calling the NOW accounts "an

---

* NOW—Negotiable Order of Withdrawal—accounts make it possible to use an interest-earning savings account like a free checking account.

ominous trend," Representative Albert W. Johnson of Pennsylvania argued that it would "completely revolutionize banking as we know it."[93] The bill also would extend to September 30, 1975, the authority of federal agencies to limit the interest rates paid to depositors. What free-enterprise banking system?

On the other hand, there are no explicit federal limits on the interest rates banks can charge borrowers. In fact, there are perhaps a hundred widely used methods of computing interest—for example, two accounts paying exactly the same rate of interest can differ as much as 171 percent in earnings over a six-month period. All fifty states have usury laws to govern interest-rate ceilings on various kinds of loans, but they are so riddled with exemptions that they are virtually unenforceable.

—Prior to 1969, commercial banks were allowed to set aside "bad debt" reserves that were twelve times higher than their real debts. The effect was to permit banks to accumulate untaxed profits in ever-increasing amounts. The "tax reforms" of 1969 changed this for some banks but allowed the banks a seventeen-year grace period of adjustment.

—Most banks base their interest rates paid to customers on a 360-day year, rather than 365, which amounts to an extra month's interest on a five-year loan. Patman has estimated that the "overcharges resulting from this calendar manipulation approach $150 million a year."[94]

—Banks and insurance companies are heavy investors in state and local tax-exempt bonds.* This is a twofold benefit: the interest paid to depositors and policyholders is tax-deductible, while the interest earned from the bonds is tax free. Commercial banks also get to write off expenses incurred in the administration of their bond departments. In 1970, the IRS ruled that banks could borrow money to buy tax-exempt bonds and deduct the loan's interest from taxes. The volume of tax-exempt bonds has passed $150 billion, with approximately 40 percent held by financial institutions. Eighty percent of the bonds are owned by 1 percent of the population.[95]

—In testimony before the Senate Subcommittee on Intergovernmental Relations on May 9, 1972, Ralph Nader detailed how "the banks get the property taxpayer coming and going." Referring to a study by the Citizen Action Project in Chicago, Nader said that "commercial banks, savings and loans, and big bond brokers have shaped the property-tax collection process to their own advantage, and are milking the taxpayers for millions

* At the time the Sixteenth Amendment was passed, in 1913, a question existed as to the constitutionality of taxing the states.

of dollars annually." Pointing to the Chicago study, Nader said that the "seven property taxing bodies in Cook County collect their taxes only once, or at most twice, every year. Most homeowners, however, have to pay their property tax to their banks in twelve monthly installments, along with their mortgage payments. The Savings and Loans put these payments into so-called 'escrow accounts' and invest them. But they pay no interest to the homeowner, nor does the homeowner get a discount for making his payment early." While the lenders are getting free use of these funds, amounting to billions of dollars nationwide, "the taxing jurisdictions to which they rightfully belong are running short of cash. What do these jurisdictions do to meet their payrolls and bills? They go to commercial banks and bond brokers for high-interest/short-term loans, called 'tax-anticipation warrants' and for longer-term 'working-cash fund bonds.'" In 1970, Cook County taxpayers paid out $37.5 million in interest on these loans, an expense that would be eliminated if the tax jurisdictions collected their own taxes on a monthly basis.* "But that is not all," Nader added. "The crowning touch is that the Federal government actually rewards this bilking of the property taxpayer. The warrants and fund bonds are forms of municipal bonds and are thus exempt from federal income taxes." Cook County is not the only bilker. "Delayed property-tax collection is the national rule, not the exception," Nader said. "In twenty-four states, local property taxes were collected only once a year [in 1971], and they were collected only twice a year in twenty-one others. In only five states were they collected quarterly. So Chicago-style diversion of property taxes to big banks may indeed be widespread."[96]

—Another Cook County banking practice with national ramifications concerns the movement of taxables out of the tax jurisdiction on assessment day each year. Either that or they are exchanged for tax-free intangibles. Called the "rollover," this gimmick cost Cook County taxpayers about $3 million in 1970.[97]

—One of the most lucrative shelters, the "real-estate investment trust" (REIT), was enacted in 1960. It was purportedly designed to encourage the channeling of risk money into real estate. The incentive—that is, the official *raison d'être* for the loophole—exempts all profits from federal income tax if at least 90 percent of the income is distributed to share-

---

* A House Banking Commitee staff report estimates that at a modest 4 percent interest rate, a medium-size lender recovers over seven times the labor costs incurred in tax collections for the government. Also figured at 4 percent interest, the staff study estimates that an average Boston family of four with an annual income of $15,000 loses $875.40 over the life of a thirty-year mortgage.

holders. With only 10 percent of the income left to be plowed back in the business, the trick was in finding a way of sustaining growth. One of the companies that solved the problem was the Chase Manhattan Mortgage & Realty Trust. In less than two years, it increased its REIT assets to almost $1 billion. The answer was in selling each issue of stock at a higher price. Its first offering in 1970 was at $25 a share, and its last issue for 1972, convertible debentures, was convertible at $55. By maintaining a rising scale, a REIT will constantly increase the book value of existing shares— each new dollar of equity capital provides an REIT with a base of $2 or more in borrowing. Chase Mortgage was paying 5.5 percent for money that was returning 9 percent. The leverage equation works like this: $1 in new equity earns 9 cents, while the $2 in borrowed money costs 11 cents but brings in 18 cents; presto, the total profit is a neat 16 cents—a hefty return of 16 percent on the equity money—AND tax-free. Because of its enviable position in the financial world, Chase Mortgage could often borrow a full one-half of 1 percent below the prime rate. The Chase Manhattan Bank created this offspring to avoid colliding with federal and state regulations. The bank runs the show. Not only does Mortgage do its banking there, it also pays the Chase Corporation a management fee equal to 1 percent of assets. There is plenty of money for everybody except the United States Treasury.[98]

—In time of tight money, banks and insurance companies often demand an "equity kicker" when making real-estate loans—in other words, they get a piece of the action, or else. The effect not only increases their control over land, housing and industry, it also provides a dandy tax shelter. By forming a wholly owned subsidiary as a 1 percent general partner in the real-estate venture, with the company itself as a 49 percent limited partner (the original developers retain 50 percent) the lending institution, in its limited partner role, pays interest on the mortgage to itself. The interest income is taxable at 30 percent, while the tax-deduction value of the interest is worth 48 percent. Depending on the amount of the equity position, it may result in canceling out any tax due on the interest.[99]

—In October 1971, the GAO reported that nine banks and eleven investment firms had reaped profits of $188.2 million in 1970 by buying and selling $738 billion—more than twice the dollar volume of the New York Stock Exchange—in bonds and other securities for the Federal Reserve System. Patman, who wants to eliminate the private handling of government securities, charged that the system "had allowed chaotic financial reporting procedures to develop . . . resulting in windfall profits for a handful of dealers. Translated, the polite language of the GAO report* clearly establishes gross negligence on the part of the Federal Reserve Bank of New York in allowing such haphazard reports to be submitted." Patman said the securities dealers were subsidized through low interest rates, giving them profits of up to 90 percent contrasted to their average five-year profit of 31 percent. Alleging that the dealers were getting valuable inside information, Patman asked for a full audit of the Federal Reserve System "because they have been avoiding an audit for fifty years." The audit would include the twelve banks and twenty-one branches of the system, which are owned by their member commercial banks but governed by the Federal Reserve Board, a governmental agency. The Fed has opposed any audit on grounds that it would lose its independence if Congress were looking over its shoulder. So far it is the only federal agency allowed to spend public money freely without any type of review.[100]

—Audits are also an oddity in the insurance business. Although some 1,800 life insurers collected more than $23 billion in premiums in 1972 on policies with a face value of more than $1.5 trillion, there is no federal regulation and no federal agency policing the industry. That is left to the states, a responsibility often shunted to political hacks. Even the states that conscientiously try to do a good job find themselves hopelessly outclassed. All major insurance companies are computerized, but only New York State has a team of examiners capable of analyzing a computer system. For example, the last full-scale examination of the Equity Funding Corporation was in 1968, by California, Illinois, and Georgia departments, while Illinois sent one examiner for a quick audit in 1970. None of them discovered anything suspicious. Before Equity Funding slid into bankruptcy on April 5, 1973, it owned four life-insurance companies, three mutual funds, a savings and loan association, and a bank in the Bahamas. It was a go-go conglomerate with $500 million in assets, claimed life-insurance sales of $2 billion a year, and a p/e of 30.

It was also a colossal swindle that left a hundred banks and other institutions stuck with some two million shares of its stock, which soared from $6 a share in 1964 to $80 in 1969. And it sold at least 56,000 bogus life policies in the reinsurance market, which produced income of about $25 million—at times it even killed one of its fictitious policyholders and pocketed the money. Equity Funding fooled modest-salaried state auditors

* The GAO report was compiled from financial statements issued by the private dealers, not from an audit of the Fed.

as well as high-priced Wall Street talent. California State Insurance Commissioner Gleeson L. Payne admitted before a State Assembly committee hearing that his department had failed to adhere to its regular three-year audit schedule but denied any attempt at a cover-up. Until January 1973, his department did not have a computer expert. "We're not the only idiots in the group," Payne said. "All of industry has assumed until now that computers were always accurate. Computer fraud wasn't expected." Meanwhile, at this writing, a federal grand jury in Chicago is investigating accusations of bribery, missing records, and other misconduct in the Illinois Insurance Department. Raymond Dirks, the security analyst who uncovered the swindle, estimated that some 140 Equity executives and other employees knew about the fraud and no one talked. Institutions' losses in the stock will probably total $100 million, but those of individual investors will add up to at least twice that much. As to the policyholders, time will tell the full story. Only nine states—Connecticut, Kansas, Maryland, New Hampshire, New York, South Carolina, Vermont, Washington, and Wisconsin—have life-insurance guaranty funds. Equity Funding was chartered in Illinois. All it takes to start an insurance company in Arizona is $25,000 in capital, which explains why 420 companies have set up shop there, and 115 more have applications on file.[101]

—Profits on automobile insurance soared 144 percent to $1.1 billion in 1972, and earnings in investment income from premiums were $2.65 billion, an increase of 23 percent. However, members' rates dropped by only 1.5 percent.[102]

—Insurance companies are expert at stashing profits in untaxed reserves. Because they are not reported as net income, dollars hidden in reserves have escaped the attention of the Price Commission and of consumer groups interested in the disparity between earnings and rates. The practice of squirreling away profits into reserves meets with the approval of insurance commissioners, who worry more about a company's solvency than its rates. For example, ITT's Hartford Fire Insurance Company boosted its 1971 untaxed reserves by $53.7 million more than it would have done at its 1969 pre-ITT rate, and it also created a $9.3-million catastrophe reserve. The motivation of the insurers is to slow down their influx of reported (taxable) earnings.[103]

Next to oil, banking is the richest industry in Texas. Few men know more about both businesses than "Big John" Connally, the conservative Texas Democrat who became a conservative Texas Republican, a conversion more in name than substance. In fact, Texas, which once belonged to Mexico, enjoys a similar one-party political system, dominated in Texas by Connallycrats, who, according to John's brother, Golfrey, reflect "the enormous disparity in the wealth of this state. It is a political process run by overwhelmingly big business money."[104]

Who among the money power's many illustrious champions is better qualified to speak for both wings of the Property Party on the merits of democracy, prosperity, and corporation profits than John Connally, the "let's kick him in the nuts"* philosopher of the Nixon Administration? Nixon stood in awe of Connally's bullyboy *savoir faire*, and soon he replaced John Mitchell as the President's alter ego within the Cabinet. It was more than a political marriage. It was a mutual admiration society. Connally lauded Nixon's "brains and self-discipline—the President is the most self-disciplined man I have ever met." Nixon said Connally was the "architect" of his new economic policy and the one who had implemented it in domestic and international arenas. "He has been a tower of strength for the President," said the President when Connally resigned in May 1972 to campaign exclusively for the President. "I refer to his service in the National Security Council. . . . Whenever I have had a very difficult decision, and I have had one or two in recent weeks that have been perhaps quite difficult, I have found that when the going is the hardest, when the going is the roughest, that Secretary Connally is at his best."†[106]

When George Meany gave Nixon a cool reception at the 1971 AFL-CIO convention in Miami Beach, Connally struck back: "We cannot permit one man to put himself above the working people of the United States. In my humble opinion, Mr. Meany's conduct reflected an arrogance, boorishness and discourtesy that ill becomes a leader of the labor movement."[108]

What fantastic persuasiveness, articulateness, and public polish! Connally, said the President, was "capable of holding any job in the United States he would like to pursue." The alter ego was a dazzling peacock in a

---

* During his eighteen months as Secretary of the Treasury, this was the offensive tactic Connally most frequently recommended in White House strategy sessions.[105]

† A year later, almost to the very day, when the going was the roughest since Teapot Dome, Connally announced his long-expected conversion to the Republican Party, and once again rushed to the President's side. "Watergate is a sordid mess," he admitted, following this minor concession with his favorite conjunction: "But it was a silly, stupid, illegal act performed by individuals. The Republican Party didn't do it." Former Democratic Senator Ralph Yarborough, who was defeated in the 1970 Texas Democratic primary by the oil interests that Connally champions, characterized Big John's conversion in more brutal language: "It's the first time in recorded history that a rat has swum toward a sinking ship."[107]

barnyard full of gray chickens. "He's full of the old crappo," a Nixon man told *Life* columnist Hugh Sidey. "On the Hill, they are too, and they love him." Sidey said Big John was known "in the back rooms of the White House as 'Lyndon Johnson with couth.' . . . One fellow watched Nixon and Connally together in the Cabinet Room and thought that despite their superficial differences they were political twins, men who liked to defy their advisers, to come down on the tough side, to rock the boat, to confound the comfortable. The bureaucratic wet blankets were always flapping around Nixon and then suddenly there was Connally at his side saying to hell with them, follow your instincts, let fly—against Congress, against labor, against the international traders."[109]

But never against money power. On that point they are Siamese twins. In late April 1972, Air Force One landed on the private airstrip of Connally's posh south Texas ranch. They said it was a nonpolitical get-together, attended by some two hundred wealthy Texans, who had been invited to come over and meet The Man. Beside a swimming pool with floating chrysanthemums, mariachis strummed gaily as the guests lined up for beef tenderloin and black-eyed peas. The President was congratulated on "four good appointments to the Supreme Court," and he took the opportunity to remind Hanoi that what was "really on the line" there was the "position of the United States of America as the strongest free world power." The two men reminisced that history was repeating itself. Former Governor Allan Shivers had led Texas Democrats to victory for Eisenhower in 1952. "There are no Republicans and Democrats any more," said one guest, "just liberals and conservatives." Another added: "We're all just Texans and we're all here."[110]

The *déjà vu* was positively eerie. Connally at the Treasury had been the best thing that had happened to the oil industry since Robert B. Anderson held the post in the Eisenhower Administration. "I firmly believe that the smartest man in this whole nation is Bob Anderson," Eisenhower told reporter James Bassett in 1963. "He would be perfect for the job [President of the United States]. Golly, that fellow can reduce the toughest problem to its bare essentials like nobody else I've ever known, and in damned short order, too. Trouble is, Bob's a Democrat." Now for more *déjà vu*: Both Anderson and Connally are Texans, attorneys, and graduates of the University of Texas. Both have been oil lobbyists and have held high state offices. Both have been close to Lyndon Johnson. Both have served as Secretary of the Navy and Secretary of the Treasury in Republican administrations, in that order, and both have received nearly a million dollars through the kindly auspices of the late Texas oil millionaire Sid W. Richardson.*

As a lawyer and attorney for Richardson, Connally was named one of the three executors of the estate when Richardson died in 1959, leaving an estate of more than $100 million. Under Texas laws, Connally's share was $1.2 million, but to avoid taxes on a lump-sum payment he settled for a smaller fee to be paid over a span of years. About a third of the money was paid to him while he was governor of Texas, in violation of the state constitution, which states that "during the time he holds the office of Governor he shall not practice any profession, and receive compensation, reward, fee, or the promise thereof." As Texas Democrats and pragmatic conservatives, both Anderson and Connally posed no threat to money power. As writer Ronnie Dugger has observed of Connally, "He wants, not to rock the boat, but to stop the yacht from rocking."

Also, because he is a man who understands the needs of the rich, it was not long before the President was seriously affirming to Connally's wealthy guests that business deserved additional tax incentives to spur plant expansion and oil exploration. In fact, he credited the lenient corporate tax policies of Japan and West Germany for their highly efficient factories and cited the need "for more jobs . . . and for American industry to be able to compete abroad." This was a page right out of Connally's tax catalogue. Earlier that month he had used his big foot on the ecology movement:

> I am not saying we should stop trying to control pollution. I am saying you can't go crazy about it and shut down your industries until you solve all your water and pollution problems. The point is that if the U.S. is going to be competitive with the rest of the world, we can only move so far ahead of the world in terms of what resources we commit to nonproductive uses. Now, say the steel industry spends $100 million a year to be sure their smoke is pure and their waste doesn't contaminate the rivers. This increases the cost of their product without affecting its quality. If Japan turns out a comparable product without the same pollution-controls costs, then we can't compete. [When it was pointed out that American steel had more serious problems than pollution, he responded:] Take refineries, then. We have the most efficient oil refineries in the world. These laws are going to make us spend hundreds of millions of dollars in almost every type of basic industry—cement, in refineries, in aluminum— and all for nonproductive costs. . . . I am not saying that cleaning the environment is not productive; in a social sense, it is. All I am saying is

---

* See Chapter Three, pages 193–198, for more detail on Anderson's role in the Eisenhower Administration.

that we can take the lead in the world trade community just so far. . . .
Look, all the other countries . . . are plagued with pollution problems, too.
[In a trade-off between pollution and productivity, Connally made it plain
that Nixon was not going to neglect productivity.][111]

Connally was equally eloquent in his defense of one of money power's
most cherished loopholes: capital gains. "Let's take capital gains," he
exploded at an AP reporter. "Anybody want to knock that out? You want
to destroy real estate values in the United States? You want to destroy the
value of insurance companies in the United States? You want to destroy
the stock market?"* This time Connally forgot to mention the plight of the
charwoman—do you want to destroy her chance for an early retirement
with dignity? The myth is that the stock market belongs to all Americans.
The facts are just the opposite. According to a recent study by the Cambridge Institute, the top 1 percent of wealthholders in 1962 directly owned
62 percent of all publicly held corporate stock, the top 5 percent had 86
percent, and the richest 20 percent held 97 percent. More than half of this
group's total income is derived from both realized and unrealized capital
gains. To a person with more than $1 million in annual income, capital
gains is worth $640,667; to one with $5,000, it is worth about one dollar.[112]

The Santa Gertrudis cattle grazed contentedly in the background as the
President continued to charm the oilmen: ". . . rather than moving in the
direction of reducing the [oil] depletion allowance, let us look at the fact
that all the evidence now shows that we are going to have a major energy
crisis in this country in the 1980s. To avoid that energy crisis, we have to
provide incentive rather than disincentive for people to go out and explore
for oil. That is why you have depletion, and the people have got to understand it."[113]

A year later, the oilmen were doing their best to shorten the President's timetable. Connally's own dire warnings before the Joint Economic
Committee had preceded the President's by fifteen months. On February
26, 1971, Connally had opposed any tampering with percentage depletion

---

* Capital gains is derived from unearned income—that is, profits gained from
capital investment in stocks and bonds, real estate, buildings, timber, and various
other kinds of property. Profits from long-term—over six months—capital gains are
taxed at no more than half the rates that apply to earned income. Needless to say,
this loophole has given birth to a series of other loopholes promoted as tax shelters
for the rich.

as he laid down what turned out to be the oil industry's game plan for
1973:

> Now, I do not at the present time view our situation with respect to
> basic fuel supplies in this country as warranting any additional changes.
> So, to that extent, I would disagree with your recommendation that we
> again go into this problem and make substantial changes in the tax struc-
> ture.
>
> I think . . . more properly perhaps, we should be concerning ourselves,
> and I mean this quite seriously, about our basic fuel supply, because I
> think we are at the point of, just at the threshold of an energy crisis in this
> country. I do not think there is any question about it.
>
> Now, we have to be quite candid in recognizing that we no longer have
> the capacity to supply the fossil fuels to completely satisfy the needs of
> this nation, and, particularly, we are now unable to assist any of our
> friends in Western Europe, in the free world. . . . There is not any
> question in my mind but that the OPEC countries, and this includes all of
> the nations of the Arab world as well as Venezuela, are determined that
> they are going to take a very strong hand in the future management of the
> production of fossil fuels from their countries, and that certainly is under-
> standable. But when you consider that Western Europe has to have those
> fuels, when you consider that Japan has to have those fuels, when you
> consider that we cannot any longer meet our needs and supply theirs, I
> think we ought to start turning our attention not to discouraging further
> development and exploration for fuels in this country but rather toward
> taking steps to encourage every type of development of energy.[114]

Cowboys on horseback moved lazily among grazing cattle and waiting
jet planes, a pastoral tableau keyed to the realities of Texas politics. The
President was still expounding on the virtue of tax incentives: "I strongly
favor not only the present depreciation rate but going even further than
that, so we can get our plants and equipment more effective."[115]

In his stint as Treasury Secretary, John Connally achieved more for
big business than any predecessor since Robert Anderson. Connally was
the fireman summoned to extinguish the small flame of tax reform ignited
in 1969. Unable to stop Congress from implementing its minor reforms,
the White House now likes to point to the 1969 act as evidence of its
populist zeal. Stanley S. Surrey knows that story well. A Harvard Law
School professor, Surrey was Assistant Secretary of the Treasury for tax
policy under Kennedy and Johnson, and it was his massive study of tax-
reform proposals that prodded Congress into action, signaling the so-called
"tax revolt" that came to a head early in 1969 with the testimony of

Under Secretary of the Treasury Joseph Barr before the Joint Economic Committee. Almost offhandedly, Barr noted that 155 people with earnings above $200,000 had not paid any income tax in 1967. Barr concluded with warnings of a "taxpayer revolt if we do not soon make major reforms in our income taxes." The lobbyists and cosmeticians went to work and the result was not even good plastic surgery.

In the fall of 1972, Surrey analyzed the White House position on tax reform:

> The Nixon administration has not made a single tax-reform proposal on its own that would end a single tax preference or close a single loophole. The few it did make were blueprinted in studies done under President Johnson, and they were prodded from the Nixon administration by Congress in 1969. Instead of backing reform, this administration has taken the path of more tax incentives for business—indefinite deferral of taxes on half of all income from exports (DISC) and even faster tax-saving write-offs for machinery. Each incentive has created a new tax escape. . . .
>
> If we were to subsidize directly those efforts the government now subsidizes through the tax system, we would quickly begin to see that in most cases the financial help given through tax preferences is neither needed nor warranted. It would be difficult to imagine, for example, that the government could justify direct payments to finance the sale of exports, or to encourage corporations to invest abroad, or to enable actors to buy cattle. But that is just what the present system does.
>
> There are those who warn that, if ever capital gains are fully taxed like other income, individual investment and risk taking will cease. They say, too, that, if business is deprived of tax write-offs for machinery far in excess of the equipment's actual decline in value, then corporate investment will greatly decline. Yet tax economists who have long studied these matters know better.[116]

The Revenue Act of 1971, Connally's contribution to the nation's prosperity, was adopted by voice vote in the House without even a quorum or roll call after a floor debate lasting all of one hour and thirty-nine minutes—only about forty Representatives out of 435 thought the measure important enough to be present on the floor for the vote. Yet the bill gave birth to two major subsidies worth about $80 billion in corporate tax relief over the next decade. Briefly, the bonanza consisted of the investment tax credit (ITC) and the asset depreciation range (ADR).

ITC, now euphemistically labeled the Job Development Tax Credit, the more lucrative of the two, was first enacted in 1962 to stimulate business expansion by allowing corporations to subtract 7 percent of all

new capital expenditures directly from their tax bill. Although it was re-
pealed in 1969 on grounds that it contributed to inflation, it was resurrected in 1971 for the same reason as before, at a time when inflation was
overheating the economy in ways undreamed of in 1969. Coupled with
ADR, which allows corporations to write off machinery and equipment 20
percent faster than normal wear, these two loopholes were tailor-made for
big business. It is estimated that 80 percent of the windfall goes to the top
one-twentieth of 1 percent of all corporations.

Critics promptly pointed out that with industry running at only 73
percent of capacity, corporations had scant reason to buy more equipment.
The tax savings would end up as a boost in profits. "Will we abandon
devices like the investment tax credit, so readily embraced as a crisis tool
theoretically designed to promote industrial expansion and job opportunities but which in reality is most often used by those who need it least?"
Wright Patman asked. "The most extensive use of the investment tax
credit has been among the largest of the nation's business and industrial
entities which have huge resources to sustain themselves." Investment decisions are based on "market feasibility," Patman said, "and little if anything else."[117]

"The President labels the scheme a Job Development Program,"
George Meany said, "but he knows well that much of industry's investment in new equipment will eliminate jobs."[118] In its study of the performance of ITC for the 1962–69 period, the Senate Finance Committee
estimated that it alone had saved General Motors $297 million and United
States Steel nearly $207 million in taxes. It had saved corporations $13.5
billion over the seven years. Senator Alan Bible of Nevada said that ADR
would save IBM about $500 million during the 1970s.[119] Few if any tax
experts would dare suggest that GM would stop retooling or that IBM
would curtail its growth without these additional tax incentives.

Writing in *Life* in June 1972, Connally talked about productivity and
growth as if they were natural offshoots of tax loopholes:

> The purposes of these two tax changes were threefold. First, they were
> designed to create new jobs by stimulating the demand for capital equip-
> ment. This they are doing and doing very well: capital spending is up 10
> percent this year over last and employment in the machinery industry is
> rising rapidly. Second, the job development tax credit and the accelerated
> depreciation allowances were designed to keep the United States competi-
> tive in the world markets and thus save jobs. Third—and this is particu-
> larly important—the only way for the real wages of working people to rise
> in the long run is for productivity to rise. One important source of produc-

tivity growth is investment by businessmen in new plants and equipment—
the very purpose of these tax changes. The program is working: new jobs
are being created at twice the normal pace.[120]

In the same *Life* article, Connally noted that "A good many miscon-
ceptions about business are transferred into the argument that there should
be no growth in the U.S. economy. Growth, say the negativists, benefits
only the rich and produces only pollution to plague the rest of the people.
This is pure poppycock. The benefits of growth have always been widely
distributed throughout the U.S. economy. The cliché that 'the rich get
richer and the poor get poorer' needs to be corrected for the American
experience, for it is a fact that as the economy grows, both rich and poor
alike make gains.* We need real economic growth to distribute more of
the fruits of our system more widely to more people. Recognizing that
need, the Nixon administration at the same time has demonstrated a firm
will to make certain that growth is not contaminated by pollution."[121]

Writing in the same issue of *Life*, Senator Edward M. Kennedy painted
quite a different picture:

President Nixon promised in 1968 to bring the economy back to
health, to end inflation without increasing unemployment.

And what did we get in the next three years? We got a President who
says wage and price decisions were none of the public's business. We got a
sick economy. We got more and worse inflation. We got soaring unemployment. We got a Nixon recession. We got the lowest Dow-Jones average in a decade. . . . We got the highest interest rates since the Civil War.
We got a hat trick of fantastic budget deficits—$23 billion last year, $26
billion this year and $25 billion next year. We got an international money
crisis and the devaluation of the dollar. We got the worst trade deficits in
our history. We got thousands of idle plants and research laboratories. . . .
Unemployment nearly doubled in the past three years, and two million
more Americans lost their jobs. We know that 6 percent is only the
beginning of the squeeze. For every person who has lost his job, another
four or five have felt the pinch. What about the shifts to part-time work,
the loss of overtime, the slowdowns in promotions? What about those who
have given up the hunt for jobs completely, and are no longer even
counted in the surveys? . . .

We need a program of comprehensive tax reform, able to bring tax
justice to the people and end the enormous distortion in the burden of
taxes that people have to pay. Tax reform is at the heart of any program,
to relieve the problem of unfair income distribution that now exists. By

* The top 100 corporations increased their sales 12.5 percent—from $280.4 billion
to $315.2 billion—between 1969 and 1971, but their employment figures dropped by
5.2 percent, or 500,000 workers.

accident and design, we have allowed the Internal Revenue Code to become America's biggest welfare bill of all. But it's the sort of welfare that only Alice in Wonderland can understand, because its welfare goes largely to the rich and to the nation's major corporations. We know that Secretary Connally speaks for oil on tax reform, but who speaks for the people?[122]

"It's a case of upside-down economics," economist Walter Heller said of ITC and ADR, "because while investment stimulus is needed, consumer stimulus is needed even more."[123]

It was money power's old trickle-down theory of prosperity that Andrew Mellon had so eloquently espoused as the economy was crashing down around the ears of Herbert Hoover.

John Maynard Keynes called profits "the engine which drives enterprise." Profits are what the corporate game is all about. Assets, sales, management, platitudes on social responsibility, all the rest are merely means to profits. Fueled by the pro-business Nixonomics of Phase II, the engine traveled at full throttle in 1972, zooming right through the fictional profit-margin ceiling of the Price Commission. With the shift to Phase III in the first quarter of 1973, the sky was the limit.

Of course there was a lot of jawboning along the way. In April 1972, a government report disclosed that 23 percent of the big companies covered in a survey appeared to have raised their profit margins illegally. The Price Commission warned that the violators might be subject to price rollbacks and civil or criminal penalties unless they could show that profit increases were within the commission's rules.[124] Two weeks later it was reported that the Price Commission had begun ordering "hundreds of millions of dollars" in price cuts and customer refunds. The commission's chairman, G. Jackson Grayson, said that customers who had paid higher prices would be entitled to refunds—that is, if they could afford to prove their case in court.

The guidelines instituted in November 1971 limited price increases to 2.5 percent annually, and set profit margins—pretax profits as a percentage of total sales—in any quarter not to exceed those of a "base period" determined by averaging the best margins of two of the past three years. Companies with annual sales of more than $50 million were required to report on productivity and profit margins on a quarterly basis, and that involved considerable jawboning as the Price Commission tried to maintain an aggressively rigorous public stance while keeping its hands off the engine's throttle. More than half of the 2,954 firms involved failed to report by the required deadline, and half of the reports of the reporting half, according to Grayson, "had to be returned because they were filled out wrong, and of the remainder about half had exceeded the profit margin ceilings." The curb on profits, Grayson explained, was a "second line of defense" in the fight against inflation. The rule was not designed to hold down profits but to restrain profit margins and "to force firms to share savings and efficiencies with customers."[125]

"The move to control profits was largely in response to complaints from the labor unions and anti-corporation forces that corporations should be made to bear the burden of controls along with workers," the *Wall Street Journal* charged in an editorial. It continued:

> Aside from the fact that this formula may tend to encourage wasteful cost rises, a fundamental flaw here is the essentially moral assumption that there should be federally regulated equity between the interests of workers and corporations, which are held to be in conflict. In fact, a corporation, as such, has no interests in the human sense, just as it has no flesh, blood or soul—it is merely a mechanism for organizing capital and human labor so as to perform work and thereby contribute to living standards and wealth.
>
> The most common result of tinkering with the profit mechanism is not equity but distortion. Managers begin making decisions that sometimes are inimical to the interests of the public and workers, not because the managers are perversely trying to defeat government aims, but because they are faced with choosing the lesser of evils or because they don't really have a choice. . . . Some corporate executives are choosing to relax their control over expenses or even to subtly encourage greater expense account spending and the like in order to keep profits below base levels.

In its attempt to provide a noble rationale for the deception, the *Journal* came up with a strangely convoluted thesis on free enterprise: "An alternative—one that the government would have desired—would have been to cut prices. But some companies are well aware that too-liberal price cutting might drive some of their weaker competitors to the wall and leave their own firms open to antitrust action. A little extra expense account fun-and-game sounds relatively harmless when compared with fighting an antitrust suit."[126]

The mad rush to hide profits, as *Newsweek* noted, had "quite a few companies setting a course that would spin Adam Smith in his grave: they are going out of their way, often down paths bordering on the frivolous, to cut profits down."[127] The evasive tactics, in addition to lavish expense accounts and new corporate jetliners, included diverting excess funds into tax-deductible expenses such as research and development, advertising and public relations, and also into "promotions" for top executives that involved salary increases and bonuses but no real change in duties.* The boost in total compensation for corporate leaders amounted to 13.5 percent in 1972, a violation of the guidelines that limited increases to 5.5 percent for wages and 0.7 percent for fringe benefits. The catch was that the rules allowed companies to set up "employee groups" for calculating percentage increases so that individuals could exceed the guidelines as long as the average conformed.

"In a sense," one executive told *Newsweek*, "people are looking for ways to get inefficient. I have some executives who, instead of looking for ways to maximize everything, which they've been trained for all their lives, are saying, 'Well, what the hell would you want to get that efficient for? The government will just take it away.' What am I supposed to tell them?"[128] Other companies were seeking mergers with low-margin companies. Waste, inefficiency, anything at all, is better than lowering prices. Monopolies and oligopolies are conditioned to charge what the market will bear. Nothing else will do.

After-tax profits of $55.4 billion in 1972 broke all records; the prior record was $49.9 billion, set in 1966. Both American Telephone & Telegraph and General Motors had more than $2 billion in profits, while Exxon exceeded $1.5 billion and IBM $1.2 billion. Eighty-five companies exceeded $100 million in profits, twenty-seven more than five years before. First pegged at an annual after-tax rate of at least $61 billion for 1973, that year's first-quarter figure was fully 23 percent ahead of the first-quarter rate in 1972 and 6.6 percent greater than the record $57.2-billion rate of 1972's final quarter. The only industry with a group-wide profit decline was the airlines, but the pattern in industry after industry was a profits gain of 20 percent to 30 percent. Profits were up by 84 percent in steel, 70 percent in paper, 65 percent in building materials, 45 percent for manufactures of farm equipment. Automakers showed whopping gains: Ford 32.5 percent, Chrysler 163.5 percent, American Motors 196 percent, while General Motors was tempted into exceeding its 20 percent targeted profit margin by 11.7 percent.[129]

Expenditures for new plant and equipment marked the greatest capital-spending binge since 1956. As expected, it reduced corporate income taxes

---

* When it reduced the top "marginal" tax to 50 percent on earned income, the Nixon Administration argued that it would reduce the "gimmicks"—stock options, expense-paid vacations, unlimited expense accounts, company cars and airplanes, special pensions, insurance policies, an endless plethora of tax-evading privileges—that corporations use to stimulate the predatory impulses of executives. All it reduced was the Treasury's tax collections.

while adding to inflationary pressures—the rate of inflation was the highest in twenty-two years. Commenting on the soaring inflation rate in May 1973, Treasury Secretary George Shultz predicted that "the pace of increase will moderate" over the rest of the year. Conceding that the economy had expanded "faster than we thought" in the past two quarters, he said the Administration's goal was to "turn [the economy] down without slamming on the brakes."[130]

"These figures are complete proof of the utter incompetence of this Administration," George Meany charged. "Its economic policies are destroying the living standards of millions of American families." But Nixon, speaking through his press secretary, continued to believe "the steps we are taking to fight inflation . . . will bring about a decrease in the rise of inflation and solve this problem and bring the cost of living index down to a reasonable level."[131]

As George Santayana once observed about those who do not know history, it is possible that Richard Nixon, who may not know of the folly of Diocletian's Edict of Prices, circa A.D. 301, may be condemned to repeat it. Determined to stop inflation during his reign over the Roman Empire, Diocletian noted in his edict that there was such "unprincipled greed" that prices of foodstuffs had recently mounted fourfold and eightfold:

> For who is so insensitive and so devoid of human feeling that he cannot know, or rather has not perceived, that in the commerce carried on in the markets or involved in the daily life of cities, immoderate prices are so widespread that the uncurbed passion for gain is lessened neither by abundant supplies nor by fruitful years, so that without a doubt men who are busied in these affairs constantly plan to actually control the very winds and weather.

The edict attempted to bring order into the chaos of rising costs by setting maximum prices for goods and labor throughout the Empire. The penalty for a violation was death. Yet the plan failed. A contemporary historian, Lactantius, wrote in 314:

> After the many oppressions which he put in practice had brought a general dearth upon the empire, he then set himself to regulate the prices of all vendible things. There was much blood shed upon very slight and trifling accounts; and the people brought provisions no more to markets, since they could not get a reasonable price for them; and this increased the dearth so much that at last after many had died by it, the law itself was laid aside.

"This Administration was elected to control
inflation . . ."—RICHARD NIXON

During his 1968 campaign, Nixon had been uncompromising on economic controls: "The imposition of price-and-wage controls during peace-
time is an abdication of fiscal responsibility. . . . Experience has indicated
that they do not work, can never be administered equitably and are not
compatible with a free economy." Three years later, the President made a
complete about-face: "Inflation robs every American, every one of you.
The twenty million who are retired and living on fixed incomes—they are
particularly hard hit. Homemakers find it harder than ever to balance the
family budget. And eighty million American wage earners have been on a
treadmill. . . . The time has come for decisive action—action that will
break the vicious circle of spiraling prices and costs." The answer was
Phases I, II, III, and IV. This last was a giant step backward to Phase II,
except that the controls were more selective and flexible, with more pressure on actual price boosts than on profit margins. The result of all controls to date has been greater inflation. The wage earner's slice of the
nation's economic pie was growing smaller every year. As for the welfare
recipient, he suddenly found himself both the victim and scapegoat of
inflation.

"It's no pleasure for a President of the United States to veto a spending
bill," Nixon told hardhat labor leaders in a "straight from the shoulder"
explanation of why he had vetoed the Vocational Rehabilitation Act. "But
if spending goes unchecked, taxes will go up, prices will rise and unemployment will increase," There were some, he said, who would curb spending by trimming the Pentagon budget. However, "Those who would slash
the defense budget today . . . and make us a second-rate power will have to
take on their hands the responsibility for sabotaging peace initiatives [with
Russia and China] that seem so promising."[132]

Only a demagogue with brass-plated hubris could so glibly sidestep
from charity to a handful of disabled poor to the nation's survival as a
world power. Much has been said by this Administration about "welfare
bums" and "cheaters." But even as the President spoke of welfare spending going unchecked and of sabotage of the nation's supremacy, Senator
Proxmire was discovering—only after a long struggle with the Pentagon's
reluctant Renegotiation Board—that defense contractors had piled up excessive profits on Pentagon contracts. In a Senate speech, Proxmire said:
"Most disturbing are the exorbitant rates of return earned by the firms on

this list even after they were forced to make sizable refunds, and the fact that some firms were found to have taken excessive profits several years in a row." On the basis of the actual investment or net worth of 131 companies, Proxmire said that after-refund profits of 94 firms exceeded 50 percent; 49 made over 100 percent; 22 made over 200 percent, and four made over 500 percent. Only four companies made a profit of less than 25 percent. One ammunition maker refunded $200,000 that had been determined to be excessive by the board but still made profits of 217 percent. Proxmire said the list contained few major corporations because their accounting practices allowed them to average profits over the year and among subsidiaries. "A giant firm that knows it can make up for losses on one contract with higher profits on another can afford to underbid the smaller companies and drive them from the field."[133]

Meanwhile, John T. Dunlop, director of the Cost of Living Council, was assuring the public that the Internal Revenue Service would investigate more than a thousand companies with annual revenues *under* $50 million to determine their compliance with the rules on profit margins. "The new regulations," Dunlop said, "say again what the council has said all along—we intend to continue the strong enforcement program with regard to profit margin violations that occurred during Phase II."[134] The possibility existed that a few small companies would eventually have to bear the brunt of Dunlop's "strong enforcement program," but big business had little to fear from Nixonomics. The economist Pierre Rinfret, a former Nixon adviser, has called the President's economic policies a joke and characterized Phase III as "everybody taking care of themselves and the hell with the rest of the United States."[135] When Citibank reported early in May 1973 that after-tax profits were rising an incredible 24 percent in the first quarter, Budget Director Roy Ash tried to cool off the overheating boom with phony figures. He claimed that the rate of inflation was only 2.9 percent, but other government studies showed that prices had shot up at a 6 percent annual rate in the first quarter. The White House publicity mill called Ash's inaccuracy a "typing error."[136]

The Administration's pipe dream of a "soft landing" from the prosperity boom went up in smoke by the end of 1973, a year that produced an unprecedented combination of corporate profits and inflation—more than $70 billion in after-tax earnings, a 27 percent boost over 1972—and with a corresponding 8.7 percent increase in the consumer price index and a 19 percent rise in wholesale prices, marking the greatest increases since the post-World War II period of inflation. Overall energy prices soared 65.1

percent, with costs of refined petroleum products up an unprecedented 125 percent—see Chapter Three for figures on oil industry profits. Farm product prices rose 36.1 percent while processed foods and feeds climbed 20.3 percent.

In terms of consumer buying power, the inflation meant that it costs $145.30 to buy the same amount of wholesale goods that $100 purchased in the 1967 base period. A middle-income family of four with a $12,614 budget had to spend an extra $1,168 in 1973 to maintain its 1972 living standard.

As always, however, inflation hits the nation's poor hardest. The Joint Economic Committee reported that the impact of higher food, housing and fuel prices had been about one-third greater for low-income consumers than for those with higher income. The Bureau of Labor Statistics reported that the average worker's weekly pay check reached $140.17 in December 1973, up $10.04 above 1972, but the cost of living increase offset any rise in average purchasing power, which was 1.5 percent less than a year ago. When deductions for taxes were figured in, an average married worker with three dependents had a pay check worth 3.3 percent less than a year earlier.

The Joint Economic Committee's report charged that the Administration "seriously underestimated the severity of inflation in 1973 and its adverse impact on the economic position of consumers. . . . To a considerable extent the nation's current economic malaise is the result of a tendency to pretend problems are not serious until a crisis occurs." The outlook for 1974 was grim: "In view of the recent slowdown in economic activity and the energy crisis, unemployment will certainly increase during 1974. This situation of higher prices and fewer jobs will further erode consumer income and confidence, which in turn will add substantially to recessionary prospects in 1974."

In detailing the figures for gross national product, the Department of Commerce said real growth—not counting inflation—was 5.9 percent for 1973 and inflation in all sectors of the economy from farms and factories to retail stores averaged 5.3 percent. Counting both real growth and inflation, the nation's GNP totalled $1,288.2 billion, an increase of $133 billion or 11.5 percent over 1972. It is sobering to recall that in January 1973, the President's soothsayers in the Council of Economic Advisers had assured the nation that the rise in the GNP deflator would be held to 3 percent in 1973—a rate that is still high by postwar standards.

The economy continues to frustrate forecasters and baffle theorists. As

Walter Heller, the incoming president of the American Economic Association, put it at the group's annual meeting in December 1973, "Economists are distinctly in a period of reexamination. The energy crisis caught us with our parameters down. The food crisis caught us, too. This was a year of infamy in price forecasting. There are too many things we really just don't know."

"Economists do learn from history," Norman Jonas pointed out in his *Business Week* column, "but they appear perpetually doomed to make new mistakes. The world of economic uncertainties they face today—dominated by the slippery political variable of the oil shortage—is far different from that of four years ago. Then, the econometricians had nothing in their computer memory banks to warn them chronic inflation would persist through the 1969–70 recession."[137]

That this recurring Nixon nightmare, stagflation, is perhaps the terminal gasp of free enterprise as it vanishes into the quagmire of oligopoly is not one of the inputs plugged into any of the models. Economics is a money-power game, replete with conflicting pronouncements by opposition team players, but nobody badmouths the owners. As chairmen of the Council of Economic Advisers, Leon Keyserling carried the ball for Harry Truman, Arthur F. Burns for Eisenhower, Heller for Kennedy and Johnson, and now Herbert Stein for Nixon. Stein's team spirit is so compelling that he even went calling on state delegations at the 1972 Republican convention to sell them on the merits of Nixon's New Economic Policy.

In the CEA's January 1973 annual report to Congress, Stein had cheerfully observed that "by the end of 1972, the American anti-inflation policy had become the marvel of the rest of the world." A year later, Stein was predicting that the rate of inflation would slow sharply when the current round of price increases for petroleum had ended and when the food supply caught up with demand. "We are now going through an essentially one-time adjustment to higher energy prices and we are still making an adjustment to relatively short food supplies. These adjustments, which are producing such skyrocketing prices, will come to end."

In a separate report to Congress, Nixon conceded that the economic picture in 1973 "was not as bright as we would have liked." The price rises reflected "increasing worldwide competition for products," but "we can be proud, however, of the way in which we have responded to the problems. We are proving that a dynamic and resilient people can meet the challenge of inflation without sacrificing the ideal of a free-market system."

The jawboners naturally try to paint a happy picture. As the troika—

Stein, Shultz and Ash—continued to tred political water in the economic maelstrom, the White House was assuring the nation that the economy was in safe hands. The American people could sleep soundly at night, assured that their President was keeping his eagle eye on big business, ready at a moment's notice to roll back prices and sweep them off that eternal treadmill. Prosperity had rounded the corner for many people, along with inflation and the energy crisis for everybody, and rampant corruption at the highest levels of business and politics. Nothing very novel about that. It was just the old system springing an occasional leak. It was, in fact, dirty business as usual and at the same old stand, all of it based on the premise that democracy owes its existence to the prosperity of the money-power elite, who control the complex mechanism of "free enterprise." The rules of the game leave nothing to chance. Dirty business is not an occasional scandal but a way of life that is practiced with consummate art by those who make up its rules. An important chapter of the game plan was written into the tax code, a subject explored at some length in the remainder of this book.

CHAPTER **2**

THE IMPERIALISM GAME

I helped make Mexico safe for American oil interests in 1914. I helped make Haiti and Cuba a decent place for the National City Bank boys to collect revenue in. I helped purify Nicaragua for the international banking house of Brown Brothers. . . . I brought light to the Dominican Republic for American sugar interests in 1916. I helped make Honduras "right" for American fruit companies in 1903. Looking back on it, I might have given Al Capone a few hints.

—MAJOR GENERAL SMEDLEY D. BUTLER,
United States Marine Corps, 1931

And indeed he might have. As it was, there were striking similarities in their *modi operandi*—and in their alibi. "All I ever did was supply a demand that was pretty popular," said Capone. The East India Company, the model for American imperialism, exported British despotism to India and Christianity (and underwear) to the African heathen. For supplying that "demand," the East India Company, established in the reign of Elizabeth I, ruled one-fifth of the world's population for more than a century, until 1858: it issued its own currency, legislated its own laws, negotiated its own treaties, maintained its own standing army, and produced more revenue than its homeland's.

In the heyday of Smedley Butler, American foreign policy toward underdeveloped countries (politely termed the "less developed countries" —or LDCs—in current tax legislation) was practiced for (and by) American business. In the first three decades of the twentieth century, Washington wielded its big stick on behalf of American economic colonialism at least sixty times in Latin America alone. The gunboat diplomacy earned American business the nickname *El Pulpo*—the octopus. One of *El*

Pulpo's most impressive tentacles, the United Fruit Company (now United Brands), once controlled a banana empire that spanned four million acres of land from Cuba to Ecuador. It also bought and sold governments in bunches, and cynically discarded those which refused to be purchased. And over in Africa, Liberia was known simply as the Firestone Republic.

Among the elaborate systems of ideologies—that is, pretexts—advanced by the United States in the conduct of its affairs, those offered for its support of American foreign investments with dollars and gunboats invoked loftier abstractions than Capone's. "If an ideology is to be effective, it must convey a vital sense of some immutable principle that rises majestically above partisan preferences," Louis Eisenstein noted in *The Ideologies of Taxation*. "Except in dire circumstances civilized men are not easily convinced by mere appeals to self-interest. What they are asked to believe must be identified with imposing concepts that transcend their pecuniary prejudices."

The exportation of American capital and technology, said the United States, was the quickest way to improve the lot of retarded nations. This, in turn, would not only increase our own foreign trade but the economic strength of the entire world. This apologia, however seemingly noble, had little bearing on the realities. The strategy of American companies in developing companies was designed to frustrate that development. The investment was almost exclusively in the extractive industries—oil, rubber, cobalt, tin, chrome, copper, iron ore, bauxite, uranium, and other minerals —which meant that huge consortia composed mostly of big American corporations were in control of every step of the operation. Capital investment in manufacturing facilities in the exploited nations was kept at a minimum, with the desired result that they failed to acquire the technology necessary for development—and competition. They were caught in a cruel trap: they sold their national treasures under terms outrageously favorable to the buyers and bought finished goods on terms equally favorable to the sellers.

Besides being provided gunboats and patriotic exhortations, American business was rewarded with generous tax concessions for venturing abroad. The treatment of foreign income has grown into a major issue of tax policy in recent years, but back in 1918 only one witness appearing before the tax-writing House Ways and Means Committee voiced any interest in the subject. He urged exemption of foreign earnings, or at least a lower rate, on the ground that double taxation resulted when a company paid both foreign and domestic taxes on the same income. On the basis of this flimsy evidence, Congress tacked an extraordinary bonanza onto the 1909 tax code (the date the modern corporate income tax was adopted) without altering the basic structure of the statute, which provides that domestic corporations be taxed on income "from all sources" and foreign corporations on income from "business transacted and capital invested within the United States."[1] Although this jurisdictional pattern was to remain substantially unchanged until 1962, lawmakers in the interim would create several layers of exceptions and qualifications—that is, loopholes—including the foreign tax credit, tax deferral, and special rates for a Western Hemisphere Trade Corporation, any corporation based in a less developed country, and any investment in a United States possession. What follows is a brief summary of the way the United States has treated these various loopholes, or "mechanisms," in the period since 1918. The mild reforms of the 1962 amendment added another layer of exceptions and qualifications.

To begin with, a domestic corporation is simply one incorporated within the United States. If it operates directly in a foreign country, it is said to be operating through a "branch" and is subject to United States taxation on the income derived from the foreign source.* When a domestic corporation conducts its foreign business through a subsidiary incorporated in a foreign country, the income of that subsidiary is exempt from United States taxation until it is repatriated—if ever—and even then the profits are not taxed as such, but as some form of receipt to the parent corporation, the exact nature depending on whether they are repatriated as a dividend, as a distribution in liquidation, or as some other form. This is the great loophole known as deferral.

Both the branch and the subsidiary are entitled to the foreign tax credit, which means that taxes paid to foreign governments are credited dollar for dollar against the U.S. tax bill. Prior to 1918, foreign taxes were treated as deductible expenses, just as state and local taxes in the United States are considered business expenses for domestic corporations. Although the foreign tax credit is limited to the U.S. tax due on foreign income, other exceptions conveniently nullify this qualification. The taxpayer may choose between two methods of bookkeeping: the per-country or overall limitations. Both offer special advantages, depending on the taxpayer's current situation. Under the per-country limitation, the "ex-

---

* Oil companies and other extractive enterprises in foreign countries are usually carried out by branches of domestic corporations because the depletion allowance is denied to foreign subsidiaries. See Chapter Three.

cess" credit earned in one country may not be offset against United States taxes due on income earned in others. With the overall limitation, the taxpayer may pool all income earned in his global operations, averaging out the high-tax and low-tax countries. No refunds are given, but excess credits may be carried forward for five years and back for two years. While this method is by far the more popular, the per-country limitation gains considerable appeal when the losses in one country must be deducted from the net income in others, particularly when they reduce the overall credit limit. It is more attractive to branches because the foreign losses of branches may be set off against the domestic income of the parent, which is not possible with foreign subsidiaries. To get the best of both tax worlds, a new foreign operation often starts out as a branch to take advantage of the initial losses; then later, as the profits begin to roll in, it is converted to a foreign-based subsidiary for the deferral benefit.

Because the foreign income base is defined in terms of U.S.-source rules and concepts of taxable income, the tax credit is not limited to foreign income taxes but includes taxes paid to political subdivisions of the foreign country, such as provinces and cities. A direct tax credit is given not only for foreign taxes paid on profits of foreign branches but likewise for foreign withholding taxes on dividends paid out by foreign corporations, whether or not they are in a subsidiary relationship. In fact, an indirect credit is permitted on taxes "deemed to have been paid." This provision permits a credit for foreign taxes paid by a foreign subsidiary of the domestic corporation's foreign subsidiary. The test for eligibility for this derivative credit requires only that the domestic corporation own 10 percent or more of the voting stock of the subsidiary and that it in turn must own at least 50 percent of the voting stock of the sub-subsidiary.*

Except for extractive companies, most branches are eventually converted to subsidiary status to qualify under Sections 881–83 of the code, which exempts foreign earnings from United States taxation unless they are distributed to shareholders who are American nationals (citizens or corporations). Thus the deferral mechanism makes it possible for the

---

* The tax credit does not apply to dividends received from portfolio investments abroad. The deduction method is used instead, which explains why very little foreign business is carried out in this form. An interest-equalization tax on foreign securities imposed in 1963 as a "temporary" measure was ended by Nixon in January 1974. Secretary of the Treasury George P. Shultz told Congress in January 1973 that the levy has helped the U.S. balance-of-payments position by "restraining outflows of capital for portfolio investment in foreign stocks and debt obligations." The tax was imposed on a sliding scale according to the maturity of the security—on stocks the tax was 11.25 percent of the purchase price.

domestic parent to escape United States taxes indefinitely on its entire global operation. Because the tax rules are shot full of loopholes, tax avoidance has become a major consideration in foreign investment. By adroit bookkeeping and pricing of transactions among subsidiaries across national boundaries, profits may be concentrated in tax-haven countries like Switzerland, where the top tax rate is about 7 percent of profits.*

There are endless devices for repatriating income free of taxes: the original capitalization of the subsidiary is set up so that the parent receives payments in the form of debt repayment and interest charges; the subsidiary pays royalties and administrative charges; the subsidiary buys its imported ingredients from the parent either at low prices to reduce import duties or at high prices to reduce local profits; the subsidiary makes long-term, low-interest loans to its parent; central-office expenditures for foreign operations are charged entirely to the parent's domestic operation; and so on ad infinitum.

Contrary to popular belief, tax havens were not conceived for the convenience of movie stars, Mafia bagmen, or deposed dictators living in expatriate splendor on loot concealed in numbered bank accounts. Tax avoidance (not evasion) on a grand scale has made the third-country arrangement—the so-called tax-haven shelter—the linchpin in the tax mechanism leading to the dizzying growth of multinational corporations in the last decade.† The reason that many foreign subsidiaries of American corporations are established in tax havens (where taxes on income earned elsewhere in the world are low or even nonexistent) to conduct operations in third high-tax countries—either directly or through "grandchild" subsidiaries—is primarily to avoid *foreign* taxes. It is the deferral loophole, not the tax haven, that permits the domestic parent to avoid United States taxes in foreign operations. Of course, the lower the foreign tax base, the more profitable it is for the parent not to repatriate subsidiary income.

In effect, the havens become fiscal siphons for global operations, creating bloated financial reservoirs that often outstrip those of the countries in which they operate. These liquid assets flow in giant waves from one country to another, on a scale beyond the power of governments to con-

---

* Although the money stays in the foreign country, the domestic parent can include the net income of its overseas subsidiaries in its consolidated public financial statements to impress shareholders.

† There is no textbook definition for a multinational company, but it is generally defined as one with sales above $100 million, with operations in at least six countries and overseas subsidiaries accounting for at least 20 percent of its assets. Some four thousand companies qualify, accounting for 15 percent of the gross world product.[2]

trol. This massive trading in currencies across national frontiers within multinational groups not only threatens but sometimes destroys national policies with regard to exchange rates, balances of payments, and the availability of credit. Meanwhile, thanks to the deferral loophole, the pool of liquid assets continues to swell, and, until the energy crisis gave the dollar a boost, so generally did the U.S. trade deficits, with the result that the dollar was in a state of chronic crisis—more later on this pernicious by-product of U.S. foreign tax policy.

The very least that can be said for deferral is that it amounts to an interest-free loan from the government for the period pending payment —taxes deferred ten years are as good as taxes saved if the investment performs well. Taxes never repatriated become a gift to be reinvested tax-free in whatever manner deemed appropriate by the foreign subsidiary. In the event the parent needs the funds, they may be repatriated as a distribution in complete liquidation, taxable under certain conditions at capital-gains rates rather than as a dividend. Since the derivative tax credit is not allowed in this maneuver, the liquidation becomes desirable only when the foreign tax rate is so low that the advantage of the capital-gains rate outweighs the advantage of the credit. A tax-free liquidation in the form of a merger, consolidation, or reorganization is possible with the approval of the Treasury—the test is to show that tax avoidance is not the principal purpose for the liquidation.

In his tax message to Congress on April 20, 1961, President Kennedy proposed the elimination of deferral in developed countries and tax-haven deferral privileges in all countries. The President took a dim view of some of the practices:

> The undesirability of continuing deferral is underscored where deferral has served as a shelter for tax escape through the unjustifiable use of tax havens such as Switzerland. Recently more and more enterprises organized abroad by American firms have arranged their corporate structures— aided by artificial arrangements between parent and subsidiary regarding intercompany pricing, the transfer of patent licensing rights, the shifting of management fees, and similar practices which maximize the accumulation of profits in the tax haven—so as to exploit the multiplicity of foreign tax systems and international agreements in order to reduce sharply or eliminate completely their tax liabilities both at home and abroad.
>
> To the extent that these tax havens and other tax deferral privileges result in U.S. firms investing or locating abroad largely for tax reasons, the efficient allocation of international resources is upset, the initial drain on our already adverse balance of payments is never fully compensated, and

profits are retained and reinvested abroad which would otherwise be invested in the United States. Certainly since the postwar reconstruction of Europe and Japan has been completed, there are no longer foreign policy reasons for providing tax incentives for foreign investment in the economically advanced countries.[3]

Congress could not have disagreed more. The bill that became the Revenue Act of 1962 left much to be desired in terms of the President's initial proposals, which by then had gone through several revisions. In fact, the act was based substantially on Secretary of the Treasury C. Douglas Dillon's final draft. What emerged was a complex piece of legislation with (as previously mentioned) a thick layer of exceptions and qualifications. If it narrowed some loopholes, mostly in the area of tax-haven transactions in developed countries, it widened others.* Deferral was eliminated only in certain categories of income made by "controlled foreign corporations"† acting as sales agents or as general clearinghouses in tax-haven countries for income earned in other developed countries. The act precluded so-called Subpart F or "base company" income from deferral where substantial tax advantages are gained through the base-company operation. Unless a company can show that its subsidiary has a legitimate management, manufacturing, or distribution function, the Internal Revenue Service may deem the subsidiary to be a tax-reducing contrivance and tax its profits along with those of the parent on a current basis, whether they are repatriated or not.

Unless, of course, certain new loopholes come into play. For example, the same controlled foreign subsidiary is permitted to operate in a tax haven if it is engaged in the manufacture of goods or some other form of production and has no tax-saving branches outside its base country, or if its income is earned by selling goods or services for use in the base country, or if it neither sells goods nor services to a related person and has no tax-saving branches outside its base country. But all income earned by a *noncontrolled* subsidiary is eligible for deferral, tax havens galore notwithstanding.‡

---

* By concentrating on transactions rather than companies, the act adroitly sidestepped the ticklish problem of differentiating between tax-haven abuses and "legitimate" benefits of deferral.

† A controlled corporation is one with more than 50 percent of its voting stock owned by U.S. shareholders, each shareholder owning at least a 10 percent interest in that voting power.

‡ A foreign corporation is considered noncontrolled when 50 percent or more of its voting stock is owned by persons (1) who each own less than 10 percent of the voting stock, or (2) who are not U.S. citizens or corporations, or (3) by any com-

And that is only the beginning. There is the "minimum distribution clause," which allows an American corporation to pool all its foreign income, whatever the source; and if the foreign taxes paid amount to at least 90 percent of the maximum U.S. corporate rate, currently 48 percent, the company is exempted from further U.S. tax. Besides benefiting from tax credits, the parent can thus cut its U.S. tax bill by 10 percent.

There is also a 30 percent rule that permits a tax-haven operation if at least 70 percent of the income is derived from legitimate sources. This generous exclusion means that a tax haven can receive 30 percent of nonoperating income from related affiliates in other countries and defer taxes on the entire amount.

To digress briefly from the provisions of the 1962 statute, the creation of the Western Hemisphere Trade Corporation (WHTC) is a prime example of tax legislation that starts out to redress equity and ends up a major loophole mindlessly spinning its largess to eternity. The apparent intent of the legislation, conceived in 1942, was to relieve American investors in the Western Hemisphere, particularly in Latin America, from any competitive disadvantages resulting from the high U.S. corporate surtax imposed during the war. The act was structured to aid extractive, manufacturing, and utility operations, but some of the largest corporations have used it to set up selling subsidiaries to handle their U.S. exports.

A domestic corporation qualifying under the 1942 legislation* receives a tax reduction of 14 percentage points in the U.S. corporate income-tax rate, so that its effective rate is reduced from about 48 percent to 34 percent. (Since the current 48 percent corporate rate is made up of the normal rate of 22 percent and the surtax rate of 26 percent, no corporation pays at exactly the 48 percent or 34 percent rates because the surtax portion is applicable only to taxable income in excess of $25,000.) Extractive companies benefit from both the 22 percent depletion allowance and the 14 percent WHTC deduction. A WHTC is not eligible for deferral, but it can function as a subsidiary and file consolidated returns with its parent without penalty. It is also eligible for the foreign tax credit.

The tax jackpot, however, goes to the less developed country (LDC)

---

bination of persons who are not U.S. citizens or who each own less than 10 percent of the voting stock.

   * To qualify as a WHTC, the domestic parent must conduct all of its business in the Western Hemisphere and derive at least 95 percent of its gross income for the preceding three-year period from sources outside the United States. At least 90 percent of that income must come from "the active conduct of a trade or business," thus disqualifying portfolio-derived income of over 10 percent.

corporation,* especially when it is a WHTC, which automatically includes all Latin-American operations. During the drafting history of the 1962 tax bill, there was considerable lobbying to give preferential treatment to LDC corporations. The rationale was that American investment would lead these poor nations to prosperity and civilization—the mighty dollar versus red tyranny. The result was something quite different.

Prior to the Kennedy reforms, a non-gross-up provision was available to all foreign subsidiaries when income was repatriated. This meant that their U.S. tax liability was estimated on the basis of net foreign income after payment of foreign taxes—*that is, taxes paid to foreign governments were both deducted from the gross income and then credited dollar for dollar against the U.S. tax bill.* The 1962 legislation eliminated one barrel of this double-barreled loophole by requiring full "grossing up" for all foreign income other than that earned by LDC corporations. The justification proffered for this exception was that the tax break would provide incentive for reinvesting earnings in plant and equipment to assist the economic development of less developed countries. The ideologists ignored the fact that the provision became effective only when profits were remitted, thus encouraging repatriation of earnings rather than reinvestment. LDC corporations are excluded from the Subpart F restrictions imposed on tax-haven transactions—income earned in one LDC may be transferred (or siphoned) to another LDC without incurring U.S. tax.

For purposes of U.S. tax laws, domestic corporations operating in American possessions are treated as foreign corporations.† Income earned within the possessions becomes subject to U.S. tax only when remitted to another domestic parent corporation or individual shareholders—corporations may claim a credit for taxes paid to the possessions. The deferred tax may be permanently forgone if dividends are distributed directly to individual shareholders. This loophole becomes especially lucrative in an area like Puerto Rico, which offers mainland corporations a seventeen-year tax-forgiveness arrangement.

---

* Less developed countries are designated by the President and currently include all countries other than the following: Sino-Soviet bloc, Australia, Austria, Belgium, Canada, Denmark, France, Germany (Federal Republic), Hong Kong, Italy, Japan, Liechtenstein, Luxembourg, Monaco, the Netherlands, New Zealand, Norway, South Africa, San Marino, Sweden, Switzerland, and the United Kingdom. For a foreign subsidiary to qualify as an LDC corporation, it must derive 80 percent or more of its income from trade or business in a less developed country in which 80 percent of its assets are located.

† The tax provision applies to the Virgin Islands, Guam, the Panama Canal Zone, American Samoa, Wake and Midway Islands, and the Commonwealth of Puerto Rico.

Finally, the so-called China Trade Act Corporations, as authorized in 1922, still provides U.S. tax exemption for income derived by American corporations in Taiwan and Hong Kong which accrues to shareholders who are residents there or who are either citizens or residents of the United States.

If nothing else, the sheer inertial complexity of the 1962 legislation raised a costly maze of legal thickets across the freeway to tax havens. More a lawyers' relief act than tax reform, it did succeed in slowing down traffic for many small and medium-sized companies. For the big multinationals, however, which look upon expensive legal and accounting fees as merely another deductible expense, the detour was short and well posted. As for financial institutions—banks, insurance, mutual funds, investment firms—and shipping subsidiaries, there was nothing in the 1962 act to impede their mad rush to hot new tax havens flaunting their tax-avoidance gimmicks from the world's most curious corners.

In the past decade tax experts have been playing musical chairs with tax havens, poring over atlases in search of the remote island or stamp-sized principality willing to make the most favorable tax-free deal. Of course, a country must offer more than tax immunity and banking secrecy to qualify as a multinational sanctuary. Political and economic stability rate high on the tax avoider's chart—democracy can be a problem here. The tax haven's currency must be freely convertible—it must be free from the sort of annoying and costly foreign-exchange controls that many European nations have enacted in recent years. Multinationals, needless to say, want to protect themselves from further depreciation of the dollar as against German and Japanese currency.

Even Switzerland, the granddaddy refuge of runaway dollars, lost some of its charm in 1972 when the Bern government imposed capital controls. There was an immediate exodus to Luxembourg, a grand duchy of 999 square miles tucked into a corner of the Ardennes Forest. Today Luxembourg is a major center for Eurocurrency banking. Some sixty "offshore" mutual funds base their operations here, and of the 1,000 international bond issues sold over the past decade, some 400 are listed on Luxembourg's modest bourse. Multinationals prefer to launch their bond issues through subsidiaries in tax havens like Luxembourg and the Netherlands Antilles because the interest on them is paid free of withholding tax— American investors could easily evade payment of the interest-equalization tax because the issuing corporations usually did not know who bought their bonds. With virtually no banking industry of its own, the city of Luxembourg is a banking boom town, with fifty-seven affiliates of foreign banks, including units of the Bank of America, First National City of New York, Wells Fargo of San Francisco, and First National of Boston. American branches are entitled to all the protection and secrecy guaranteed by the laws of the tax haven in which they operate. The total banking assets rose from $1.8 billion in 1968 to $11 billion in 1972.

The biggest can of corporate worms is buried in a small pocket of Alpine scenery called Liechtenstein. Because of low taxes and favorable corporation laws, this mountainous sixty-two-square-mile principality has become the Delaware of Europe. It has 21,000 citizens, half that many cows, and five times that many foreign corporations and foundations. It offers everyone, from superstars to supermultinationals, the ultimate in secrecy. As the writer Roger Beardwood phrased it in a *Fortune* article on tax havens, "The Swiss are merely secretive; the Liechtensteiners have their lips sutured together. When they do talk, it is often to boast of their superior secrecy."

Besides providing secret banking with numbered accounts, Liechtenstein does not oblige companies to publish financial statements; the government provides no information services to foreign countries, nor does it assist in the enforcement of judicial decisions in tax matters—it has no diplomatic relations with the United States.* Other pluses: holding companies pay a basic tax of one mill (one-tenth of 1 percent) on capital and assets; only one Liechtenstein resident must be a member of a company's board of directors, whereas Swiss law demands a majority must be locals; and it takes one man less than a day to complete the formalities of setting up a corporation.

It is the home of the *Anstalt*, that most versatile of corporate tax-evading devices. Svetlana Alliluyeva used an *Anstalt* to shelter the millions gained from the worldwide sales of *Twenty Letters to a Friend*. Anybody can set one up; Swiss lawyers do it by mail order. The usual procedure for an individual—movie star, author, anyone with a large income—who is setting up an *Anstalt* is to assign all his earnings to it and list himself as a salaried employee. The *Anstalt*, at his direction, will control his investments, building up his capital tax-free, and he will be liable for taxes in his own country only on the salary paid to him there.

Of the thirty or so tax havens currently flourishing, about a dozen are

---

* Liechtenstein has a customs and economic union with Switzerland, but its banks are not subject to the Swiss Bank Act.

really impressive performers in this shadowy world of high finance. The latest and fastest-growing new entrepôt in the competition for tax-haven dollars is the New Hebrides, a Y-shaped archipelago of eighty islands under joint Anglo-French rule some five hundred miles west of Fiji. Before their instant conversion from an economy based on fish and copra to the heady world of international finance, the islands were best known as the setting for James Michener's *Tales of the South Pacific*. Since the French and British could never agree on fundamentals, the islands never adopted a tax code. The inertia of the stalemate promises an eternity of political stability. Even more important for American interests, the islands are a "less developed country." As previously noted, LDC corporations are excluded from Subpart F restrictions imposed on tax-haven transactions. Earnings can flow from one haven to another without incurring U.S. taxes, and repatriated funds are entitled to the non-gross-up provision.

The influx to the New Hebrides has been overwhelming. An estimated five hundred companies had moved in by late 1972, including Exxon. The Bank of America joined with Japan's Sumitomo Bank, Australia's Bank of New South Wales, and Britain's Hill, Samuel Group, Ltd., in forming a trust company called Pacific International Trust Company (PITCO). The Irving Trust Company of New York and the Crocker National Bank of San Francisco had an interest in the Melanesia International Trust Company, which tacked some two hundred phony company nameplates on its walls, the only public announcement required—many of the names were the invention of the Melanesia manager, a Monopoly enthusiast. The rush for office space was so frantic that many companies, including Price Waterhouse, were operating out of hotel bedrooms and in walkups over grocery stores.

The New Hebrides' stiffest competition comes from halfway around the world. Curaçao, an island forty miles off the coast of Venezuela and the largest of the Netherlands Antilles, plays host to perhaps two thousand foreign-owned companies. An old-timer at the tax-avoidance game, it got a new lease on life in the late 1960s when a number of major multinationals (Royal Dutch/Shell, Gulf & Western, LTV, American Tobacco, John Deere, Teledyne, Pan American) established financing subsidiaries to tap the Eurobond market. Although much of this business still moves through Luxembourg's banks, with the issues being quoted on its bourse, there are advantages in the convolution. For one thing, the costs are lower and a Curaçao company can lend to a business in which it has no equity participation or to its U.S. parent without losing tax benefits.

Another competitor is Grand Cayman, largest of the three Cayman Islands, lying between Jamaica and Cuba. Besides being accessible to the United States, it is a British colony, which means that it has a stable government and a legal system based on common-law concepts of equity, trusts, and contracts familiar to U.S. businessmen. Of even greater attraction is the government's willingness to make tax-free deals lasting from thirty to fifty years.

Popularity in tax havens is as volatile as the Eurodollar market. The slightest political tremor sends hip-pocket operators as well as giant multinationals back to the atlases. Several tax havens in the Western Hemisphere went on the skids in the early 1970s, the most notable example being the Bahamas. The reelection in 1972 of Prime Minister Lynden O. Pindling, a black nationalist, assured the islands that final independence from Great Britain would come in 1973. The fear of what freedom would bring promptly plunged the world's most permissive tax haven into an economic tailspin.

A slow starter in the tax-haven race, by 1969 the Bahamas rivaled all those in the Western Hemisphere. Bay Street, which runs through downtown Nassau, was touted as the Wall Street of the Caribbean. It boasted 269 financial institutions (a phenomenal gain of 232 in six years) among its occupants. There were nearly a hundred mutual funds, many of them hotshot promotions like Investors Overseas Services and Gramco, then fronted by such former political luminaries as Pierre Salinger and Walter Jenkins, and most of them serving as vehicles for foreign investment in U.S. securities and real estate. The 11,000 companies registered were represented mostly by nameplates covering the walls outside local law offices. Business was booming. It was a tax dodger's paradise. Besides secrecy and freedom from taxes—income, sales, capital gains, dividends, corporate excess profits, you name it—the Bahamas offered U.S. banks a major international market for Eurodollars—U.S. dollars on deposit in foreign banks, including foreign branches of U.S. banks. U.S. banks could hold Eurodollars offshore in tax-free accounts and make corporate loans without worry of exchange controls. Since the Johnson Administration first began limiting the export of dollars in 1964, the Eurodollar market has grown at a frenetic pace. Not only were foreign subsidiaries of U.S. corporations borrowing Eurodollars to finance expansions abroad, but in times of tight credit, U.S. banks borrowed Eurodollars from their overseas branches.

The greatest impetus to the Eurodollar market came in 1968, when

President Johnson, in a move to bolster the U.S. balance of payments, limited the amount of money American banks could lend to foreign customers and the amount American corporations could remit for investment abroad. As always, there was a loophole—foreign branches of American banks were excluded from the restriction. They could make all the foreign loans they wanted, provided the funds used came from overseas. Unlike their mainland parents, they were not restricted in the rates they paid on deposits they solicited overseas. This privilege carried a reverse twist on the balance-of-payments argument: by offering interest rates above the U.S. level, the branches have diverted dollar deposits that otherwise might have flowed to the United States. (In January 1974, Nixon dropped all controls on foreign investments. Along with the equalization tax, the Administration abandoned the voluntary foreign credit restraint program imposed by Johnson which limited foreign lending and investment by commercial banks, and also the foreign direct investment controls that restricted fund raising for overseas investment.)

The first flush in the boom of Eurodollar loans was enjoyed mostly by a handful of giant U.S. banks with branches in London, the center of the Eurodollar market. But the smaller banks, which could not afford a London operation,* quickly latched onto the "shell" branch gimmick. Of the eighty branches that quickly set up shop in the Bahamas, most were of the hole-in-the-wall "shell" variety. James L. Robertson, vice chairman of the Federal Reserve Board, is one of two members who have consistently opposed the board's perpetuation of this shell game. "My primary objection is that they aren't branches in any sense of the word," he has said. "They are simply desk drawers in somebody else's desk. Why make a bank go through a sham proceeding to obtain certain privileges?"[4]

Sham or not, in 1969 alone the shells, with the approval of the U.S. Treasury, sent $10 billion in Eurodollars skittering through Nassau ledgers on the way to foreign subsidiaries of U.S. corporations. While the *modus operandi* is to create the illusion that the shell is a fully operating branch bank, the actual transfer of funds takes place at the parent bank in the United States, with the transaction dutifully recorded in a set of books by a part-time agent of the Nassau shell.

The exemption of financial and shipping companies from the 1962 restrictions imposed on tax havens has led tax attorneys to punch huge loopholes in the law. Set up as holding companies for other foreign opera-

---

* British authorities require that branches maintain full-service facilities, with an initial cost of at least $250,000.

tions, they have been used to shelter the global income of their parents from U.S. tax.

The record is replete with examples of elaborate tax dodges contrived by even the most prestigious American corporations. Yet few have found more ingenious ways to balk the revenuer than the billionaire Daniel K. Ludwig. A tanker tycoon with a Howard Hughes complex, Ludwig has mysteriously managed to metamorphose a small salvage company into a vast shipping empire without having to share more than a pittance with the United States Treasury. A client of the Nixon law firm of Mudge Rose, Ludwig has cleverly registered his numerous fleets, including his flagship National Bulk Carriers, in "flag of convenience" countries like Liberia, Bermuda, and Panama, which impose no taxes on earnings and allow complete freedom from seamen's unions and stringent safety regulations. And, as in the case of the Nassau bank shells, the registering process conveniently takes place in New York. Touching all tax bases, Ludwig underwrites his fleets through a captive insurance company incorporated in Bermuda. The entire operation, ships and insurance, is staffed by one full-time director and a part-time secretary.

On a smaller scale, U.S. Steel owns two shipping subsidiaries (Navois and Navigen) in the Bahamas. As of 1969, some thirty ships, most of them under the Liberian flag, plowed the seas for U.S. Steel and other customers. Any American corporation is free to invest in new ships, register them in Liberia, and charter them to itself at whatever rates it wishes—the ships need never appear on its books, and their earnings are entirely free of taxes until repatriated.

> See the great tanker gliding majestically into harbor.
> It is one fifth of a mile long. It was built in Japan for a German syndicate and brings Middle East oil to a New Jersey refinery on long-term lease to a Dutch oil company, flying a Panamanian flag. The master is a Swede, it is manned by a Hong Kong crew—a short-term operation financed by New York banks and insured by Lloyds of London.
> What nationality is this?*

There is one serious drawback to incorporating an American ship in a foreign country. Under maritime law, it cannot engage in coastal shipping between United States ports, a prohibition that can depress a ship's market value. This was the predicament facing the New York investment house of Dillon, Read & Company when it tried to sell the *Sansinena*, one of three

---

* By Richard L. Strout ("TRB"), *Christian Science Monitor* News Service, April 9, 1972.

tankers it owned through Barracuda Tanker Corporation, which was incorporated in Liberia and had its registered headquarters in a Bermuda desk drawer. Under the Liberian flag the estimated value of the *Sansinena* was $4.5 million, but its value would leap to $11 million if it were permitted to engage in coastal shipping. The procedure was to get the Treasury Department to grant it a waiver on grounds that it was essential to national security.

Few companies were better equipped to square this problem with the Nixon Administration than the firm of C. Douglas Dillon. Although Dillon was Secretary of the Treasury under Presidents Kennedy and Johnson, he was a Republican who had generously contributed to his party both in 1960 and 1968—understandably, in 1964 he favored the Democrats, with $42,000. One vice president at Dillon, Read was Peter M. Flanigan, a fund raiser for Richard Nixon in 1968, who also was president and managing director of Barracuda. Flanigan was one of the original twenty-seven investors in the 1950s who put up a grand total of $20,000 to organize the company, which borrowed $51 million, bought three tankers, and leased them to Union Oil for a period of twenty years. The deal was calculated to net a cool million in tax-free profits: if repatriated, the earnings would be subject only to 25 percent capital-gains tax.*

The request for the waiver had been in the works since 1967, but nothing much happened until after Peter Flanigan moved over to the White House in 1969 as the President's staff expert on business and oil. For his first assignment he compiled a White House code of ethics to help guide staffers in their relationship with regulatory agencies. On February 25, 1970, Flanigan sold his Barracuda stock to others in the venture. One week later, March 2, the Treasury granted the waiver, ruling that the national security required increased tanker capacity in coastal shipping.

Senator Joseph D. Tydings of Maryland disputed the ruling in a Senate speech on March 9, pointing out that four American tankers had been forced to switch over to the grain trade because they could not find oil cargo. Tydings said that merely "by the stroke of a pen," Treasury had increased the value of the *Sansinena* by $6.5 million. Following the Tydings speech, when it appeared that the Senate would launch an investigation, Secretary of the Treasury David M. Kennedy, who accepted "full responsibility for the waiver decision," was summoned to the White House for a conference. When the waiver was canceled the next day, Press Secre-

---

* Another of Barracuda's tankers, the *Torrey Canyon*, lathered the English coastline with crude oil when it split open on a reef in 1967.

tary Ronald Ziegler explained that Flanigan had been "unaware" of the waiver. Nothing more was said about national security.[5]

Few tax havens have been associated with more fiscal skulduggery than the Bahamas. Until the Bay Street Boys, a minority of wealthy white businessmen who ruled a majority of impoverished blacks, discovered the value of illegal money, the islands were mainly noted for their white beaches, tourist weather, and colorful history. Nassau's banking reputation in the 1950s and early 1960s was a joke—that is, a joke played on depositors who could never locate the right desk drawer when they tried to make withdrawals. Even the Mafia, spearheaded by the ubiquitous Meyer Lansky, organized its own banks in Nassau to launder its dirty money skimmed from Las Vegas casinos, along with the profits from illegal gambling, narcotics, loan sharking, extortion, and other rackets.

Long before black nationalism gained political ascendancy in the islands, Mafia power had helped pave the way for legalized gambling. In the beginning, however, the power belonged to the Bay Street Boys. They, in turn, took their lead from a triumvirate that exercised almost feudal power over the land and the people. Each of the three members contributed an essential ingredient in the composition of that power: Wallace Grove, an ex-convict from the States, was the brains; Sir Stafford Sands, leader of the Bay Street Boys, was the clout; Daniel K. Ludwig, mysterious financier, was the banker. The Lansky–Mafia–Bay Street Boys take-over of gambling in the Bahamas in 1963 provided the *Wall Street Journal* with the kind of investigative challenge that won it a Pulitzer Prize in 1966. The newspaper's account was officially confirmed a year later by a Royal Commission of Inquiry. The late Sir Stafford Sands, who was charged with taking a $1.8-million payoff, decamped for a castle in Spain. Grove took his profits and also cut out. Only Ludwig, mysteriously (again) excluded from complicity, remained. He built the luxurious King's Inn on Grand Bahama and leased it to Morris Lansburgh and Sam Cohen, who in 1972 were indicted with Lansky and five others on charges they had skimmed more than $36 million in gambling profits at the Flamingo Hotel in Las Vegas between 1960 and 1967. The money was deposited in various banks in New York, Florida, and the Bahamas for transmittal to Swiss banks. Both Lansburgh and Cohen, the Flamingo's owners of record during that period, pleaded guilty to two counts of impeding the collection of taxes. The penalty for each count is $10,000 in fines and/or five years in prison. After failing to gain sanctuary in Israel, Lansky returned to the United States to face a series of trials. He was convicted of contempt of a federal grand jury and sentenced to a year and a day in prison but was acquitted by a jury on a charge of income-tax evasion; at this writing, he was awaiting trial in the Flamingo skimming case.

The exposé in the *Wall Street Journal* convinced Lansky and Vincent ("Jimmy Blue Eyes") Alo, Lansky's official link with the Mafia, that it was time to reconsider their position. They had learned a costly lesson in Cuba. Now they wanted a leader with grass-roots support, and they turned to Pindling, a London-educated attorney, who headed the black Progressive Liberal Party. Mike McLaney, a Lansky gambling associate in Cuba and later in Haiti, became the liaison between the Mafia and Pindling. Besides money and advice, McLaney provided Pindling with air transportation for the campaign. Since Pindling's election in 1967, the Mafia has taken root in the islands. Columnist Jack Anderson reported in 1972 that Moncrieff J. Spear, the U.S. consul general, had filed a secret report with the State Department alleging that "recently there has been evidence suggesting that some Government of the Bahamas leaders are getting criminal financing and are playing politics with security at the casinos." Meanwhile, Mafia scandals and Black Power expectations have created disastrous economic tension. Desk-drawer corporations and illegal money are nothing if not mobile. The exodus, now in progress, will be hard to stop.[6]

Canada may not have secret bank accounts, but for multinationals enjoying the 14 percent WHTC tax discount, it is the United States' greatest colony. The statistics are staggering: nearly two-thirds of all factories operating in Canada are U.S.-owned, nine of every ten plants big enough to hire more than 5,000 persons are owned by foreigners, mostly Americans, who also control 62 percent of Canadian petroleum and natural gas, 52 percent of mining and smelting, 97 percent of the auto industry, 78 percent of chemicals, and 77 percent of the manufacture of electrical apparatus. In fact, about $35 billion of the country's $58 billion in total corporate assets is American-owned. Americans have more money invested in Canada than in any other foreign country. It therefore came as a shock in 1971 when President Nixon remarked at a news conference that "Japan is our biggest customer in the world and we are their biggest customer in the world." Actually, the two-way flow between Canada and the United States is the greatest trade volume between any two nations in all history.

The President's remark "scared hell" out of Allan Grossman, minister of trade and development for Ontario Province: "The mere thought that the President of the United States should be so poorly advised, that he could make such a statement so factually incorrect, worried me about the sort of advice he might be getting on other matters."[7]

As far as tax havens are concerned, it makes little difference whether the money is dirty or hot, whether it comes from a mafioso, a multinational, or a dentist, for money is money. The old cliché never had greater meaning: money has no odor, nor does it have nationality, politics, race, or religion. Nobody loves a money smuggler more reverently than a tax-haven banker.

The laundering process is fairly simple. From the United States, the money may flow to several tax havens to cool the trail, but eventually most of it will get its final rinse in the snows of the Alps, for Switzerland is the ultimate illegal money haven. It is the most stable country in the world, free from the fears of war or even civil disorder; it is the only known country where the banks are more powerful than the central government—they are so powerful that they can virtually guarantee depositors against any changes in the banking laws. The Swiss franc is as solid a currency as any in the world.

The very magnitude of the Swiss operation diminishes all others by comparison. A country of 16,000 square miles and six million people, with a gross national product equal to less than half of General Motors' net sales, Switzerland currently supports more than 500 banks with 4,400 branches and total assets of $40 billion. The nation's three largest banks—the Union Bank of Switzerland, the Swiss Credit Bank, and the Swiss Bank Corporation—would each rank among the top ten in the United States. Of even greater significance from the standpoint of laundering illegal money —and the basic reason the United States government is so interested in Switzerland—is that Swiss banks are permitted by law to act as stock-brokers. Swiss banks account for about 20 percent of all trading on the New York Stock Exchange. They take the final step in the laundering process. The money, now washed clean, is plowed back into legitimate investments, portfolio and direct corporate interests, in the United States or anywhere else in the world. Of vital importance here is that Swiss banks illegally buy securities on 10 percent margin, whereas Federal Reserve margin rules now require American investors to come up with 50 percent.*

---

* It was lowered to 50 percent, from 65 percent, on January 2, 1974. The reduced margin requirement applies to stocks listed on all U.S. stock exchanges, plus a selected

To protect the identity of investors, Swiss banks use omnibus accounts at U.S. brokerage houses, with all trades made in the bank's name. This means that American banks with branches in Switzerland—the Bank of America, Chase Manhattan, First National City, among many others—can play the same game. It is no secret that in many Swiss cities, the largest volume of business is done by American branches. On this side of the Atlantic, an increasing number of Swiss banks have set up shop in New York and Los Angeles, with representatives in strategic mother lodes like Miami and Las Vegas. Their standing omnibus accounts with Wall Street brokers do a thriving business in bonds and securities, far more than their domestic clientele would indicate. They are popular because they offer investors a chance not only to evade margin requirements and taxes on profits but also to indulge in forbidden insider trading.

Much has been written about the tenacious though fruitless attempts by the United States to pressure Switzerland into signing a judicial assistance treaty that would force the banks to furnish secret information in cases involving gangsters. The impression created is that only gangsters use secret bank accounts. It is either that or the United States makes a distinction between dirty and hot money.

Robert M. Morgenthau did not see it that way. As former U.S. Attorney for the Southern District of New York, he was the most persistent advocate of disclosure laws, the one man who gave Swiss bankers cause for alarm. In testimony before the House Banking and Currency Committee in 1968, Morgenthau revealed that many people besides hoodlums were interested in secret bank accounts. They included, he said, "sophisticated international financial operators, stock market swindlers and manipulators, corporate officers making illegal profits from their inside information, businessmen who hide profits from the tax authorities, and enormous numbers of stock market investors who through foreign banks evade income taxes on their trading profits."[8]

For a while in 1969, Morgenthau turned hot money into a hot potato for the Nixon Administration. It bounced all over the lot, from the White House to Justice, Treasury, the Fed, and the Securities and Exchange Commission, but nobody could hold onto it for very long. Meanwhile, on Capitol Hill that rambunctious chairman of the House Banking and Currency Committee, Wright Patman, was beginning to make threatening

---

list of Over-the-Counter issues. The requirement has fluctuated through the years. During most of 1946, it was 100 percent, the only time that the maximum level has been imposed.

sounds about new legislation to make life more difficult for respectable tax dodgers. Among a long list of prohibitions, he proposed to ban stocks purchased through foreign banks from being voted in U.S. corporations unless the identity of the owner was revealed to the satisfaction of the SEC.

In New York, Morgenthau persuaded federal grand juries to indict seventy-five businessmen for financial crimes involving secret bank accounts, and then referred scores of other cases to the Internal Revenue Service for action. Going after gangsters was one thing, but this was an unexpected switch in tactics. And there was more. Morgenthau began looking for pretexts to freeze securities accounts of Swiss banks in the United States on grounds that some of the money was smuggled to Europe to evade taxes—that is, it was American money masquerading as European money—or that the banks cooperated in evading margin requirements. "We're working on a number of cases where there's been violation of margin requirements," he told newsmen. "Last December we indicted the Arzi Bank of Zurich for purchasing securities on margins of as little as 10 percent. We seized the bank's securities in several New York brokerage houses and the bank's director came over to plead guilty."[9] Morgenthau's strategy impaled Swiss bankers on the horns of a painful dilemma: to defend themselves against his charges, they would have to appear in court and answer his questions, which they could not do without violating their bank's code of secrecy, in which case their silence in defiance of court immunity would place them in contempt.

By copping a plea, the Arzi bank director had left the door open for a far more illustrious violator to slip through. As we shall see, however, it was not the kind of case that gladdens the crusading heart of a political appointee.

The story begins in July 1968 as two major economic events were dramatically unfolding on the American scene: Richard Nixon, then a full-fledged Wall Street lawyer, was campaigning for the presidency, at a time when Wall Street conglomerators were partaking in the most succulent cannibal feast in history.

Following his defeat in the 1962 gubernatorial race, Richard Nixon fled California to "bury the corpse" in New York. In analyzing his motives for the move, he told Robert J. Donovan of the Los Angeles *Times* that New York was "very cold and very ruthless and very exciting, and therefore an interesting place to live. . . . The main thing, it is a place where you can't slow down—a fast track. Any person tends to vegetate unless he is moving on a fast track. New York is a very challenging place to live. You have to bone up to keep alive in the competition."

Nixon was introduced to the Wall Street law firm of Mudge, Stern, Baldwin and Todd by two old friends: Elmer H. Bobst, chairman emeritus of Warner-Lambert Pharmaceutical Company, who met Nixon in 1952 and reached instant rapport—and Donald M. Kendall, president of Pepsico, who offered the firm a large retainer if it would make the services of the former Vice President available to his company, which was then in the throes of a drag-out sales battle with Coca-Cola for the cola championship of the world. As Kendall envisioned it, the former Vice President would charm world leaders into sponsoring his product, an assignment that would dovetail perfectly with his desires to maintain an international image.*

The law firm was happy to welcome Nixon into the fold. With a fast reshuffling of senior partners and a chopping away of deceased partners from the title, the company was renamed Nixon, Mudge, Rose, Guthrie, Alexander & Mitchell.

Of all the new partners Nixon acquired by this move, it is reliably reported by those who were intimately acquainted with the situation that none was closer to him than Randolph H. Guthrie, a specialist in corporate law and international finance. In *The Superlawyers*, Joseph Goulden tells a story—perhaps apocryphal—about the time Guthrie paid a first visit to a Midwestern company that was about to be raided by a competitor he represented. "Gentlemen," Guthrie began, "you are about to be raped. Now, why don't you lay back and enjoy it?"[10] In the rampage years of the go-go conglomerators, Randolph Guthrie must have made capital of that persuasive proposition. Yet the rape he threatened oftentimes relied more on the element of surprise than brute force. At least, that was the situation in the case in point.

The eager rapist, Liquidonics Industries, Inc., of Westbury, New York, was a small engineering firm with annual earnings of $4 million and a net worth of $6.1 million. The reluctant victim, UMC Industries, Inc., of St. Louis, was a large manufacturer with a product line ranging from matches to missile warheads, and with earnings of $22 million and a net worth of $54.5 million. At first glance, the impending corporate rape appeared ludicrously implausible—can a pilot fish impregnate a shark? Even the head strategist at Liquidonics, N. Norman Muller, became discouraged after several months of futile thrusts. Then early in 1969 Muller met

---

* One of the first rulers to succumb to Nixon's charm was Chiang Kai-shek, who gave Pepsi-Cola an exclusive franchise arrangement in Taiwan.

Guthrie and discovered that Mudge Rose was the U.S. representative for the Banque de Paris et des Pays-Bas (Suisse) S.A., in Geneva. His request for a $40-million loan was approved within a matter of days.

But UMC refused to "lay back and enjoy it." It charged that Liquidonics violated the Securities and Exchange Act when it failed to satisfy the 80 percent margin requirement in purchasing the stock—at that time a company had to post 80 percent of the purchase price in order to borrow 20 percent.

In *The Superlawyers*, Goulden printed a "memorandum of a telephone conversation" dictated by Patrick J. Griffin, an official of the Securities and Exchange Commission, which summarized his talk with James Sargent, attorney for Liquidonics. Dated February 12, 1969, less than a month after President Nixon's inauguration, it said:

> UMC has raised the question as to whether or not the two brokerage firms, who were acting as dealer-managers for Liquidonics in the tender offer, were not in violation of Regulations G, T or U with regard to arranging a loan with a foreign bank which was collateralized by stock where the loan exceeded 20% of the value of the stock. I conveyed this information to Mr. Sargent's secretary in his absence and he telephoned today and advised that the loan was arranged by a lawyer who was a former partner of President Nixon and the Attorney General and who is still in the name of the firm. He stated that *under the circumstances there was no violation of the law in the arranging of the loan.*
>
> Mr. Sargent will send us a letter regarding the status of the loan under the Federal Reserve regulations and the legality thereof.[11]

No regulatory agency ever intervened on UMC's behalf, yet Liquidonics failed to pull it off because it could not raise the long-term funding required to cover the Swiss bank loan. In the ensuing debacle, Liquidonics lost about $16 million in a forced sale of its UMC stock to the Swiss bank, which in turn gave the stock to its Luxembourg subsidiary, Overseas International Corporation, the ultimate ravisher of UMC. And behold! From that misdirected seed was born the new chairman of UMC Industries: Randolph H. Guthrie.

As a reminder of its position in the legal firmament, Mudge Rose charged Liquidonics $200,000 for the use of its financial expertise over a three-month period.

Morgenthau, who had successfully prosecuted the Arzi Bank director on a similar charge, never got the opportunity—assuming he ever really wanted it—to try his luck with Guthrie. On the other hand, Guthrie was convinced that margin requirements did not apply to foreign banks. He stressed that point in an interview with Goulden. The Federal Reserve, he said, "was never intended to cover loans made by European banks—that's a lot of crap. As a matter of fact, we consulted with the Federal Reserve Board before we made the loan. If it was not a first-class loan, we didn't want to make it. So I call up and find out—I tell them all the facts. 'Why are you calling me on this?' the man asked. Based on that conversation, and what we know of the law, we gave the opinion the loan was all right." Asked about the Presidential name-dropping quoted in the memo, Guthrie replied, "That's the sort of thing we keep running into."[12]

That sort of thing was not totally distasteful to all the partners at Mudge Rose. In the four years that Nixon headed the firm,* it expanded from fifty-seven lawyers to a hundred and twenty. Following his election in 1968, the Washington office of Mudge Rose grew instantly from one man to twelve. Asked by Goulden why the firm had included the President's name in its listing in the 1969–70 Washington phone book, Guthrie said they had a "big estate and trust practice, and we deal with people who don't come into the office but once every ten years. Old ladies will come into the building and look for the previous firm name. They don't know our firm by the name of individual lawyers, the one who drew the papers, but by the firm itself, and that has changed many times over the years. . . . What I'm trying to say is this: We have to keep all these old listings in the phone book so that people can find us. It's a very, very practical problem that we face all the time . . . Nixon's name was there so people can find our firm. What is someone to do if he knows us as Nixon, and so forth? He's got to have some place to look."[13] Guthrie did not say how often Mudge Rose changed addresses. As noted in other chapters, Penn Central and El Paso Natural Gas, among a long list of farsighted companies, never had any trouble finding a law firm with clout in the White House.

Robert Morgenthau lasted until December 1969. Although he was named the most effective United States Attorney in the nation by a Republican study group, he was still a Democrat occupying the most powerful prosecutive seat outside of Washington. And there was his prosecution of Roy Cohn, the second in five years, which did not sit well with the Director of the FBI. J. Edgar Hoover and Cohn had been intimate friends since the old days of the McCarthy committee. Finally, his probing of foreign bank accounts, as he expressed it, "was making the Administration nervous."

* According to a tax return made available to the writer Fletcher Knebel during the 1968 campaign, Nixon earned about $150,000 a year.

For a grand finale, Morgenthau went to Washington early in December to give his blessings to Wright Patman's proposed legislation. The House Banking Committee hoped it was concluding interminable public hearings and private discussions with Nixon Treasury officials on a bill designed to tighten the rules on foreign financial transactions. At that very moment, however, State and Treasury officials were meeting behind closed doors with a delegation of irate bankers, including representatives of America's three largest banks: Bank of America, Chase Manhattan, and First National City Bank of New York (Citibank)—among them, they controlled more than eight hundred foreign branches.

Following two lengthy sessions with the bankers, Treasury official Eugene T. Rossides experienced a change of heart. He told the banking committee he could not support the measure as written because it went too far. IRS Commissioner Randolph Thrower thought the bill was too strict. Rossides even tried to neutralize the testimony of Assistant Attorney General Will Wilson, who had given the measure his unequivocal approval on the day of Morgenthau's appearance. Wilson, said Rossides, had meant to say that he favored the bill's objectives but not the bill itself. This came as a surprise to Patman, since Rossides and Thrower had both helped write the legislation.

An emasculated version of the bill was finally signed into law in October 1970, but renewed lobbying by the banks twice forced the Treasury to change the effective date it would issue its final regulations—from August to November 1971 to July 1972. "It's just a matter of priorities," a Treasury spokesman explained. Nobody, however, tried to explain the department's softened approach: the final regulations were not nearly as sweeping as originally proposed.

Under the new rules, financial institutions are required to keep records of all domestic checks and deposits for five years, except for depositors who write at least a hundred checks a month. In addition, they are required to report to the Treasury all "unusual currency transactions"—the interpretation of "unusual" is as good a loophole as any—involving $10,000 or more, and to keep for five years records of all money transfers in or out of the United States in amounts greater than $10,000. The original proposals had required records on all transactions exceeding $1,000. It was left to the individual to report to the Customs Bureau all foreign transfers of money exceeding $5,000. A domestic financial institution that violates the law is subject to a civil penalty of $1,000, but the criminal penalties for an individual range from $1,000 and five years in prison up to $500,000 for engaging in illegal transactions exceeding $100,000.

The lobbying forces, of whom hundreds testified over a two-year period, could chalk up another victory. Except for creating an avalanche of paperwork—some forty billion separate items to be recorded annually—the merits of the bill remained a mystery even to Patman. At one point the Pentagon had supported the bill. It seems the Defense Department wanted Patman to do something about the spy network financed by secret Swiss bank accounts—a notion the military brass had perhaps neglected to clear with the CIA. "Foreign numbered accounts pose a security threat to the Department of Defense in that they may be used to support foreign agents targeted against the military establishment," a Pentagon official revealed, "or they may be used to conceal payments to U.S. personnel recruited by foreign intelligence services." Better still, he could have directed the attention of the lawmakers to "The Late Late Show."

"The multinational corporations have come to consider it part of their self-interested duty to shareholders to minimize world wide-tax liability."* There is nothing very astounding about this observation. The maximization of profit has always been the *sine qua non* of any business. A United Nations study arrived at a similar conclusion: "The number of potential participants in international tax escape has drastically increased."[14]

In the respectable world of multinationals, tax havens become tax-minimization territories. The older havens also like to play the euphemism game and call themselves profit oases or taxation sanctuaries. The goal, by any other name, is strictly tax avoidance on a monumental scale. Of the eight thousand U.S. companies involved in foreign operations, it is impossible to even guess the number participating in this international tax ripoff. The fact that the Internal Revenue Service has legal and administrative sanctions against many of the more blatant practices has had little effect on the players. IRS audits of foreign subsidiaries are few and far between, and even when loopholes are challenged in Tax Court, the gobbledygook of tax language makes enforcement difficult, if indeed not impossible.

The osmotic growth of American multinationals has hit the world economic community with the impact of a tidal wave. In a single generation, the book value of American direct investment† abroad leaped from

---

* From a study by the Economist Intelligence Unit, an international business consulting firm associated with the magazine *Economist* in London.

† Direct investments are those made to acquire ownership of a company or factory, as opposed to portfolio investments and short-term assets and claims.

$7.2 billion in 1946 to $84 billion in 1972, and the market value is probably closer to $250 billion. It is estimated that the total before-tax foreign profits in 1970 were $17.5 billion, or about 20 percent of total U.S. corporate profits. The U.S. taxes paid, however, were not the $8.4 billion due under the 48 percent corporate tax rate but a miserly $900 million, for a *tax rate of 5 percent.*[15]

In consideration of these extraordinary tax subsidies, what are the broader implications of multinational economics? Theoreticians, from so-called monetarist economists to payola columnists, have woven a deceptive literature. A few samples follow:

> . . . U.S. direct investment abroad, after all, is now the only significant money-maker on the balance-of-payments books. The net surplus on the account last year was more than $5 billion, and if one wants to count the U.S. trade surplus in the flow of goods and services between U.S. companies and their affiliates abroad, the total positive impact of U.S. foreign investment on the balance of payments is close to $10 billion [sheer fantasy].
>
> With due regard for the good intentions of George Meany, Sen. Hartke, and Rep. Burke, who believe otherwise, it should be clear enough that the U.S. multinational corporations—which hold roughly 90% of the roughly $86 billion in U.S. direct investment—are the best thing that ever happened to the U.S. balance of payments. If their earnings are to continue to multiply thereby giving the United States the wherewithal to buy its way through its energy problems in the years ahead, the companies must continue to modernize, to expand, to share in growing markets abroad.
>
> That takes capital. And with the U.S. controls on capital outflow [imposed by Johnson in 1968], along with requirements that a share of overseas earnings be repatriated, the multinationals are carrying the burden of a U.S. policy that is patently not in American interests.—*Wall Street Journal*, October 18, 1972.

The reference to Indiana Senator Vance Hartke and Massachusetts Representative James Burke was directed at the Hartke-Burke bill, generally labeled in the press as protectionist legislation:

> Organized labor's attitude is set forth in ominous terms in the Hartke-Burke Bill. In bluntest terms, the intent of this bill is to kill or maim the present U.S. based multinational operation. The bill would subject foreign earnings of U.S. corporations to double taxation by eliminating foreign income taxes as a credit against U.S. income taxes, and by subjecting the foreign earnings to U.S. taxes even when the earnings aren't brought home. Other wild proposals of the bill would clamp controls on investment capital going overseas and ban the use of U.S. technology abroad.

The bill would set quotas on all goods coming into the U.S., limiting them to 1965–1969 levels. A ridiculous bill? Don't laugh. It attracted 70 co-sponsors in the House, including congressmen from such normally liberal states as New York and Connecticut.—*Forbes*, March 1, 1972.

A. W. Clausen, president of the Bank of America, one of the world's largest multinationals, warned California businessmen that their state would be among the first to suffer the consequences of a trade war if the Hartke-Burke bill became law. To him, it was "the worst piece of legislation introduced in the last forty years." Its "protectionist arguments" were not new to him. "You find them century after century, like so many bits of refuse on the scrapheap of human folly." The bill "could hardly avoid igniting a trade war as other countries retaliated against the closing of our markets. At immediate stake would not just be the profits of American international businessmen, but the 2.7 million American jobs which depend directly or indirectly on the export trade." In response to a question, Clausen said his bank's investment in foreign branches was about $10 billion.[16] Meanwhile, Henry Ford II was predicting that any effort to improve the balance of payments by limiting imports and restricting U.S. investment abroad would have catastrophic effects on the economy.

A study by the Federal Reserve Bank of New York, released in July 1972—just when the Democratic platform was calling for the closing of tax "loopholes" that "encourage the export of jobs"—said the "evidence seems clear that U.S. direct investment is a long-run positive factor in the balance of payments." However, the report conceded that its conclusions "must be considered tenuous" since it was impossible to judge the effect of multinationals on the country's exports and imports without knowing how trade would have flowed if they did not exist. Yet the report said it was reasonable to assume that most of the changes in exports and imports would have occurred even in the absence of U.S. foreign investment, at least in the long run. As an example of the quality of the statistics quoted in the report, it said that "available statistics don't support the claim that there are very significant imports from affiliates in the areas frequently cited as low-wage countries, such as Mexico, Taiwan and Korea."[17]

The report completely ignored the fact that General Electric, RCA, Admiral, Motorola, Zenith, and Philco-Ford were all busily manufacturing electronic equipment in low-wage countries such as Taiwan, Spain, Mexico, Japan, Hong Kong, Singapore, Macao, Korea, Indonesia, South Africa, and Latin America, with the result that 96 percent of the tape recorders used in this country, 92 percent of the radios, and almost 42 percent of the television sets are now made overseas. Quality cameras, electronic calculators, and a long list of labor-intensive items produced by multinationals are no longer manufactured in the United States. Imports of shoes and textiles, along with steel and machine tools, are currently flooding the American market.

"This flood of imports is not an innocent reflection of just and normal fluctuations of free trade as some would have us believe," said Senator Hartke. "This flight of investment abroad has a three-fold purpose: 1) to avoid U.S. corporate income taxes; 2) to buy cheaper labor abroad; and 3) to sell back on the world's best market—the American consumer—products which paid nothing, by way of manufacture, into the average American wage earners' ability to pay for it."

> The labor leaders who are pushing Burke-Hartke are not acting out of caprice, or malice, or simple bullheadedness. They are not, in the main, economic illiterates. They simply operate with a parochial frame of reference, rather than an Olympian perspective of the national interest. . . .
>
> Labor considers it a self-evident proposition that if production facilities and technical know-how remained at home, the same volume of goods could be manufactured here and sold abroad. The motive for setting up shop abroad, in labor's view, has generally been to exploit tax advantages, as well as benefit from cheaper labor.
>
> The multinationals, of course, heatedly dispute that view. Indeed, they maintain that in most cases their motive for going abroad was to jump trade barriers. Thus if they had remained at home, they would have sacrificed some foreign markets. . . .
>
> The burden of proof that multinationals are depriving American workers of jobs should be on the labor movement, for the Burke-Hartke bill would impose a drastic therapy. For one thing, foreign taxes paid by the multinationals would be treated as a deduction from taxable income and could no longer be taken as a direct credit against U.S. taxes due. The changes in tax law would cost the companies billions—heavy punishment indeed for a mere suspicion of guilt. But when an A.F.L.-C.I.O. staffer was asked for his evidence, he said, "Let the government get the data. Why is it up to us?"—Irwin Ross, *Fortune*, March 1973.

Hartke deplored the lack of international controls on multinationals:

> I talk about world order, not protectionism. I say without it, U.S. corporate giants have advantages no other American citizen or American business has. The big multinational can roam the world like a Barbary pirate, setting up a plant in Spain, wholly tax free, fully protected by dictatorship from organized labor and strikes. Henry Ford just visited Madrid.* He wanted to put in Spain a $235 million, 300,000-car-per-year

* December 1972.

plant. Spain, according to newspaper accounts of the visit, affords Ford "labor peace" and low wage scales. Strikes are illegal. The only trouble is that Spain wants to join the Common Market. But if she does, she will have to allow labor to organize and mount economic strength, just as Ford himself does. Neither Ford nor Spain apparently want that. To call my bill a backward step, a return to Smoot-Hawley or a labor protectionist idea, is to fly in the face of the economic facts of life around the world today. There is, for a few corporations, a flight from tax at the water's edge. Big business did not grow in a share-cropper economy. Nor will it be a credit to America abroad, as the plantation owner and wheeler-dealer among poor nations, buying and selling their governments and their peoples as it never could or would do in this country.

On March 1, 1973, the *Wall Street Journal* again seized its editorial cudgel and pummeled the nemeses of multinationals:

> Senators [Frank] Church, Hartke, [Gaylord] Nelson and a few others of like disposition are again making threatening noises towards American multinational corporations, but the basis for whatever it is that concerns them is murky indeed.
>
> Senator Church heads a Foreign Affairs subcommittee which may spend the next three years or so "investigating" the MNCs. Senator Nelson, in some of the most awesome Senate rhetoric heard in a long time, describes them as a "new and dark power."
>
> Senator Hartke, of course, is co-sponsor of the Burke–Hartke bill, which would deliver a karate chop to the MNCs by taxing their unrepatriated earnings, putting new limits on their ability to transfer capital and attaching some other fetters. Burke–Hartke also offers some new and dangerous trade protectionism.
>
> The only Americans with much reason to have a grievance against the principle of multinational corporate operation are labor union leaders— the leaders, that is, not the members. Union leaders feel that their bargaining power is weakened by the flexibility of multinational firms. If the unions get too tough in Detroit, a multinational company, theoretically, can transfer production to Taipei. . . .
>
> Some of the MNCs have grown large indeed. Senator Nelson observes that only 23 of the world's nations are larger than General Motors if their GNPs are compared to GM's net sales. But the Senator seeks to equate size with power and to jump from the mention of power to the suggestion that the power poses some sort of vague threat.
>
> Power and size do not equate naturally. The MNCs, unlike nations, command no armies and make no law. What power they have exists in their ability, largely economic in origin, to sometimes influence the decisions of governments. . . .
>
> The MNCs currently return some $8 billion to the U.S. in interest, dividends and earnings and that also could be affected.

Still fantasizing, same old tune, but considerably toned down from the statistics offered on October 18, 1972, as previously noted: ". . . the *total positive impact* [emphasis added] of U.S. foreign investment on the balance of payments is close to $10 billion." Figures are thrown around every which way. In its warning against the perils of the Hartke-Burke Bill, *Forbes* came up with its own numbers: "Last year [1971] they earned an estimated $10 billion on those assets and remitted $6.5 billion in dividends to the U.S., while direct new investment was only $5.5 billion. Such legislation could knock much of this investment into a cocked hat."[18]

One of Senator Hartke's solutions to the "unlicensed piracy" of the giant multinationals is to find ways to encourage big labor to export "organizing know-how in the field of collective bargaining, in union organization, in the technology of the labor movement. Why should not the AFL-CIO export labor organization massively to Japan, Mexico and South America? There would be no automobile parts assembled across the borders for sales back to this country. What could be fairer, less isolationist than that? I don't hear the multinational giants saying they will invest in world standards for anything. Not even for open elections and worker rights under some of the dictatorships they love to do business with. They don't even pay enough taxes in many countries to cover municipal garbage collections."

Presidential adviser Peter Flanigan disagreed with Senator Hartke on all counts. On February 26, 1973, Flanigan told the Senate Finance Subcommittee on International Trade that it was fortunate Congress had not acted on the Hartke-Burke Bill. "It is difficult to find much evidence that the multinational corporations, as a group, have damaged the U.S. economy or its workers." In fact, studies by both the Tariff Commission and the Commerce Department, he said, suggested quite the opposite. "The evidence appears conclusive that the multinational corporations exert a highly positive influence on our trade and payments balance." Turning the U.S. trade deficit around, he said, could best be achieved by Congress giving the Administration broad powers "to allow the President to offer a combination of encouragements and discouragements" in negotiations with trading partners scheduled to begin next fall." Other than the power to impose tariffs and import quotas, he said, the President's only negotiating tool would be a threat to withdraw U.S. commitments for military assistance abroad. This power was important because the multinationals were losing popularity "not only among less developed countries, but among some of our most prosperous trading partners." He denied that the companies were exploiting low-wage countries. It was his opinion that facilities were not moved abroad to take advantage of labor costs unless competitive circumstances forced them to it. "The proper role for the multinational corporations is to be good citizens in the countries in which they operate. This implies the duty to conduct operations within the constraints of good citizenship, plus the responsibility to accept all the obligations of citizenship."[19]

But Hartke said it was "still cheaper to support slaves in squalor than buy a cotton gin." How did that square with Flanigan's concept of good citizenship? Which was closer to the reality of South Africa? General Motors and Ford began assembling cars there in the 1920s, coexisting very profitably with its government's later pervasive "white supremacy" policy of apartheid. There are critics who say that most of the three hundred or so American multinationals currently operating there have gone beyond mere coexistence with apartheid and actually entrenched it. It is a fact that between 1960 and 1972 American direct investment in South Africa more than tripled, growing from $286 million to about $900 million. Coincidentally or not, it was in 1960 that police killed sixty-nine black South Africans after a demonstration in Sharpeville.* World reaction to the massacre made South Africa an international pariah. The United Nations condemned it, passing two scores of censuring resolutions against it, including an arms embargo. It withdrew from the British Commonwealth, and its trade unions were banned by the International Labor Organization. Even the Olympics are closed to its athletes.

None of this, however, had discouraged the American businessman. The Republic of South Africa offers precisely what a multinational prizes most of all: political stability, a convertible hard currency, a booming market, and an inexhaustible pool of slave labor. For years now, the after-tax returns on investment have been gamboling in the 19 percent range. That alone will buy plenty of rationalization. Ford set the tempo many years ago. "The Ford Motor Company," one of its spokesman has pointed out, "believes that U.S. corporations should not interfere in the domestic affairs of the countries in which they do business."

"Would apartheid disappear if American investments were with-

---

* A similar incident took place at the Western Deep Level Mine at Carletonville in September 1973 when black miners rioted against low wages and working conditions. A squad of policemen opened fire, killing eleven and wounding twenty-seven.

drawn?" a Los Angeles *Times* editorial inquired. "The answer is no. More than that, the heaviest burden would fall on the 100,000 nonwhite workers connected with the 308 U.S.-controlled companies in South Africa."[20]

The truth of the matter, as a 1969 market-research survey revealed, is that most American executives like the system just the way it is. Eighty-three percent approved of apartheid as "an approach that is, under the circumstances at least, an attempt to develop a solution." Less than one in ten felt it was "altogether incorrect." In an interview conducted by a member of New York's Council for Christian Social Action in 1970, Jim Hatos, then managing director for the International Harvester subsidiary in South Africa, did not mince words: "I am sympathetic to what the South African Government is trying to do. I don't want hundreds of Africans running around in front of my house."

Under apartheid, not only are nonwhites forced to live in segregated areas, but companies are required to maintain separate sets of facilities for each race,* including cafeterias, drinking fountains, toilets, and plant entrances. Certain jobs are reserved for whites only; nonwhites may not supervise whites. What this means is that the whites at the top of the totem pole get all the best jobs and the blacks at the bottom only the worst. The pay scales really tell the story. The average *monthly* wage paid to blacks by manufacturing companies in 1972 was $69, while the whites received $419. The "poverty datum line" for a family of five was $103 a month in Johannesburg, Pretoria, and Port Elizabeth; $89 in Capetown, and $93 in Durban. Among the multinationals that paid below the poverty datum line were John Deere, General Electric, International Harvester, FMC/Link-Belt, Sterling Drug, and Firestone.

And there are ways of circumventing even these basic requirements. Firestone built a new plant in Brits, a "border area," which exempted it from paying the rock-bottom minimum scale of 35 cents an hour. Its cafeteria was so filthy that nobody could use it. The tables and food were covered with soot.

The O'okiep Copper Company, a subsidiary of Newmont Mining Corporation, is said to be operating a regular mining operation in South Africa. It employs two thousand blacks, recruited from the most impoverished tribal areas, on one-year contracts at wages averaging $40 a month, plus bed and board in the company compound, where it is doubtful that

---

* In 1972, there were 4,000,000 whites, 15,000,000 "Bantu" (blacks), 2,000,000 "Coloured" (mulattoes), and 600,000 "Asiatics" (mostly Indians).

the living conditions could be visualized by even the most fertile imagination.

The disparity between white and black is perhaps widest in gold mining, the country's most crucial industry. The privileged position of the 42,000 white miners is protected by a powerful trade union—wages for whites start at $475 a month and can rise to $1,100. The 42,000 black miners, by contrast, have no workers' organization,* and their wages start at $32.50 a month and can only on rare occasion rise to $157.50. According to a study by a South African economist, wages for black miners were no higher in real terms in 1969 than they were in 1911 and possibly were even lower, while those of whites had increased by 70 percent. The total black wage bill of the mining industry was $150 million in 1972, whereas the industry's profits before taxes were $850 million—$332.5 million or 63 percent greater than in 1971. The profit increase, ascribable to the rise in the price of gold, was alone more than double the amount spent on black wages.[21]

What is slave labor? In a *Fortune* article (July 1972), John Blashill, *Time* bureau chief for Africa, came as close to defining it as anybody without actually coming out and saying so:

> Given their choice, many employers would rather hire blacks than whites. The whites, pampered and protected by tradition, tend to be unreliable and shoddy workers. They often wander from job to job, quitting on the slightest pretext. Sometimes they refuse to work at all unless management provides then with African "assistants," who do everything for them—brew their tea, hand them their tools, and even fill in for them when they play hooky. In one American heavy-equipment plant, where welding jobs are reserved for members of the white union, the managing director reports that the welders seldom come to work more than two days a week, and go fishing—without pay—the other three. When they're absent, the welding is done by their supposedly untrained African assistants —who work twice as fast at one-third the pay. "I get six times the production per dollar out of my Bantu," the manager says.
>
> I.T.T.'s Peter Loveday calls this indefensible exploitation. "In practically every situation where you've got whites and nonwhites doing the same job," he says, "you're dealing with the cream of the coloreds and blacks, and the dregs of the whites." Yet the blacks cannot afford to be

---

* Although not specifically illegal, black trade unions are not recognized in law in South Africa and have no collective bargaining rights—even the token "works committee" system permitted in secondary industry is not allowed in the mining industry.

prima donnas, for there is a vast pool of unemployed African labor. Once an African lands a job, he does his best to keep it. If he quits or gets fired, he runs the very serious risk of being shipped back to his "homeland," or reservation. In most American subsidiaries the only employees with twenty years' service are Africans.

It took Ford about fifty years to recognize the medical needs of its nonwhite employees. Whites were covered by its medical plan after three months' employment, nonwhites only after ten years. In January 1972, all employees were given coverage after three months. There are still no Coloureds or blacks in the top two of its eleven labor grades, and Coloureds—who are rated higher than blacks—with fifteen years' experience get the same pay as whites starting out. With a labor force of nearly six thousand, Ford is the largest American employer in South Africa. Its lowest rate is 53 cents an hour, slightly below the poverty datum line, which makes Ford considerably above average as an employer. Chrysler and General Motors are not quite that generous.

Beginning in 1971, General Motors has been criticized soundly from American pulpits. The Episcopal Church, which has a sizable investment in GM, has joined with five major Protestant denominations in denouncing the company's role in South Africa. After a tour of inspection in the fall of 1971, the churchmen issued a damning report, asserting that "any cooperation with or strengthening of apartheid is contrary to the fundamentals of Christianity." Their report added: "Most of us believe that American corporations should totally disengage from Southern Africa; that the presence of American corporations in which we are shareholders undergirds the systems of racial colonialism and apartheid which prevails in Southern Africa. . . . While every American company visited stated that they felt themselves to be 'good' and 'progressive' employers, we found that American companies as a general rule are not more enlightened in their employment practices nor in their sensitivity to the South African situation than are other companies in South Africa."

GM's immediate response was to label the group political revolutionaries in clerical garb. But after a meeting of the board, the corporation assumed a more pragmatic stance: "The board of directors believes this pattern of united, concerted action further evidences that the basic intent of these proposals is to alter the political, racial and social practices of the countries involved and that safeguarding the stockholders' investment in these target companies is the secondary, if any, interest to these church groups."[22]

Balance the above with another passage from the March 1, 1973, editorial in the *Wall Street Journal*.

> They [multinationals] of course do have major importance. And many of them have attained great economic efficiencies through their ability to apply the benefits of division of labor and mass production on a global scale. These efficiencies, which have contributed to a general rise in the world standard of living, stem very much from the flexibility multinational operation permits.
>
> It is hardly a misfortune for the United States that its workers have had the best of things in the multinational division of labor. Since a very large proportion of the large MNCs are headquartered here and since the U.S. has for years made a strong commitment to higher education and other forms of human resource development, Americans tend to hold the best jobs in the MNCs. They are the headquarters staffers, the computer technologists, the engineers, etc.
>
> But this privileged status is by no means guaranteed. Nothing could destroy it faster than unwise and unnecessary regulation of American-based MNCs. For good economic reasons, the MNCs are training citizens of other countries to step into higher-level jobs. Almost inevitably, more of these workers will find their way to headquarters management jobs.

In his *Fortune* article, John Blashill concludes with these words:

> Only top management in U.S. headquarters can take the steps necessary to improve the lot of their nonwhite employees in South Africa. "The direction for change must come from the boardrooms back home," says Bill Marshall Smith of Caltex. "And let's face it, we could all be moving faster." Too often, however, home-office decisions must be made on the basis of faulty or misleading information from the field. An auto-company executive, resident in South Africa, explains the danger: "Corporate decisions are made from tiny slips of paper with maybe just the figures written on them. The slips are the distillations of reports from the field. But no subsidiary tells its home office the truth. We all lie about figures, so you can imagine how much we lie about everything else. If anybody back there really knows what we're doing, it's certainly not our fault."
>
> Top managements that want to protect the future of their companies in a changing South Africa will face a difficult, and perhaps painful, task. One important step would be to quit judging local managers solely by the size of their current profit margins. Instead, they should be encouraged to act in the longer-term interest of the company, with power to increase wages and improve the benefits of African workers. In most cases the profits from South African operations are so substantial that the increased labor costs would not be overly burdensome—especially since productivity would be likely to improve.

Yes indeed, as one of Hemingway's heroes once expressed it, "Isn't it pretty to think so?" Gunnar Myrdal, writing about South Asia, said, "Optimism, and therefore approaches that make optimism seem more realistic, is itself a natural urge for intellectuals. . . . All [economic] planning . . . tends to err on the side of optimism."

At those rare moments when the profit motive fails to suffice, there is always the magic shibboleth of national security. Union Carbide and Foote Mineral found themselves at that crossroads when the United Nations, supported by Great Britain and the United States, imposed a ban on chrome imports from the white-supremacist government of Rhodesia, a good neighbor of South Africa's. As it happened, Carbide and Foote owned Rhodesia's main chrome mines, with annual returns upward of $28 million on their investment. While the dispute raged in the councils of governments and on the front pages of newspapers, Rhodesia continued to operate the mines and market the chrome through a false-front company called Univex. Meanwhile, back in Washington in 1971, lobbyists drew up legislation to remove the ban on the basis that chrome was vital to national security and ramrodded it through the conservative Armed Services Committees of both the House and Senate. The gimmick, a rather ingenious one, prohibits the President from banning imports of any strategic commodity the United States is also buying from a Communist country—the U.S. was getting about half of its chrome from Russia. "What they [the companies] did was legitimate," a high State Department official told Henry Simmons of *Newsweek*. "It was a powerful but essentially phony argument, because we have all kinds of short-term supply; there just wasn't any national-security element to the argument."[23]

The pristine hands-off policy advocated by Ford in South Africa is not automatically *de rigueur* around the world. Exceptions come rapidly when the status quo is threatened. That, in a nutshell, explains why the United States government will join forces with businessmen in either scuttling or shoring the ship of state of any ruler. The test is not whether the ruler is benevolent or despotic, or, for that matter, white, black, or red. The test, more precisely, is whether he recognizes the sanctity of the balance sheet.

There are times when intervention takes on ludicrous aspects. In 1971, for example, Washington backed American fishermen in protesting Ecuador's self-proclaimed two-hundred-mile offshore territorial limit by cutting off military aid at a crucial moment. Then when a military regime grabbed power, the oil-rich Ecuadorian Andes were opened up to American oil interests and U.S. military aid was quickly resumed over the angry protests of the fishing lobby.

It is a question of muscle, and nobody has larger political biceps than the oil industry. It is no big secret that in many parts of the world, particularly in the Middle East and Latin America, U.S. oil companies include CIA agents among their staff aides. In 1971, when the feudal policies of the Sultan of Oman endangered the status quo at a time when leftist rebels were gaining popular support, the oil companies were instrumental in dethroning the Sultan and installing his son in his place.

There have been numerous incidents of international muscle leveraging in recent years, from the landing of the Marines in the Dominican Republic to the fiasco of the Bay of Pigs, but none has received more acrimonious publicity than the ITT-Chile episode. International Telephone and Telegraph Corporation is the world's largest multinational conglomerate. The statistics are impressive: it controls more than 200 primary divisions and subsidiaries—between 1964 and 1971, it absorbed no fewer than 98 companies*—and countless sub-subsidiaries (one directory lists 284 subsidiaries of ITT subsidiaries, but many of the subs-subs-subs and subs-subs-subs-subs are untabulated); it operates in 67 countries, employs 400,000 people, and counts world sales of more than $8 billion.

It was Jack Anderson who first uncovered the ITT-CIA plot to block the 1970 election of Marxist President Salvador Allende Gossens in Chile. That extraordinary disclosure early in 1972—along with ITT lobbyist Dita Beard's memo and the charge that the Nixon Administration had settled antitrust suits against ITT in return for pledges of $400,000 in cash to bring the Republican convention to San Diego—earned him a Pulitzer Prize. Anderson published two articles and gave newsmen eighty pages of confidential documents (surprisingly, they had escaped shredding) allegedly from ITT's files. Both the State Department and ITT denied they had conspired to keep Allende out of office, but neither challenged the authenticity of the documents.

The picture presented by this material shows ITT brass working feverishly to defeat Allende. Latin-American Marxists have a habit of expropriating gringo assets, and ITT had $153 million tied up in the Chile Telephone Company, plus other Chilean investments. If nothing else, the *dramatis personae* again points up the special entree of big business in top

---

* It is now barred, by an antitrust settlement worked out in the Hartford Fire Insurance Company case, from acquiring any more U.S. firms with annual sales of $100 million or more, but there are no limitations on foreign acquisitions.

echelons of government. It appears that ITT was not only willing to spend millions to defeat Allende but even considered fomenting a military coup.

The strategy was worked out by William Broe, then the CIA's chief of Clandestine Services for Latin America.* His scheme was to create economic chaos: "massive unemployment and unrest might produce enough violence to force the military to move." Broe later flew to New York to explain the scheme to ITT Senior Vice President Edward J. Gerrity, Jr. Meanwhile, ITT's man in Washington, J. D. ("Jack") Neal, detailed his own efforts on behalf of the Chilean affair in a September 14, 1970, memorandum, in which he began by mentioning a telephone conversation with a White House aide in Henry Kissinger's office:

> I told [the aide] Mr. Geneen (ITT president Harold S. Geneen) is willing to come to Washington to discuss ITT's interest and that we are prepared to assist financially in sums up to seven figures.
> Early Saturday morning, I telephoned Assistant Secretary of State for Latin American Affairs Charles A. Meyer, at his office. I repeated the same run-down. . . . Chuck said he could understand Mr. Geneen's concern [and] appreciated his offer to assist. . . . He said "this is a Chile problem" and they have done a good job in "screwing up their own dessert."
> I went to a wedding reception at the Korean Embassy late Saturday. I ran into Attorney General Mitchell, so decided to mention Chile just in case the subject reached him in a cabinet meeting or otherwise. Mr. Mitchell mentioned Mr. Geneen's recent visit with him. He said he could understand Mr. Geneen's concern over ITT's Chile investment.

A paper dated September 17, 1970, and carrying the names of Hal Hendrix and Robert Berrellez, two former newsmen hired by ITT as public-relations officials, shows that the plot was now on the rails: "Late Tuesday night [U.S.] Ambassador Edward Korry [in Santiago] finally received a message from the State Department giving him the green light to move in the name of President Nixon. The message gave him maximum authority to do all possible—short of a Dominican Republic-type action—

---

* This is merely supposition, but is it not possible that ITT's telecommunications and telephone networks now spanning the globe are as invaluable a resource to friendly spies as to stockholders? Among other things, ITT operates the hot line between Washington and Moscow. In a speech before the third United Nations Conference on Trade and Development on April 14, 1972, Allende warned of a "formidable danger" in the present international telephone communications system. He foresaw a moment less than a decade ahead when "our homes will be flooded by information and publicity directed from abroad by means of high power satellites and which, unless they are counteracted by timely measures, will serve only to increase our dependence and destroy our cultural values."

to keep Allende from taking power." In another memo, Korry is described as "a male Martha Mitchell" who often made undiplomatic remarks to newsmen. Yet he was a hard worker. According to the same PR men, he had already "started to maneuver" with Chilean politicians to try to block Allende's election in the Congress. The ambassador, the report added, "has never let up on [Chilean President Eduardo] Frei, to the point of telling him to 'put his pants on.' "

Following his meeting in New York with CIA agent Broe, Gerrity outlined the strategy for his boss, Geneen, in a confidential telex dated September 29:

> 1. Banks should not renew credit or should delay in doing so.
> 2. Companies should drag their feet in sending money, making deliveries, in shipping spare parts, etc.
> 3. Savings and loan companies there are in trouble. If pressure were applied they would have to shut their doors, thereby creating pressure.
> 4. We would withdraw all technical help and should not promise any technical assistance in the future. Companies in a position to do so should close their doors.
> 5. A list of companies was provided, and it was suggested that we approach them as indicated. I was told that of all the companies involved, ours alone had been responsive and understood the problem. The visitor [Broe] added that money was not a problem. He indicated that certain steps were being taken but that he was looking for additional help aimed at inducing economic collapse.

At this point it is not clear who was captaining the team. The next day, Gerrity notified ITT's Washington office that advice from an anti-Allende source in Chile had cautioned to "keep cool, don't rock the boat, we are making progress. . . . This is in direct contrast to what Broe recommended. I will call you later to discuss HSG's [Geneen] reaction to my telex in some detail. He agrees with me that Broe's suggestions are not workable. However, he suggests that we be very discreet in handling Broe."

The next actor to step center stage in this bizarre drama was John McCone, an ITT director and once the head of the CIA. A memo to McCone from ITT Vice President William Merriam indicates that some preliminary steps to implement the Broe plan were actually taken:

> Today I had lunch with our contact at the McLean agency [the CIA is headquartered in McLean, Virginia], and I summarize for you the results of our conversation. He is still very, very pessimistic about defeating Allende when the congressional vote takes place on October 24.
> Approaches continue to be made to select members of the Armed

Forces in an attempt to have them lead some sort of uprising—no success to date. . . . Practically no progress has been made in trying to get American business to cooperate in some way so as to bring on economic chaos. GM and Ford, for example, say that they have too much inventory on hand in Chile to take any chances and that they keep hoping that everything will work out all right.

Also, the Bank of America had agreed to close its doors in Santiago but each day keeps postponing the inevitable. According to my source, we must continue to keep the pressure on business.

One of the "approaches" may have been directed at former Chilean Brigadier General Roberto Viaux Marambio, a political foe of Allende's. "Clearly," Hendrix reported in mid-October, "Viaux was gearing up to launch a move. . . . It is a fact that word was passed to Viaux from Washington to hold back last week. It was felt that he was not adequately prepared, his timing was off, and he should cool it for a later unspecified date."

As the presidential candidate of the Marxist coalition, Allende had received 37 percent of the vote in a three-cornered race. According to Chilean custom, the election was thrown into Congress, which despite the ITT-CIA conspiracy chose Allende because he was the leading vote-getter. Also the Christian Democrats, who are themselves a left-leaning party of social reform, supported much of Allende's program. There was no coup in 1970, but the head of Chile's army, René Schneider, was assassinated, and Viaux was imprisoned for taking part in the murder conspiracy.[24]

Once in power, an angry President Allende promptly confirmed ITT's worst fears. The Chile Telephone Company was nationalized and there was no mention of compensation. Ultimately, of course, the U.S. taxpayer will have to absorb the lion's share of ITT's Chilean misadventure. Internal Revenue Service regulations stipulate that in cases involving nationalization of a foreign company in which a U.S. firm owns stock, the take-over will be treated as an involuntary conversion of the stock resulting in an ordinary loss. If the stock is exchanged for bonds of the foreign country under threat of expropriation and the country later refuses to make payment, the company is then entitled to a business bad-debt deduction. But before this provision comes into play there is the Overseas Private Investment Corporation (OPIC), a U.S. agency that insures American investment abroad against expropriation. ITT claimed $92.6 million from OPIC as partial compensation for the loss of its telephone holdings. Kennecott Copper Corporation was awarded $66.9 million and Anaconda Company is demanding $154 million from OPIC for its Chilean mines. Kennecott has filed lawsuits to block shipments of Chilean copper headed for foreign ports.

In his speech before the third U.N. Conference on Trade and Development, Allende accused the private business interests of wealthy nations of plundering and exerting "powerful corruptive influence on public institutions in rich and poor countries alike: The corporations have gone as far as seeking to upset the normal functioning of the government and institutions of other nations, to start worldwide campaigns against the prestige of a government, to make it the victim of an international boycott and to sabotage its economic relations with the rest of the world."

Charges of *Yanqui* imperialism and neo-colonialism were leveled at Washington from nations around the world. The State Department issued a blanket denial, declaring that "any ideas of thwarting the Chilean constitutional process following and before the election of 1970 were firmly rejected by this Administration."

The Senate Foreign Relations Committee announced it was launching an immediate investigation into the overseas operations and political machinations of multinationals. "ITT was the catalyst," Senator Frank Church of Idaho told the press. "What they did in Chile was so brazen, or seemed so brazen, that responsible people could not ignore them."[25] Church said he wanted to know if companies were throwing their weight around in international politics. Also he was increasingly dubious about the Overseas Private Investment Corporation: "We'll look at it to see whether it's necessary, or for that matter desirable, for the taxpayer to assume the risk of losses for big corporations."

Church's promised investigation got sidetracked in 1972, an election year, by behind-the-scenes Republican pressure. It was rescheduled for the spring of 1973, and by then Church was assuring the press that his inquiry "is not meant to be a vendetta against ITT or the multinationals. . . . I'm going to conduct well-balanced hearings—no inquisitions but no cover-up either."[26]

The subcommittee's lead-off witness, ITT Vice President William Merriam, admitted that ITT people had bombarded the White House, the State Department, and the CIA with letters, phone calls, and visits in an attempt to get the government to intervene on their behalf: "If Allende was faced with economic collapse, he might be more congenial toward paying us off." Merriam said Allende "had stolen our property without compensation." The Washington pressure was supposed to force Allende "to pay us off. That's all we wanted."

What is most remarkable about this testimony is the blatant distortion of facts. The ITT-Washington pressure was applied in September and October 1970, immediately following Allende's narrowly won popular election, at a time when it was being considered by the Chilean congress, which decided in Allende's favor in November that year. The expropriation did not take place until a year later.

Merriam said that ITT President Geneen introduced him to CIA spy boss William Broe in July 1970. Geneen instructed him to "stay in touch" with "our man." "I had no idea then that he was clandestine," Merriam told the Senators. "We had luncheons in places with 300 to 400 people. . . . I talked to Mr. Broe many times, just when we had something to tell each other." Merriam made it clear that the CIA was impressed with political reporting on the Chilean situation by ITT's operatives in Latin America. Broe sent CIA messengers to his office to get the reports. "The highest people we went to," Merriam said, were Arnold Nachmanoff, then chief adviser to Kissinger for Latin America, and Charles Meyer, Assistant Secretary of State for Latin America.

On the very next day (March 21, 1973), ITT director John McCone testified that he had personally relayed Geneen's offers of $1 million to Kissinger and CIA Directer Richard Helms for U.S. help to prevent Allande's election. (McCone was not only Helms's predecessor but also a consultant to the agency.) "Mr. Kissinger thanked me very much and said I would hear from him," McCone said. "I did not." It was after McCone's meeting with Helms that Broe met secretly with Geneen. Although ITT had offered financial support, the corporation, said McCone, had not devised a plan to stop Allende: "It was not a plan generated by ITT." McCone denied suggestions by Senator Clifford Case that the plan was designed to use the money in order to bribe members of the Chilean congress. There was nothing surreptitious about the plan, McCone insisted. In fact, the idea was to supply housing, technical, and agricultural assistance to Chile. The objective, he said, was to placate Allende into forestalling expropriation. In other words, $1 million for housing as compensation for a $153-million telephone company.

On the following day, United Press International reported that a special Senate panel had met with CIA officials and was satisfied with the agency's explanation that it had merely exchanged information with ITT. "There is nothing unusual about the CIA exchanging information with representatives of American corporations abroad," a Senator, who asked to not be identified, told the UPI. There was nothing wrong, the Senator added, with the CIA's attempting to effect changes in a foreign country to the advantage of the United States.

But the subcommittee had evidence of far more serious charges. According to new memos in the hands of the subcommittee, one ITT official had asked the White House to "take a neutral position, or not discourage, in the event Chile or others attempt to save the situation." Later a message from ITT agents in Latin-American headquarters coldly assessed the chances for a coup led by the outgoing President Frei: "The armed forces boss, René Schneider, is fully aware of the danger of Allende moving in. But he will not budge an inch without Frei's okay . . . [and Frei] won't move unless he is provided with a constitutional threat. That threat must be provided one way or another through provocation." Still later there is another memo from the head of ITT's Washington office, William Merriam: "Today I had lunch with our contact at the McLean agency [CIA]. . . . Approaches continue to be made to select members of the Armed Forces in an attempt to have them lead some sort of uprising—no success to date."

The frantic lobbying by ITT to enlist the White House in its effort to stop Allende was more fully documented in the subcommittee's lengthy report issued in June 1973. Contrary to testimony that Kissinger had kissed off McCone's proposal, the subcommittee reported that Chile was the subject of a meeting in June 1970 of the top-secret Forty Committee in the White House.* Presided over by Kissinger, the membership of this committee includes the chairman of the Joint Chiefs of Staff, the Deputy Secretary of Defense, the Deputy Secretary of State, the director of Central Intelligence, and, until 1972, the Attorney General. This means that in the summer of 1970, when the Nixon White House was drawing up its secret domestic intelligence plan, Mitchell was attending the committee's hearings. According to the subcommittee's report, McCone had three conversations with Richard Helms, then CIA director, and had expressed his fears of an Allende victory, asking Helms "whether the U.S. intended to intervene in the election to encourage the support of one of the candidates who stood for the principles that are basic to this country." The report went on to add: "Mr. Helms told Mr. McCone that the matter had been considered by the Forty Committee. Helms indicated that some minimal effort would be mounted which 'could be managed within the flexibility of

---

* An organ of the National Security Council, the Forty Committee is in charge of studying and approving plans for covert action abroad by the U.S. intelligence community.

the CIA budget,' that is without seeking additional funds. Mr. Helms was very pessimistic about the chances of Mr. [Jorge] Alessandri [ITT's rightist-backed candidate] and was of the personal opinion that Dr. Allende would win. This opinion was contrary to the official reports of the U.S. Embassy. Based upon polls commissioned or undertaken by the CIA, the Embassy was reporting that Alessandri would win a plurality." Helms's "minimal effort" consisted of an expenditure of $400,000 in CIA funds for anti-Allende propaganda. It was Helms who arranged the meeting between Geneen and Broe, the agency's Western Hemisphere chief for clandestine operations, who cooked up the economic-chaos plan.

Assistant Secretary of State Charles A. Meyer testified that "shortly after the September 4 election [of Allende], the Forty Committee, at a meeting which he attended, met for the express purpose of discussing U.S. policy in connection with Chile; but he refused to inform the Committee what precisely was said at the meeting, what decisions, if any, were taken and what instructions were communicated to Mr. Korry, the U.S. Ambassador in Chile. Because neither Mr. Meyer nor Mr. Korry would communicate to the Subcommittee the content of the instructions which Mr. Korry received, and because the State Department would not permit the Subcommittee to have access to the cable traffic between the U.S. Embassy in Santiago and the State Department, it is not possible to determine whether Ambassador Korry did in fact receive a cable, which, in substance, authorized him in the name of the President to do everything possible, short of a Dominican Republic type intervention, to stop Allende from being elected President of Chile."

In its report issued in late June 1973, the subcommittee charged that the company had "overstepped the line of acceptable behavior." If the scheme had succeeded, says the report, it could have resulted in "bloodshed and possible civil war." The report scored Geneen's million-dollar offer to the CIA, noting that if such actions came to be accepted as normal, "no country would welcome the presence of multinational corporations." In the opinion of the subcommittee, "the attitude of the company perhaps was best summed up" by Gerrity when he asked: "What's wrong with taking care of No. 1?"

Three months later the generals that ITT looked to for salvation suddenly seized power in Chile and Allende was dead—whether he committed suicide or was murdered is of little moment at this point. What is important is that the coup ended forty-two years of strict constitutional neutrality on the part of Chile's military, converting a middle-class democracy into a dictatorship and reducing the number of nonmilitary governments in South America to four—Argentina, Venezuela, Colombia and Guyana. As in all Latin-American countries, the disparities of wealth have persisted in Chile although the socialist tradition is an old one. A small minority enjoys affluent splendor while a large majority lives in abject poverty in shack belts around the cities. One single statistic illustrates this poverty: When Allende raised wages, the consumption of powdered and canned milk used for feeding children increased tenfold in a year.[27]

Many factors contributed to the success of the military coup, not the least of which was economic chaos. Writing in the London *Observer*, Neal Ascherson reviewed some of these factors:

> Allende was able to achieve much in his three years. In the face of American attempts to subvert the regime, he nationalized the copper mines and the great foreign corporations like ITT. The Popular Unity government carried through widespread nationalization of Chilean firms and successfully reformed land tenure by breaking up the large estates and distributing land to the peasants. As recently as March, the coalition surprised even itself by increasing its vote in the congressional elections to nearly 44 percent.
>
> Why, then, was it overthrown?
>
> The immediate reason was an economic crisis that was exploited by the extreme right. Allende raised popular living standards and created a huge increase in demand: At the same time, Western financial aid was almost cut off and revenue from exports of nationalized copper fell. Violent inflation—endemic in Chile—set in, imports were reduced, and there were acute shortages of consumer goods and food. . . .
>
> Many Marxists will be persuaded that it is impossible to overcome the middle classes by peacefully winning control of "their" state and "their" army, because at the last moment the bourgeoisie will use this apparatus to destroy its enemies. . . .
>
> Allende did not mobilize the slum-dwellers and landless peasants who might have fought for him, they will say, and look what befell him. Unwittingly, the Chilean generals have made a formidable case for armed revolution rather than for peaceful evolution towards socialist democracy.[28]

Scholars will long argue the deeper reasons for Allende's failure. Whether the CIA or the White House had a hand in the coup will also be a subject for debate. Yet there is no question that Washington laid a heavy hand on Chile's economy. As Latin-American Experts James F. Petras and Robert LaPorte, Jr., noted in *Foreign Policy* magazine, "Dominican style 'gunboat diplomacy' has been replaced by 'credit diplomacy.' " The

Nixon Administration did its best to light an economic brush fire under Allende, not only through financial pressure on institutions like the World Bank and the Export-Import Bank—they wrote off Chile as a poor credit risk—but also by deliberately isolating Chile in the world money market. "The only thing we did," said one former high Nixon aide, "was to cause problems for them when they tried to borrow money."[29] This policy was so effective that when Allende appeared before the United Nations in 1972, he accused the United States of raising an "invisible blockade" aimed at undermining his government. U.S. exports to Chile declined 50 percent during Allende's three years, a move that contributed disastrously to shortages and inflation. Meanwhile, the Pentagon remained on solid terms with the anti-Allende military brass. Arms shipments and military loans continued without interruption.

Chilean Ambassador Hugo Vigorena Ramírez, a career diplomat who resigned his post in Mexico City after the coup, claimed to have seen documents outlining what he called the "CIA's war against Allende." Code-named Centaur, the plan allegedly involved economic and psychological subversion of the Allende government, including such dirty tricks as introducing counterfeit money and upsetting the rhythm of crops. "The CIA plan prepared for the coup," Vigorena charged. "It was a systematic campaign of torpedoing the government."[30]

Was ITT involved? Was the White House? The CIA? The Forty Committee? One of the questions raised by the Church subcommittee in its report goes directly to the heart of the White House's policymaking processes vis-à-vis the Forty Committee: Does the White House, through the Forty Committee, grant broad policy mandates to the intelligence community, empowering it to implement and improvise, with the proviso that credit for failure or success of specific projects be laid, when exposed, at its own doorstep and not the President's?

The roles, if any, played by the Nixon White House and its various intelligence appendages in the coup will undoubtedly remain a dark secret. What is without dispute is that Nixon sent no message of condolence to Allende's widow—a traditional gesture on the death of an elected head of state. In fact, the death of democracy in Chile was welcomed by the Administration. "We will have to work with the generals," a State Department spokesman told *Time*, "and it makes no sense to issue some moral statement about democracy." Particularly when the Pentagon's rapport with the military junta was so close that Reuters reported that Washington officials knew about the coup at least forty-eight hours in advance and took no action to alert Allende.

It is no secret that the imperialists in the White House viewed Allende as an enemy of American business interests. On September 16, 1970, only eight days after the Forty Committee determined the strategy of its opposition to Allende, Henry Kissinger held a White House press briefing to explain the Administration's attitude:

> Now it is fairly easy for one to predict that if Allende wins, there is a good chance that he will establish over a period of years some sort of Communist government. In that case you would have one not on an island off the coast which has not a traditional relationship and impact on Latin America, but in a major Latin American country you would have a Communist government, joining, for example, Argentina, which is already deeply divided, along a long frontier, joining Peru, which has already been heading in directions that have been difficult to deal with, and joining Bolivia, which has also gone in a more leftist, anti-U.S. direction, even without any of these developments. So I don't think we should delude ourselves that an Allende takeover in Chile would not present massive problems for us, and for democratic forces and for pro-U.S. forces in Latin America, and indeed to the whole Western Hemisphere . . . It is one of those situations which is not too happy for American interests.

It is sad that this half-baked Monroe Doctrine Domino Theory was propounded by Nixon's Prince Metternich, the architect of the détentes with China and Russia, the original Domino players. Yet Kissinger's evaluation of Chile under Allende is typical of his recorded opinions on Third World nations, to wit: Bangladesh, Cuba, South Vietnam and most other Southeast Asian countries. Like Metternich, Kissinger's sympathies tilt in favor of great-power interest. (Hailed as the most astute statesman of his age, Metternich became the actual head of the Austrian government, under the nominal rule of Emperor Francis I, a weak and procrastinating man. Metternich's own weakness, as historian Carlton J. H. Hayes noted, was that "his detestation of revolution from below made him fearful of reforms from above, and he preferred to bring honor and prestige to Austria by means of successful foreign diplomacy rather than through what always seemed to him the more uncertain means of internal changes in society and political organization." As a reactionary, Metternich believed "that a strong reactionary Austrian Empire was a most necessary bulwark against the divisive and disturbing forces of revolution.")

Right or wrong, past, present or future, power is its own reward. In the case of Allende, the events themselves demonstrate the blatant hypocrisy of Kissinger's prediction. Most of Latin America was then, and is now, in fascistic hands. Nothing has changed except Chile has now joined the ranks. Writing in *The Progressive*, Laurence Stern noted that "In the thirty-three months of Allende's tenure as President, all of Chile's parties survived, a free press continued to flourish, and Allende never succumbed to the strong temptations to suspend constitutional government. . . . Yet within two weeks after the junta took over in Santiago the Marxist parties were outlawed and other parties 'recessed'; labor unions were suppressed; books were put to the torch; thousands of Allende loyalists were arrested and untold numbers were killed throughout the country; aliens were rounded up for deportation—some to homelands in which they face certain imprisonment or death; the press was muzzled, and normal constitution process suspended. This is precisely the fate that was to overtake Chile after Allende's accession to power, in the misguided view of those who opposed his election."

The White House, Kissinger, ITT and others with a multinational stake in Chile were hardly misguided. Scarcely a week after the coup, while Santiago's Moneda Palace was still smoldering and squads of book burners were purifying the land of Marxist literature, the leaders of the junta were reassuring U.S. multinationals that some four hundred companies would either be handed back or full payment would be made for expropriated property. In the area of copper mining, the Chilean government suggested joint ventures in developing new properties. The response from the United States was demure enthusiasm—after all, a few thousand bodies were still warm.

Perhaps the more important question is whether ITT would have participated in the coup if given the opportunity. Given its druthers, would ITT prefer a dictatorship to a democracy? In *The Sovereign State of ITT*, Anthony Sampson traces the success of Sosthenes Behn, the founder who parlayed a tiny Puerto Rican telephone company into a supranational monster by hedging his bets on both sides of the Spanish civil war, World War II, and the cold war. Sampson carefully documents Behn's dealings with various dictators, including Hitler. In fact, when Hitler took over in 1933, Behn appointed Kurt von Schroeder, later to be an SS general, to promote ITT's interests. He was enormously successful, acquiring a 28 percent interest in Focke-Wulf, which made bombers. While ITT bombers carried the war to Europe, England, and Africa, Behn never once protested the use of his companies in the Nazi effort. In a display of rare chutzpah, ITT not only kept the profits earned during the war but ultimately received $27 million in reparations for the wartime damage to its German factories, including the Focke-Wulf plants. "It was a notable reward for a company that had so deliberately invested in the German war effort," Sampson wrote, "and so carefully arranged to become German. If the Nazis had won, ITT in Germany would have appeared impeccably Nazi; as they lost, it re-emerged as impeccably American." Geneen took over the company in 1959 following the retirement and death of Behn.

One ITT man, Sampson writes, has a passage from Lord Keynes's "Economic Possibilities for Our Grandchildren" framed on the wall of his office:

> For at least another hundred years we must pretend to ourselves and to everyone that fair is foul and foul is fair; for foul is useful and fair is not. Avarice and usury and precaution must be our gods for a little longer still. For only they can lead us out of the tunnel of economic necessity into daylight.

Who knows what foul deeds now lie hidden in the files of the CIA? In what was perhaps his last interview, Lyndon Johnson told Leo Janos that he "never believed that Oswald acted alone, although I can accept that he pulled the trigger." Johnson said that when he had taken office he found that "we had been operating a damned Murder Inc. in the Caribbean." A year or so before Kennedy's death, a CIA-backed assassination team had been picked up in Havana. Johnson speculated that Dallas had been a retaliation for this thwarted attempt, although he couldn't prove it.[31]

Johnson was referring to a CIA plot to assassinate Fidel Castro prior to the Bay of Pigs invasion. With Cuba leaderless, the invasion was expected to touch off a general uprising that would result in the defeat of the Communist militia. The plot was first exposed by Jack Anderson in January 1971, ten years after "the CIA enlisted Robert Maheu, a former FBI agent with shadowy contacts,* who had handled other undercover assignments for the CIA out of his Washington public relations office. . . . Maheu recruited John Roselli, a ruggedly handsome gambler with contacts in both the American and Cuban underworlds, to arrange the assassination."†[32]

---

* Maheu was later associated with Howard Hughes in his Las Vegas ventures.

† A Chicago mafioso who played "godfather" in Las Vegas during the 1960s, Roselli sought reduction of a federal prison term in July 1971 on the ground of his alleged "heroic" mission to kill Castro.

Anderson named the two CIA agents who rubber-stamped the various plans Roselli devised in six attempts on the life of the Cuban leader. The last attempt failed early in March 1963. "Nine months later," Anderson observed, "President Kennedy was gunned down in Dallas by Lee Harvey Oswald, a fanatic who previously had agitated for Castro in New Orleans and had made a mysterious trip to the Cuban Embassy in Mexico."[33]

The Senate Finance Committee, responding to pressure from the AFL-CIO, announced its own investigation of multinationals. By the time hearings began early in 1973, every superlawyer in Washington was in one or another multinational camp, ready to unload a barrage of dizzying technical minutiae on the committee—they filled most of the panel's 968-page compendium of papers:

> . . . Arguments of the spreading corporate giants against crippling increases in taxes on their overseas earnings seemed to have won considerable support in Congress as a Senate finance subcommittee [on International Trade] headed by Abraham Ribicoff (D-Conn.) opened hearings this week on activities of the multinationals.
> An array of corporate executives told the panel that multinational operations on balance create jobs in the U.S. and bolster the U.S. balance of payments. Their testimony was backed up by a broadside of studies by the Commerce Dept., trade associations [lobbies], and a number of individual companies. . . .
> The Finance Committee will be writing tax and trade bills later this year and against such evidence legislators appear particularly unsympathetic to protectionists' proposals for ending or reducing the tax credit that corporations get in the U.S. against taxes paid to foreign countries. A committee staff study shows that multinationals already pay taxes to foreign governments at the rate of 51 percent on earnings abroad. Abolition of the tax credit would virtually wipe out their foreign operations, the companies fear.—*Business Week*, March 3, 1973.

There is no telling where the staff got its statistics. The 51 percent foreign tax rate sounds more like something concocted by Presidential adviser Peter Flanigan than by a so-called "reform-minded" subcommittee. The Nixon Administration has been outstanding at the numbers game. Of course, all Administrations and Congresses have pulled figures out of thin air—President Johnson was a genius at it.

For the moment, however, the 51 percent deserves close scrutiny. According to the same staff study, the multinationals received a $4.6-billion tax credit in 1971, which reduced their U.S. tax liability to only

$640 million, or 6 percent. In very basic arithmetic, how could even that minuscule amount be due if the companies were already paying 3 percent (51 percent minus 48 percent) more taxes to foreign governments than required by the U.S. Treasury?

First of all, viable statistics in the area of multinationals are more than scarce. In a 1972 study for the Joint Economic Committee, Professor Peggy B. Musgrave discovered that the Internal Revenue Service was a decade behind the times. The most recent published issue of the IRS's Supplemental Reports to the Statistics of Income on Foreign Income and Taxes Reported on Corporation Income Tax Returns was for the 1961–62 period, though a later issue including material up to 1966—still in its preparatory stages—was made available to her. "While this material is of considerable value in providing statistics on the volume and characteristics of U.S. investment abroad as well as its tax treatment, there is room for improvement in terms of the time lag before publication . . . and the coverage of the material itself," she wrote in her report. "While the Statistics of Income give flows and taxes paid, statistics on capital flows and assets values abroad must be obtained from the Department of Commerce series on Direct Investment Abroad. While the former are derived from tax returns, the latter are derived from questionnaires submitted on a regular basis to a sample of U.S. corporations with foreign investments. Again, the material is not as comprehensive as students of foreign investment would like, and it is difficult to reconcile the two sets of statistics where they overlap. . . . Unfortunately, the most recent available data on the earnings of, and foreign profits taxes paid by, U.S.-controlled foreign corporations on a country-by-country basis are for 1962. There also seem to be no plans for updating the country-by-country statistics in the next Supplementary Report to the Statistics of Income."[34]

On the basis of the only statistics available to anybody, Professor Musgrave extrapolated the *effective* foreign tax rates paid by American multinationals on 1970 earnings—rates that in her judgment have not changed substantially in the intervening years. Japan, at 52 percent, had the highest corporate tax rate of the countries surveyed. The lowest, at 7 percent, was Panama. Others included Canada and Great Britain, 40.5 percent; West Germany, 35.3; Australia, 38.4; Switzerland, 12.3; assorted Latin-American countries, 20.5; France, 42.8; Belgium, 31.0; Netherlands, 28.2; South Africa, 22.0; Argentina, 28.7; Chile, 22.7; Peru, 36.2; Italy, 45.3; Spain, 31.0; Venezuela, 22.3; and 43.3 percent for the Middle East, but this rate is based on "royalty taxes"—that is, the royalties paid for oil-land rights are disguised as taxes. The average effective rate for all subsidiaries abroad was 36 percent.[35]

But even if one were to take the committee's 51 percent at face value, it is still a whopping bargain, particularly for a less developed country operation. Let us assume that a branch of an American multinational earned $1,000,000 in Mexico and paid the 51 percent rate for a total foreign tax of $510,000. Further assume that the parent also earned a million at home, for a total income of $2,000,000. Now deduct the $510,-000 for a non-gross-up balance of $1,490,000 to be taxed at the U.S. rate of 48 percent, or a tax of $715,200 before a foreign tax credit of $480,000 (it cannot exceed the U.S. rate) is applied, reducing the amount due the U.S. Treasury to $235,200. The total taxes paid on the $2,000,-000 ($510,000 plus $235,200) are $745,200. That comes down to an effective tax rate of 37.3 percent. The example, of course, does not consider multiple possible loopholes available to the company, such as accelerated depreciation, investment tax credit, and percentage depletion, *ad infinitum*. There is also $30,000 in unapplied foreign tax credits floating around somewhere in search of a profit.

Unfortunately, that is not the full story, either. It does not take into account the billions that vanish into tax havens by sleight-of-hand operations. Little is known of the internal pricing policy used by multinationals to inflate the profits of their tax-haven subsidiaries—as noted before, tax havens generally do not tax income not generated in their country. Sophisticated computer and communication systems facilitate the routing of invoices through paper-shuffling subsidiaries in tax havens to reduce U.S. taxable profits and boost low-taxed foreign income. The IRS seldom tampers with pricing policies because it is nearly impossible to legally determine a fair market price. Even when a tax haven acts only as a profit-siphoning middleman, as in the case of PPG Industries (formerly Pittsburgh Plate Glass) a few years ago, the courts have invariably ruled against the government. In the PPG case, the U.S. parent had set up a "selling" subsidiary in a Swiss desk drawer for the sale of plate glass to various customers, including two PPG subsidiaries in Canada. The fact that the Swiss unit never handled the glass did not deter the Tax Court judge from ruling that the subsidiary's selling efforts entitled it to the profits.[36]

In *Invisible Empires*, Louis Turner observes that "profits are easier to make in countries where the taxation authorities are inefficient. Italian company accounts are notorious for their very tenuous connections with actual events. Selling an Italian firm poses problems, since it may well be worth far more than accounts actually show. . . . So long as tax authorities exert differing degrees of pressure, the ruthless multinational will find it pays to manipulate prices, even if few firms go so far as to have all their transfer prices set by tax lawyers and international accountants—a known practice."[37]

In its heyday, for example, Bernard Cornfeld's Investors Overseas Services (IOS) had at least a billion dollars in its investment funds. It took money from anywhere and placed it wherever it did the most good, which meant taking full advantage of all possible international tax concessions. On some days IOS accounted for as much as 4 percent of the action on Wall Street. In 1966, with $6 million in profits, it paid a tax bill of $375,000.

Many American companies were enticed to foreign shores by the promise of "tax holidays." The scenario differs little from what happened in this country after World War II when the South stole the textile industry right out from under New England—the same industry that has now gone to greener pastures in Asia. Far from paying 51 percent, these companies do not pay any taxes at all. IBM is the queen bee in that international set. Nearly all nations want its technology and hence offer it tax exemptions.

There are other inducements to foreign operations. The Colgate-Palmolive Corporation stopped disclosing the geographic breakdown of its profits after 1966. That year it earned $26 million abroad as compared with only $4.5 million at home. Yet its total sales were roughly equal: $514 million foreign and $417 million domestic.[38]

An interesting item appeared in the *Wall Street Journal* of February 12, 1973: "Pssst! Here's an investment tip: The 'smart money' is going into black-eyed peas in Nicaragua, African palm trees in Honduras and pompons in Guatemala. Those things may not sound exactly like the proverbial pot of gold, but some big U.S. companies, including Bank of America, Chase Manhattan Bank, Ralston Purina, Gerber Products, Deere, Monsanto and Dow Chemical, think there's money to be made from these and other commodities grown in Central America." And why not? The companies, each chipping in $200,000, formed a joint venture called Latin American Agribusiness Development Corporation (LAAD), for the purpose of financing promising Latin-American agricultural ventures. "There's an enlightened self-interest here," one LAAD official pointed out. "We view Latin America as an important market. If it prospers, this certainly will help us." The plan is as simple as it is foolproof. LAAD makes interest-bearing loans to farmers for exclusive contracts on their crops, which they sell to United States customers like Safeway Stores and Southland Frozen Foods. The farmer pays 9 percent interest on the loan, but LAAD gets its money from the Agency for International Development, an arm of the State Department, at about half the cost.

On October 22, 1933, President Roosevelt took to the radio to prepare the nation for the first major devaluation of the dollar in its history:

> Because of conditions in this country and because of events beyond our control in other parts of the world, it becomes increasingly important to develop and apply the further measures which may be necessary from time to time to control the gold value of our own dollar at home. Our dollar is now altogether too greatly influenced by accidents of international trade, by internal policies of other nations, and by political disturbances in other countries. Therefore, the United States must take firmly into its own hands the control of the gold value of our dollar. This is necessary in order to prevent dollar disturbances from swinging us away from our ultimate goal, namely, the continued recovery of our commodity prices.

His scheme was to raise the price of gold from $20.67 per troy ounce —a price that had prevailed since 1837—to $35 almost slicing the value of the dollar in half.* Al Smith, whom Roosevelt had easily defeated at the Democratic National Convention in 1932, expressed the sentiments of many when he said, "I am for gold dollars as against baloney dollars." John Maynard Keynes called the plan "puerile" and "rubbish." Yet it worked pretty well. It made American products more competitive by making them cheaper to buyers in foreign markets. Exports recovered and continued to climb for many years. Only farm prices refused to perform as expected. Years later Roosevelt was to ponder over the ambiguity of economics. "It was funny how sometimes they [farm prices] seemed to go against all the rules."

The problems facing President Nixon in December 1971 were the reverse of those in 1932. Roosevelt was trying to heat up the economy while Nixon wanted to cool it down. Since the late 1940s the United States has been living beyond its means in the world. American consumers, tourists, businessmen, and the government have papered the world with untold

---

* Devaluation increases the value of the Treasury's gold hoard by creating that much more real money in its checking account at the Federal Reserve banks, where it keeps its gold.

billions of the once almighty dollar. The United States has lavished an estimated $150 billion on guns and butter around the world since the Truman Doctrine "saved" Greece and Turkey from Communist subversion in 1947—$837 million in two years to those countries. Since then, America, that stalwart arsenal of democracy, has been playing supercop, a role that eventually led to Korea and Vietnam.

Under the laudable rubric of "foreign aid," the government does not distinguish between guns and butter. The Marshall Plan brought economic aid to a war-ravaged Europe, but it also supported France militarily in Indochina and provided "defense support" in the Korean War. The Eisenhower years spread the U.S. defense umbrella over forty-two nations on the periphery of China and Russia. The 1960s placed more emphasis on counterinsurgency than on formal alliances. Petty tyrants and corrupt juntas were propped up by "economic aid" because they maintained the status quo against incipient insurrections by reform groups. Billions were spent for the now defunct "Decade of Development" crusade to develop the hungry nations of Asia, Africa, and Latin America, because "we cannot live as an island of affluence in a sea of poverty": to achieve stability, poor nations must be "developed."

The emissary charged with this trust was the American businessman. Fanning the dying embers of the Industrial Revolution, he filled his civilization kit full of patents, advanced technology—hundreds of billions' worth of it acquired at government expense under research and development contracts—and plenty of dollars to buy land, build factories, and pave easy-access roads to carry his "developed" products to the nearest exits leading to world markets.

The international financial policy of the United States was based on the idea of "benign neglect": the egocentric belief that the dollar, once the central trading currency of the world, was sacrosanct no matter how overvalued it became—America could create industrial powers in West Germany and Japan,* buy all the foreign goods and factories it wanted, subsidize investment abroad with tax money, and station troops around

---

* While enjoying virtually tariff-free access to the United States for its supercharged export drive, Japan continues to cling to the protective import restrictions imposed with America's blessing to aid her industrial postwar recovery. The European Economic Community also continues to raise protective walls around its Common Market. In recent years, France, Germany and other EEC countries have written exclusive two-way trade pacts with former African colonies and Mediterranean countries.

the globe. The rest of the world would absorb the dollars because they were as good as gold—the government was pledged to redeem dollars with gold whenever foreigners wished to cash in.

The gold hoard had melted down to $10 billion by the time Nixon embargoed gold shipments* in August 1971 and floated the dollar, which was left to seek its own rate against the Deutsche mark and yen.

"This is the end of Western civilization," Budget Director Lewis Douglas intoned as Roosevelt signed the 1934 devaluation bill. But in December 1971 Nixon hailed the Smithsonian agreement, which devalued the dollar by raising the price of gold to $38 an ounce,† as "the most significant monetary agreement in the history of the world." When he had to do it all over again in February 1973, raising the price of gold to $42.22 an ounce—a 10 percent devaluation of the dollar‡—the President was not grandiloquent in his appraisal: he did not proclaim it the most significant monetary agreement in the history of the last fourteen months. Instead he warned that devaluation was "at best only a temporary solution" to the massive U.S. trade imbalance that had produced a shocking $6.4-billion deficit in 1972, nearly tripling the $2.6 billion of 1971, when the nation suffered its first trade deficit in this century.

Without getting hopelessly mired down in an exploration of economic mysteries—which, like religion, are best taken on faith—the most remarkable development of the entire fiasco was the Administration's almost paranoid defense of multinationals. There were a thousand and one contributing factors for the dollar crisis, but none were ascribed to the mammoth foreign investment and monetary machinations of America's economic ambassadors.

Following the second devaluation, Peter Flanigan, whose imposing title was executive director of the President's Council on International Economics, made a strong plea before the Senate Finance Subcommittee on International Trade on behalf of the status quo. He was adamant in refuting charges that speculation against the dollar by multinationals had helped precipitate the latest currency crisis. Basing his defense on statistics culled from current studies by the U.S. Tariff Commission and the Com-

---

* This meant the United States would no longer redeem foreign-held dollars for gold. The use of gold as domestic currency was ended by Roosevelt in 1934.

† Depending on how one looks at it, the dollar was devalued by either increasing the price of gold 8.6 percent, or decreasing the value of the dollar by 7.9 percent ($38 is 8.6 percent more than $35, but $35 is only 7.9 less than $38).

‡The dollar was worth 20.6 percent less than it was before the Smithsonian devaluation.

merce Department, Flanigan said the Administration had the "impression" that "most of those movements [of currencies] were not connected with American firms." Yet he conceded under questioning that nobody really knew. And apparently did not want to know. The Administration's efforts, he said, were aimed not at finding culprits but at correcting conditions that encourage holders of dollars to speculate.[39]

It is conceivable that even the most diligent scholar may miss significant details when thumbing through 930 pages of statistical data. With that thought in mind, here are a few more items from the commission's study. It estimated that some $268 billion of short-term liquid assets were held at the end of 1971 by "private institutions on the international finance scene," and that the "lion's share" of this money was controlled by American multinational companies and banks. The $268 billion "was more than twice the total of all international reserves held by all central banks and international monetary institutions in the world at the same date. . . . These are the reserves with which the central banks fight to defend their exchange rates. The resources of the private sector outclass them." In February 1973, when this report was released, the Federal Reserve Bank of New York reported that the nation's money supply in the week ended February 21 had jumped to a seasonally adjusted high of $258.4 billion. This amount represented the total private demand deposits, or checking-account deposits, plus cash in the public hands—less than the money floating around the international market.

In analyzing the impact created by the multinationals' control of these enormous assets, the study adds: "It is clear that only a small fraction . . . needs to move in order for a genuine crisis to develop." It "can focus with telling effect on a crisis-prone situation—some weak currency which repels funds and some strong one which attracts them." Which was precisely what happened prior to both devaluations as speculators dumped dollars and bought marks and yen in hopes of profiting on future changes in their exchange values.

But the study strives mightily to absolve the multinationals of any "destructive, predatory motivations" because only a small proportion of the multinationals' money is needed "to produce monetary explosions." Therefore predatory practices "don't characterize the sophisticated international financial activities of most multinational corporations, even though much of the funds which flow internationally during the crisis doubtlessly is [sic] of multinational corporation origin." The study offered two possible conclusions: either the multinationals "react protectively" with moves to protect the value of their assets, or they "hardly react at all, while a small minority, capable of generating heavy disruptive movements of funds, do so." The latter group includes companies that may actually "speculate" in the sense of betting on exchange-rate changes in hopes of a swift profit.[40]

And so the commission evaluates its own incriminating evidence and concludes that there might perhaps be a few bad apples—but nothing endemically rotten in the system.

Senator Hartke wants to scrap the Tariff Commission and replace it with a newly created Foreign Trade Investment Commission. "The present Tariff Commission is nothing more than a means of importing new welfare payments into this country on a unique tax support base for corporations. It is part of a tax incentive system to force companies that may not wish to leave this country to establish manufacturing and processing plants in other countries."

The Tariff Commission had multiple-choice answers for Senator Hartke and other detractors. It estimated that the presence of American-owned plants abroad represents a net loss of 1.3 million jobs in America, if it is assumed that foreigners would otherwise import the plants' entire output from the U.S. If foreigners imported only half of such output and produced the rest themselves, the job loss would be calculated at 400,000. If one rejected these figures, there was a third set of assumptions which indicated that multinationals have created a net gain of about 500,000 jobs in the United States.

Treasury Under Secretary Paul A. Volcker, the official who negotiated the second devaluation with Japan and the Common Market, told the House Banking and Currency Committee on March 6, 1973, that the massive buildup of dollars abroad "is a source of concern" to the government. He estimated the Eurodollar holdings of foreign central banks and multinationals at about $80 billion. This pool of Eurodollars, the result of excessive U.S. spending abroad, trade deficits, and repatriated profits is the prime source of the speculative funds that have plunged currency markets into a state of chronic turmoil in recent years.

> Exchange rate planning is becoming a highly developed art in many multinational enterprises. But few have gone as far as Ford Motor Co. Since it is extensively involved with less-developed countries, which devalue frequently, it feels the need to take systematic steps to protect its exposed position. But the company seeks only to cover, not speculate. A Ford economist regularly scans the international financial statistics to

determine which countries have the highest rates of inflation; these are obviously prime candidates for devaluation. He then examines patterns of trade. If a country is running more of an inflation than its chief trading partners and competitors and its reserves are limited, it is more than a candidate, it is a shoo-in. His most difficult problem is to determine exactly when the devaluation will take place. Economics determines whether and how much, but politicians control the timing. So the analyst maintains a complete library of information on leading national officials. He tries to get "into the skin of the man" who is going to make the decision. The economist's forecasts have been correct in sixty-nine of the last seventy-five crisis situations.—*Fortune*, September 15, 1968.

This is like saying that customers of Jimmy the Greek's morning line are more interested in advance information than in gambling. In any event, as with all good things, the system improves with age:

The finance ministers are years behind the times. Look, we are programing a computer right now, which can take floating rates, fixed rates, any kind of foreign exchange data you can conceive of, and it will tell us in a matter of seconds where we should be buying or selling, where our funds should move. They just can't invent regulations or controls or a system which can beat the computers.—Anonymous bank executive, Los Angeles *Times*, July 23, 1972.

Money in the Eurodollar market may be transferred fast into a strong currency in any money crisis. Because any such money goes through commercial banks, it is almost impossible for any outsider to evaluate totals. A Middle Eastern nation, for instance, may have funds with a dozen different banks from First National City Bank to Union Bank of Switzerland in Zurich and from Bank of America to Deutsche Bank in Frankfurt.

If there is any dollar dumping, a foreign-exchange dealer may not know the source of it; he is usually dealing with commercial banks. Incoming dollars may be received by the dealer as if they were holdings of the banks rather than of their clients. Moreover, banks, mindful of the huge amounts of business that may be coming their way in the future from the Mideast, fear being connected in any way with discussions of customer habits and inclinations.—*Wall Street Journal*, March 1, 1973.

For a far more accurate picture of the fabled gnomes-of-Zurich game depicted above, substitute "multinational corporation" for "Middle Eastern nation." The problem here is that you will find more gnomes who practice this currency brinkmanship on a Long Island commuter train than on the Orient Express. During the first seven days of February 1973, the West German central bank was flooded with an estimated $6 billion of dumped greenbacks. That panic culminated in the closing of most foreign-exchange markets on February 12 and the second devaluation of the dollar that night.

The catalyst was the announcement of the horrendous $6.4-billion U.S. trade deficit. The multinationals reasoned that with the United States in deficit and West Germany in surplus, the mark would go up in any currency realignment, and the dollar down. So they balanced their exchange risks by purchasing dollars on the open market and selling them to German banks. By the end of the week, it would have been interesting indeed to find any multinational operation that was not more than "protected." "We were modestly long in our position on foreign currencies," said Paul L. Smith, executive vice president of Los Angeles' Security Pacific National Bank. "And we would be surprised if any major bank would have been short."[41] In fact, the multinationals were so long that it was their volume of purchases which forced their bet into a winner. The Nixon Administration decided that the only way it could stop the run and restore confidence in the dollar was by another devaluation.

"We don't believe in gambling against the U.S. dollar," said Richard Thompson, European financial director for Johnson Wax, "but with assets in Germany, England, and Japan, we made a handsome profit."[42]

> Almost in spite of themselves, many U.S. multinationals have found the last few weeks of currency speculation very profitable indeed. Upon the devaluation of the dollar, the value of both the large foreign exchange holdings and the extensive overseas operations held by multinationals jumped anywhere from 5 percent to 20 percent.* Sellers of dollars for marks last week alone made an estimated $330-million. . . . A Frankfurt banker estimates that corporate treasurers alone were responsible for "about 50%" of the $6-billion in dollars that flowed into Germany.— *Business Week*, February 17, 1973.

Confidence in the dollar lasted about a week before speculators began dumping massive amounts of dollars on international currency markets on the bet that the dollar would be devalued again. The Frankfurt bank sopped up $2.5 billion of unwanted greenbacks in one day. That panic

---

* Once again the big loser was the American consumer. Senator Proxmire estimated that devaluation would cost Americans at least $3 billion in higher prices. Considering its multiple impact, that is a conservative figure. For example, the increase in import prices lessened foreign competition, making it possible for American manufacturers to jack up domestic prices as they filled the trade gap. Also, the reduction in food prices for exports created such a demand in foreign markets that domestic supplies fell far below demand, giving inflation another shot in its most vulnerable mainline.

culminated in the closing of most foreign-exchange markets for two weeks. On March 12, six Common Market countries, including France and West Germany, retaliated with a joint float of their currencies—a move that signaled a "dirty float." In diplomatic jargon, the snake finally got out of the tunnel. This refers to the formula established at the Bretton Woods Conference in 1944, when the International Monetary Fund and the World Bank were created, which stipulated that foreign governments were supposed to accept dollars in unlimited amounts at a fixed parity, or price. The parity set by Common Market countries permitted their currencies (the snake) to move up and down in line with each other in a "tunnel" with percentage limits only half as wide as the 4.5 percent fluctuation provided in the Smithsonian agreements. Great Britain, Italy, and Switzerland were the first to break out of the tunnel—they floated their currencies and stopped supporting the dollar. With the joint float of March 12, all Common Market countries were saying enough is enough. Thenceforth, the dollar would have to seek its own level in the market place, except as some governments might intervene and maneuver the rate—the "dirty float." The fall of the almighty dollar has left the world without a stable international currency—that is, a currency that maintains a fixed value in terms of other currencies.

By January 1974, the dollar was rebounding strongly in the wake of the turmoil created by the oil crisis on the major economies of the world. Most bankers and economists were convinced that the dollar's recovery was due to the belief by currency speculators that the U.S. economy was in a relatively strong position to ride out the oil crisis because of its own energy reserves. The theory goes that as oil becomes scarcer and costlier, European and Japanese industries will have to spend proportionately more than the U.S. for imported petroleum. This will damage their payments balances and weaken their currencies. As foreign currencies decline, the dollar should become relatively stronger.

However, the forecasters were overlooking the fact that the fate of many multinationals depends on the economics of their adopted countries. Investors may not realize it, but from 25 percent to 30 percent of the profits of American corporations come from foreign operations. In its evaluation of what it called "The foreign recession factor," *Business Week* noted that "Not only might foreign sales drop, but companies aren't likely to benefit from a dollar devaluation this year—which made U.S. products more competitive in foreign markets in 1973 and made profits in foreign currencies fatter when converted back to dollars. Indeed, the opposite may happen this year if countries begin devaluating relative to the dollar—as Japan did this week. States . . . Provident National Bank's investment guru, Charles F. O'Hay: 'Foreign earnings are going to get kicked in the teeth.' "[43]

Another minus factor was the oil import bill. As estimated by the Department of Commerce, it would soar to $19 billion in 1974, as compared to $7 billion in 1973. It could mean a whopping deficit in the U.S. trade balance, which surprisingly was running in the black the last three months of 1973.

Taking the long view, it seems doubtful that the dollar will ever completely recover from its fall into disrepute. Its era of world predominance is over. The game of devaluation, so popular in parts of Latin America, feeds upon itself. Each devaluation reminds speculators of the currency's vulnerability. As one gnome observed, "The United States is no longer a virgin."

"There has been a certain breakdown in discipline," Federal Reserve Board Chairman Arthur F. Burns told the House Banking Subcommittee on International Finance on March 7, 1973. "And if we don't watch our step, we will have currency wars, political uncertainties, and businessmen will have great uncertainty about their future. . . . We live in a world now where confidence in paper currencies has greatly declined. Not long ago the U.S. dollar was the great sign of safety and stability and strength around the world. But something has happened."

Whatever that was, in the view of the Nixon Administration it had nothing to do with the great exodus of multinational wealth to foreign shores. As further inducement, the President phased out the three controls the government maintains on the movement of capital abroad: the 11.25 percent interest-equalization tax on the purchase of foreign securities, the restrictions on U.S. bank loans to foreigners, and the limits on dollars that corporations can send out of the country for investment abroad—imposed by Johnson in 1968.

The hearings of the Senate Foreign Relations Subcommittee on multinationals were expected to drag on for perhaps three years. Millions of words would be spoken, recorded, printed, distributed, and, most likely, promptly forgotten. Among the questions to be raised: How much influence do global corporations exercise on U.S. foreign policy decisions? Do their operations dislocate national economics? What effect do they have on world trade and currency flows? Have they grown too big to handle without international controls?

There is much to be discovered, but how much of it will surface is uncertain. As noted in these pages, here briefly are a few possible answers: Giant multinationals enjoy complete freedom in the operation of their global empires. They behave as if they were above local laws. They employ sharp accountants and attorneys who know how to price transactions among subsidiaries across national boundaries to realize the highest profit and the lowest taxes. They smuggle hard cash into the United States to avoid taxes and to make political payoffs.* They reap windfalls from the dollar crises which they trigger by their tactics of money manipulation. The bulk of their foreign income is never repatriated and therefore remains tax-free, and what is remitted comes in at bargain rates. They operate just as cynically in less developed countries in the 1970s as in the old days, but are far more circumspect about it than ITT. The contemporary corporate style runs to suave denial, Madison Avenue euphemism, legal trickery, and, when all fails, wounded protests.†

They pay bribes to local officials, depositing large sums in Swiss banks, to obtain economic and tax concessions. They encourage American aid to countries where corrupt officials "cream off" a large proportion of the money for their private use. The exportation of American industrialization to less developed countries makes the local establishment richer while worsening the plight of the poor. They employ all tools and weapons at their disposal to protect the status quo, from economic coercion to CIA and military intervention. They flaunt their wealth with haughty arrogance

---

* When the House Banking and Currency Committee discovered that Nixon's re-election committee had received at least $30,000 from a secret Luxembourg bank account and about $89,000 from some wealthy Texas Democrats who channeled it through a Mexican bank to assure anonymity, Chairman Wright Patman concluded that it was "reasonable to assume that the total amount is substantially higher."[44] It was not until months later that the General Accounting Office reported the secret $200,000 donation from Robert Vesco, who at the time was under investigation by the Securities and Exchange Commission for the alleged "wholesale looting" of no less than $224 million from Investors Overseas Services. Vesco's chief administrative assistant from the time he began his looting of IOS up to this writing was Donald A. Nixon, Jr., nephew of the President—see Chapter Five, page 358. In August 1973, ABC News reported that the Senate Watergate committee was investigating a report that Nixon's re-election committee "laundered" $2 million in illegal contributions through Bahama's banks, including some used or owned by Charles G. ("Bebe") Rebozo, the President's closest friend. ABC said the money was run through gambling casinos in the Bahamas before being placed in several Miami area banks, including Rebozo's Key Biscayne Bank and Trust Company. The allegations were still under investigation at this writing.

† When Anaconda was accused by a Chilean congressional commission of having financed a propaganda "campaign of terror" against Allende, the company's lawyer dismissed the charges as an "enormous farce" and challenged the constitutionality of the commission.

in the midst of heartbreaking squalor. There is a strong belief in poor countries that the colonial control of Western nations has been passed on to the multinationals. They are the new imperious imperialists. There is a growing acceptance of Jean-Jacques Servan-Schreiber's prophecy that "The third industrial power, after the United States and the Soviet Union, could easily be in 15 years not Europe, but American industry in Europe."*

Finally, there is the theory of Howard V. Perlmutter, a professor at the University of Pennsylvania's Wharton School of Finance and Commerce. He predicts we are "moving towards a world of very large multinational firms and very small entrepreneurial firms of the 'one man show' variety. . . . I come out with a round number of 300 giant firms." The "super-giants" will benefit from "the absence of effective countervailing forces in the world community." Consumers "are at best unorganized" and trade unions "have enough difficulty at the national level." Individual governments are at a disadvantage. "Any given nation-state, acting alone, has limited bargaining power." Giant multinationals can play one country off against another until they get the freedom they want. "What guarantees are there that the key executives of the 300 geocentric super-giants will show a social responsibility to the world community of consumer and citizens?" There is a "need for laws at the world level . . . because the quality of life of the world's citizens and their survival cannot be made to depend on the policies of international firms."[45]

Science fiction or fact? How much has already come to pass? More, surely, than most people suspect. Gargantuan greed and respectable corruption have created a Frankenstein monster perhaps already advanced beyond the point of no return. And now, in the age of Nixonomics, it is fattening up in this best of all possible tax worlds, growing strong for the day when it will own it.

* In his book *The American Challenge*, published in 1967 (English translation 1968).

CHAPTER **3**

THE NATIONAL SECURITY–
ENERGY CRISIS GAME

The most spectacular of all tax games is played by the superstars of the international oil cartel. These good ole boys from the black gold country really know how to hone an edge. Not only are they better at the game than anybody else, they get to umpire and write their own rules as they go along. Oilmen, it should be noted at the outset, are not just ordinary businessmen. Congress has anointed them to a more exalted status, one that transcends the domestic realm. As providers of an exhaustible natural resource, one that is the very lifeblood of that industrial vampire called progress, they are not mere players in another lucrative game but esteemed guardians of our national security, the last stout bulwark against the burgeoning energy crisis.

This is not to say that oilmen exist in a state of benign public indulgence. There are critics around, their numbers growing geometrically in recent years, but their voices are lost in the great wilderness of government. Yet with all that money and power at stake, oilmen are not insensitive to criticism. They are quick to justify their tax and monopoly privileges, presenting the public with an elaborate catalogue of patriotic arguments prepared by expensive lobbyists.

There is no question that the oil lobby is the most awesome single political force in Washington. It is so powerful that it is in itself a subgovernment, with roots planted deep in the soil of the real government. The network of its roots runs throughout the federal bureaucracy, while up on Capitol Hill well-tempered champions of oil control all the committees that affect it by legislation. In fact, oil is so crucial to the present Administration that following his election in 1968 Richard Nixon quietly announced that the White House, not the Interior Department, would thenceforth make oil policy.[1] The presidential assistant picked for this assignment was Peter M. Flanigan, a generalist well versed in the philosophical merits of oil in politics. This includes international politics. In recent years, the imperialist image has been dimmed, with the old gunboat diplomacy of the State Department replaced by the more sophisticated palace intrigues of the Central Intelligence Agency.

Oil is the largest and richest industry in the world. It is so mammoth in the United States that it accounts for one-fifth of all manufacturing *profits* —more than the automobile, aircraft, steel, basic chemicals, and drug industries combined—while accounting for only 9 percent of the sales. This impressive performance is a tribute, not to its great operational efficiency, but rather to the very special tax dispensations woven into the fabric of the industry by grateful politicians over the past sixty years.

The oldest and most sacrosanct of these tax subsidies is the percentage-depletion allowance. With the adoption of the income tax in 1913, oil producers were allowed to deduct up to 5 percent of their gross income when computing taxable income. Although it was a modest beginning—the corporate tax rate was low and the 5 percent was comparable to the depreciation allowance granted other industries—a valuable accounting principle was introduced into the law. An oilman's venture capital, it was explained, was not the same thing as his capital investment. Oil became a capital asset, which meant it was not to be taxed as income. The lawmakers defended their action on the ground that exploration was costly and risky and that, once discovered, oil provided a limited quantity of an irreplaceable substance that was gradually being exhausted. The depletion allowance would make it possible for the producer to recoup his cost for the consumed portion of his property. The explanation seemed logical enough to them. After all, since the intent of the income-tax law was to tax income, not capital, it should not apply to that portion of the income derived from oil which was a wasting capital asset. The result was that 5 percent of the oil pumped from the well, actually the raw material of the industry, was shifted over to the capital side of the ledger. The normal way for a business to compute gain or loss is to offset the cost of the raw materials against receipts. By excluding the oil industry from this basic accounting procedure by even that small percentage, Congress initiated a subsidy that would grow like Topsy and eventually cost the Treasury countless tens of billions of dollars in lost taxes.*

The theory advanced for this remarkable inspiration was that it would serve as added incentive for exploration so that new discoveries would keep pace with national requirements. What is even more astounding about this rationale is that it was offered at a time in history when the oil boom had reached its greatest peak since 1859, when the drilling near Titusville, Pennsylvania, had started the first oil boom in the familiar pattern—the rush for leases, the frantic wildcatting, the overproduction, the wars among refiners, the enormous waste, and always, of course, the dream of instant wealth—the great legend of "Coal Oil Johnny" Steele, the lowly oilfield teamster who struck it rich and blew it in grand style. As one story went, when a hotel clerk in Pittsburgh refused him a room because of his grimy teamster's garb, Coal Oil Johnny bought the place and evicted everybody but himself. Those were the days when the mad scramble was to supply oil for the lamps of China.

Fifty years later it seemed to many that the wildcatters had punched enough holes in the earth to squeeze it dry. The conservation movement begun in the days of Teddy Roosevelt was at loggerheads with the formidable forces of "predatory" oilmen who looked upon the whole movement as a limp-wristed effort by a bunch of effete wealthy Easterners more interested in scenery than in jobs and progress. Oil was the "liquid gold" that would someday power the industries and navies of the world.

The conversion of the United States Navy to oil brought warnings from geologists that the earth contained only a limited supply of oil and that the Navy's future was in jeopardy unless it was carefully safeguarded. It was this warning that prompted President Taft in 1909 to withdraw public lands in California and Wyoming for this purpose. Elk Hills and Buena Vista Hills in California were set aside in 1912, and in 1915 President Wilson established Teapot Dome in Wyoming as a reserve. By the outbreak of World War I the public sector had come to occupy an eighth of the nation's oil lands. Eyed hungrily by oilmen and zealously guarded by the Navy, the battle over the preserves went on for years. The problem was not how to motivate oilmen to drill but rather how to stop them. Congress haggled endlessly over whether the public oil lands should be leased or sold. And whether there was a danger, as expressed by the Navy, that

---

* Oil accountants use this special method only for computing taxes; in reporting profits to stockholders, they figure them in the ordinary way.

private wells placed strategically close to the Navy's precious reserves were draining away the government's oil.

"Oil was money, and the struggle for it was earnest and relentless," wrote W. L. Connelly, a Sinclair Oil associate.[2]

Old Progressives like Gifford Pinchot and Robert La Follette, the Easterners led by Harvard's President Charles W. Eliot, head of the National Conservation Association, and the naval men gathered around Secretary of the Navy Josephus Daniels were pitted against the superior forces of the oil lobby, which included the Interior Department, a close ally throughout most of oil's history, and an overwhelming majority in both houses of Congress, all of whom enthusiastically asserted the oilman's "natural right" to government land. The shadow of war added a note of hysteria to the struggle. Now they wanted access to the preserves to increase production for "patriotism and national need." The call to "national security" was not far away.

Meanwhile, another fight was raging in Congress to increase the depletion allowance. It seems that the oilman's drilling morale during World War I needed added incentive. Leading the fight in the Senate was the oil lobby's top gun, Boies Penrose, a corpulent dandy from Pennsylvania and one of the most powerful Republicans in the country. His philosophy of government, as he expressed it to an associate, was to "control legislation that means something to men with real money and let them foot the bills."[3] It was Penrose who persuaded President Harding to appoint Andrew W. Mellon Secretary of the Treasury, a reign that was to span three Administrations. Mellon was the kind of ruthless operator the cynical Penrose admired. Born into a wealthy Pittsburgh banking family, Mellon maneuvered his way into more than a hundred corporations by demanding a "piece of the action" whenever the promoter of a promising enterprise wandered into his bank for a loan. His *modus operandi* in Gulf Oil was typical. When Anthony F. Luchich, the Yugoslav prospector who brought in Texas's fabulous Spindletop gusher in 1901, came to Mellon for a loan to buy needed equipment to handle the flow, he ended up selling his prospector's interest for $400,000. Colonel J. M. Guffey, who held the Spindletop lease, was given the presidency of the new company, paid a million dollars, and promised a half million in future dividends. Mellon and his brother, Richard, took 40 percent of the stock in the new corporation and sold the remaining 60 percent to six Pittsburgh capitalists. Then Guffey Petroleum was renamed Gulf Oil and the colonel was soon sent packing.[4]

The original intent of the legislation passed in 1913 was to limit the benefit to the cost of the investment. By 1918 the oil lobby was ready to dump "cost depletion" for more liberal legislation. Testifying before the Senate Finance Committee, oil spokesmen warned that high taxes imposed during the war were discouraging wildcatters from discovering new fields. All they were asking for was a "reasonable allowance for depletion without statutory restrictions." Senator Thomas Gore of Oklahoma, an oil lobbyist himself in later years (a popular occupation with many former members of Congress), was the first to propose this new formula. As one lobbyist put it, the oilman "sells his capital assets from the day he begins producing." It just was not fair, he said, to treat his operation like "other going industries."

On December 17, 1918, Senator Penrose spelled it out for his committee colleagues in a statement that took only twenty-one lines in the *Congressional Record*. It was his opinion that depletion should not be limited to the capital actually invested. As an alternative he proposed that the deduction on wells not brought in "proven fields" be based on the market value of the discovered oil "instead of the cost."

La Follette, who argued in favor of retaining cost depletion, warned that under the Penrose plan the cost of a well might be deducted ten times. His plea got him exactly seven votes. However, his estimate of the tax bonanza in the making was most conservative. The cost of some wells in recent years has been deducted a thousand times—in some cases, perhaps more than ten thousand times. Mellon's Gulf Oil was one of the first to take advantage of the new amendment. A study revealed that Gulf's depletion allowance in 1919 had been 449 percent of its net income. Two years later a Treasury official, speaking out of turn, called discovery depletion "really a gift in the form of tax-free income." He charged that the proven-field requirement was being ignored and that thousands of unqualified wells drilled practically on top of each other in proven fields were being classified as "discovery," making it "unquestionably one of the greatest loopholes of escape from taxation to be found in the entire statute."

By the mid-1920s it was getting pretty obvious to critics that discovery depletion was too complex for the Mellon Treasury to administer. A Congressional study in 1924 showed that of 13,671 wells granted discovery depletion to the tune of millions of dollars, only thirty-five had actually found new oil pools, and that wildcatters, who historically have been responsible for nearly all discoveries, were receiving only 3.5 percent of the benefits. The lion's share of tax-free dollars was flowing to the giant oil companies, the companies whose entire holdings were in proven fields.

The next development in the evolution of this historic Golconda came in 1926. As the story goes, percentage depletion was born during lunch one day when the president of the Mid-Continent Oil and Gas Association got the undivided attention of Senator David Reed of Pennsylvania, whose father was one of the original six capitalists brought into Mellon's Gulf Oil. Senator Reed rushed back to Capitol Hill to tell his colleagues on the Senate Finance Committee about the awesome burden imposed on the oil industry by the rising costs of exploration. As related by his luncheon companion, the oil industry had spent more for exploration in 1925 than its total income. This morsel of prandial intelligence proved conclusively to the Senator that "the industry can truthfully say that it has not made a cent on all its business of last year."[5]

Thus was launched the great debate between those in the Senate who favored a depletion allowance of 30 percent on gross income and those in the House who thought that 25 percent was more equitable. Finally, the conferees, rising to the wisdom of Solomon, halved the difference and the oil industry got its infamous 27.5 percent. With La Follette dead, resistance to the measure was sporadic at best. One of the few Senators to speak out against it was William King of Utah. He accused the Senate of "gross favoritism . . . under the guise of simplifying the law. . . . I cannot understand this great solicitude for the Standard Oil Company, the Shell Oil Company, the Sinclair Company, and the other great organizations, whose annual profits are many hundreds of millions of dollars. . . . I am afraid we are blinded because of the power and the bigness of great corporations and sometimes deal unjustly with the people."[6]

Treasury Secretary Mellon was at the side of President Coolidge when he signed the bill into law. Gulf Oil more than doubled its assets during Mellon's tenure in office. A small man with sad, dark-circled eyes, Mellon was second only to John D. Rockefeller as the world's richest man. Harding called him "the ubiquitous financier of the universe."[7]

As noted in Chapter One, Mellon was the decade's greatest exponent of laissez-faire economics. His rule over the Treasury assured businessmen of low taxes and fat profits. When the bottom finally dropped out, Mellon escaped unscathed. The historian Arthur M. Schlesinger, Jr., wrote years later:

> Through family corporations, the Mellons shared in the grand barbecue. The *New York Times* reported in 1926 that the Secretary of the Treasury's relatives had made $300 million in the bull market on alumi-

num and Gulf Oil alone. Nor did this exhaust the possibilities of family corporations. "Pursuant to your request for a memorandum setting forth the various ways by which an individual may legally avoid tax," wrote the Commissioner of Internal Revenue to the Secretary of the Treasury, "I am pleased to submit the following." The following consisted of ten possible methods of tax avoidance, five of which Mellon in time admitted under oath he actually employed.

The arbitrary depletion deduction of 22 percent (reduced from 27.5 percent by the Tax Reform Act of 1969), which applies to gross income from oil and gas up to 50 percent of net income, means that it can be used through the full producing life of the property regardless of its classification. With the 1926 law, restrictions on new fields and cost depletion went out the window. In his excellent report on the oil industry, Ronnie Dugger concluded that "the killing off that year of the restriction of the privilege to wildcatters' newly discovered wells was a change at least as important as the percentage system. The original idea of a special incentive to expand U.S. oil supplies was blurred, and a new privilege began to generate its adaptable new reason for existing."[8]

To further lighten the oilman's burden, Congress decreed the "intangible drilling and development deduction," which makes it possible for oilmen to deduct immediately from other *income* more than three-fourths of all costs for exploration. This includes all expenditures for wages, fuel, repairs, hauling, and supplies, right along with the cost of tubing, casing, pumping equipment, and other tangible items normally capitalized and recovered through depreciation deductions taken throughout the useful life of the property.

Having pulled the door off its hinges for oil and gas producers, Congress soon succumbed under pressure from other extractive industries. In subsequent years, starting in 1932, percentage depletion at lower rates was extended to all the natural resources of the earth, except, as Congress finally stipulated, "soil, sod, dirt, turf, water, or mosses or minerals from sea water, the air, or similar inexhaustible sources.* The cumulative cost

* Some of the rates currently in effect include the following: 22 percent for sulfur, uranium, molybdenum, and an extended list of minerals from domestic deposits; 15 percent for domestic gold, silver, copper, iron ore, and oil shale; 14 percent for rock asphalt, vermiculite, and certain types of clay; 10 percent for coal and a limited group of other minerals; 7.5 percent for clay, shale, and slate used for specified purposes; and 5 percent for such items as gravel, peat, sand, and certain minerals from brine wells. In addition, a 14 percent rate applies to a final category which contains an extended series of minerals and includes all other minerals (unless sold for riprap, ballast, road material, rubble, concrete aggregates, or for similar purposes, in which case the rate is 5 percent).

of this benefit to the Treasury has to be astronomical. For example, a survey taken in 1960 showed that the depletion deductions on a group of products, including silver, copper, and iron, were ninety-one times cost depletion each year. As C. Wright Mills has pointed out, "The important point of privilege has less to do with the percentage allowed than with the continuation of the device long after the property is fully depreciated."[9]

The point to remember about the oil percentage-depletion deduction is that it does not relate to the capital invested in drilling the well (the intangible deduction takes care of that expense), but rather to the capital invested in the oil in place in the ground—that is, the money spent to acquire rights to the oil land. The distortion in the accounting procedure arises because of a very clever distinction: percentage depletion is computed as a percentage of the *selling price* of the minerals produced from a property, rather than by reference to the capital actually invested in those minerals. For example, if an oil producer invests $10,000 in acquiring rights to oil lands, hits a gusher, and sells the oil for a million dollars a year for ten years before the well runs dry, his tax-free benefit computed at the 22 percent rate would total $2.2 million. His deduction would be 220 times as large as his original investment. This is not an atypical example. The usual procedure, however, in acquiring rights to oil lands is for the oil producer to assign a one-eighth royalty to the property owner, who, incidentally, is entitled to percentage depletion on his royalty income. The fact that he does no drilling and bears none of the risks is immaterial. This is what has made oil and gas such popular tax shelters for investors in high income brackets, and such a lucrative gimmick for hotshot promoters.

But that is far from the full story. These benefits, the intangible deduction and percentage depletion, created on the pretext that they would stimulate domestic production, are also available to American producers in overseas operations. The logic here is elusive. But then logic has never been a legislative requisite in negotiations with the money elite.

It is with the foreign operation that the third major tax benefit enjoyed by oilmen comes into play. In the beginning, when they first ventured overseas, oilmen operated under the traditional one-eighth royalty arrangement used in the United States. The royalty was treated as income by the holder and excluded from income by the oil producer, with the net result that the oilman's gross income was seven-eighths of the well's total earnings. Oftentimes governments rather than private individuals owned the mineral rights and the royalties were paid to them. This was particularly true in republics south of Mexico and in Middle Eastern feudal sheikdoms where a barrel of oil (42 gallons) was produced at a cost of about a dime. The bonanza here was manifold. So when the Arab potentates began to press for higher royalty payments after World War II, the oilmen hit upon another brainstorm. It was perfectly simple: why not call a royalty a tax? American businesses operating overseas can deduct from U.S. taxes any taxes they pay to foreign governments. The oil companies deny that there was any collusion with foreign governments, but informed critics believe otherwise.

In testimony before the Joint Economic Committee, Thomas F. Field, a former Treasury expert,* outlined the background of the conspiracy for the committee:

> Of course, foreign governments would have to cooperate in this charade, and the U.S. Government would have to disregard the realities and pay attention only to the external form of the transaction. Both these tasks proved quite easy. The Saudi Arabian government adopted an income tax statute—which, I am told, was drafted by oil company lawyers in a New York City law office. The statute effectively excused everyone except oil producers from paying the tax.
>
> Armed with this "income tax statute," oil company representatives descended on Washington to induce the Internal Revenue Service to allow U.S. companies operating in Saudi Arabia to credit this "tax" against their U.S. income tax liabilities. The result was an Internal Revenue Service ruling, I.T. 4038, holding that the Saudi Arabian "tax" was creditable, dollar for dollar, against U.S. tax. This left both the Saudi Arabians and the U.S. oil companies better off; the U.S. Treasury was left holding the bag. Within the next few years, virtually every foreign country in which U.S. minerals producers operate had adopted "royalty type taxes" so as to take advantage of this I.R.S. ruling.
>
> The net effect has been to relieve U.S. firms that produce oil in foreign countries of one of their major costs of doing business in the U.S. U.S. producers, such as the independent domestic wildcatter, must continue to pay royalties to land owners in return for drilling rights. U.S. firms operating overseas must also make substantial payments to landowners—that is, foreign governments—in return for drilling rights, but they are able to pass these costs along, dollar for dollar, to the U.S. Treasury.

Field estimated that the "taxes" currently constituted better than 50 percent of the selling price of foreign oil: "Since U.S. companies realize about $4 to $5 billion per year from the sale of oil, a conservative estimate would place the cost of these 'royalty type taxes' at from $2 to $2.5 billion per year."[10]

* Field, who testified before the committee on January 10, 1972, is the executive director of Taxation with Representation, a nonpartisan public-interest tax group.

Although the tax benefits enjoyed by oilmen are more generous than those of any other industry, there is more to the politics of oil than taxation. Big oil, as Robert Engler noted in his comprehensive study, *The Politics of Oil*, "has learned to operate within the entire spectrum of the political processes of the society, reaching out to mold law, the bureaucracies, political machinery, and public opinion."[11]

The instrument created to carry out these goals was the American Petroleum Institute, a trade association founded in 1919 by officials of Standard Oil of New Jersey. The original board of directors was made up of the former members of the defunct National Petroleum War Service Committee, organized during World War I to serve as a liaison between the government and the oil industry in a common effort to increase the supply of oil necessary for war. The board consisted of the presidents of the major integrated oil companies. Through the years the API has served as the voice, the brain, and the muscle of the industry. As a trade association, it works as a forum for solving conflicts within the industry. For example, in the area of competition, the API has worked out a code of trade practices to control production and marketing. In the public sector, it operates as a high-intensity lobby to fight against unpopular tax and anti-trust legislation.

In terms of the hazards of competition, the API was created not a day too soon. With the cessation of World War I, the industry's problem was suddenly reversed, the fear of a scarcity of oil shifting to one of overabundance. The mad scramble to pump the world dry was having a disastrous effect on the stability of prices. The major integrated companies, which pumped, refined, transported, and sold their petroleum products in their own service stations, were being challenged by a bunch of ragtail independents in costly competition. Free enterprise and immunity from antitrust legislation were inalienable rights, but when the supply exceeded the demand, it was time for the "clerks in Washington" to protect business. What was needed were controls at the source. The government, taking the cue from conservationists, was only too happy to oblige.

The first step in the government's intervention in the marketplace on behalf of big oil was taken in 1924 with the creation of the Federal Oil Conservation Board. Calling attention to the wastefulness of oil production on both public and private lands, President Coolidge said the purpose of the board was "to study the government's responsibility and to enlist the full cooperation of representatives of the oil industry in the investigation. . . . The oil industry itself might be permitted to determine its own future.

That future might be left to the simple workings of the law of supply and demand but for the patent fact that the oil industry's welfare is so intimately linked with the industrial prosperity and safety of the whole people, that government and business can well join forces to work out this problem of practical conservation."[12]

The board was made up of four Cabinet members and an advisory body of API representatives. Together they persuaded the oil states to reexamine and intensify their conservation efforts. In 1929 they proposed the following law: "Federal legislation which shall (a) unequivocally declare that agreements for this cooperative development and operation of single pools are not in violation of the Federal Antitrust laws, and (b) permit, under suitable safeguards, the making in times of overproduction, of agreements among oil producers for curtailment of production."

Federal action was aborted when the Attorney General ruled that the plan was nothing more than an attempt to win immunity from the antitrust laws. But the board had better luck with the states. Matters came to a head in 1930, when the price of oil dropped to ten cents a barrel following the discovery, largely by independents, of the lush East Texas oil field. Actually, this economic crisis was engineered by big oil to force independents to the wall. The underlying fear of the large integrated producer is of competitively set prices. Conservation was a legal means of achieving an orderly and predictable flow of petroleum to protect industry-set prices and investments. The end result was the birth of the oil industry's second government-guaranteed privilege: prorationing—the setting by states of monthly production quotas based upon market estimates controlled by the major companies. Known today as maximum efficient rates (MER), the quotas are set for all rigs drilling into a single reservoir.

Texas led the way, but not before there was a change in Austin. The money power of the giants was being challenged by a small army of wildcatters, dirt farmers with royalty holdings, and independent refiners who had broad grassroots support in local governments. In the words of W. J. Crawford, the tax administrator for Humble Oil (Humble Oil was Jersey Standard's largest domestic subsidiary), "We had to let a president of Humble quit to become governor to establish proration." Once in office, Governor Ross S. Sterling ordered the state militia into the oil fields to shut down all that wasteful *competitive* production. The commander of the troops was moonlighting from his job as chief counsel for the Texas Company (Texaco).[13]

With the Market Demand Act of 1932, the Texas Railroad Commission became the administrative arm of proration. Other states soon followed suit. It remained finally for the federal government to get into the act. Something had to be done about independents who were shipping "hot oil" (produced in excess of state quotas) to other states. To prohibit interstate shipments of hot oil, Congress passed the Interstate Transportation of Petroleum Products Act, written by Texas Senator Tom Connally, who steered the measure through the Senate in 1935 without hearings.

The law placed production and consumption in balance. State prorationing laws were now backed by the federal government. A joint industry-government committee, dominated by API oilmen, was created to serve as a continuing liaison in implementing the new regulations. Secretary of the Interior Harold L. Ickes said the oilmen were only advisers, but, as it turned out, the industry was to control the policies as well as the day-to-day operation of the entire program.

Twenty years later the program was declared a rousing success by Assistant Secretary for Mineral Resources Felix F. Wormser in a speech to oilmen in 1954. "I asked the Bureau [of Mines] to give me a total figure covering all of the forecasts made monthly from July 1935, when it started, through July 1954, and the actual crude oil production reported for the same period. I was astonished to find that the total amounted to approximately 32 billion barrels and the difference between the forecast and actual production has been less than one percent."

If the elimination of waste looked promising to the government and conservationists, it looked even better to the oil industry, which had neatly sidestepped the one-two knockout combination of competition and anti-trust action. With the support of government, the giants were ready to exercise their own muscle in controlling every phase of the business. Included among their vast resources was the control of storage tanks, tankers, barges, privileged access to railroad tank cars, and, most importantly, interstate pipelines. When on rare occasions the state agencies approved more production than the giants authorized, the companies simply refused to take the excess—this is called "pipeline proration."

Proration is a hangover from the New Deal's NRA codes, which were designed to cure an economy diagnosed to be suffering from the "free play of a self-regulating market." The remedy suggested was government control over production, wages, working conditions, and prices. It is ironic that President Roosevelt's New Deal Administration would be the first to welcome oilmen into the councils of government since World War I. The NRA petroleum code was worked out by a Planning and Coordination

Committee whose membership included the presidents of Socony-Vacuum, Jersey Standard,* Indiana Standard, Standard of California, the Texas Company, and the API.

During the two-year life of NRA, the oil industry was dominated by this committee. In assessing its role, Robert Engler wrote: "The committee's deliberations were closed, and the financing came from the major oil interests. There was less need now to run continually to Washington on each issue of public policy that might affect the industry. Big oil had arrived in government on an official basis. Independents were to complain repeatedly that they were being regulated and judged by their giant competitors who, as government servants, were now gaining vital competitive information, fixing production and refining quotas, and generally implementing trade practices that limited competition."[14]

World War II brought more oilmen into the government. Although Secretary Ickes was in favor of this policy, he had certain reservations. An entry in his diary in 1933 concerning a meeting in his office with Harry F. Sinclair shows that he was fully conscious of the sensitive nature of his position: "I kept wondering whether the ghost of Albert Fall carrying a little black satchel might not emerge from one of the gloomy corners of this office."[15] As Secretary of the Interior in the Harding Administration, Fall was later sentenced to prison for receiving $400,000 in bribes from Sinclair and Edward L. Doheny in the Teapot Dome scandal. Ickes confided to his diary in 1936 that "an honest and scrupulous man in the oil business is so rare as to rank as a museum piece."[16] And he likened dollar-a-year men serving on the War Production Board to crawling maggots looking out for their private interests.

In 1949 the Senate Small Business Committee concluded that proration forms "a perfect pattern of monopolistic control over oil production and the distribution thereof . . . and ultimately the price paid by the public."

William J. Murray, Jr., former chairman of the Texas Railroad Commission, told the Senate Subcommittee on Antitrust and Monopoly that "market demand proration simply means that the production of crude oil will be restricted to that amount which, when refined into petroleum products, will supply the needs of all the consumers of the nation for each and

---

* Since Standard Oil of New Jersey (Jersey Standard), which distributed the Esso and Humble gasoline brands, formally changed its corporate name and brand names to Exxon in November 1972, its new name will be used in these pages wherever possible. (With the outbreak of the Watergate investigation in the spring of 1973, Shana Alexander suggested in her *Newsweek* column that Nixon change his name to Nixxon.)

all of the multitude of petroleum products." However, he conceded that as the commission lowered the amount of production, prices tended to go up. "If we let the stocks (storage tank supplies) run up, we would create waste, and you would also break the price." The giant companies were very much in favor of proration, he said, and "became the biggest policing agents of all. They even had their own detectives."[17]

It was inevitable that proration, as exercised by the giants, would lead to other evils in the marketplace. Domestic price fixing was relatively simple when the United States produced more than two-thirds of the world's crude oil and owned one-third of the world's proved reserves. The trend in world oil prices was set by the United States—more specifically, by the Texas Railroad Commission.

The situation was to change drastically in the 1950s. The world's oil reserves were tripled in that decade, from an estimated 100 billion barrels to nearly 300 billion. The United States reserves, failing to respond to tax incentives, remained constant at 33 billion barrels. The most significant discoveries were in the Middle East, with proved reserves of 60 billion barrels in Kuwait, 50 billion in Saudi Arabia, 35 billion in Iran, and 25 billion in Iraq.* Suddenly the United States was producing only one-third of the world's oil and possessed only one-ninth of the reserves. Proration was keeping U.S. prices up but world prices were plunging into a tailspin.

Once again the giants were faced with the specter of an uncontrolled abundance of cheap oil. Whereas an American well on proration produced about fourteen barrels per day, the average output of an Arab well was around 5,000 barrels. In 1956 the 175 wells of Kuwait were producing one-sixth of the daily yield of the United States' 500,000 wells. Middle East oil cost from ten to twenty cents a barrel to produce and could be delivered to the East Coast at about half the domestic price and still earn a handsome profit. A study by the Secretariat of the United Nations Economic Commission for Europe in 1955 calculated that the net profit on a barrel of Saudi Arabian oil selling at $1.75 was $1.40. And that was about $1.50 cheaper than the domestic product.

The challenge could have been catastrophic had it not been for the fact that the international market was in the capable hands of a consortium of seven integrated giants: five American companies (Exxon, Mobil, Gulf, Texaco, and Standard of California) and two foreign organizations (Royal Dutch/Shell, British- and Dutch-controlled, with large holdings in the United States, and the British Petroleum Company, with a majority of its

* Later, of course, some of these figures would double and triple.

stock government-owned). Their combined holdings equaled no less than two-thirds of the world's proved reserves, and their monopolistic control involved every phase of the business—production, refining, cracking, transportation, and marketing—from the moment the crude appeared at the wellhead until the ultimate consumer purchased it in the form of oil, gasoline, heating fuel, antifreeze, plastics, tires, sweaters, detergents, or whatever in an endless line of products.

By 1959 the five American companies had a gross investment in overseas fixed assets estimated at $9 billion. Their control of global reserves included 64 percent of Middle East reserves (the British and Dutch companies had 31 percent, for a total of 95 percent), 70 percent of Canada's production, and 68 percent of Venezuela's, which then accounted for 16 percent of the world's supply. The staggering value of these holdings was beyond Croesus's wildest dream. Exxon alone controlled proved reserves equal to those within the United States, and 80 percent of its crude-oil production and about 75 percent of its net income were derived from its overseas investments. Two-thirds of Gulf's income came from foreign operations.

Their overseas holdings were paying off handsomely. For years the government, fearing the prospect of foreign domination of new crude sources, had spurred their predatory ventures, urging greater effort at every turn with generous tax incentives, favorable trade treaties, dollar diplomacy, military intercession when dollars failed—and, if that did not work, CIA sculduggery was called into play. In 1953 the CIA helped give Premier Mohammed Mossadegh of Iran the old heave-ho when he decided that the nationalization of the oil fields would be beneficial to his country. The consortium promptly imposed an economic blockade, threatening legal reprisals against any violator. The real fear of the consortium members was not the loss of Iran's oil fields but the possibility of a large quantity of oil flowing into world markets outside of their control system.

Washington's position was made crystal clear when President Eisenhower cut all economic aid to Iran:

> There is a strong feeling in the United States that it would be not fair to the American taxpayers for the United States Government to extend any considerable amount of economic aid to Iran so long as Iran could have access to funds derived from the sale of its oil and oil products if a reasonable agreement were reached with regard to compensation whereby the large-scale marketing of Iranian oil would be resumed. Similarly, many American citizens would be deeply opposed to the purchase by the

United States Government of Iranian oil in the absence of an oil settlement.[18]

The army that backed the Shah who deposed Mossadegh was American-trained and -equipped. In testimony before the House Foreign Affairs Committee in 1954, Major General George C. Stewart described what took place:

> . . . when this crisis came on and the thing was about to collapse, we violated our normal criteria and among the other things we did, we provided the army immediately on an emergency basis blankets, boots, uniforms, electric generators, and medical supplies that permitted and created an atmosphere in which they could support the Shah. . . . The guns that they had in their hands, the trucks that they rode in, the armored cars that they drove through the streets, and the radio communications that permitted their control, were all furnished through the military defense assistance program. . . . had it not been for this program, a government unfriendly to the United States probably would now be in power.[19]

President Eisenhower assured the new government of "sympathetic consideration"—the Shah received $85 million of mutual security and technical assistance program funds in 1954, $76 million in 1955, and $73 million in 1956.*

From the beginning, the oil companies have viewed themselves as representatives of the United States abroad. Since mineral rights in most areas where they operate belong to governments rather than private property holders, oil's diplomatic corps works closely with American embassies in their negotiations with the heads of political states. In a search that has taken them to every corner of the world, the oil companies have received the fullest protection of the flag. In summing up their profitable activities in China in an earlier period when local warlords sometimes failed to recognize property rights, a State Department official told a Senate committee:

> A study of the cases in which requests for aid were made and of the action taken in such cases by representatives of this government would reveal that the latter consistently did their best to render effective assistance to oil companies; that measured in terms of dollars and cents, the cumulative value of such assistance would reach a very impressive figure. . . .[20]

---

* Reportedly instrumental in the coup was Richard M. Helms, then a CIA agent in Tehran, who later came to head the agency and—at this writing—is ambassador to Iran.

"Some oil representatives fought within American Government circles against the cutting off of oil supplies to Japan as she prepared for World War II," Robert Engler wrote in *The Politics of Oil*. "They also resisted or ignored efforts to prevent indirect shipments by way of 'neutrals' or 'independent brokers,' and even were reluctant to stop the refueling of Axis ships. Earlier, during the Ethiopian War when the League of Nations was testing its strength by attempting to apply sanctions against Italy, the companies won in their efforts to enjoin the State Department against placing an embargo on oil to the aggressor."[21]

Forty years later the companies would turn against their own country. When the Arab–Israeli war erupted in October 1973, King Faisal of Saudi Arabia and other Arab leaders promptly ordered American oil companies to cut off all petroleum shipments to the U.S. Sixth Fleet operating in the Mediterranean and to other overseas units. The companies obediently complied, forcing the military to institute a massive air and sea lift to meet the needs of the Mediterranean fleet. Following Senate hearings in January 1974, Senator Henry M. Jackson angrily observed that "We're not going to knuckle under to any tin-horn colonel or sheik over in the Middle East. . . . What I want to know is whether there was any corporate patriotism or whether they knuckled under." By their behavior, the companies had jeopardized the "nation's security at a critical time. I don't think it was an excuse to say 'we were under orders.' This was oil that was in their stocks. The critical thing was the time factor"—cutting off the military at a moment of crisis.

J. K. Jameison, chairman of Exxon, which alone supplies about 60 percent of the petroleum contracted by the military, said that Exxon "vigorously denies the charge of disloyalty and believes the facts fully confirm this position. As is generally known, the Saudi Arabian government in late October imposed an embargo on the export of crude and products to the United States and certain other countries. Included in this embargo were deliveries to the U.S. Military of products derived from Saudi Arabian crude. Those developments and the actions taken by Exxon were promptly reported to the Department of Defense and the Defense Fuel Supply Center."

The same American firms in Saudi Arabia* sold Arabian crude to the U.S. Navy in World War II for $1.05 a barrel—its cost, including royalty,

---

* The Arabian American Oil Company (Aramco) is a joint venture consisting of Exxon, Texaco, Mobil, Standard Oil of California and the Arabian government—it is the biggest and most profitable oil operation in the Middle East.

was 41 cents.[22] Engler went on to write: "After World War I the State Department had ardently advocated the full implementation of the 'open door' policy. When it appeared that the Netherlands Government was planning to turn over to Shell the German concessions in the Netherlands Indies, ignoring Standard Oil (New Jersey), which was also in the area, American diplomats argued for equal opportunity. At first they were unsuccessful. But a reciprocity clause in the newly passed Mineral Leasing Act and the knowledge that Shell was searching for crude oil in the western parts of the United States provided weapons."[23]

To put pressure on the Netherlands government, the State Department, according to one of their memorandums, "took steps to block the issuance of further concessions to the Royal Dutch Shell in public lands in the United States. The final result was that the New Jersey company was given additional producing concessions in the Indies which turned out to be some of the richest in the islands."[24]

The State Department used similar tactics to get Exxon and Mobil into the oil fields of the old Turkish Empire. "Coveted by the Germans," Engler wrote, "these were eagerly being divided by the British, French, and Dutch, for earlier successes in Persia had made geologists alert to prospects in neighboring Iraq. 'This Government has contributed to the common victory [said the State Department], and has a right, therefore, to insist that American nationals shall not be excluded from a reasonable share in developing the resources of territories under mandate . . .' "[25]

But once the companies got their piece of the Iraq Petroleum Company, they quickly joined in exclusive agreements with their foreign partners to keep others from the region. And when the pro-Western, reactionary dictatorship in Iraq was overthrown in 1958 by a middle-class-dominated coup, the American marines landed in Lebanon and British paratroopers dropped into Jordan in an effort to contain the revolt. The United States said it was trying to protect American lives and prevent the "indirect aggression" of "assassins in plain clothes" seeking to place Lebanon under the domination of Gamal Abdel Nasser's United Arab Republic. A New York Times dispatch quoted a "highly experienced military analyst" as saying that the job of smashing the headquarters of the opposition to the Government "might be done with two light tanks alone." In the United Nations, the Soviet delegate said he detected "an acute smell of oil," and the Times reported a series of conferences at which President Eisenhower, Secretary of State John Foster Dulles, and Foreign Secretary Selwyn Lloyd of Britain had agreed to limit their military action in the Middle East for the time being to Lebanon and Jordan: "Intervention will not be extended to Iraq as long as the revolutionary government in Iraq respects Western oil interests." Confronted by this gunboat diplomacy, the new Iraqi government agreed to respect the properties and concessions of the Iraq Petroleum Company.[26]

Always on the alert for threats to its dominion, the API moved quickly that same year when the United Nations General Assembly received Soviet-backed resolutions proposing that the U.N. provide aid to nations wishing to develop their own petroleum resources, and for study of international cooperation in such development. "In no time at all the oil lobbyists were swarming around the United Nations," the St. Louis *Post-Dispatch* reported. "There were so many conferences between the oil men and members of the United States delegation that one American diplomat said he told the oil people to 'let us alone so we can protect your interests.' " Speaking for the United States and on behalf of the API's defense of private enterprise, Senator Mike Mansfield ridiculed the resolution: "If the General Assembly starts with the oil industry today, where shall we stop? Will there be a separate resolution on the steel industry, the flour milling industry, poultry raising, cement manufacturing, automobiles, synthetic fibers or the hula hoop business?"[27]

The State Department was put on notice by the API against accepting the United Nations' proposed Covenant on Human Rights because of a provision asserting the right of peoples to self-determination including "permanent sovereignty over their natural wealth and resources." "Governments may change, rulers may be deposed, and feudal social systems overturned," Robert Engler wrote. "But the right granted by an existing state to a company to take out the oil wealth of a people should not be interfered with—even where the investment has been paid off many times over."[28]

The State Department, in its fulfillment of the manifest destiny of the nineteenth century, has paved the diplomatic path of oil from China to South America, where their forays into Mexico, Venezuela, Argentina, Guatemala, Colombia, and Bolivia received "the closest collaboration" in safeguarding their investments and profits. When countries like Brazil and Argentina insisted on developing their own resources, the United States assumed a hostile posture, refusing to extend loans and technical advice unless American corporations were given entry. The policy of gunboat or dollar diplomacy has played a large role in the propping up of corrupt regimes more interested in Swiss bank accounts than in the welfare of their people.

It was from this framework that the private international conspiracy of oil evolved into what is perhaps the first world government. It drew up "treaties" and marked off regions as open, closed, or postponed for concessions, and developed systems of cooperation in obtaining leases and in drilling. Monopolistic grants from feudal potentates were shared by the group, and individual operations were converted into joint affairs: united we stand against an oil-inundated world, divided we fall into competitive ruins. They called their effort a consortium to take the onus off what their critics charged was a cartel.

In a report provocatively entitled *The International Petroleum Cartel,* the staff of the Federal Trade Commission concluded that a cartel by any other name exudes the same potent odor. The carefully documented report, which covered 378 pages, complete with charts and diagrams, meticulously detailed the monopolistic practices of the seven members of the consortium in their dealings around the world, charging that they limited production, divided up markets, shared territories, and followed a system of pricing that eliminated price differences among themselves to any buyer at any given destination point.[29]

The report, which became the *cause célèbre* of 1952, the last year of the Truman Administration, was promptly suppressed by a shocked bureaucracy, consisting, no less, of the CIA and the Departments of Defense and State. It remained for President Truman to get the cartel off the hook in a farewell gesture that was impressively oblique.

The most shocking aspect of this unprecedented report was the sheer perfidy of the Federal Trade Commission. To think that a regulatory agency, an organically business-oriented institution, would have the colossal temerity to . . . well, it was beyond comprehension. The joker in the deceptively stacked deck was the commission's acting chairman, Stephen J. Spingarn, an intellectual with a capricious sense of humor. His response to the censure was to submit the report to the Senate's Select Committee on Small Business, which later made it public, but not before a careful editing, on grounds of national security, had blurred the sharp edges.

Exxon, the kingpin of the cartel, warned that the release of the report would prejudice "American petroleum interests in the Middle East. The prestige and respect which the companies in the Middle East have so earnestly worked to establish have been damaged by the challenge to the ventures. The allegations of antitrust violations are interpreted in the Middle East as official and outright repudiation by the United States of the behavior of its own nationals in the conduct of their business in that area. What is incorrectly thought to be a profound lack of confidence by the United States Government in its own companies has created grave distrust of the companies in the countries where they do business. Deserted and repudiated by their own Government, as they appear to be in the Middle East, the American companies are marked as fair game for attack and hostile acts by different nationalist, Communist, or religious factions, which would not occur if the companies were thought to have the full backing and confidence of their Government."[30]

The Middle East, Secretary of State Dean Acheson concluded, was a powder keg ready to go off in favor of a Kremlin victory. The release of the report would only hasten the confrontation.

Senator Thomas C. Hennings, Jr., of Missouri suggested that the report was "an American powder keg," startling only to an American public uninformed of the machinations of an Anglo-American oildom that "strikes at the heart of the American free-enterprise system." In a letter to Acheson, the Senator said: ". . . It perhaps ill behooves this nation, on the one hand, to talk of democracy and the development of backward countries and to make promises of assistance to peoples throughout the world still living under feudal conditions and, on the other hand, to refrain from disclosing information possibly indicating the efforts of large financial interests to hamper and defeat the attempts of the peoples in various parts of the world to free themselves through their own efforts from feudalism and economic imperialism."

Meanwhile, as a grand-jury investigation of the five American companies got under way, Exxon's law firm, Sullivan and Cromwell, whose senior member was John Foster Dulles, strongly objected to turning over any documents to the Justice Department. "If it were not for the question of national security, we would be perfectly willing to face either a criminal or a civil suit," the law firm explained. "But this is the kind of information that the Kremlin would love to get its hands on." Finally, after months of haggling, it agreed to submit certain documents, but only after it was agreed that they would be classified and that government personnel handling them were cleared for "top secret" material. No such requirement, however, was made of the industry, which apparently was better qualified to protect national security than the government.

Early in January 1953, just when the grand jury was about to meet to review the government's case, President Truman proposed "in the interest of national security" and "for foreign policy reasons" that civil proceedings be substituted in place of a criminal indictment.

Spingarn, who had been a White House adviser before going over to the FTC, observed that the cartel was "moving heaven and earth" to have the charges quashed. A brilliant and dynamic administrator, Spingarn became the cartel's principal scapegoat. He quickly found himself buried under an avalanche of media vilification. Typical of the viciousness of the attack was an *Oil Forum* editorial, widely circulated to news media by the high-powered public-relations firm of Hill and Knowlton, which recalled the influence of Alger Hiss in the government and asked "if there were any communist-inclined officials" in the FTC responsible for the report. It then suggested that "it might be well to play safe, and have the FBI investigate every man who participated in its preparation and writing." The Congressmen who had favored the report's release were denounced as cheap and venal politicians. When Spingarn tried to defend his motives and patriotism, the Hill and Knowlton firm concluded it was evidence of his guilt: "He appears as if he doth protest too much when he refers so much to his loyalty." A brochure, *As U.S. Editors View the Oil Charges*, portraying the FTC as a hotbed of radicalism, was circulated to American and foreign newspapers and government officials.[31]

Eventually, of course, nothing happened to the oil cartel. The incoming Eisenhower Administration, with Sullivan and Cromwell's senior member in the seat of power at State, clutched at Truman's suggestion and quickly dropped the criminal case. The civil suit that was instituted alleged that the five American companies violated the Sherman Antitrust and the Wilson Tariff Acts by conspiring to divide and control foreign production and distribution while fixing prices and limiting competition. An inadequate staff was assigned to the case and the action finally petered out a decade later with a couple of meaningless consent decrees.

As often happens when the forces of might collide with the forces of right, the roles of the participants are conveniently reversed, the defendants turning into prosecutors, with the latter becoming their victims. In this instance, the FTC was allowed to lapse into premature senility, and Stephen Spingarn, in the prime of life, was transformed from a vigorous, dedicated public servant to an odious leper, never again allowed into the sanctums of government.

The introduction of the nation's security into the economics of oil has had a titanic effect on the profits of the industry. It is an inspired concept —arrived at through the osmosis of money-power politics—that equates the security of a whole people with the compulsive greed of a few Goliaths bent on apportioning for their own private gains the exclusive ownership of one of nature's most precious resources. In the name of this bogus ethos, many crimes have been applauded by duped patriots.

One of the most heinous crimes, certainly in terms of its cost to the American public, was the Mandatory Oil Import Program decreed by executive fiat in 1959. Packaged in the flag and labeled national security, it was presented to the oil barons by President Eisenhower, who ranks first as their greatest White House benefactor, more generous even than the present occasional occupant.

To gain perspective on the magnitude of this crime, compare the evidence in this case with what until recently was this century's most infamous scandal—Teapot Dome.

Some fifty miles north of Casper, Wyoming, prairie winds have eroded a huge mass of sandstone, which sits atop a dome of oil, into the shape of a teapot. During the twenties, Teapot Dome came to symbolize the corruption of an age, and Albert Fall was its archvillain, the public servant who sold out his country for cash in a little black bag.

A month before becoming Secretary of the Interior in Harding's Cabinet, Fall wrote his wife that the President "thinks the Interior Department is second only to the State Department in importance and that there is more opportunity for graft and scandal connected with the disposition of public lands, etc., than there could be in any other department and he wants a man who is thoroughly familiar with the business and one he can rely upon as throughly honest."

The first step, in what was later portrayed as a sinister conspiracy, was the transfer of the Naval Reserves at Elk Hills, Buena Vista Hills, and Teapot Dome to the jurisdiction of the Interior Department. Fall later explained that when Secretary of the Navy Edwin N. Denby, "at the door of the Cabinet office, asked me, as Secretary of the Interior to take over administration of the naval oil reserve lands, and when, afterward, at Denby's request, President Harding directed me to do so, I became officially an agent for the Navy Department. The authority I exerted was executed in cooperation with the Secretary of the Navy and under the direction of the President of the United States."[32]

Fall's own views on conservation were not secret. He thought the whole Department of the Interior should be abolished. Except for national parks, he advocated private ownership of all public lands, including oil reserves.

A poor boy who had made good, Fall owned one of the largest ranches in New Mexico, three-quarters of a million acres, but he was in financial trouble, never having recouped from the loss of his Mexican mine holdings in the 1910 revolution. When he took his seat in Harding's Cabinet in 1921, Fall was $140,500 in debt and eight years in arrears in his taxes.

The question of whether the reserves should be sold or leased was still being heatedly debated. In February 1920, President Wilson had signed a bill that gave the Secretary of the Interior authority in leasing the general public oil lands as well as the naval reserves. The same month it was passed, Secretary of the Interior Franklin K. Lane resigned to take a position at $50,000 a year with the Pan-American Petroleum and Transport Company, the corporate name for Edward Doheny's oil interests.

By the end of Wilson's second term, the problem of drainage had reached a crisis. The reserve at Buena Vista Hills was almost fully depleted, and the loss of oil at Elk Hills was so serious that Navy Secretary Josephus Daniels called for bids to drill twenty-one offset wells on the western edge of the reserve to tap the underground oil flow.

It was these bids that arrived on Fall's desk shortly after his appointment. He awarded the lease to Doheny, the high bidder, who offered the government 55 percent of the oil taken from "strip leasing." Fall and Doheny had sweated together as hard-rock miners in the old days and their friendship had endured through the years. Settling in Las Cruces, New Mexico, on the bank of the Rio Grande, Fall had busied himself with real estate and reading law. By the time of New Mexico's constitutional convention in 1910, Fall was one of its most influential delegates. Two years later he was elected to the United States Senate by the legislature of the new state. Although vehemently anticonservationist, Fall became closely associated with Teddy Roosevelt, who was to praise Fall in 1916 as "the kind of public servant of whom all Americans should feel proud."

Another old friend was oilman Harry F. Sinclair, who had excellent contacts among the Navy's top brass, many of whom were convinced that war with Japan was inevitable. But their warnings and request for funds to build storage tanks for refueling stations on both coasts and at Pearl Harbor had failed to arouse Congress from its antimilitarist postwar lethargy. It was at this point in the spring of 1922 that Fall and Sinclair joined forces to help the Navy—and themselves. Fall leased the entire Teapot Dome Reserve for twenty years to Sinclair, who agreed to pay royalties to the government based on rates ranging from 12.5 to 50 percent, depending on the productivity of the wells, but in certificates to the Navy instead of money to the Treasury. The certificates were exchangeable for petroleum products at twenty-seven seaboard points on the Atlantic and Gulf coasts and in Cuba. Of even greater importance to the Navy was Sinclair's agreement to accept certificates in exchange for steel storage tanks to be constructed wherever the Navy requested.

Although Fall was empowered by the Navy's transfer agreement to lease the reserves without competitive bidding, he kept the contract a close secret. His next mistake was in accepting money from both men. The $100,000 in cash from Doheny—Fall called it "mortgage money" for the purchase of an adjoining ranch—was delivered to his hotel suite in a little black bag.

Before the Sinclair deal was consummated, the oilman was to travel to Fall's Three Rivers Ranch, arriving on New Year's Eve (1921) in his private railroad car, *The Sinco*, with his lawyer and their two wives. Francis Russell vividly described his visit in his fascinating biography of Harding, *The Shadow of Blooming Grove*:

> . . . Sinclair and his party remained three days, exploring the ranch and hunting deer and quail and wild turkeys with the cowpunchers. On New Year's Eve Emma Fall took them to a cowboy dance. During the evenings, Fall and Sinclair sat before a log fire in the main ranch house discussing the terms of the Teapot Dome lease. When Fall remarked offhandedly that he would like to have some milch cows on his ranch but could not afford such expensive cattle, Sinclair said he had more than he needed at his Rancocas Farm. After returning to New Jersey he sent Fall six heifers, a yearling bull, two six-month-old boars, four sows, and an English thoroughbred horse for Fall's foreman. For a man of Sinclair's means it was a picayune gift, although in later years much was made of it by Fall's enemies. More was made of the improvements at Three Rivers following *The Sinco's* visit. Neighbors observed a new hydroelectric plant, miles of new wiring, irrigation and power projects, road building and landscaping, new fences, a refurbishing of the ranch house. Fall also bought an additional 6,500 acres to round out his domain.
>
> Six weeks after signing the Teapot Dome lease Fall told his son-in-law, Mahlon Everhart, in Washington, that he was selling Sinclair a third interest in the [ranch] . . . with Fall and Everhart each having a third and with Everhart acting as Sinclair's trustee. Sinclair's name did not appear on the company books, nor was there any documentary evidence that he owned a third of Fall's ranch.

On May 8, 1922, Everhart met Sinclair on *The Sinco* on a siding in the Washington railroad yards and picked up $198,000 in Liberty Bonds in thousand-dollar denominations. Two weeks later he received an additional $35,000 in bonds. . . . Everhart was instructed by Fall to ask Sinclair for a separate loan of $36,000 to cover operational expenses and improvements. Sinclair paid it, and . . . [later] gave Everhart another $10,000. The following January Everhart called on him at the Wardman Park Hotel and received still another payment, this time for $25,000.[33]

Fall, the archvillain, was found guilty of taking a bribe from Doheny, who in a separate trial was found not guilty of giving it. Suffering from arteriosclerosis, myocarditis, arthritis, tuberculosis, and pleurisy, Fall was driven to prison in an ambulance, to serve one year of a three-year sentence. Though ruined and shunned, he remained hopeful of vindication to the end. "My borrowing the money may have been unethical," he admitted after his conviction. "I certainly did not realize it at the time, and my employing a falsehood to prevent a volcano of political abuse pouring upon the administration that had honored me deserves condemnation; but neither one nor the other justifies the charge that I was disloyal or dishonest as Secretary of the Interior and as a member of Harding's Cabinet." His justification for secrecy in the Sinclair lease has a familiar ring: "to call attention to the fact that the contracts providing for enormous storages for future use in a crisis of oil were being made off the coast or in certain parts of the country" would have been a breach of national security.

There are striking evidentiary parallels in the two cases. Both Fall and Eisenhower enjoyed the companionship and generosity of oilmen, both had large properties in need of funds for improvement and maintenance, and both were publicly concerned with the nation's security.

President Eisenhower's relationship with three wealthy oilmen was unquestionably the most flagrant example of conflict of interest in high places on record. The exact terms of the arrangement were never revealed. Two of the oilmen—W. Alton Jones, chairman of the executive committee of Cities Service, and B. B. ("Billy") Byars of Tyler, Texas, an oil producer and close associate of Texas oilmen Sid Richardson and Clint Murchison—have been dead for some time, and were followed in 1973 by the third, George E. Allen, a professional crony of Presidents and a superlawyer in Washington when Clark Clifford was still in knee pants. His services were so extraordinary that he sat as a director on the boards of some twenty major corporations. He was a heavy investor in oil and was associated in that business with Major Louey Kung, a nephew of Chiang Kai-shek.

In a book cockily entitled *Presidents Who Have Known Me*, Allen assured the reader that he would not learn anything important from him. "Anyone looking for a balanced assessment of the man and the President will do well to spare himself irritation by closing this book at this point. . . . But anyone who likes Ike, as I do—and there seem to be quite a few of us—is cordially invited to stay with me for an admirer's-eye view, close up and distorted by proximity in time and space. Since he is my next-door neighbor at Gettysburg, I should hesitate to criticize him even if I felt critical. To do so would be to violate my own Good Neighbor Policy."[34]

Few neighbors were ever more dedicated to this policy than our three wise oilmen. To make it all perfectly legal, they signed a secret lease agreement in which they assumed financial responsibility for the operation of the President's Gettysburg farm in return for a share of the profits. The fact that there were no profits did not seem to disturb them overmuch. They kept their end of the bargain, splurging more than $500,000 on livestock, equipment, and construction: $30,000 on a show barn; $22,000 on three smaller barns; $10,000 to remodel a schoolhouse as a home for the President's son, John; $110,000 to remodel the main house; $6,000 to landscape ten acres; plus substantial sums for the staff and a $10,000-a-year farm manager. Other expenses included a John Deere tractor, an all-electric kitchen, ponies, and Black Angus steers.[35]

A letter dated January 28, 1958, written by General Arthur S. Nevins, the farm's manager, and addressed to Allen and Byars, reveals that Ike's method of collecting was not very different from Fall's. The letter, which began "Dear George and Billy," quickly briefed them on the farm's operation before putting on the bite:

> *New subject*—The funds for the farm operation are getting low. So would each of you also let me have your check in the usual amount of $2,500. A similar amount will be transferred to the partnership account from W. Alton Jones's funds.[36]

Was this a legitimate business transaction? After checking into it, the Internal Revenue Service could find no evidence that the oilmen had attempted to operate the farm as a profitable venture. It disallowed their deductions as business expenses and ruled that the expenditures were an outright gift.

In their book *The Case Against Congress*, Drew Pearson and Jack Anderson took a close look at Eisenhower's relationship with oilmen:

During his eight years in the White House, Dwight Eisenhower did more for the nation's private oil and gas interests than any other President. He encouraged and signed legislation overruling a Supreme Court decision giving offshore oil to the Federal Government. He gave office space inside the White House to a committee of oil and gas men who wrote a report recommending legislation that would have removed natural-gas pipelines from control by the Federal Power Commission. In his appointments to the FPC, every commissioner Ike named except one, William Connole, was a pro-industry man. When Connole objected to gas price increases, Eisenhower eased him out of the commission at the expiration of his term.[37]

The big payoff, the one the oilmen were in mortal fear of losing until 1973, was the import-quota system, granted by executive order on March 10, 1959, and worth to date more than $100 billion to the industry. The President's authority was vested in the 1958 Trade Agreement Act, which empowered him to establish mandatory controls over oil imports if he found that they *threatened to impair* the national security. In other words, it was the threat and not the impairment that was the key to the hidden treasure. Senate Majority Leader Lyndon Johnson had said the year before that the imports were "an immediate threat to national security." The advocates of national security created a vision that saw the nation under attack, surrounded by enemies, and quickly "running out of oil."

Meanwhile, however, the tariff on a barrel of oil was still only a dime. The doomsayers did not speculate on this contradiction to their protectionist solution. The Kefauver Antitrust Committee had suggested a sharp increase in the tariff, but except for Texas Senator Ralph Yarborough (now departed from those hallowed halls), who proposed 84 cents a barrel, there was no interest on the Hill in that approach to the problem.

Nor did Congress speculate on the peculiar application of the industry's tax incentives. The extension of the intangible-development deduction and percentage-depletion allowance to overseas production, coupled with the royalty-tax credit and low production costs, has had a reverse effect on domestic exploration. The result was a great windfall for the five integrated giants. They reaped the benefits of a system of market-demand prorationing that made it possible for them to import all the cheap crude they wanted for their refineries, which they then peddled at industry-pegged prices. The only fly in that soothing ointment was that they did not control all the imports. Some 30 percent of the annual billion-plus barrels of imported crude was coming in through other channels. Also, domestic producers were up in arms. "The torrent of foreign oil robs Texas of her oil market," they charged. They were particularly incensed by the unloading of Middle Eastern oil in Texas ports. They warned that imports were adversely affecting the incentive for the search of new domestic sources of oil. The giants' response was that the domestic companies had been crying wolf about the dangers of imports for nearly thirty years, beginning with the Venezuelan shipments. The domestics, in turn, charged the importers with raising false alarms about supposedly dwindling domestic reserves over the same period. At the height of the dispute, the president of one of the giants gave the industry a piece of advice: "Even the Hatfields and the McCoys had enough sense to team up and present a united front when the 'revenooers' came around. To you oilmen I should like to say, 'Since you are so rich—why ain't you smart?' "

Of course, in their own self-interest, the giants were protective of their smaller brethren. They kept their cheap crude on a parity with domestic prices. And during the Suez crisis when President Nasser of Egypt seized the canal, they even raised the price in open defiance of an appeal by President Eisenhower in his 1957 State of the Union message for business to "avoid unnecessary price increases." The annual cost to the consumer of the price rise that followed was estimated at $1 billion.

In expressing his concern over the price rise, Secretary of the Interior Fred A. Seaton said that he had not made an appeal to the industry for cooperation because obtaining an agreement from the oilmen to hold prices would flout the antitrust safeguards built into the voluntary plan.

A subsequent investigation by the Justice Department into charges of collusion among the major oil companies resulted in the indictment of twenty-nine firms, including the big five, for having violated the Sherman Act by conspiring to raise and fix crude oil and gasoline prices. The companies issued the usual disclaimers as more than a hundred attorneys began preparing the defense. "If we lose this," one company official was quoted as saying, "we're well on the road to becoming a public utility." A federal district court in Tulsa subsequently acquitted the defendants, holding that the price increases were rooted in "terrific economic pressures" rather than in any concerted industry action.

By the fall of 1957, Texas wells were operating at a record low of twelve days a month. Domestic producers renewed their assaults upon imports, citing the recent Suez crisis as further proof of the unreliability

and costliness of foreign crude. The giants, also plagued by imports outside their control, finally joined forces with the domestics in asking for
government quotas.

Martin Lobel, a former legislative assistant to Senator William Proxmire, has made a study of prorationing and import quotas. In an article in
the *Washington Monthly*, he wrote: "The oil industry realized that domestic prices could not be kept high without protection from inexpensive
foreign oil. Having built market demand proration on the back of conservation measures, the crowd from Texas determined that yet a third form of
government intervention was required—import quotas to make sure that a
free market would not operate. This was sold to the public . . . on the
grounds that domestic production was essential to national security and
high prices stimulated the discovery of new oil reserves."[38]

During the Eisenhower years, oil money flowed copiously through
conduits controlled by that powerful pair from Texas, the late Sam Rayburn and his protégé Lyndon Johnson. As Speaker of the House from the
beginning of 1955, Rayburn was in the seat of power—no one was ever
appointed to the tax-writing Ways and Means Committee without first
giving Rayburn the right answer to one question: "Do you favor the oil-
depletion allowance?" Senate Majority Leader Johnson was equally selective in his appointments to the Senate Finance Committee.

Oil has been traditionally bipartisan in its politics. It is true that Republicans like Eisenhower and Nixon have been favored far more generously than their campaign opponents, but in Congressional races the sole
criterion is the candidate's voting record on oil legislation. For example,
the late House Republican Leader Joseph W. Martin, Jr., Speaker from
1947 to 1949 and 1953 to 1955, was from Massachusetts, but he ranked
high enough with Texas oil millionaires in 1958 for them to throw a fund-
raising dinner in his honor at the Rice Hotel in Houston, where many of
the same sponsors had gathered a few weeks earlier to attend an appreciation dinner for Lyndon Johnson. The banquet invitation lauded Martin's
record:

> Joe Martin has always been a friend of Texas, especially of the oil and
> gas producing industries. He mustered two-thirds of the Republican votes
> in the House each time the gas bill passed. . . . As Speaker of the 83rd
> Congress, he led the fight for adoption of the tidelands ownership bill. It
> will be up to Joe Martin to muster at least 65 percent of the Republican
> votes in order to pass the gas bill this year. He had put Republican
> members from the Northern and Eastern consuming areas on the spot

politically, because the bill is not popular due to the distortion of the facts by newspaper columnists and others.[39]

The oil industry spends an estimated $50 million every year for lobbying and in promoting its role in the defense of the nation's security—more recently in publicizing the alleged energy crisis. Millions of dollars are funneled to political campaigns, with millions more going into sophisticated payoffs such as law fees and stock options. In times of great corruption, the artifices are discarded and the cash goes out in straight, unadulterated graft—cash in a black bag, or even in a paper sack. But bagmen, like pimps in an open city, tend to get bold and sloppy when the heat is off. And, like pimps, sooner or later they proposition the wrong mark. That was precisely what happened in 1956 when bagman John Neff thrust a brown paper sack containing $2,500 at South Dakota Senator Francis Case with the request that he vote for a bill to free natural gas from federal price control. Neff was carrying out orders from his boss, Superior Oil lobbyist Elmer Patman (a cousin of Wright Patman), who in turn was following instructions from John B. Connally, who was directing the lobbying campaign for the gas industry. It was reported by Pearson and Anderson that on the day Senator Case sounded off about the bribe offer, Connally "sat white-faced, for hours, in his Mayflower Hotel room."[40]

Connally was not called as a witness in the probe that followed. His mentor, Lyndon Johnson, quickly maneuvered the investigation into the hands of the gangbuster from Arkansas, Senator John McClellan, whose Little Rock law firm represented Exxon, Seaboard Oil, Tidewater Associated Oil, and Carter Oil. His curiosity did not carry his committee beyond the Case incident. Patman and Neff pleaded guilty of failing to register as lobbyists and received suspended one-year jail sentences.

As noted in Chapter One, there are interesting similarities in the careers of Robert B. Anderson and John B. Connally. Although both were bootstrappers, they had amassed considerable fortunes by the time they arrived in Washington. As Secretary of the Navy (1953–54), Anderson was sympathetic to the opening up of the federal lands in Alaska for private development. In 1950 Anderson testified before the House Ways and Means Committee against reducing the depletion allowance. He saw this as cutting the ground from under wildcatting:

> I think that I know almost every independent oil operator in Texas and
> a great many in other states of the Union. I know most of those who are
> engaged in the management of . . . the major companies. They are adven-

turesome people. . . . They represent to me something in the nature of the folks who were the pioneers of this republic. . . . I do not know why, but the oil industry has come to be thought of as a highly lucrative business.[41]

Anderson identified himself to the committee as an educator—he was chairman of the Texas Board of Education—rather than as president of the lobbying Texas Mid-Continent Oil and Gas Association. At the time of his appointment as Secretary of the Treasury in 1957, he had been manager of the $300-million W. T. Waggoner estate with its extensive oil operations, a member of the National Petroleum Council, and a director of the American Petroleum Institute—he was seriously considered for its presidency. Questioned concerning the fitness of the depletion allowance at his confirmation hearing, Anderson assured the Senate Finance Committee that he would approach the issue "as objectively as I possibly can" and would be pleased to cooperate with Congress in a review of this tax abatement.[42]

The real story behind Anderson's appointment was not told for thirteen years, until Bernard D. Nossiter carefully rewove one of the weirdest plots in recent history into a Washington *Post* (July 16, 1970) exclusive. Back in 1956, said Nossiter, President Eisenhower wanted Anderson, whom he greatly admired, to replace Richard Nixon, whom he did not greatly admire, as his running mate in his re-election bid. Anderson was willing, but not having his own oil wells to sustain his Texas style of living, he told the President that he would first have to raise a million dollars to carry him over the next four years. Ike was not deterred by this obstacle. As the story goes, the President consulted Sid Richardson, another rich friend in oil, who obligingly devised an elaborate million-dollar finder's-fee payment for Anderson. The deal, which Anderson later described to Nossiter as "ordinary, normal," involved some properties, chiefly in Texas, that were under leasehold to Stanolind, a subsidiary of Indiana Standard. Anderson's task was to find a driller for Stanolind. After searching about he found his friend Sid Richardson, whose office in Midland, Texas, was only one block away from Stanolind's. Richardson agreed to drill and the deal was signed. Later, when Nixon's own influential friends persuaded Ike to keep him on the ticket, the President rewarded Anderson with the Treasury post.

It was Anderson, as head of a Cabinet committee, who designed the Mandatory Import Quota Program, which not only restricted the amount of crude oil allowed to enter the country but also gave the profit differential to domestic refiners instead of to the government. Again the explanation was "national security." If foreign oil were allowed to be imported in a free market, argued President Eisenhower, it would drive out noncompetitive American companies and make this country dependent on "unreliable sources" for its essential energy requirements. The quota system, like all other incentive systems devised for the oil industry, was established to encourage domestic exploration. Only by increasing domestic reserves would the nation meet the threat of any shortage caused by an interruption in the flow of foreign oil. This was another way of saying that domestic producers could not compete with imported oil. The reasons for the industry's inability to compete, such as price fixing backed by prorationing, which increased cost by reducing production, were not discussed. In fact, a barrel of domestic crude oil cost East Coast refiners roughly $3.75, while a barrel of comparable oil from the Middle East could be delivered for about $2.25, including freight and tariff. By 1963 the delivered price of Arabian crude had dropped to $2.08, and in 1966 it was $1.87, while the domestic kept going up.

The profit differential of about $1.50 per barrel between foreign and domestic crude oil made quota assignments ("tickets") a valuable commodity. The tickets were allocated to all domestic refiners, including those too far inland to use foreign oil economically. Forbidden to sell their tickets, some inland refiners traded them to the giant integrated importers on the East Coast in exchange for an equivalent value in domestic oil (usually oil produced by an inland affiliate of the giant). Provoked by this incredible gift, Representative Charles A. Vanik of Ohio observed that "free enterprise is indeed a wonderful thing for these refiners when the President creates an asset which they can sell at a handsome profit with no risks involved."[43] With foreign imports then at a billion barrels, the bonanza to oilmen was worth $1.5 billion a year. If the price fixing was in the interest of national security because it stimulated exploration, then the incentive to search for oil would have been better served if this money had been collected by the government in the form of a tariff. The line of reasoning offered for this extraordinary gift was that the extra revenues would be largely devoted to the quest for cheap domestic oil. The fact that the tickets were allocated to refiners, not to producers, creates a serious credibility gap. For years nearly 80 percent of onshore exploratory drilling was done by nonintegrated independent producers. "Giving import tickets to refiners," one independent observed, "is like giving a grain subsidy to the miller." If anything, the quota system (along with prorationing) further diminished the independent's incentive to increase production. The independent was not able to compete with integrated companies that were being capitalized by the quota subsidy.

By making foreign oil more profitable to refiners, the government encouraged all integrated companies, large and small, to seek their fortunes overseas. There was an immediate exodus of drilling teams to Canada, Latin America, Africa, and any other region not already staked out by the cartel. The clamor for more quotas and greater profits has led to a growing dependence on foreign sources, which provided 25.4 percent of the petroleum consumed in this country in 1971. The domestic industry had three million barrels of excess daily crude production capacity as recently as 1967. What it has now is anybody's guess. By 1972 Americans were consuming more than one-third of the annual 14-plus billion barrels of oil used in the world. Each year we use one-ninth of our reserves, at high prices, while the rest of the world uses only 1/39th of its collective reserves, at low prices. For example, the United States is still the world's biggest producer of crude oil, but in Japan, which has almost no oil wells in its home islands, the price in 1972 was about $1 a barrel cheaper than in this country. This artificial suspension of the law of supply and demand, erected behind a barrier against low-cost foreign oil, was a high price to pay for a policy doomed to failure. In his research, Martin Lobel discovered that the United States is "now using oil more rapidly than it is being discovered. Seismographic crew time, a measure of the basic oil seeking activity in the industry, has declined from about 7,000 crew weeks per year in the middle Fifties to 3,337 crew weeks in 1967. The success ratio of wildcat drillings has declined."[44]

The quota program limited imports east of the Rockies to 12.2 percent of estimated domestic production (proration schedules). For the five states west of the Rockies, the limit was the estimated difference between demand and domestic supply. (In 1966, residual oil, a cheap crude product used by utilities, industrial plants, office buildings, and other large users, was exempted from restrictions, which was a tribute to their own political clout.) One significant aspect of the program was that it retained the quotas on a company rather than a producing-country basis. This provision enabled the titans of oil to maintain their cartel patterns. It gave them the flexibility of playing one producer nation against another. If Venezuela, for example, increased its tax, the cartel could shift its purchases to more amenable countries.

Robert Anderson's consideration for the industry did not go unrewarded. As to his million-dollar finder's fee, Nossiter wrote that of "this amount, $270,000 was scheduled to be paid during his term in office. His chances of receiving some $450,000 of the rest depended in part on the price of oil." Anderson told Nossiter it "never crossed my mind" that there was a conflict of interest. "I think anybody who comes into these things tries to think of the national interest."

"One of the biggest inland refiners is the Standard Oil Co. of Indiana," Nossiter wrote. "Its subsidiary, Stanolind, held the lease on the Texas property for which Anderson served as a broker. Since its birth in 1959, the quota system has given Standard of Indiana what amounts to [in import tickets] a windfall estimated at $193 million."

The windfall of the quota system to the large integrated oil companies cannot be overestimated. Small wonder that Eisenhower was their favorite President. Perhaps there was nothing personal, no *quid pro quo*, involved in any of this. And perhaps Anderson, who cut his teeth on an oil drill, was only thinking of the nation's interest. A more scholarly approach might conclude that the alliance between the private government of oil and the public government of the United States was based in part on common needs, with the assumption that the historic premise of antitrust as a way of preserving a competitive economy must give way to the expediency of an integrated approach when the exploitation of a fundamental resource is concerned; that government sanction of a world cartel system which protects oil's imperial commitments serves the nation's best interest in an age of escalating global responsibilities. But even if the supposition were valid, would it explain the incestuous nature of the partnership and oil's dominant position? Why must public access to oil always be equated with private profits from oil? Is the government policy based on naïveté or institutional calumny?

Whatever the conclusion, the fact remains that in Eisenhower's case, his personal relationship with rich oilmen was far more mutually beneficial than anything conceived by the archvillain of Teapot Dome. It was a heady game, with billions at stake, and the good ole boys calling the shots were sharpshooters from way back. Even in his last hour in office, Ike did not forget his friends. The President's thoughtfulness was recorded by Pearson and Anderson in *The Case Against Congress*:

> On January 19, 1961, one day before he left the White House, Eisenhower signed a procedural instruction on the importation of residual oil that required all importers to move over and sacrifice 15 percent of their quotas to newcomers who wanted a share of the action. One of the major beneficiaries of this last-minute executive order happened to be Cities

Service, which had had no residual quota till that time but which under Ike's new order was allotted about 3,000 barrels a day. The chief executive of Cities Service was W. Alton Jones, one of the three faithful contributors to the upkeep of the Eisenhower farm.

Three months later, Jones was flying to Palm Springs to visit the retired President of the United States when his plane crashed and Jones was killed. In his briefcase was found $61,000 in cash and travelers' checks. No explanation was offered—in fact none was ever asked for by the complacent American press—as to why the head of one of the leading oil companies of America was flying to see the ex-President of the United States with $61,000 in his briefcase.[45]

The first cost analysis of the import program was not made until 1969. That year the Office of Emergency Preparedness estimated that the total cost to consumers was $5.2 billion a year in higher petroleum prices. By supporting the price structure of the cartel, the government had indirectly levied a tax on the American public amounting to $96 for a family of four, with the state-by-state cost varying from a high of $228 in Wyoming to a low of $44 in Hawaii.

This estimate was conservative compared to the figures of Dr. John M. Blair,* then chief economist of the Senate Subcommittee on Antitrust and Monopoly. Blair's calculations, based from data on comparative prices of Arab and American crude delivered at East Coast ports, placed the cost of the program at $7.2 billion a year. At the time this devastating indictment was delivered, the press tables were almost deserted. No reporter broke a leg trying to get this news to the people who paid the bill.

One of the most amazing developments of the quota program, aside from its immaculate conception, was that its contorted economics survived virtually unscathed a full decade. The first hairline crack in the high-price dike appeared at Machiasport, Maine, early in 1968. Occidental Petroleum Corporation, one of the companies driven overseas by the program, had discovered enormous reserves of low-sulfur oil in Libya, but, not having its own refineries, it lacked access to the rich American market. Occidental offered Maine an irresistible proposition. If the government would permit the company to import 100,000 barrels of crude a day in excess of quotas allowed, it would build a refinery at Machiasport (whose

---

* As assistant chief economists for the Federal Trade Commission during the Truman Administration, John Blair and Stephen Spingarn were the two men most responsible for the controversial study of the international petroleum cartel. Like Spingarn's, Blair's government career faltered in the Eisenhower years; later he became chief economist to the Senate Antitrust and Monopoly Subcommittee, then chaired by Estes Kefauver of Tennessee and later by Philip A. Hart of Michigan.

natural harbor can accommodate the world's largest tankers) and pledged a 10 percent price reduction on home heating oil, residual oil, and gasoline sold in the New England market. And it would donate about $7 million a year to a conservation fund. On behalf of the company, the state that summer asked the Department of Commerce to establish a "free trade zone" at Machiasport.

A senatorial contingent from New England that included Edmund S. Muskie of Maine, Thomas J. McIntyre of New Hampshire, and Edward M. Kennedy of Massachusetts took up battle stations on the Senate floor in support of anxious constituents. The opposition from the oil states, some thirty hard-core oil Senators, was led by Russell B. Long of Louisiana, son of the late Kingfish Huey Long, who personally owns substantial oil and gas interests. As chairman of the Senate Finance Committee, which handles tax and trade legislation, Long is in a strategic position to render yeoman service to the industry and to his own Win or Lose Corporation.

The contingents battled frequently on the Senate floor, but the most important forums early in 1969 were provided by Senator Proxmire's Joint Economic Committee and Senator Hart's Subcommittee on Antitrust and Monopoly with its hearings on "Government Intervention in the Market Mechanism." By then, of course, oil was already in plenty of trouble. Besides Machiasport, the grievances were rapidly multiplying: the leaking oil well in the Santa Barbara Channel; President Johnson's unpopular 10 percent surtax to further escalate the controversial Vietnam War, followed by the oil companies' price increases; the chronic shortage of home heating fuel in Northeastern states; and, finally, the "tax revolt," conceived and seemingly aborted early in the Kennedy Administration, which was gradually gaining momentum. It was a time of social unrest, of student and ethnic protest, but the catalyst was not a mass demonstration on the steps of the Treasury. The revolution got its biggest impetus from inside the Treasury in the last days of the Johnson years in Washington. It came in a statement by Secretary of the Treasury Joseph Barr before Proxmire's committee.

"I will hazard a guess that there is going to be a taxpayer revolt over the income taxes in this country unless we move in this area," Barr told the panel. The revolt would not come from the poor, who did not pay very much in taxes, he said, but from the middle class, "who pay every nickel in taxes at the going rate. They do not have the loopholes and the gimmicks to resort to." People believed that everyone should pay his share, but "this does not happen," Barr said, "when you are running a corporation and you look at the international oil companies and see they pay little or no taxes. They pay huge taxes including royalties to other governments, but not to this government."[46]

Meanwhile, before the Hart Subcommittee, John Blair was engaged in a colloquy with M. A. Wright, a top official of Exxon. After presenting facts that showed the company had lowered its price for Arabian oil in Japan after it had raised gasoline prices in the United States four or five cents a gallon, Blair asked: "Are we to conclude therefrom that at the same time that you were raising the price to the American consumer, your company was reducing the price to foreign buyers?" To which Wright replied: "You are working in two separate worlds when you speak about what you do in the U.S. compared to what you do abroad—and what you say is exactly right."[47]

Asked if it would seem to weaken, not strengthen, national security to sell basic materials to foreign competitors at lower prices, Wright said the purpose of the system was to assure ourselves of an adequate supply of oil within the United States. "And when we have controls," he added, "we naturally are supporting a price situation. That is true."

The petrochemical industry was also restive. Represented by the Chemco Group (an alliance of nine companies: Union Carbide, Celanese, Dow Chemical, Monsanto, E. I. duPont, Eastman Kodak, Olin Mathieson, National Distillers, and Publicker Industries), the industry said it was paying 60 percent more for petroleum feedstocks (crude oil and natural gas) than their foreign competitors. Being realists, they asked for an exemption (their own Machiasport) rather than the abolishment of the program. They warned that unless something was done immediately, world competition would force them to build new plants abroad at the rate of $2.5 billion a year.*

In no time the oil lobby was manning the import barricades. Michael L. Haider and Frank N. Ikard, chairman and president respectively of the American Petroleum Institute, were dispatched to reconnoiter the terrain.

---

* Although its content was suppressed by the White House, a memorandum from the Justice Department's Antitrust Division had urged the President to exempt the petrochemical industry from the quota program. "The use of petroleum as a chemical raw material is different in kind than its use for energy," the document said. "No presumption of security importance can attach to a product by reason of its manufacture from petroleum. A trash bag or a plastic toy is no more essential to national security because it is made from petroleum rather than from paper or metal." The memo, which was made available to the press by Senator Proxmire in January 1972, was distributed on March 15, 1971, to several key officials. Two days later it was recalled by order of Peter Flanigan from all persons to whom it was sent.[48]

Both men were superbly qualified for the assignment. Haider was a retired board chairman of Exxon and Ikard was a former Texas Congressman who served on the House Ways and Means Committee and was a close friend of Wilbur J. Mills, the committee's chairman. Their proposed solution was an old political ploy—have the problem studied into oblivion.

Wasting no time, Haider and Ikard proceeded to the White House for a conference with Arthur F. Burns, then Counselor to the President. On March 25, 1969, barely two months after his inauguration, President Nixon announced the creation of a Cabinet Task Force on Oil Import Control to study the program. It was composed of the Secretaries of the Treasury, Defense, State, Commerce, Interior, and Labor, plus the director of the Office of Emergency Preparedness. Secretary of Labor George Shultz, a noted economist, was appointed chairman, and Harvard Law School Professor Philip Areeda was chosen to head the staff, which consisted of a number of lawyers and economists not connected with the oil industry.

One look at that staff and the API knew instantly that something had gone awry. The next trauma came when the Justice Department's Antitrust Division, headed by Assistant Attorney General Richard W. McLaren, attacked the quota system: "The import quotas themselves do nothing to preserve this nation's domestic oil reserves" and the program "intensifies the effect of the existing lack of competitive vigor in various domestic oil markets." After that, the API pulled out all the stops. It had created a Frankenstein monster that had to be destroyed before he destroyed them. All the IOUs were called in. Its many friends in Congress inundated the White House with fervid expressions of support for the program. Ikard paid a call on Wilbur Mills, who in turn sent a telegram to the task force urging leniency. Four governors—Preston Smith of Texas, Robert B. Docking of Kansas, Stanley K. Hathaway of Wyoming, and Richard D. Ogilvie of Illinois—assembled in the White House office of Peter Flanigan for a meeting with Shultz and three other members of the task force.[49] Their advocacy was echoed by telegrams (with suspiciously similar phrasing) from thirteen more governors. Michael Haider went directly to the President. Following a private audience, Haider emerged "feeling more optimistic," *Oil Daily* reported, after "a very good conversation." Haider "believes Nixon has a good grasp on the problems surrounding oil-import controls and is more confident that the outcome will be favorable." Finally, when the task force held its last full meeting in December (theoretically in secret) to consider the staff recommendations, they were confronted by the awesome presence of John N. Mitchell, who was not only the Attorney General (going against his own Antitrust Division) but also the President's closest adviser, his former law partner, and the manager of his 1968 campaign—he knew intimately every branch of the political money tree. His counsel to Shultz was cryptic but direct: "Don't box the President in."[50]

The White House released the task force report on February 20, 1970. Of the thirteen Cabinet officers and other government officials who participated as members and official observers on the task force, ten agreed with the following key finding on the question of national security:

> The present import control program is not adequately responsive to present and future security considerations. The fixed quota limitations that have been in effect for the past ten years, and the system of implementation that has grown up around them, bear no reasonable relation to current requirements for protection either of the national economy or of essential oil consumption. The level of restriction is arbitrary and the treatment of secure foreign sources internally inconsistent. The present system has spawned a host of special arrangements and exceptions for purposes essentially unrelated to the national security, has imposed high costs and inefficiencies on consumers and the economy, and has led to undue government intervention in the market and consequent competitive distortions. In addition, the existing quota system has left a significant degree of control over this national program to state regulatory authorities. If import controls are to serve the distinctive needs of national security, they should be subject to a system of federal control that interferes as little as possible with the operation of competitive market forces while remaining subject to adjustment as needed to respond to changes in the overall security environment. A majority of the Task Force finds that the present import control system, as it has developed in practice, is no longer acceptable.[51]

Opposed to this conclusion were the heads of agencies that traditionally have been weighted on the side of big business: Secretary of the Interior Walter J. Hickel, Secretary of Commerce Maurice H. Stans, and Federal Power Commission Chairman John N. Nassikas, who was a task-force observer.[52] The majority recommended that the quotas be replaced by tariffs that would let oil prices fall about thirty cents a barrel, at a saving to consumers of billions of dollars. Plus, of course, the billions going to oil refiners as a reward for price fixing that would now be collected by the government. This was as far as the task force would go. The professional staff, however, recommended a tariff that would let the price of oil sink from $3.90 to $2.50 a barrel, which really would have blown the lid off the industry's monopoly game. Shultz was the only member to go along with the staff.

Incensed by what they felt was a betrayal, the oil lobby pressured the Administration into a concrete show of good faith. Seizing on the fact that the report was not unanimous, President Nixon appointed a new Oil Policy Committee to "restudy" the issue. The committee was composed of all but one of the Cabinet members who served on the task force: Shultz was replaced by Mitchell.

Few voices were raised in outrage by this obvious flimflam. "The consumers have been sacrificed once again to the interests of big oil," Senator Proxmire observed. A New York *Times* editorial pointed out the hypocrisy of "an Administration that prides itself on being a great inflation fighter when it comes to trimming outlays for health, education and welfare [but] does not mind letting consumers pay out more than $60 billion in extra oil bills over the coming decade."[53]

Under the chairmanship of General George Lincoln, head of the Office of Emergency Preparedness, the committee, said the Washington *Post*, reached its decision to retain the quota program "without any formal discussions or working papers by the responsible officials involved." The news story continued:

> In response to reporters' questions, Lincoln said that his fellow Oil Policy Committee members only discussed the issue "now and then, casually" and "my staff didn't prepare writers papers on this."
> Lincoln also disclosed that Peter Flanigan, a White House aide, sits in regularly on the committee's meetings and was present at the crucial "principals only" session last Thursday when the Lincoln letter [on August 17, 1970, the White House released a letter, bearing Lincoln's signature, urging there be no relaxation of the quota system] was adopted. Lincoln, however, denied reports that Flanigan had dictated the letter's essence. Lincoln acknowledged that he had discussed it in advance with White House figures whom he declined to name.[54]

The President was delighted with the committee's change of heart. He was so delighted, in fact, that he did not seem aware of the incongruity of his position when, on the same day that he joined the committee in assuring oildom of the sanctity of its $20-million-a-day gratuity, he also berated the Democratic Congress for ignoring economy proposals on welfare legislation that would have cut $2 million a day from the budget. The oil industry's response was to raise the price of gasoline by one cent a gallon, at an added cost of $800 million a year to the consumer. (The task force estimated the annual cost of the quota program would reach $8.4 billion by 1980.)

As a further demonstration of his good faith, the President slapped import controls on Canada, which had been exempted from restriction because the industry had failed to convince previous Administrations that Canada was a likely candidate in the event an international conspiracy tried to dry out this nation's foreign oil sources.

The task force, which studied this problem from every conceivable angle, could not envision a single situation in which foreign oil could be cut off long enough to cause serious damage to the nation's defense posture. If the major oil nations joined in a conspiracy, the boycott would have to include all U.S. allies, which means most of the major world markets. The conspirators could not sustain such a boycott for very long without destroying their own economies.

Another study, the Charles River Report for the Office of Science and Technology, estimated that the removal of quotas and tariffs would lower the price of crude petroleum to about $1.75 a barrel and boost annual domestic consumption to 5.9 billion barrels, with 3.4 billion barrels produced here and 2.5 billion imported—1.3 billion from the Middle East and North Africa, 1.0 billion from Venezuela, and 0.2 billion from Canada. The task force found that if the Middle East were to shut off oil for one year in 1980, the United States could still supply 104 percent of domestic oil needs without rationing. Senator Proxmire's staffer Martin Lobel concluded after a study of the various reports that "the national security argument may be classified as idiocy."[55]

Back in 1969, with their errant monster still on the loose, the antics of the oil lobby grew so manic that at one point Haider and Ikard actually appeared willing to accept a cut in the percentage depletion allowance in return for support in saving the quota program. Thus they went from Frankenstein's monster to a Trojan horse. They killed the monster but only wounded the horse.

At the time it seemed like a safe enough gambit. The purity of the 27.5 percentage figure had remained inviolate forty-three years. Except for Roosevelt and Truman, no President had dared denounce it. Even President Kennedy, who proposed certain reforms to increase the industry's share of the tax burden, equivocated on depletion. His Treasury Secretary, Douglas Dillon, in response to a question on whether it should be changed, told the Senate Finance Committee, "We have studied that matter at some length. We probably have not studied it enough. I do not know how to study it enough."

Richard Nixon was not yet on record as President, but in his 1968 campaign he had vowed to a group of Houston oilmen: "As President, I will maintain it." The oil tycoons responded with heavy contributions to the GOP cause.* Nixon's stand was far bolder than Ike had dared assume. Pressed by reporters for an opinion at a news conference in 1957, he had cryptically replied: "Now, the 27.5 percent depletion allowance I am not prepared to say it is evil because when we find, while we do find I assume that a number of rich men take advantage of it unfairly, there must certainly be an incentive in this country if we are going to continue the exploration for oil and gas that is so important to our economy."[56]

Nixon kept his word. He told his chief tax "reformer," Assistant Secretary of the Treasury Edwin Cohen, that the Administration would not support any change in the depletion allowance. The President explained that the tax privilege encouraged investors to explore for the new oil that was so vital to the nation's security. Needless to say, Cohen's tax package omitted any mention of oil reform.

The President's emphasis on tax incentive was in contradiction with a technical study by the CONSAD Research Corporation, entitled "The Economic Factors Affecting the Level of Domestic Petroleum Reserves." Commissioned by Johnson's Treasury, it was kept under wraps by Nixon's Treasury until March 1969, at which time it was reluctantly released (upon request) to the House Ways and Means Committee. It was forwarded by Under Secretary Charles E. Walker with this notation: "This report, which has not been reviewed by this Administration, is forwarded without comment."

The purpose of the CONSAD study was to develop "numerical estimates of the changes in liquid hydrocarbon and natural gas reserves which would occur if the percentage depletion allowance were reduced (or eliminated) and if the option to expense intangible drilling costs were removed,

---

* At a private meeting with oilmen in Midland, Texas, during the 1968 campaign, Spiro Agnew promised to block the Machiasport plan if the oilmen would back Nixon financially. In the spring of 1969, Agnew turned up in New England with an executive of Sinclair Oil handling his public relations. "Would someone please tell us why Vice President Agnew—with the administrative appropriation he gets—needs someone from Sinclair Oil to handle his relations with the press?" the Portsmouth, New Hampshire, *Herald* inquired in an editorial. "The reader with a memory will recall that it was Sinclair Oil that threatened to bring an injunction against the foreign trade zone for Machiasport. . . ."

and the resultant tax increase was absorbed by the petroleum producers."
The major conclusions were:

1. The elimination of percentage depletion as an option would reduce
existing reserves levels by 3 percent and result in an additional $1.2
billion* in tax revenue at current production levels.
2. Eliminations of the option to expense intangible drilling cost would
reduce existing reserve levels by from 1.9 percent to 4.0 percent, depending on the alternative tax policy.
3. Percentage depletion is a relatively inefficient method of encouraging exploration and the resultant discovery of new domestic reserves of
liquid petroleum. This is in part due to the low sensitivity of desired
reserve levels to the price subsidy represented by percentage depletion, and
in part to the inefficiency of the allowance for this purpose, since over 40
percent of it is paid for foreign production and non-operating interests in
domestic production.[57]

The report further concluded that for every dollar's worth of new oil
discovered, the Treasury loses ten dollars in taxes.

Meanwhile, Wilbur Mills, who labored under the impression that the
oil industry was amenable to a small reduction, was already on record as
supporting a cut to 23.5 percent. This did not sit very well with oilmen.
"Oilmen had felt they could count on Mills' allegiance," Pearson and
Anderson noted in their column. "In the past, he had always comported
himself as if he had been baptized in oil. So when word of this heresy
reached the oil overlords, the Petroleum Institute's Frank Ikard hurried up
to Capitol Hill to set Mills straight. . . . For two hours, Ikard lectured
his old colleague from Arkansas on the inviolability of the 27.5 percent
oil depletion allowance. Sternly the oil lobbyist warned that the tax exemption couldn't even be whittled down half of one percent without injuring
the industry."[58]

But Mills was too far downstream to change horses. The public clamor
would not be denied. The big boys, cried the critics, are getting away with
murder. Even the ranking Republican on Mills's tax committee, John
Byrnes of Wisconsin, another faithful friend of oil, was appalled when he
learned that Atlantic Richfield, which had earned $797 million in net
income for the period 1962–68, paid no federal tax in the first six years
and then only at a rate of 1.2 percent in 1968. "Frankly," Byrnes said, "I
no longer know what to write to my constituents." What made it even
more appalling was that it was perfectly legal. And, said a New York

* This is a conservative estimate. Most economists place the saving at $1.3 to
$1.6 billion.

Times editorial, the president of Atlantic Richfield, without a sign of emotion, would argue that the oil depletion allowance should be higher.

J. P. Morgan laid down the code many years ago: "Anybody has a right to evade taxes if he can get away with it. No citizen has a moral obligation to assist in maintaining the government. If Congress insists on making stupid mistakes and passing foolish tax laws, millionaires should not be condemned if they take advantage of them."

J.P. was telling it the way it always is. Except, of course, that foolish laws are passed by legislators who are stupid like a fox. It was not a stupid mistake when Congress made it possible for giant oil companies to pay a smaller tax rate than that paid by gas-station attendants. A quick look at some dizzying statistics tells the story. The five American member firms of the international cartel earned a combined net income of $21 billion for the years 1963–67 and paid $1 billion in federal taxes—or a tax rate for the five-year period of 4.9 percent. The individual rates for the same period were: Exxon, 5.2 percent; Texaco, 2 percent; Gulf, 8.4 percent; Mobil, 5.2 percent; California Standard, 2.5 percent.* Figures in *U.S. Oil Week* showed that for the same period, the nation's twenty-three largest companies, including the big five, paid an aggregate rate of about 7.2 percent.

Representative Charles A. Vanik of Ohio estimated that since it was first introduced, depletion had cost about $140 billion, "paid at the expense of almost all of the other taxpayers of the country." And, he might have added, at the expense of 99 percent of the oil industry. Three dozen companies, comprising 1 percent of the industry, received 87 percent of oil's corporate depletion in 1960; 4 percent of the companies got 9 percent; and 95 percent, some twenty-nine hundred companies, got 4 percent of the depletion. A previously unpublished federal study† found that the total amount of depletion deductions claimed in 1967 was $3.6 billion. Of this amount, $3.1 billion, or 88 percent, was claimed by just twenty-two companies.

Beginning in the early 1950s, the foreign tax credit has had a tremendous impact on the low tax rate enjoyed by the giants of the industry. For example, through 1953 the federal income tax paid by Exxon was about 16 percent, while its payments to foreign governments averaged another 19 percent of its pretax income. Five years later, as foreign royal-

---

* When computing their taxes for press releases, oil companies include the domestic excise and sales taxes paid by the consumer.

† It was made public in 1972 by Senator Proxmire's Joint Economic Committee

ties became standardized as "taxes," Exxon's U.S. tax payments had dropped to 1 percent, while its foreign tax had ballooned to 40 percent. Aramco experienced a more rapid reversal. In 1950 it paid taxes of $50 million to the United States and $66 million to Saudi Arabia. The next year it paid $6 million to the United States and $110 million to Saudi Arabia.

In January 1974, Senator Walter F. Mondale of Minnesota said that a new Treasury report showed that American oil companies had used foreign tax credits to cut their 1971 U.S. tax bill by more than 75 percent—from $3.2 billion to $788 million. The tax writeoff, he said, "reinforces the longstanding suspicion that the big multinational oil companies have worked out special deals with the Arab sheiks to jack up their foreign tax credits."

"The artificiality of this [tax] system is obvious and well known, but it has not been challenged by the IRS." This comment was made by an oil official in a secret cablegram made public in January 1974 by Senator Church's subcommittee on multinational corporations. Written in 1971, it was one of several cablegrams exchanged between oil executives proposing ways to protect tax advantages in the face of growing demands by Arab nations for higher oil prices. According to the Church hearings, the tax credit has been used to funnel millions of dollars from the U.S. Treasury to the purses of Arab producers. Launched by the Truman Administration in 1950, the program was supposedly initiated to fight the Cold War. "Fearful that the oil rich nations of the Arabian Peninsula might 'slip behind the Iron Curtain,'" Church explained, "the Department of State made a basic foreign policy judgment that the rulers of these countries should receive increased revenue at the expense of the U.S. Treasury." The Treasury was persuaded to accept "a system in which the companies would increase their payments to the oil producing governments, and the American government would permit them to reduce their U.S. tax payments correspondingly." In other words, for twenty-four years the oil companies and the federal government have jointly manipulated the tax rules to fund a mammoth foreign aid program for Arab rulers—secretly and without congressional approval. The key to the arrangement is the "posted price" system, also created in 1950, and presently under attack—more later on this loophole and the secret cablegrams.

Even with all their tax advantages, oilmen are constantly seeking new ways to evade taxes. One of the more ingenious contrivances cooked up in the 1960s was called "ABC transactions" which evolved into a number of intricate variations. Without getting too technical, one method worked this way.* Big A was the owner of an oil property that produced a gross wellhead profit of $100 million in 1967. With his pre-1969 depletion allowance of 27.5 percent, it meant that he could deduct tax-free $27.5 million right off the top, but there was a dangerous complication created by his other privileges—that is, a conflict of gimmicks. Big A's intangible deductions and foreign tax credits had pushed his operating expenses up to $80 million, reducing his net income to $20 million. This was all wonderful, except that the depletion allowance may not exceed 50 percent of net income. Big A faced the incredible possibility that his $27.5 million deduction would be slashed to $10 million. What to do? Well, Big A sells a production payment (an interest in the oil and gas still in the ground), called a "carve-out," to Big B for $80 million, which increases his total income for the year to $180 million. Since his expenses have remained the same, Big A's net income is now $100 million, but the depletion allowance applies to the full gross income—27.5 percent of $180 million, or $49.5 million, which is deducted from the net income of $100 million leaving Big A liable for taxes on the remaining $50.5 million. At the 52.8 percent rate of 1967, the tax bite is $26,664,000. That is more in taxes than he would have had to pay without the carve-out, but the payoff comes in the following years. With identical income and expenses in 1968, Big A must now pay back the $80 million to Big B, cutting his income to $20 million, which gives him a paper loss for the year of $60 million. This eliminates his federal tax liability for the second year and offsets the $50.5 million income for 1967, entitling Big A to claim a refund of the $26,664,000 in taxes he paid and to provide a carry-over of $9,500,000 to be applied against future taxes.

There is more. Big B, we discover, is none other than Big A's straw foundation, created for this sole purpose. Since banks are discouraged by law from direct purchase of production payments, Big B borrows the money from a bank and either buys the production payments itself or lends the money to any Big C who wants to buy a carve-out. Then Big B charges Big C a fraction more in interest than it is paying to the bank.

Scores of oil foundations were created in Texas and Louisiana during the 1960s. Known in the courts as bootstrapping, the gimmick became a favorite with tax-avoidance attorneys, who predicted, accurately, that the courts would uphold the technique. The Treasury Department estimated

* This practice was sharply curtailed by the 1969 Tax Reform Act, whereby production payments are treated as the repayment of loans.

the turnover of money amounted to $217 million in 1965, $750 million in 1967, $703 million in 1968, and $814 million in 1969.

Only a token percentage of the profits earned by the oil foundations has trickled down to charity. The Bright Star Foundation of Dallas (mentioned in Chapter Four), the nation's thirty-second largest foundation, with total assets at market value of $109 million in 1968, is a shining example of the charitable bent of the oil foundation. Its gross profit from oil production payments for the fiscal year ending March 31, 1967, was $9,933,119. Its contribution to charity was $100 to the Children's Medical Center of Dallas. When the Internal Revenue Service challenged Bright Star's tax exemption, Federal District Court Judge T. Whitfield Davidson, an octogenarian Dallasite, ruled in favor of the foundation. His reasoning was limited to the observation that "the foundation was organized by some wealthy outstanding citizens of Dallas, some of them engaged in the banking business." In an almost identical case, the Fifth U.S. Circuit Court of Appeals said: "A taxpayer is entitled to take any legal course with his property or business which lightens or lessens his tax load . . . and . . . the fact that an arrangement reduces his taxes is of no moment in determining its validity . . ."

It was a series of ABC transactions which made it possible for Atlantic Richfield to avoid paying any income taxes at all from 1962 through 1967. There are complex variations on the ABC deal. For example, A sells his mineral interest to B for a reserved production payment, but then sells the production payment to C. A gets capital gains, B excludes the production payment from his income, and C gets the benefit of depletion to offset his taxable income.

Continental Oil Company, using the ABC scheme, bought Consolidated Coal, the world's largest coal company in terms of sales, and not only escaped income taxes on its $460 million of profits from operating the coal company—profits with which it was buying the company—but also was permitted to deduct its $128 million in coal-mining costs. As for the coal company, it paid no taxes on its income from the sale because it was liquidated under a certain section of the tax code.

Other extractive companies have used the production payment to spectacular advantage. Take U.S. Steel Corporation and its subsidiary, Orinoco, which mines iron ore in Venezuela. In the finest tradition of oilmen economics, U.S. Steel was paying high Venezuelan "royalty taxes" for the privilege of bleeding that underdeveloped country of its national wealth. The idea, of course, was to shift the entire cost of this privilege to the U.S.

Treasury, but because of the restriction to 50 percent of net income, the company got caught with more tax credits than it could use—and time was running out. The solution devised involved the sale of $85 million in future Orinoco iron ore production, through an intermediary, to a group of U.S. banks. The new income generated by the sale was saved by the otherwise expiring tax credits, and the big losses in future years as Orinoco repaid the banks was used by U.S. Steel to offset more U.S. income taxes.

Somewhat reminiscent of 1926, the great debate of 1969—between those in the House who favored a reduction to 20 percent in the depletion allowance and those in the Senate who thought 23 percent was low enough —was resolved by conferees. This time, however, they invoked the wisdom of Nixon rather than of Solomon. The result was that the House gave up twice as much as the Senate.

Yet the final figure of 22 percent was more deception than remedy. By simply raising the prices of crude oil to their own refineries, the major integrated companies were able to nullify the effect of the rate reduction. Thanks to the clever wording of the legislation, an increase in the price of crude oil produces a bigger tax deduction and, in turn, more after-tax profits, even though there is relatively little change in the prices and profits on the refined products. The top twenty-one integrated companies control 85 percent of the refinery capacity.

In a prepared statement to Senator Proxmire's Joint Economic Committee in 1972, former Treasury official Thomas Field elaborated on this convenient feature of the law:

> The tax incentive to raise prices is particularly strong in the case of those vertically integrated petroleum producers who extract from their own properties most of the crude oil they need for their refineries, and who buy only a small proportion of their needs from unrelated producers. For many years, the Internal Revenue Service has been pricing the oil that these firms produce for themselves in terms of the prices paid to outsiders for similar crude. This IRS practice seems plausible at first, but it fails to take note of one very important fact: When an integrated oil company produces the bulk of the oil needed for its refineries, and purchases only a small amount of crude from outsiders, *it is better off, after tax, if it pushes crude oil prices upward.* . . .
>
> The effect of using an unrealistically high transfer price for "self-produced crude oil" is to move profits from the refining to the producing side of an integrated petroleum firm. Every extra dollar "paid" by the refinery for crude oil, means one less dollar of refinery profit and one additional dollar of product profit. Every dollar transferred in this way also

means a 22¢ increase in the firm's percentage depletion deduction. In effect, profits are being transferred from a "high tax jurisdiction" (refining) to a "low tax jurisdiction" (production). This tax incentive to raise crude prices has another desirable effect from the point of view of large, vertically integrated firms; it makes it more difficult for independent refiners to survive, because these refiners must pay higher prices for all their crude needs, not just a portion, and these higher prices bring no corresponding increase in percentage depletion.

Thus at least some major petroleum producers are in the happy position of being able to drive their competition to the wall and at the same time increasing their after-tax profits—by simply paying more for a small portion of their crude oil needs.[59]

In his testimony, Field noted that the oil industry "is one of the very few industries that still collects, without much governmental supervision, most of the statistics that relate to the industry." Taking a stand similar to that of Wright Patman in his criticism of the Treasury Department, Field said it was time for the Internal Revenue Service to

push hard for better reporting of petroleum data. Quite frankly, the IRS has some of this data now, because the service required form O and form M to be filed by all companies claiming percentage depletion with respect to the year 1967. Those data have been compiled by the IRS with respect to a limited number of companies—the 25 largest—but the data have not been published. Petroleum economists and attorneys studying the petroleum industry certainly can't do anything constructive with unpublished data. . . .

If the IRS decides to study crude petroleum prices, I do have one recommendation to make, and that is that the existing IRS offices in the petroleum area not conduct this study. Although I have good friends who are solid people in some of these offices, the fact is that I regard many of the people who staff the IRS petroleum and minerals groups as superannuated and as people about whose loyalty to the service and to the public interest I sometimes have had questions.[60]

The price of crude oil was increased by 25 cents a barrel in 1970. Oil-industry profits survived unscathed not only the cut in the depletion allowance but also the economic slump that sent profits for all manufacturing companies plummeting by 14 percent. The price of crude went up another 6.9 percent in 1971 and profits soared to record heights. The combined net earnings of the big five reached $4 billion, up from $3.6 billion in 1970. Total profits for the eighteen largest companies topped $10 billion, and their aggregate tax rate was 6.7 percent, down by 0.5 percent from the 1963–67 period. The big five paid a rate of 4.2 percent, down by 0.7

percent. As one marketing expert told the Joint Economic Committee, the oil industry, by virtue of its power to raise crude prices, "restored to itself what Congress saw fit to take away."

Because of percentage depletion, the international companies have always looked for their biggest profits "upstream" at the wellhead, rather than in refining and marketing, although the quota program has made refining a lucrative business at home. The seven members of the international cartel, popularly known as the Seven Sisters, actually accounted for well over half of the total world production of 48 million barrels per day. This upstream output, together with "downstream" operations in refining and distribution, brought them combined revenues of $62.7 billion and profits of $5.2 billion. Two-thirds of their crude, nearly 20 million barrels per day, comes from the nations of the Organization of Petroleum Exporting Countries (OPEC), dominated by Persian Gulf and North African states.

The awesome growth of the five American Sisters was made possible by the tax-giveaway program. By 1972 Exxon had combined sales of $18.7 billion, greater than the gross national product of Austria, and its earnings of $1.5 billion was more than the sales of 424 of the 500 largest U.S. industrial corporations. The $851.5 million it paid out in dividends in 1971 was more than Ford Motor earned that year. In fact, its dollar earnings in 1971 were fifteen times as great as those of John D. Rockefeller's old Standard Oil trust in 1911, the year before it was broken up into thirty-four "competitive" units by the Supreme Court. These figures were to change even more dramatically in 1973—more later on this.

While Americans were worrying about national security, the oil biggies were growing in geometric ratio. "What do you consider to be our national security?" Senator Edward Kennedy asked M. A. Wright of Exxon. "National security against what? A ground war in Western Europe . . . a land war in Asia . . . guerrilla wars . . . ?"

"We're not thinking about protection from atomic war," Wright replied. "The thing we are endeavoring to guard against is the termination of imports abroad due to political emergencies." He alluded to strikes, turnover in political parties, and boycotts against shipments to the United States—and that was all. "These kinds of things we want to be able to survive," avoiding some other country having control over "our economic destiny," he said. Senator Long suggested the possibility of war in the Middle East and even with Canada. Senator John Tower of Texas, one of oildom's greatest champions, pointed to rising Soviet power in the Persian

Gulf and the Mediterranean. "We could conceivably get in conventional war with Russia, although I don't foresee it," Tower conceded.

Oil lobbyists and their political defenders were not impressed by the argument that "proved reserves" were sufficient to keep the nation operating at present levels of consumption for many years without a single new discovery. Nor were they impressed by the findings of the Interstate Oil Compact Commission, which estimated that the nation's proved reserves could be increased by more than half simply by installing additional equipment, and that more than 60 billion barrels were recoverable by the application of new methods, including injecting steam or hot water into the reservoirs. These well-known techniques would raise the reserves to about 110 billion barrels, enough oil to sustain the nation through a ten-year national emergency. By then scientists should have perfected the necessary technology to process the oil-shale deposits of the Rocky Mountain states, which are said to contain the equivalent of more than a trillion barrels of oil. Even with present technology, shale oil can now be extracted from the best shales for about $6 a barrel, a price that by 1974 was closely competitive with domestic oil. If the national emergency should span a millennium, there is always 1.9 trillion tons of coal waiting to be mined and converted to gas and oil. That alone is enough fuel to meet *all* energy needs for about 650 years at the current rate of use.

Meanwhile, many other sources of energy are on drawing boards. The fast-breeder reactor converts useless rocks into nuclear fuel uranium-238. The fact that it breeds more atomic fuel than it consumes makes it a promising source of almost inexhaustible energy. There are several truly inexhaustible sources of energy already in various stages of research. Hydrogen is the most abundant and energetic and the cleanest of all elemental fuels in the world. It is manufactured by a process known as electrolysis, the passing of a strong electric current through water, which decomposes it into its main gaseous elements—hydrogen and oxygen. Scientists envision processing plants on great floating platforms in the oceans. Plans to tap the heat from molten basalt deep in the earth are already in operation at several locations. A Rand Corporation report said that if the Imperial Valley were to be tapped over a fifteen-year program, California would need no other new power plants between 1985 and 2000, assuming that power demand grew at 3 percent a year. Solar power has long fascinated and eluded scientists. Its source of energy, the sun, will outlast the human race. Although the problems appear monumental, some scientists believe it could be utilizable by 1990.

The old chestnut of national security was reroasted so often during the 1969 debate that it finally went up in smoke. It soon became crystal clear to oil lobbyists and their political troops that a new banner was needed if their crusade to save America—if not from its enemies, then from itself—was to succeed. Thus was born, full grown, the theme for the 1970s, the *energy crisis.*

It was an inspiration worthy of the great P. T. Barnum himself. No huckster's snow job ever knocked America off its pivot faster than the energy crisis. The stratagem was executed with exquisite finesse. The trial balloon was natural gas, the cheapest and cleanest of all fossil fuels, the one most coveted by environmentalists. It was like killing a whole gaggle of pesky birds with one load of buckshot. Another strategic plus for the new banner was its adaptability to an old scenario: incentive was still the only alchemy powerful enough to solve the problem. Spelled out in oilskrit, it meant higher prices, lower taxes, fewer restrictions, more import quotas, and greater profits.

One thing to remember about the energy crisis is that oilmen come naturally to the mechanics of the squeeze play. The oil business has always been an international poker game in which the cartel giants hold all the aces. For half a century the companies have practiced muscle flexing on a global scale. More than one monarch has been brought to heel. No oil-exporting country could afford a showdown with the cartel, which played the countries off against one another, often driving hard bargains home with threats of boycotts (Mossadegh of Iran was toppled by one in 1953) or reduced production in their oil fields, which could mean almost instant fiscal disaster in underdeveloped countries with oil-based economies.

It is perhaps more poetic justice than irony that through the cartel's collusive effort the Organization of Petroleum Exporting Countries (OPEC) was formed in 1960. The aim was to fix the world price of oil by restricting its members' oil production. Although OPEC included all major oil-exporting countries except Canada, the world price of oil continued to drop throughout the 1960s. However, the oil countries, notably the Arab states, were growing fabulously wealthy as the energy hungry world became hopelessly addicted to oil. The situation was analogous to a drug pusher who waits for his customer to get hooked before raising his price. The turning point for OPEC came at the Tehran Conference held in January 1971. It was OPEC's demand for a 50-cent-per-barrel price rise that precipitated the flurry of secret cablegrams referred to earlier. It looked as though the new alliance of oil nations was starting out with a sealed deck, but the oilmen still had more aces up their sleeves, to wit: the exclusive ownership of the downstream operation—the apparatus for refining and distributing petroleum products in the world market.

At this point it became important for the cartel to have its traditional joint effort sanctioned by the government. A single bargaining team to discuss prices and costs with OPEC nations was approved by the Justice Department, which presented the cartel with a letter granting special dispensation from antitrust laws. According to Senator Church's Subcommittee, the letter was drafted in the New York law offices of John J. McCloy, who represented twenty-three oil companies. James E. Akins, who headed the Office of Fuels and Energy in the State Department, and a representative from the Justice Department sat in one room, while in another room oilmen were meeting behind closed doors to prepare the letter. Periodically, an emissary would emerge to show them drafts of the letter they would eventually sign. At this writing, Akins is United States ambassador to Saudi Arabia.

As William Pitt observed back in 1770, "Unlimited power is apt to corrupt the minds of those who possess it." Oilmen and Arab despots would be among the last to be excluded from this wise dictum. When the inevitable confrontation came in the spring of 1972, it had a familiar ring for those Americans who viewed the energy crisis with growing suspicion. If nothing else, the head-on collision between the Iraq Petroleum Company (owned by Exxon, Mobil, Shell, British Petroleum, Française des Pétroles, and the Gulbenkian Foundation) and Iraqi President Ahmad Hasan Bakr proves that oilmen are not infallible in assessing their limits of power.

In an attempt to force the Iraqi government to grant certain concessions, the cartel cut back the daily production in the rich Kirkuk fields in northern Iraq to 600,000 barrels a day from the normal 1.1 million. The showdown began with an emotional speech by Saddam Hussein Takriti, vice chairman of the ruling Revolutionary Command Council, who gave the cartel three days to restore normal production. If they refused, he said, the third day "will be a day of victory for the Iraqi people, the day when the company will be brought down on its knees, bowing to the legitimate rights of the Iraqi people."[61]

The third day was stretched to two weeks before President Bakr seized IPC's holdings and nationalized the northern oil fields. "We have decided to go on the offensive against the oil companies," Bakr told a nationwide radio and television audience. "You know that the oil companies are the symbol of colonialist policy of robbing a country, and any true national liberation would have been incomplete without imposing national sovereignty on the companies." The reduction in March and April cost the Iraqi treasury $85.8 million. The power play backfired on the cartel when the other Persian Gulf nations supported Iraq. Some of the oil nations have since gained participation shares in their own oilfields. After years of being ruthlessly exploited, the OPEC nations were asking for a fair shake, which was promptly interpreted as aggression. On April 1, 1973, in an article praising Exxon, *Forbes* noted that when the United States first devalued the dollar late in 1971, the OPEC nations "wrung out another tax increase to compensate for it. They will probably get another to make up for the latest dollar devaluation. Result: The tax and royalties on a barrel of Saudi Arabian crude will have risen from 88 cents in 1970 to over $1.70 by 1975. Such is their strength now that the OPEC nations will undoubtedly win further big increases." *Forbes* continued:

> The latest wrinkle dreamed up by the OPEC nations is the concept of participation. To date, Saudi Arabia, Qatar, Kuwait and Abu Dhabi have taken over 25 percent ownership of the crude produced within their borders, with an option to raise their shares to 51 percent by 1982. Iraq will probably follow suit later this year or next with the rest of its crude. The present government of Libya, the wildest-eyed of the lot, is now demanding an immediate 50 percent participation from companies operating its wells, one of which is Exxon.

Of course, the royalty taxes that oil companies pay to OPEC nations are deductible dollar for dollar against U.S. taxes, so that the U.S. Treasury is bearing the brunt. The fact remains that Middle East oil is the cheapest to develop and produce. It still costs around ten cents a barrel to produce, or one-fifth of a cent per gallon. Compare this to about $1.30 a barrel in this country. Prior to the formation of OPEC the ratio of income favored oil companies by 82 to 18. The balance of profit is shifting, but with the present U.S. tax structure, the oil giants are far from hurting.

The picture was to change even more dramatically in the next few months. On October 6, 1973, Egyptian and Syrian forces invaded Israeli-occupied territory, and for the fourth time in their struggle against Israel—previously in 1948, 1956, and 1967—the Arabs, who account for roughly 55 percent of OPEC's sales, tried to use oil as a weapon. Suddenly a handful of medieval shiekdoms were virtually in a position to dictate to industrialized nations and the oil companies that were once their colonialist "oppressors." The Arab position was based on experience. Having worked closely with the oil cartel, they naturally assumed that extortion was an essential element of the political game. Their thesis was simple: now is the perfect time to attack. The United States is in the middle of an energy crisis. Cut off its source of Arab oil and it will abandon Israel, its protégé, which will then be forced to withdraw from the occupied territories.

The invasion was preceded by a series of political and publicity moves in the United States on the part of the oil cartel to pave the way for the Arabs. On August 1, Standard Oil of California asked its stockholders and employees to urge the government to support "the aspirations of the Arab people" and "their efforts toward peace in the Middle East." The reason given was that Arab oil reserves were vital to "the future welfare of the Western world." Israel was not mentioned by name, nor did the company disclose its strong dependence on Saudi Arabia, which alone in 1972 supplied more than three times as much oil as all of Standard's wells in the United States.[62]

If nothing else, this bold stroke illustrates the collusion that exists between the oil companies and the exporting countries—both were striking while the iron was hot. Even the angry reaction from Jewish organizations did not dissuade the oilmen from their precarious position. In fact, Frank Jungers, board chairman of the Arabian American Oil Company— Aramco, the world's largest single oil-producing enterprise, consisting of Exxon, Texaco, Mobil, and Standard of California—took to the publicity circuit to promote the "Arab cause." Aramco has the exclusive concession to operate in Saudi Arabia, which sits on top of 138 billion barrels of oil, making its reserves greater than those of the United States, the Soviet Union, and China combined.*

The significance of Aramco's position was assessed by *Petroleum Intelligence Weekly*: "As Aramco goes, so goes the world oil supply picture. For the next few months. For the next few years. And as far ahead as anyone dares project. Put simply, no other oil exporter—nor, in fact, all other exporting areas of the world put together—can begin to meet the growth in oil requirements during the next couple of years, much less over a longer term."[63]

"If a new war broke out in the Mideast," Jungers said in an interview

---

* Exxon, Texaco, and Standard of California each owned 30 percent and Mobil had 10 percent, but in January 1973 Saudi Arabia cut itself in for 25 percent, leaving the principal shareholders with 22.5 percent and Mobil with 7.5 percent. According to the agreement, the Saudi interest will rise to 51 percent by 1980.

on September 4, 1973, one month before the Arab attack, "American interests would be thrown out of the Arab world because the Arabs would figure America is one hundred percent behind Israel." It was not that Jungers was anti-Israeli, he himself assured Los Angeles *Times* reporter Jerry Cohen, but he thought it important to promote a climate of public opinion that might move the American government to "more aggressively seek a settlement of the Arab-Israeli dispute." Picturing Aramco as a powerless servant, Jungers recalled how King Faisal had kept him waiting "three or four days" when Jungers had asked for an audience early in May of 1973. "I knew something was cooking," he said. His worst fears were confirmed when the king began speaking in "a quiet, measured way." The king wanted to know, said Jungers, "why American companies doing business in Saudi Arabia and in other Mideast countries weren't doing their share to attempt to cause a settlement. He said he felt we should be doing more than we were. He said he realized the problems that existed. But he felt the American government was the key to this thing [a settlement]. Of course, from his point of view, continued overbalance of support of Israel was what was keeping the Israelis from wanting to settle. His approach was one of despair and frustration at what seemed to be the American position. He felt that, to be more specific, the company—Aramco—should do what it could to bring this thing into better focus in the United States. With the energy crisis being what it is, the oil crisis in particular, one had to agree that more should be done to properly inform the American public on the whole Mideast situation and on the energy situation."

There was another dimension to Faisal's position. Besides being under constant attack from his more radical Arab neighbors "for being pro-American," Jungers added that the Saudis "no longer need the money that additional growth and production will bring, and one must ask: 'What's in it for Saudi Arabia to allow an American country to grow and operate?'"

Jungers promptly conveyed Faisal's message to Aramco's four American partners. "And all the companies," Jungers said, "readily agreed that the only chance we had to keep our production growth was to recognize what the interests of America were—namely that there had to be stability in the Mideast. Another way to say it would be: Up until now, before there was a crisis, we all tended to keep quiet, thinking that was in the interest of stability. We were aware that people would say, 'You're just taking this position because of your business interests.' We felt to speak out would be counterproductive. But now, while the business interest remains, Mideast stability also has become an American national interest. . . .

I don't want to get into the merits of the Israeli case or the Arab cause. That's not our business. But we must look at what the American interests are and stick with that."

Although Jungers did not define what he meant by stability, events moved rapidly after the companies apparently failed to stabilize the situation. The Persian Gulf nations began boosting prices, but the real catalyst came in mid-September when President Muammar el-Qaddafi suddenly nationalized all foreign oil companies operating in Libya. Already in the vise of the Watergate investigation, Nixon was in no mood for an Arab squeeze play. The United States, he pointed out, was not without recourse of its own. In fact, it might "be in a position to influence them [the Arabs] for this reason: Oil without a market, as Mr. Mossadegh learned many, many years ago, does not do a country much good. We and Europe are the market and I think that the responsible Arab leaders will see to it that if they continue to up the price, if they continue to expropriate . . . without fair compensation, the inevitable result is that they will lose their markets, and other sources will be developed." The United States, he said, was aiming for energy self-sufficiency in three to five years, but he did not explain the basis for this prediction.

The United States placed the "highest priority on seeking a Mideast settlement," he said. "Both sides are at fault. Both sides need to start negotiating. That is our position." To demonstrate his sincerity, he promised to send John Connally to the Mideast and to the Soviet Union in the future. Later, however, he sent Henry Kissinger.

By mid-October, six Arab countries had lifted the posted price of crude oil by a stunning 70 percent, to $5.11 per barrel. Joined by four other Arab states, the ten decided to reduce oil output at least 5 percent below the preceding month, with the cutbacks to continue "until an Israeli withdrawal is completed, and until the restoration of the legal rights of the Palestinian people." In a final desperate move, Saudi Arabia, Libya, Algeria, Kuwait, Dubai, Bahrain, Qatar, and Abu Dhabi embargoed all oil shipments to the United States in rataliation for its continued arms support of Israel.

Joining in the chorus of strident imperialist voices raised in horror at the sheer audacity of the Arabs, William F. Buckley, Jr., flicked his eighteenth-century rapier across the Arabs' jugular. In his syndicated column of October 10, 1973, Buckley laid it squarely on the jingoist line: "It is an axiom of Christian social thought that the individual human being has the right to live. Translated, let us say into a community in which on the one hand there is abundance and on the other hand starvation, the starving man is not—according to Christian principle—guilty of theft when he takes a loaf of bread from the man who has a loaf to spare." Buckley went on to draw a distinction in national practice between "the words 'nationalize' and 'confiscate.' The former is acceptable moral practice, the latter unacceptable. We come then to focus these points on Mideast oil. As a matter of morals, an industrial nation dependent on oil to avoid instant mass unemployment, the immobilization of its defense, and ultimately the starvation of its people, has the moral right to force a supplier to sell it the oil it needs. . . . What if the Mideast countries should say no? . . . If Western Europe has to have the oil, then it has to take whatever means are necessary to acquire it. Yes, that means that the Western military must, at the margin, be prepared to, let us say, land an expeditionary force in Libya. But having done so, and having turned the faucets back on, the morally distinguishing feature of their enterprise is that they must buy the oil, not take it."

Simple. Just like Korea and Vietnam. Just walk in and turn on the faucets. The Soviet Union, which had mounted a massive airlift of military ammunition and equipment to the Arab forces, would politely cease and desist in the face of such irresistible Christian logic: it is morally right to take something by force—if you pay for it.

For forty years, the Arab nations were little more than peasants groveling at the foot of the giant oil companies. Now, suddenly, they were in a position to get a piece of the action, with or without Buckley's blessings. Between 1970 and early 1973, they managed to double their posted prices, and in the last nine months of 1973, they quadrupled it, from $2.59 a barrel to $11.65. Venezuela and Ecuador, both members of OPEC, raised their posted prices per barrel to $14.08 and $13.70, respectively.

The first thing to remember here is that the actual price of oil is always far less than the posted price. The arithmetic is not all that complex, either. In Persian Gulf countries, the oil companies operate under concession agreements with a fixed royalty rate of 12.5 percent and corporate income taxes set at 55 percent. Under this formula, for example, Saudi Arabia's goal of earning $7 per barrel from oil produced from its rich oilfields merely placed a floor under the price Aramco's customers—that is, Exxon, Texaco, Socal, and Mobil—must charge for crude they sell. Add to this figure a generous production cost of 13 cents per barrel, plus the 45 cents the Saudis have ruled mandatory for shareholder-customer's profit per barrel, and you arrive at a market price of $7.58, a far cry from the inflated $11.65 posted figure the oil companies were complaining about. At that juncture in the energy crisis, any increase—real or rigged—in foreign crude oil could only mean corresponding increases in the price of domestic oil. The oilmen never had it so good. Their profit from foreign oil had not decreased, and by paying slightly higher prices for a small percentage of imported oil, they would eventually double and triple the value of their domestic oil reserves. Only that wide Texas was the limit.

If the oilmen had not orchestrated OPEC's moves, then they still deserve the credit, for there is no question that the exporting countries learned plenty from the oilmen, who know all about the strategy of cutting production and falsifying records. That is all part of the oil game, particularly at home, where the rules are more relaxed and sovereignty is often measured in terms of campaign contributions. It was the same group who were in control of the energy crisis, pushing the panic button and wringing their hands as they pleaded for more incentive. Some forty million customers, ranging from powerful utilities to indigent ghetto dwellers, bought about $11 billion worth of natural gas in 1971. The gas traveled through the pipelines of 116 interstate companies, with twenty companies, including such familiar names as El Paso Natural Gas Company, United Gas, and Tenneco, accounting for 80 percent of the volume. They, in turn, bought the gas at the wellhead from thousands of producers—but the five giants, along with eighteen of their associates, accounted for about 70 percent of all wellhead sales.

Add this information to the fact that the only data available on gas reserves are published by the American Gas Association, an industry trade organization that gets its figures from the producers themselves, and you begin to get an inkling of what is involved. Nobody knows anything about the energy crisis beyond what the oil industry wants the public to know.

In hearings before the Oil Policy Committee held in June 1973, J. Roy Goodearle, associate director of the Interior Department's Office of Oil and Gas, admitted that the federal government got its figures from the American Petroleum Institute. Asked if there had been any independent audit of the API figures to test their accuracy, Goodearle said there might have been one.

"That will come as news to the Federal Trade Commission," said Senator Adlai E. Stevenson III of Illinois, who stated that the FTC had informed members of his staff that there were in the entire country "at best two inspectors" from the federal government who could be made available to check up on the oil companies' figures.[64]

But the Federal Power Commission, relying entirely on industry-supplied data, granted billions of dollars in rate increases "in an effort to coax gas producers to explore, drill, and develop new gas supplies," the House Subcommittee on Special Small Business Problems concluded after hearings in the spring of 1972. "Presently, this FPC regulatory experiment appears to have netted few additions to the nation's dwindling gas reserve base," said Neil Smith, the subcommittee's chairman.[65]

Finally succumbing to organized pressure from critics, the FPC initiated the National Gas Survey, which purportedly would provide the public with an accurate estimate of gas reserves. The survey would use random samples of gas-field data submitted by the AGA and selected by the survey's accounting agent. The samples were to be made on a minimum basis in order to expedite it—after all, there was a crisis going on.

The director and deputy director of the survey's Supply-Technical Advisory Task Force-Liquefied Natural Gas (LNG) were executives of El Paso Natural Gas Company, which was then engaged in an LNG proceeding at the Commission. "It would appear," said Neil Smith, "that the results of the LNG task force study could be shaped to a large degree to substantiate the legal positions urged by El Paso Natural Gas Company, as well as other gas companies on the survey." The task force conducted secret meetings for three months before FPC Chairman John Nassikas got around to appointing representatives from environmental and consumer groups to the panel.[66]

El Paso won its case before the commission. "The Federal Power Commission, reacting to intense pressure from the national gas industry, made major revisions in an earlier decision allowing El Paso Natural Gas Company to import massive, long-term supplies of liquefied natural gas from Algeria," the *Wall Street Journal* reported on October 6, 1972. The agreement allowed El Paso to import one billion cubic feet of gas daily from Algeria under a twenty-five-year contract valued at more than $8 billion. The FPC approved rate increases of almost 400 percent (from an interstate rate of about 26 cents to more than a $1 per thousand cubic feet) and certified the new prices without qualification for the length of the contract even if lower-cost sources were developed in the interim.*

El Paso has had considerable success in getting governmental bodies to reverse earlier decisions. One of its most controversial legal hassles has been an antitrust action to dissolve the 1957 acquisition by El Paso of

* The federal government will subsidize about 25 percent of the construction cost of liquefied natural gas tankers.

Pacific Northwest Pipeline Company. Initiated by William M. Bennett, then a member of the California Service Commission, the case has been bouncing around in the courts fifteen years. On four separate occasions, the United States Supreme Court has ruled that the merger violated anti-trust laws and ordered divestiture. Two months after leaving the Wall Street law offices of Mudge, Rose, Guthrie and Alexander (Nixon's former law firm), the newly appointed Attorney General John Mitchell announced, without explanation, that the Justice Department would not appeal any lower-court decision it lost in the El Paso case. Bennett provided what he thought was a good explanation, charging that between 1961 and 1967, El Paso had paid Mudge Rose legal fees of more than $770,000.[67]

El Paso took refuge on Capital Hill. Warren G. Magnuson of Washington, chairman of the Senate Commerce Committee, sponsored legislation that would overturn the Supreme Court order and allow El Paso to retain Pacific Northwest. This effort in 1971 looked promising until it disintegrated into charges of bribery and political donations. Bennett, who, as a "consumer advocate," has dogged El Paso through the years asked the committee to investigate "lobbying activities of El Paso, past, present and future, promises of political contributions to public officials and the reasons prompting Governor Ronald Reagan of California, whose Administration record of consumer protection is miserable, to support your bill."[68] Bennett said the merger gave El Paso a lock on the Western market, costing consumers countless millions of dollars in higher gas rates. In his letter to the committee, Reagan said: "Legislation providing for congressional approval of this merger would improve the assurance of an available natural gas supply and would result in lower costs, to the benefit of gas consumers in our state."[69]

A month after Bennett testified, John M. Klas, a Salt Lake City banker and Utah Democratic chairman, told the committee that Daniel Berman, an attorney representing El Paso, had offered to arrange a $100,000 interest-free deposit with his bank. The offer was made over drinks at a private club. Berman told Klas he was on the "wrong side" in the El Paso case and "something to the effect . . . 'and we are going to beat the hell out of you on the Magnuson bill.'" Berman asked if Klas had any banking relationship with El Paso, and when Klas said he had tried unsuccessfully to enter into one in previous years, Berman allegedly told him he could be helpful in getting a deposit from El Paso, adding that he was talking about $100,000 interest-free.[70]

Despite powerful backing from a bipartisan Western coalition of twelve Senators and nine governors, Magnuson was forced by the dispute to shelve the bill until 1972. In the spring of that year, a colleague, Representative Brock Adams of Washington, sponsored a House version of Magnuson's bill, but before either one could gain any headway, the Washington *Post* revived the dispute with facts and figures culled from a report El Paso had filed with the FPC in April.* In an exclusive story on September 20, the *Post* disclosed that El Paso had "spent nearly $900,000 last year drumming up public support for a bill that would have let it keep control of Pacific Northwest Pipeline division." The gas company's report described the $893,862 as "expenditures relating to participation in activities connected with congressional consideration of legislation designed to preserve the merger . . ."

A Washington law firm that lobbied for the bill in Congress was paid $353,113; the public-relations firm of Hill and Knowlton received $179,555; attorney Daniel L. Berman was listed for $13,433; former Republican Governor Robert E. Smylie of Idaho was paid $16,975; and $16,556 went to the law firm of former Democratic Governor Albert D. Rosellini of Washington.

At one point in the hearings, Senator Magnuson facetiously observed: "If divestiture occurs, El Paso will continue to serve California as the overwhelmingly dominant gas supplier—it just won't be allowed to serve consumers of the Northwest. Apparently, California wants to keep El Paso for itself and not allow the Northwest consumers to share in its service."[71]

Both bills died in committee, and on March 5, 1973, the Supreme Court again ordered El Paso to get rid of Pacific Northwest. The ruling marked the eighth appearance of El Paso before the court in the past sixteen years. It is estimated that El Paso paid close to $16 million to lawyers and public-relations men during its losing fight.[72]

The Natural Gas Act of 1938 charged the Federal Power Commission with the responsibility to ensure consumers both a reasonable and an abundant supply of natural gas. To curb the greed of newly built interstate pipelines, the act instructed the commission to regulate rates charged by pipelines. As is often the case when the oil industry is involved, the language was ambiguous and the FPC chose to ignore that part of the act

---

* The FPC requires all natural-gas pipelines to file annual reports under a uniform system of accounts so that it can determine whether certain expenses should be borne by the companies or by consumers.

which requested it to regulate wellhead prices, until a Supreme Court decision in 1954 ruled that it had to. But the FPC was still reluctant to assume jurisdiction. For several years it agonized over what constituted a "just and reasonable price," one that would allow enough profits to attract new capital. The method finally adopted was to take up rate cases company by company; by 1960 it found itself with what it estimated to be a 250-year backlog. "Producers of natural gas cannot by any stretch of the imagination be classified as public utilities," it argued. "The traditional method of regulating utilities is not sensible or even workable."

In 1961 President Kennedy appointed Joseph C. Swidler, a New Dealer with a distinguished record as a TVA administrator, chairman of the FPC, and announced that the commission would thenceforth assure consumers of an abundant supply of low-priced natural gas. Swidler promptly scuttled the backlog and divided the country into twenty-three producing areas, with a price ceiling for each based on its average costs. This system not only provided consumers with a cheap supply of natural gas but also gave producers the incentive to explore for new fields by placing higher ceilings on new gas. Total gas production in the 1960s rose at an average of 7 percent a year. In 1971 it dropped to 2.6 percent.

Two factors greatly affected the decrease in production: the Tax Reform Act of 1969, which convinced the giants of the need for a new strategy, and the appointment that year by President Nixon of John N. Nassikas as chairman of the FPC, an event that was celebrated in executive suites from Houston to Baghdad. It is the consensus of the Nixon commission that the Supreme Court erred in 1954 and that wellhead prices should be deregulated, leaving the nation's energy needs to the play of free enterprise. It has defined a fair return to producers as whatever it takes to revive exploration and development. Commissioner Rush Moody, Jr., a Texas lawyer with oil and gas clients (a Nixon appointee), has said that he wants an immediate "return to the discipline of the marketplace as the basic tool of consumer protection."

Nassikas was not that gung-ho about it at first. He was apprehensive of what he calls the "sudden jolt" of quick deregulation in a shortage. "If we don't get the necessary response from the gas industry in the next two years," he has said, "we may ask Congress to return producers to a free market, subject only to antitrust laws."[73] With such a promise in the wind, was there any chance that oilmen would do anything to delay that happy day? There was no question that the major producers could prolong the energy crisis over many years without damaging their profit structure.

Data control is a vital factor in the integrated company's monopolistic hold in the market place. New discoveries must be understated to maximize the illusion of a shortage.

In a column on June 14, 1971, Jack Anderson charged that Nassikas had "conspired . . . to conceal evidence and mislead Senators about . . . the amount of natural gas available . . . in a vast Louisiana reservoir. . . . Their figures make the risk and expense of sinking new wells appear to be far higher than is true." According to Anderson:

> The American Gas Association, which speaks for the producers, estimated one part of the Louisiana reserves to be 24 trillion cubic feet. But the FPC's own experts, after careful calculation, came up with a 34 trillion figure. The difference of 10 trillion cubic feet would seriously weaken the producers' case for a rate increase.
>
> Yet Nassikas not only accepted the producers' figures but suppressed estimates that were damaging to the producers. This shocking malfeasance, which could cost the consumer a staggering $4 billion, should be grounds for impeachment.
>
> We know from the suppressed Nassikas Papers that the Federal Power Chairman was fully informed as early as February, 1970, by both his Economics and Producers division that the industry's figures were suspect. Yet he concealed, the discrepancy and sided with the gas producers in public statements, Senate hearings and congressional correspondence.

Nassikas rejected an appeal by his economics division to amend the legal brief to show that it had objected to the figures, and also took the case away from a tough hearing examiner. "The supressed evidence," said Anderson, "in the form of studies, letters and memos—has been kept under lock by Nassikas."

Two years later Nassikas would report that the completed National Gas Survey indicated that recoverable proven natural-gas reserves totaled 261.6 trillion cubic feet at the end of 1970, about 10 percent below estimates by the American Gas Association. On the basis of these findings, the FPC continued to grant huge rate increases to stimulate exploration and forestall the apocalypse. In May 1973 the commission approved a 73 percent increase in the sale of gas produced from offshore Louisiana to the Tennessee Gas Pipeline Company, a division of Tenneco, which operates a pipeline system in fifteen states from southern Texas to New England. The producers favored were Belco Petroleum Corporation, Texaco, and Tenneco Oil Company, another unit of Tenneco.[74]

By late summer of 1973, the commission had abandoned all pretense of regulating prices. It permitted sales of gas at unregulated prices for periods of six months, renewable ad infinitum. In response to an action brought by the Consumer Federation of America and three other groups, the Federal Court of Appeals issued an order in mid-October blocking the agency's new policy. In their complaint, the groups charged that if allowed to stand, the FPC policy would permit gas prices to skyrocket to double their present regulated prices or even higher.

Two months later the Supreme Court overturned the lower court's ruling. In its appeal to the high court, the government had argued that only pipelines that could show they were short of supplies would be permitted to shop for gas at whatever price they could obtain it. With this ruling, the new Nixon court cleared the way for natural gas prices to go unregulated before Congress could act on Nixon's request to deregulate the industry.

In June 1973 the Federal Trade Commission, the agency that had taken such a walloping from the oil industry in the early 1950s with its report on *The International Petroleum Cartel*, suddenly leaped back into the arena, ready for another knee-groin session. Awakened from its stupor by the militant prodding of consumer advocate Ralph Nader and John W. Gardner of Common Cause, the FTC, in its new activist consumer-protection role, decided to take another close look at the old cartel. A two-year staff study under the direction of James T. Halverson, the commission's antitrust chief, resulted in the filing of a massive antitrust complaint against the nation's eight largest oil companies, charging them with unlawfully monopolizing the refining of crude oil into petroleum products, driving competitors out of business, aggravating recent gasoline scarcities, and reaping excessive profits. The eight vertically integrated companies cited in the complaint were Exxon, Standard of Indiana, Mobil, Atlantic Richfield (Arco), Standard of California,* Gulf, Shell, and Texaco, but the allegations were not limited to those eight companies. The combined assets of the eight firms were listed at $76 billion, and their after-tax profits in 1972 totaled nearly $4.6 billion.

The complaint alleged that at least since 1950 the firms have been "pursuing a common course of action [to] maintain and reinforce a noncompetitive market structure." The companies have been controlling supplies of crude oil and refined products through a complicated series of pricing and production decisions. The nation's petroleum shortage was the

---

* The first five companies named were originally created by the breakup of Rockefeller's Standard Oil trust in 1911. Instead of carving the empire into its functional parts—production, refining, and marketing—Harvard economist Marc J. Roberts points out, "the Government split it along geographical lines, thus making every successor company vertically integrated."

result of anticompetitive practices fostered by government regulations and manipulated by the major oil companies to protect their profits: "In the many levels in which they interrelate, the majors demonstrate a clear preference for avoiding competition through mutual cooperation and the use of exclusionary practices." The companies use oil-depletion allowances and other tax benefits to reap huge profits at the production level— that is, upstream at the wellhead—while running their refining, distribution, and marketing operations so cheaply that other companies cannot compete effectively. They "have behaved in a similar fashion as would a classical monopolist: they have attempted to increase profits by restricting output." Through cozy exchange agreements among themselves and with certain independent refiners, they have ensured a sufficient supply of crude and refined products for their own refineries and service stations, while refusing to sell to other refiners and service stations.

The only effective competition to survive has come from independent gasoline stations, the report noted, but an estimated 1,200 of them had closed in the first five months of 1973.* "What has happened here is that the majors have used the shortage as an occasion to attempt to debilitate, if not eradicate, the independent marketing sector." If the majors' attempt "is at all successful in diminishing the market shares of independents the consumer will pay dearly for this advantage." The companies "have obtained profits and returns on investments substantially in excess of those they would have obtained in a competitively structured market." Actual and potential competition "at all levels" of the industry has been "hindered, lessened, eliminated and foreclosed."[75]

As to natural-gas reserves, Halverson told the Senate Judiciary Committee's Antitrust and Monopoly Subcommittee that company documents examined by his investigators showed gas reserves as much as ten times higher than the figures given to the American Gas Association. The procedure of reporting reserves through an American Gas Association committee composed of employees of major producers "could provide the vehicle for a conspiracy among the companies to falsify the data." Halverson added that the FTC found large discrepancies between figures reported for fields by the AGA and data that companies filed with the FPC.[76]

The counterattack from within and without the Administration was not long in coming. A staff analysis by the Office of the Energy Adviser at the Treasury Department, then headed by William E. Simon, bluntly charged

* By year's end, the number of independents closed had spiraled to 10,000.

that the FTC report was "inaccurate" and "biased": "Although perhaps unintentional, the FTC report is biased against the largest integrated oil companies. Nothing in the report supports restricting the FTC's complaint to the eight largest oil companies." The Treasury said integration of the producing, refining, transporting, and marketing of crude oil and petroleum products had proved to be an efficient method of operation. Without alluding to the predatory temperament of oilmen, the study warned that divestiture would cause the integrated oil companies to consider foreign investment and/or operations as their best course of future action, thus aggravating domestic shortages and balance-of-trade problems. The Treasury study could not have stated the oilmen's case better if John Connally himself had written it.[77]

Simon, who would soon become Nixon's energy czar, even wrote to FTC Chairman Lewis A. Engman to again express the view that the commission's action would deter the building of much-needed refinery capacity. His effort earned him a stinging rebuke from Engman's assistant, who replied that it would be improper for the chairman even to read the letter.

In a lengthy editorial, the *Wall Street Journal* took the FTC to task. "This may look like monopoly to the FTC," the *Journal* said, "but to us it looks like efficiency." In conclusion, it added:

> Our own reading of the whole matter is that the FTC is playing games with us, that it has taken two years to discover there is really no conspiracy among the major oil companies, but that it hates to admit it. Pressed by Congress and others to find a scapegoat for the present shortages, it has come up with a report and complaint in which loaded rhetoric is used to describe inexorable economic forces at work.*

Although the FTC complaint did not charge the companies with conspiracy in achieving their dominant market position, it did seek to make illegal a form of antitrust behavior known as "conscious parallelism": by their oligopolistic practice of keeping close watch on one another, the companies were able to coordinate their pricing, production, and marketing decisions in ways that restrained trade. The new attack against the FTC was not as virulent as the old one, but the agency's chances for success were no more promising than before.[78]

At the Interior Department, meanwhile, Secretary Rogers C. B. Morton was tilting at ecological windmills in a frantic effort to get the oil

---

* Some of the oil companies were so delighted with the editorial that they mailed it to their customers.

industry "to achieve domestic reliability." In a speech at the annual convention of the American Petroleum Institute in 1971, Morton had vowed to speed up the leasing of offshore acreage in the outer continental shelf. At the same convention, oil lobbyist Frank Ikard leveled a caustic attack at environmentalists, whom he called "the new prophets of doom." The United States, he said, needs a dependable flow of oil "to maintain diplomatic and political options in international affairs and in the cause of world peace and freedom."[79]

Using geophysical data derived by the government and the oil companies, Morton put several undersea territories on the auction block, all of which were snapped up by major producers. For example, an auction on September 12, 1972, on seventy-four oil-rich offshore tracts lying beyond the mouth of the Mississippi in the Gulf of Mexico, brought in $586.3 million, and the five giants, along with their various subsidiaries, ended up with about 95 percent of the 346,000 acres sold.[80]

Environmentalists did not oppose the auction because Morton persuaded them that to do so was not in the national interest during the energy crunch. The oilmen, their appetites whetted, were jubilant when Morton announced a new schedule of two auctions a year. Expressing the viewpoint of most oilmen, Ray W. Heggland, vice president of exploration for Continental Oil, said: "Environmentalists view the cleanliness of gas as important, and since blocking the lease sales is worsening the gas shortage, and leading to increased use of alternative fuels that are not as clean, they should be less opposed to the sales."[81]

Nothing churns an oilman's bile quicker than concern for ecology. The following excerpt from the *Wall Street Journal* spells out the industry's theme:

> Growing concern for environment and ecology is a major reason the industry isn't enlarging supplies in pace with demand, oilmen contend. Environmental controversies have stalled development of the Alaskan North Slope and offshore oil fields, they say, and ecological battles have blocked the building of U.S. supertanker ports, which would open the way to big savings on transportation costs for imported oil."[82]

Even without the supertankers, the President boosted import quotas twice in 1972, an increase of 15 percent in May and 35 percent in September, for an extra total of almost a million barrels a day—a daily bonus of about $1.5 million in refiner tickets. At this rate of increase, oilmen were gleefully predicting that by 1980 the United States would be importing about $20 billion worth of oil annually, almost a tenfold increase in the oil balance-of-payments deficit. Their prediction was supported by the Interior Department, which estimated that by 1985 the balance-of-payments deficit from importing crude oil and refined products could total $27.5 billion. No allowance was made for domestic discoveries or the development of alternative fuels. Yet the U.S. Geological Survey estimated the total potential supply of natural gas available in this country, including resources yet to be discovered, at 6,600 trillion cubic feet, enough for three hundred years at the current rate of use. The Survey's estimate of oil was even more impressive—enough for five centuries at the present rate of consumption.

Meanwhile, except for Alaska, oilmen were looking for oil everywhere but in the United States. Billions of dollars were spent in foreign countries in search of high-profit oil. Negotiations were open with China and the Soviet Union. President Nixon endorsed one of the largest potential trade agreements in history, a deal to buy $45.6 billion worth of natural gas from the Soviet Union. The agreement would also involve expenditures of about $10 billion for pipelines, liquefaction plants, port facilities, and supertankers. Two American consortiums (Tenneco, Texas Eastern Transmission, and Brown & Root versus El Paso, Bechtel Corp., and Occidental Petroleum) were negotiating for various pieces of the deal. For example, the El Paso-Occidental group was interested in piping gas from Yakutsk to the Vladivostok area for delivery to the West Coast of the United States. The Tenneco group was focusing on natural gas deposits in the Urengoi area that would be piped to the European Russian Arctic port of Murmansk, and from there to the Eastern Seaboard of the United States. Much of the construction work in Russia would be done by Brown & Root, and the twenty special LNG carriers would be built by Newport News Shipbuilding & Dry Dock Company, a subsidiary of Tenneco, and by Texas Eastern, at a cost of about $100 million apiece. They—along with the supertankers needed for the Alaskan pipeline—would be subsidized by the American taxpayer at a cost estimated eventually to run to several billion dollars. A large percentage of the money for construction in Russia would come from the U.S. Export-Import Bank. The architect of this superdeal was none other than John B. Connally. Although it means better relations with the Soviet Union, doesn't it, to borrow a phrase from George Lincoln, throw the national security gambit into a cocked hat?

Representative Les Aspin called it an "all-time bad deal" that would make the 1972 "fleecing in the Russian wheat deal look like a Sunday school picnic. . . . If the Arabs, many of whom are rabid anti-Communists, feel free to cut off the United States from supplies," Aspin said, "the Russians during any international crisis would do the same." Not only was it "plain stupid to become so dependent on the Soviet Union for our energy resources," but the price contemplated for the Soviet gas amounted to $1.25 to $1.50 per thousand cubic feet, compared with the domestic wellhead price of about 20 cents then in effect—by December 1973, the price had spiraled to 50.7 cents per thousand cubic foot. While the price of natural gas was expected to rise, Aspin said, "it is simply silly to get boxed into a price from the Russians that is 500 percent higher than we are currently paying."

Interior Secretary Morton was perfectly willing to spend billions on a Siberian pipeline, but he strongly opposed building one across Canada because the trans-Alaskan route, which is fraught with potential ecological disasters—it will traverse one of the most active earthquake zones in the world—is more in "our interest."* The Alaskan pipeline would stretch 789 miles, from Prudhoe Bay on the Arctic Ocean to the port of Valdez, on the state's southern shore. The trans-Canadian pipeline would proceed east from the North Slope, across the Yukon Territory to the Mackenzie River delta, then south to Alberta and on into the midwestern United States. It would be about four times longer, but it could be integrated with pipelines already connecting Alberta and the Midwest. Of even greater importance, it would parallel a pipeline planned to carry natural gas from the North Slope. For several years, environmentalists, who proposed the alternate Canadian route, successfully challenged the oil companies in the federal courts, but that came to an abrupt end with the Arab embargo in October 1973. The *coup de grâce* was executed a month later when Nixon signed the Alaskan pipeline bill, which removed all legal and environmental barriers.

Morton conceded that the ecological risks were greater across Alaska, but he joined with the oil companies in stressing national self-sufficiency. Oilmen said they feared a political clash between the United States and Canada. Mobil chairman Rawleigh Warner, Jr. warned that it was "a real possibility that the Canadian Government might very properly say to us: 'When we have as much oil as we want, you can put yours in.'" Morton supported this viewpoint, arguing for "a secure pipeline located under the total jurisdiction and the exclusive use of the United States." Donald S.

---

* Oilmen speak of the Alaskan pipeline as a greater achievement than the Great Wall of China. Aside from its technological elegance, the pipeline will form a barrier to animal migration that will forever change the ecological balance of the region.

Macdonald, the Canadian Minister of Energy, Mines and Resources, scoffed at the idea, pointing out that "the Americans could shut down all of Eastern Canada."[83]

"It has been known for some time that President Nixon personally leaned toward the speediest possible development of Alaskan oil," the *Wall Street Journal* reported on May 12, 1972. "National security considerations and a desire to hold down the adverse impact on the U.S. balance of payments that would result if equivalent oil supplies had to be obtained from the Middle East have influenced Mr. Nixon's opinion."

At the time of President Nixon's concern, 3 percent of all imported oil came from the Middle East. "Administration sources also suggest that Mr. Nixon, heeding the urgings of Treasury Secretary John B. Connally, was anxious to end the uncertainty that has confronted U.S. oil companies since they initially approached Washington with the pipeline proposal in 1969," the *Journal* continued. "Their investment in exploration for construction of the pipeline itself probably represents an investment of $2 billion or more at this point."

Even when viewed as an economic equation, the Canadian pipeline seemed a better way to go. An independent study found that it might even be more profitable because the companies could get at least 45 cents per barrel more for their crude oil in the Midwest than on the West Coast; it would also eliminate the need for costly port facilities, LNG plants, and tankers. Environmentalists could understand the oilmen's disregard for the fragile ecological balance of the Arctic region, but they puzzled over their lack of concern for profits until John M. Houchin, deputy chairman of Phillips Petroleum, prematurely tipped their hand before a congressional committee. Houchin said the consortium might want to sell some of the North Slope oil to Japan, a plan that would be ruled out by the Canadian route. The fact that the price of oil was lower in Japan was immaterial, Houchin said, because they were working on an "export-for-import" program.[84]

A spokesman for Phillips Petroleum later explained that Houchin's proposal was "made at a time when it appeared the West Coast would not be able to absorb the entire production of oil from the North Slope." New projections, however, indicated that Alaskan oil would just about make up the difference between supply and demand on the West Coast in the next decade. This raises an important question: How much United States oil are the giants pouring into world markets at low prices as they import foreign oil at high prices? The answer will not be found in API press releases.

For the better part of a year, through the shortages of the fall and winter of 1972 and the early spring of 1973, the nation patiently awaited the President's energy message. Throughout this period, the oil industry was adroitly molding public opinion in a massive tax-deductible advertising campaign—the API and AGA alone spent $12 million on three rapid splurges. The emphasis was on the industry's "good track record" in predicting likely disruptions of supply, as proclaimed in a Mobil ad: "Oil companies knew the shortage was coming. We knew how it could be averted."

"Corporate energy advertising improved self-fulfilling prophecy to the point where corporations predicted what their own behavior would be if they did not receive adequate incentives to act in a specific way," Emma Rothschild wrote in *The New York Review*, "and this confused but commercially effective prediction was, of course, not a prophecy but a threat."[85]

The oil industry's messages vacillate between insufficient refinery capacity created by the constraints of "doomsday" environmentalists, and the insufficiency of crude oil resulting from a lack of tax incentives. The companies took turns in selecting different sides of the coin. The ambiguity of the messages pointed up the flexibility of the oil industry's position.

By late fall of 1973 the campaign had snowballed into the oil industry's biggest propaganda blitz in history. Just four companies alone— Exxon, Shell, Texaco and Gulf—spent $22 million on corporate "image" ads—that was exclusive to the $115 million they spent on product advertising that year. This did not include the millions more spent by the other oil companies, or the expenditures by the API and AGA.

Representative Benjamin S. Rosenthal of New York told reporters that the oil companies were "spending millions of dollars in a not-so-subtle attempt to defuse public indignation over their price-gouging profiteering and attempts to discredit the environmental movement." Rosenthal, who was joined by five other Democratic members of Congress—Senators Birch Bayh of Indiana, Frank E. Moss of Utah and Thomas J. McIntyre of New Hampshire, and Representatives Andrew Young of Georgia and Les Aspin of Wisconsin—asked the Federal Trade Commission to make the companies substantiate their advertising claims.

The FTC investigation concentrated on five general claims:

—Congress and environmentalists have prevented drilling for oil and gas and have delayed construction of pipelines, refineries and deep-water ports.

—Government pollution restrictions, price controls, antitrust laws and tax policies must be changed to provide greater incentive for oil and gas production.

—The oil industry is doing all it can to provide fuel.

—The oil companies are doing their best to protect the environment.

—The fuel shortage in the United States is part of a worldwide crisis.

The FTC found all of these claims subject to challenge. Typical of the blatant distortions presented as facts by the companies was a Mobil ad entitled "An Open Letter (to lawmakers) on the Gasoline Shortage." It claimed: "The U.S. is short of refining capacity, and will be critically short in a year or two, as a result of erratic government import policies, environmental constraints, and inability to bring the largest, most economical tankers into U.S. ports. Oil companies had no control over this."

The facts are that the companies stopped building refineries in the United States because it is more profitable to build them overseas closer to rapidly expanding markets, particularly in tax-exempt sanctuaries such as the Caribbean, and because it affords them greater latitude in determining how much crude oil and petroleum products each country will receive. The Seven Sisters have not lost their control in the downstream operation—the Arabs play no role in the distribution process. The companies, which ultimately decide how much oil the United States receives, sell far more oil in foreign countries than at home. As to the "erratic import policies," it was the industry's lobbies, sparked by Michael Haider and Frank Ikard, that killed Nixon's first Cabinet Task Force when it voted to abolish the import quota system.

A Gulf advertisement, entitled "We Can't Talk Our Own Way Out of the Energy Crisis," clearly spelled out the provisions of the ransom to be paid for redemption. It proposed giving the oil industry a free hand to solve the energy crisis. It said in part: "Price controls over fuels should be eliminated. . . . Tax incentives are needed in the form of credits for research . . . tax-free bonds for environmental protection facilities. . . . Public lands should be made available for mining and drilling. . . . We must permit offshore drilling. . . . We must construct the Alaska pipeline. . . . Strip mining must be permitted. . . . A free market price system would encourage conservation. . . . As supply decreases, prices will increase. Increased prices will, in turn, stimulate more production. . . ."

Exxon's advertising slogan was "We'd like you to know," and Texaco's was "We're working to keep your trust." However, when the FTC suggested that the companies consent to opening a prehearing conference to the public, Exxon was not that anxious for the public to know, and Texaco thought it could best keep the public's trust by working behind closed doors.

The Administration's position, meanwhile, was notoriously familiar. Even before his promotion as energy czar, Deputy Secretary of the Treasury William Simon was complaining that "at present there are no new refineries underway," and that "this is in a period where all the refineries are operating at 100 percent of their effective capacities." This remark was followed by a sharp exchange with a reporter:

> Q. If the refiners are at 100 percent capacity, of what value and what will happen to the new crude oil that comes in here for refining?
> A. There are refineries inland that are not operating at 100 percent.
> Q. So your 100 percent was a very vague number?
> A. No, it wasn't vague. A great majority of them are functioning at 100 percent. . . .

"The energy crisis could well serve as a smoke screen for a massive exercise in picking the pockets of the American consumer to the tune of billions of dollars a year," charged S. David Freeman, director of the Ford Foundation's Energy Policy project and a former White House energy adviser, in an address to the Consumer Federation of America. "Energy is going to cost much more in the future . . . yet I hear few voices in Government raised to assert the consumer's concern in this critical area."[86]

Soon after the 1972 election, Secretary of Commerce Peter G. Peterson was proclaiming that "the energy strategies and programs the President presents next year will be fully equal to his initiatives to the Soviet Union and the People's Republic of China."

And why not! Henry Kissinger's staff had organized "paperwork" on the strategic aspects of energy policy, the *Wall Street Journal* reported, and planned to "float it around the State Department, Pentagon, CIA and other concerned agencies." Energy policy was presented as a major endeavor for the period "after Vietnam." "Suddenly, we've realized we should worry about energy problems," one Kissinger aide revealed. "We've been pondering which matters to stress over the next four years, and this is certainly one." The entire resources of the federal government was brought into play, including some sixty government reports, a Cabinet supercommittee, an energy overlord, and a White House energy coordinator trained by the U.S. Navy, plus Kissinger's secretariat.[87]

One of the prime movers behind the scenes was John Connally. "It was worth literally millions to Connally when Mr. Nixon, at his news conference of March 2, indicated that Connally would serve him as an unofficial adviser in the energy field," Joseph Kraft wrote in a *New York* magazine article.

The long-awaited message contained few surprises for the oil industry. The nineteen-page White House message offered a bundle of expected incentives designed to improve industry profits *now*—supply would come later. "In the years immediately ahead, we must face up to the possibility of occasional energy shortages and some increase in energy prices," Nixon said. Elsewhere in his message, he observed that if energy prices rise to reflect their "true costs" to consumers, it will be the "single most effective means of encouraging energy conservation."

Delivered on April 19, 1973, the President's message came at a time when oil industry profits were surging to record heights. First-quarter earnings were up 69.5 percent for Occidental, 24 percent for California Standard, 21 percent for Indiana Standard, 49 percent for Shell, 52 percent for Atlantic Richfield, 28 percent for Union Oil, 43.1 percent for Exxon, 25 percent for Amerada Hess, 20.6 for Getty Oil—in fact, all majors posted sharp gains. When Gulf Oil profits soared to 82 percent in the second quarter, the company's chairman observed that "our profits margins are getting back to levels that will again make investment in the oil industry attractive." When Freeze Two was imposed in June 1973, gasoline prices were at a level sometimes nine cents a gallon higher than they were in January that year. And the prospect for still higher prices looked promising, as shown in the remark of a Cost of Living Council official that "if our regulations [against oil inflation] are causing a supply problem, we'll change them. We don't want to aggravate the situation." Phase Four solved that problem by permitting increases in wholesale prices while denying commensurate increases in retail prices. This placed the burden of controlling inflation on retailers, the lowest bump on the economic totem pole. Who could object when the Cost of Living Council approved a series of retail price increases that prevented massive service-station closings? Behind the scenes, of course, it was the same old hassle between the oil companies and the dealers over profit margins. One thing was certain. The energy crisis had brought a quick cease-fire in the gasoline price wars. An independent with a dry pump is not competitive.

Responding to the threat of a "genuine energy crisis," Nixon urged Congress to end the Federal Power Commission's regulation of new natural-gas prices at the wellhead. Also to be decontrolled was the production of gas from wellheads on which contracts have expired. This would allow interstate gas prices to rise to marketplace levels, costing consumers billions in rate increases in the years ahead. All quotas and tariffs on imported oil were removed effective May 1, 1973, and a scaled system of "license fees" was substituted. Builders of new refineries will be allowed to import 75 percent of their crude-oil requirements free of the usual license fee of 21 cents per barrel for five years—an 18 percent subsidy that sent most majors into a constructive frenzy. Exxon immediately announced plans to increase its refining capacity by about 30 percent at a cost of $400 million.

Big oil did not mourn the death of the oil-import quota system. The system, which these many years had protected the giants from being inundated by cheap foreign crude, had finally reached the point of diminishing returns. As Secretary of the Treasury Shultz explained in a press briefing, foreign oil was no longer cheap, and so there was no longer a need to keep it out. There was no mention of national security.

Of particular delight to the oil industry was Nixon's order to the Interior Department to triple by 1979 the annual acreage leased on the federally owned Outer Continental Shelf, which may contain as much as 49 percent of the country's undiscovered oil and gas reserves. The expanded lease sales would include the Gulf of Mexico, the Santa Barbara Channel, the Gulf of Alaska, and the region off the Atlantic Coast. It was estimated that by 1985 this chain of drilling rigs could be supplying 16 percent of the nation's oil requirements and 20 percent of the natural gas needs. Michael McCloskey, executive director of the Sierra Club, called it a "drain America first" policy. "We should conserve our offshore oil resources until we know how to develop them and also protect the environment. There is nothing in the President's message to suggest this is what he intends to do."[88]

As an added incentive, Nixon proposed new tax deductions that would permit companies to write off 12 percent of the cost of producing wells and 7 percent of the cost of dry holes—this was above and beyond all other tax subsidies already in effect. The *Wall Street Journal* quoted the opinion of an oil analyst that "The tax credit was the only surprise in the energy message."

Point by point, the President's message adhered closely to the exhortations expressed in the oil industry's advertising campaign. He touched all bases, including ecology, with a request that the standards of the Clean Air Act be eased to permit greater use of high-sulfur coal which could not otherwise be used in 1975. The message warned that the 1975 deadline could prevent the use of up to 155 million tons of high-sulfur coal annually, threatening an estimated 26,000 coal-mining jobs. Moreover, it would take an additional 1.6 million barrels daily of foreign fuel oil to replace the coal, adding $1.5 billion to the nation's balance-of-payments deficit.

This was directly in line with Assistant Interior Secretary Hollis M. Dole's advocacy of a return to the use of coal as a source of energy. In December 1972, in a speech before a seminar on "Energy as a Scarce Resource," Dole had recalled that in 1920 coal provided 75 percent of the country's energy but by 1970 accounted for only 20 percent. For each ton of coal used, the United States could cut importation of four barrels of oil and would have 25,000 cubic feet of gas that could be put to other uses. "We have not run out of energy resources," he said. "We have run out of the initiative to exploit them and because we ran out of initiative a good many years ago we have at this point run out of time."[89]

Dole may have believed that the country had run out of time, but he knew that the oil companies had not run out of energy resources. For several years, the oil companies have been quietly buying up mineral and surface mining rights from the federal and state governments and private owners in an area designated by geologists as the Powder River Basin and the Fort Union formation, which covers, all told, 250,000 square miles, sprawling across the Old West (Little Big Horn, the Black Hills, the Cheyenne and Crow Indian reservations, Teapot Dome) from North Dakota to New Mexico. This tract holds the richest deposits of coal ever discovered, plus oil and uranium, and up to now the oil companies have sewn up 5.5 million acres at prices that environmentalists charge were a giveaway. "The whole deal smells like Teapot Dome," says a high official of the Environmental Defense Fund. "The energy companies got the Federal coal for peanuts—as little as $1 an acre from two national administrations. Now they are sitting back and laughing as people discover what has happened."[90] By late 1972, the companies (Continental Oil, Occidental Petroleum, Ohio Standard, Exxon, Mobil, Atlantic Richfield, Sun Oil,

Shell, Westmoreland, Peabody, Gulf, and Kerr-McGee*) held rights to strip-mine some 30 billion tons of coal, as much as the entire nation has produced since coal first came into use in 1702—and that is a modest beginning. The rape of Appalachia will seem benign by comparison to what is in store for this incredible trove of nature's bounty during the energy crisis of the 1970s.

"I can foresee a situation, not far off," former Senator Albert Gore warned in 1969, "when we will no longer have an independent coal industry. We will have all major energy sources—petroleum, coal, uranium—under the control of a very few powerful corporations."

At least eighteen oil companies are involved in the production and processing of uranium; the oil industry controls 45 percent of all known uranium reserves and accounts for one-sixth of uranium production. Atlantic Richfield and Kerr-McGee have exclusive rights in the conversion of "yellow cake," which produces UF6, used as nuclear fuel. The processing of uranium to fissionable isotope U-235 is done at government-owned gaseous diffusion plants at Oak Ridge, Tennessee, Paducah, Kentucky, and Portsmouth, Ohio, but there is a strong possibility that before the end of President Nixon's second term, these facilities will be sold to oil companies. The President announced his intentions during his first year in office. The plants will be sold "at such time as various national interests will best be served." Republican Senator George D. Aiken of Vermont observed, "The President probably feels indebted to those who helped elect him."[91]

In terms of what we know today, Nixon has every right to feel indebted to oilmen. As Representative Les Aspin revealed in January 1974, oilmen kicked in some $5 million of the $60.2 million *known* to have been raised for his reelection in 1972. That sum would not include the $268,700 contributed by Nelson A. Rockefeller and his brothers, all major stockholders in Exxon, or gifts by other principal stockholders of oil companies. "The big oil companies have Mr. Nixon in a double hammerlock," Aspin said. "After their massive contributions there is little he can do to control them."[92]

There is no question that Nixon has worked hard in their interest, leaving few cornerstones unturned in the process. In a special message to

---

* The late Oklahoma Senator Robert Kerr, a partner in Kerr-McGee, once remarked to his friend Bobby Baker that he was opposed to all monopolies unless he had a piece of them.

Congress in September 1973, one month before the Arab embargo, Nixon asked Congress to open up the Elk Hills naval reserve to commercial oil and natural gas production. To sweeten the deal, he proposed an exchange that would cancel leases for production in the Santa Barbara channel, making its underwater fields a naval oil reserve in return for operating Elk Hills.*

Nixon was not the first president since Harding to push a plan that would turn over to private interests the nation's naval oil reserves. His mentor, President Eisenhower, slipped a proposal into his 1959 Budget Message to Congress, suggesting a study to consider "the advisability of disposing of the anachronistic naval petroleum reserves." Eisenhower wanted "legislation to streamline procedures . . . for disposing of such obsolete [military] facilities and real property." Petroleum was an "inappropriate responsibility" for the Navy. Reminding the lawmakers that such federal lands were "exempt from state and local taxes," the President suggested that his plan would restore the property to the tax rolls.

At his press conference the following day, Eisenhower played down the significance of the proposed gift: "The whole problem of the naval reserves really belongs a long time back about into the Teapot Dome thing. It is really not an important matter today, as I see it." The constant bickering over the drainage of reserves into adjacent private fields, as well as the fact "that the nationwide, even worldwide, petroleum industry must be relied upon to provide efficiently for our petroleum requirements in both peace and war," had made the "worthwhileness of these reserves" questionable.

Writing about Eisenhower's plan in *Frontier* magazine, Gabriel Kolko noted that "The similarities between the recent problems of the oil reserves and those of the 1920s are striking. No evidence for bribery in the present case exists. But the threat of drainage into nearby fields has been effectively used as a bogeyman to open the fields to more intensive drillings in both instances. . . . But other than the bribery of high government officials, it is likely that the effect and intent of the President's recent proposal will be remembered by future historians more unfavorably than the Harding debacle. After all, even Fall, Sinclair, and Daugherty did not have the

---

* The 46,000-acre Elk Hills reserve near Bakersfield contains an estimated 1.3 billion barrels of oil, making it the richest known oil resource in California, and the third richest in the United States—the two richest are Alaska's Prudhoe Bay and the East Texas field. The Navy Petroleum Reserve consists of four reserves: Elk Hills and Buena Vista, California; Teapot Dome, Wyoming; and Northern Alaska, as well as three oil-shale fields in Colorado and Utah—a total of 24 million acres.

audacity to suggest the sale of the naval oil reserves, especially under the pretense of their being worthless real estate. Nor did the Harding regime militantly seek to lease the valuable public domain for pittances. . . . The real issue is the conservation and protection of the public lands, the wildlife refuges, and the common heritage of the American people from those business interests seeking profit from them. . . . It is still a historical fact that the quickest and often the easiest way to build a fortune in America has been by political means—land grants, government subsidies and contracting, tax depletion, and the like."[93]

Although Eisenhower's proposal failed, the oil companies stand a far better chance of realizing this multibillion-dollar bonanza during this latest squeeze play. Congress responded quickly to Nixon's call that "we act now to draw upon the oil available" in the Elk Hills reserve. Conservatives and liberals alike immediately jumped on the Administration's bandwagon. The Senate, voting sixty-seven to ten, adopted a resolution authorizing production of 160,000 barrels a day, and the House appropriated $65.5 million for its development and production.

John A. Love, then serving as presidential energy adviser, told the House Armed Services subcommittee that he was no military expert, but he doubted that there would be a conventional war of the kind that required special reserves: "To save the oil for some future contingency at a time when jobs may be lost, when some parts of our economy could suffer—this seems to me to be less than a perfect approach for the nation to take."

Secretary of Interior Morton, also appearing before the subcommittee, said that it would take several years to develop other energy resource programs. "Until they can make their impact," Morton said, "an immediate means of developing usable energy is sorely needed. The only domestic resource which matches this job description is Naval Petroleum Reserve No. 1 [Elk Hills]."

Morton took the opportunity to remind the lawmakers that the development of new energy sources was being held up partly because of cumbersome procedures required by the environmental law, and he urged Congress to revamp the procedures while avoiding "any real degradation of the environment." The proposal was greeted warmly by the panel members. "Basically, we're all environmentalists," Representative Leslie C. Arends of Illinois reminded his colleagues, "but maybe we have come to the time when we have to forgo some of that. Do we want to stay warm or look pretty?"

At this writing the only obstacle standing in the way of the oil companies was the panel's chairman, F. Edward Hebert of Louisiana, who had the resolution bottled up in his committee. A staunch defender of the military position, Hebert has vowed that "not one drop of oil will be taken from Elk Hills." However, a source on the committee said Hebert was going into the hearings "with an open mind."

If Hebert fails to stop the Nixon juggernaut, perhaps another scandal will—if it comes along in time. There were some glimmers early in January 1974 when Lieutenant Commander Kirby Brant, deputy director of the Naval Petroleum and Oil Shale Reserves, resigned because, as one congressional source quoted him as saying, "I have written my last lie" in support of White House policy on the reserves. Brant was known to believe that the energy crisis was one in a series of ploys by the Administration and the oil industry to open the naval reserves.

Yet there are still a few outspoken critics left in Congress. Representative John E. Moss of California, for example, testified before the Senate Commerce Committee that Elk Hills was a $10 billion property:

> The oil industry lusts for these riches. In no way can we depend upon the Interior Department to safeguard the public interest, for it has shown itself to be an adjunct of industry in such a matter as to constitute a public disgrace.
>
> The Navy is too intimidated to act aggressively against encroachers. The Justice Department is at best today a bulldog with rubber teeth, frightening only to those with an infinite capacity to rationalize.[94]

Finally, who will pay for the ravages to the land in the crisis years ahead? "Society has to pay for it," says S. A. Jagnoli, president of Gulf Mineral Resources Company, a division of Gulf Oil. "We passed on the short-term benefit of cheap fuels to the consumer. We've been on a fifty-year drunk. Natural gas and coal have been given away. Now society has to make a choice. If it doesn't want it, fine. But if it wants the fuels, it has to pay."

That is the way oilmen think. The "cheap fuels" brought them untold billions in profits, but the future would bring them rewards beyond their wildest dreams. There was no question that the Nixon Administration was opposed to cheap fuels. And no one was more in agreement with the oilmen and the Administration than William E. Simon, who headed the new super-agency, the Federal Energy Office, which was staffed with hundreds of oil company executives. A former Wall Street bond trader who amassed a personal fortune estimated at $34 to $38 million, Simon, like George Shultz, his boss at Treasury, is a dedicated believer in the conservative principles of free market economics. This belief has blinded him to the realities of oil economics, says Martin Lobel. "He thinks of the oil industry as being freely competitive. Look at that letter to the FTC. The fact is, we do have an oligopoly, an oil cartel."

Both Shultz and Simon have long stressed higher prices as the key to restraining energy consumption. Anybody who has bought gasoline or distillate products recently knows that they are men of their word—between January and December of 1973, prices of gasoline, diesel fuel and heating oil increased at least 50 percent, and jet fuel rocketed 345 percent. They believe that the only solution is to offer more economic incentives—that is, greater oil profits. It alone can lead to the increased domestic production of energy that will free this nation from future Arab blackmail. "I consider the consumer interest in this country of prime concern," Simon said, and that was why he declined to champion the continuation of relatively cheap fuels. The answer was simply higher energy prices. "Haven't we learned that by now?" he said. "I hope so. I suggest this is in the long-term interest of the public and the consumer."

His remarks were published in the Los Angeles *Times* on January 12, 1974, one day after the United States Export-Import Bank had approved a loan and financial guarantee of $100 million to five Arab nations—Egypt, Saudi Arabia, Kuwait, Abu Dhabi, and Qatar—to build two pipelines from the Gulf of Suez to the Mediterranean, by-passing the closed Suez Canal and enabling oil companies to avoid lengthy tanker voyages around Africa. How did this fare with Nixon's vow for energy self-sufficiency in three to five years? Representative Thomas M. Rees of California thought the arrangement gave the Arabs "even more leverage than they now have in their stranglehold on the individual oil-consuming nations of the world." If anyone needed a loan, at 6 percent interest, it was not King Faisal, et al., whose vast accumulations of major currencies were currently threatening the international monetary system.

Contradictions do not confuse oilmen or politicians. For example, in the abortive haggling over the emergency energy bill just before Congress adjourned for Christmas, Simon aggressively lobbied to kill provisions in the bill that would have required oilmen to disclose their reserves—even though Simon had often complained that the lack of independent information was a primary problem in the energy crisis. Three weeks later Simon ordered investigators to begin "auditing price, profit, and supply records of every petroleum refiner in the country." All of thirty-five IRS agents were assigned to conduct field audits. The desk audits, carried out in Washington, involved checks of company reports, not original records. "The program in no way reflects on the refiners," Simon said, "but it will assure us that they understand and are abiding by FEO regulations." That was fine, as far as it went, but what did refiners have to do with the shortage of crude oil and natural gas?

Was there really a shortage? Consider these facts. According to the Census Bureau, oil and gasoline exported from the United States in September and October, 1973, were five times the normal export traffic. The Bureau's records conveniently omit the identity of the sellers and buyers, nor do they list the selling price. The figures do not include the oil cargoes that were literally sold while the tankers were still on the high seas. Many tankers bound for the United States were diverted to Northern Europe, where the oil was sold at a higher price. As far as the Arab embargo was concerned, it appeared as phony as the rest of the energy crisis story. An analysis of statistics on tanker sailings compiled from Lloyd's of London shipping reports covering six large Arab ports picked at random showed that total sailings during the final quarter of 1973 were up 31 percent over the same period in 1972.[95] According to the *Economist*, an authoritative British magazine, tankers loading at Persian Gulf oil terminals in late November and early December rose 23 percent to 43 percent over a year earlier. United States Customs records showed that imports of foreign oil in Los Angeles, which was really put through the energy wringer, were 50 percent greater in 1973 than in 1972.

"Storage tanks are, in fact, full to the brim in northwest Europe, the east coast of the United States and in Italy," Platt's Oilgram, a daily price reporting service that monitors the worldwide activities of the oil industry, reported in mid-January 1974. It quoted a European oil trader as saying that the last three months had shown the " 'Arabs either cannot, or really didn't want to, pull off their embargo.' Even singled-out Holland has ended up with the fullest tanks of any of us, in short, the panic factor has ironed out the market." The Italian police had seized dozens of telegraph messages in a Rome refinery that were sent to oil tankers bound for that country. The messages urged tankers to go elsewhere because there was no more storage space for crude oil in Italy. In Genoa, Italy's largest oil port, Antonio Orlando, press office for the Genoa Port Authority, expressed the opinion that "the oil companies played a great deal on the Arab embargo to close off the taps of petroleum and get an increase in prices." Statistics for the Genoa port showed that imports for the last three months of 1973 were up 19 percent over the same period in 1972.

"If these and other reports we are getting are accurate, it could represent a conspiracy far greater than anything in the Teapot Dome scandal," Senator John V. Tunney told reporters early in 1974. "The figures lead one to believe that the oil companies are withholding oil from the market to jack up prices and maximize profits."

It was not long before Simon put a lid on government statistics concerning the importation of foreign oil. Basing the decision on grounds of national security, his edict stopped newsmen from tracing the massive leakage of Arab oil to the United States through previously available Commerce Department data. Simon, of course, surrounded as he was with oil executives, believed deeply in the energy crisis. "There is a real crisis," he pronounced early in January 1974, "and it has been brought home to the American people by the embargo and, as I have said quite often, my most difficult task will be once the embargo is over, to keep the American people awake to the fact that we are going to continue to have shortages, and subject ourselves to the economic and political blackmail of any foreign nation, both on the supply side and the price side."

This scenario, as columnist Ernest B. Furgurson has pointed out, might run into problems around April when the House Judiciary Committee approaches its vote on impeachment. "Stand by for a dramatic rescue," Furgurson wrote. "The hero, according to the White House scenario, is going to be none other than Richard M. Nixon, starring in yet another comeback role—Henry Kissinger, the co-star, already has tipped off the climax: The President, through valiant individual effort, is going to pacify the mustachioed villains of the energy crisis. Even now he is sending personal messages to the Arab chieftains and leaders of other major oil-producing and consuming nations. . . . Meanwhile, we can reasonably conjecture, the White House also is directing the supporting staff. William Simon, the energy czar, is to sow maximum confusion about how much gasoline prices are going up, and when—so that however much it is, it will be less than everybody feared. . . . Along about the vernal equinox, if not sooner, all these sacrifices and virtues are going to come together and the President is going to preempt 'Wild Kingdom' or some other show to tell us he has whipped the energy crisis and we and he can all live happily, if frugally, ever after. . . ."[96]

Time alone will tell the accuracy of Furgurson's prediction. As of January 19, 1974, Nixon was still promising to "do everything in my power to avoid rationing" and "with continued cooperation by everyone, we all have good reason today to hope for the best" but "if we should choose to believe that our efforts in fighting the energy crisis are unnecessary, if we permit ourselves to slacken our efforts and slide back into the wasteful consumption of energy, then the full force of the energy crisis will be brought home to America in a most devastating fashion and there will no longer be any question in anyone's mind about the reality of the crisis."

In a quarter-hour live radio broadcast from the Oval Office, Nixon promised to "do everything in my power to prevent the big oil companies from making unconscionable profits out of this crisis." In fact, if the FEO audit was "not satisfactory, I shall ask the heads of the major oil companies to meet with me personally in Washington so I can get the facts I need to make decisions." He would not, he said, "allow the American people to be victims of a snow job in a crisis which affects the jobs, the comfort and the very way of life of millions of Americans."

By the second week of January 1974, four congressional committees had announced plans to force the oil industry to prove that the energy crisis was real.* Senator William Proxmire urged Attorney General William B. Saxbe to take antitrust action against the eighteen integrated major oil companies. "There may be ample evidence of joint efforts by the major oil companies to share markets, restrict outputs, raise prices, deny crude to independent refiners and deny products to independent marketers, evidence to constitute an illegal conspiracy in violation of the Sherman Act. As the courts have held, there need not be a showing of an overt act to sustain such a criminal suit; circumstantial evidence may suffice. All that is required is that proof of such conscious concerted efforts existed beyond a reasonable doubt." The big oil companies, Proxmire complained, could "manipulate prices at various stages of the producing process" because they "control the production of oil from the time it comes out of the ground until the time it reaches the ultimate consumer."

Instead of responding directly to Proxmire's proposal, Saxbe told CBS-TV's "Face the Nation" that it would be reasonable to change laws or make other arrangements to allow oil companies to cooperate on improving the situation: "We've got some conflicts going on that are really—if they weren't so serious would be amusing, because Mr. Simon says to the oil companies, 'Now you get together and do this,' and they say, 'Get to-

* Senate Permanent Investigations Committee, House Small Business Select Committee, and subcommittees of the Senate Foreign Relations Committee and the Joint Economic Committee.

gether? If we even tip our hats to each other, why we're in big trouble with the attorney general.' So if we want them to get together, we're going to have to get together under a man from Mr. Simon's office or we're going to have to pass a law to give them some freedom to work together."[97] Saxbe's response did little to dispel Moss's description of the "bulldog with rubber teeth."

In December 1973 the Administration classified all oil extracted above the 1972 volume level as "new" crude and freed it from price controls. At the same time, "old" oil—that is, all domestic oil produced below the 1972 volume level—was permitted to rise $1 a barrel. The rationale was not all that original: the price increase would provide the incentive necessary to raise production in the fields. But the Administration was offering a different kind of incentive when it promised oilmen that it eventually would allow domestic prices to equal higher world prices.*

Representative John D. Dingell of Michigan, chairman of one of the investigating committees, blasted the decision. "The major oil producers," he said, "who are already getting record profit increases, have gotten a bonanza from this old oil price increase to the tune of $13 million a day, or $4.75 billion per year."

In testimony before Dingell's committee, John C. Sawhill, deputy administrator of the Federal Energy Office, admitted that there was a total lack of independent, verified information on energy matters. "The information we now have to work with is not adequate and its reliability cannot be checked," he said. "Today and in the years ahead we need better data on every aspect of energy—reserves, refinery operations, inventories and production costs."

Asked if they had proof that there was a conspiracy, Sawhill said: "No. I've heard these charges of rascality and other things. . . . We need more information." On the other hand, he had no evidence that there was a conspiracy to rig prices and violate antitrust laws.

"The American people have a right to know the truth about the energy situation," said Senator Henry M. Jackson, chairman of the Senate Permanent Investigations Committee. "We cannot expect people to line up for gasoline when there are allegations that storage tanks are full and there are

---

* On January 30, 1974, the Cost of Living Council lifted most price controls on petrochemical feedstocks, with the result that retail prices for most plastic, rubber and synthetic fiber products would soon reflect the change. "These price and profit increases are necessary," the council said, "to provide incentive to expand production and decrease the rate of exports of these vital products."

fully loaded tankers lying off many ports. . . . The public is about to revolt."

With some of the top officials of the seven largest oil companies lined up before the members of the Subcommittee on Permanent Investigations, Senator Abraham A. Ribicoff of Connecticut let fly with some direct language:

> You are reaping the whirlwind of thirty years of arrogance. . . . You have embarked on a program of redistributing the sale of oil, using the conditions we have, the shock and the fright, to squeeze out the independent dealers and smaller franchises throughout the nation. You have created a panic situation [and with respect to taxes and royalties, have formed] a conspiracy with the Middle Eastern states [to avoid $3 billion in U.S. taxes]. The time has come for Congress to move against the major oil companies.[98]

Joining in the rebuke, Senator Jackson, the committee's chairman, said:

> The American people want to know why oil companies are making soaring profits at a time when the government contends that only costs of production are allowed to pass through to the consumer [and] whether major oil companies are sitting on shut-in wells and hoarding production in hidden tanks and at abandoned service stations.[99]

Unfazed by the charges, the seven oil moguls blandly turned aside attacks, denied charges and asserted their need for even greater freedom and income. As to their current profits, they argued that they were far from being out of line. Profits in 1973 only looked high because 1972 had been a bad year. In fact, their chief lobbyist, Frank Ikard, told NBC's "Meet the Press" that the oil profits "have not been above the middle group of the business in America." When one of the interrogators noted that a Federal Trade Commission report showed that 1972 return on sales was 50 percent above the average for U.S. industries, Ikard replied, "I would exclude from any gauge, then, return on sales."[100]

What should be excluded from any gauge is any return based on invested capital. With oil computed as a capital asset, the figures on capital investment are so far out of line as to be ludicrous. As to the fiction that 1972 was a bad year, it should be recalled that profits soared to record heights in 1971. Net income for the seven companies (Exxon, Mobil, Texaco, Gulf, California Standard, Indiana Standard and Shell) as represented by their officials before Jackson's Subcommittee decreased only slightly in 1972, which was by any standard a very good year. Computed in terms of sales, and even those figures are dubious since oil companies are in the habit of including excise taxes collected from consumers in their totals, compare the profits of the seven oil companies with the profits of the top seven industrial firms (General Motors, Ford Motor, General Electric, IBM, Chrysler, ITT and Western Electric) as listed in *Fortune*'s Directory of the 500 Largest Industrial Corporations:

	1971		1972	
	SALES ($000)	NET INCOME ($000)	SALES ($000)	NET INCOME ($000)
OIL	54,502,642	4,564,941	58,820,843	4,374,309
OTHERS	83,796,157	4,821,962	95,384,862	5,828,774

If the above figures are impressive, the ones for 1973 are simply dazzling. With modest increases in sales, the net income of the seven oil giants zoomed to $7 billion. Exxon, the king of the hill, earned $2.4 billion, actually double its 1969 profits. Most of the others could boast of comparative increases. Figures for the other industrial firms were not available for comparison at this writing.

"Unpopular as it perhaps sounds today," Z. D. Bonner, president of Gulf Oil, told Jackson's panel, "profitability levels, in fact, will have to increase."[101]

"There is a total lack of public confidence in the oil industry," Jackson said, "in the federal agencies charged with regulating the industry, and in the validity of the spiraling costs of gasoline and heating oil."

Then, in typical political fashion, Jackson went from the sublime to the ridiculous, warning that "unless we make rational moves now, we are going to see in 1974 the most punitive legislation ever adopted by Congress affecting any one industry."

What the public could expect in 1974 was more of what it got in 1973. Whatever the outcome of the investigations, or, for that matter, the fate of Richard Nixon, oilmen will continue to get bigger, stronger, richer and even more politically pervasive.

CHAPTER 4

THE CHARITY GAME

It is the ultimate irony that the charitable foundation, that most prestigious of American institutions, was conceived in nothing more inspired than deathbed greed. Under the banner of philanthropy, great fortunes, amassed in ruthless exploitation of human rights and natural resources, were literally plucked from the clutches of the tax collector. With the palsied scratch of a pen, old robber barons grudgingly passed on their financial empires intact to heirs and in the bargain achieved corporate immortality.

Early in the century, in the days before high income and estate taxes, Mark Twain wrote: "Remember the poor—it costs nothing." How true then and how much truer today when the uncharitable rich man is faced with the loathsome alternative of having to bequeath to federal and state governments the lion's share of his worldly goods as he departs this best of all possible worlds.

No one ever accused Henry Ford I of being a soft touch. Biographers pretty much agreed that he was a crusty old man with an incredibly narrow and rigid point of view. He was abysmally ignorant, stubborn, bigoted, dictatorial, and miserly, totally unsympathetic to the welfare of his workers. For example, his pronouncement in 1937 that "We'll never recognize the United Auto Workers Union or any other union" was backed by a "service department" composed of six hundred goons armed with guns and blackjacks. Referring to this service department, the late Governor of Michigan Frank Murphy said: "Henry Ford employs some of the worst gangsters in our city." There is ample testimony in the records of the National Labor Relations Board of broken heads and limbs to prove that the boys in the service department earned their keep.[1]

The death of Henry Ford at the age of eighty-three in 1947 posed a unique dilemma for the company's experts in fiscal legerdemain. Henry's only son, Edsel, had died in 1943. Together they owned 96.5 percent of the stock of Ford Motors. The remaining 3.5 percent was held by Mrs. Henry Ford.[2] The elder Ford's death came at a most inopportune time. The New Dealers had jacked up the inheritance tax to 91 percent in the top bracket, and today's loopholes for marital deduction and estate splitting were not yet on the books. Edsel, whose share of the stock was equal to 41.5 percent, had the foresight to establish trust funds for his four children, but tightfisted Henry had successfully resisted all attempts to dilute his majority control of the company he had nurtured from a small-town bicycle shop into an industrial behemoth worthy of a king's ransom —and then some.

As matters stood at that crucial juncture, the government waited anxiously in the wings for its whopping 91 percent chunk of the estate— unless, of course, the experts should conjure up an eleventh-hour loophole.

Thus was born the Ford Foundation for Human Advancement.

As it happened, the Foundation was already in existence, having been incorporated by Edsel in 1936 with a $25,000 grant, but its impact had been minimal, its small grants going mainly to community projects in and around Detroit that were beneficial to the Ford Motor Company.[3] Even so, Henry had pointedly ignored his son's peculiar aberration. The Foundation's charter proclaimed lofty goals: "The purpose or purposes of this corporation are as follows: To receive and administer funds for scientific, educational, and charitable purposes, all for the public welfare, and for no other purpose . . ."

And so in the final analysis it was Edsel who provided the escape hatch to the tax problem. Consistently overruled by his father in life, Edsel gained his most important victory in death. His Foundation provided the means for the family to retain absolute control of the company, saving it from outside factions seeking control. Even more importantly, as far as Henry was concerned, it kept the money from the grasping hands of the hated New Dealers in Washington.

For Henry Ford, who spoke out freely against public benefactions, charity became the least of several far more odious evils. In this last desperate move (a model for thousands of smaller foundations), the Ford

Foundation received 88 percent of Ford Motor Company assets in the form of a new issue of convertible nonvoting stock, with the family retaining the voting stock. In his study of the Ford Foundation, Dwight Macdonald wrote: "On the Foundation's books, this [stock] was given the value, for tax purposes, of $416,000,000, but its real value, as measured by the earnings of Ford Motors, was at least $2,500,000,000."[4]

By this maneuver the family retained control of both Ford Motors and the Foundation. The two have worked hand in glove ever since. It is the family, wearing the company's hat, that decides how much dividends it will pay out to the Foundation for its stock holdings each year. And it is the family, wearing the Foundation hat, that selects the causes worthy of its largess, making sure in the process, of course, that the fabled goose's feathers are stroked, not ruffled.

The most sensitive point of controversy in foundation circles goes to the heart of the matter: Whose funds are the foundations dispensing— private or public money? A closer look at Ford economics might provide a clue. If Henry and Edsel Ford owed the government ninety-one cents on the dollar and through the creation of a foundation were able to deposit eighty-eight cents of that same dollar into the Foundation's till and the remaining twelve coppers into the company's, the answer is not really puzzling. Tax figures show that Henry and Edsel paid a combined inheritance tax (paid on property other than Ford stock) of approximately $30 million on total assets with a market value of more than $3 billion—a flat rate of 1 percent. Bear in mind also that no capital-gains tax was ever paid on the appreciation of the Ford stock that grew from zilch to its staggering capital assets under the aegis of Henry 1.[5]

After two decades of dispensing charity around the world at a cost of some $3.5 billion, the Ford Foundation still had assets of $3.2 billion at the end of fiscal 1971. Beginning in 1956, the Foundation decided to diversify its portfolio. Large blocks of stock were sold back to the company, which converted it to voting securities and gradually sold it to the public. There have been negotiated exchanges of stocks with other corporations, and some stock was used for the company's executive retirement plan. By 1969 the Foundation had reduced its share of Ford's outstanding stock to 25 percent. At that time it listed its holdings of stocks, bonds, and securities in 171 companies—only eleven of its holdings were valued at less than a million dollars. A quick look at some of the holdings, which covered seventeen pages in the Foundation's financial statements, clearly demonstrates its economic muscle: $118,369,438 in oil stocks, $122,-

701,600 in utilities stocks, $88,567,263 in business and electrical equipment, $70,524,675 in banks and finance, $49,019,876 in chemicals, $81,387,621 in consumer products, $8,994,375 in the New York *Times*, $2,917,688 in Time Inc., $2,200,000 in the Columbia Broadcasting System; plus shares in seven major airlines, and a small piece of the military-industrial complex, with $6,254,750 in the Boeing Company, $6,714,583 in Litton Industries, Inc., and $1,496,000 in Lockheed Aircraft Corporation. Included among its holdings were $350,656,969 in government and other bonds. Its portfolio is so enormous that market fluctuations can shave off as much as four-fifths of a billion in a single year (from $3,846,-000,000 in 1965 to $3,051,400,000 in 1966); market declines in 1969 cost it $678,000,000.[6]

Who is more beloved than the philanthropist? His beneficence is fantasized in the press with mindless repetition. Nothing quite touches the heart of the poor like the charity of the rich. It is an act of faith, a public absolution, a final reaffirmation that the free-enterprise system still works, that the American dream lives on in the reflected magnanimity of men like Rockefeller, Mellon, Pew, Carnegie, and Ford. That these same men spewed their life juices in the cannibalistic ritual of amassing corporate profits at incalculable cost to the world around them is of little moment in the face of such overwhelming personal sacrifice. This myth, like all popular myths, defies rational explanation.

Wherever Howard Hughes hangs his cloak, that is where charity begins —and ends. In the words of Noah Dietrich, the accountant who supervised the Hughes dominion for thirty-two years, Hughes "never had any friends. He didn't want any friends. He never did a humane act to my knowledge, except with an ulterior motive."[7] In his review of Dietrich's book on Hughes,[8] Rich Thomas criticized the biography for not coming to grips with Hughes's misanthropy: "His role in Hughes's strange story was hardly a pretty one, and he lists a weird melange of reasons for turning Boswell as well as henchman. . . . But Dietrich and his collaborator, Bob Thomas, seem to have missed their own most obvious central fact about Howard Hughes: an appalling lack of humanity. If he is a recluse, it is not only because of phobia; it is mainly because he doesn't care about people. The horror is that at the center of the mystery, there is no one. The heart of darkness is an empty hotel room."[9]

Now consider the Howard Hughes Medical Institute, a bona fide tax-exempt charitable foundation organized "primarily" to do medical research. Incorporated on December 17, 1953, it has had a fascinating history, one that was completely ignored until Representative Wright Patman cast a curious and suspicious glance in its direction.

Patman was born in Patman's Switch, Texas, on August 6, 1893. His fiery Southern Populist zeal against Wall Street bankers and Big Business has not cooled in forty-five years in Congress.[10] As chairman of the House Subcommittee on Small Business,[11] Patman launched not only the most exhaustive but actually the only meaningful probe of foundations ever conducted by Congress, or, for that matter, by any other investigative body. Patman began his crusade with an ambitious premise:

> I am . . . concerned with, first, foundation-controlled businesses competing with small businessmen; second, the economic effect of great amounts of wealth accumulating in privately-controlled, tax-exempt foundations; third, the problem of control of that capital for an undetermined period—in some instances perpetuity—by a few individuals or their self-appointed successors; and fourth, the foundation's power to interlock and knot together through investments, a network of commercial alliances, which assures harmonious action whenever they have a common interest . . .[12]

For Patman, who also served as chairman of the House Banking and Currency Committee, the study of foundations was a natural evolution in his lifelong opposition to the monopolistic practices of the economic royalists, the "pious phonies" who controlled Wall Street and the banking community. As far as he was concerned, foundation trustees and bank directors were cut from the same cloth: "You can't tell Brand X from Brand Y, they're the same people."[13]

Before long Patman had verified his worst fears. At the end of 1962, he published his findings in a 135-page report, the first in a series to follow over the next ten years.[14] There was nothing timid about his first report:

> On the basis of our discoveries thus far, and in view of the rapidly increasing number of tax-exempt foundations, I strongly urge the Secretary of the Treasury to declare an immediate moratorium on granting exemptions to foundations and charitable trusts until such time as the Congress has an opportunity to consider and develop new laws and procedures to fit present day economic circumstances and needs. . . . How can the Treasury Department possibly justify continuing to wring heavy taxes out of the farmer, the worker, and the small businessman, knowing that people of large means are building one foundation after another, and—for all the Treasury knows—for the purpose of decreasing their taxes, eliminating competition and small business, subsidizing antidemocratic propaganda, and otherwise working a hardship on the Nation?[15]

It was a devastating indictment, considering the magnitude of the investigation. Assets of the 534 foundations included in the study totaled more than $10 billion at the end of 1960, and their aggregate untaxed receipts averaged more than a billion dollars a year. And it was only the tip of the iceberg. The Internal Revenue Service had reported an increase in numbers of foundations from 12,295 at the close of 1952 to a total of 45,124 at the end of 1960. The list was revised down to 30,262 in 1968, a figure disputed by the Foundation Center, the trade organization for foundations, which placed the total at 22,000. Then in 1972 IRS again revised its figures, back upward to 42,000, and estimated their total assets at about $50 billion. The fact of the matter was that nobody knew for certain just what was out there, although all the foundations enjoyed tax-exempt status. Any serious attempt to estimate their total assets tends to border on the ridiculous. Few foundations carry assets on their books at market value. For example, just to name two: the Hearst Foundation, Inc., of New York, listed its holdings in Hearst Corporation stock at $1—a dollar that produced $500,000 in dividends. The James Irvine Foundation recorded the value of its stock in the Irvine Co. at $2, yet it represented 53 percent of the common stock in a company whose holdings included 88,000 acres of prime land in Southern California reportedly valued at $1 billion.[16]

In the beginning for Howard Hughes, there was only the Hughes Tool Company ("Toolco" to the initiated), which he inherited in 1924 at the age of eighteen. Although the company's market value was fixed at only $1.3 million, his legacy included something far more valuable. In 1908 his father had devised and patented a conical drill bit with 166 cutting edges that could bore through rock shale as though it were cardboard. The patent was the capstone of the Hughes empire. The patent expired in 1953, but not until the bit had been used for approximately 75 percent of all drillings throughout the world. It was available for lease only at a fee per well, wet or dry, of $30,000. "We don't have a monopoly," Hughes once said. "People who want to drill for oil and not use the Hughes bit can always use a pick and shovel." This was obviously an ideal position. Having started out with a monopoly, Howard Hughes would strive his whole life to dominate all within his reach. He was a natural-born capitalist.[17]

Still his legacy was certainly a far cry from the $2-billion financial complex he ruled in 1972. There is no rational explanation for this phenomenon. A gambler would say he had that magic touch. Everything he touched turned to gold, regardless of the chaotic conditions prevailing at the management level. His rule at Trans World Airlines was once characterized by a departing company president as comparable operationally to the government of Honduras. Those were the days when Hughes was frustrating corps of engineers, scientists, and executives with his procrastination, fanatical obsession with minutiae, incessant meddling, and extraordinary inaccessibility, and when he was also playing the role of the eccentric to the hilt. There were people "standing by" in various places throughout the world collecting fabulous fees, waiting for his summons, day or night, which never came—though there were occasional checks on their ready availability. There were business conferences in men's rooms and nocturnal rendezvous by flashlight in deserted parking lots, along country roads, and even in a city dump. There were nightclub appearances in baggy pants and sneakers to order a sandwich. There were germs everywhere, and employees who wore rubber gloves (one pilot was wrapped in a cellophane suit two weeks while awaiting the call) and a boss who shuffled around with his feet stuck in empty Kleenex boxes. And finally there were invisible enemies, like germs, out to destroy him. He did not like to go outside.

The Hughes Aircraft Company was a classical example of Hughes's magic touch. Founded as a sort of glorified hobby shop for tuning up racing planes, it got its impetus as a going concern during World War II. It was one of the great boondoggles of the war. Though it received $60 million in government warplane contracts, it produced not a single plane for the war effort. However, there was more than magic involved here. Hughes's eccentricity never clouded his capitalistic judgment on politics— there was no question in his mind that everybody had his price, a premise he proved many times over.

In 1947 Hughes's wartime "public-relations man," Johnny Meyer, was asked to explain his *modus operandi* before the Senate's Special Committee to Investigate the National Defense Program, chaired by Senator Owen Brewster of Maine. His job, Meyer said, was to "pick up the check" for Hughes when army officers came into town: hotel suites, restaurants, nightclubs, racetracks, women, booze, coast-to-coast transportation, outright gifts, anything that could be squeezed under the heading of public relations. The tab from 1942 to 1945 was $169,661.17 in itemized expenses, plus untold thousands of dollars never explained.

Hughes's own response under cross-examination was plaintively simple: "All the aircraft companies were doing the same thing," he said in defense of his entertainment policy. "I believe Meyer patterned his work after what he saw in other companies. I don't know whether it's a good system or not. But the system did obtain. And it certainly did not seem fair for all of my competitors to entertain while I sat back and ignored the government and its officials. . . . You, Senator, are a lawmaker, and if you can pass a law that no one can entertain army officers and you can enforce it, I'll be glad to abide by it. I never wanted to bother with it. If you can get others to do business that way, I'll be glad to do so, too."

After the war Hughes Aircraft gave up on airplanes to specialize in electronics. It hired a platoon of retired generals and staffed its research department with a regiment of young scientists (more than 3,300 Ph.D.s at one time) headed by Dean Wooldridge and Simon Ramo. By 1953 the company had grown into one of the largest electronics firms in the world, its resources devoted almost exclusively to government contracts—the backlog was an astonishing $600 million. Yet chaos prevailed at every level of management. Finally, in July of that year, unable to get any satisfaction from Hughes, Wooldridge and Ramo left to form their own company—Ramo–Wooldridge. Charles "Tex" Thornton and Roy Ash, as noted in Chapter One, left at about the same time to start a small firm that grew into Litton Industries.[18]

The exodus of executives caused alarm in Washington. Noah Dietrich explained what happened next: Secretary of the Air Force Harold E. Talbot gave Hughes a "dressing down such as Howard had never heard before. 'You personally have wrecked a great industrial establishment with gross mismanagement! I don't give a damn what happens to you, but I am concerned for this country. The United States is wholly dependent on Hughes Aircraft for vital defense systems. It would take at least a year to set up alternative sources of supply. That could be a national tragedy. It was a terrible mistake entrusting the nation's security to an eccentric like you!' "[19]

And there was more trouble, equally disturbing to Dietrich. Suspecting there had been overcrediting of the inventory accounts, Dietrich discovered in a special audit that the government had been overcharged by $43 million.

It was at this point in time that Howard Hughes ventured into the charity business. It was a bold and brilliant move. The plan was devised by his Houston attorney, Tom Slack, and the idea was to create the illusion that a public trust, the Howard Hughes Medical Institute, was in control of Hughes Aircraft. Among other things, it would remove the objectionable element (to wit, Howard Hughes) from under the guns of the Pentagon establishment.[20] (To simplify matters, hereafter the three entities will be referred to as Toolco, Aircraft, and Institute.)

If the transactions that follow appear complicated, it must be remembered that fiscal clarity was probably not Hughes's first consideration. As noted before, in the beginning there was only Toolco. All of its stock was owned by Howard Hughes. It was the vehicle by which Hughes controlled everything else. On December 17, 1953, the Institute was incorporated, and it, in turn, on the same day, incorporated Aircraft. The Institute's charter vested control in a single trustee, Howard Hughes, with life tenure and power to name his successor. As outlined by Patman, a series of intricate steps were executed on December 31 that year:

1. Toolco contributed to the Institute the patents, trademarks, and goodwill of Toolco's aircraft department, including the name Hughes Aircraft Co. These items were on Toolco's books for $37,000.

2. Toolco leased to the Institute for 10 years and 6 months certain real estate of the aircraft department and certain tangible fixed assets costing Toolco $26 million. The rental was to be primarily the amount of depreciation Toolco is allowed for tax purposes on the leased assets. The lease is carried on the Institute's books at $1.

3. Toolco sold to the Institute $74 million book value of assets of its aircraft department. These assets consisted primarily of cash, receivables on U.S. Government contracts, and inventories. Contracts with the U.S. Air Force were transferred by Toolco to the Institute. Toolco owed on these assets $56 million [up from the $43 million found by Dietrich in 1952], most of which was for renegotiation of Government contract prices. To pay for the $74 million of assets, the Institute assumed the $56 million of liabilities, gave Toolco a note for the balance of $18 million. The note was payable in 3 years with interest at 4 percent. The Institute put up all the Aircraft stock as collateral for the note.

4. The Institute contributed to Aircraft the patents, trademarks, and goodwill that Toolco contributed to the Institute.

5. The Institute subleased to Aircraft the assets the Institute leased from Toolco. The sublease term was likewise 10 years and 6 months. The sublease rent called upon Aircraft to pay an aggregate of $33,600,000, of which $4,700,000 a year was to be paid in the first 3 years, and $2,600,-000 a year in the next 7½ years. These terms were patterned after terms Toolco had previously been negotiating with Lockheed, but that deal fell through.[21]

As to Hughes's ever selling out to Lockheed or anybody else, Dietrich had his doubts: "Howard's pride of ownership seldom allowed him to part with any of his holdings. . . . The trouble was that he enjoyed negotiating. He loved to hold clandestine meetings and discuss deals in the hundreds of millions of dollars. He enjoyed the negotiating so much that he didn't like it to end. And so the talks would go on and on until the exhausted negotiator finally had to conclude that he wasn't really serious about selling. He was simply "counting his chips"—determining how much Hughes Aircraft was worth."[22]*

> 6. The Institute transferred to Aircraft the $74 million book value of assets bought from Toolco. Aircraft assumed the $56 million of liabilities that Toolco originally owned on those assets. For the other $18 million, Aircraft issued its stock to the Institute. Cutting through all this paperwork, the Institute books showed the end of the road to be as follows: Its "capital" was the $37,000 initially contributed to it by Toolco. It carried at $1 the leasehold from Toolco. The Institute also had the Aircraft stock, carried at $18 million, but pledged against a corresponding note liability to Toolco of $8 million.[23]

The first thing that happened was that Toolco claimed a tax deduction of $2 million in 1953 for its charity to the Institute—that is, Toolco saved more than a million dollars in corporate taxes on the very day (December 31) the Institute was born. Many other good things were to follow, but first there was the question of the Institute's application for tax exemption, filed with the Internal Revenue Service on June 1, 1955. Much depended on that piece of paper. The bad news came on November 29, 1955, when the IRS denied the exemption on grounds that the "whole setup was merely a device for siphoning off otherwise taxable income to an exempt organization, and accumulating that income." On March 26, 1956, the Institute filed a protest to that ruling.[24]

Without getting unduly mired down in the machinations of the Hughes-Nixon "loan," consider these basic facts. In December 1956, only weeks after the landslide re-election of Vice-President Richard M. Nixon, Noah Dietrich got a telephone call from Frank J. Waters, a Hughes attorney and Washington lobbyist. "I've been talking to Nixon," he said. "His brother Donald is having financial difficulties with his restaurant in Whittier. The Vice-President would like us to help him." "Help him in what way?"

---

* Hughes surprised his watchers in late 1972 by selling the Oil Tool Division of the Hughes Tool Company in a public offering of five million shares at $30 apiece for $150 million cash. The company was then renamed the Summa Corporation.

Dietrich asked. "With a loan." "How much?" "Two hundred and five thousand dollars."[25]

Although he was used to Hughes's "penchant for dabbling in political favors," Dietrich was uneasy about the request. Even when Hughes called and told him, "I want the Nixons to have the money," Dietrich still did not like it, especially when he learned that the collateral for the loan was a small parcel of land in Whittier, assessed at $13,000 for tax purposes. No one was to be held liable for the repayment of the loan if it went into default; the Nixons would simply surrender the property.[26]

Thoroughly convinced that the loan was a serious mistake, Dietrich took matters into his own hands and flew to Washington for a meeting with the Vice President.

"About the loan to Donald," Dietrich began. "Hughes has authorized it, and Donald can have it. I realize that it involves a loan to your brother and not to you. But I feel compelled to tell you what's on my mind. If this loan becomes public information, it could mean the end of your political career. And I don't believe that it can be kept quiet."

Nixon's response was immediate: "Mr. Dietrich, I have to put my relatives ahead of my career."[27]

On March 1, 1957, only three months after Don Nixon got his loan, the IRS reversed itself and ruled the Institute was indeed deserving of its desired tax-exempt status.[28]

How many coincidences is a politician entitled to before two and two add up to four? Until Noah Dietrich wrote his book in 1972, no one knew for certain whether Richard Nixon had been personally involved in the loan scandal. In his book, *Six Crises*, published shortly before his ill-fated attempt at the California governorship in 1962, Nixon offered this gentle tug at the heartstrings in explanation of the episode:

> Now, it really was all over [the 1960 presidential campaign]. Pat, Julie and Tricia, and I walked together down the corridor to the elevator. On the way, we stopped to say good-by to my mother and my brother, Don. Over and over again in the days and weeks ahead I was to find that the hardest thing about losing is not how it affects you personally but to see the terrible disappointment in the eyes of those who have been at your side through this and other battles. It was particularly hard for Don. During the last days of the campaign, the opposition had resurrected the financial trouble which had forced him into bankruptcy two years before and *had tried to connect me* [emphasis supplied; notice that no denial was offered] with a loan he had received from the Hughes Tool Co. during that period. They had, of course, conveniently ignored the fact that my

mother had satisfied the loan by transferring to the creditor a piece of property which represented over half her life savings and which had been appraised at an amount greater than the loan.[29]*

Asked by a Los Angeles *Times* reporter at the outset of the 1962 California campaign what he would do if the Hughes loan were raised against him in the fall, Nixon's reply was grim: "I'll dump a load of political bricks on anyone who tries to use it." Advisers to Governor Edmund G. Brown counseled a delicate approach. They were convinced that Nixon was deliberately laying the foundation for another Checkers speech, this time with his mother as Exhibit A. As one politician observed, "He will don the robes of a righteous, avenging son, rushing to defend the honor and good name of his mother."

Nixon got his opportunity on October 1 before a televised meeting of United Press International editors and publishers in San Francisco. It was the only joint appearance of Nixon and Brown in the campaign. When asked by a reporter whether it had been "proper . . . morally and ethically" to have permitted his family to receive a secret loan from a major defense contractor, Nixon was advised by the moderator that he did not have to answer the question. But Nixon was ready for it:

> As a matter of fact, I insist on answering it. . . . I welcome the opportunity of answering it. Six years ago, my brother was in deep financial trouble. He borrowed $205,000 from the Hughes Tool Company. My mother put up as security for that loan practically everything she had—a piece of property, which to her, was fabulously wealthy and which now is producing an income of $10,000 a year to the creditor.†
>
> My brother went bankrupt six years ago. My mother turned over the property to the Hughes Tool Company.‡ Two years ago at the presidential election, President Kennedy refused to make a political issue out of my brother's difficulties and out of my mother's problems, just as I refused to make a political issue out of any of the charges made against the members of his family.
>
> I had no part or interest in my brother's business. I had no part whatever in the negotiation of this loan. I was never asked to do anything by the Hughes Tool Company and never did anything for them. And yet, despite President Kennedy refusing to use this as an issue, Mr. Brown, privately, in talking to some of the newsmen here in this audience, and his

---

* This appraisal estimate was sheer fantasy.

† Don Nixon used $40,000 of the loan money to build a gasoline station on the land which was leased to Union Oil at $800 a month. No interest was charged, but even so the $9,600 annual repayment was still less than a normal interest rate.

‡ Los Angeles County tax records at that time still showed Mrs. Hannah Nixon as the legal owner of the property—the deed had not been recorded by Toolco.

hatchetmen have been constantly saying that I must have gotten some of the money—that I did something wrong.

Now it is time to have this out. I was in government for fourteen years as a Congressman, as a Senator, as Vice-President. I went to Washington with a car and a house and a mortgage. I came back with a car and a house and a bigger mortgage.*

I have made mistakes, but I am an honest man. And if the Governor of this state has any evidence pointing up that I did anything wrong in this case, that I did anything for the Hughes Tool Company, that I asked them for this loan, then instead of doing it privately, doing it slyly, the way he has—and he cannot deny it—because newsmen in this audience have told me that he has said, "We are going to make a big issue out of the Hughes Tool Company loan."

Now, he has a chance. All the people of California are listening. Governor Brown has a chance to stand up as a man and charge me with misconduct. Do it, sir![30]

Brown could only sputter inanely in return. It was the high point of the Nixon campaign. Polls taken immediately afterward showed him leading on the basis of his answer to the loan question. Like Howard Hughes, Richard Nixon had an uncanny ability for turning defeat into victory. In retrospect, his defeat in California was the turning point in his inexorable journey to the White House.

As far as Howard Hughes was concerned, he had what he wanted. The tax exemption was retroactive to December 31, 1953, saving him the million-plus dollars for 1953, plus savings in actual taxes of $275,078 in 1954 and $207,619 in 1955. And, naturally, all that the future would allow. The $18-million note payable by the Institute to Toolco, due on December 31, 1957, was not paid. Its maturity was extended until 1959, at which time a new note, bearing 4.5 percent interest, was issued, and it has been extended on a year-to-year basis ever since.

From 1954 through 1961, the Institute collected $26 million in rent from Aircraft, and it in turn paid Toolco $11 million in rent, plus $6 million washed back to Toolco as interest on its $18-million note.[31]

---

* This was true in 1962. Nixon's first Washington home cost $40,000, paid in part with money from the $18,000 secret fund the "millionaires' club" had donated for his personal use and which culminated in his famous Checkers speech. His next home was the palatial residence of the late Attorney General Homer S. Cummings, assessed at around $75,000. But in 1962 his home in Truesdale Estates, a subdivision in Beverly Hills developed by the Murchison brothers of Texas with a Teamsters pension fund loan, was a $250,000 "Hollywood" monstrosity with a colonnade one hundred and ten feet long and twelve feet high.

Throughout this period, Aircraft was involved primarily in government contracts, under cost-plus-fixed prices that were subject to renegotiation. "I wonder whether the ring-around-rosy that took place on December 31, 1953," Patman inquired, "really didn't have something entirely different behind it, and that is, renegotiation. Through the lease and sublease, Aircraft wound up paying $15 million more in rent than Toolco would have had in depreciation and other charges for the leased assets if Toolco had stayed put. The $15 million will become a higher figure by the time the sublease expires. Aircraft has big contracts from the Government. Wasn't the effect of these transactions to step up costs on Government contracts for Aircraft by this $15 million? To put it another way, by the steps taken on December 31, 1953, didn't Howard Hughes save $15 million from renegotiation?"[32]

According to the law, a foundation must be organized "exclusively, and operated exclusively," for charitable purposes. The wording in the Hughes charter states it was organized "primarily" for charity (medical research). Addressing himself to this problem, Patman concluded that the foundation did not qualify for tax exemption:

> Does a charity start off with buying $75 million of commercial business assets and assuming liabilities of $56 million, plus becoming directly liable for $18 million on its own note? This sounds more like high finance to me than charity. . . . The charter does authorize conducting a business, provided that the business is substantially related to the charitable purpose. No one will seriously contend that the business of Aircraft is substantially related to medical research. . . . The law says that exempt organizations must pay a tax on unrelated business income. The leasing to Aircraft is certainly unrelated to medical research. Rentals from real property are exempt from this law. The Institute does not own real property. It merely owns a leasehold. That would make the $15 million net rentals between 1954 and 1961 taxable to the Institute. Even if real property was involved, I think there would still be a tax because the Aircraft sublease is a business lease and the Institute has indebtedness against it. While on paper there were separate transactions of gift, lease, and sale by Toolco to the Institute, the tax law approaches things in a practical way. All transactions on December 31, 1953, were obviously a package deal, interdependent and concurrent. . . . In other words, every asset acquired by the Institute carried with it a corresponding indebtedness.[33]

It was Patman's contention that the Institute was taxable on 100 percent of its rental income until the $56 million (75 percent of the indebtedness) was paid off or renegotiated. It would then be taxable on 25 percent of the rental income.

During this eight-year period no dividends were ever paid by Aircraft to the Institute. Accumulated earnings after taxes amounted to $76,-955,000, plus $3,300,000 that the Institute accumulated from its rent income after expenses. With Hughes in sole control of both Toolco and the Institute, he could keep the Institute locked in that way as long as he wanted. "Certainly," Patman charged, "Congress did not intend to permit, through the simple device of a 100 percent owned subsidiary, that there be an end run around the restriction on unreasonable accumulation of income."[34]

Whether Congress intended it or not, the fact remains that foundations offer one of the greatest dodges in the long list of tax-game loopholes. Howard Hughes was not alone in milking the blessings of charity for personal gains. He was in elite company. But first a final word on the Institute.

By the end of fiscal 1968, the latest date that comprehensive figures were available, the accumulated earnings held by Aircraft amounted to $134 million. No dividends were paid in the fifteen years of its existence. And except for expenses incurred in maintaining the Institute, not one red cent was spent on charity.[35]

Hughes was more generous with politicians. Dietrich estimated his annual contributions at between $350,000 and $400,000. It took in the whole gamut of political offices, from tax assessor to President. In an effort to circumvent the Corrupt Practices Act, which prohibits American corporations from making political contributions in national elections, Dietrich funneled the funds through a Canadian subsidiary set up for that specific purpose—the law does not apply to foreign subsidiaries of U.S. corporations. "It was a curious operation," Dietrich recalled. "Money from the use of Hughes drills in Canada flowed to the Bank of America branch in West Hollywood and thence to politicians' coffers from Sacramento to Washington." That was the precise route taken by the $205,000 loan.[36]

Robert Maheu, Hughes's surrogate during his four-year stay in Las Vegas, also learned something about his boss's affinity for politicians. On March 14, 1968, Hughes was already focusing on the presidential election. "Bob, as soon as this predicament is settled," he wrote, alluding to the license application for the Stardust Hotel then under consideration by the Nevada Gaming Control Board, "I want you to go to see Nixon as my special confidential emissary. I feel there is a really valid possibility of a Republican victory this year. If that could be realized under our sponsorship and supervision every inch of the way, then we would be ready to follow with [Governor Paul] Laxalt as our next candidate [for Howard Cannon's Democratic Senate seat in 1970]."[37]

Two months later, with the presidential primaries in full swing, Hughes and Maheu were carefully looking over the field of local and national candidates. "Please don't have any apprehension about any of these items," Hughes wrote Maheu. "I am very realistic and you may be sure we will do more than any of these men had hoped for from us. I will give you the detailed numbers to permit an outright firm commitment whenever you tell me you feel like it is time to do so. I am sort of anxious to know whom we are going to support for President and how much, because I believe these others you mention should bear some relationship to our contribution toward the White House candidate."[38]

Because of the Watergate committee and the $17.3-million libel lawsuit filed against Hughes by Maheu,* many of the rumors concerning the "detailed numbers" of Hughes's political generosity have now been confirmed by sworn testimony. In a deposition made in connection with his lawsuit, Maheu unloaded more information than Hughes's attorney could reasonably appreciate. "One time in 1967 I showed Mr. Holliday," Maheu said, referring to Raymond M. Holliday, executive vice president of the Hughes Tool Company, "a handwritten memorandum from Mr. Hughes wherein Mr. Hughes was asking me to make a million-dollar payoff to a President of the United States. Mr. Holliday fainted, dropped the yellow sheet of paper on the floor and requested of me whether or not his fingerprints could be taken off the piece of paper. Subsequent to gaining his composure . . ."

"Excuse me," said Howard W. Jaffe, attorney for Hughes's Summa Corporation, "I wish you would give a responsive answer, without all the elaboration."

Without further elaboration on the million-dollar payoff, Maheu went on to detail a series of political contributions:

—He personally gave $50,000 in cash to Vice President Hubert H. Humphrey in a limousine in front of the Century Plaza Hotel in Los Angeles during the 1968 presidential campaign. Hughes, who was then in the midst of his hotel-buying spree in Las Vegas, was also engaged in his celebrated opposition to the Atomic Energy Commission's testing program

---

* With charges that Maheu "stole me blind," Hughes fired Maheu in December 1970 and moved to the Bahamas.

in Nevada, and he wanted to enlist Humphrey's support. His donation to Humphrey allegedly made it possible for Humphrey to have Lawrence O'Brien as his campaign manager. "I never personally received any funds of any kind at any time from Howard Hughes or any of his emissaries," Humphrey said in a statement. "If Mr. Hughes made a campaign contribution in 1968, which he may very well have done, it was not to me."[39]

—Two $50,000 contributions were delivered to Bebe Rebozo, one in late 1969 and one in the summer of 1970. The courier was Richard G. Danner, a former FBI agent and onetime city manager of Miami, who was then the manager of the Hughes-owned Frontier Hotel in Las Vegas. Danner was selected because he was a friend of both Rebozo and Nixon.

In his own deposition, Danner said that Rebozo and Nixon first met in 1950 when Danner borrowed Rebozo's yacht at Vero Beach, Florida, to take Nixon fishing. (Former Senator George Smathers, now a Washington lawyer and lobbyist, claims the honor of having introduced Nixon to Rebozo: "I took him [Nixon] to Florida the first time he went, to Vero Beach [in 1950]. I introduced him to Bebe Rebozo, who is now his very best friend"—see Chapter Five, pages 337–342).

Washington attorney Edward P. Morgan sounded out the Hughes organization in 1968 and found that a $50,000 contribution could be obtained by Nixon. "Bebe Rebozo and I learned," said Danner, "that Donald Nixon and John Meier [a Hughes aide] were in New York in this connection—that is, to make the arrangements for the campaign contribution. Rebozo, of course, became alarmed when he heard the name Don Nixon . . . and at that time he said that he didn't want it handled that way, and best just to drop it, forget it and that was the end of it."

—Although Hughes wanted the $50,000 paid before Election Day, Maheu said it was not done because "there was a difficulty in establishing a contact with Mr. Bebe Rebozo, who had been chosen by Mr. Nixon as the person to whom the money should be delivered." Following the 1968 election, Maheu tried to deliver the money to Nixon personally. The plan called for two intermediaries, Maheu explained: "After the election there was a convention in Palm Springs of Republican governors—at which President-elect Nixon made an appearance. Through Governor Paul Laxalt [of Nevada] and Robert Finch [a key Nixon aide], arrangements were made for an appointment with . . . Nixon in Palm Springs at which time . . . Laxalt and I were to deliver the money personally to . . . Nixon. Unfortunately, something happened during the day that scuttled the President-elect's schedule and Governor Laxalt reported to me that it would be impossible for us to make the delivery of the money." Laxalt, now an attorney in Nevada, confirmed that he had dealt with Finch in behalf of Maheu, but he could not recall that the money was to be given to Nixon personally. Finch's recollection was even more disappointing—he could not recall talking to Laxalt, let alone talking with him about a contribution to Nixon from Hughes.

(To digress, it was Robert Finch who precipitated the publication of the Hughes-Nixon loan story two weeks before the 1960 presidential election. Unaware that the story was safely buttoned down by the media because it would not have allowed Nixon enough time to reply, Finch released a bogus "exclusive" story to columnist Peter Edson. Captioned "V.P. Bares Story of 'Kin's 'Deals,' '" the story made no mention of the Hughes Tool Company, nor of the fact that Frank J. Waters was a Hughes attorney and lobbyist. Vice President Nixon, it said, "has never had any part or investment in his brother's business enterprises. Most of the deals he made in the name of his now defunct company, Nixon's Inc., were not even known to the Vice President until after their completion." Frank Waters was identified only as the lender: "Mrs. Waters and Donald Nixon's wife had been in high school together and the two families were and still are good friends. So it was natural that Mr. Waters should have assisted in financing Don's business ventures. Frank Waters then deeded the property back to [Phillip] Reiner [a Waters intermediary], one of the creditors who had threatened foreclosure. The deed contained an option of absolute conveyance, giving complete satisfaction for the indebtedness." Edson concluded: "This is the story on which it is claimed the Vice President's opponents are trying to make political scandal." It was more than Drew Pearson could bear. The facts, he wrote, "boil down to this. Four years after Nixon had given his famous TV explanation of the $18,000 expense fund to American voters and flown across the continent to receive his 'clean as a hound's tooth' blessing from General Eisenhower, his family received a much bigger financial benefit from the Hughes Tool Co., wholly owned by Howard Hughes . . ." Finch labeled the Pearson story "an obvious political smear," and repeated the claim that the money had come from Waters and not Hughes. Then on October 21, only eight days before the election, with most of the damaging facts already before the public, Don Nixon issued a written statement, saying that he was "deeply grieved and concerned to think that any individual would use my business misfortune to influence the outcome of the Presidential election." His brother's campaign headquarters, he went on to say, had misinformed the public about the source of the loan, which had been made by a "client" of Waters, "the Hughes Tool Company." The following day Finch told the press he had been "misled" by Thomas Bewley, the Nixon family lawyer. "I guess," said Edson, "they made a sucker out of me.")

—Danner said the first $50,000 in $100 bills was handed to Rebozo in his bank offices at Key Biscayne. "I handed the money over and said, "This is the money that we promised to raise for the forthcoming campaign, the congressional campaign [of 1970], particularly the Senate."

—The second installment was paid to Rebozo at Nixon's San Clemente home on July 3, 1970, with virtually the same instruction concerning the mid-term elections. On the same date, according to Watergate committee sources, Rebozo and Robert Abplanalp, another Nixon confidant, were concluding a deal for the purchase of 2.9 additional acres for Nixon's lavish San Clemente estate—the purchase price of that parcel was exactly $100,000. Documents released by the White House in August 1973 revealed that Nixon purchased the 2.9-acre parcel on October 13, 1969, for $100,000, and that on July 15, 1970, he borrowed $175,000 from Abplanalp to pay off the note plus $75,000 in interest due on other loans—see Chapter Five, pages 342–350.

—The first $50,000 came from a Hughes personal bank account in Los Angeles, and the second payment from the cash cage of the Silver Slipper Casino in Las Vegas. During this period, when Hughes, as usual, was having problems with various governmental agencies, two major federal cases were expeditiously decided in his favor. One was a Civil Aeronautics Board decision in July 1969 allowing him to buy Air West, a small California-based passenger line;* the other was a Justice Department cancellation in the late summer of 1970 of an antitrust action that sought to prevent him from purchasing additional gambling casinos in Las Vegas. Danner was vague as to when in 1970 he first met with Attorney General Mitchell in Washington. "It wasn't winter," he said, "so it could have been spring or fall. I don't remember it being unusually hot, so I imagine it was spring or fall. Now, which, I couldn't say." Danner said he gave Mitchell

* In December 1973, Hughes and four others, including Maheu, were indicted by a federal grand jury in Las Vegas on charges of perpetrating a stock swindle in the purchase of Air West. Seven days before the indictment was handed down, Hughes moved his hermitage to the Bahamas, which happens to have a limited extradition treaty with the United States. A few weeks earlier the Bahamian government had refused to extradite Robert Vesco on similar charges. A month later, a federal judge in Reno dismissed the indictment, calling it the "worst criminal pleading I have ever encountered." At this writing, prosecutors contend they will take the matter before another grand jury.

the figures on the percentage of Las Vegas hotel rooms Hughes then operated and was told that adding a thousand rooms would not violate antitrust laws. "Never was [there] any discussion, nor any intimation," Danner recalled, "that this was a *quid pro quo*, that if they would do something for us we would do something for them. Absolutely not."

—According to his testimony to Watergate investigators, Rebozo was under the impression that the funds were earmarked for the 1972 Presidential campaign. Yet Rebozo claimed that he kept the money stashed in a safe-deposit box in his Key Biscayne bank until Maheu mentioned the contributions in his deposition in the spring of 1973. It was at this point that Rebozo finally decided to return the money to Hughes attorney Chester Davis without explanation.

If Nixon is to be believed, Rebozo kept the money secret even from him. Here is the way the President fielded a question on this subject in his press conference of October 26, 1973:

> Q. Mr. President, is it credible, can the American people believe that your close friend Mr. Rebozo, for three years, during which time you saw him weekly sometimes, kept from you the fact that he had $100,000 in cash from Mr. Howard Hughes? What campaign committee was he an official of?
>
> A. Well, it is obviously not credible to you, and I suppose that it would sound incredible to many people who did not know how I operate. In terms of campaign contributions, I have had a rule, Mr. Deakin, which Mr. [Maurice H.] Stans and Mr. Rebozo and every contributor will agree has been the rule—I have refused always to accept contributions myself. I have refused to have any discussion of contributions.* Now, with regard to Mr. Rebozo, let me say that he showed, I think, very good judgment in doing what he did. He received a contribution, he was prepared to turn it over to the finance chairman when the finance chairman was appointed. But in that interval after he received the contribution, and before the finance chairman was appointed, the Hughes company, as you all know, had an internal fight of massive proportions, and he felt that such a contribution to the campaign might prove to be embarrassing. At the conclusion of the campaign, he decided that it would be in the best interests of everybody concerned, rather than to turn the money over then to be used for the 1974 campaign, to return it intact.

* There is irrefutable evidence that Nixon violated this rule in the milk-fund case (see Chapter Five), and quite possibly in this instance, too. According to several newspaper accounts, Danner told Watergate committee investigators that Nixon had personally asked him for a $50,000 contribution from Hughes. The Baltimore *Sun* reported that Rebozo had made Danner swear that he would never disclose that he had discussed the money personally with Nixon. Both the White House and Danner denied the reports.

The President did not explain why those particular funds were different from the additional $150,000 Hughes contributed to the Nixon campaign during 1972. Nor did he explain any of the other obvious questions. Later on in the press conference, Nixon further elaborated on the "very good judgment" of Rebozo: "I would say that any individual, and particularly a banker, who would have a contribution of $100,000 and not touch it— because it was turned back in exactly the form it was received—I think that's a pretty good indication that he is a totally honest man, which he is."[40]

Chester Davis confirmed that the money had indeed been returned, but he refused to say when Rebozo had given it back and whether it came in the original bundle of $100 bills. As for Rebozo's memory, Watergate sources say he was tardy in recalling that he had taken the money out of the box and replaced the original wrappers with rubber bands. That admission left the door wide open for the investigators.[41]

Also of interest to the Ervin committee were the adventures of "Big Don" Nixon: "They call me 'Big Don,' " he once said, "I'm larger than Richard. I'm not a public figure—I'm just a fellow trying to make a living. I don't want to be in the limelight at all."

Two years younger than Richard, portly F. Donald Nixon is full of easy-money ideas. The bad luck that dogged him most of his life has improved considerably with the passage of time. Whittier was abandoned long ago and the wheeling-dealing has gone international. His new goal, as expressed to friends following the 1968 election, was to make a million dollars in the next four years.[42] In no time he was well on his way, having held several important jobs before accepting a vice presidency with the Marriott Corp., a Washington-based hotel, restaurant, and airline catering firm with worldwide operations. His boss, J. Willard Marriott, headed the committee for Dick's inauguration in 1969, and his wife was National Republican committeewoman for the District of Columbia. According to a Marriott spokesman, Don's thirty years in the food business was going to be a tremendous asset to the firm—particularly when he called on airline executives to ask them to shift their in-flight food-catering business to Marriott. Some competitors regarded him as "unfair competition," but Don differed with them. "It's nothing new," he says. "Dick's been in politics many years. I've had to lead a careful life, to completely stay out of anything to do with politics, which is my brother's concern."[43] Meanwhile, he was jetting around the world, promoting a whole bunch of big-buck schemes besides the Marriott line. He went to Greece in 1972 to discuss "Hallamore Homes" with Aristotle Onassis and the Greek military junta, then away to Spain, Portugal, and Brazil, and everywhere he got the red-carpet treatment—Onassis sent him roses with the longest stems he had ever seen. "They [Hallamore] have promised me 25 percent of their stock," he told George Clifford, an associate of columnist Jack Anderson. "And I'm going to be a director of San/Bar." This corporation, he said, would handle foreign sales of the modular homes. Asked by Clifford if he would accompany his brother on the presidential trip to Peking, Don said, "Oh, no. Only my brother and his closest advisers will go." Then he grinned, and his left forefinger jabbed the air. "But remember this," he said. "Don't overlook the possibility of trade with China. And with Russia. There is an opportunity there. Someone has to do business with them." Later, fixing his gaze on a visitor connected with Hughes Air West, Don wanted to know how he could get the airline to switch to Marriott. "We ought to do their catering," he said. "They owe me that."[44]

It is alleged that it was because the President was worried about Don's involvement with John Meier and others in the Hughes empire that he decided to have him placed under electronic surveillance by the Secret Service. A White House request to Hughes officials led them to forbid Meier to associate with Don. When it was discovered that Meier "was talking over a big real estate deal" at the Orange County Airport, near Huntington Beach, with Don in September 1969, Meier was forced to resign under threat of dismissal.

The question of Meier's tenure takes a curious turn in Maheu's deposition. Maheu said he wanted to fire Meier because of his "irresponsible actions" but that he had received word from the "penthouse" [the top floor of the Desert Inn in Las Vegas where Hughes was secreted for four years] that Hughes opposed the firing. "On the one hand, President Nixon had offered to either see or converse on the telephone with Mr. Hughes in order to explain the posture of the United States government vis-à-vis the Atomic Energy testing. Mr. Nixon offered to send Mr. Kissinger to Las Vegas to discuss the matter with Mr. Hughes, either in person or on the telephone . . . [but] Mr. Meier kept saying that he was seeing Mr. Hughes regularly, that he was talking to Mr. Hughes regularly [which] made it very difficult for us to explain to Dr. Kissinger and the President of the United States that they could not talk to Mr. Hughes." In August 1973, Meier was indicted by a federal grand jury on charges that he failed to report $270,000 in income for 1968 and 1969. Without mentioning Don by name, Meier's attorney argued that the reported wiretapping of "an associate" of his client indicated "this prosecution is politically motivated and based on illegally obtained evidence."

On January 14, 1974, Meier and three others were indicted by a federal grand jury on charges of conspiracy and tax evasion in the sale of mining claims to Hughes. The indictment, which superseded the first one, accused him of evading more than $1.6 million in taxes in 1969 and 1970, and of conspiracy in the funneling to a Dutch company of some $4.8 million in profits from the sale of claims to the Hughes Tool Company. The case was awaiting disposition at this writing.[45]

More than a century ago, Henry David Thoreau placed two truths in opposition. "Philanthropy," he said, "is almost the only virtue sufficiently appreciated by mankind," but, he added, there "is no odor as bad as that which rises from goodness tainted."

The ambivalent pull of these truths seriously blurred the focus of foundations almost from the beginning. For the first half-century of their existence, however, from the time of the old John D. Rockefeller kerosene trust and the gospel of Andrew Carnegie that the "man who dies rich, dies disgraced," the foundations, except for an occasional attack, operated in a rarefied atmosphere.

This is not to say that all people looked upon them with benign gratitude. The social activists of the Progressive Era were hard on philanthropists. When the Rockefeller Foundation petitioned Congress in 1909 for a federal charter to administer its initial gift of $35 million in Standard Oil of New Jersey stock, groups led by Edward T. Devine and Jane Addams denounced it as a "new form of the dead hand." They raised such a clamor against "tainted money" that after three years of stormy debate in Congress, Rockefeller finally backed off and turned to the New York legislature, where a state charter was unanimously awarded within a week.

The first inquiry into the behavior of foundations authorized by Congress began in 1912, at a time in history when the trust-busting fervor of Teddy Roosevelt against the financial freebooting of America's foremost tycoons was at a fever pitch. John D. Rockefeller, one of Roosevelt's prime targets, was desperately searching about for ways to preserve his huge fortune—and his reputation. He had gone through a decade of virulent attack by the muckrakers and the New Populists. When Ida M. Tarbell had begun digging into his past for a series of articles that began to appear in *McClure's Magazine* for November 1902, Rockefeller had quickly organized the Rockefeller Institute for Medical Research and the

General Education Board to great public acclaim in a press controlled by "predatory wealth."

The odor of "goodness tainted" permeated Miss Tarbell's history as she detailed how Standard Oil "openly made warfare on business, and drove from the oil industry by any means it could invent all who had the hardihood to enter it." She charged that Rockefeller "worked with the railroads to prevent other people getting oil to manufacture; or if they got it he worked with the railroads to prevent the shipment of the product. If it reached a dealer, he did his utmost to bully or wheedle him to countermand his order. If he failed in that, he undersold until the dealer, losing on his purchase, was glad enough to buy thereafter of Mr. Rockefeller."

In 1905, again writing in *McClure's Magazine*, Miss Tarbell had more to say about her subject:

> No candid study of his career can lead to other conclusion than that he is a victim of perhaps the ugliest . . . of all passions, that for money, money as an end. . . .
>
> This man has for forty years lent all the power of his great ability to perpetuating and elaborating a system of illegal and unjust discrimination by common carriers. He has done this in the face of moral sentiment, in the face of loudly expressed public opinion, in the face of the law, in the face of the havoc his operations caused. . . . He has fought to prevent every attempt to regulate the wrong the system wrought, and . . . turned his craft and skill to finding secret and devious ways of securing the privileges he desires. . . .
>
> He has turned commerce from a peaceful pursuit to war, and honeycombed it with cruel and corrupt practice; turned competition from honorable emulation to cut-throat struggle. And the man who deliberately and presently does these things calls his great organization a benefaction, and points to his church-going and charities as proof of his righteousness. To the man of straight-forward nature the two will not tally. This, he says, is supreme wrong-doing cloaked by religion. There is but one name for it—hypocrisy.

This image would fade with the years. But in his times, the old man was the nation's greatest ogre. In the summer of 1907 Standard Oil was convicted of receiving rebates from the Chicago and Alton Railroad. A fine of $29,240,000 was imposed on the company by Federal Judge Kenesaw Mountain Landis on 1,462 specific counts. However, the verdict was annulled on appeal and the case dismissed. In another attack, the Hearst press revealed that Standard Oil vice president John D. Archbold had transmitted almost $100,000 to Senator Joseph B. Foraker of Ohio with a note referring to antimonopoly legislation that "needs to be looked after." Somebody apparently slipped up. On May 15, 1911, after a court battle that had lasted four years, the Supreme Court handed down the decision ordering the dissolution of the Standard Oil Company. Whether the court believed that the thirty-eight "independent" companies created by the judgment would actually "compete" with one another, the muckrakers entertained no such illusion. The Rockefeller group controlled the companies severally as thoroughly as it had controlled them combined. The only difference was that an investor would receive a number of small dividend checks instead of a big one for the aggregate amount.

The charter of the Rockefeller Foundation proclaimed its desire to "promote the well-being and to advance the civilization of the peoples of the United States and its territories and possessions and of foreign lands in the acquisition and dissemination of knowledge, in the prevention and relief of suffering, and in the promotion of any and all of the elements of human progress."

Almost before the ink immortalizing that lofty sentiment had a chance to dry, Rockefeller was once again propelled into the public spotlight. The Presidential Commission on Industrial Relations, headed by Frank P. Walsh, was formed in 1912 to investigate the "general conditions of labor in the United States." Its immediate mandate, however, was to explore the connection between the Rockefeller Foundation and the Ludlow Massacre in the Colorado coal fields.

Touched off by a strike of the United Mine Workers against the Colorado Fuel and Iron Company, a Rockefeller enterprise, the incident was one of the bloodiest in union history. The massacre took place on October 7, 1913, when a company of National Guard troops, mostly company guards in militia uniforms, staged a surprise foray on the strikers' camp at Ludlow. Five men and a boy were killed by machine-gun fire; the troops then set fire to shacks and tents, and eleven children and two women were burned to death.

Although John D. Rockefeller and three Foundation trustees were directors of Colorado Fuel and Iron, they denied any knowledge of the labor conditions at the camp and the militia action.

"It is not customary in any corporation that I have ever been connected with as director to receive regular information regarding labor matters," Rockefeller told the commission.

Walsh then promptly produced a letter written by Rockefeller to company officials after the massacre:

You gentlemen cannot be more earnest in your desire for the best interests of the employees of your company than we are. We feel that what you have done is right and fair and that the position which you have taken in regard to the unionizing of the mines is in the interest of the employees of the company. . . . Whatever the outcome may be, we will stand by you to the end.

At this point in the proceedings, Walsh asked: "Have you ever had a description prepared for you, Mr. Rockefeller, of what might have been accomplished if the sums which have been given through your benefactions of various kinds, had been given in increased wages or increased the conditions of labor and standards of living in the communities from which the investments of Mr. Rockefeller have drawn the profits?"

"I have not," Rockefeller replied.

"Do you consider that 12 hours work in steel works in the rolling mills is a hardship to employees?"

"I am not familiar enough with the work to know," Rockefeller said.

Among its various discoveries, the Walsh Commission learned that the president of Colorado College and the dean of the College of Liberal Arts at the University of Denver had circulated a "public manifesto" that placed the responsibility for the violence on the strikers and called for them to return to work. The Rockefeller Foundation and the General Education Board showed their appreciation with unrestricted grants of $100,000 to each school. The Foundation's next effort to refurbish its founder's image was to sponsor a general study of labor conditions under the direction of William L. Mackenzie King, later Prime Minister of Canada. But when Walsh pointed out that King had not interviewed any members of the United Mine Workers or the State Federation of Labor on his visit to the Colorado coal fields, the Foundation was embarrassed into canceling the project.

In its findings the Walsh Commission recommended the dissolution of the Rockefeller Foundation and asked that its funds be spent to relieve unemployment and to curb sickness and accidents. The report charged that the Foundation's assets consisted of money that should have gone to workers in the form of wages: "These wages were withheld by means of economic pressure, violation of law, cunning, violence practiced over a series of years by the founder . . . and his business associates."

The Walsh Commission then turned its attention to the "concentration of wealth and influence" held by foundations. The majority report agreed that "the domination by men in whose hands the final control of a large part of American industry rests is not limited to their employees but is being rapidly extended to control of the educational and social service of the nation." Foundation funds, the report argued, were heavily invested in the shares of corporations, which gave them enormous power in the formulation of corporate policies.[46]

Fifty years later Wright Patman would issue this warning:

> Unquestionably, the economic life of our Nation has become so intertwined with foundations that unless something is done about it they will hold a dominant position in every phase of American life.

> The forerunner of modern antitrust enforcement was the successful prosecution in 1907 of the Rockefeller-controlled monopoly, Standard Oil Co. As a result, competition was restored in the industry by the creation of a number of oil companies; e.g., Standard Oil Co. (New Jersey), Standard Oil Co. (Kentucky), et al. Additionally, an atmosphere was created wherein other companies could and did enter and compete in the field.

> Now, the multimillion-dollar foundations have replaced the trusts which were broken up during the Theodore Roosevelt administration.

> It is a well-known fact that the Rockefeller family controls Standard Oil Co. (New Jersey),* and the Rockefeller-controlled foundations own a substantial part of the corporation. At the close of 1960, 7 Rockefeller-controlled foundations owned 7,891,567 shares of common stock of Standard Oil of New Jersey with a market value of $329,946,110. The same 7 foundations owned 602,127 shares of the common stock of Socony Mobil Oil Co. with a market value of $23,610,770. Two Rockefeller foundations owned 306,013 shares of Continental Oil capital stock with a market value of $17,060,224 (the Rockefeller Foundation itself held 300,000 of these shares with a market value of $16,725,000); 4 Rockefeller foundations owned 468,135 shares of Ohio Oil common stock with a market value of $17,998,495; 5 Rockefeller foundations owned 1,256,305 shares of the common stock of Standard Oil Co. of Indiana with a market value of $59,736,991; and the Rockefeller Foundation, itself, owned 100,000 shares of the capital stock of Union Tank Car Co. with a market value of $3,100,000.

> If Standard Oil Co. (New Jersey) were to attain substantial ownership in its competitors, it would certainly tend to eliminate competition and again tend toward monopoly, and engage the Department of Justice in inquiry.

> The use of subterfuge—in the form of Rockefeller-controlled foundations—in effect produces the same result as if Standard Oil Co. (New Jersey) owned substantial stock interest in Continental Oil, Ohio Oil, Standard Oil Co. (Indiana), et al.[47]

* Exxon.

The big question today, of course, is that nobody, including Patman, knows precisely the degree of control the Rockefellers exercise over the old Standard Oil empire that was supposedly dissolved in 1911. Or, for that matter, over the entire industry. How much oil stock has been secreted in personal trusts? Securities and Exchange Commission regulations state that any holding of a publicly offered stock by any individual or enterprise in excess of 10 percent of the issue must be reported. But this obstacle is easily circumvented by limiting the holding of each trust to 9 percent. The number of secret trusts you control is your business.

Back in 1929, Colonel Robert W. Stewart, chairman of Standard Oil of Indiana, tried to bypass the Rockefellers in a move for control of the company. His appeal to general stockholders resulted in a devastating defeat.

The Walsh Commission concluded that the concentration of wealth and power created "creeping capitalism." The foundations were tools of conservative reaction, dedicated to forwarding the cause of Big Business in its dominance over the labor force and colleges. Congress, for its part, completely ignored the Walsh Report. No legislation followed.[48]

By the mid-1930s the fears of creeping capitalism had turned to creeping socialism. The first ban on political activity imposed on foundations was passed in 1934. Title 26 of the U.S. Code defines the qualifications for tax exemption of an organization as follows:

> Section 501(c)(3)—Corporations and any community chest fund or foundation, organized and operated exclusively for religious, charitable, scientific, testing for public safety, literary or educational purposes, or for the prevention of cruelty to children or animals, no part of the net earnings of which inures to the benefit of any private stockholder or individual, no substantial part of the activities of which is carrying on propaganda, or otherwise attempting to influence legislation, and which does not participate in, or intervene in (including the publishing or distributing of statements), any political campaign on behalf of any candidate for public office.

The key words "substantial," "propaganda," and "influence" required the kind of interpretations that paralyzed the courts, making the act all but unenforceable. It was not until the Red hunt of the early 1950s, at the apex of the McCarthyite delirium, that the act gained importance in Congress. The perjury conviction of Alger Hiss, in a case involving Communist espionage, electrified the country. Hiss was president of the Carnegie Endowment for International Peace, one of the nation's most prestigious foundations.

The clarion was surrounded by the *American Legion Magazine* in an article entitled "Let's Look at Our Foundations." It charged that foundations constituted a danger to society because they were financing "outright communists, fellow travelers, socialists, do-gooders, one-worlders, wild-eyed Utopians and well-meaning dupes."

The man behind the Legion article, Representative Edward E. Cox of Georgia, chaired the next committee authorized by Congress to investigate foundations. The committee's mandate was to inquire into activities not in the "interests or tradition of the United States." Foundation trustees, educators, and Communist informers testified at public hearings for several weeks in 1952. It began as a wild fishing expedition and closed with surprising results. The committee's report hailed the importance of foundations in American life and noted that "their most significant function had been the supplying of venture capital for advancing the frontiers of knowledge." As to their undermining of the capitalist system, it concluded that "on balance the record of the foundations is good" in resisting Communist efforts to infiltrate their organizations.

Two years later, following the death of Cox, Representative B. Carroll Reece of Tennessee got up on the floor of Congress and proposed a new investigation of foundations. As a member of the Cox Committee, Reece had attended only one session, but he had ideas of his own, as his remarks indicated:

> Some of these institutions support efforts to overthrow our government and to undermine our American way of life. . . . Here lies the story of how communism and socialism are financed in the United States. . . . There is evidence to show that there is a diabolical conspiracy back of all this. . . . Organizations which are primarily committed to a given ideology have received large grants from big foundations over many years.

If possible, the Reece Committee accomplished less than its predecessor. For one thing, it played second banana to Joe McCarthy's center-ring spectacular, a circumstance that led committee members to indulge in grandstand plays and stormy exchanges until finally the committee recessed and never reconvened. The majority report recommended legislation to unseat trustees who made grants to "subversive organizations." It warned that foundations "might eventually control a large part of the American economy" and charged that they had led education "toward the promotion of collectivism" and had supported subversion. The minority report attacked the majority for an "unseemly effort to reach a predetermined conclusion." Both could have saved their energy, for, as usual, no legislation resulted.

The first great mass exodus of wealth into foundation havens began in 1936, when Congress passed a law permitting business firms to deduct 5 percent of their taxable income for charity. An individual could deduct 20 percent for contributions to private foundations, and an additional 10 percent for gifts to publicly supported institutions such as churches, schools, hospitals, and the Red Cross. All donations by individuals or corporations to reduce gift and estate taxes were fully deductible.

After 1936, the foundation, which before had been the exclusive preserve of aging tycoons (convinced finally they could not take it with them), went public. It became everybody's loophole. Postwar excess-profits taxes, coupled with the permissive tax "reforms" of 1950, sent their numbers soaring. In effect, Congress that year told the foundations they could regulate themselves. The sole imposition was a meaningless ban on the use of foundation funds to purchase businesses. In no time at all, tax attorneys had polished the foundation into a sophisticated device for wholesale tax avoidance. It became standard financial doctrine for the "living" rich, and the not-so-rich, more interested in minimizing income (instead of estate) taxes than in advancing "human welfare."

Its popularity contributed to a tremendous surge of interest in tax-avoidance literature. A few random titles will illustrate the point: "The Tax Blessings of Charitable Giving," "How to Get Maximum Tax Benefits from Charitable Contributions," "How to Make Money by Giving It Away: Tax Consequences of Creating a Charitable Trust," "Possible Tax Bonanza in Giving Property Instead of Cash," "How to Draft the Charter or Indenture of a Charity so as to Qualify for the Federal Tax Exemption," "How to Use Gifts to Take Earnings Out of a Corporation Tax Free." And for fifteen cents the Government Printing Office will forward an IRS pamphlet, "How to Apply for Exemption for an Organization."

For incipient philanthropists with an extra $10,500 to spare, the Americans Building Constitutionally, of Barrington, Illinois, conducted do-it-yourself seminars for physicians, dentists, and other wealthy professionals interested in the tax blessings of charitable giving. ABC's motto was "to help citizens of the United States make full use of the rights guaranteed them under the Constitution." Its premise, as expressed to students, was marvelously simple: "A foundation may, under most state laws, own anything and everything that is ownable in the world. Once a foundation owns the world it may sell it." In a span of two years, 1966–67, ABC graduated eight hundred applicants. What actual benefits were derived by its graduates was illustrated by the case of Dr. Michael B. Saxon of Aurora, Illinois. Under the guidance of ABC, the Saxon Foundation was set up to receive all fees derived from the general medical practice of its founder. In turn, the foundation paid Saxon a salary, plus full expenses for his house, offices, car, retirement plan, and insurance. There was testimony before the Patman Committee that his four children attended college on educational grants from the foundation, but the doctor failed to respond to a subpoena on the final day of the hearings and the committee did not pursue the matter further.[49]

If the older foundations, as a rule, knew how to perform their legerdemain with a degree of decorum (but not always, as Patman illustrates time and again), the newer foundations often slipped into a form of low comedy. According to the Washington *Star*, the Playboy Foundation, granted tax-exempt status in 1964, immediately contemplated using part of its funds for a "study of the effect of smut on public morals."

Spencer R. Collins conducted his own research with funds from his St. Genevieve Foundation. A millionaire in his late sixties, Collins supported twin sisters "through several years of parties and gay living, spending an estimated $100,000 on them." One of the twins lived in a posh duplex, while the other was ensconced in a five-bedroom mansion on Lake Oswego, and received $36,000 as "caretaker of the house." Tried and convicted for tax evasion, Collins' defense was that he needed companionship and knew no other way to obtain it.[50]

The "primary function" of the Julian S. Eaton Educational Foundation "is to aid the University of Miami football team by helping recruit prospective players and making loans to needy students," or so stated one of its mailing pieces. Once a year, the team's boosters, who pay annual $100 tax-deductible dues, get together for a big blowout, free and tax-free, with the taxpayers picking up the tab.[51]

But compared to the National Football Foundation, the Eaton operation was small potatoes. Incorporated in 1949 by a group of gridiron enthusiasts, the objective was to create a Hall of Fame to honor the nation's outstanding college football players, complete with statuary and memorabilia of designated heroes. As envisioned lo these many years ago, the Hall of Fame was to be erected on the hallowed grounds of Rutgers University, only a stone's throw from the field where the first college football game was played in 1869. In the interim, with the support of men like Presidents Hoover, Eisenhower, Kennedy, and Nixon, Supreme Court Justice Byron ("Whizzer") White, a former All-American from Colorado, and General Douglas MacArthur, all of whom have accepted awards in person at the annual bash at New York's Waldorf-Astoria Hotel, the Foundation raised more than $5 million in donations.

Shortly after its customary $30,000 annual Waldorf-Astoria blowout in December 1971, with California Governor Ronald Reagan as featured speaker, the Foundation's startled philanthropoids were summoned to a meeting at the Charity Frauds Bureau of the New York Attorney General's office. The bureau wanted to know why the Foundation had not yet launched its project. When Chester LaRoche, the man most prominently identified with the Foundation, explained that there was only $2 million left in the coffers, the Frauds Bureau began going through the Foundation's books. Although LaRoche, a former advertising executive, is the prime mover, the man routinely toasted at banquets as the one "without whom the Foundation wouldn't be where it is today," the president is ex-entertainer and ex-Senator George Murphy, who receives a $15,000 salary, plus expenses, for "part-time" work. Out of national expenditures of $243,425 in fiscal 1971, the total spent on "gifts and grants" was $7,500. Yet its interest in the gridiron has not diminished. A few years ago it paid $50,000 for a study on "The Impact of Athletic Participation on Academic and Career Aspiration and Achievement." The handsomely printed forty-four-page report was adorned with seven photographs of Chester LaRoche. Of the thirty-seven Hall-of-Famers inducted by LaRoche, himself a Yale man (second-string quarterback for one season in 1916), thirty-three are from Ivy League schools and one each from Texas, UCLA, Oklahoma, and Michigan State. Pressed by the Frauds Bureau for an early launching, the Foundation finally purchased a sixty-five-room house in Manhattan for a reported $800,000. What action the Frauds Bureau proposes to take is not known at this writing, but, as *Sports Illustrated* magazine asked, "Will anyone really care to go to East 80th Street to see Red Grange's helmet?"[52]

Another example of charitable hocus-pocus was provided by the Government Affairs Foundation, Inc., of Albany, New York, which between 1961 and 1964 received $310,469 in gifts from its founder, Governor Nelson A. Rockefeller, and paid out exactly zero dollars to charity. The stated purpose of the Foundation was to "improve quality and reduce quantity of government." During those four years the Foundation paid out

$120,000 in salary and $40,000 in expenses to Frank C. Moore, former Lieutenant Governor of New York, an amount equal to 57 percent of the Foundation's total expenses of $284,193, with the rest of the money going for administrative costs. The result, said Patman, was a politician's dream come true. An important politician had found a "method by which he could hire a full-time liaison man, and be able to deduct that expense as a charitable item."[53]

Charity is currently paving the way to this politician's perennial dream of occupying the White House. Following his resignation after fifteen years as Governor of New York, Nelson Rockefeller organized the National Commission on Critical Choices for America to study the nation's problems into the next century. "I have concluded that I can render a greater public service to the people of New York and the nation by devoting myself to the work of two bipartisan national commissions,"* he told a news conference. "My only regret is that my undertaking these tasks has been interpreted as a political maneuver to seek the Presidency or for any other political office. Whether I will become a candidate in the future, I do not know. I should like to keep my options open. . . . This is not a gimmick. This is not a political trick. This is a fundamental study. Hopefully, it will benefit mankind."

Rockefeller was working hard to erase the old "liberal" stigma, embracing Barry Goldwater and hanging tough on welfare cheaters, drug users and law-and-order. Dick, that clever chameleon, had pulled off a new image in 1968, why not Rocky in 1976? If the title of the commission seemed grandiloquent (Rocky thinks its report will rival the Federalist Papers in historic importance), its mandate was no less ambitious.

"I hesitate to quote the exact, and rather pompous, words of the prospectus," Kermit Lansner wrote in his *Newsweek* column on December 17, 1973, "but I think that we can say that by July 4, 1976, on the very anniversary of the 200th year of the Republic, a short time before the national convention of the Republican Party, this *summa*, this distillation of three years of work by the most knowledgeable, hard-working and ambitious minds will be ready for the next President of the United States."

The cost, estimated at $20 million, will be borne by the Third Century Corporation, a tax-exempt umbrella for the commission, which is funded by grants from a half-dozen foundations and several governmental agen-

---

* He was also chairman of the National Commission on Water Quality, established by Congress in 1972 to recommend criteria for carrying out the amended Pure Waters Act.

cies. This time around, Rocky did not intend to be left vacillating at the picket fence. The blessings of charity are manifold.

And still another type of charity, although on a lower level of greed, was practiced by a family foundation in Oregon. It donated beef carcasses to the city's soup kitchen, but minus the steaks, tenderloins, prime ribs, and other choice cuts. They were diverted to the family's deep freeze, providing them with tax-free and, for the most part, cost-free meat.

The tax advantages of foundations are indeed limitless. In an article in the *Cleveland-Marshall Law Review*, Berman and Berman, tax attorneys, listed some of the highlights of controlling property without ownership:

What can be accomplished by creating a foundation?
1. Keep control of wealth.
2. Can keep for the donor many attributes of wealth by many means:
    a. Designating the administrative management of the foundation.
    b. Control over its investments.
    c. Appointing relatives as directors of foundations.
    d. Foundation's assets can be used to borrow money to buy other property that does not jeopardize its purposes. Thus, foundation funds can be enhanced from the capitalization of its tax exemption.
3. The foundation can keep income in the family.
4. Family foundations can aid employees of the donor's business.
5. Foundations may be the method of insuring that funds will be available for use in new ventures in business.
6. We can avoid income from property while it is slowly being given to a foundation by a combination of a trust and the charitable foundation.
7. We can get the 20 percent charity deduction in other ways:
    a. By giving away appreciated property to the foundation, we escape a tax on the realization of a gain.
    b. We can give funds to a foundation to get charitable deduction currently in our most advantageous tax year.
    c. Very often local personal and real property taxes can be avoided.
    d. We can avoid speculative profits.
    e. We can give away valuable "frozen assets," white elephant estates, residences, valuable works of art, and collections of all arts.[54]

The years from 1950 to 1969 were a golden era for tax attorneys specializing in foundations. They stretched the language of the tax code to lengths undreamed of by even the most permissive legislator. Financial abuses proliferated as rapidly as foundations. It was inevitable that Wright Patman, last of the old-time populists in Congress and lifelong foe of bigness in government and business, would elect to probe beneath that crazy quilt of piety and piracy. That he found more piracy than piety was almost as inevitable. Yet his findings raised an unholy ruckus in establishment circles. This was only to be expected, since the foundation is the philanthropoid's final and greatest bastion of bureaucratic survival. The typical philanthropoid (a term coined to distinguish between an administrator, the philanthropoid, and his boss, the philanthropist) is an ex-academic or high-level government bureaucrat, mixed here and there with an occasional Wall Street banker or Washington lawyer. The traffic between Ivy League schools, foundations, investment houses, corporate law firms, and the government is brisk. Some examples:

John Foster Dulles from the Carnegie Endowment for International Peace to Secretary of State under President Eisenhower; Dean Rusk from Assistant Secretary of State in 1952 to the Rockefeller Foundation and back to government in 1960 as Secretary of State for Presidents Kennedy and Johnson—in 1969 the Rockefeller Foundation awarded him a one-year "transitional grant" to give him time to compile his papers (foundations have had a leasehold on the Secretary of State's office for many years, with other holders including Edward R. Stettinius, Jr., Henry L. Stimson, Frank B. Kellogg, and Charles Evans Hughes); W. Willard Wirtz remained with the Stern Family Fund while Secretary of Labor under Kennedy and Johnson; Clifford M. Hardin from the Rockefeller Foundation to Secretary of Agriculture under President Nixon; Arthur Burns remained with the Twentieth Century Fund while counselor to Nixon and chairman of the Federal Reserve Board; C. Douglas Dillon from Secretary of the Treasury under Kennedy to the Rockefeller Foundation; John Connally from the Sid W. Richardson Foundation to Secretary of the Treasury under Nixon; Adlai Stevenson remained with the Field Foundation while U.S. permanent representative to the United Nations; Ralph J. Bunche remained with the Field Foundation while U.N. Undersecretary; McGeorge Bundy from presidential adviser to Kennedy and Johnson to the Ford Foundation; John W. Gardner from the Carnegie Corporation to Secretary of Health, Education and Welfare under Johnson. Four members of the Nixon Cabinet had their own foundations: Maurice H. Stans, Commerce Secretary; Winton M. Blount, Postmaster General; John A. Volpe, Transportation Secretary; and George Romney, Secretary of Housing and Urban Development. The precedent was probably set by Robert S. McNamara, who headed a personal foundation while serving as Defense Secretary under Kennedy and Johnson.

In Congress, Senator George McGovern of South Dakota was a trustee of the Danforth Foundation; Senator Edward W. Brooke of Massachusetts was a trustee of the Council on Religion and International Affairs; Senator Edward M. Kennedy and Representative F. Bradford Morse of Massachusetts were directors of the Pan American Development Foundation; Representative Jonathan B. Bingham of New York was a trustee of the Twentieth Century Fund; Representatives John P. Saylor of Pennsylvania and Frances P. Bolton of Ohio were with the Accokeek Foundation; and so the list goes.

In the judiciary, Chief Justice Warren E. Burger was a trustee of the Mayo Foundation while a judge of the U.S. Circuit Court of Appeals—he resigned several months after his appointment to the Supreme Court; Supreme Court Justice Abe Fortas was forced off the court when it was revealed that he had accepted a $20,000 check from the Wolfson Family Foundation, Inc., at a time when Louis Wolfson was under investigation by the Securities and Exchange Commission, later being indicted and convicted; Supreme Court Justice William O. Douglas was finally persuaded to resign from the Albert Parvin Foundation, created by Las Vegas money, after a decade on its payroll at $12,000 a year.

On the other side of the ledger, hundreds of government officials, from every crevice of the Administration, both elected and appointed, have collected consultant fees, honorariums, travel expenses, and even straight salaries from foundations. Much of it, of course, has been sub rosa. The old robber barons must have held a rose over the roof of their foundations, indicating as in ancient custom that all within were sworn to secrecy. When Eduard C. Lindeman began research in the late 1920s for a book on foundations, he discovered to his surprise that "those who managed foundations and trusts did not wish to have these instruments investigated. Had it occurred to me then that it would require eight years of persistent inquiry at a wholly disproportionate cost to disclose even the basic quantitative facts desired, I am sure that the study would have been promptly abandoned."[55]

Other writers had equally frustrating experiences. The head of the Carnegie Corporation, Frederick P. Keppel, complained in his 1930 book *The Foundation* that "I myself, who am professionally interested in such matters and ought to be in a position to secure available information, have been able to obtain nothing whatever regarding three foundations, the announced capitalization of which aggregates seventy-five million dollars."[56]

The situation had not improved greatly by 1956 when F. Emerson Andrews, president of the Foundation Library Center, admitted that he could find only 107 foundations that issued reports. Ten years later, J. Richard Taft, editor of *Foundation News*, raised the count of reporting to 212. The problem prevailed despite the fact that the Revenue Act of 1950 for the first time permitted public inspection of annual forms filed by foundations with the Internal Revenue Service. Even for those who complied with the act, the forms filed revealed very little. With the prodding of Wright Patman, the form was revised in 1962, requiring that more facts be made available to the public, including officers' salaries, investment holdings, accumulation of capital gains and other income, relationship with contributors, names and addresses of donees, and amounts and types of grants. Additional information, such as the names of donors and facts surrounding unrelated business income of more than $1,000, was collected but was not available for public inspection. That most foundations failed to comply, and that others filed only partially completed forms, did not seem to disturb the IRS.[57]

"When it comes to the proper policing of tax-exempt foundations, the IRS appears to be totally impaled in the quicksands of absolute inertia," Patman charged during hearings in 1964.[58] If the metaphors were scrambled, the message was not. It was not the first time Treasury had felt the old warrior's wrath. Right from the start of the investigation, Patman had blamed the Treasury for "laxness and irresponsibility" in its supervision of foundations.

There were many points of contention. In 1962, for example, the lack of "statistics was appalling." The required tax form (990-A) used by foundations "omits vitally important facts." No description of the foundation's business activities was required. There was widespread disregard of Treasury regulations: "Uneducated sharecroppers are presumed to know the law, but many of the foundations under study and their well-paid, well-educated advisers are apparently exempt from this ancient presumption, in practice, if not as a matter of strict law. Singling out the shortcomings of each individual foundation would fill countless pages." The prohibition against "unreasonable" accumulation of income was ignored. Many foundations were being used for purposes not related to charity: "The laws of the past are no longer effective. Congress could not envision the gigantic proportions that the foundation business would reach." Capital gains was not considered income and the foundations were permitted to place them in the principal account instead of the income account: "Many foundations have become a vehicle for trading in securities and dodging the capital gains tax. This type of activity by foundations—with huge, untaxed funds at their disposal—poses some big questions in the light of the recent sharp breaks in the market. In my view, tax-exempt foundations—all of whom are supported by the taxpayers—should not be permitted to use public funds for speculation in the stock market." Although capital gains were not considered income, capital losses were deducted from income: "Thus, the coin has only one face and the foundations cannot help but win."

The Treasury was "perfectly willing" to permit foundations to reinvest and speculate with income: "One of the oddest of the Treasury oddities is that it does not require foundations to maintain separate accounts for income and principal; both can be thrown into the same bag, shaken up, mixed, and confused until it is impossible to separate income from principal funds. Hence, the setup is uniquely favorable to a foundation's profiteering by obtaining non-distributable capital gains through investing income which was supposed to have been distributed" to charity. Tax-exempt foundations operated wholly-owned enterprises in competition with taxpaying enterprises. Foundation grants to universities were used in *applied*, profit-making research for enterprises connected with the foundation rather than in *basic* research available to everybody, thus placing taxpaying competitors at considerable disadvantage. Some foundations were devoted exclusively to applied research without any pretense of a charitable purpose. Patman inveighed against a long list of shoddy practices in which donors exploited their tax-exempt privileges with self-dealing schemes that often placed their foundations in direct competition with taxpaying enterprises. And the "foundations of America, which as a whole make up one of the most powerful economic and propaganda forces in modern times, are virtually unregulated."[59]

In 1963, Patman renewed his attack on the Treasury. His findings showed "that the Internal Revenue Service record—in terms of supervision of foundations—is a dud, a dismal failure." While Mortimer M. Caplin, then IRS commissioner, "deplores the lack of such supervision prior to 1961 and has released torrents of words during the past two years assuring the Congress and the public that the Internal Revenue Service is engaged in intensive examination of tax-exempt foundations, there is no recognizable sign of progress in this area." Of the 546 foundations (the original sampling of 534 was increased by twelve) involved in the study, the IRS had failed to conduct field audits in 433 cases, including the ten largest ones, for the ten-year period from 1952 to 1962.

As to the audits performed, there were "sufficient grounds to doubt"

the agency's "competence and effectiveness. . . . One conclusion is inescapable . . . Treasury officials lack the zeal for reform and the know-how
necessary for thorough supervision of tax-exempt foundations." "To date,
the granting of Federal tax exemption to foundations has been a mere
formality. The record proves that, as far as the Treasury is concerned, an
organization becomes 'charitable' by merely describing itself as such. Once
the exemption has been granted, there is little or no check on the foundation's operations. Perhaps significantly, the Commissioner has indicated
that he favors a minimum of Federal control over tax-exempt foundations.
. . . At another point, we asked the IRS to submit a list of tax-exempt
foundations holding 10 percent or more stock of corporations. The Commissioner replied that such information was not available. This leads to
the inevitable conclusion that the Treasury prefers to remain arrogantly
ignorant of the enormous concentration of economic power among foundations. The ever-increasing drift of wealth into such organizations does
not seem to bother the Department one bit, even though the result is an
erosion of our tax base imparing the revenues of the Federal government."[60]

By 1964, Patman was finding "indications of deliberate obstructionist
tactics on the part of top Treasury officials." Stanley S. Surrey, who took
leave from Harvard to join the Kennedy Administration as the Treasury
Department's tax expert, seemed "to be much more in tune with the tax-
exempt foundations than with the taxpayers. His conversations with me
have given me the impression that he is one of the principal apologists for
the large foundations." When early in 1963 Treasury appointed an Advisory Committee on Foundations, it took Patman nearly nine months to
get the names of the members from Surrey, and then only "after an alert
Associated Press reporter had unearthed the fact that the Treasury had
appointed—amid great secrecy—an Advisory Committee, composed of
fourteen persons, to counsel the Department respecting possible legislation
and administrative changes in the supervision of tax-exempt foundations."
The innately suspicious Patman's apprehensions were confirmed when he
discovered that ten of the committee's fourteen members were wired in
directly to foundations. They were F. Emerson Andrews, director of the
Foundation Library Center, supported largely by the Rockefeller Foundation, the Ford Foundation, the Carnegie Corporation, the Alfred P. Sloan
Foundation, the W. K. Kellogg Foundation, and the Russell Sage Foundation; Leigh Block, president of the Inland Steel-Ryerson Foundation of

Chicago; Morris Hadley, chairman of the Carnegie Corporation of New York, treasurer of the Rubicon Foundation, trustee of the Grant Foundation, director of the Milbank Memorial Fund and trustee of Arthur Vining Davis Foundation; Barklie M. Henry, vice president of the John Hay Whitney Foundation of New York, vice chairman of the Carnegie Institute of Washington, trustee of the Vincent Astor Foundation, and director of the Milbank Memorial Fund; Henry A. Moe, retired president of the Guggenheim (John Simon) Memorial Foundation of New York; James Patton, president of the National Farmers Union of Denver; Walter M. Upchurch, Jr., vice president of the Shell Companies Foundation of New York; Donald Young, president of the Russell Sage Foundation of New York. The remaining six members were attorneys, of whom two were foundation consultants and one was a Harvard law professor.[61]

On July 21, 1964, Secretary of the Treasury C. Douglas Dillon (a board member of the Rockefeller Foundation) testified before the Patman Committee:

> The Chairman is quite right in saying that the Treasury does not know how many foundations there are. Because of the growth of this area, I think that is knowledge that we should have, and we are in the process of acquiring it. . . . Now, with the advent of electronic data equipment the Internal Revenue Service is in the process of asking all exempt organizations, which are many hundreds of thousands, for statistical information which will enable classification into foundations, fraternal orders, religious orders, or whatever it is, and they intend to put all this information on a master electronic tape which will be kept up to date currently so we will have that information. But that will not be completed for about a year.[62]

Many years were to pass before Treasury would come up with any kind of viable statistics. But Patman was indefatigable. No quixotic idealist tilting at windmills, his quest for information was as cynically hard-nosed as that of a big-city vice cop—both know damned well that the world is not the way they tell you it is.[63]

"The attitudes of far too many of the foundations under study suggest an unmatched arrogance and contempt for the Congress and the people whom we represent," Patman noted in 1966. "They appear to have adopted the attitude that tax exemption is their birthright—rather than a privilege granted to them by the people, through the Congress, for a public purpose. The reluctance to cooperate takes many forms. Some only furnished information under subpoena, demonstrating something less than a charitable attitude toward public knowledge and democratic processes. Others have sent us incomplete, or partially or wholly illegible, documents. Frequently, principal officers seemed to be in Europe when our letters arrived, leaving no one in the office with access to the records."[64]

It has been suggested by Ferdinand Lundberg that what looked like arrogance was perhaps only a genuine misunderstanding by adverse parties of the nature of political reality. Patman believes that the United States government is a supreme entity, while persons of great wealth are convinced that it is they who are supreme. The Patmans come and go, but great fortunes roll on forever under the protection of regressive tax laws. When they are challenged by a man like Patman, the reaction is no more than the amused contempt of a French duke of the time of Louis XIV when accosted by a minor official. "Is the man mad?" The challenge is something to be brushed aside and quickly forgotten.[65]

Finally, in 1965, Stanley Surrey, "after much prodding" from the Patman Committee, presented the Treasury's recommendations for reforms to the House Ways and Means Committee and the Senate Finance Committee. The department's 110-page report concentrated on six categories of major problems, with accompanying proposals. One of Treasury's top priorities was to prevent loans and other financial transactions between a donor and his foundation. It suggested that some foundations were keeping cash on hand rather than putting it to charitable use on the presumption the donor might in the future want to borrow some of it.

The Treasury recommended that private foundations "be prohibited from engaging in any transaction with a donor or parties related to the donor involving the transfer or use of the foundation's assets." Among such forbidden dealings would be loans, more than reasonable compensation for personal services actually rendered, any "preferential" services, selling or leasing foundation property to the donor, or purchasing or leasing property from him. A few minor exceptions would be made, such as an interest-free loan for bona fide charitable purposes from the donor to the foundation.

That a number of private foundations had become "deeply involved in the conduct of active business enterprises" was singled out by the Treasury. Of the 1,300 foundations sampled, about 180 owned 10% or more of a corporation's stock. One foundation had controlling interests in eighteen businesses, including a large metropolitan newspaper with annual receipts of $17 million, the largest radio station in its state, a lumber company, several banks, three large hotels and other enterprises concentrated largely in one city that gave it "an economic empire of substantial power and influence."*

Pointing to the Revenue Act of 1950, which subjected "unrelated business income" of foundations to ordinary income taxes, the Treasury noted that some were making use of exceptions that "can frequently shield their commercial enterprises from tax." Foundations, the report said, could lease business assets owned free of debt to operating subsidiaries and "siphon off most or all of the business profits by means of rent which is deductible by the subsidiary but not taxable to the parent foundation." This procedure made it possible for a foundation to "accumulate large reserves of untaxed capital which could be used to support the future operations of the business." Thus, with some exceptions, the Treasury would limit a foundation's ownership of a business unrelated to its charitable activities to less than 20 percent.

The third area of abuse the Treasury wanted closed was "trading or speculation" by foundations with any of their assets. It proposed that they specifically be prevented from such "inherently speculative" operations as trading in commodity futures or selling borrowed stocks "short" with a view toward buying them back later at a lower price. Although speculation could lead to "spectacularly successful" gains, it could also lead to "financial empire building." And there was always the risk of losing the foundation's assets altogether, not to mention the time consumed in the management of such transactions. Along this same line, Treasury requested that foundations be prohibited from all borrowing "for investment purposes." Also it asked that they be limited to making loans that are clearly "necessary, safe and appropriate for charitable fiduciaries." It found that sometimes a loan was made because the foundation managers had some "particular private reason" to want to benefit the recipients: "The same personal considerations which impel the foundation's director or donor to cause the loan will quite probably dissuade him from enforcing its terms with vigor and dispassion when collection difficulties arise."

Because of frequent "undue delay" between a donor's obtaining a tax deduction and a foundation's actually putting the money to charitable use, it proposed a timetable for spending. It would not directly include contributions or long-term capital gains (those derived from sales of assets held six months or more), but it would require a private "non-operating" foundation to spend all its net income from one year by the end of the

---

* Although the report did not name this foundation, it was the Houston Endowment Inc., of Houston, Texas. See page 301 for more details.

following year. This would apply to all foundations which do not operate their own charities but donate to others. "Income" would be that derived from investments, such as rents, interest and dividends, and short-term capital gains.

Since families have commonly established private foundations to maintain control of corporations while "substantially diminishing the burden of income, gift and estate taxes," the Treasury would prohibit a tax deduction for donating a part interest in a family business to a foundation until the foundation disposed of the donated property or devoted it to active charitable operations, or until the donor's control over the property ended.

The "proliferation and perpetual existence" of private foundations itself posed a problem. It estimated that twelve hundred new ones were formed annually, and many went on year after year "without achieving any of the external indicia of unique advancement of philanthropy." Because an individual could dominate his foundation throughout his life and then pass its management to family members on his death, "all the dangers of narrowness of view and parochialism can persist in perpetuity." To eliminate this problem, it proposed to limit donor control of a foundation to 25 percent after 25 years.[66]

If the Treasury proposals were a step in the right direction, the tone and spirit of the report flew in the face of the massive documentation of across-the-board abuses presented by the Patman Committee. There was one particular paragraph that must have had the old firebrand biting down hard on the bullet:

> Private philanthropy plays a special and vital role in our society. Beyond providing for areas into which government cannot and should not advance (such as religion), private philanthropic organizations can be uniquely qualified to initiate thought and action, experiment with new and untried ventures, dissent from prevailing attitudes, and act quickly and flexibly. Private foundations have an important part in this work. Available even to those of relatively restricted means, they enable individuals or small groups to establish new charitable endeavors and to express their own bents, concerns and experience. In doing so, they enrich the pluralism of our social order. Equally important, because their funds are frequently free of commitment to specific operating programs, they can shift the focus of their interest and their financial support from one charitable area to another. They can, hence, constitute a powerful instrument for evolution, growth and improvement in the shape and direction of charity.[67]

In appraising three general criticisms made by Patman, the Treasury study concluded that foundations had been guilty of unnecessarily delaying the use of funds donated for charitable purposes, *but* they had not become a disproportionately large segment of the national economy, and no substantial data were discovered to confirm the contention that "foundations represent dangerous concentrations of economic and social power." While conceding that "serious abuses do exist among a minority of private foundations," the Treasury found that most of them operated "responsibly," and defended its proposals as ones that would not only counter shortcomings but would "stimulate and foster the active pursuit of charitable ends which the tax laws seek to encourage." Any restraints its proposals might exert on the inflow of foundation funds, the Treasury said, "will be far outweighed by the benefits which will accrue to charity from the removal of abuses and from the elimination of the shadow which the existence of abuse now casts upon the private foundation area."

Was "the elimination of the shadow" the first order of business? In other words, were the proposals aimed at better public relations or at genuine tax reforms? There is no question that the Patman crusade was catching fire in liberal circles. Writers, and certain law professors not beholden to foundations, were suddenly pointing an incriminating finger at this crescent avalanche of privileged wealth, adding fuel to the "taxpayers' revolt" then slowly gathering momentum across the country. Some critics charged that large foundations were a benevolent-aid society for the Eastern establishment. Even John D. Rockefeller III had his doubts. "Philanthropy generally is not attuned to the tempo of the times," he said. "We are prone to be too complacent."[68]

One reason given for the discontent was that foundations no longer enjoyed a monopoly in philanthropy. The Great Society had usurped nearly all the traditional foundation fields—education, health, international aid, and research—and was outspending the private foundations, with a large percentage of the money going for research and development of new ideas. The government's National Foundation on the Arts and the Humanities, established in 1965, was already taking the initiative away from foundations. The Treasury Department's claim that foundations provided the venture capital in a pluralistic economy was disputed by critics who believed the government had captured the lead in innovation as well. In short, the Federal government was making better grants than private foundations, with the result that foundations were being forced to search for new competitive purposes for their tax-free billions.

Patman called the Treasury report "wishy-washy," and in a veiled attack on Secretary Dillon, Senator Albert Gore of Tennessee said the proposals by the department's legal experts must have been "altered and softened" by Treasury higher-ups. The best that can be said for the study is that it was perfunctory, conducted with a small sample and with statistics from a single year's operations. These restrictions could have distorted the conclusions. Although the report strongly stressed the value of venture capital, it failed completely to deal with the issues of the internal, public, and political factors inhibiting meaningful innovation by foundations.

Meanwhile, back in Congress, the House Ways and Means and the Senate Finance Committees, which had requested the Treasury study at Patman's insistence, yawned very quietly through it all, not wanting to alarm anybody unduly.

However, the government's attempt to soften the indictment was short-lived. After five years of strategic pounding at the foundations' front door, Wright Patman seemed to have located some hidden public nerve. Not that it would produce any instant legislation. Not yet. But the stench raised from his relentless dissection of the bloated corpus could not be sweetened with a dab of GI toilet water.

His own critics notwithstanding, and they were legion, Patman's study was a monumental undertaking and could not be easily dismissed. It could be ignored, of course, because who besides a writer or professor interested in the subject would bother plowing through six thousand pages of evidence and testimony?

As to Treasury's conclusion that serious abuses existed in a minority of cases, it should be added that all the pages of this book could not begin to cover the documentation of abuses presented by Patman against the whole gamut of foundations, from the smallest and most frivolous to the largest and most highly respected. It was not a question of pouncing on a few bad apples in a grab for headlines. In the final analysis, they were all pretty much the same, each practicing its own brand of tax avoidance to the best of its ability.

Perhaps the best way to illustrate this point is to present some pertinent statistics. By 1968 the Patman study had been broadened to include 20,616 foundations—almost half the number then known to exist by Treasury. Their book assets for that year amounted to nearly $29 billion, but again this was merely a vague approximation of their market value. Still it represented an awesome concentration of tax-free wealth, dwarfing the committee's earlier findings. The leverage of their economic force in the marketplace alarmed Patman: "There is reason for concern when such power is held by a relatively small and select group who can perpetuate themselves in office, and who never have to face scrutiny of a public that is affected daily by their autonomous actions." The study revealed that only 1 percent of the group had assets in excess of $10 million, but they in turn controlled more than 63 percent of all assets reported. In fact, less than 7 percent owned 90 percent of the total wealth—a rather significant correlation with the general distribution of wealth in America.[69]

Considering the horrendous erosion of the tax base caused by this vast pool of tax-exempt wealth, it is only fair to inquire into the nature of the philanthropic bounty bestowed upon the land by this horde of professional almoners. The measurement of a foundation's ability and willingness to provide charitable services must logically begin with its effort to invest its holdings so as to achieve a maximum return on its investments with a prudently minimal degree of risk. Because of the obvious undervaluation of assets reported (book value assigned by benefactor as opposed to market value),* the percentage arrived at by Patman was grossly distorted —that is, grossly inflated. The aggregate rate of return for 1968 was 7.17 percent, or $2,051,567,000 in income from an investment of $29 billion. It was Patman's estimate that the actual total market value of the reported assets was more like $40 or $50 billion, which would reduce the rate of return to 5.1 and 4.1 percent respectively.[70] Compare this with the total return, in 1968, of 15.3 percent for so-called common-stock mutual funds, and 14.9 percent for balanced funds.[71]

Patman linked their poor earning performance directly to their holdings of passive and nonproductive assets. An article in a financial journal entitled "Foundations: The Quiet $20 Billion," raised the question of whether there was "a place yet untouched by the revolution on money management," a place "where the winds of performance are not felt." It answered that "such a place does exist," and it is called "foundation land," where a tax-exempt twenty billion dollars, "one of the biggest pools of capital in capitalism" is "still run the way money used to be. The way it used to be, that is, for Widows and Orphans, before currency began to depreciate." In foundation land, "the managers do not often buy their stocks, because they already have them—they were given them many years ago, and now they sit, quietly watching."[72]

An analysis of the fifty largest foundations with holdings in excess of 5

* The variance in book and market values of the top five foundations in 1968 were as follows: Ford Foundation, book value was $2,975,418,695, market value $3,658,860,807; Rockefeller Foundation, $332,142,604 and $890,561,643; Duke Endowment, $169,655,466 and $634,411,587; Lilly Endowment Inc., $29,454,546 and $579,659,692; Pew Memorial Trust, $4,454,173 and $541,342,369.

percent of any corporation produces even more dismal figures. With aggregate holdings of $6.5 billion, the group's percentage point of return on investments in 1968 was 2.6 percent. To take only a handful of the top ones, here are some illuminating performances: Ford Foundation, 4.41 percent; Lilly Endowment Inc., 1.17; Duke Endowment, 3.40; Pew Memorial Trust, 1.26; Kresge Foundation, 0.88; Moody Foundation, 2.58; Howard Hughes Medical Institute, 0; Henry J. Kaiser Family Foundation, 0; Henry Luce Foundation Inc., 2.31; Richard King Mellon Foundation, 0.55; William Randolph Hearst Foundation, 1.67; Houston Endowment Inc., 0.30. The tragic fact here is that each added percentage point of return on total investments would yield additional hundreds of millions of dollars for charity—assuming, that is, that charity is the "exclusive" objective of foundations, a fact yet to be uncovered by any objective research.[73]

An additional $1,270,947,000 in revenue was gained through contributions and gifts by the 20,616 foundations reporting for 1968. This figure is not entirely reliable because foundations are in the habit of exchanging contributions and gifts among themselves. But taken at its face value, this brought their gross receipts for the year up to $3,322,514,000.[74]

So what happened to the $3.3 billion? Even with a poor earning performance, that is still a sizable bundle of alms to sprinkle upon the land. Before we get overly optimistic, there is another important item to consider: the cost factor! "The cost of producing and distributing charitable benefits by private foundations is staggering by any standard," Patman said in his report. For every *two dollars* distributed to charity, the foundations spent *one dollar* in administrative expenses. Total expenses amounted to more than $715 million, with more than 38 percent going for salaries and wages.[75]

Being a president or trustee of a foundation can be a rewarding experience, both in prestige and money. For example, the Duke Endowment paid twelve trustees $43,000 each for part-time work, and two who acted as officer and trustee received $88,000 and $70,000; the Booth Ferris Foundation paid three trustees $59,000 each for "whatever time is required to discharge their responsibilities"; the chairman of the board of the Kellogg Foundation received $120,000 for 90 percent of his time, plus expenses—his salary was raised to $130,000 in 1970; the administrative trustee of the Richard Mellon Foundation received $74,750 for 80 percent of his time; McGeorge Bundy's salary at the Ford Foundation was $65,000; the president of the Rockefeller Foundation received $67,500; and the Glendale Trust Company, the sole trustee of the Pew Memorial Trust, was paid a fee of $131,639.[76]

Interest on debts accounted for $25 million; $15 million went for rent, almost $130 million for depreciation and depletion, $225 million in miscellaneous expenses. In the miscellaneous column, the Houston Foundation spent $730,000 for "hotel laundry and garage supplies," $125,000 for "hotel guest parking," $905,000 for "food and beverages," and $126,-000 for "advertising." The Richard King Mellon Foundation paid $145,-000 in pension costs on salaries of $184,000; the Guggenheim (John Simon) Foundation had pension costs of $188,000 for $254,000 in salaries. The Robert A. Welch Foundation had expenses of $71,000 for ranch operations.[77]

The total amount contributed to charity in 1968 by the 20,616 foundations was $1,444,068,225—less than 43 percent of gross receipts. Even this low percentage was not an accurate picture of their philanthropy. The payouts included substantial amounts that were given to "conduit" foundations and paid out in the same year. For example, during the four years 1961 through 1964, the Standard Oil (Indiana) Foundation of Chicago made charitable grants totaling $5,459,967, but $2,059,736 of it was lateraled to the American Oil Foundation of Chicago, which is controlled by Standard Oil Company of Indiana. These "pass-through" funds inflated the proportion of payouts on actual endowments. At any rate, this left more than $1.1 billion in the kitty, undistributed funds on which to grow fat, or about 48 percent of net receipts retained as accumulated income. The Ford Foundation retained $67.4 million in accumulated funds, and the Rockefeller Foundation $41.8 million.[78]

If the performance of the group was lamentable, there were individual performances that by comparison lent luster to the former. The Bright Star Foundation of Dallas, with total assets at market value of $109 million and income of $17.7 million, paid out 0.3 percent to charity. The James Irvine Foundation, with assets estimated in the neighborhood of $1 billion and income of $1.8 million, paid out zero dollars to charity. The Houston Endowment, the one with the fancy miscellaneous expenses, paid out 7.9 percent. The Carnegie Institute of Washington paid out 8.1 percent; the Kresge Foundation, 14 percent; the Sid W. Richardson Foundation, which was brought into being by the tender care of John Connally, with total assets of $106 million and income of $9.4 million, paid out 16 percent.[79]

Finally, after we have examined the quantity, there remains the ultimate question: Who gets the money and why? To begin this brief survey with the Houston Endowment is to rush in where even old populists fear to tread. A victim of the regional malaise that afflicts so many of his Southern colleagues, Wright Patman steered clear of the large Texas foundations. Except for the language of statistics, he had nothing critical to say about the three largest foundations in his state—the Moody Foundation, ranked fourteenth in the nation in total assets; the Houston Endowment, ranked seventeenth, and the Bright Star Foundation, ranked thirty-second—even though their records on return-asset ratios and payouts were as invidious as any in the top fifty.

The closest Patman got to actual criticism was the inclusion in his first report of a story from the Dallas *Morning News* of December 15, 1962:

> Austin, Tex.—Attorney General Will Wilson, ending six years as attorney general Jan. 1, Friday recommended strong new laws to regulate charitable trusts.
>
> "This is an unbridled field for tax evasion and public trust violation," Wilson said in his final report to Gov. Price Daniel. . . . Wilson's staff located names of 1,629 known foundations . . . about 850 complete reports have been assembled and for 675 of them there had been tabulated $403,370,000 in assets . . . listed at acquisition value and thus were grossly undervalued. . . . "The flight of capital into charitable trusts and foundations is rapidly increasing," wrote Wilson in his report. "As of the present time, there is no registration of assets or liabilities and no accounting for the administration of trusts. This is a prolific field for conflict-of-interest situations and misconduct, and I feel that a great deal more basic supervision of actions of trustees is in the public interest. . . ."
>
> Wilson cited several trusts which his staff had investigated and in which he had intervened to halt what he termed misconduct and conflict of interest. . . . One example he cited was a trust first investigated in 1961 for alleged misconduct and conflict of interest. It involved a drilling company, life insurance companies, a large company not otherwise identified, a shopping center, a building and ranches, and the foundation board chairman. At one time two life insurance companies were involved in loans amounting to 90 percent of their assets. Filing a suit was considered but abandoned because it might have caused their collapse, said Wilson, which would have had a disastrous effect on the Texas life insurance industry. Reforms in operations were accomplished through agreements, he reported, preventing the collapse of insurance companies licensed to do business in many states.[80]

Patman had the opportunity but failed to identify the Moody Foundation as the maverick trust. Nor did he express interest in its future "reformed" performance. If he had followed its progress in succeeding years, he would have found that Moody family businesses, including American National Insurance Company, were as reluctant as ever to pay dividends to the foundation that sheltered them from the revenuer.*

Jesse H. Jones came to national prominence during the Administration of Franklin D. Roosevelt, first serving as chairman of the Reconstruction Finance Corporation and later as Secretary of Commerce. But long before he came to Washington, Jesse Jones was a man of considerable substance in his home town of Houston. He was a banker, publisher, industrialist, hotelier, politician, and, naturally, a philanthropist.

In defense of the poor earning performance of Southwestern foundations, Jesse Jones's grandson, John T. Jones, Jr., the man now straddling the empire, offered this description of first-generation wealth contributed to foundations:

> Our founders were the opportunists, the wheelers and dealers of the frontier. They were hard rock individualists who started from scratch and made their money whenever, wherever, and however they could. Southwest foundations have precious little AT&T stock, for these were mostly men deeply suspicious of New York with its top-hatted bankers and smooth talking brokers. Instead of the stock, there may be three or four short grass ranches where oil might or might not be found some day, and that are always well stocked with hungry cows. It is likely that the corpus may include not only ranches but also office buildings, pine lands, oil royalties, theaters, maybe a fleet of leaky shrimp boats, real estate in places no one ever heard of, a string of hotels or motels, and God only knows what all else.[81]

That was not exactly the case with John T. Jones, Jr. As president of the Houston Endowment, he reigned over assets that included a 28 percent interest in the Texas National Bank of Commerce, and outright ownership of a long list of properties: six real-estate and "properties" companies, which in turn controlled the Rice Hotel, one of Houston's finest; two smaller hotels; a downtown department store; a medical building; seven office buildings; and various tracts of land both in Houston and in New York. It owned the Banker's Mortgage Company; the Jones Lumber Company; the Houston Terminal Warehouse and Cold Storage Company;

---

* The Moody family was in more trouble in 1972. A federal district judge permanently enjoined W. L. Moody & Company, Bankers, from violating registration and antifraud provisions of federal securities law. A receiver was appointed. The Moody bank, the largest private bank in Texas, was not a member of the Federal Deposit Insurance Corporation or the Federal Reserve System, and was not regulated or examined by any state or federal banking authority.

and, most importantly, the Houston Publishing Company, publisher of the Houston *Chronicle*, the city's only afternoon newspaper, with the largest daily circulation in Texas.[82]

That the *Chronicle* enjoyed an enviable competitive advantage because of its unique tax-exempt position was illustrated in the 1965 Treasury report. Since it could defer indefinitely the payment of dividends to the foundation, it utilized those funds to modernize and improve its "competitive posture." For example, the *Chronicle* had seven wire services: "Other newspapers of similar size have from one to three"; it published "seven separate editions each day," the Houston *Post* but five, and "no comparable evening newspaper in the country publishes seven." Its subscription rate was $2 per month; the *Post*'s had been "forced down to $2.25." At the time of the Treasury study, the *Chronicle* purchased—and then killed —its only afternoon competitor, the Houston *Press*. The Treasury concluded that the *Chronicle*'s advertising rates "appear to remain substantially lower than those of any similar newspaper in the country."[83]

The bottom line to this happy vignette leaves little doubt of the benefits awaiting anyone with a bent for philanthropy. With assets in 1968 at a market value of $169,982,248 and a gross income of $50,445,450, the foundation received dividends of $3,972,919. The tax-free accumulation of income that year, less expenses of $11,362,775, was a whopping $35,109,756. Figured at the 52 percent federal tax rate then in effect, the foundation saved Mr. Jones's conglomerate at least $18 million in corporate federal taxes alone.[84]

If Patman was remiss in the above instances, he was only a little more valiant when he inadvertently got entangled with the Central Intelligence Agency. The date was August 31, 1964, and Patman was questioning in private session acting IRS Commissioner Bertrand Harding and his assistant, Mitchell Rogovin, about why the government had failed to pursue its investigation of the J. M. Kaplan Fund of New York, which had engaged in so many stock deals that the IRS had considered revoking its tax exemption as far back as 1957. Patman made Rogovin's response public on a day when few people were present in the hearing room. "Mr. Rogovin," he said, "informed us that J. M. Kaplan Fund has been operating as a conduit for channeling CIA funds and hence . . . would rather not discuss the matter for the public record. He also indicated that the fund's operations with the CIA was the reason for the lack of action on the part of IRS." Patman demanded information on eight foundations which, he said, had channeled nearly $1 million into the Kaplan Fund.

Apparently it was not as much a mystery as the CIA believed. F. Emerson Andrews, who was present at the Hearings, testified: "Persons close to the foundation field had known for some years that the CIA was sending agents abroad as presumed scientists from invented foundations and that funds for certain conventions and projects abroad were being channeled through a few legitimate foundations."[85]

It was estimated later that as many as seventeen foundations were being used as CIA conduits, but Patman slammed the lid shut after he ran into what he called "a hint that I had better not touch this because it involves foreign operations of the CIA." And when, in 1967, it was suggested that Congress investigate revelations that the John Hay Whitney Trust Fund was being funded by the CIA, Senator Everett Dirksen quashed the idea, saying, "I can't imagine the British Parliament investigating the British intelligence system."[86]

Although it is beyond the purview of this book to delve into the ideological escapades of the CIA, it should be noted in passing that millions of government and tax-free corporate dollars were funneled into ultra-right-wing propaganda foundations in the alleged pursuit of shaping foreign policy. Credit for penetrating behind the CIA-IRS curtain belongs to Group Research, Inc., a fact-finding organization based in Washington, whose efforts in 1966 revealed an intricate web of fund-swapping among groups of politically oriented foundations dedicated to rightist anti-Communist smear campaigns, some with smudges of racism and anti-Semitism on their banners. At least seven of the foundations were spawned by the philanthropy of Texas oilmen. Two had particularly close ties to President Johnson. One was the Hobby Foundation, established by Oveta Culp Hobby, publisher of the Houston *Post* and Secretary of Health, Education and Welfare under Eisenhower, and by her son, William Hobby, Jr., executive editor of the newspaper. The other was the Brown Foundation of Houston, founded by George and Herman Brown of the big government contractors, Brown & Root, the original and lifelong financial angels of Lyndon B. Johnson.

Among the recipients of their oblations were the American Friends of the Middle East, an anti-Zionist, pro-Arab foundation, and the Cuban Freedom Committee, sponsor of Free Cuba Radio and, according to Robert G. Sherrill, writing in the *Nation*, "the most belligerent anti-Castro radio series broadcast out of this country, whose advisory board includes several galloping right wingers."[87]

It follows that good politics with Arab nations is good business for oilmen with sizable interests in that area. Whenever the American Friends of the Middle East, which spends money like a drunken sheik,[88] entertains in Washington, the most prominent guests are Senators and Representatives from oil states. Kermit Roosevelt of the Gulf Oil Company was on AFME's board. The suspicion that the CIA was funding AFME gained substance in 1963 when Bushrod Howard, Jr., an agent for the Yemeni royalists, told the Senate Foreign Relations Committee: "Some are putting all the blame for the problem of the Middle East on Israel and American Jews. To counter these alleged evils they have, over the years, put some $4 million of government funds into an anti-Israel organization." The committee conveniently forgot to ask who "they" were, and the State Department issued a memorandum saying, "There is no factual basis for Mr. Howard's charge that U.S. officials support an anti-Israel organization.[89]

With or without the CIA's assistance, Texas foundations were pouring money into AFME. The Brown Foundation gave it $50,000 in 1963 and $150,000 in 1964.[90] Other contributors included the Dearborn Foundation, believed to be a CIA dummy; the Jones-O'Donnell Foundation; the Marshall Foundation; and the San Jacinto Foundation. These foundations, in turn, received large contributions from several other foundations.[91]

A study in the mid-1960s by the Anti-Defamation League of B'nai B'rith estimated that the cost of ultrarightist propaganda was "in the neighborhood of $14,000,000 a year." A substantial portion of this money came from "70 or more foundations . . . 113 business firms and corporations, 25 utilities, and some 250 individuals who can be identified as having contributed at least $500 each in recent years."[92]

One of the big spenders for right-wing causes was J. K. Lilly, scion of the drug firm of Eli Lilly & Company and sponsor of the Lilly Endowment Inc., the nation's fourth largest foundation. Lilly was one of the original backers, with a $25,000 grant, of the Committee for Constitutional Government, which between 1937 and 1944 distributed the staggering total of 82,000,000 pieces of literature, 750,000 books, 10,000 radio talks "on national issues," 350,000 telegrams to citizens "to arouse them to action on great issues," "many thousands" of releases to daily and weekly newspapers, and "full-pay" advertisements in 536 different newspapers with a combined circulation of nearly 20,000,000. And yet it also boasted, at the same time, "Throughout its seven years, the committee has not spent one dollar for lobbying." This monumental barrage was directed at discouraging "welfare legislation" such as the forty-hour week, collective bargaining, and Social Security.[93]

When the House Select Committee on Lobbying Activities, chaired by Representative Frank Buchanan of Pennsylvania, investigated corporate lobbying in 1950, the committee's counsel, Benedict F. Fitzgerald, Jr., remarked: "Of particular significance is the fact that Dr. Edward A. Rumely and the Committee for Constitutional Government, Inc., in recent years have devised a scheme for raising enormous funds without filing reports pursuant to the provisions of the Federal Regulation of Lobbying Act. This scheme has the color of legality, but in fact is a method of circumventing the law. It utilizes a system whereby contributions to the CCG are designated as payments for the purchase of books, which are transmitted to others at the designation of the purchaser, with both the contributor of the money and the recipient of the books totally unaware of the subterfuge."[94]

The Buchanan Committee wanted a list of the subscribers, but Dr. Rumely refused to comply for fear of exposing them to "the pressure of the labor bosses or the smear of left-wingers."

During this period Dr. Rumely's friends in Congress, including Senators Harry F. Byrd, Sr., and James O. Eastland, sent out millions of free mailings under their franks. Referring to the CCG as "that fascist group," Wright Patman called it the "most sinister lobby ever."[95]

Lilly also supplied much of the initial financing when the National Foundation for Education in American Citizenship (NFEAC) was incorporated in 1940, with this lofty statement of purpose: "To make better known the American way of life among adults, college, high school and elementary school children by grants to writers of books, pamphlets, and addresses dealing with the American theme; by fostering observation of patriotic holidays, by bringing outstanding speakers on education and political subjects."[96]

Through the years NFEAC has found many enthusiastic backers. And it, in turn, has been generous with its contributions to *Human Events*, one of the more rabid propaganda publications of far-out right-wingers.

For a number of years, *Human Events* was closely linked with the Life Line Foundation of the Texas oil billionaire H. L. Hunt, who holds the distinction of being one of the very few benefactors ever drummed out of the eleemosynary corps by the Treasury Department. After a three-year investigation, Treasury revoked Life Line's tax-exempt status on the ground that it was engaged principally in the production of a radio propaganda program, and that its newsletter, *Facts Forum News*, was a propaganda sheet.

In this instance, Patman displayed no regional trepidation in exposing Hunt's operation. He showed where Life Line "subscribers" (mostly Texas oil companies and foundations) had contributed more than $3 million. Expenses over a period of years ran to $4.9 million, and the amount of charity dispensed in the same length of time was an even $1,000.

Another favorite charity of the Lilly Endowment was the Christian Anti-Communist Crusade of Dr. Fred Schwartz, whose dramatic warning on the approaching Red Armageddon has stirred the restless soul of many a patriot: "Christian! To arms! The enemy is at the gate! Buckle on the armor of the Christian and go forth to the battle! When they come for you, as they have for many others, and on a dark night in a dank cellar, they take a wide-bore revolver with soft-nose bullet, and they place it at the nape of your neck . . ."[97]

J. Howard Pew of Sun Oil, who controls the Pew Memorial Trust, the nation's fifth largest foundation, was an avid supporter of the far-out Far Right. Among his favorite charities were the intercollegiate Studies Institute of Philadelphia, the Christian Freedoms Foundation, Dr. Schwartz's Christian Anti-Communist Crusade, the Foundation for Economic Education, and the American Economic Foundation.[98]

Large chunks of General Motors money in the form of grants from the Alfred P. Sloan Foundation, eleventh largest in the nation, have gone into right-wing coffers. One of the beneficiaries was the National Education Program, brain trust of the ultra Right, which was set up by Dr. George S. Benson on the campus of Harding College in Searcy, Arkansas.[99]

The list could go on for countless more pages. Left-wing groups would take up some space too, but, considering who holds the purse strings, not nearly as much. The Ford Foundation has poured funds into the Institute for Policy Studies (IPS), a New Left think tank in Washington. IPS codirector Marcus Raskin ran the presidential campaign for Dick Gregory in 1968, and was a codefendant in the Dr. Benjamin Spock draft-conspiracy trial. Arthur I. Washow, an IPS senior fellow, helped organize the demonstration at the 1968 Democratic national convention in Chicago. IPS is perhaps the most extreme of the left-wing groups funded by foundations.

There was a time when Paul Hoffman and Robert M. Hutchins were *les enfants terribles* at the Ford Foundation. The Chicago *Tribune*, that great bastion of civil liberties, was quick to lead the attack in 1951 under the banner headline "LEFTIST SLANT BEGINS TO SHOW IN FORD TRUST." It was a natural assumption for the *Tribune*, considering that Hoffman, as head of the Marshall Plan, had "given away ten billion dollars to foreign countries." While right-wingers were enjoying a moveable feast in the early 1950s, Hearst columnists, backed by the radio commentator Fulton Lewis, Jr., and others, were cannonading the Left from every point of the perimeter. "Many books and various studies have been financed by tax-free grants from these foundations," Lewis charged. "In effect, the American people are paying more taxes to finance so-called scholars who work diligently to beat out our brains and change our traditional way of life into something more Socialistic." With a punch line worthy of Marie Antoinette, George Sokolsky summed it up in a neat little package for his confreres: "Henry Ford . . . made nearly all his money in this country, but Paul Hoffman, who is spending that money, seems to prefer to pour it into remote bottomless pits and to expend it for meaningless purposes, such as an investigation as to why the world is full of refugees, when, as a matter of fact, it always has been. . . . Why cannot some of the money the Ford Foundation is piddling away on trivia be used constructively for the saving of opera?"

Westbrook Pegler foamed at the mouth: the Ford funds "are in reckless hands. . . . That is the way queer international things get going." In one story, headlined FORD FOUNDATION IS FRONT FOR DANGEROUS COMMUNISTS he found some connection between the Foundation and President Eisenhower, Henry ("China Boy") Luce, and "the Marshall Plan squanderbund." "I find it beyond my ability at the moment to establish the master plan of these strange associations and activities. I will continue, however, to offer you verified facts and my best efforts at interpretations." Later he wrote: "There is a very important and sinister political mystery concealed in the mixed activities of the Ford Foundation under Paul Hoffman and Robert Hutchins, the *Time-Life* propaganda empire of Henry Luce, and the political works of William Benton, the Social-Democratic Senator from Connecticut." This was comparable to charging the leaders of the Politburo with being secret "international bankers"—an occupation, incidentally, very much suspect in *Tribune* aeries. As noted earlier, this was part of the smear campaign that culminated in the Cox and Reece investigations.

The irony of the right-wing barrage is that it was directed at a house of cards. Hoffman and Hutchins did not last long. "Every now and then the newspapers would pick up some wild grant," one Ford staffer observed, "and Henry [Ford II] would come in and roar 'Jesus Christ, why can't we be a nice foundation like Rockefeller?' "[100] Hoffman lasted from 1951 to 1953, which was all the liberalism and innovation Henry could stand. As

Hoffman recalled: "Every time we got a dozen letters objecting to something we'd done—a radio show or an overseas program or what not—I'd
have to spend hours reassuring the board."[101]

For a while Hutchins enjoyed an enviable position in the world of big-
time charity. His Center for the Study of Democratic Institutions, an
intellectual think tank outside Santa Barbara, California, which pays Congressmen fees up to $500 per day for brainstorming sessions, was sup-
ported exclusively by the Ford Foundation. Although aging like everybody
else, Hutchins remained an *enfant terrible*, immune to the forces of conformity, until finally Henry angrily severed the hawser and Hutchings found
himself adrift in a cruel world.

Writing about the Ford Foundation in 1966, Hutchins delivered some
typically tart observations: "Once I achieved, briefly, the ambition of
every right-thinking man, I became associated with a very large sum of
money. I refer to the Ford Foundation. My experience during that period
and my observations before and since convince me that thorough examination of the foundation in American life is overdue."

Hutchins quoted from Gilbert and Sullivan's *Iolanthe* the words of the
Lord Chancellor as he sings: "In my court I sit all day/Giving agreeable
girls away." "If you substitute millions for girls," Hutchins wrote, "you get
the popular picture of the foundation executive. But it is not as idyllic as
all that. The foundation officer knows very well that the money he is giving away would have gone to the government if it had not gone into the
foundation."

Hutchins said the government was preempting the field of philanthropy: "And I have not heard any serious suggestion the governmental
subsidy is less efficient or discriminating than foundation grants. Governmental subsidy results from consensus. But so do foundation grants. The
notion that an enormous foundation can be the 'risk capital' of philanthropy has been refuted by the history of the Ford Foundation. It cannot
be accused of being venturesome. The foundations have in fact accepted
the soporific advice given by one of the congressional investigating committees: 'They should be very chary of promoting ideas, concepts and
opinion-forming material which run counter to what the public currently
wishes, approves and likes.' "[102]

As it turned out, Hutchins was not wary enough of his next sponsor,
the Albert Parvin Foundation. For a while in 1969 it was a toss-up in the
press between the Wolfson and Parvin foundations as to which was the
more sinister. The pall that it cast over the entire field of philanthropy

brought tremendous pressure to bear on certain members of Congress. For others it offered an ideal opportunity to get rid of a couple of Warren Court disciples. The resignation of Justice Abe Fortas, followed by Senate rejection of two Southern judges—Clement Haynsworth and G. Harrold Carswell—triggered an attempt to begin impeachment proceedings against Justice William O. Douglas. The attack was launched on April 15, 1970, in a speech in the House of Representatives by then Republican Minority Leader Gerald R. Ford, who obviously had paid close attention to his homework before trying to persuade his colleagues. His charges ranged from inciting anarchy to conflict of interest, from alleged dealings with "known criminals" to permitting publication of an article under Douglas's name in *Evergreen Review*, a magazine that Ford said contained "hard-core pornography."

Excerpts from the Ford speech dealing with the Parvin Foundation are presented here to illustrate the complex nature of the case:

> Albert Parvin was born in Chicago around the turn of the century, but little is known of his life until he turns up as president and 30 percent owner of Hotel Flamingo, Inc., which operated the hotel and gambling casino in Las Vegas, Nevada. It was first opened by Bugsy Siegel in 1946, a year before he was murdered.
>
> Bugsy's contract for decorations and furnishings of the Flamingo was with Albert Parvin & Company. . . . After the gangland rub-out of Siegel in Los Angeles . . . the Flamingo passed into the hands of Gus Green-baum . . . [who] was later murdered. Next Albert Parvin teamed up with William Israel Alderman—known as Ice Pick Willie—to head the Flamingo. But Alderman soon was off to the Riviera [Hotel], and Parvin took over [in 1955].
>
> On May 12, 1960, Parvin signed a contract with Meyer Lansky, one of the country's top gangsters, paying Lansky what was purportedly a finder's fee of $200,000 in the sale of the Flamingo . . . for a reported 10.5 million dollars to a group including Florida hotelman Morris Lansburgh. . . . His attorney in the deal was Edward Levinson, who has been associated with Parvin in a number of enterprises. . . .
>
> In November of 1960, Parvin set up the Albert Parvin Foundation. Accounts vary as to whether it was funded with Flamingo Hotel stock or with a first mortgage on the Flamingo taken under the terms of the sale. At any rate, the foundation was incorporated in New York and Mr. Justice Douglas assisted in setting it up, according to Parvin. . . . There is additional evidence that Mr. Justice Douglas later, while still on salary, gave legal advice to the Albert Parvin Foundation on dealings with an Internal Revenue investigation.

A later inquiry by the House Judiciary Subcommittee revealed that

IRS had investigated Parvin himself (as well as the Foundation), and that Parvin was on the Justice Department's Organized Crime Drive list. Even the FBI had begun investigating the foundation on March 28, 1961, which was two years before the foundation was awarded its tax-exempt status. The subcommittee's report said that Douglas and other foundation officers permitted Parvin to handle all the institution's finances, including the purchase and sale of stock, without prior consultation. Published minutes of the directors' meetings showed that transactions were approved after they had already been made, sometimes after periods of several months.[103]

One particularly interesting transaction approved by Douglas as president of the Foundation involved a loan of $250,000 from the City National Bank in Los Angeles at 5.5 percent interest. The Foundation then turned around and deposited the entire amount in the Long Beach Federal Savings & Loan and collected 4.75 percent interest. The money stayed in the account from April 6, 1962, to January 2, 1964. The matter was not brought up before the Foundation's board of directors* until January 23, 1963. The minutes read: "On motion of Mr. Parvin, seconded by Mr. Hutchins, the directors authorized the opening of an account with the Long Beach Federal Savings & Loan." The minutes were signed by Douglas.

As the subcommittee discovered, the transaction was not as stupid as it appeared on surface. Parvin was one of a number of people seeking to gain control of Long Beach Federal through a merger with a group known as Equitable Savings and Loan Association. Some seventy-seven accounts, totaling more than $20 million, were opened on or shortly after April 2, 1962. The purpose was to dilute the interest of small and regular shareholders in the association's net worth. The ploy failed when the Federal Home Loan Bank Board rejected the merger plan. Parvin, who had $60,000 of his own funds invested in Long Beach Federal, plus ten thousand shares of Equitable stock, promptly joined with other shareholders in bringing a court action to reverse the order. When the issue reached the Supreme Court in February 1968, Douglas did not disqualify himself, but since the petitions for certiorari were denied automatically, the subcommittee ruled there had been no need for him to do so.[104]

Ford further told his colleagues:

---

* In addition to Parvin and Douglas, sitting on the Foundation's board of directors were Robert Hutchins; Robert F. Goheen, president of Princeton University; William J. Campbell, chief judge of the U.S. District Court in Chicago; and Harry Ashmore, an executive with the Center for the Study of Democratic Institutions.

The ostensible purpose of the Parvin Foundation was declared to be educating the developing leadership in Latin America. This had not previously been a known concern of Parvin or his Las Vegas associates, but Cuba, where some of them had business connections, was then in the throes of Castro's Communist revolution.

In 1961 Mr. Justice Douglas was named a life member of the Parvin Foundation's board, elected president and voted a salary of $12,000 per year plus expenses. There is some conflict in testimony as to how long Douglas drew his pay, but he did not put a stop to it until last May [1969], in the wake of public revelations that forced the resignation of Mr. Justice Fortas. . . .

In April, 1962, the Parvin Foundation applied for tax-exempt status. And thereafter some very interesting things happened.

On October, 22, 1962, Bobby Baker turned up in Las Vegas for a three-day stay. His hotel bill was paid by Ed Levinson, Parvin's associate and sometime attorney. On Baker's registration card a hotel employe had noted: "Is with Douglas."

Bobby was then, of course, majority secretary of the Senate and widely regarded as the right hand of the then Vice President of the United States. So it was unclear whether the note meant literally that Mr. Justice Douglas was also visiting Las Vegas at that time or whether it meant only to identify Baker as a Douglas associate.*

Ed Levinson, a former Florida and Kentucky bookmaker, got his start in Las Vegas as a front for Joseph ("Doc") Stacher, the New Jersey gangster who was the power behind the building of the Sands Hotel—he was deported to Israel in 1965. In 1967, Levinson, who by then was a principal owner of the Fremont Hotel in downtown Las Vegas, was indicted with Edward Torres and five others on federal charges of skimming casino profits to evade corporate income taxes. After Levinson filed a $2-million invasion-of-privacy suit against four FBI agents whom he accused of having bugged his office, the government quickly lost interest in the case. Levinson pleaded no contest in March 1968 and was fined five thousand dollars.† Conviction on the charge could have got him three years in prison.

Representative Ford next embarked on a Caribbean excursion:

In December, 1962, I have learned, Bobby Baker met with Juan

---

* The Judiciary Subcommittee established that on that date Baker was registered at the Beverly Hills hotel. The bill was indeed paid by Levinson, but Douglas was out of the country at the time.

† On October 1, 1971, the Internal Revenue Service imposed a $1.4-million levy for back taxes, fraud penalties, and accumulated interest against the Fremont Hotel, which was to be paid out of a contingency fund set aside in 1966 when the hotel was sold to Parvin-Dohrmann Company.

Bosch, soon-to-be President of the Dominican Republic, in New York City.

In January, 1963, the Albert Parvin Foundation decided to drop all its Latin-American projects and to concentrate on the Dominican Republic. Douglas described President-elect Bosch as an old friend.

On February 26, 1963, however, we find Bobby Baker and Ed Levinson together again—this time on the other side of the continent in Florida —buying round-trip tickets on the same plane for the Dominican Republic.

Since the Parvin Foundation was set up to develop leadership in Latin America, [Rafael] Trujillo had been toppled from power in a bloody uprising and Juan Bosch was about to be inaugurated as the new liberal President. Officially representing the United States at the ceremonies February 27 were the Vice President and Mrs. Johnson. But their Air Force plane was loaded with such celebrities as Senator and Mrs. Humphrey, two Assistant Secretaries of State, Mr. and Mrs. [Jack] Valenti and Mrs. Elizabeth Carpenter. Bobby Baker and Eddie Levinson went commercial.

Also on hand in Santo Domingo to celebrate Bosch's taking up the reins of power were . . . Albert Parvin . . . and . . . William O. Douglas. . . .

Again there is conflicting testimony as to the reason for . . . [their] presence. . . . One story is that the Parvin Foundation was offering to finance an educational television project for the Dominican Republic. Another is that Mr. Justice Douglas was there to advise President Bosch on writing a new constitution for the Dominican Republic.

There is little doubt about the reasons behind the presence of a singularly large contingent of known gambling figures and Mafia types in Santo Domingo, however. With the change of political regimes, the rich gambling concessions of the Dominican Republic were up for grabs. . . . This brought such known gambling figures as Parvin and Levinson, Angelo Bruno and John Simone, Joseph Sicarelli, Eugene Pozo, Santa Trafficante, Jr., Louis ["Sleep-Out"] Levinson [Ed's brother], Leslie Earl ["Killer Kane"] Kruse and Sam Giancana to the island in the spring of 1963.

Bobby Baker, in addition to serving as go-between for his Las Vegas friends . . . was personally interested in concessions for vending machines of his Serv-U Corporation, then represented by the Washington attorney Abe Fortas. Baker has described Levinson as a former partner.

Mrs. Fortas [Carolyn Agger], also an attorney [with the Washington law firm of Arnold and Porter], was subsequently to be retained as tax counsel by the Parvin Foundation. . . . In April, 1963, Baker and Levinson returned to the Dominican Republic, and in that same month the Albert Parvin Foundation was granted its tax-exempt status. . . . In August, President Bosch awarded the [gambling] concession to Cliff Jones, former Lieutenant Governor of Nevada who, incidentally, also was an associate of Bobby Baker's. When this happened, the further interest of the Albert Parvin Foundation in the Dominican Republic abruptly ceased.

I am told that some of the educational-television equipment already delivered was simply abandoned in its original crates. . . .

Meanwhile, through the Parvin-Dohrmann Company which he had acquired, Albert Parvin bought the Fremont Hotel in Las Vegas in 1966 from Edward Levinson and Edward Torres, for some 16 million dollars [they remained on the payroll]. In 1968, Parvin-Dohrmann acquired the Aladdin Hotel and Casino in the same Nevada city, and in 1969 was denied permission by Nevada to buy the Riviera Hotel, and took over operation of the Stardust Hotel. This brought an investigation which led to the suspension of trading in Parvin-Dohrmann stock by the SEC, which led further to the company's employment of Nathan Voloshen. But in the interim Albert Parvin is said to have been bought out of the company and to have retired to concentrate on his foundation. . . .

When things got too hot on the Supreme Court for Justices accepting large sums of money from private foundations for ill-defined services, Mr. Justice Douglas finally gave up his open ties with the . . . Foundation. . . . [But he] moved immediately into a closer connection with the leftish Center for the Study of Democratic Institutions. . . .

A long time "consultant" and member of the board of directors of the center, Mr. Justice Douglas was elevated last December to the post of chairman of the executive committee. It should be noted that the Santa Barbara Center was a beneficiary of Parvin Foundation funds during the same period that . . . Douglas was receiving $1,000 a month salary from it and mobster Meyer Lansky was drawing down installment payments of $25,000 a year. In addition to Douglas, there are several others who serve on both the Parvin Foundation and Center for Democratic Studies boards, so the break was not a very sharp one.

Parvin's brief retirement, as it was called, was arranged by Sidney Korshak, a peripatetic Chicagoan with underworld ties every bit as mysterious as Lansky's—if not more important, at least he was certainly less notorious about it. His background is pretty much a blank, except that he grew up on Chicago's West Side in the days when Al Capone ran the show in that town. As a young attorney, Korshak got to know a number of the Mob's captains and lieutenants, earning a reputation as a shrewd legal adviser, but there is no record of his ever being arrested. His close link to the gang was first revealed in 1943 during the celebrated movie extortion trial that sent seven of Chicago's top hoods to prison—Frank Nitti escaped prosecution by committing suicide. Willie Bioff, the stool pigeon in the melodrama (later murdered by a bomb), testified that he had been introduced to Sidney Korshak by Charles "Cherry Nose" Gioe, one of the defendants, as "our man." "Pay attention to him [Korshak]," Gioe had warned Bioff. "Remember, any message he may deliver to you is a message from us."[105]

A lot of messages have slipped through the keyhole since that day. In fact, Korshak has been so busy that a news story described him once as a man who "seldom stops long enough in one place to get a wrinkle in his suit." Chicago columnist Irv Kupcinet, who hangs on his every word, asserted that Korshak was undoubtedly the highest-paid attorney in the United States.

This is especially impressive considering that Korshak does not practice law. He calls himself a labor-relations man, but the two most descriptive words would be "finder" and "fixer." Which was precisely what he did for his good friend Albert Parvin when he sat him down across a table from Delbert W. Coleman, a Chicago go-go conglomerator, who had merged his J. P. Seeburg Corporation, the old jukebox outfit, to the point where its annual sales exceeded $100 million. This was the season when the passions of corporate raiders had reached a frenzy, and Coleman was one of the most gravely infected. In the space of a few months, he had made passes at five heavyweights, including Warner Brothers-Seven Arts, without success. By the time he sat facing Parvin, with Korshak at his elbow, he was hot to trot.

To shorten a long, incredibly involved story, Coleman agreed to purchase from Parvin and his partner, Harry Goldman, some 300,000 Parvin-Dohrmann shares, a controlling interest equal to about 22 percent of the outstanding stock. The total price was to be $10.5 million, or $35 a share, slightly below the trading price of the previous month.

What happened next is a nightmare known best to those who fabricated it. Yet the record shows that on October 11, 1968, Parvin signed an agreement selling the 300,000 shares to Coleman, pending approval of a gaming license by Nevada authorities, which meant that control of the company would not officially pass into his hands until the license was granted in January 1969. Parvin took off for an extended safari in Africa, and Coleman promptly got to work. In no time at all, or so it seemed, Coleman and Korshak had boosted the company's stock from $35 to $141.50 a share.

The method employed was a fancy version of the old boiler-room promotion. Here is the way it worked. Coleman arranged to redistribute 143,200 of his shares to twenty-one individuals or groups, all at the same price of $35 a share. Korshak supervised many of the transactions, signing up his brother, Marshall, who was the city treasurer of Chicago, for a thousand shares, and his good friend the actress Jill St. John for another thousand. Korshak himself drew an allotment of 12,500 shares. But most of the shares were parceled off in blocks to pivotal figures in the market game like FOF Proprietary Fund, Ltd., of Geneva, Switzerland, part of an overseas complex of mutual funds run by Bernard Cornfeld, which acquired 81,000 shares. Cornfeld had something else in common with Parvin: he too was a supporter of Hutchins's Center in Santa Barbara.

Of the $5 million he retrieved from this sale, Coleman plowed $4 million right back into the market, buying Parvin-Dohrmann shares through ninety open-market transactions in which he acquired more than 51,000 shares at prices ranging from $68 to $107 a share. These purchases, enhanced by the touting of the pivotal figures, the SEC later charged, created a false appearance of active trading in the stock on the American Stock Exchange and hence tended to induce unwitting public investors to buy. The purchase of the Stardust for $15 million in January, 1969, and rumors that the Riviera Hotel was next on the list of acquisitions also helped produce the desired results.

Suddenly things started going sour. On April 24, 1969, the American Stock Exchange suspended trading in Parvin-Dohrmann stock over-the-counter as well as on the exchange. It was then that Korshak gave Coleman the telephone number of Nathan P. Voloshen, the influence peddler who operated from the office of House Speaker John McCormack. For an alleged fee of $50,000, Voloshen quickly set up a meeting between Coleman and SEC Chairman Hamer Budge, who agreed to lift the suspension if Coleman would prepare a detailed press release of all his transactions. This was done and trading was resumed on May 12. On that day and the next, the stock soared to $141.50 per share. According to the SEC report, Coleman and his associates did not intend to stay with the company: "After the stock was driven up to a price of about $150, the company was to be unloaded to a merger partner." The SEC filed a massive lawsuit, charging seven company officials with manipulating the stock and making misleading statements about proposed mergers. After that the whole operation gradually collapsed. By May 1970, the price had dropped to $12.50. Parvin reclaimed his company, changed the name to Recrion Corp., and Sidney Korshak pocketed his finder's fee, a cool half million, for his efforts, which was more than double what Lansky got.[106]

In drawing a comparison between the Douglas and Fortas cases, Gerald Ford presented some interesting parallels:

Why, even the cast of characters in these two cases is virtually inter-changeable. Albert Parvin was named a co-conspirator but not a defen-dant in the stock-manipulation case that sent Louis Wolfson to prison. Albert Parvin is again under investigation in the stock-manipulation action against Parvin-Dohrmann. This generation has largely forgotten that William O. Douglas first rose to national prominence as Chairman of the Securities and Exchange Commission. His former law pupil at Yale and fellow New Dealer in those days was one Abe Fortas, and they remained the closest friends on and off the Supreme Court. Mrs. Fortas was retained by the Parvin Foundation in its tax difficulties. Abe Fortas was retained by Bobby Baker until he withdrew from the case because of his close ties with the White House.

With all that wheeling-dealing whirling about him, Robert Hutchins thought Patman was on the right track. In the same column in which he knocked the Ford Foundation, Hutchins had some kind words for the old crusader: "Congressman Wright Patman has lately been on a line of in-quiry that must be taken seriously. He has been doing noble work in trying to find out whether the foundations are really foundations. He has been asking to what extent they are tax dodges, vehicles of financial manipula-tion, public relations devices and instruments of private aggrandizement rather than public service."

It must have seemed ironic to Patman that it was not his awesome detailing of fiscal irresponsibility that finally led to the inclusion of founda-tions in the Tax Reform Act of 1969, but rather a series of controversies like the Fortas case, described by the New York *Times* as the "biggest scandal ever to hit the Supreme Court," and the emotional debate over the "moral fitness" of Douglas. William F. Buckley, Jr., was for impeaching Douglas forthwith, not for his association with Parvin (Buckley had no interest in corruption, only in competitive ideologies) but for his views as expressed in his book *Points of Rebellion*.[107] On the other hand, the Los Angeles *Times*, which had first exposed the jurist's link to Parvin, could not wait that long: "The impeachment attempt has a long way to go, with no promise of success. That is irrelevant, however, to the question of Douglas' suitability to remain on the Supreme Court. We believe strongly that he should resign his position."[108]

Nixon believed in the constitutional process of impeachment. This whole plethora of information was made available to Ford through his auspices. On May 13, 1970, Nixon wrote to the House Judiciary Com-mittee, saying, in part: "The power of impeachment is, of course, solely entrusted by the Constitution to the House of Representatives. However, the executive branch is clearly obligated, both by precedent and by the necessity of the House . . . having all of the facts before reaching its decision, to supply relevant information to the legislative branch . . . to the extent compatible with the public interest." Nixon added that he would "authorize and direct appropriate officials of the executive branch to furnish information within the jurisdiction of their departments and agencies relevant to the charges against Justice Douglas and otherwise to cooperate with the House . . . in this matter." Not only were the files of the Department of Justice, the Internal Revenue Service, and the Security and Exchange Commission made available, but investigators were allowed to read, but not copy, secret CIA documents. Needless to say, the President has since experienced a change of heart. In the impeachment drive against himself, he has rejected House requests for information by invoking executive privilege. The difference this time, as one House member observed, is that "the President's ox is being gored."

There was a whole string of surefire episodes that turned the heat on in Congress:

· The Ford Foundation gave $175,000 to the Cleveland chapter of the Congress of Racial Equality (CORE) to help finance a voter-registration drive in black wards at a time when Carl Stokes, a black, was running for mayor.

· Brooklyn Congressman John Rooney was opposed in a Democratic primary by a businessman who financed his campaign with funds from his personal foundation.

· McGeorge Bundy, shaping his "new look" at Ford, made sizable grants to three New York school districts, located in black slums, to experiment with decentralization. Several teachers were subsequently dismissed by the local school board in the Ocean Hill-Brownsville district, and the teachers' union struck, demanding the virtual abolition of the entire experiment.

· Congressman Henry B. Gonzalez of Texas blasted the Ford Foundation for support of the Mexican-American Youth Organization, a group run by young militants.

· McGeorge Bundy gave $131,069 in Ford travel-study grants to eight aides of Robert F. Kennedy, "who had been uniquely stricken in a moment of terrible tragedy" following the Senator's assassination.

In a piece in *Harper's* (July 1969), entitled "The Very Expensive Education of McGeorge Bundy," David Halberstam suggested that the establishment discovered the race problem in the mid-1960s "when a commuter train to Manhattan from Greenwich was fired on by black youths as it waited at the 125th Street station."

It is a fact that the venture into "high risk" ghetto areas was minimal at best. Foundation investment directed toward "high social yield" has gone to the moderate middle—that is, the solidly middle-class Urban League and the NAACP. Ford subsidiaries involved in "civil rights" areas, according to two Washington *Post* writers, are "run by essentially the same class of people that run Ford," men with sterling establishment credentials, who are not predisposed by temperament and education to understand or fight the deepest-rooted problems of the ghetto. The slums of Watts, Harlem, or those only a few blocks from the White House have remained conspicuously immune to the impact of venture capital.[109]

In the heated Congressional debate over foundation tax reform in 1969, the questions asked most often by politicians were directed not at correcting fiscal abuses but rather at what the anthropologist Robert Ardrey has called the territorial imperative—"the inward compulsion in animate beings to possess and defend . . . an area of space . . . which an animal or group of animals defends as an exclusive preserve."[110]

That a Congressman's job goes on the auction block every two years makes for deep-seated insecurity. Voters are fickle, fame fleeting, and what had happened in Brooklyn or Cleveland or Texas could easily be repeated in their district. Lobbyists and contributors are always-present helps, but there is no security blanket like a good press. In a session of crisis, Congressmen can be stampeded to run right over their fat-cat backers. The spring of 1969 had all the appearance of being such a season. With not a second to waste, the House Ways and Means Committee opened its hearings with their biggest gun: Wright Patman. Whatever else may be said about Patman, he is first and foremost a political animal. No one had to tell him the direction of the reform wind blowing over Capitol Hill that day.

After having pounded the ear of Ways and Means Chairman Wilbur Mills for nigh on nine years without arousing a scintilla of interest, Patman changed the order of priorities in his scenario from fiscal abuse to social change. Following a quick recapitulation of the political tribulations brought on by foundation grants (Rooney, Cleveland, etc.), Patman got down to the business at hand:

> I am hopeful that this committee will agree that there is an urgent need to redefine the role of the privately controlled charitable foundation.

Are the giant foundations on the road to becoming political machines? . . .
The Ford Foundation had gross income of $252 million in 1967. . . .
The Rockefeller Foundation had gross income of $53 million. . . . I need
not tell you gentlemen what can happen in a local, state, or national
election where this kind of money is turned loose, directly or indirectly, in
behalf of their favorite candidates. . . . Does the Ford Foundation have a
grandiose design to bring vast political, economic, and social changes to
the nation in the 1970s? Is this what Congress had in mind when it
granted tax exemption to privately controlled foundations?[111]

"When you introduce a wild card into the actual business of elections,"
one newsman observed, "then you are on life-and-death territory for these
guys."[112]

Having made his point, Patman went on to score the foundations on
grounds he knew best:

In the coming weeks, the foundation lobbyists will be emitting predictable cries that they can't "afford" taxation because it would divert
funds from their "vital activities" in public welfare, educational and other
fields.

Let us dispense with this nonsense in a hurry, for the bloated foundations would benefit greatly from forced attendance at a financial weight
watchers' class. . . . While the Congress and the administration searched
feverishly for funds to finance essential urban rebuilding programs, the
Richard King Mellon Foundation sent $50,000 to Ireland for the "preser-
vation of historical buildings." While thousands of Puerto Rican young-
sters drop out of New York schools because they can't master English, the
Agriculture Development Council, Inc., of New York, one of the thirteen
Rockefeller-controlled foundations in our study, sends $311,280 to Japan
to "improve English language teaching in Japanese schools."

The list is seemingly endless—one could call the examples ironic, but I
think "tragic" is the better adjective. The shortage of physicians in America is critical, so the Commonwealth Fund of New York sends $208,141
to Canada for medical education. The Bollingen Foundation of New York
City, a creation of the Mellon banking family of Pittsburgh, an organization that seems to specialize in sending thousands of dollars abroad for the
development of trivia into nonsense, disbursed $212,113 in foreign grants
during the period January 1, 1965–November 15, 1967, including grants
for the following: Archaeological research . . . [for] a study relating to
the remains of rural chthonic traditions which existed in Europe during
the Middle Ages. . . . [The] study of a Roman mystery cult of the second
and third century A.D. . . . Acquisition of data on important proto-historic
entrepôts and on maritime activities of peoples of Southeast Asia in proto-
historic times. . . .

Congress certainly cannot complain if the entire Mellon banking family assembles in one of their Pittsburgh mansions each evening for a

roundtable discussion on the origin and significance of the decorative types of medieval tombstones in Bosnia and Herzegovina. If the Mellons are more interested in medieval tombstones than in Pittsburgh poverty, and care to spend their money studying 12th and 13th century church construction, that is the Mellons' affairs. However, there is no obligation upon either the Congress or the American citizenry to give the Mellons tax-free dollars to finance their exotic interests.[113]

Although Patman delighted in detailing these exotic trivia, the point that foundations had a free hand in the disbursement of what many believed were "public" funds was not lost on the public. And there were more serious charges. For example, the Ford Foundation had 357 employees in the United States and 920 in foreign countries. The Rockefeller Foundation, which had 211 employees in the United States and 112 abroad, spent $17.8 million for the benefit of foreign institutions or persons, and only $10.9 million for similar goals in this country. It spent half as much just running its New York office—$5.4 million—as it spent throughout the entire nation in 1966. Other Rockefeller expenses cited in the Patman report: "$1,693,762 in India, but not a penny in Arkansas; a half-million dollars in Uganda, but not a cent in Idaho; over a $1 million in Nigeria, but only $1,000 in Kentucky; $2 million in Colombia, but nothing at all in South Carolina, Wyoming, Maine or Delaware."[114]

Twenty-two foundations in the study disbursed $70.4 million in foreign countries, purchased $91 million in foreign securities, and sent $15.2 million to foreign branch offices during the period from January 1, 1965, to November 20, 1967.

During this same period, the Ford Foundation made direct grants in U.S. dollars to at least twenty-five foreign governments or regions, including the United Arab Republic, Jordan, Lebanon, Zambia, Nigeria, Northern Nigeria, Midwestern Nigeria, Eastern Nigeria, Pakistan, India, Republic of the Ivory Coast, Syrian Arab Republic, Iraq, Tanzania, Mexico, Kenya, Tunisia, Antigua, Cameroon, West Bengal, Chile, Brazil, and Nepal.[115]

"Thus far, the relationship between the tax-exempt foundations and the U.S. Government has been a one-way street—with the foundations doing all the 'gittin,' " Patman told the committee. "For example, three of the Rockefeller-controlled foundations have received Federal funds totaling at least $18 million during the past thirteen years, in part from the Agency for International Development."[116]

Patman did not further develop this point, but it goes without saying that funds spent abroad in the name of humanity by foundations owned by American multinational corporations were not unappreciated by the favored governments. If a hardheaded businessman chooses to silently bury a quid in the sand under some sheik's tent instead of opting for a Harlem project with the usual public-relations "splash value" in the New York *Times*, is it unreasonable to presume that perhaps somewhere in his financial future a quo may be in the offing? After all, Big Business is not a game played for Brownie points.

On balance, the money spent on "social experiments" in this country by all the foundations was a pittance. The Commission on Foundations and Private Philanthropy, a private study group headed by Peter G. Peterson, then chairman of Bell & Howell, found that less than 1 percent of all foundation grants went to projects in any way political, that slightly more than one out of ten foundations had recently made grants they considered experimental, and not one in a hundred admitted making any controversial grants.[117] And yet it was the only catalyst hot enough to bring the Congressional blood pressure to a reform boil. In the final analysis, the foundations were punished, not for their blatant fiscal violations and antitrust machinations, but for the very thing they were not doing enough about in the first place. Foundations have no more reason to exist as simple piecemeal conduits to established philanthropies than they do as tax dodges or stock shelters.

In his book *The Rich and the Super-Rich*, Ferdinand Lundberg summed it up this way:

> As to giving money away, it is evident that these endowments could have been transferred in one original move to extremely capable hands. In education they could have been turned over to the Association of American Universities and similar bodies, in science to the American Association for the Advancement of Science, in medicine to the American Medical Association, and so on. But this would be the end of it all. The donor and his heirs would have no more participation in it.
>
> By making serial gifts each year out of income from a perpetual principal fund the donor can keep prospective worthy recipients sitting around forever like a circle of hungry dogs, awaiting the next handout. In such an arrangement prospective institutional recipients are not likely to voice unwelcome socio-economic or politico-economic ideas. They are more likely to be careful to give utterance only to impeccably sound ideas, the kind one might hear in the top clubs. The general foundations, then, with their serial gifts, function pretty much as a carrot, rewarding those who are cooperative and constructive, passing over the unworthy, the carping, the critical, the nonadmiring, the unsound.[118]

James W. Armsey, who administered the Ford Foundation's matching-grant program for colleges, ruefully told a reporter in 1966 that "every phrase I write is scrutinized and dissected for meaning." And one college president admitted, "There are a lot of us who would run down Fifth Avenue naked if Jim Armsey said it would help get one of his grants." Peter Caws, a former officer at Carnegie, observed, "Wherever you go you are welcome, every suggestion you make is regarded as a special kind of illumination from above. When I went to Carnegie, a friend told me, 'You'll never have another honest conversation again in your life.' " Alan Pifer, president of the Carnegie Corporation of New York, said that he frequently made recommendations for college presidents and deans, and that foundations tend to nominate those they know. The anatomy of a grant follows pretty much the same configuration at all large foundations. At Ford it begins with a "discussion paper" prepared for the staff officers in a particular program. It moves through all the officers, and up through the president to the trustees, who, according to Patman, are the same "pious phonies" who dominate the Wall Street banking community. "Given this world," one Ford staffer admitted, "We don't make a grant seem like a breaking-down-the-barricades proposition."[119] Another critic contended, "The influence of the rich in philanthropy focuses on the established institution, tends to maintain the *status quo*. It is rare, indeed, that major donations are made to encourage basic change or even minor dislocation of any aspect of established society."[120]

There was very little the foundations could not live with in the tax bill by the time it was signed into law on December 30, 1969. The foundations had staged the most intensive lobbying and publicity campaign in their history. Financed by their philanthropic funds, the campaign easily defeated the more stringent features advocated by Patman in preference to a softened version of the Treasury's 1965 proposals. A distinguished coterie of spokesmen was paraded before the congressional committees, prophesying doom and bankruptcy for foundations. Countless editorials in magazines and newspapers pounced upon the rabble-rouser Patman in particular and Congress in general, with wild charges of recklessly endangering the freedom and prosperity of American philanthropy. One foundation consultant, writing in a national magazine without identifying his biased role, warned that if the reforms should become law, "the golden age of the private philanthropic foundation will come to an end."[121]

The strongest sanctions in the 1969 Tax Reform Act (Public Law 91-172) were imposed in the areas of legislative and political activities. The act prohibited *any* lobbying activities except for certain specific activities that might be classed as requested,* nonpartisan, analytical, educational, or related to the organization itself. Voter-registration drives were limited to those conducted in at least five states with support from five or more organizations. Grass-roots campaigns to affect the opinion of the general public on legislation were also prohibited. The law provided strong penalties, in the form of extra taxation, for any violation. Although the restrictions were quite specific and detailed, there were still many gray areas to be resolved in the courts.

As to the financial provisions, one of the most controversial proposals was a Senate Finance Committee amendment that would have required foundations after forty years (Patman wanted the limit set at twenty-five years) to distribute all assets to charity or to pay a regular corporate tax on income. After a meeting in his office with McGeorge Bundy and Alan Pifer, Senator Walter F. Mondale of Minnesota agreed to sponsor an amendment to kill the forty-year rule. The amendment was adopted by roll-call vote.

One of the provisions imposed by the act was a 4 percent tax on net investment income—Patman had asked for 20 percent on gross profits. The rate was set merely to cover the cost of auditing by the Internal Revenue Service.

Self-dealing between foundations and disqualified persons was banned. In this context, "disqualified persons" include just about anyone having a "substantial" interest in the foundation, relatives of persons in this category, and government officials in most circumstances.

The combined holdings of voting shares by a foundation and its contributors and officers was limited to 50 percent of any single business and for the foundation itself to 25 percent, requiring divestiture of holdings in excess of 50 percent but not in excess of 75 percent within a ten-year period. If the holdings are more than 75 percent, the reduction to 50 percent need not occur for a fifteen-year period, which is extended to twenty years if the foundation itself holds more than 95 percent of a corporation's stock (this provision looks tailor-made for Howard Hughes).† The ownership of companies obtained after May 26, 1969, is not limited until it reaches 20 percent (in some instances 35 percent),

* Foundation officials would be permitted upon request to testify before Congressional committees in areas of their expertise.

† Yet it was not good enough. To circumvent this restriction, Hughes asked the IRS to rule in 1973 that the Hughes Medical Institute be classified as a medical research institute rather than a private foundation.

which means the trustees and managers will be allowed to continue to exert powerful influence over the foundations: in most American corporations, 20 percent is a controlling interest. Patman's proposal was far more realistic. He would not permit a foundation to own more than 3 percent of the outstanding shares of any class of stock of a corporation or to own more than a 3 percent interest in the capital or profits of a partnership.

All net income (gross income less expenses incurred and long-term capital gains) must be distributed on a current basis. Beginning with 1972, foundations with assets invested in low-income "growth stock" or unimproved real estate with no current income will have to spend either their net income or an amount equivalent to 4.124 percent of the market value of their assets, whichever is greater. Although the rate was scheduled to increase to a maximum of 6 percent by 1975, it was left to the discretion of the Secretary of the Treasury to adjust it to conform with changes in the money rates—it was lowered to 5.5 percent in April 1972, to conform with the decline in interest costs since 1969.

Had this provision been in effect in 1968, the 20,616 foundations surveyed by Patman would have been required to make $665 million in additional contributions. The Lilly Endowment Inc., would have had to contribute $27 million more to charities than it did in 1968, the Pew Memorial Trust would have increased its contributions by $23 million, the Duke Endowment by $17 million, Kresge by $13 million, and Rockefeller by $10 million.[122]

In August 1972, Patman warned there was "already a serious effort being put forth to reduce this minimum payout provision from 6 percent to 5 percent and to extend the transitional period in the act. These legislative and administrative efforts are receiving strong support from the foundations who will have to divest control in corporations which paid little or no dividends. If their legislative efforts are successful, charity, the intended beneficiary of the tax-exempt activities of private foundations, will stand to lose hundreds of millions of dollars in contributions by 1975 and the Internal Revenue Code will once again serve as a shield to protect the real beneficiaries of private foundations—the foundations themselves."[123]

As an instrument of philanthropy, the private foundation has been a costly failure in this century. It is true that foundation money *helped* eradicate hookworm, yellow fever, malaria, and polio in many areas of the world; it supported rocket research when the military could not see a need for it, improved agricultural techniques, sponsored educational television, developed the new math, supported artists and scholars, advocated better salaries for college teachers, and brought new contraceptive techniques to villages in India.

But at what devastating cost to the taxpayer! And at what fantastic benefit to the philanthropist! The 1969 Tax Reform Act was not the loophole-closing measure necessary to immunize the avarice in philanthropy. The private foundation is still the best game in town for the wealthy man with stock holdings up in the millions, for eventually estate taxes would force him to sell most of his holdings, with the possibility of breaking the market in the process.

Meanwhile, the game goes on without interruption. While Nader's Raiders waited endlessly for tax exemption to help defray costs of the campaign they waged against General Motors (GM deducted the millions it spent in the fight), the National Dividend Foundation obtained its tax preference posthaste. The charitable objective of the National Dividend Foundation is to promote a constitutional amendment to make stock dividends tax-free. Its advisory board includes Elmer Bobst, chairman emeritus of the Warner-Lambert Pharmaceutical Company and the man President Nixon has affectionately described as his second father.[124]

CHAPTER **5**

THE REFORM GAME

If I were a visitor from another planet, by the way, here is how I would explain Mr. Nixon's actual malice toward Losers: I would say that it was because his family was poor during the Great Depression and it was a humiliation to them to be lumped with other poor people. It was as though the Nixons had all been locked up in a dog pound by mistake.

—KURT VONNEGUT, JR.[1]

Except for an occasional Mellon or Rockefeller—genuine money-power brokers who have participated directly in government—the trustees of our democratic institutions are mostly bootstrappers, dreamers of the impossible dream, fugitives from the mean labyrinths of the dog pound, Losers who have finally made it into the elite circle of Winners.

It is Vonnegut's theory that the "two real political parties in America are the Winners and the Losers. The people do not acknowledge this. They claim membership in two imaginary parties, the Republicans and the Democrats, instead. Both imaginary parties are bossed by Winners. When Republicans battle Democrats, this much is certain: Winners will win."[2] This is another way of saying that most incumbents of the Property Party, whether of liberal or conservative cant, are automatically classified Winners, no matter which wing controls the White House.

By the time a congressional Winner arrives in Washington, he is so much dressed meat on the hook of money power, having been bought and paid for several times over with campaign funds; further, his own public stipend alone is greater than the income of 99.5 percent of all American taxpayers.* What he gets in private gratuities, the true measure of the

---

* Representatives and Senators receive $42,500 in base pay, plus a minimum of $8,500 in fringe benefits. In July 1973, the Senate unanimously passed a bill to raise its base pay to $50,000, up from $22,500 in 1963.

quality of his service, is a secret shared only with his creators, the money power elite who have made the Property Party indivisible under God. The real trick of stewardship is to make it appear that one is serving God and not money power—but if a politician honestly believes that his sovereignty emanates from God, then anything is possible, including a nuclear holocaust. Needless to say, money power prefers good actors to fanatics. Hollywood still holds the best patent to the impossible dream.

This is not to imply, however, that there is no real competition in the memberships of both wings, or that they are immune to that infectious strain of animus which feeds on greed and vanity and which is so virulent among prima donnas, or that there are no mavericks in the flock, but whatever the origin or ambition of individuals, the system is powerful enough to crush all dangerous opposition. Even money power has its factions. It is no longer the exclusive monolith of Eastern wealth. The cowboys, as Kirkpatrick Sale describes the new-money establishment from the Southern-rim "sunbelt" states—from southern California to the Florida Keys—have been steadily chipping away at the Yankee power base.[3] With vast fortunes made in oil, natural gas, real estate, and postwar industries such as aerospace and defense contracting, the cowboys have been rooting deep in the, pork barrel ever since 1952. From Eisenhower to Nixon, with a heavy assist from Johnson, they have increased their influence in the bedrooms of government power to the point where they are now almost on an equal footing with the Yankees.

The cowboys, too, are bootstrappers, and their fortunes were created in the exploitation of natural resources and government largess: lucrative contracts, favorable regulations, generous subsidies, and big tax breaks. Their politics reflect the same malice toward Losers. They are not only right-wingers, but retrograde reactionaries, and their malevolence knows no bound. They are anti-everything that remotely suggests the agony of Losers: anti-black, anti-Mexican, anti-union, anti-consumer, anti-liberal, anti-regulation, anti-taxes, anti-welfare, anti-ecology, anti-aged, anti-youth, anti-intellectual, anti-Catholic, anti-Semitic, anti-competition, anti-Communist, and, certainly, anti-democracy.

Kirkpatrick Sale believes that "because of the newness of their position, their frontier heritage, or their lack of old-school ties, they tend to be without particular concerns about niceties of business ethics and morals, and therefore to be connected more than earlier money would have thought wise with shady speculations, political influence-peddling, corrupt unions, and even organized crime." The truth, of course, is that they are the spitting image of the old robber barons—both being endowed with the morals of a spider. And both have always been up to their wallets in crime—organized or otherwise—whether they were hiring hoods to break the heads of strikers or concealing Mafia loot in legitimate enterprises. As Francis Ford Coppola, director of *The Godfather*, aptly put it: "Men of power and the criminals in our society are distinguished only by their situation, not their morality."

Because many big-city political machines have been Democratic, the Democrats have historically enjoyed closer ties to organized crime. Adlai Stevenson owed his political career, governor of Illinois and twice presidential candidate, to Jake Arvey, who began his own career as a political stooge for Al Capone's West Side Bloc and continued his close alliance with the Chicago mob throughout his long career. Arvey's brightest protégé, Paul Ziffren, migrated to southern California, where he soon became the state's Democratic National Committeeman, a post he held seven years, until a national magazine unveiled his shadowy ties, including his business partnership with Alex Greenberg, the Chicago mob's financial wizard. When Greenberg was slain gangland-style, the Chicago *Tribune* suggested that his autobiography might have been called "My 46 Years With Chicago Gangsters." Ziffren bounced back into national politics in the 1960s, first as a backer of Johnson-Humphrey, then Humphrey-Muskie, and finally as chairman of Muskie's southern California committee in 1972.[4]

Many Presidents have indulged in the Christmas spirit (at various times of the year) by commuting the prison sentences of notorious Mafia bosses and associates. Truman created a national scandal when he commuted the sentences of the entire hierarchy of the Chicago Syndicate—seven top-ranking mobsters were paroled after serving only three years of ten-year sentences for their role in the infamous Browne-Bioff movie-extortion case.

Late in 1962 the United States Immigration and Naturalization Service ordered John ("Jake the Barber") Factor deported, but only eight days later John F. Kennedy granted him a full presidential pardon on a mail-fraud conviction, which is something on the order of a marriage annulment; it pretends the act never happened. Immediately after the pardon was granted, Factor applied for United States citizenship, and the Immigration Service, which only three months earlier had sought his ouster, now filed a petition in support of his application, with the declaration that

Factor had "clearly established his moral rehabilitation." Although no one stepped forward to accept public hosannas for pile-driving the pardon through the White House against the vociferous objections of Bobby Kennedy, three men stood taller in certain private circles because of it, whether they deserved it or not. They were James Roosevelt, Edmund ("Pat") Brown, and Pierre Salinger.*

One of Richard Nixon's most notable commutations freed Angelo ("Gyp") DeCarlo, a New Jersey Mafia boss who was characterized by one federal prosecutor as "violent . . . homicidal . . . and a man who orders executions."† His business was gambling, stolen securities, loan sharking, and narcotics. There was no scandal in connection with his release in 1972 from a 1970 twelve-year sentence for loan-sharking and extortion because it was accomplished without the knowledge of even those responsible for his conviction. "Before we even knew he was up," said one Justice official, "he was out again." DeCarlo's petition for executive clemency was based on claims that he was suffering from terminal cancer. An Administration spokesman said that it tried to avoid having prisoners die in prison: "It's considered detrimental to prison morale."[5]

The commutation on December 20, 1972, was at a time when the President and the Attorney General were talking tough on crime. "The time has come," said the President, "for softheaded judges . . . to show as much concern for the rights of innocent victims of crimes as they do for the rights of convicted criminals." Nixon's solution was to revive the death penalty and impose stiff mandatory minimum terms for certain kinds of crimes. "In a study of 955 narcotics drug violators who were arrested by the Bureau of Narcotics and Dangerous Drugs [the no-knock, middle-of-

---

* For a more detailed account of the bizarre career of Jake Factor, see Note 4A, p. 420.

† As an indication of DeCarlo's reputation, the FBI provided the government's chief witness, Gerald M. Zelmanowitz, with a new identity to protect him from DeCarlo's executioners. In mid-July 1973, Zelmanowitz testified before Senator Henry Jackson's Subcommittee on Permanent Investigations that in his former role as a securities racketeer for DeCarlo he had bribed bankers and brokers for their signatures on blank IRS forms certifying previous U.S. ownership of foreign securities, and that he had paid IRS agents up to $1,000 a week to obtain fraudulent exemptions from securities taxation. When Zelmanowitz's cover was inadvertently broken early in 1973, the IRS tried to reimpose a 1969 tax assessment against him. "The men who were assigned to review and resolve once and for all this assessment problem were none other than the same individuals whom I have identified as officials whom I have bribed," he said. "However, the most bizarre aspect to me in regards to this entire matter is the fact that Angelo DeCarlo is freely associating with his old associates and carrying on the exact same illegal activities he did prior to my testimony. He is free and I am hiding." DeCarlo died of cancer on October 21, 1973.

the-night raiders], and convicted in the [federal] courts," the President asserted in his message to Congress on March 14, 1973, "a total of 27 percent received sentences other than imprisonment. Most of these individuals were placed on probation. . . . This situation is intolerable." For the ghetto kid or college student caught experimenting with drugs supplied by DeCarlo and his colleagues, the President recommended a rigid uncompromising five- or ten-year minimum term because anything less is "intolerable."

The late Murray Chotiner, the Los Angeles lawyer who fashioned the young Nixon into the old Nixon, and from there many times into the new Nixon, publicly took credit for springing Jimmy Hoffa from prison. "I did it, I make no apologies for it," he said, "and frankly I'm proud of it."[6] It was Chotiner who taught Nixon the value of words like "Communist" and "traitor" and the magic of the poisonous dart and slanderous innuendo that earned him the sobriquet "Tricky Dick." All who crossed his path were smeared with the same red brush. Even Senator Robert A. Taft, the arch-Republican, was appalled by Nixon's tactics. After the 1952 convention, Taft confided to Joseph Polowsky, a friend and supporter, that Nixon was "a little man in a big hurry . . . [with] a mean and vindictive streak." Summing up his personality as one tending to "radiate tension and conflict," Taft expressed the hope that circumstances would never permit Nixon to accede to the Presidency.[7]

Between 1949 and 1952, while he was charting Nixon's course from the House to the Vice Presidency, with a brief stop in the Senate, Chotiner handled some 221 gambler-bookmaker cases in Los Angeles.[8] With his young protégé one heartbeat from the presidency, Chotiner elevated his clientele. He interceded successfully on behalf of Marco Reginelli, a Philadelphia hoodlum up for deportation,[9] and in 1956 the McClellan Rackets Committee scored Chotiner's role as attorney for a convicted clothing racketeer and exposed his influence-peddling activities in Washington.[10]

Chotiner, however, could not claim full credit for Hoffa's premature release. As it turned out, the commutation was only one of many capitulations in a complex entente cordiale worked out between the Teamsters and the White House. It is not clear who masterminded it, but things began happening soon after John Connally took over at Treasury in the spring of 1971. The President desperately needed at least one union to support his wage-price guidelines. For many reasons, most of them illegal, Teamsters President Frank Fitzsimmons seemed the logical choice. Fitzsimmons' pal

Dave Beck, Hoffa's predecessor and the first Teamsters boss to serve time for playing games with the union's pension fund, needed a big favor in a hurry. He owed the government $1.3 million in taxes, penalties, and interest, which was immediately due and collectible by IRS seizure of his properties. Instead of paying the obligation, Beck, according to the Seattle *Post-Intelligencer*, "got on the phone and began to collect from top Teamsters for past favors. What he collected was time. The Teamsters bought it for him." In "an unprecedented written agreement," the newspaper reported, the government—i.e., Connally—granted Beck a five-year moratorium on his debt.[11]

On December 23, 1971, four months after the U.S. Parole Board had rejected Hoffa's parole application for the third time, Nixon commuted Hoffa's sentence, but with the proviso that Hoffa could not engage, directly or indirectly, in the management of any labor organization prior to March 6, 1980—the theory is that Fitzsimmons had a hand in nailing down this restriction. In June 1973, Hoffa announced that he was going to regain the presidency of the Teamsters. The law, said Hoffa, "does not give the President the right to add something to your sentence that a judge does not add." With John Mitchell rapidly vanishing into the quagmire of Watergate, Hoffa had no problem in finding a scapegoat: "I have my own suspicion that the President signed in blank my commutation orders . . . and I think that Mitchell filled in and without the President's knowledge put in the 1980 restriction. And I think he did it deliberately to keep me out of the labor unions . . . because he thought he could manipulate Fitz better than he could talk to me. . . . They knew the economy was upside down and I think they wanted to have Fitz in there who would be more amenable to going along with controls than I would be."

Six weeks after his release from prison, an amenable Hoffa had told a national television audience that "President Nixon is the best qualified man at the present time for the Presidency of the United States in my own personal opinion."

Then there was the problem of Fitzsimmons' son Richard, a Detroit Teamster official, who was up on federal charges for misappropriating union funds. Soon after the entente was negotiated, the U.S. attorney in Detroit was told by the Justice Department to drop the case because the evidence was "thin."[12]

It was the McClellan Rackets Committee, under the leadership of Robert F. Kennedy, its chief counsel from 1955 to 1959, which first exposed the awesome corruption thriving at every level of the Teamsters union. No one who reads that blood-chilling record can long doubt that it is the most infamous union in history. The imprisonment of two of its presidents has had absolutely no effect on its present leaders, an impressive indication of the depth of its corruption. The fact that the Nixon White House has given it its seal of approval is as reprehensible as anything produced by Watergate.*

"This whole thing of the Teamsters and the mob and the White House is one of the scariest things I've ever seen," an FBI agent observed recently. "It has demoralized the bureau. We don't know what to expect out of the Justice Department."[13]

Here, briefly, are some of the scary facts as developed by reporters Jack Nelson and Bill Hazlett in a Los Angeles *Times* story headlined "Teamsters' Ties to Mafia—and to White House."[14]

To begin with, it should be noted that hoodlums, like cowboys and old people, are nuts about year-round sunshine. In recent years they have migrated to the sunbelt by the thousands, setting up shop mostly in southern California, Nevada, Arizona, Texas, and Florida, states considered in Mafia circles as "open territory." A large number of their sunbelt front operations have been financed by the Teamsters Central States, Southeast and Southwest Areas Pension Fund, a $1.4-billion cache located in Chicago. Next to personally receiving pension-fund loans, a mafioso likes nothing better than collecting illegal finders' fees—usually about 10 percent of the total loan, plus additional kickbacks—for setting up the connection between the lender and the receiver. In the words of one federal investigator, "the Teamster fund is sort of an open bank to people well connected in Las Vegas and well connected in organized crime." The infusion of Teamster money in underworld projects has been overwhelming, not only in Las Vegas but also in Palm Springs, Los Angeles, Orange County, San Diego County, Tucson, Phoenix, Dallas, Houston, New Orleans, Orlando, Fort Lauderdale, Miami, the Bahamas, and throughout the Caribbean.

The latest Mafia-Teamster schemes, as confided by FBI agents to the Los Angeles *Times*, include a "prepaid health care plan, a similar dental care program, a prepaid legal service and a series of real estate transactions involving more than $40 million in commercial property in Orange

---

* At a time when organized crime has stepped up its infiltration of legitimate business, both the Justice Department and Congress are backing off from further investigations—at least three committees have consigned the topic to the back burner.

and San Diego Counties—all financed by pension fund loans." The health plan, described as "a possible $1 billion-a-year business," would provide medical service to Teamsters covered under the union's welfare program. The program would be administered by a Los Angeles physician selected by the hoodlums.

On February 8, 1973, Frank Fitzsimmons, who was in Palm Springs to play in the Bob Hope Desert Classic golf tournament, discussed the health plan with Sam Sciortino, Peter J. Milano, and Joe Lamandri, all identified by the FBI as members of the California Mafia. In the next two days, Fitzsimmons met with Anthony Spilotro, a Chicago enforcer; Marshall Caifano, also known as Johnny Marshall, another Chicago hit man; Tony Accardo, the aging Chicago Mafia boss; Lou ("The Tailor") Rosanova, a former gofer who recently made the FBI's "top 300" mobster list in the Chicago area—he is currently executive director of the Teamster-owned Savannah Inn and Country Club, "the mob's Southern watering hole"— and with three friends and associates of Rosanova: Lloyd J. Pitzer of Los Angeles, Charles E. Greller of Chicago, and Richard Strummer. To handle the series of commissions or kickbacks to be paid under the health-care plan, Rosanova set up an office called People's Industrial Consultants in Beverly Hills.

How did the FBI know all this? For one thing, it was using wiretaps, the Nixon-Mitchell chief get-tough-on-crime weapon, along with no-knock and its random search-and-seizure technique. From a tap at People's Industrial Consultants, the FBI overheard Raymond ("Rocky") DeRosa, a Mafia enforcer-collector, brag that he was to receive $50,000 "in front" when the Teamsters signed up the health-care plan. Of the 10 percent P.I.C. would receive, three-tenths would go to Chicago hoodlums and one-tenth was earmarked for two unidentified Teamsters.

On February 12, Fitzsimmons met with Rosanova at the Teamster-financed, mob-operated La Costa Country Club, located a few miles north of San Diego, and known in police circles as the West Coast rest and recuperation center for top-rated organized-crime troops. The following morning, Fitzsimmons drove to the El Toro Marine Air Station and there boarded Air Force One with Nixon for the flight to Washington.[15]

A few days later the Justice Department rejected the FBI's request to continue the court-authorized wiretaps, which, according to a supportive FBI affidavit, "had begun to help strip the cover from a Mafia plan to reap millions of dollars in payoffs from the welfare funds."

As chief of the Justice Department's Criminal Division, Henry E.

Petersen again took the rap for Attorney General Richard G. Kleindienst —or the White House.* A Democrat and career public servant, Petersen had demonstrated his loyalty during the ITT investigation by trying to absolve Kleindienst and Harry Steward, U.S. attorney in San Diego, of any wrongdoing in squelching a grand-jury investigation of C. Arnholt Smith on charges that he had conspired to violate federal tax law and the Corrupt Practices Act by illegally funneling contributions to Nixon's 1968 campaign.

(An influential backer of the President since the beginning of Nixon's career, C. Arnholt Smith was one of southern California's richest and most powerful cowboys for some forty years before the bottom fell out of his elaborately constructed financial empire. On May 31, 1973, the Securities and Exchange Commission filed a civil suit against Smith and his associates on charges that "an egregious fraud [was] perpetrated on the stockholders" of Westgate-California Corporation and the U.S. National Bank (with sixty-nine branches and assets over $1 billion), the two pillars of Smith's financial empire. Once dubbed "Mr. San Diego of the Century" by the San Diego *Union*, whose publisher, the late James Copley, was another cowboy who rated high around the Nixon campfire—he contributed several top hands to the Administration, including former Director of Communications Herbert Klein and Deputy Press Secretary Gerald Warren— Smith is a classic bootstrapper and freebooter. In asking for the appointment of a receiver, the SEC told the court that the case "involves serious questions of mismanagement, misappropriations, possible defalcations and other misconduct by those in charge of Westgate and other entities. . . . Where, as here, those in control of a vast corporate empire have demonstrated an almost total disregard for their obligations under the securities laws and for their obligations as fiduciaries to the public stockholders by engaging in a scheme to divert corporate assets for their own use and benefit and to falsely inflate Westgate's earnings over a number of years, this commission cannot now stand by and assume that those responsible for the disaster can be expected to objectively assess the effects of their activities and further to take whatever measures are appropriate to correct the situation. . . . Any action short of removing the culpable individuals would be inadequate . . . since there remains a great deal of uncertainty [over] a large number of Westgate assets." Smith's conditioned reaction

---

* Petersen's predecessor, Will Wilson, also a Mitchell appointee, was forced to resign when his name was linked to the banking scandal that has since dragged half of the Texas political establishment into court.

was to hire Nixon's old law firm, Mudge Rose, to defend the case. But it was too late—for many reasons, not least of which was Watergate—for anybody to help. Three months later the Internal Revenue Service filed a $22.8-million personal income-tax lien against him. Then on October 18 the U.S. Comptroller of the Currency declared insolvent the U.S. National Bank of San Diego, with all its branches and $1.2 billion in assets. The collapse was the biggest in United States banking history. Specifically, the bank had lent more than the legally permissible 10 percent of its assets to companies controlled by Smith, and it was estimated that his companies' bad debts constituted a large percentage of the $143 million in outright losses and possibly uncollectible loans carried on the bank's books.)[16]

Petersen denied that Kleindienst had anything to do with turning down the FBI's Teamsters-Mafia wiretap request, and went on to say that in his own judgment the wiretaps had been unproductive in obtaining evidence and there was no "probable cause" for their continuation. When the New York *Times* suggested that the FBI's investigation "was reportedly producing disclosures potentially damaging" to Fitzsimmons, "the Nixon Administration's staunchest ally within the labor movement," Petersen said the story advanced "spurious allegations."[17] But in light of the promiscuous use of *illegal* wiretaps and burglaries to monitor the domestic Left, as an instance of what Senator Sam J. Erwin has called the Administration's "Gestapo mentality," the Petersen explanation now appears far more spurious than the allegations.* (When questioned by the newspaper, Rocky DeRosa replied that it was "all part of this harassment of people with Italian ancestry.")

The *quid pro quo* in the entente required more from Fitzsimmons than his public support of Nixon's economic policies. The big payoff came on July 17, 1972, when Fitzsimmons and his executive board met at La Costa Country Club; for the first time in its history, the union pledged that its two-million membership would support a Republican presidential campaign. The word went out to other Teamster officials to contribute $1,000 each, which was later reduced to $500. It was estimated that the total would amount to at least a quarter-million dollars, and perhaps much more. Happy with their decision, Fitzsimmons and other board members drove up the Pacific Coast to San Clemente for a meeting with the President. Asked by the press if the endorsement was part of a deal for Hoffa's

---

* Petersen was initially in charge of the Watergate investigation and the first trial.

commutation, Press Secretary Ronald Zeigler heatedly responded, "This is untrue and absolutely absurd."[18]

Not much was said when the Administration suddenly lost all interest in pushing a bill to prevent strikes in the transportation industry. Fitzsimmons campaigned for Nixon: ". . . We believe America needs in these perilous times a man of President Nixon's courage, vision and experience." McGovern, on the other hand, was pictured as the champion of abortion, amnesty, marijuana, and "Big Brother" government. "George McGovern is no friend of American labor." A rambler and mumbler, Fitzsimmons, like Mayor Richard Daley of Chicago, is a master of *le mot injuste*. When Nixon appointed him to the Pay Board, Fitzsimmons said: "We intend to do what we can to implement the problem that is at hand today."[19]

When a news report charged that Chotiner had funneled $875,000 to the Nixon campaign from Teamsters officials and Las Vegas gambling interests, Chotiner responded that it was a "pack of vicious lies." The contributions were not reported, the story alleged, and some of the funds were used to finance the Watergate conspirators. The "gambling interests" provided $400,000 of the amount after Chotiner "interceded on behalf of Fitzsimmons to stave off prosecution of any official or friend of the Teamsters," the story said. Interviewed in his Washington office, one floor above the offices of the Committee to Re-elect the President, Chotiner labeled the report "a scurrilous story"; "Unless there is an immediate retraction, I plan to sue or take whatever action the law allows against whoever is responsible for this horrible libel."[20] Faced with a multimillion-dollar lawsuit, the newspaper filed a retraction.

There was more to the entente's *quid pro quo*. Presidential assistant Charles W. Colson intervened on behalf of Daniel F. Gagliardi one week after a Justice Department memorandum announced the imminent indictment of Gagliardi for alleged Teamsters Union extortion activity. A White House memo to Colson from one of his aides told of Gagliardi's personal plea that he be "gotten off the hook." In a handwritten response at the bottom of the memo, Colson wrote: "Watch for this. Do all possible." The word "all" was underlined. Gagliardi was not indicted and the case was dropped, but Justice Department prosecutors denied they had been subjected to pressure. Gagliardi, who was business manager of Local 137 of the International Union of Operating Engineers in Briarcliff Manor, New York, was described in the Department's files as a close associate of John ("Buster") Ardito, a member of the Mafia family once headed by the late Vito Genovese.

When Charles W. Colson left the White House staff to join the Washington law firm of Morin, Dickstein, Shapiro and Galligan, Fitzsimmons transferred the Teamsters' $100,000-a-year legal business to that law firm. Fitzsimmons was appointed a national vice chairman of Democrats for Nixon, which was financed by the Re-election Committee and headed by Connally. As a final macabre gesture of retribution for the Kennedys' dedicated prosecution and exposure of Teamster corruption, Nixon, in a splendid display of gallows humor, named Fitzsimmons' wife to serve on the Arts Committee of the Kennedy Center for the Performing Arts.

On December 30, 1971, one week after Hoffa was paroled, the Washington lobbyist George A. Smathers telephoned Colson to urge that the White House expedite the parole of Calvin Kovens, a codefendant of Hoffa in a pension-fund fraud case. Colson's response was to shoot a memorandum to presidential counsel John W. Dean III, along with a transcript of the conversation. In the transcript, Smathers is quoted as telling Colson: "I was talking with Bebe [Rebozo] about it and said, 'Bebe, it looks to me that this would be a pretty good thing to do.' . . . He's [Kovens] the most popular Jew in Dade County, south Florida. . . . This I know would at least give the President, and those who are going to help in this area, a very strong basis of going to the Jewish community and saying, 'For God sakes, the one guy that went to bat for him (Kovens) was the President.' . . . Bebe said, 'I think he [President Nixon] ought to do it.' I said, 'I agree, there's no negatives on this side, it's all pluses.' "

In the covering memo, Colson told Dean: "The attached is much too hot for me to handle. Smathers called me, I assumed, just to talk politics. The moment he began to get into the subject I turned on the recorder. Hence you have the full transcript attached. Obviously he makes a very good point and I would assume if there is anything we can do properly, we should. On the other hand, in view of the personalities involved here, I would think this has to be handled with extreme care. . . . I would appreciate your earliest advice as to what we should do. Please discuss with me before getting this too far along. I do think, however, in view of Smathers' decision to support the President next year that we had better attend to this and not let it slip. . . ."*[21]

The records of the U.S. Parole Board indicate that Kovens was released for medical reasons, but the fact remains that the parole was

---

* The transcript and covering memorandum were among four sets of documents that Dean turned over to the Senate Watergate committee.

granted eight days after Smathers' call.* As a Washington lawyer and lobbyist, George Smathers holds impressive credentials. He spent twenty-two years in Congress, with eighteen of those years in the Senate—from 1950 to 1969—and in that span of time devoted himself exclusively to two interests: money and power. In his book *Gothic Politics in the Deep South*, 1968, Robert Sherrill wrote that Smathers had "yet to put his name on a single important piece of legislation that was not designed to help a special interest." Tall, dark, and dandyish, Smathers is a politician's politician. He can talk turkey with anybody, especially Presidents. From the beginning, he cultivated only the rich and powerful. He played poker with Truman, played golf with Ike, double-dated with Jack Kennedy when both men were Senatorial bachelors, dog-robbed for LBJ, a distant cousin, and, most importantly, introduced Nixon to Charles G. ("Bebe") Rebozo back in 1950, a relationship that has seen all three men—Smathers, Rebozo, and Nixon—become millionaires.

"I took him [Nixon] to Florida the first time he went, to Vero Beach. I introduced him to Bebe Rebozo, who is now his very best friend."[22] While in Florida, Nixon, who also wanted a promotion out of the House in 1950, paused long enough to study Smathers' primary tactics as he brutally destroyed his former friend and mentor, Claude Pepper, then the Democratic incumbent. A supporter of labor unions and corporate-tax reforms, Pepper was a marked man in both camps of money power. Yankee money power, as represented by the vast duPont enterprises in Florida, joined forces with the local cowboys in Associated Industries of Florida, and their choice was Smathers. Wrapping himself in the flag, Smathers told his audiences that he was for "the sanctity of the home and the kinship of God and man."[23]

"You will not find in me an apologist for Stalin," he thundered, "nor an associate of fellow travelers, nor a sponsor of Communist-front organizations." According to Smathers, Pepper had lifted a proposal for government medical care for the aged bodily from the Communist Party platform. Not only was Pepper advocating closer relations with Russia, but he was also willing to give the Commies A-bomb secrets. "The leader of the radicals and extremists is now on trial in Florida."[24] Smathers was proud of the orange and blue of the University of Florida: "Thank God, thank God, I don't have to wear the crimson of Pepper's and Felix Frankfurter's Harvard Law School. Alger Hiss is no classmate of mine."[25]

* Kovens made a $30,000 secret cash contribution to Nixon's campaign.

Claude Pepper became "Red" Pepper, and out in California Nixon's opponent, Helen Gahagan Douglas, who had a faultless anti-Communist record, was accused by Nixon of having a "soft attitude toward communism. . . . How can Helen Douglas, capable actress that she is, take up so strange a role as a foe of communism? And why does she when she has so deservedly earned the title of 'the pink lady'?" And so Red Pepper and the Pink Lady went down to defeat, and the two patriotic Senators became business associates and golfing buddies. Two years later, the new Vice President took the Florida senator to England to be royally wined and dined, and in turn Smathers introduced Nixon to fishing, boating, and the pleasures of the Caribbean. Among Smathers' good friends and clients were two dictators, Rafael Trujillo of the Dominican Republic and Fulgencio Batista of Cuba. When both rulers were deposed, Smathers' shrill solution was to dispatch the Marines to "destroy the armed bastion of communism."[26]

The low point in Smathers' political career came in 1966 with the indictment of Robert G. ("Bobby") Baker, Senate secretary to the Democrats and a Lyndon Johnson protégé. When Bobby's bubble burst, Smathers was the only Senator identified as one of his business partners. Yet the Senate Rules Committee, which had promised to pursue the Baker investigation wherever it led, curtly announced that its mandate did not include the investigation of Senators. The day before the grand jury returned its indictment, Smathers checked into Georgetown University hospital and predicted that frail health would end his career. President Johnson sent him a get-well note, flowers, and a red-leather photo album with "To GS from LBJ" in gold on the cover—inside were twenty enlarged pictures of Smathers at White House breakfasts. When the grand jury indicted Baker only on tax charges, demonstrating its own limited appetite for scandal in high places, Smathers said he was feeling much better. But his reputation as the man to see was badly damaged. Also, Republicans were looking for a live target and the quickest way to short-circuit their strategy was to remove the target.

"I'm going to be a Clark Clifford," Smathers told his Senate colleagues. "That's the life for me." Members of the Florida congressional delegation charged that he had more than a million dollars' worth of business lined up prior to his retirement. "I've found the pastures outside are a lot greener than I had presumed," he told a reporter in 1969. "A fellow with my background can make more money in thirty days out here than he can in fifteen years as a Senator." In his role of lawyer-lobbyist, he

said, "you don't sneak around, playing the footpads.* You know you can
be helpful and you talk with them right out in the middle of Pennsylvania
Avenue if that is convenient." Smathers speaks proudly of his "sophisticated lobbying." In his opinion, there is more "dignity" in it than in being
a Senator who is always being "picked at."[27]

His approach to lobbying is as uncomplicated as his expertise on foreign affairs. As an open advocate of A-bombs for Korea, Smathers was
"not sure it wouldn't be a good idea to carry some of them to the Kremlin
where the orders for the Chinese Communists are coming from." A master
of cloakroom buttonholing and negotiations, Senator Smathers worked
quietly behind the scenes while his Miami law firm of Smathers & Thompson represented powerful clients before regulatory agencies and congressional committees—conflicts of interest never seemed to worry George
Smathers. There are endless examples on record to testify to his lack of
concern. Take Winn-Dixie Stores, one of the South's largest grocery
chains. As a member of the Senate Finance Committee, Smathers was able
to successfully delay a Treasury proposal to plug a tax loophole that
permitted appreciations in convertible stock to be taxed at a capital-gains
rate—that is, at about half the rate applicable to dividends from common
stock. The delay made it possible for Winn-Dixie to push through a refi-
nancing plan ahead of deadline at a saving to its shareholders of millions
of dollars. Later it was discovered that Smathers was the secret owner of
two Winn-Dixie stores, purchased under an arrangement that earned him
an estimated half-million-dollar profit. Upon his retirement from the Senate, Smathers was elevated to the Winn-Dixie board. In a brilliant 70,000-
word exploration of the Smathers-Rebozo-Nixon alliance, the Long Island
newspaper *Newsday* quoted Winn-Dixie board chairman James Davis,
"Smathers was the best goddamn senator we ever had here."[28]

A long list of clients would secretly second this endorsement. Aerodex,
Inc., for example, one of the nation's hundred largest defense contractors,
fell upon evil times in the mid-1960s when the Air Force charged that its
"poor quality" work on an engine-overhauling contract was "endangering
Air Force pilots and aircraft." In fact, the Air Force had traced the
cause of three jet-aircraft crashes to failures of Aerodex-overhauled J-57
engines, and had concluded that "numerous operational failures by Aerodex-overhauled engines have created unacceptable safety hazards to aircraft
and crew . . ." The Air Force contract was only one of several problems

* Webster's Third New International Dictionary (unabridged) defines "footpad"
as a "(highwayman): one who robs a pedestrian: HOLDUP MAN."

Aerodex was having with the military. The Justice Department was suing the corporation for overcharges on Army helicopter-engine repairs, and there was a debarment action stemming from the discovery that the company had used reworked bearings stamped with counterfeit serial numbers in overhauling Navy helicopter engines. Enlisting the support of an impressive array of political and military figures, Smathers saved Aerodex from being blacklisted by the Pentagon. Two months after leaving the Senate, Smathers joined Aerodex as a director and was allowed to purchase $435,000 worth of stock for only $20,000. His Washington law firm, Smathers & Merrigan, received a $25,000 retainer from Aerodex.[29]

The beauty in this type of operation, whether it is called a payoff, a bribe, or a legal fee,* is that the money is not taxable until the stock is sold, and then only at a capital-gains rate. Aerodex board chairman Raymond M. Tonks told *Newsday*: "I thought if he could do us any good, what the hell. . . . I figured he had clout, and that it would be worth it for us." Commenting on his use of lobbyists, Tonks said, "I never used any of those political guys to do anything I didn't think that I was rightfully entitled to. . . ."[30] (The Los Angeles gambling racketeer Mickey Cohen once told an interviewer that he had never killed anybody who "didn't deserve it.")

One final sophisticated deal from the juicy Smathers file should illustrate his expertise in keeping tax loopholes unplugged. Back in 1968, Senator Lee Metcalf of Montana launched a campaign against "tax-dodge farmers." Movie stars and professional people with large personal incomes were abusing a tax incentive that was originally designed to help the working farmer. In fact, in many instances the tax benefits to "tax-dodge" nonfarmers exceeded economic losses to the point where it became profitable to invest in unprofitable farms and breeding operations. Briefly, the farmer enjoys a dual benefit. Whereas the businessman may deduct expenses only after sales, and must then pay the regular tax rate on profits, the farmer may deduct costs as they occur, often years in advance of sales, and his income on the sales of many products, including livestock, falls into the capital-gains category. The Treasury Department under Johnson endorsed the Metcalf Bill, which simply denied this tax break to persons with more than $15,000 in nonfarm income. Early in 1969, the Nixon Treasury proposed its own complex plan to plug the loophole. Any farmer

---

* "If you had it all to do over again," Lincoln Steffens once asked a dying boodler, "would you still want to be a boodler?" "No," he replied. "I'd become a lawyer and charge legal fees."

or horse breeder who incurred losses (or expenses) totaling more than $5,000 in any given year would be required to open an excess-deductions account, and the proceeds of sales from this account would be treated as ordinary income rather than capital gains.

The first to panic were wealthy businessmen with racing stables. Ogden Phipps, chairman of the New York Jockey Club, quickly formed the American Horse Council, Inc., with former Senator and Republican National Chairman Thruston B. Morton as president and former Senator George Smathers as counsel. To earn his $75,000-a-year retainer, Smathers began arranging meetings between Horse Council officials and various power brokers, including Agriculture Secretary Clifford Hardin, Treasury Secretary David Kennedy, Senate Finance Committee Chairman Russell B. Long, and Representative Sam Gibbons of the House Ways and Means Committee. The bargaining at "intimate dinners" culminated, according to the Horse Council's Washington Newsletter for June–July 1969, with "two days of very fruitful meetings in Washington," climaxed by a White House session on June 18: "The President evidenced considerable interest in equine industry problems during the 40-minute meeting . . ." Not mentioned in the newsletter was the interest the President later evidenced over the horsemen's donation list. This was Smathers's brainstorm. The members were asked to calculate the amount each had contributed to GOP candidates during the previous five years, and the total came to $6 million. According to Newsday, Smathers later told a Horse Council staffer: "I slid the list to Bebe to show to the President. They both understand this type of thing." Without going into further details, it is enough to note that the Treasury Department, along with the two tax committees, promptly lost interest in closing that particular tax loophole. When asked if he would appear before committee hearings, Smathers replied: "Oh, no. Personal contact with senators, congressmen. Showing them all the bad things that will happen if they change the law. . . . I guess you would call it sophisticated lobbying. . . . All this talk about tax reform has got the wealthy people in this country scared to death. Of course, up on the Hill, I was always on the other side, urging tax reform. Now I represent the people who don't want anything changed."[31]

Nixon, who bought his first Key Biscayne house from Smathers, was an apt pupil when it came to enhancing his own fortune. After his 1968 election, he sold his 185,891 shares in Fisher's Island, Inc., a Florida land company controlled by Rebozo's business associates, for $2 per share—double what he had paid for them, at a time when other stockholders were still paying $1 per share. Yet Nixon was furious that the company's board of directors would not triple the par value of his holdings. When Hoke T. Maroon, the largest stockholder, tried to reason with him, he got only as far as "But Dick . . ." when Nixon exploded: "Don't you dare call me Dick. I am the President of the United States. When you speak to me, you call me, 'Mr. President.' "[32] The next time Mr. President offered property for sale in Florida, he did considerably better. In 1972 he sold two vacant lots in a Cape Florida subdivision to William E. Griffin, Jr., who was general counsel and a director of Robert Abplanalp's Precision Valve Corporation. In a public statement of his finances made on May 12, 1969, Nixon listed the total value of both lots as $37,600—Griffin paid $150,000.

As of May 31, 1973, Nixon still owed $160,934 on his two Key Biscayne houses, which he purchased for a total of $252,000. As for the other three houses in the Presidential compound on Key Biscayne's Bay Lane, one is owned by Robert Abplanalp, one by Rebozo, and one by A. Edward Campbell, a stockholder in Rebozo's Key Biscayne bank. The Abplanalp and Campbell houses are rented by the White House and the General Services Administration for a total annual rent of $37,643. Nixon has no qualms about commandeering Rebozo's home whenever the size of the presidential entourage requires it.

Meanwhile, on a bluff in San Clemente, California, high above the blue Pacific, the arithmetic became a little more complex. It took three years to get the White House to release any details of Nixon's purchases. In fact, it was not until the Santa Ana *Register* charged that Nixon had misappropriated $1 million in unreported 1968 campaign funds to pay for his San Clemente estate that the White House reluctantly began revealing pieces of the transactions put together by Abplanalp and Rebozo. After a series of misleading releases, the White House made public a special audit on the purchase of his California estate as well as of his two less ostentatious Florida houses. The aim of the White House was "to put to rest once and for all the false allegations that campaign funds were used to acquire" any of the President's properties.

According to the six documents released by the White House, the San Clemente estate consisted of two properties. The purchase price of the Hamilton Cotton estate was $1.4 million. At the time of the purchase— July 15, 1969—the parcel was said to be 21 acres, but a subsequent survey added five acres to it. It included a ten-room Spanish-style house that Nixon dubbed Casa Pacifica. The Elmore tract, a 2.9-acre parcel adjacent to the estate, was bought on October 13, 1969, for $100,000, which brought the total cost to $1.5 million for 28.9 acres. Nixon made a cash down payment of $399,609 on the Cotton estate four days after he received a $450,000 loan from Abplanalp, at 8 percent interest. That left him with $1 million in promissory notes payable to the original owners, with interest accumulating at the rate of $75,000 annually. As to the Elmore tract, Nixon paid $20,054 down and gave the sellers a note for $80,000, payable in five installments of $16,000 each.

On July 15, 1970, the date that has intrigued Watergate investigators, Nixon borrowed an additional $175,000 from Abplanalp,* again at 8 percent interest, and paid $100,000 on the Cotton note plus $75,000 of related interest. On October 13, 1970, he paid $16,000 on the Elmore note and $6,000 interest. So far his payments had not exceeded the Abplanalp loans—that is, the property had not cost him a single dollar of his own money. Then on December 15, 1970, he sold 23 acres of undeveloped Cotton property to Abplanalp and Rebozo, described in the audit as "co-partners doing business under the firm name and style of B & C Investment Company." The total purchase price was $1,249,000. This left Nixon with the choice 5.9 acres surrounding his Casa Pacifica and 600 feet of ocean frontage. When the dust finally settled, his total indebtedness was $251,000 plus related interest. Before the audit was made public, Abplanalp bought out Rebozo in an attempt to shield him from publicity.

The entire plot is held in trust by the Title Insurance and Trust Company—headed by Rocco C. Siciliano, a former Nixon appointee—which means that what B & C actually bought was a "beneficial interest" in the trust. This might make it difficult for Abplanalp to develop his share of the property. Meanwhile Nixon is free to enjoy the luxury of this natural sanctuary around his property. Abplanalp's enthusiasm for the deal has run hot and cold. When asked by one reporter about his plans for the property, he snapped: "I'm going to build a ten-story whorehouse on it." To another newsman, he said: "If they had been able to unload it on somebody else, I would have been happy as a clam. But I have no regrets —except for the speculative stories in the press." It was Herbert W. Kalmbach, the President's personal attorney, he said, who recruited him for the deal.

The air of suspicion surrounding Nixon's finances was not entirely dissipated by the audit report. For one thing, three former officials of the

---

* Both loans from Abplanalp were secured by typed documents on paper without letterheads and without notary seals or signatures of witnesses.

accounting firm chosen, Coopers & Lybrand, formerly Lybrand, Ross Bros. & Montgomery, who were convicted of mail fraud and distribution of false financial statements in 1968, were subsequently given a presidential pardon by Nixon in 1972. And when reporters asked Ronald Ziegler to explain why the White House had said in October 1972 that no land had been sold, contrary to its new statement that it was sold in 1970, he replied that to have put it in the previous year's statement would have been "not appropriate." No one asked Ziegler about the White House's 1969 statement on San Clemente which listed the purchase price of the entire estate at $340,000, with Nixon reportedly paying $100,000 down and the remainder to be paid within the next five years at 7.5 percent interest.

There have been so many lies that nobody knows the truth any more. Take the so-called "security" improvements at the various nest-feathering compounds. The White House spoon-fed the press a whole series of "inoperative" statements concerning the amounts spent by the General Services Administration. At first the cost was announced as $39,525. Then, with each new shocking revelation, the official cost went up to meet the new charges, until finally by late August of 1973 the price tag had climbed to $10.5 million. There is a good chance that by the time this book is published the above figures will be "inoperative."[33]

> The Big Lie is a strategy for concealing the truth by putting forward a story so audaciously false that it disarms ordinary skepticism, which is ready to cope only with petty distortions and deceptions. The White House, in its Watergate maneuverings, has apparently adopted another strategy: that of the Big Snarl. Instead of putting forward a single, easily grasped false story that routs all other stories, including the complex true story, from the field, one who resorts to this strategy puts forward—and then often retracts—numberless clashing, mutually cancelling stories, so that before long the integrity of all the facts and the logic of all the justifications are destroyed beyond reconstruction. Instead of advancing a phony story that pushes aside the truth, one assails the very idea of a single truth and effaces from the public mind the memory of what truth is. In this way, a public figure can in effect shred a bothersome issue while working to debase public standards to the level of his own conduct.—The *New Yorker*, December 17, 1973.

This strategy was particularly successful in obfuscating Nixon's finances. However, on October 3, 1973, after years of rumors followed by denials that became inoperative in the wake of more speculation, the Providence (Rhode Island) *Journal-Bulletin* reported that Nixon had paid a total of $1,670 in federal income taxes in 1970 and 1971 and received refunds totalling $131,503 for the two years. In his November 17 appearance at Disney World before the annual meeting of Associated Press managing editors, Nixon again resorted to exaggerations, half-truths and outright distortions. Asked why he had paid less than $2,000 on earned personal income of more than $500,000 for those two years, he said it was "not because of the deductions for interest or all of these gimmicks." It came about, he said, because Lyndon Johnson "came in to see me . . . and he told me that under the law, up until 1969, presidential and vice presidential papers given to the government were a deduction and should be taken, and could be taken as a deduction from the tax."

> The . . . story is told by a southern Republican lawyer who visited Mr. Nixon at his New York apartment in 1968, before he was nominated. Mr. Nixon said he assumed that the lawyer was visiting New York on clients' business and would charge the trip to them or, at the very least, would deduct the charge on his tax returns as a business expense. The visiting lawyer said he probably wouldn't; it really was a personal trip. Mr. Nixon looked as if he were shocked, made the visitor repeat that he did have some clients in New York, and finally extracted an admission that his visitor could, if he worked at it, concoct a passable excuse for either a charge to clients or a tax deduction. Mr. Nixon cocked his right thumb and forefinger at the visitor, winked, and made a *chucking* sound. The visiting lawyer, telling this story to a partner who told it to me, said he found the episode embarrassing and never afterward had much respect for Richard Nixon.—John Osborne, The *New Republic*, December 22, 1973.

Having laid the onus on Johnson—he usually prefers using Kennedy in such instances—Nixon told the editors that he turned his papers "over to the tax people. . . . They appraised them at $500,000." So when the tax people prepared his returns, they "took that as a deduction."

It was not all that pure and simple. To begin with, the tax-deductible gift of so-called private papers was one of the oldest gimmicks alive—that is, before it was killed by the Tax Reform Act of 1969, which became effective July 25, 1969. For years, famous persons, especially politicians, had donated their private papers to libraries and received tax deductions equal to the appreciated value a collector placed on them. In fact, Nixon had received an $80,000 deduction on his income tax return for 1968 by donating his congressional correspondence and papers about his work for fellow Republicans in the 1964 campaign.*

The appraiser of that gift was Ralph Newman, chairman of the Chi-

---

* Like everything else in Watergate, this information was acknowledged by the White House only after it was widely reported in the press.

cago Public Library, who had performed this service for every President since Herbert Hoover. In an interview with Tony Fuller of *Newsweek*,* Newman said he was summoned to the New York law offices of Mudge Rose in late December 1968, and was ushered into a room piled high with Nixon's memorabilia. "Let me tell you what sort of tax deduction we want," a Nixon lawyer said, naming a figure. Newman flipped open a few crates, riffled some papers and agreed. "I just kind of carved it out for them in round numbers. I shoved a few boxes aside and said, 'There's what you need.' Maybe to be on the safe side, we shoved aside a couple more." Time was of the essence, of course, still it was a touching gesture for Nixon to sign the deed turning over the twenty-one cartons of papers to the United States government on Christmas Day 1968—there was a clause, however, which reserved to the donor the right to limit access to the papers during his Presidency to persons designated by him.

On April 6, 1969, Newman was asked to certify some of Nixon's vice-presidential papers for $576,000.† "The second examination was equally cursory," *Newsweek* reported, and the donation, according to Newman, included fifty-six boxes of 27,000 "invitations and turndowns" for 1954 to 1961. In explaining how he arrived at that precise figure, Newman said, "They tell you what they want when they're going to give a gift and you certify it for them." But, he added, his estimate on the papers was "very conservative. They are worth easily $1 million and probably more than that."‡ It is curious that when Newman told Nixon of his appraisal at a White House prayer service, the President shook his head "in sort of disbelief" and said that he would never have thought his papers were worth so much. Yet at his AP press conference at Disney World, Nixon said, "I'll be glad to have the papers back. I think they're worth more than that."

It is quite possible that Nixon will get them back. At this writing, there is every indication that the gift was not only invalid but that a criminal act was involved. The grounds are that the gift was made after the cut-off date of July 25, 1969. On that date, according to a General Services Administration investigation conducted at the request of Senator Lowell Weicker of Connecticut, the papers were on deposit at the National Ar-

---

* The *Newsweek* story was published December 17, 1973.

† This means that his private papers have earned him to date $656,000 in tax deductions.

‡ Newman said he estimated the bulk of Lyndon Johnson's papers to be worth between $20 million and $40 million, but instead of taking the deduction, Johnson left them to the LBJ Library in his will.

chives in an area reserved for "courtesy storage," and they were not even sorted until November 1969. That month Newman reportedly separated out 1,176 National Archives boxes that he valued—for tax purposes—at $576,000. It was not until April 6, 1970, that Newman drew up his appraisal of the 1969 gift, in which he asserted that "from the sixth to the eighth day of April 1969," he or his employees did "examine the papers of Richard Milhous Nixon Part II." But Sherrod East, a retired member of the National Archives staff, told GSA investigators that in April 1969 most of the material later selected was in unidentified cartons and packing cases—no description of contents was possible. Nevertheless, a deed dated March 27, 1969, which included a list of the specific papers that made up the gift, was delivered to the National Archives on April 10, 1970. What intrigues investigators, who suspect the deed was predated, is the fact that Edward L. Morgan, then the President's deputy counsel,* signed it on behalf of Nixon. No power of attorney document from the President accompanied the deed. Instead there was an affidavit notarized by Nixon's personal tax attorney, Frank DeMarco, Jr., who was a senior member of the law firm headed by Herbert W. Kalmbach—Kalmbach, DeMarco, Knapp & Chillingworth. After Kalmbach's appearance before the Watergate committee, the White House said he was no longer the President's personal attorney, but in December 1973 the White House grudgingly admitted that Kalmbach was still signing checks on the President's personal account.

> I've made my mistakes but in all my years of public life I have never profited from public service. I have earned every cent. . . . People have got to know whether their President is a crook. Well, I'm not a crook. I've earned everything I've got.—Nixon at Disney World.

On December 8, 1973, some three weeks after his Disney World performance, the White House released more than 150 pages of complicated tax records and summaries. It was, in Nixon's opinion, the most "comprehensive and exhaustive" disclosure of its kind in Presidential history. It would "lay to rest such false rumors as that campaign funds were used in the purchase of my home in San Clemente, that I have hidden away a secret $1 million investment portfolio, that I sheltered income on which my daughter, Tricia, should have paid taxes, and that $10 million in

---

* Morgan, who later became an assistant secretary of the Treasury, resigned on January 18, 1974, after he was questioned by the staff of the Congressional Joint Committee on Internal Revenue Taxation. "It's not directly related, but I can't say it's totally unrelated," he said. "Obviously, I'm questioning what I did." Morgan refused to discuss whether he had signed the deed prior to the cut-off date.

federal funds were spent on my homes in Key Biscayne and San Clemente."

There is no question that Nixon took advantage of every conceivable tax dodge to minimize his taxes—including a $1.24 deduction for interest on a department store charge. His returns were so loaded down with deductions that the IRS computer automatically targeted his 1971 and 1972 returns for inspection, an event that nearly caused IRS Commissioner Johnie Walters to have a stroke. As required by law, a special audit was conducted and upon its completion, the IRS district director in Baltimore, William D. Waters, wrote the Nixons a personal note. "Our examination of your income tax returns for the years 1971 and 1972 revealed that they are correct," it said. "I want to compliment you on the care shown in the preparation of your returns."

During the first four years of his presidency, Richard Nixon tripled his net worth, becoming almost a millionaire. His "net assets" increased from $307,141 to $988,522. The gimmicks produced deductions totaling $988,-963.43 on a gross income of $1,122,266.39. This explains why he paid taxes of only $72,682 in 1969,* $792 in 1970, $878 in 1971, and $4,298 in 1972. His tax rate for the four years averages out to about 7 percent, less even than the 10 percent supposedly made mandatory by the new minimum tax requirement.

He tried to prepare the press at Disney World: "I wasn't a pauper when I became President. . . . When I left office after . . . eight years at $45,000 as Vice President . . . my net worth was $47,000 total after 14 years of government service, and a 1958 Oldsmobile that needed an overhaul." Nixon knows how to pull the heartstring. "I have no complaints. Over the next eight years I made a lot of money . . . $250,000 from the serial rights on a book . . . as an attorney . . . between $150,000 and $200,000 a year. I sold all of my stock for $300,000, my apartment in New York for $300,000, I'm using round figures . . . and $100,000 the law firm owed me."

Obviously, if his net worth was $47,000 in 1960, his stock and apartment were purchased from the royalties on his book and his income from the law firm. At any rate, he did not say anything about a possible capital gain from the sale of the 23 acres of his San Clemente property to the B & C Investment Company, owned jointly by Abplanalp and Rebozo. Nor did

---

* It is alleged that he received a $30,000 refund on this amount, but since his long-awaited "full disclosure" did not include his 1969 return, the allegation remains just that.

his income tax returns reflect such a profit. Although it appeared that his good friends had given him a substantial gift, his tax accountant, Arthur Blech, was equal to the challenge. Blech began, he said, by arbitrarily valuing the 5.9 acres and house at $376,000, from which he deducted $96,000 in improvements, reducing the original value of the parcel to $280,000. By subtracting this amount from the $1,529,000 originally paid for the entire estate, he arrived at a happy coincidence: $1,249,000—the exact amount paid by B & C for the 23 acres. That meant the Nixons had realized no capital gain on the sale, and so, alas, would pay no taxes. The White House announced that Blech's calculations were made "concurrently" with the B & C negotiations, but when the heat was turned on, Blech later admitted that he did not begin his work until the sale price was fixed.

Blech, with the aid of DeMarco, was equally successful in evaluating the California tax code. It was true that San Clemente was Nixon's legal, voting residence, they argued, but the President visited it only "for brief periods of time [that] would not aggregate more than a few weeks in each year." His principal residence was the White House. This opinion saved the Nixons an estimated $64,000 in state taxes over the four years.

On the other side of the same tax coin, however, was the $142,912 profit Nixon made on the sale of his Manhattan co-op apartment. The only way a homeowner can avoid paying tax on such a profit is by reinvesting it within a year in another "principal residence." Nixon claimed this exemption, saying that he had used the $142,912 to help buy his San Clemente home, which meant that he was claiming two principal residences. In other words, he played it both ways. Also, it should be remembered, Nixon purchased the San Clemente property without spending a single dollar of his own money. His finances involved many other questionable practices— especially $56,954.97 claimed for "costs incurred in use of property for official purposes" at San Clemente and Key Biscayne—but one would have to be a tax magician to completely unsnarl it all. At this writing, the Congressional Joint Committee on Internal Revenue Taxation had agreed to review "the whole tax strategy that has helped make him a millionaire," a task, according to Time, "that should make them busier than an accounting firm in April."

This leads to another question. What are the proper perquisites of the President? There is no question that the imperial life style of Richard Nixon is the most costly in history. The true cost of running the Nixon presidency has been estimated by a veteran official of the Office of Management and Budget to be as high as $100 million a year.[34] But there is no easy way of verifying this figure because much of the funds for equipment and personnel used by the White House come from other agencies—these funds are not reported and they are not traceable in their budgets. This leaves the White House in the enviable position of having a non-accounting system. This questionable practice is justified by a 1968 statute that obliges all other federal agencies to comply with *any* request from the Secret Service for assistance in carrying out its protective mandate.

The payroll for Nixon's personal White House staff is $10 million, but again this figure does not include personnel carried on other payrolls. However, the actual White House staff is known to be at least three times larger than even in Johnson's years, and some of its members, as Don Cordtz noted in a *Fortune* article, "have little function other than to smooth the President's path. One aide walks beside the President to tell him in advance whether to turn left or right at a corner or warn of the number of steps in a staircase."[35] The White House has a full-time domestic staff (paid by government funds) of seventy-five butlers, cooks, stewards, maids, and technicians; twenty-one gardeners who are assisted by several National Parks Service employees; more than one hundred Secret Service agents; and three hundred uniformed White House police.

Other Presidents have established second official residences, but Nixon is the first one to maintain ten "White House" offices: three in Washington, two at Camp David, two in San Clemente, one at Key Biscayne, one on Grand Cay, an island in the Bahamas owned by Abplanalp, and one on Air Force One as he flies from office to office. Some two hundred people usually accompany the President on a routine trip.

Beside the flight crews and Secret Service agents, there is the White House staff and couriers, with their wives, Nixon's valet and dog handler, Mrs. Nixon's hairdresser, White House switchboard operators, Navy mess stewards, and chauffeurs. There is a backup plane with newsmen and a C-141 Star Lifter packed with communications gear. Several days prior to the takeoff, advance men check out airport security; a physician arranges for emergency medical procedures, making sure that local hospitals have an ample supply of Nixon's blood type. On the day of the flight, both airports are placed on alert for his departure and arrival, with firefighting teams, rescue helicopters, an Army bomb-disposal squad, and Navy frogmen if it is near water. At the point of destination a fleet of limousines awaits to whisk the impressive entourage to its luxurious government-paid lodgings.

Nixon has five lavishly appointed Boeing 707 jetliners at his disposal, plus sixteen helicopters,* eleven Lockheed Jetstars complete with Air Force crews, two bulletproof Continental limousines at a cost of $500,000 apiece (which are flown to the various White Houses), and thirty other limousines manned by military drivers—King Timahoe, Nixon's Irish setter, rides to Camp David in solitary grandeur.[36] The cost of maintaining this mountaintop retreat has quadrupled in five years, from $148,000 in 1968 to $640,000 for fiscal 1973. As for Nixon's personal income, he receives a salary of $200,000, an expense allowance of $90,000, $40,000 of which is nontaxable, and a $1.5-million "special projects" fund.†

Nixon is *the* biggest spender of all time. Bess Truman used to pay for her own transportation when she traveled from Washington to Independence. Lady Bird Johnson rode the Eastern Airlines shuttle on shopping trips to New York. None of that for the Nixons. Even the daughters and sons-in-law travel by government plane. Ziegler has been known to use the official helicopter to fly from San Clemente to a party in Hollywood. By contrast, the total income of the Prime Minister of Great Britain is $57,500 a year, out of which he must pay all of his domestic bills, including the wages of the solitary housekeeper at 10 Downing Street. His travel expenses are defrayed by the same $20 per diem paid to all civil servants. Prime Minister Kakuei Tanaka of Japan rides to work in his own Dodge sedan and travels by commercial airliner.

Besides the tremendous waste of funds and resources, there are obvious perils from this type of imperial isolation. In his book *The Twilight of the Presidency*, George E. Reedy, press secretary to President Johnson, gives interesting advice: "No nation of free men should ever permit itself to be governed from a hallowed shrine. Government should be vulgar, sweaty, plebeian, operating in an environment where a fool can be called a fool."

Representative Jack Brooks of Texas, chairman of a subcommittee now checking into the federal funds spent on Nixon's private homes, believes that all agencies providing services, personnel, and equipment to the White House should bill the President, who should then present a line-by-

---

* The entire fleet was replaced in 1973, with the Army spending $6 million for six Presidential helicopters and the Marine Corps putting out $31.5 million for eleven more. And for 1974, the White House was planning to spend another $30 million for four medium-range jets.

† Besides banking large chunks of his salary, Nixon's tax returns showed that he had saved $91,000 from his expense account.

line budget to Congress for approval the same way other federal agencies do.

Meanwhile, the suspicions of Watergate investigators concerning the Hughes contributions to Rebozo give rise to other darker speculations. How many other contributions did he keep secret? As with the Watergate buggers and White House plumbers, is it reasonable to believe that this was an isolated instance? Yet even if all the details were truly stated in the audit, the President's propensity for sponging on his rich cronies borders perilously on the edge of criminality. Rebozo and Abplanalp have been well rewarded by a generous government for their thoughtfulness—but that is another story.

> When the national chairman of the party in power intervenes in behalf of a client, such action is influence itself, regardless of whether he goes further and advocates the merits of the case. . . . The top official of both parties should set an example of propriety and ethics which goes beyond the strict legal minimum required by law.—Richard M. Nixon, circa 1951[37]

Nixon was talking about President Truman, accusing him of disgracing the White House by "condoning unethical practices by members of his own official family," practices that had done "more than anything else to encourage the decline of morality among government employees." The talk got tougher in Oil City, Pennsylvania, in 1952. Eisenhower as President, Nixon said, would have only one test: "Is it good for America? Compare that with Harry Truman, Harry Vaughan, R. F. C. Dawson, O'Dwyer, and all the rest of these crooks and these incompetents."[38]

In terms of political time, that was many billions of campaign dollars ago. An army of big and little crooks have since trampled through the corridors of power, leaving their stains on an invisible record and their dollars in bottomless pockets. Money power works both sides of the street. Myer Feldman, Peter Flanigan's counterpart in the Kennedy White House, was so successful at his job that a colleague once hung a red light outside his office, an unsubtle implication that he was the call boy of business.[39] Lyndon Johnson, who became a multimillionaire on the salary of a public servant, spread the fiction of Lady Bird's "inheritance," metamorphosing a modest dowry into a very big cover story.

The Yankees were more circumspect than the newly arrived cowboys in their dealings with the White House. Hugh Sidey took note of the new men's *modus operandi* in a *Time* essay back in April 1972, long before Watergate was a national scandal:

Nixon has gathered the power to himself and his few trusted men. The action is in the White House; the rest of the bureaucracy is paralyzed with fear of those White House aides. More corporate representatives find their way into the White House back rooms than in the two previous Administrations. Nixon's public entertainments embrace more big businessmen than his predecessors ever saw. John Mitchell, acting probably as an old acquaintance, has referred people to certain lawyers and influence men who stand the best chance of getting the job done.[40]

From the very beginning of Nixon's first term, on up to Watergate, the cowboys have managed to wangle a preponderance of choice Administration posts for their top hands. From the ultra-super Cabinet right down to the lowest White House courier, most have been cynical men, pragmatic and manipulative, uninterested in "issues" beyond their own special interests. Governing became merely an extension of campaigning. The survival of their own cushy power positions depended on the reelection of the President, which in turn depended on campaign dollars. At least $60.2 million—perhaps no one will ever know the real bottom line—flowed into Nixon campaign coffers from the spring of 1971 through the end of 1972, perhaps as much as half of it collected before April 7, 1972, the date the new campaign-fund reporting law went into effect.

While McGovern stood on the sidewalks of New York exchanging his autograph for dollar bills, the President's personal lawyer, Herbert Kalmbach, and his former Commerce Secretary, Maurice Stans, were bluntly demanding that corporate executives donate stock or cash up to 1 percent of their personal net worth. And while the President was piously assuring the voters that the new disclosure law would "guard against campaign abuses and work to build public confidence in the integrity of the electoral process" by giving "the American public facts about political financing," his surrogates were frantically counseling contributors on the importance of avoiding disclosure by beating the April 7 deadline—they raised $11.3 million in the four weeks prior to the deadline, and $5 million in the last two days. As Secretary of Commerce, Stans had been the Cabinet's business spokesman for three years, going right down the line for business, a zealous fighter against strict consumer protection and antipollution standards, or any other program not endorsed by money power. As far as contributors were concerned, Stans would be back at the same old stand in the second-term Cabinet.

This covert fund-raising operation was described as a businesslike campaign organization—"With a $250 billion government at stake," one Nixon aide observed, "it was time [the presidential campaign] became businesslike." Being such great business enthusiasts, they tried to fashion the Committee to Re-elect the President—CRP, or more appropriately, CREEP—into an impersonal corporate-type structure, a buffer between the President and the National Republican Committee, the political apparatus designed to serve all Republicans.

Conceived by the advertising mentality of Bob Haldeman, who once helped popularize Disneyland, this furtive cabal promptly superannuated the National Committee: "We've got enough politicians," one CREEP aide said. "What we need are communicators." It included seventy high-priced media experts, who crystallized the "Selling of the President," technique initiated in 1968, the campaigning via public relations cum advertising that bases its appeal on cute slogans rather than on debate of the issues. In his Nixon biography, Jules Witcover revealed some of the "non-campaign" Madison Avenue phrases used by CREEP managers. The strategy, for example, was identified as "an outgrowth of the extensive program for merchandising the Nixon administration to the press of Middle America that had been developed since 1969." On the plus side of Watergate, Witcover said that it inspired Henry Kissinger's famous television appearance ten days before the election. Until Watergate, Nixon had successfully concealed his commitment to a military resolution in Vietnam by having Kissinger announce a phony negotiated political settlement. In response to Witcover's question on what was done to divert attention from the scandal, one Nixon campaign manager said: "Try 'peace is at hand.' We can thank Watergate for that." Until then Nixon had been opposed to a compromise settlement, and in fact was prepared to bomb North Vietnam into surrender or annihilation.[41]

Those were the days when the Washington *Post* was pushing hard to get the facts of Watergate before the public, and the White House was equally determined to discredit the newspaper. When the *Post* connected Haldeman with a "secret" GOP cash fund on October 25, 1972, only days before the election, Ziegler became hysterical: "This is the shabbiest type of journalism. This is a vicious abuse of the entire journalism process by the Washington *Post*, well conceived and coordinated to discredit this Administration, and individuals in it." Asked by a reporter why he thought the *Post* was trying to discredit the Administration, Ziegler replied: "You have a man who is the editor over at the Washington *Post* by the name of Ben Bradlee. I think anyone who would honestly want to assess what his political persuasions are would come quickly to the conclusion that he is not a supporter of President Nixon."[42] In the world of public relations and advertising, it is a normal assumption that reporters and editors play the same game they do.

"Incidentally, when I am the candidate, I run the campaign," Nixon said during a televised interview on January 4, 1971, a statement borne out in the creation of CREEP. From its first director, John Mitchell, to his successor, Clark MacGregor of the White House staff, and from Jeb Stuart Magruder, Haldeman's protégé, to Fred Malek, the President's chief personnel recruiter, and, of course, fund raisers Stans, Kalmbach, and Chotiner, the President had found surrogates who would give him the complete control that he always exercised in his campaigns. Contrary to the devout protestations of loyalty by worshipers, the businesslike operation was based on more substantial ground:

> Gone are the Washington headquarters volunteers; gone are the handful of paid workers; gone are the informal groups operating on their own. In their places sit a paid staff of more than 350 with dozens of $30,000 per year specialists and almost a hundred more in the $20,000 category—salaries larger than any heretofore known in a presidential race. John Mitchell, perhaps, set the pattern during his short tenure as chairman. He was taking down $5,000 per month (a $60,000 a year salary) from the campaign group while, according to another report on file, his old law firm paid him $15,000 a month in both April and May and $10,000 in June, July and August. . . . The monthly payroll for the re-election committee alone topped $400,000 by August. . . . Murray Chotiner, who is said to be running the ballot operation, never appears on its payroll. Yet hardly a week goes by that he fails to collect $1000 or more for travel expenses.*— New Republic, September 23, 1972

From his second-floor quarters at the White House, the President could almost watch the men from CREEP line up only two blocks away to deposit funds in their favorite bank, the First National Bank of Washington, which occupied the ground floor in the same building with CREEP, Mudge Rose, and Chotiner's law firm. As director of CREEP, Mitchell, who had returned to Mudge Rose, occupied two offices in the building.

The little black bag became a museum piece in 1972 as millions in cash moved in and out of CREEP headquarters in suitcases. Roy Winchester, a Pennzoil executive, flew in a private aircraft to Washington with $700,000 in cash donated by Texas Democrats for Nixon, including four Mexican checks totaling $89,000 plus another $11,000 in cash from Gulf Re-

---

* Chotiner also collected $12,000 in expenses for a so-called ballot security operation survey.

sources and Development Corporation, a Texas company with pollution probems, which had surreptitiously funneled the $89,000 through an inactive Mexican subsidiary. The subterfuge was designed to circumvent the Corrupt Practices Act, which makes it illegal for corporations to contribute their own funds in a federal election. The "hot" Mexican checks, along with a $25,000 check from Dwayne Andreas, were converted into cash through the Miami bank account of Bernard Barker, one of the convicted Watergate burglars and a business associate of Bebe Rebozo. The Andreas check, which was made out in the name of Kenneth Dahlberg, a CREEP fund raiser, was dated April 10, three days past the deadline and also hot unless reported, a fate that Andreas, a Humphrey supporter, wanted desperately to avoid. What Andreas wanted from CREEP was not the reelection of the President—he donated $75,000 to Humphrey—but a new bank charter, which he received with dizzying dispatch. When questioned about the charter's speedy approval, Comptroller of the Currency William B. Camp agreed that the decision was quick but went on to explain that "this is one of the cleanest cases I've seen." Any implication that his approval was related to the fact that both Andreas and Dahlberg were directors of the new bank was "without any foundation and wholly unwarranted."[43]

On April 6, 1972, one day before the reporting deadline, Roger Milliken, president of Deering-Milliken Inc., stuffed $363,112.50 in cash and cashier checks into a satchel and personally flew to Washington to deliver the funds directly to Stans. At that time the textile industry was having problems meeting new federal flammability standards in textile products— the death of thirty-two persons in an Ohio nursing home had been attributed to flammable carpeting. In October 1972, the responsibility for enforcing the new federal standards was switched from the Federal Trade Commission to a newly formed Product Safety Commission. A year later the new commission was reported still "gearing up."

Robert Vesco stuffed two thousand $100 bills into a black attaché case and had it carried by hand to Washington by two emissaries on a private plane. That Vesco was then under investigation by the Securities and Exchange Commission for the alleged "wholesale looting" of no less than $224 million from Investors Overseas Services (IOS) did not deter the President's brother Edward from arranging the contribution. In sworn testimony, Harry Sears* said that Edward made a sudden helicopter flight

---

* A Vesco associate and head of the Nixon fund drive in New Jersey, Sears was indicted along with Mitchell, Stans, and Vesco for attempting to stop the SEC investigation.

to the Vesco headquarters in New Jersey to verify that the $200,000 contribution was wanted in cash.

Edward was not the only Nixon involved with Vesco. Donald Nixon's son, Donald Jr., was Vesco's personal business aide from the time he began his looting of IOS. When Donald Jr. first went to work for Vesco, his father admonished him not to say that he was going to work for IOS: "If that gets around, he's going to be in a lot of trouble. I told him to say he was going to work for International Controls. IOS and International Controls are allied companies, but he's not supposed to say he's working for IOS. . . . That dumb so-and-so," Donald said of his son, "John Ehrlichman talked to him for a couple of hours and told him to behave himself over there. You know, he told him he was the President's nephew and couldn't do anything to embarrass the President." When the scandal broke, Donald Jr., who had spent time in the mountains with hippies before joining IOS, observed that "It's a heavy trip that we're all on now, I'm afraid."* Meanwhile, the President's nephew continued living the good life in the Bahamas and Costa Rica, "one of the most spectacular places you've ever seen," he says, and flying around in Vesco's plushly refurbished Boeing 707 jet, complete with sauna and discotheque.[44]

During his press conference at Disney World, Nixon was so anxious to give his version of the "milk fund" embroglio that he repeatedly invited questions about it. "Would you mind asking me about the milk?" he pleaded with one interrogator. When no one obliged, the President proceeded to answer his own question, an effort that carried the hour-long news conference into overtime. "Television, keep me on," he said, pointing a finger at the cameras. "There are some awful nice people getting a bad rap about it," he said. "The charge is basically this: that this Administration in 1971 raised the support price for milk *quid pro quo* for a promise by the milk producers that they would contribute substantial amounts, anywhere from $100,000 to $2,000,000 to $10,000,000 to our campaign. Now that is just not true. I was there."

Secretary of Agriculture Clifford Hardin had told Nixon in the spring of 1971 that the support prices were high enough, but within three weeks, Nixon said, "Congress put a gun to our head. Let me tell you what it was. Republicans? Uh-uh," he said, shaking his head. "One hundred and two

---

* The man dispatched to "rescue" the President's nephew from a California hippie commune was Anthony Ulasewicz, who was later named as the bagman in the payoff of Watergate conspirators.

members of Congress signed a petition demanding not 85 percent of parity, but a 90 percent support price."

Federal milk price support is another government intrusion in the marketplace. The support level is set by the government through its own purchase of surplus commodities and other devices that are designed to keep domestic prices high enough to guarantee farmers an "adequate" income. In 1970, a point not raised by Nixon, his Administration had increased milk support levels by 38 cents per hundredweight to $4.66, one of the most spectacular boosts in the program's history.

"I talked to my legislative leaders and I said, 'Look here. What I am concerned about is what people will pay for that milk and I don't want to have that price jigged up here if we can keep it and get the supply at the present support price.' " But he was told, he said, that "with the kind of heat that we're getting from the Congress" there was "no way" he could avoid a bill to raise the support price to 90 percent. "We said 85 percent and that's why it was done. And that's the truth."

There are different truths. One is that no committee of either house had cleared a dairy bill at that time. Another is that Nixon's ability to triumph over Congress was an established fact. Not only had he successfully impounded billions in appropriated funds, but of his nine vetoes in the current session, in only one, his war powers, was Congress strong enough to muster the necessary two-thirds vote to override. There is still another truth in the "milk deal," one fashioned from the records of the Senate Watergate committee, court depositions on pending lawsuits, and other existing evidence. The story begins, as it should, with the election of Richard Nixon in 1968.

The Associated Milk Producers Inc. (AMPI), a giant Texas-based dairy cooperative, supported Humphrey that year, a mistake the dairymen were anxious to rectify when Nixon took office. The first move was to dispatch AMPI attorney Milton P. Semer to the Justice Department to inquire from John Mitchell just how the dairy industry could get a more "sympathetic understanding of [its] problems within this Administration." Semer wanted to know who the Administration had assigned to handle dairy industry problems, and Mitchell referred him to Herbert Kalmbach. Semer's law partner, Jake Jacobsen, a former aide to President Johnson and a close friend of John B. Connally, has testified that "Kalmbach said that he [Semer] ought to make a contribution." On August 2, 1969, Semer picked up an attaché case in Dallas filled with $100,000 in cash and flew to Newport Beach, California, for a restaurant rendezvous with the President's personal attorney. "We had breakfast," Semer told investigators, "And then we walked over to his office. He showed me around . . . opened the case on a desk and counted the money."

Three weeks later, Semer and two AMPI officials were ushered into the office of White House counsel Harry Dent. The dairymen, who had started out to find a "friend in court," suddenly found themselves wheeling and dealing in the White House. On September 9, 1970, two AMPI officials were invited into the Oval Office for a chat with the President and Colson. By that time, the dairymen had contributed an additional $500,000 to Republican causes. The money came from AMPI and two other large dairy cooperatives—Mid-America Dairies and Dairymen Inc. —through three political "trusts." According to federal court records, these trusts were formed for the expressed purpose of raising and disbursing funds to political candidates of both parties. AMPI established TAPE (Trust for Agricultural Political Education), Mid-America set up ADEPT (Agriculture and Dairy Educational and Political Trust), and Dairymen created SPACE (Trust for Special Agricultural Community Education). As noted before, it was in 1970 that Nixon raised support levels by 38 cents per hundredweight.

On December 16, 1970, the White House received an intriguing letter. It was addressed to the President and signed by Patrick J. Hillings, a partner in the Washington law firm of Reeves & Harrison, Murray Chotiner's outfit, which represented AMPI. A former Congressman from Nixon's old California district, Hillings was hardly a stranger around the White House. After reminding Nixon of his meeting with the two AMPI officials, Hillings asked Nixon to impose import quotas on certain dairy products. The letter opened by saying "this letter discusses a matter of some delicacy and of significant political impact." It read in part:

> The time is ripe politically and economically to impose the recommended quotas [on imports]. AMPI has followed our advice explicitly and will do so in the future. AMPI contributed about $135,000 to Republican candidates in the 1970 election. We are now working with Tom Evans [a partner in Mudge Rose] and Herb Kalmbach in setting up appropriate channels for AMPI to contribute $2 million for your reelection. AMPI is also funding a special project.
>
> The Dairy and related industries have great faith in your personal leadership. At the same time they are shaken by the economy. The right kind of proclamation, issued quickly, would dramatize your personal interest in a large segment of agriculture.

> We write you both as advocates and supporters. All that is necessary is a simple proclamation implementing the four specific tariff commission recommendations.

On December 31—was that fast enough?—Nixon signed a proclamation drastically reducing import quotas on cheese, chocolate products containing butterfat, ice cream and animal feeds. containing milk. In addition, the new Nixon budget the next month recommended raising dairy subsidies by nearly 10 percent. Delighted with their good fortune, the milk industry soon began an intensive lobbying campaign to again raise the price support level of milk. It was this effort that Nixon referred to in his Disney World comment. Secretary of Agriculture Hardin, who had set the $4.66 price, saw no justification for another increase. His decision was backed by the Council of Economic Advisers and by George Shultz, then head of the Office of Management and Budget. It was at this point that Chotiner and Connally went into action. According to his sworn statement, Chotiner used his White House contacts to lobby extensively for the price increase. He spoke to John Ehrlichman and Colson, among others. Evidence given to Ervin committee investigators indicates that the milkmen found a good friend in Connally. He met with representatives of the three milk co-ops—AMPI, Mid-America and Dairymen Inc.—some time between March 12 and March 23, 1971. There is testimony that Connally told the milkmen that "new money will have to come" if they wanted to see price supports boosted. Either that same evening or shortly thereafter, Robert Lilly, the secretary of AMPI's political group, and several milk executives met Connally by accident at a small private airport adjacent to Washington's National Airport. Lilly has testified hearing Connally say something like "Go ahead with the new contributions because it's in the bag." Connally conceded to investigators that he supported the dairymen but denied he was involved in any actual deal trading price supports for campaign funds.

At this meeting, the three co-ops agreed to divide the $2 million among their groups. On March 22 TAPE contributed $10,000 to a "Salute to the President" dinner, channeling the funds through Chotiner's law firm. This was part of an eventual $527,000—this sum includes the $100,000 donated in 1969—the milk industry contributed to Nixon's campaign coffers. The very next morning, Nixon, Hardin, Connally, Shultz, Hillings and Chotiner met in the Cabinet Room with a dozen dairy farmers and executives. Prior to the meeting, Colson reminded the President in a staff memorandum that the milk industry had pledged $2 million to his reelection campaign, and suggested that he acknowledge AMPI's support.* According to a transcript in a Nader suit, Nixon obliquely thanked the milk producers for their pledge, saying in part: ". . . Others I get around this table, they yammer and talk a lot, but they don't do anything about it. But you do and I appreciate that. I don't need to spell it out . . ."

That afternoon Nixon held a follow-up session with Hardin, Connally, Shultz, Chotiner and Ehrlichman, and that evening, Connally again met with co-op executives at a private home in Washington. There is multiple testimony that Connally discussed contributions vis-à-vis price supports. The next morning—March 24—SPACE contributed $25,000 to the Nixon campaign. The very next day, Hardin reversed himself and boosted milk support prices up to $4.93 per hundredweight, or 85 percent parity.

In August 1971, as President Nixon was addressing the AMPI convention, a dairyman handed a $5,000 check to a Colson aide. The money was used to repay a loan Colson had received from a friend to finance the break-in at the office of Daniel Ellsberg's psychiatrist. The check was made out to a Nixon committee entitled People United for Good Government.

Were the milk men contributions a payoff?[45]

Read the letter William A. Powell, president of Mid-America Dairy, wrote to a member, and judge for yourself:

> The facts of life are that the economic welfare of dairymen does depend a great deal on political action. If dairymen are to receive their fair share of the government financial pie that we all pay for, we must have friends in government. I have become increasingly aware that the sincere and soft voice of the dairy farmer is no match for the jingle of hard currencies put in the campaign funds of the politicians by the vegetable fat interests, labor, oil, steel, airlines and others.
>
> We dairymen as a body can be a dominant group. On March 23, 1971, along with nine other dairy farmers, I sat in the Cabinet room of the White House, across the table from the President of the United States, and heard him compliment the dairymen on their marvelous work in consolidating and unifying of our industry and our involvement in politics. He said, "You people are my friends and I appreciate it."
>
> Two days later an order came from the U.S. Department of Agriculture increasing the support price of milk to 85 percent of parity, which added from $500 to $700 million to dairy farmers' milk checks. We

---

* In a press conference statement on October 26, 1973, Nixon said he had always "refused to have any discussion of contributions." On January 14, 1974, in response to the disclosure of the Colson memo, Deputy Press Secretary Gerald L. Warren said that "Occasionally people break rules," but denied that it had influenced the 1971 decision to boost milk price supports.

dairymen cannot afford to overlook this kind of economic benefit. Whether we like it or not, this is the way the system works.[46]

There is another curious angle to the milk deal. On September 9, 1971, Richard W. McLaren, who later gained such notoriety in the ITT case, asked Mitchell to authorize a grand jury investigation of AMPI to determine the possibility that it was engaged in a conspiracy to eliminate competition in milk marketing in the Midwest. McLaren has since testified in an affidavit that on November 30 Mitchell suggested that the antitrust division "proceed along civil rather than criminal lines." Except for his communication with Mitchell, McLaren said he "did not at any time have any direct or indirect communication with anyone in the White House, the Republican National Committee, any fund-raiser for President Nixon, or any fund-raiser for any political committee . . . relating to the investigation of or suit against AMPI. I deny that I directed the investigation of AMPI or the filing of the suit for any improper purpose." AMPI has charged that the Justice Department brought the action to force it to continue making Republican campaign contributions.

The civil suit, which was filed February 1, 1972, charged the 40,000 member cooperative with forcing haulers to refuse to deal with non-members and forcing dairies to buy only from members. It was at this point that John Connally, who then was still Secretary of the Treasury, came back into the picture. Participants in a meeting at Connally's Treasury office on March 16 have testified that he telephoned Mitchell at his new CREEP office to warn him that the antitrust suit might jeopardize further contributions from the milk industry. According to AMPI executives, Connally demanded and received another $50,000 for his own Democrats for Nixon group.

> This Administration has proved that it is utterly incapable of cleaning out the corruption which has completely eroded it and re-establishing the confidence and the faith of the people in the morality and honesty of their government employees. The investigations which have been conducted to date . . . have only scratched the surface. For every case which is exposed, there are ten which are successfully covered up and even then this Administration will go down in history as the "scandal-a-day Administration."
>
> It is typical of the moral standards of the Administration that when they are caught red-handed with pay-off money in their bank accounts the best defense they can give is that they won the money in a poker game, a crap game, or by hitting the daily double.
>
> A new class of royalty has been created in the United States and its princes of privileges and pay-offs include the racketeers who get conces-

sions on their income tax cases, the insiders who get favorite treatment on government contracts, the influence peddlers with keys to the White House, the government employee who uses his position to feather his nest. The great tragedy, however, is not that corruption exists but that it is defended and condoned by the President and other high Administration officials. We have had corruption defended by those in high places. If they won't recognize or admit that corruption exists, how can we expect them to clean it up?—Richard Nixon, November 13, 1951.

Nixon is a shifty-eyed goddamn liar, and the people know it. I can't figure out how he came so close to getting elected in 1960. . . . They say Nixon has changed, but they'll have to prove it to me. Where that fella is concerned, you might say I'm from Missouri.—Harry Truman, circa 1961–62.*

Scandals like Watergate focus attention only on the tip of the political iceberg, an occasional jarring note in a long unwritten history of corruption. Conflicts of interest, in myriad forms, exist at all levels of government. Sometimes it is as devious as the grain sale to the Soviet Union. The Agriculture Department (USDA) made it possible for the six largest grain shippers to make enormous windfall profits at the expense of farmers, who were not apprised of the sale in advance and sold their harvest at depressed going prices. "There is nothing remarkable in wealthy agribusinessmen getting wealthier," said the New Republic in an editorial, "but the pattern of job shifting that took place while negotiations were in progress was remarkable":

Businessmen and officials changed jobs as follows: 1. an assistant secretary of agriculture quit the government to become vice president of a grain firm that later had the largest sales to Russia; 2. he was replaced at USDA by a former executive of another grain firm involved; 3. another USDA official left to become the Washington agent for yet another of the grain firms; 4. replacing a man who had quit the firm to work at USDA five months before. The vice president of a fourth grain firm quit a month before to work at the White House. Conflict of interest? An insulting question, according to the administration.†47

Or sometimes it is in the form of a juicy plum for top insiders. The

---

* From conversations with Harry S. Truman as recorded in Merle Miller's book, *Plain Speaking*, published in 1973.

† On July 11, 1973, the Justice Department exonerated the grain dealers of any criminal wrongdoing. It found no evidence warranting prosecution of traders accused of manipulating grain prices so that they could qualify for larger government subsidies, nor was there evidence that two former USDA officials who joined grain companies at that time disclosed confidential information to grain dealers or violated conflict-of-interest laws.

transformation of the Post Office Department into an independent government corporation in 1971 presented such an opportunity. The sale of $10 billion in bonds, which could have been marketed through the U.S. Treasury at savings of many millions of dollars in interest and legal costs, was turned over to five underwriters—selected without competitive bids—including Dillon Read, Peter Flanigan's old firm, and Kidder, Peabody, which retained Jack E. Gleason, a fireball Republican fund raiser, for the express purpose of getting the postal-bond business. Nixon's old law firm, Mudge Rose, handled the legal work for a fee that may total more than $1 million.[48]

The eternal search for campaign funds, in the words of Senator Edward Kennedy, "is the most flagrant single abuse in our democracy, the unconscionable power of money." Larry O'Brien—it seems incredible that only yesterday the spark plug of the winning party was still being shunted to the Post Office—thinks "There's a smell, an odor about it and unless things change the system cannot survive." "The way we nominate and elect people is the heart of representative government," says Maryland Senator Charles McC. Mathias, Jr. "If you have to be rich or have rich friends and backers to reach high office, then democracy is a fraud. This is the most undemocratic flaw in our system, and yet nothing is done about it."[49]

How expensive a business is campaigning? Herbert E. Alexander, the leading authority on this subject, estimated that candidates for elective offices spent some $400 million in 1972, with about $100 million going to the presidential race—the split was nearly three to one in favor of the Republican Party.* The lion's share of this bounty came from the private vault of money power. McGovern, too, received large sums from a few maverick contributors, but the windfall reaped by the Nixon campaign was the most spectacular in history. One contributor gave $2 million, another gave $1 million, ten gave more than $4 million, and the top one hundred gave $14 million. All of it in violation, either in spirit or letter, of tax and election laws.[50]

The Federal Corrupt Practices Act, on the books since 1925, is the most abused law since the Volstead Act. It is an impressive document of almost impenetrable jargon, which has been amended so many times, including by the Federal Election Campaign Act of 1971, that the titles alone run for two pages. As with the tax laws, the amendments, alleged efforts to plug loopholes, have only inspired greater secret evasion. The

* Traditionally, the GOP has maintained a two-one edge in contributions.

political answer, of course, is always more amendments, that is, reform, which is the most deceptive of all political games. When the people catch on to the game being played, the automatic answer is more reform. Nothing is said about compliance with the laws already on the books.

Here, briefly, are some of the stipulations and the evasions that have evolved from the Corrupt Practices Act. For example, a candidate for the House of Representatives may not spend more than $5,000 and a candidate for the Senate may not spend more than $25,000 on an election campaign. The loophole provided, which is large enough to slip the Capitol dome through, requires every candidate to report all receipts and expenditures that were incurred in his campaign "with his knowledge or consent." So candidates let others handle the money and then officially report their financial outlay as "None." According to Alexander, $100 million was spent on House and Senate candidates in 1972, about fifty times more than the law allows.

The act limits contributions from individuals to $5,000* per candidate through a committee operating in two or more states, but the insinuation of the interstate-commerce clause gave rise to another gaping loophole. Only fund-raising committees operating in two or more states, which are limited by the act from spending more than $3 million on an election campaign, need divulge their transactions on federal reports. Thus candidates may set up any number of committees in various states on the pretext that they operate autonomously within state borders. Since some states require full disclosure, the drafters conveniently omitted the District of Columbia, creating a sort of lawless DMZ where campaign managers could set up hundreds of committees and report nothing.

To evade the limitation on both spending and giving, contributors wanting to give more than $5,000 can easily do so by giving to such nonreporting committees. The phony committee has the additional advantage of enabling large donors to avoid paying the required gift tax—under the law, no taxpayer may give more than $3,000 annually to any person or organization without incurring gift taxes—once the taxpayer has exhausted a $30,000 lifetime exemption.† But with the contributions funneled through separate dummies, often consisting of just a name and a mailing address, the contributor gets as many $3,000 exclusions as he needs to

---

* The 1971 act removes this limit—a wealthy contributor may now give as much as he wants, but the gift-tax limitation remains, and so the subterfuge continues.

† Married couples in community-property states such as California may double their gift.

avoid the tax. In 1972, for example, Richard Mellon Scaife, an heir to the Mellon fortune, gave the Nixon campaign $990,000 by writing 330 separate checks, each for $3,000, to 330 separate committees.

Contributors who donate appreciated securities also get to evade capital-gains taxes, making it possible for candidates to run for public office partly at Treasury expense.

> One day last February a group of imaginative financiers sat down in secrecy to dream up fancy titles for a batch of phony organizations.
> The men were experienced in this sort of work, so it didn't take long to compile a big list of names: Better America Council, Loyal Americans for Effective Government, Dedicated Volunteers for Reform in Society, United Friends of Good Government, and so on. Fifty organizations were created, and copies of the list were quickly sent across the country.
> Next, solicitors speaking in urgent, patriotic tones ("The future of our country is at stake!") induced citizens to part with securities bought at low prices long ago. This stock was carefully divided into blocks worth a few thousand dollars each. Then title to the stock was transferred to the impressive-sounding organizations. In a twinkling, the stock was sold and, once the cash proceeds had been safely deposited at four banks, all 50 groups vanished.
> A stock fraud preying on gullible Americans?
> By no means. This is the novel way in which the Committee to Re-Elect the President collected millions of campaign dollars this year. The idea is to make political giving relatively painless through avoidance of taxes—both capital gains and gift taxes.—*Wall Street Journal*, September 27, 1972

The act makes it "unlawful for any national bank, or any corporation . . . to make a contribution or expenditure in connection with any election to any political office." Through amendments, this stipulation now applies to any individual working under a federal contract, which automatically includes workers in defense and aerospace plants. The Taft-Hartley Act of 1947 extended the stipulation to labor unions. The maximum penalty prescribed by the act is two years in prison and a $10,000 fine, but other penalties, particularly in the areas of conspiracy and tax evasion, come into play in the myriad loopholes created by both "soft" and "hard" contributions. In a probing *New Yorker* article entitled "A Fundamental Hoax," Richard Harris included an excerpt from a political action memorandum prepared by the Washington State Bankers Association and distributed to bank executives around the state:

> A frequent device used by companies is for an officers' fund to be administered by some committee. The officers and employees make con-

tributions to this fund, sometimes even by an automatic payroll deduction plan. Such contributions are sometimes indirectly coerced through intracorporate memos by superior officers pointing out that they have made contributions and inviting action memos from subordinates. Sometimes the voluntary contributions are encouraged by the corporations' providing some other fringe benefit of significant value, such as group life insurance. Sometimes employees are encouraged to pad expense accounts as a device for reimbursement for their "voluntary" corporate contribution. . . . Devices which are illegal and clearly prohibited but difficult to detect are sometimes used by corporations. Examples of these are donations of stamps to candidates with the expense hidden in the general corporate expenditure for postage. Sometimes loans are made which are subsequently written off as uncollectible. This activity for banks is clearly prohibited and would be immediately suspect. Another device sometimes used is for advertising agencies to render bills for services . . . to the candidate's campaign and sending the invoice to the corporation without specific detail for what services were rendered. Similarly, printing bills or, in some cases, even lawyers' fee bills are used. . . . A frequently used device is the loan of employees or other facilities of the corporation, such as duplicating facilities, computer facilities, telephone networks, and the like. In addition to contributions of postage stamps, [there are] often contributions of envelopes or other products of a company which might be usable in the campaign, such as lumber for signs, stationery, or other paper. . . . All of the foregoing probably constitute a prohibited expenditure, though indictment and prosecution are infrequent.[51]

Other tax-evading schemes include, as Harris noted, "turning over billboards" to a candidate; "giving employees cash bonuses, which are then passed on, minus a proportion set aside for income taxes, to the candidate; retaining public-relations or advertising men with the proviso that part of their fee and part of their work go to the candidate; lending automobiles, airplanes, credit cards, [hotel suites], and office space; and turning over entire computer systems for use at night." Also corporations permit their employees to work in campaigns while still on the payroll, and they pay attorneys' professional fees with the understanding that a percentage will be contributed to a designated candidate. "Most of these indirect donations are handled surreptitiously," Harris observed, "and many are deducted as ordinary business expenses in figuring federal corporation taxes.* Since the Corrupt Practices Act does not prohibit backers

---

* The fund-raising dinner, still a mainstay of politics, offers an excellent opportunity for a firm or individual to spend thousands on whole blocks of tickets and not be listed as a major contributor. Better yet, the price of the tickets—or ads in local dinner journals—are easily disguised on tax returns as a business expense.

from picking up a candidate's political debts after a campaign,* this is often arranged beforehand so that no record exists; expenditures of this kind have been deducted as bad debts. Both deductions are outright violations of the Internal Revenue Code, but so far no Administration has prosecuted any person or any company for taking them, probably because every Administration has benefitted, and has hoped to go on benefitting, from this form of crime." Harris concludes that the "Corrupt Practices Act assures that the financial practices of practically everyone who attains national office will be corrupt."[52]

Besides the millions coveted in "soft money" contributions, it takes plenty of cash or "hard money" to run a political campaign. The *modus operandi* here is no less criminal. For example, Maurice Stans assigned "quotas" to corporations, with specific amounts he expected their executives to contribute. For years corporations have systematically dunned their executives for "voluntary" campaign contributions. Other corporations openly operate employee and executive "citizenship committee" campaign contributing funds. But none disclose or report the amount they raise or distribute. Labor unions, which also collect political donations from individual members, report their contributions. Yet corporations, professional groups, and industry-wide associations say their own political-action committees were inspired by the success of union committees such as COPE (AFL-CIO) and DRIVE (Teamsters). Some companies go so far as to use their payroll-deduction system to collect campaign contributions from employees, but the final decision on distribution of the funds is made by corporate executives.

On September 25, 1970, the organizers of BankPAC—Bankers Political Action Committee—drafted a solicitation letter that was distributed to banking-industry leaders across the country: "The purpose is to support financially the campaigns of those candidates for the U.S. Congress who have demonstrated and expressed a real understanding of the proper function and structure of our banking system and its necessary part and contribution to our society and our economy."[53] According to reporter Walter Pincus, who investigated the contribution practices of several corporations, the gadfly in the bankers' bonnet was Wright Patman, chairman of the House Banking and Currency Committee. "The banking industry, which

---

* By campaigning on the cuff, candidates actually force telephone companies, airlines, hotels, and others into making involuntary and illegal contributions. Many companies are quick to discount or write off the delinquent bills of successful candidates, while aggressively dunning losers.

for years had faced little if any interference from Congress," Pincus wrote, "suddenly found itself in 1970 with critical pieces of legislation on the House floor, such as the Bank Holding Company Act, and little, if any, leverage with a majority of the individual House members":

> Determined to prevent that from happening again, national BankPAC and 47 state organizations were established with the help of sophisticated legal advice on how to operate within the letter, if not the spirit, of the campaign fund reporting laws. "Conveniently," suggested the BankPAC solicitation letter, "you and your associates can get together and remit for all by one personal check (not more than $99 in any individual check to avoid Federal reporting requirements)* to BankPAC and mail to me. It will take only a dollar or two per person—'Peanuts'—and still be a combined effort we can practically and effectively contribute to proper legislation and supervision for the financial system which can best serve our people and our communities."[54]

In October 1970, Patman got wind of the bankers' concern for *their* people and communities, and his reaction was to write a letter to Attorney General Mitchell asking that he "immediately launch an investigation to determine the extent of political fund-raising activities carried on by individual commercial banks and banks acting within associations and committees." That is where matters comfortably rested until only days before the 1970 election, when Washington *Post* reporter Morton Mintz revealed that twenty-one members of the House Banking and Currency Committee and four members of the Senate Banking Committee had received about $200,000 in BankPAC funds. Caught with their contributions showing, thirteen recipients promptly returned the money. Commenting on the debacle, a BankPAC official characterized its distribution procedure as "naïve": "They [the campaign contributions] were sent in the mail with no time to write letters in advance with an explanation." Looking forward to 1972, the spokesman said the organization was "in pretty good shape financially," and he expected to do "a more thorough job this year."[55]

Industry-wide associations have taken on major political significance in recent years. Bankers, milk producers, doctors, lawyers, truckers, oil producers, airlines, road builders—just about everybody has gotten into the act. It takes seven yellow pages in the Washington telephone directory to list all the associations. What they are looking for is their own private

---

* The new election law requires that all candidates and their committees report the name, address, and vocation of anyone contributing more than $100, and the name of anyone receiving more than $100 from the committee.

piece of the government—not for the benefit of people and communities but for their own special profitable interest. "Few, if any, large campaign contributors are motivated entirely by altruistic considerations," Joseph A. Califano, Jr., formerly chief aide to President Johnson and counsel to the Democratic National Committee in 1972, told a Senate subcommittee during hearings on campaign financing. "Money unquestionably is the most debilitating and corrupting force in American politics today."[56]

There is a lot of delicate waltzing around this topic in the media. The system is riddled with criminal loopholes, but many reporters still prefer to accept the pious rationalizations of public-relations specialists rather than admitting that it is hopelessly corrupt. Except for Kennedys and Rockefellers, few politicians like to spend their own money in election campaigns.* It is cheaper to hustle special-interest groups, which deal in investments, not contributions. Stripped of euphemism, a large contribution may be called many things, but a gift it is not. At best it is a gratuity from a predator, given in anticipation of special consideration, usually at the expense of the general public; at worst, it is an outright bribe, designed to pervert judgment and corrupt conduct—in other words, a specific quid for a specific quo, a deal. Smaller deals, but no less invidious, are conducted at the ambassadorial auction. It has long been a common practice to sell ambassadorships to the highest bidders, the incubating source of Ugly Americans who spread the foul word around the world. Ruth Lewis Farkas donated $200,000 to CREEP *after* the November election and was nominated ambassador to Luxembourg by Nixon and approved by the Senate Foreign Relations Committee. The committee chairman, J. W. Fulbright, who cast the lone dissenting vote, said: "I don't believe in paying this kind of money for these appointments. It is demeaning of the office."[57] Demeaning or not, the committee rubber-stamps appointments. One of Eisenhower's big contributors, Maxwell H. Gluck, was approved as ambassador to Ceylon even when he could not name that nation's Prime Minister during the confirmation hearings.[58]

Before the ink was dry on the election law, there were forces at work to emasculate it. A literally inside joke on Capitol Hill during the 1972 election went like this: "The top priority on the agenda when the 93rd Congress convenes is reserved for prison reform—because that is where we'll all be if the new campaign finance law is enforced."[59]

---

* The new election law limits what a politician or his family can give to his own candidacy—$50,000 in campaign for President or Vice President, $35,000 for Senator, $25,000 for Representative.

According to Richard Strout, who writes the column signed "TRB" in the *New Republic*,

> Members of Congress, particularly those in the House, have discovered that they really didn't know what they were doing when they passed a law that requires comprehensive public disclosure of all campaign income and expenses by all candidates for federal office—and that just happens to include members of Congress seeking reelection. . . . The Congress stepped into this quagmire because the House and Senate focused almost all attention on the sections of law which would limit, for the first time, expenditures for radio and television, while little interest was displayed in the new reporting requirements.
>
> Those requirements now emerge as a problem for the incumbents because they are the recipients of potentially embarrassing donations from interest groups seeking to influence legislation. As a rule, the dispensers of that "smart money" don't like to deal with a challenger because they don't know what committee assignments he will receive, how "cooperative" he will be and how long it will take him to gain influence in Congress. Besides, most challengers lose anyhow, and the money is wasted.[60]

The major impact of the new law was to precipitate a paper crisis. Ten thousand separate committees (all those spending more than $1,000) submitted reports consisting of some 200,000 sheets of paper filled with names and numbers, enough to reform the most rabid reformer. The report of just one Texas committee for Republican Senator John Tower ran nearly 1,400 computer readout pages on microfilm.[61] The handwriting on the wall is indelible. The prime targets of the rollback effort include the provision banning indirect contributions by government contractors, and the affiliated political funds,* which were virtually outlawed by a Common Cause lawsuit. The attempt to repeal the section failed only after Senator Proxmire threatened a filibuster. The AFL-CIO joined money power in a massive lobbying effort in support of the repealer. It sailed through the House without committee hearings shortly before adjournment, but Proxmire stopped it before it reached the Senate floor. Representative Morris K. Udall of Arizona praised the "Active Citizenship Fund" at Hughes Aircraft Company, a government contractor if there ever was one, as "one of the finest programs in America. They appoint a Democrat and a Republican chairman in their plant and they go through the assembly line getting small contributions from the employees and urging employees to vote."

---

* Funds collected by corporations and unions from employees and executives.

But an examination of the Hughes fund showed that executives and engineers uniformly donated $150 each. The wife of a Hughes employee complained in a letter to Common Cause of the "company's request for $150. No ifs, ands or buts about it. We had been underlined to give $150 with no designation possible." A Hughes engineer wrote, "Most of us feel it is a political slush fund. First we are asked to contribute a specific amount of money. Of course we are told it is 'voluntary' but there is the subtle suggestion that if you don't contribute your chances for promotion or a salary increase may be jeopardized. They never say this, but we feel it."[62]

In a deposition and affidavit written in 1964, John T. Naylor, a former ITT vice president, alleged he had been pressured by ITT executives into contributing $1,200 to Johnson's vice-presidential campaign in 1960. William Marx, who was then an ITT senior vice president, had solicited the contribution in the name of the company's chairman, Harold S. Geneen. Naylor quoted Marx as saying, "Hal [Geneen] and the board have a program that is very important to political protection and business development. Hal has given me a selected list of top executives to contribute to the election campaign. You are down for $1,200. This can be financed for you by the company if necessary; Jim Lillis [controller] will handle it. You will be expected to recover the amount by covering it up in your traveling expense account. The board of directors wants us all to cooperate."[63]

Another big push is being directed at modifying the reporting requirements to protect the identity of shy Yankees and cowboys. Lawmakers are afraid that too much publicity might dry the well that nourishes them. But that is unlikely, considering the economic clout generated by the "natural aristocracy" in its benevolent mandate to rule over the plebeian majority. How viable is the concept of "one man, one vote" when candidates are manipulated and bankrolled by those who have the most to gain from their election? "The relationship between money and politics is so organic that seeking reform is tantamount to asking a doctor to perform open-heart surgery on himself," *Newsweek* concluded in an essay entitled "The $400 Million Election Machine." "The overhaul of the system is unavoidably dependent on the very men who have risen to power by the old rules."[64]

Election reform, or any other kind of reform that effects the welfare of politicians and money power, will invariably turn out to be more loophole than reform. "Most of the political process has become—behind the scenes—a vast game of barter and purchase involving campaign contributions, appointments to office, business favors, favorable legal decisions, favorable locations of defense installations," John Gardner has said. "It is a game that is going on all the time at every level of government. And it is paid for, ultimately, by you and me."[65]

A harsh judgment? Perhaps. But follow the Washington *Post* as it traces the twinkling footsteps of Maurice Stans through the resplendent aeries of money power:

> —Stans's conversations with corporate executives sometimes combined the subjects of campaign solicitation and the corporations' problems with the federal government. For example, Stans reminded steel executives of his continuing efforts on their behalf to avoid harsh remedies to their industrial pollution problems. He asked a Greyhound Corporation official for a contribution in a conversation that included mention by Greyhound of its interest in legislation to permit wider buses. . . .
> —Stans urged corporations to use a so-called "conduit system," in which the chief executive solicited others in his company and then turned in all the money at one time to Stans. Many of the companies sent the campaign money to Stans via their Washington representatives who handled corporate business with the federal government.
> —Stans urged pre-April 7 contributions to insure secrecy and furnished donors with names of dummy committees so they could divide up their contributions to avoid gift taxes.
> —Stans called a meeting in August of officials from about thirty major corporations to urge them to continue the "conduit system" of soliciting employees even though some thought the new law prohibited it. When a Westinghouse executive and others still questioned the legality of such corporate fund-raising efforts, the Nixon Administration furnished the corporations with an "advisory" Attorney General's opinion to reassure them on September 15.
> —Stans got the funds from corporations whose chief executive officers he had placed earlier on government advisory committees on industrial pollution [National Industrial Pollution Control Council] and consumer protection [National Business Council for Consumer Affairs]. He organized and led the committees while serving as Secretary of Commerce until early in 1972. He told the committees that their purpose was to give business "an input at the White House."[66]

The campaign money game, as played by the lackeys of money power, reduces democracy to a government of the rich, by the rich, for only the rich. Legislation and administrative decisions are made according to the amount of money involved. It is government by exquisite blackmail.

Although a long parade of repentant corporate executives passing before the Watergate committee were quick to lay the blame on the defunct Nixon Administration, none charged that Nixon's fund raisers had to get tough. George S. Spater, former chairman of American Airlines, testified that his firm gave Kalmbach an illegal $75,000 donation* because he feared the unknown. The situation reminded him of "those medieval maps that show the known world and then, around it, *terra incognita* with fierce animals." But Kalmbach, over dinner at Manhattan's posh "21" Club, was "a very soft-sell, a very congenial gentleman."

All the executives appearing before the committee strongly protested that their firms had received no special favors—and no promise of favors —in return for their gratuities. They donated because they were afraid not to. As Claude C. Wild, Jr., of Gulf Oil phrased it, his firm gave $100,000 because it might otherwise end up on "a black list or bottom of the totem pole."

The devious ways the companies concealed their gifts vividly demonstrates their expertise in fraudulent operations. Asked by the committee if he knew he was acting illegally in using corporate money for a political contribution, Orin E. Atkins, board chairman of Ashland Oil, replied: "To be precise to your question, I did. I guess I viewed it as somewhat analogous to the situation in Prohibition—the Volstead Act—where it was more honored in the breach than by observation."

Then Atkins described how the donation was laundered through a foreign subsidiary and a Swiss bank. A company official traveling through Europe was asked to withdraw $100,000 in cash from a Geneva bank. The withdrawal was listed as "investment in land" on the books of Ashland Petroleum Gabon, a subsidiary exploring for oil off the coast of Africa. Asked to explain the reason for the subterfuge, Atkins said: "Well, $100,000 in cash is a commodity which U.S. banks, I do not believe, normally deal in from day to day. But I think the Swiss, being a more sophisticated financial society than ours, I believe are used to dealing in such numbers, and it does not excite anybody's curiosity if you walk in and ask for $100,000 out of a Swiss bank. If you did that in the United States, everybody and his brother would be wondering what you did with it."

Gulf Oil, Wild told the committee, made two withdrawals from Baha-

---

* Others known to have made illegal contributions were Ashland Oil Inc. ($100,000); Braniff Airways Inc. ($40,000); Goodyear Tire & Rubber Company ($40,000); Gulf Oil Corporation ($100,000); 3M Company ($30,000); Phillips Petroleum Company ($100,000); American Ship Building Company ($26,500). The legal penalty in most cases was a $1,000 fine and a gentle reprimand.

mas Exploration, Ltd., a wholly owned Gulf subsidiary, and charged it off to "miscellaneous expense account." American Airlines hid its contribution in phony invoices routed through a Lebanese subsidiary and a Swiss bank. American Ship Building issued "bonuses" to eight trusted corporate officials along with instructions to forward the money to specific GOP committees. This method was also popular with the dairy industry. Stuart H. Russell, a former AMPI attorney, has sworn that he received at least $176,828 in phony "legal fees" from the dairy cooperatives, which he returned to a milk lobbyist in a series of transactions between December 1969 and December 1970.

The National Industrial Pollution Control Council is only one of 1,500 industry advisory committees now functioning within the Executive Branch of government. Senator Lee Metcalf of Montana, who has made a study of their operations, discovered that the committees "exist inside most important federal agencies, and even have offices in some":

> Legally, their function is purely as kibitzer, but in practice many have become internal lobbies—printing industry handouts in the Government Printing Office with taxpayers' money, and even influencing policies. Industry committees perform the dual function of stopping government from finding out about corporations while at the same time helping corporations get inside information about what government is doing. Sometimes, the same company that sits on an advisory council that obstructs or turns down a government questionnaire is precisely the company which is withholding information the government needs in order to enforce a law.[67]

The National Industrial Pollution Control Council was conceived in 1970 for the purpose of advising the President and the chairman of the Council on Environmental Quality, through the Secretary of Commerce, on industrial pollution problems. The sixty-three "pollution experts" named to the committee were the top executives of "Companies that have the greatest experience in spewing filth and poison into our environment . . . including the chief officers of airlines and electric utilities, and producers and manufacturers of steel, automobiles, detergents, coal, petroleum, chemicals, beverage containers, and paper and wood products."[68] Charged by the President with collecting data and evaluating "programs of industry relating to the quality of the environment," the council was not hampered in its deliberations by a single representative from conservation or consumer groups, universities, or other public-oriented groups. The analogy that came to mind, said Metcalf, was that of sending the rabbit to fetch the lettuce. The council's chairman was

Bert S. Cross, chairman of the board and chief executive officer of Minnesota Mining and Manufacturing, a company that had been under a four-year edict from Wisconsin authorities to stop discharging sulfurous wastes into the municipal sewers of Prairie du Chien.[69]

Further to avoid unwelcome static from environmentalists, the council shrouded its performance in secrecy. Its "public" meetings were either not announced or held in government buildings closed to the public. At its meeting of October 14, 1970, held at the Commerce Department, representatives of environmental and consumer groups were denied entrance and their request for a transcript of the proceedings was turned down. The data collected by the council that day included a ten-minute discussion of national pollution standards by Russell Train of the Council on Environmental Quality, while a round-table exploration of tax breaks and incentives as a means of promoting pollution controls lasted one hour and forty-five minutes.

After its February 1971 meeting, held at the security-tight State Department, the industrialists stood on the White House lawn with the President for a demonstration of new pollution-abatement equipment being tested on a Boeing 727. When the first 727 took off from National Airport, sharply rising over the Jefferson Memorial, it emitted a heavy trail of black smoke. The second 727, moving at a slower rate of speed and climbing at a reduced angle, produced cleaner exhaust, which prompted Nixon and his visitors to hail the test as evidence that industry was moving swiftly on its own to control pollution. "This little episode on the White House lawn," Metcalf observed in 1971, "demonstrates the industrial pollution council's function as a massive, government-established public relations arm of the world's worst polluters. Little more than one year after its inception, the council has published approximately 25 reports printed at public expense by the Government Printing Office, including a 'Casebook of Pollution Cleanup Actions.' These cleanup actions are 'drawn from published accounts of individual company environmental accomplishments throughout American industry'—most of them reprinted from such highly unimpeachable sources as industry trade association publications and house magazines."

What would happen if representatives of public interest groups asked for the same quasi-official status accorded industry advisory committees, which not only have direct access to government files and officials but are permitted to sit in while government policy is formulated? Would the public interest groups pose a threat to national security if let loose in the

Pentagon? This is precisely the privilege enjoyed by some of the nation's top defense contractors serving on the Defense Industry Advisory Committee—the euphemism "Defense" was dropped in 1968 in deference to public sentiment and the committee now simply refers to itself as IAC. Except for the Deputy Secretary of Defense, who serves as chairman, all twenty-four members of IAC are corporate executives, with about half representing the nation's top defense contractors. According to Metcalf, the committee's influence in government is so powerful that it even prevailed over the General Accounting Office, the independent auditing arm of Congress:

> When the IAC advises the Pentagon on defense profits, it advises from experience. It has negotiated both for changes in procurement rules and for higher profits, and its success can be measured by a recent General Accounting Office questionnaire that last year [1970] found an average 56 percent profit based on equity invested in 146 negotiated defense contracts examined.
>
> The IAC, wanting to minimize its success in the area of profits, worked to convince the GAO to write another draft of its report, highlighting new information voluntarily and unselfishly provided by industry, showing a lower profit margin of 21 percent. The IAC prevailed—the final version of the GAO report de-emphasized the government's independent conclusions and upgraded the industry's data showing the lower figures.[70]

It is a cozy arrangement. The Pentagon can privately resolve conflicts between contractors, shortstopping disgruntled contractors from complaining to Congress or the press. For industry, of course, it means top-secret briefings on the technology of foreign powers and advance information on the Administration's economic "game plan." No wonder IAC is known as the "board of directors of the military-industrial complex." It was at IAC's insistence that the Pentagon changed its policy in contracting, providing for more cost-plus contracts and less competition. Low profits, IAC argued, imperiled national security. The nation's defense posture, as one IAC spokesman phrased it succinctly, will best be served "without cutthroat competition."

Following in the footsteps of bureaucracy, IAC has created subcommittees to oversee the entire Pentagon operation. The subcommittee on military exports, for example, has "as its prime objective the selling of the Pentagon abroad by promoting overseas military sales and mini-arms races. Small countries provide a lucrative market for second-hand arsenals, and IAC's subcommittee helps convince them they need to be the first on their continent to have a surplus destroyer or an obsolete jet. . . . Their approach seems not unlike a weapons' sale roadshow, including a more favorable policy on profits so as to stimulate export expansion; a combined effort by industry and the Departments of State, Commerce, and Defense to solicit foreign sales; and upgrading of 'industrial-educational institutions' in the instruction of problems of military hardware export."[71]

It is an odds-on bet that when former Secretary of State Rogers told the Senate Foreign Relations Committee that this nation should sell jet fighters to Arab nations—"If we don't, others will"—the IAC had a hand in it, along with advisory committees at Interior (oil), Commerce, State, and all others with a stake involved. Advisory committees have been around a long time. As noted in Chapter Three, President Coolidge created the Federal Oil Conservation Board so that "the oil industry itself might be permitted to determine its own future. That future might be left to the simple workings of the law of supply and demand but for the patent fact that the oil industry's welfare is so intimately linked with the industrial prosperity and safety of the whole people, that government and business can well join forces to work out this problem of practical conservation." It was this decision that permitted oilmen to introduce prorationing of oil to protect industry-set prices. It was the Planning and Coordination Committee, composed exclusively of executives from the major oil companies, that worked out the NRA petroleum code, designed to cure an economy diagnosed to be suffering from the "free play of a self-regulating market."

Oilmen abound throughout the bureaucracy. For example, in the area of providing statistical information on the energy crisis, William Simon relies primarily on the Department of Interior and the Federal Power Commission. The Department of Interior has two principal sources: the Office of Oil and Gas and the Bureau of Mines, which in turn rely on two advisory groups made up of oil-industry executives, the Foreign Petroleum Supply Committee, which recently empaneled its smaller Emergency Petroleum Supply Committee to consider the impact of the Arab embargo, and the National Petroleum Council. The FPC has the Bureau of Natural Gas, which tabulates and publishes information on natural gas reserves and production based on questionnaires filled out by the gas industry. The FPC also publishes as government statistics estimates made by the American Gas Association, the industry's lobby. To monitor the lobby's data, the FPC has one employee on its ten-man Committee on Natural Gas Reserves, the rest are oilmen.

The floodgates of money-power inputs were officially opened by Congress in 1942 when it legislatively deflected to the Budget Bureau the flood of clarification requests from small businessmen confused by the mounting paperwork required in the administration of rationing and wage-price controls. Charged with coordinating the collection of information, Budget promptly turned to industry for assistance in administering the new law. It created the Advisory Council on Federal Reports, which consisted of sixteen advisory committees, covering all fields from banking to equal employment and staffed, of course, with the leaders of those same industries. Today there is no limit to the degree of supervision exercised by industry. For example, proposals by federal agencies requiring Budget approval (now the Office of Management and Budget—OMB) are automatically listed on "birdwatcher sheets" forwarded to dozens of industry and association representatives for possible advisory action. Metcalf points out that a "critical national inventory of industrial water wastes was delayed more than seven years by a filibuster of OMB and the advisory committees" consisting of representatives from such polluters as U.S. Steel, Consolidated Coal, and American Pulp and Paper, who challenged the inventory on grounds that the information might fall into the hands of "news media and opportunistic politicians."[72]

After so many years of leadership, it was only natural that the Civil Aeronautics Board Finance Advisory Committee would decide to hold its first meeting at One Chase Manhattan Plaza, as prestigious a money-power address as one is likely to find. These men felt no compulsion to continue the charade. Why bother playing the game when no one is watching? It was a convenient decision. The committee's chairman, James P. Mitchell, was also Chase Manhattan's vice president in charge of airline finances. In fact, the committee, which was created by CAB to deal with the liquidity problem of airlines, was staffed by the airlines' major lenders. Their astute recommendation was for greater government subsidies to help the airlines pay their bills.

Metcalf believes that the advisory committees, instead of benefiting society through increased information, have "closed off the flow of information and reserved key governmental access points for the leaders of the corporate world. The widespread and pervasive influence of these committees marks the emergence of the American corporate state, where dominant political power is officially and quasi-officially invested in the massive industrial and financial conglomerates."[73]

What is even more remarkable about advisory committees is that in most instances they are advising government officials who come from their own world of big business, banking, foundations, and Wall Street law firms. Even the Labor Department, the working man's putative ombuds-man, is topheavy with former corporate executives from such illustrious employers as Lockheed, Ford, Cities Service, American Motors, Bethlehem Steel, and Olin.[74]

Before Ralph Nader and John Gardner came on the scene, one of the money power's most widely accepted myths was that the people retained sovereignty over the economic structure through government regulations. In *The Vital Center*, reissued as recently as 1962, Arthur M. Schlesinger, Jr., confirmed this myth: "The capitalist state . . . far from being the helpless instrument of the possessing class, has become the means by which other groups in society have redressed the balance of social power against those whom Hamilton called the "rich and the well-born. . . ."[75]

Nothing could be further from the truth. Ironically, the greatest advocates of "corporate socialism" are to be found in the regulatory agencies, that bureaucratic apparatus supposedly designed to "redress the balance." In fact, Nader quite accurately views the regulators as monopoly makers: the government, which is "a bustling bazaar of accounts receivable" for industry and commerce, is a captive of corporate power.[76]

Nicholas Johnson, a former member of the Federal Communications Commission and one of the few liberals to have escaped after seven years with his liberal hymen intact, soon discovered to his chagrin that citizen participation in the decision-making process "is virtually non-existent," with the "necessary but unhappy result . . . that the FCC is a 'captive' of the very industry it is purportedly attempting to regulate."[77]

The watchdog is nothing but a declawed pussycat. This has been the story from the beginning. Back in 1894, Attorney General Richard Olney, a former railroad attorney, articulated this concept in a letter to President Perkins of the Chicago, Burlington & Quincy. The letter, which reads like something cooked up by an ITT or Watergate conspirator, was written to dissuade Perkins from lobbying to dismantle the new Interstate Commerce Commission:

> My impression would be that, looking at the matter from a railroad point of view exclusively, [the abolition of the ICC] would not be a wise thing to undertake. . . . The attempt would not be likely to succeed; if it did not succeed, and were made on the ground of the inefficiency and uselessness of the Commission, the result would very probably be giving it the power that it now lacks.
>
> The Commission, as its functions have now been limited by the courts, is, or can be made, of great use to the railroads. It satisfies the popular clamor for a government supervision of railroads, at the same time that

the supervision is almost entirely nominal. Furthermore, the older such a Commission gets to be, the more inclined it will be to take the business and railroad view of things. It becomes a sort of barrier between the business corporations and the people and a sort of protection against hasty and crude legislation hostile to railroad interests. . . . The part of wisdom is not to destroy the Commission but to utilize it.[78]

It is only fitting that the ICC, the oldest regulatory agency in the U.S. Government, is still the most abysmally inefficient and corrupt. Founded in 1887 to regulate railroads, it has "clung to the notion that transportation is inherently unsuited to competition in spite of the development of new competitive modes," Dan Cordtz wrote in *Fortune*. The commission "still bears the marks of its origin," Cordtz concluded. "It started out to oversee railroad cartels, and it still oversees the U.S. transportation system, or large parts of it, in the cartel spirit."[79] The financial disaster of today's railroads flows from the original sin of the ICC's creation. Its mandate was to stop destructive competition between large railroads, which practiced collusive rates and pooled traffic, and small branch lines, not subject to cartel rules. Rate wars, secret rebates, and declining profits finally forced railroad magnates into seducing their congressional catamites into birthing a commission that would protect the cartel system.

It began as a conspiracy against free enterprise, and as the concept caught the imagination of robber barons, it quickly spread to other monopolistic industries at the first threat of competition. When the Bell patents expired around the turn of the century, for example, Theodore Vail of American Telephone and Telegraph was quick to demand regulations to protect his empire. By December 1971 the Federal Communications Commission was forced to admit that it lacked the resources to investigate the Bell Telephone System's investment and operating expenses. This means that whenever AT&T, with $40 billion in assets, demands a rate increase—a semiannual event, at least—the government's decision is made without specific information on how the company spends its money. "Because we're copping out" on financial study "doesn't mean we're copping out on regulation," said Bernard Strasser, chief of the FCC's Common Carrier Bureau, which has 165 employees and a $3-million budget to regulate not only AT&T but a $70 billion-a-year industry, including all independent telephone and telegraph companies, plus international and satellite communications.[80]

In the area of television, the FCC has refused to set minimum license-renewal performance standards for television stations. Early in July 1973, in a farewell blast at the commission, Nicholas Johnson released a 264-page study that proposed a set of standards and rated the nation's big-city TV stations according to quality. "The major hope is simply that the mere publishing of this data will, standing alone, provide reinforcement for the better stations and an incentive to improvement by the worst," Johnson said in the study's introduction. Among a long list of critical observations, Johnson scored the commission for doing nothing about overcommercialization "because its knee-jerk response tends to be to protect the industry's profits rather than the public interest."[81]

The Federal Aviation Administration has catered to the "profit motive of the airlines" instead of protecting the public from aircraft noise. This charge by the Environmental Defense Fund in 1972 was followed by a demand that the FAA be relieved of its mandate to enforce noise control because the agency operates under "a conflict of interest" since it is required by law to promote development of air commerce. Judging from its performance to date, said the EDF, "the protection of the public has been subordinated to the profit motive of the airlines."[82]

"One of the biggest frauds perpetrated on the public" is the claim made by the Federal Housing Administration and communities that their property standards and building codes assure the adequacy of new homes. Writing in the *Ladies' Home Journal*, Ralph Nader said that home buyers often found a "frightening number of hidden hazards" in new homes "because there is virtually no effective system for regulating home safety requirements." The FHA, said Nader, abdicated "its potential leadership" in establishing meaningful building codes because of "the agency's belief that influential builders, not home-owners, need its protection." Restrictive measures in many building codes "are designed to give manufacturers of certain building materials a monopoly within specific geographic markets." A study by the Department of Housing & Urban Development of five major "model" building codes (including FHA's) "discovered 178 home safety hazards for which no standard existed in any of the codes. Of the standards that did deal with identified hazards, 45 were judged adequate to prevent injury while 49 were judged inadequate."[83]

The Environmental Protection Agency has ten employees to monitor the entire annual production of all domestic and foreign automobile manufacturers. According to a *Wall Street Journal* study, the agency is virtually helpless: "As it stands now, the auto makers themselves, at great cost in time and money, are ultimately the chief enforcers of the standards they are supposed to meet, and federal regulators, hopelessly outgunned, can do little more than monitor the industry's self-regulation."[84]

There is no need to run through the full gamut of regulators. Basically understaffed and underbudgeted, regulators are in no position to take their work seriously, even if they wanted to. Their basic information comes from the regulated, and their own regulations are limited by the will of Congress. Yet there are some differences between agencies. The worst is still the ICC, and the best *was* the Securities and Exchange Commission, which now lies in a shambles at Nixon's feet. Nader goosed the Federal Trade Commission out of what seemed terminal apathy, and the sounds emanating these days from its once cloistered chambers have the shrill ring of militancy. Before Nader, the FTC was so hopelessly moribund that even a special committee of the American Bar Association recommended that it be dismantled unless drastic reforms were implemented.

In terms of protecting the public, the regulators present a dismal record. A study of their performance only proves what has been common knowledge for a very long time: federal regulation begins with Congress— it is far less expensive for money power to sway it and the federal bureaucracy than fifty state legislatures. The end result of federal regulation has been the creation of a system that caters almost exclusively to giant industries. It encourages existing monopolies by approving mergers and excluding new entrepreneurs from entering controlled fields, it sets price floors, makes minimal inspections, and ignores illegal practices, hazardous products, unsafe conditions, fraud, corruption—in fact, a plethora of transgressions goes unchallenged, at a cost to the consumer and taxpayer in the tens of billions of dollars a year.

There is no simple solution. Or a complex one, for that matter. Considering the magnitude of the problem, there is no solution possible under the existing structure of government. The new populist vision of Nader-Gardner and their followers has dispelled the optimism of old Schlesinger-type liberals, but their new orthodoxy is equally fraught with perils. Considering the awesome dimension of the problems, their proposed reforms are simplistic to the point of naïveté. Two bright-eyed apostles, Jack Newfield and Jeff Greenfield, authors of *A Populist Manifesto: The Making of a New Majority*, presented the 1972 Democratic candidates with a purified populist manual on how to reform the government—from top to bottom, and vice versa. As for regulatory agencies, it was their opinion that they offered "one area where results can come quickly." New laws or new institutions were not necessary because "they are designed for what may be the most radical notion of all: the idea that agencies that were *created to protect the public interest* [emphasis added] should protect the public interest." Beginning with a false premise, they went on to suggest that the way to "break the industry-agency-industry cycle" was to "appoint men whose concern for fairness is paramount, even at the expense of technical expertise.[85] In a review of their book, Harvard Professor James Q. Wilson bluntly rejected this notion: "I'm sorry, but that sounds like a proposal to reform prostitution by putting virgins into brothels."[86]

Although Nader and Gardner have squeezed countless consumer and environmental protection laws out of Congress, the question remains whether anything lasting will come of their efforts. What Congress proposes today it can depropose tomorrow. And while Congress proposes, the President disposes. Recalcitrant virgins seldom begin as madams. Unfortunately, Nader is likewise hung up on grandiose reform schemes. He has called his proposed "independent" Consumer Protection Agency, which would watchdog all other agencies in the interest of consumers, "the most important consumer legislation ever considered by the Congress." Yet by the summer of 1973, Chet Holifield, chairman of the House Government Operations Committee, had sat on the legislation nearly three years. California Democrat Holifield's views are similar to the Administration's on limiting the power of a consumer protection agency: "I refuse to give a new agency unlimited subpoena power over every agency of government and every corporation, foundation and labor union."[87] Even if such an agency were created, it is unrealistic to think that any President would appoint relentless, independent commissioners with a mandate to expose the shenanigans of his other appointees.

Even more unrealistic, if possible, is Nader's proposed Federal Corporation Agency, which would supervise the activities of the nation's five hundred largest corporations. The agency would have the power of licensing, which means that it could dissolve any corporation that did not shape up and fly right. Imagine telling General Motors to ship out. The idea of a federal licensing agency is not new. John D. Rockefeller and other robber barons proposed it many years ago as a means of escaping from conflicting (and expensive) state regulations.

The above examples are not meant to minimize the tremendous impact of Nader's genuine achievements, truly one of the most remarkable records in our history, but rather to point up the bewildering problem of reform. This game can be played only from the inside. Nader knows better than anybody else that the money power's scale of priorities begins with legislators, not regulators. "We were created to grant exemption from the antitrust laws," says the confidential assistant to the chairwoman of the Federal Maritime Commission. "That was and is our only reason for existence."[88]

The pernicious influence of the money power is not secured simply by a few large campaign contributions at the top. The dairymen, who contributed $422,500 to Nixon for price-support increases, hedged their investment with an additional $1.6 million in contributions to congressional leaders.

The reform game can prove dangerous for sincere reformers by backfiring and producing the contrary result. A specific example concerns the Wholesome Meat Act of 1967, which shifted the responsibility for meat inspection to the states. It relieved meat packers from meeting the federal standards first enacted in 1906, which were inspired by Upton Sinclair's *The Jungle*, a novel that vividly described the filthy conditions existing in Chicago plants. The 1967 act was motivated by an intensive barrage of press reports depicting the filthy conditions that still existed in processing plants. Concerned finally that the reports would result in people eating less meat, the powerful American Meat Institute, with the support of Swift and Armour, backed a compromise bill to quiet the reformers. Congress complied, the press turned its attention to other matters, state-inspected meat began flowing into interstate commerce without federal approval, and the Department of Agriculture went back to taking orders from the industry.

John Gardner is convinced that political corruption can be cured by public financing of election campaigns, which will free politicians from the clutch of money power. The point overlooked is that incumbent politicians hold the key to their own golden servitude. Only they have the power to unlock the system, and to date there has been no indication, beyond rhetoric, that they are ready for emancipation. Even if they were persuaded into severing this financial cord, the money power, as the master of industry, controls millions of votes plus many postelection perquisites. Campaign contributions help the candidate to get to the seat of power, but that is only the first step in the money-power game. Few men can hope to improve their political or financial position without playing the game, which has little if anything to do with redressing "the balance of social power."

As noted earlier in this chapter, forces are at work in Congress to emasculate the Federal Election Campaign Act of 1971. What is happening—at this writing, at least—portends ominous results.

> The only thing more dangerous to democracy than corrupt politicians may be politicians hell-bent on reform. We have had a large dose of corruption in Watergate and now, by God, they mean to make us take our medicine. Waving the banner of reform, they have already pushed through the Senate, with a minimum of debate or public attention, a bill that would basically alter the American political calendar.

Writing in his syndicated column, David S. Broder was referring to two bills described in the "noblest, most altruistic rhetoric as measures to purify politics" but which would make it "virtually impossible ever again to defeat an incumbent for federal office." Besides scrapping the provision banning indirect contributions by government contractors and the requirement that contributors be listed by name, address, and occupation (the new version would require only that the name of the donor be reported), the reform measure would shorten federal election campaigns and reduce campaign expenditures—it would prohibit any congressional or senatorial primary before the first Tuesday in August, and the presidential nominating convention could not begin until the third Monday of that month. Broder goes on to observe:

> Noble and desirable, right? The only problem is that there is precious little reason to think that any challenger, limited to an eight-week campaign, would stand a snowball's chance in hell of defeating an incumbent representative, President or senator who has had two years, four years or six years to gain name recognition and familiarity at public expense and to organize his reelection campaign.[89]

The bill includes an overall spending limit of 20 cents per eligible voter for the general election, with a maximum limit of $90,000 for House races. "What these two bills amount to is the Incumbents' Guaranteed Reelection Act of 1973," says Broder. "Since it is in the incumbent senators' and representatives' power to vote themselves this boon, there is no reason to doubt they will do so. Lord save us from such reformers."[90]

Of all "such reformers" the Lord should save us from, the tax reformer heads the list. Talk about noble, altruistic rhetoric! Beware legislators who start talking tax reform. "Our tax system has become a house of horrors which needs rebuilding from the ground up," Wilbur Mills told

Life readers in 1959, after his first year as chairman of the House Ways and Means Committee.[91] Thirteen years later, the 1972 *Almanac of American Politics* would rate Mills "one of the most powerful men in the United States," with "authority in tax matters—social security, welfare, medical care, tariffs, and import quotas—second only to that of the President. And sometimes it is not second." Mills has flourished but the tax system is still "a mess and a gyp," with various taxpayers coddled as "pets" and others treated as "patsies."[92] In 1959 Mills was quick to criticize the inequities of the tax system:

> Our tax laws—revised each year, with something added here, something subtracted there—are like some fantastic building on which a dozen contractors have been working at once, each from a different blueprint. The laws have long since lost sight of the real purpose of taxation, which is simply to raise the money the government needs to pay its bills. They are full of contradictions and inequities and are totally inadequate to do the job of raising the tremendous revenues our government needs. Bringing order out of the chaos is as important to our national survival as is our defense program—which in the long run can only be as good as our tax revenues permit it to be.[93]

Included in the loopholes Mills then thought "we must investigate" were the oil and mining depletion allowances and "the various fast write-offs of capital investment" which were excluding about $7 billion of corporate income from federal taxes. At times Mills sounded as if he were running for President:

> If we kept the $600 personal exemption but taxed *all* other income, we could reduce the individual income tax rate by about 40 percent and still raise just as much money. Our tax system would be a model of simplicity and ease of enforcement. It would no longer discriminate between Mr. Smith and Mr. Jones. It would no longer put the government in the awkward position of pushing its citizens into one kind of economic activity instead of another. It would let the rules of the free market operate once again. . . . I hope that the Congress will try in every way possible to hold spending to the very least amount that is compatible with good government. But I hope we will not delay a realistic examination of our tax system because of any vague hope that our government expenditures can at any time soon be reduced much below their present $81 billion a year. I believe that a really efficient tax system can raise this $81 billion, which is less than a fifth of our gross national product, without putting the present undue burden on any citizen or upon the growth of our economy. . . . As I see it, a fair and equitable tax system is not only desirable for itself but may well be an element in our national survival. Naturally the

job the Ways and Means Committee is now tackling is a tremendously complex and difficult one, and it will probably force us to step on a few toes. I hope that we can rally a majority of our citizens to support us, because everybody will be better off in the long run—and our nation more secure—if we can improve our tax system.[94]

In the next fifteen years, as government expeditures rose from $81 billion to $304.4 billion a year—a $50 billion increase in the 1975 budget —Wilbur Mills discovered that not everybody wants a "fair and equitable tax system." When his powerful—the press's favorite adjective—Ways and Means Committee was considering the Tax Reform Act of 1969, Jack Anderson reported that Mills "cautioned oilmen privately to acquiesce to the public mood and accept a symbolic cut in the 27½ percent depletion rate. He suggested a reduction to, say, 23½ or 22½ percent. The 27½ percent figure has taken an almost religious significance to oilmen, and hitherto Mills had treated it as Holy Writ. Oilmen had felt they could count on Mills' allegiance. In the past, he had always comported himself as if he had been baptized in oil."[95]

As noted in Chapter Three, the Petroleum Institute waged an intensive lobbying campaign on Capitol Hill, with particular emphasis on the twenty-five members of Ways and Means. The plan, Anderson reported, was to "work through fourteen big Committee members who have always been faithful friends of oil." In addition to Mills, they included:

Hale Boggs of Louisiana, John Watts of Kentucky, Phil Landrum of Georgia, Richard Fulton of Tennessee, and Omar Burleson of Texas, all Democrats; with John Byrnes of Wisconsin, James Utt of California, Jackson Betts of Ohio, Herman Schneebeli of Pennsylvania, Harold Collier of Illinois, Joel Broyhill of Virginia, George Bush of Texas and Rogers Morton of Maryland, the GOP National Chairman, all Republicans.

On November 20, 1969, Anderson reported that Mills "was gifted with a $6,000 luxury cross-country trip by jet from the biggest gas transmission company. This was shortly after his committee gave gas transmission firms a whopping loophole in the tax reform bill." Mills "was also provided with a limousine by the company, Tenneco Inc., while he was in the Los Angeles area." The "pipeline sweetener" in the tax-reform bill allowed gas-transmission firms to "reap investment tax credits long after other industries begin paying through the nose. . . . Six thousand dollars in company airplane tolls for any ordinary Congressman and a lobbyist to ride across the country and back is a good deal of money. . . . But a prize fish like the hard-working and powerful chairman of the Ways and Means

Committee is easily worth every penny of luxury and comfort he can be persuaded to accept from a corporate giant. This is an old axiom of the Washington game, even though the House bars any 'substantial' gift to a Congressman handling bills affecting the donor."[96]

There is no question that lobbyists prefer doing business through the tax laws. The importuning is limited to the two revenue committees, Mills's Ways and Means and Russell Long's Senate Finance. Once a loophole becomes law, the only thing the beneficiary has to do to cash in is file a tax return—its secrecy is protected by law—and the subsidy runs uninterrupted into perpetuity.

The revenue committees possess about all the influence there is in the federal government to redistribute wealth and income in America. Promises of tax reform by presidential candidates are meaningless without the consensus of these two chairmen, who exercise a degree of control over the members of their committees and the legislative process that other chairmen only dream about. Both committees operate under a cloak of secrecy and anonymity. The composition of the committees is rigidly controlled by the leaders of both parties in the House and Senate, and the memberships have traditionally been confined to conservatives in taxation, without regard to party affiliation. Since all tax-reform proposals must first receive the blessing of these committees, special-interest groups have had little reason to be concerned.

All tax legislation originates in Ways and Means, which gets most of its publicity from public hearings devoted almost exclusively to the biased proposals of lobbyists and their paid economists and academicians. When it comes time for the members to vote, "the key tallies of both these committees," says former congressional aide V. O. French, "are usually wired up in advance by Mills, Long, other committee members, the lobbyists, and the Treasury—official approval of any bill is a foregone conclusion registered by grunts, winks, and nods. . . . Nobody is present, of course, except the committee itself. Neither Long nor Mills permits even personal staff members to attend meetings." No one except Ways and Means Committee members is allowed to read the records of executive sessions, and the Finance Committee offers the ultimate in document security—no records at all.[97]

Ways and Means reports its complex legislative recommendations—sometimes several hundred pages long—to the full House under a "closed rule" restriction that bars floor amendments. In effect, the committee's handiwork is presented to the other 410 House members on a take-it-or-leave-it basis.* Being a compulsively cautious man, Mills's *modus operandi* has been not to report a bill unless he has the required votes. As chairman of the Democratic Committee on Committees, Mills has been in a position to accumulate IOU's from friends and foes alike. He lost two bills in his first year as chairman but since then has lost only one other bill. "Mills is so cooperative and helpful with fellow congressmen," one writer observed, "that they impose their own limits on what they ask of him." Inordinately vain and pompous, Mills is a thin-skinned egotist who has fortified himself by digesting whole reservoirs of inert materials that would drive most legislators up the wall. Much of his power derives from the simple fact that he knows more about the complex terrain of federal tax law than anybody else in Washington, and at times, like a revival preacher, he is wont to recite chapter and verse on entire sections of the tax code without faltering. Conceding his awesome expertise, the majority of the committee has cheerfully abdicated its responsibility to Mills. But when Mills, the compleat politician, is pressed in interviews for his position on pending legislation, he shifts the responsibility back to the committee: "Of course, it's not me, you understand—it's the committee, and I just don't know what the committee's going to do on that yet." At other times it is the blame that gets shifted: "I am just chairman of the committee. I am bound by what the committee decides."[98]

After the House has passed the legislation, the bill is sent to the Senate, where it goes directly to the Finance Committee, popularly known as "the citadel of conservatism" and the "happy hunting ground" for tax pressure groups. Since Senators can tack on riders and amendments to revenue bills reported by the Finance Committee, Senator Long likes to wait until the end of the session to take up such bills, catching liberals when they are fatigued and eager for adjournment.

If the Senate proposes amendments to the House bill, the differences are ironed out by a House-Senate conference committee, whose membership, selected by Mills and Long, consists of the conservative senior members of both tax committees. Although Long is wont to associate himself with his father's populist views, the fact remains that progressive Senate floor amendments inevitably vanish in conference while special-interest bonanzas just as inevitably survive. When a conference report returns to the Senate floor, the "closed rule" applies—Senators vote it up or down, but no amendments are entertained. The last resort available to a dissent-

---

* This procedure was modified in 1972 to enable Democrats to force votes in the full House on amendments if such amendments receive broad support within the party.

ing lawmaker is the filibuster—a "bludgeon," says French, "where a scalpel is required."[99]

Finally, after months of being buried in what is known as the salt mines of Congress, the members of Ways and Means get a chance to feather their own nests. The twenty-five members seclude themselves behind closed doors and each is allowed to write special tax amendments—usually expensive tax loopholes for the rich and special-interest groups—disguised in innocuous language, which all other members naturally approve and bring to the floor of the House on the "consent calendar." Unless a lawmaker specifically objects, the bills are automatically passed. Known as "members' bills," they have traditionally sailed through Congress with no hearings, no floor debate, and no detailed information concerning their beneficiaries or their impact on the Treasury.

Since most legislators take turns in sponsoring members' bills originated by committee members, hardly anyone ever objects to the pork-barreling. It took the irascible Wright Patman to throw a monkey wrench into Mills's sacred domain. The battle that ensued took on the dimension, as one Congressman phrased it, of a fight within a feudal family.

It began on February 29, 1972, when Mills tried to zip twenty-two members' bills through the House without a recorded vote. Patman objected, blocking the "unanimous consent" needed for suspension of the rules. This meant that Mills would have to marshal a two-thirds vote for passage. In his objection, Patman stated:

> These bills contain broad questions of public policy as well as parliamentary procedure of a representative government. . . . We must not have bills like this, with no hearings, no adequate reports, no compliance with rules. . . . Members of Congress do not know how far-reaching they are and what they will do. It is costing us billions and billions of dollars. . . . Now is the time we must stop this procedure.[100]

Wisconsin Representative Les Aspin joined with Patman in blocking the bills. "Some of them were clearly just incredible boondoggles for people in particular situations," Aspin said. "No wonder our tax laws are just like Swiss cheese with these coming in here like this. The whole process stinks anyway."[101]

Of the twenty-two tax bills, only one would have provided additional revenue. Bills that were blocked involved tax breaks amounting to $70 million for banks, $120 million for the cigar industry, $25 million for four large timber companies, $3 million for the olive industry, $500,000 for private foundations, and $250,000 for owners of offshore oil-drilling and oceanographic vessels, shrimp boats, and barges, which was retroactive to 1967.

Shrewdly assessing the mood of Congress, Mills brought up the least objectionable bills first to avoid total defeat. One of the bills that was passed prohibited the government from disclosing information about persons who paid a federal gambling tax, creating another legislative impediment in the enforcement of antigambling laws against organized crime. Retreating from the confrontation, Mills quietly promised: "If we do not pass them this way, we will have to get another way to pass them." The bills came up again on April 17, but this time Mills, conveniently out of town, was not there to lead the floor fight. When it appeared that the bills simply did not have the necessary two-thirds vote, they were withdrawn from the day's calendar.

In October 1972, still frustrated by Patman and a coalition of tax-reform organizations, a Ways and Means staff attorney said that some end runs would have to be attempted, and suggested that the members' bills might be appended to House-passed bills then under consideration by the Senate Finance Committee.

"They'll have a helluva time getting around us, I'll tell you that," said Patman, who claimed he had been unaware of members' bills for forty-four years in Congress because they usually came up only once a year at an off hour—actually on Christmas Eve one year.[102]

There is no telling how many thousands of these private tax bills were enacted in the past. Even the 1969 Tax Reform Act, as Senator Edward Kennedy pointed out, was loaded down with special dispensations involving millions in tax breaks to Mobil Oil, Uniroyal, Lockheed, Litton, Transamerica, McDonnell-Douglas, half a dozen private foundations, and nineteen oil-pipeline companies.[103]

"What's the good of being on this committee if you can't get through a little old amendment now and then?" one lawmaker is reputed to have remarked.

Through the years some of these little old amendments have saved a privileged few a great deal of money. The United States Chamber of Commerce, one of money power's most prestigious lobbies, was responsible for the notorious Mayer Amendment, which saved the movie mogul Louis B. Mayer and another executive of Loew's Incorporated about $2 million in income taxes; superlawyer Clark Clifford was instrumental in persuading lawmakers and the IRS to grant the dispensation that saved duPont stockholders some $2 billion in capital-gains taxes. Other mem-

bers' bills awarded American Motors Corporation $20 million in tax re-
bates; Harvey Aluminum Company got a $2-million windfall; Mrs. Gerard
Swope saved some $4 million in estate taxes. The tax laws are riddled with
these special provisions hidden in massive tax legislation. For example, the
Uniroyal provision consists of thirty-seven words squeezed into the middle
of a vaguely worded paragraph on page 420 of the 585-page Tax Reform
Act of 1969. It saved the company $3 million in taxes, or $81,000 per
word. Four words saved McDonnell-Douglas $6.5 million, or $1,625,000
per word. The fact that these beneficiaries have been identified is no reflection on the skill of the writers. The beneficiaries of thousands of members'
bills still remain invisible, lost forever in the matrix of the tax code.

Besides the tax committees, the Treasury itself may favor a single
taxpayer with a special dispensation. When Eisenhower sold his memoirs
for a lump-sum payment of $635,000, the Treasury generously ruled that
he was entitled to capital-gains treatment, a privilege not available to any
other writer, composer, or artist in similar circumstances.

"Sen. Russell Long, D-La., whose Finance Committee oversees the
Treasury Department, has bullyragged Treasury into giving his cronies in
the cement industry a multi-million dollar tax loophole," Jack Anderson
reported in his syndicated column. Long was opposed to a Treasury ruling
to tax certain transportation costs: "I frown on the tax proposal," Long
wrote to Secretary of the Treasury Henry H. Fowler on December 5,
1967. He urged Fowler "as strongly as I know how to remedy your proposed regulations." But Fowler resisted and Long had to wait until the
Republicans took over the Treasury. Even before Nixon was inaugurated,
Anderson reports, Long had a letter in the mail: "The cement industry
[and] the sulphur industry have been in touch with me," he began, once
again repeating his demand for the loophole. On the day after Long confirmed Randolph Thrower as head of the IRS, the Treasury quietly printed
a proposed regulation to grant him his loophole.[104]

The Nixon Administration has been good to Russell Long. In June
1970, a federal grand jury in Baltimore returned a sealed draft indictment
in which Baltimore contractor Victor Frenkil and his firm, Baltimore Contractors, Inc., were charged with conspiring with Bernard Shephard, a vice
president of the company, and other persons to defraud the government of
"its right to have the disinterested services of its officials and employes
unimpaired by the exertion of improper pressure and influence."[105]

Frenkil, through congressional contacts, had allegedly sought to convince the Architect of the Capitol and his staff that their employment was

in jeopardy unless he was awarded an extra $5 million, over his $11.7 million contract, for building two underground parking garages in the Rayburn Office Building. As part of the conspiracy, the jury said, the defendants offered money to Long, Hale Boggs, and former Maryland Senator Daniel B. Brewster, as an inducement "for them to bring the prestige, weight and influence of their respective offices to bear upon officials and employes of the architect" to promote the defendants' interest.

The indictment was first recommended by U.S. Attorney Stephen Sachs, a Democrat, and the jury voted for it after ten months of investigation. Attorney General John Mitchell stepped in and asked for additional study. Sachs resigned and his replacement, George Beall, a Republican, after reviewing the case, concurred with the jury, which again voted to indict Long, Boggs, Brewster, et al. At this point, Mitchell flatly refused to authorize the U.S. Attorney to sign the indictment, which automatically killed it.

"This matter was reviewed by the professional staff and criminal division, which raised some question about the nature of the case," Mitchell asserted. "In view of the questions, the staff asked that it be allowed to review the case again . . ."[106]

Mitchell released a memorandum from six Justice attorneys, including Will Wilson, then head of the Criminal Division,* and Henry Petersen, which recommended that the indictment not be returned on grounds of insufficient evidence. The attorneys believed that while the conduct of Frenkil and his associates "may be considered by some to have been heavy handed, taken as a whole and viewed in the context of the substantive controversy between architect of the Capitol and Baltimore Contractors, Inc., neither Frenkil's conduct nor that of his other associates can be proven to be a violation of any criminal statute."

This must have come as a surprise to the grand jury, which, among a long list of stipulated violations, had charged that Frenkil offered Long and Brewster one-third of whatever he recovered in exchange for their assistance. As for Boggs, Frenkil remodeled his house at a price "substantially below cost."

"Moreover, the evidence developed by the grand jury is insufficient to show any instance of corruption on the part of any federal officers or employes of any branch of the government," the attorneys maintained. The actions Long had authorized his administrative aide, Robert

---

* A year later, Wilson was forced to resign when he became implicated in the Sharpstown Bank scandal, one of the biggest stock frauds in Texas history.

E. Hunter, to take in behalf of Frenkil's claim were not illegal, and Boggs's "few contacts with the architect . . . cannot be shown to have been undertaken for any improper motives."

The grand jury was of a different mind. The jurors prepared a present-ment that named Frenkil and half a dozen present and former members of Congress, including Long and Boggs, and cited forty-five overt acts in furtherance of the conspiracy. Then it asked the judge that it be made public. Their move precipitated a panic. Lawyers for the accused peti-tioned the court to suppress the report, and the judge complied by releas-ing a watered-down summary of his own. Then he expunged the presentment from the court records.[107]

The upshot was that everybody concerned got a pass except Brewster, the has-been Democrat, who was indicted by another grand jury on differ-ent charges. On February 2, 1973, he was convicted of accepting an "illegal gratuity" for favorable votes on postal legislation, and received a maximum sentence of two to six years in prison and a $30,000 fine.[108]

George Beall promised to continue his investigation. "I would like very much to hit pay dirt on this thing," he said. Three years later Beall would have somewhat better luck with Vice President Spiro T. Agnew, although not all that much better. He still had to compromise a case with approxi-mately fifty counts of bribery, extortion, and tax evasion, settling for a "no contest" plea on a single charge of income-tax evasion. Agnew resigned, paid a $10,000 federal fine, and was placed on unsupervised probation for three years. Many Agnew supporters were convinced that he was the vic-tim of a monstrous conspiracy and that one day, when all the evidence was in, it would be proved that he was framed by his political enemies. Others, while appalled by his plea bargaining, were quick to praise the system that brought about his downfall.

What is truly appalling about the Agnew case is that it took a Water-gate climate to make it stick. There was nothing new in the charges against Agnew, nothing that was not public knowledge during the 1968 presiden-tial campaign. In fact, on October 28, 1968, the New York *Times* charged in an editorial that Agnew had engaged in banking and real-estate dealings that conflicted with his official duties as governor of Maryland, and through these practices his financial worth had "risen sharply." The edi-torial went on to detail five areas of improper activities, precisely the same allegations that five years later Beall would present to a federal grand jury.

Nixon was quick to attack. He called the *Times* editorial "the lowest

kind of gutter politics that a great newspaper could possibly engage in."
Agnew demanded a retraction, calling the charges inaccurate and distorted, and threatened to file a libel lawsuit. The *Times*'s response was to
reprint the editorial and then follow it up with a new one. "The *Times*
unequivocally rejects the charge of libel," it said, adding that Agnew's
denial of conflict-of-interest charges "underscores his inability to perceive
the ethical judgments demanded of persons in high positions of public
trust."

> Mr. Riddell is a brash Washington lobbyist. And Mr. Mills, of course,
> is the chairman of the House Ways and Means Committee. Mr. Riddell,
> aided by Mr. Mills, got the IRS in early 1971 to stop massive tax investi-
> gations of several big shoe companies. The IRS retreat saved the com-
> panies and others on the verge of similar audits many millions of dollars
> in taxes (over $100 million by one informed estimate) that a number of
> senior IRS people had determined they owed.
>   Subsequently, Mr. Riddell lent $17,000 and gave another $2,702 to Mr.
> Mills' abortive campaign for last year's Democratic presidential nomina-
> tion. These aren't particularly large sums by Watergate standards. But,
> according to General Accounting Office records, Mr. Riddell's loan and
> gift add up to far and away the largest contribution Mr. Mills received
> from an individual.*—*Wall Street Journal*, 14 June 1973

Even before Wilbur Mills had declared his availability in the presidential race, several influential tax and trade lobbyists—including a registered
foreign agent for the Japanese government—were trudging through the
snows of New Hampshire in support of his write-in campaign. The lobbyists included James W. ("Dick") Riddell, a former tax counsel with Ways
and Means, who in the past ten years had registered as a tax lobbyist for a
score of major firms and trade associations in the banking, insurance, air-
transport, and footwear fields; J. D. Williams, a registered lobbyist for
groups in the utilities, health care, and security fields; Carl F. Arnold, a
former lobbyist for the American Petroleum Institute, who then represented the Gas Supply Committee; and Michael Daniels, a registered foreign agent of the embassy of Japan, who was a Washington representative
for several Japanese and European textile and industrial exporters.[109]
    The Draft Mills for President Committee went to work in 1971. The
pitch was that "America needs Wilbur Mills in the White House." Full-
page newspaper ads proclaimed that "America needs a President who is

---

* It should be stated that all parties concerned—Mills, Riddell, and the IRS—
emphatically denied any wrongdoing. "If you're implying someone tried to buy me,"
Mills told the *Journal*, "you would be completely mistaken."

inclined toward quiet action, not grandstand plays." Mills was pictured as a tower of "strength, wisdom, intellect and common sense." As chairman of Ways and Means, he "has authored and provided the leadership necessary for enactment of more meaningful legislation for the economic well-being of the individual citizen than any man in Congress. His action has demonstrated the rare understanding of national economics that is necessary to cure our economic ills."[110]

With all the other Democratic presidential aspirants hitting hard at the inequities in the tax code—Mills's baby—the chairman was forced to retaliate in kind, or at least to appear to retaliate. The trick was to do it without antagonizing either "reform" or "anti-reform" groups. Without even consulting high-ranking Democrats on his committee, Mills introduced H.R. 15230, entitled "Tax Policy Review Act of 1972," which at first glance appeared to eliminate fifty-two mighty loopholes, ranging from oil depletion to capital gains and charitable contributions. On closer examination, however, it turned out that the legislation would force Congress merely to review the preferences, one-third at a time, over a period of three years.*[111]

In a press release explaining the measure, Mills called the voters' attention to the 1969 act, which "was clearly the most comprehensive tax reform measure in our history." That is not the opinion of most tax reformers. Instead of reforming the tax code, the act added enough complexities to give the tax courts ten years of work in interpreting the revisions. In fact, the Revenue Act of 1969 is known on Capitol Hill as "the Lawyers' and Accountants' Relief Act of 1969."

In his press release, Mills said he was glad to see "the continuing interest in tax reform which has been expressed so widely in the public press and also by a number of my colleagues through the introduction of their notions of what constitute desirable tax reforms. . . . Only by holding extensive hearings on the various aspects of the tax laws, including the economic effects of any change, will it be possible for us to do the type of job a task of this dimension deserves."[112]

Hearings are for legislators what commissions are for Presidents—lots of sound and fury signifying nothing. Hundreds of so-called experts have testified before Mills's committee in the last fifteen years to help him, in his words, "develop specific legislative proposals for extensive revision of the income tax." Since nothing specific has developed, it must be concluded

* See Note 111, page 423, for a complete listing of the loopholes as described in the bill's table of contents.

that the hearings served either as pablum for the press or as a catalyst to motivate lobbyists to desirable reactions.

In New Hampshire, the Draft Mills for President Committee spent $84,700 for radio and television advertising, plus an undisclosed amount for an extensive direct-mail and telephone effort.[113] Following the convention in July, the defunct committee still managed to raise $75,000 to pay off campaign debts. The list of contributors, as reported in the Washington *Star-News*, reads "like a Who's Who of big business," including Henry Ford II, the president of Bank of America, the chairman of 3M, the executive vice president of Standard Oil of New Jersey, and the head tax accountant at General Electric.[114] The milk co-ops gave him $54,000, which was more than any other Democrat received; Humphrey got $13,000; Wallace, $2,000; Muskie, $750; McGovern, zilch.

H.R. 15230 died a natural death. Although tax reform continues to a popular pitch among politicians, it is not now and never has been a prime issue in national politics. People who have the impression that the Democrats are out to soak the rich should remember that the liberalization of corporate taxes in 1962 and in 1971 was enacted by Congresses controlled by Democrats. The National Committee for an Effective Congress made this observation in its *Congressional Report*:

> When the Democrats put Richard Nixon on the spot on tax reform, they put themselves on the spot. One reason the issue of unjust taxation has languished so long is because complicity in the treasury raid is bipartisan. Recalling the 1969 attempt at tax reform which turned into a "Christmas tree," one Democrat says in disgust: "After all the palaver about 'New Priorities for the Seventies,' we gave away over a hundred billion dollars in tax cuts, mainly for the wealthy."
>
> In contrast with Republican "benign neglect" on social issues, Democrats—like Tammany politicos—have always provided "food baskets" for the poor. These tax turkeys have been accompanied by an ever growing number of welfare assistance programs financed by federal borrowing. Now many of these programs have lost their economic impact and their political lustre. Many Democrats still harken back to the old nostrums and incantations, however, forgetting that the original New Deal was not an expression of *noblesse oblige*—a philanthropic gesture to the poor—but an assertive movement rooted in the legitimate self-interest of a desperate middle class.[115]

Even for progressive Democrats, tax reform has always been mired down in ambivalence and hypocrisy. The graduated income tax enacted in 1913 was at least an attempt to create a valid instrument for promoting social equity. Ever since then politicians of both parties have lost few opportunities to punch loopholes into it, until the law is a sieve, and the gap between rich and poor has nearly doubled in the last generation alone.

No one in recent memory better epitomizes the money power's antipathy for tax reform than John Connally. In his vocabulary, "loophole" is nothing more than a dirty word invented by wild-eyed radicals. During his whirlwind *coup de théâtre* for Nixon, Connally had many opportunities to articulate the money power's old trickle-down theory of prosperity. He let it all hang out in one session with members of the Business Council:*

> I sit before Congressional Committees and without fear, embarrassment or shame say that I think profits are too low in this country. I think the Congress has gone too far in reducing individual income taxes, $36.4 billion over the last five years, while raising corporate taxes $3.2 billion. I think it is basically unfair and unwise to overdo what you promise and give to the individual when it reduces our ability to build a plant and equipment to provide jobs. . . . We want to create many jobs and be competitive with other nations who I assure you are working six days a week, ten hours a day and at wages about one-fourth of our own. This nation must reappraise its policies with respect to nations around the world who first entice and then expropriate American business interests without adequate compensation.†116

Connally's blatant manipulation of facts and figures is part and parcel of the "old crappo" technique that has made him the Administration's most persuasive con man. Evidence to refute him is overwhelming. Loopholes for corporations and the rich have so eroded the so-called progressive tax system that it is now almost totally regressive. In just two decades, the percentage of taxes collected from corporations in terms of the total revenue pie was sliced nearly in half—from 30 percent in 1954 to 16 percent in 1972, and this during a period when corporate income achieved enormous growth. Contrary to Connally's figures, the cuts in federal income taxes since 1964 have reduced the 20 to 91 percent range to the current 14 to 50 percent. Basic arithmetic will show that a reduction of 41 percent on $1-million income will save the rich taxpayer $410,000, and a reduction of 6 percent on $5,000 will save $300. Add to this tragic story the fact that state and city income taxes, sales taxes, property taxes,‡

---

* A group of a hundred corporate chieftains who meet periodically to confer with government leaders—the money power keeps close tab on its servants.

† This is an intriguing interpretation of imperialism.

‡ Corruption and favoritism in property-tax assessments have resulted in generous exemptions for business. In most large cities, fully 50 percent of all taxable property is exempt because of special concessions to churches, colleges, foundations, airlines,

Social Security taxes, excise taxes, unemployment taxes, and "sin" taxes on liquor and tobacco actually doubled between 1960 and 1970—from $711 to $1,348 for each American man, woman, and child. As recently as 1968, corporate taxes and Social Security taxes were producing about equal income for the federal budget. By 1973 Social Security was producing almost twice as much revenue as corporate taxes. The most regressive of all federal taxes, Social Security rates have tripled in a decade. The drift in recent years has been inexorably toward what is in effect a flat rate of taxation. In this way the poor get a greater opportunity to subsidize the rich. The overall effective tax rate on a poor family ($2,000 a year) and a rich family ($50,000 a year) is currently just about the same—around a third—when the burden of sales and similar taxes is considered. Because of all the loopholes, income distribution after taxes is almost unchanged—the spread between average rates for the poor and those for the rich is only 8 percent.[117]

In their report to the Joint Economic Committee, the Brookings Institution economists Joseph Pechman and Benjamin Okner identified $77 billion of special provisions (loopholes) in the individual income-tax law and pinpointed the beneficiaries by income class. In summarizing their findings, the committee reported that 18 percent of the poorest families, with annual income below $5,000, received only 1.4 percent of the loophole benefits. At the other end of the totem pole, the top 1 percent of the richest families, with annual income over $50,000, enjoyed 24.3 percent of the special provisions. In fact, 47 percent of all loophole benefits go to the top 8 percent of families with incomes over $25,000. The committee went on to note:

> Despite the distorted distribution of tax benefits, the erosion in the income tax system might be acceptable if the special provisions efficiently achieved the specific social or economic goal toward which they are aimed. A somewhat distorted distribution of benefits might be the price that must be paid for an oil depletion allowance to stimulate oil exploration or for an excess depreciation provision to stimulate the production of rental housing. In fact, there is no body of significant evidence showing that these special tax provisions achieve their objectives efficiently.[118]

In testimony before the Subcommittee on Priorities and Economy in

---

real-estate speculators, and business factories and buildings. The inequities of the property tax in financing local communities has shifted the burden most heavily on those least able to pay. No wonder local governments are in a state of perpetual bankruptcy, unable to provide adequate education, welfare, health care, garbage collection, waste and pollution control, and police and fire protection.

Government, former Treasury expert Stanley Surrey offered this evaluation of tax benefits:

> I think you can also say that less critical analysis is paid to these tax subsidies than almost any direct program that the Congress considers and these tax subsidies simply tumble into the law without any supporting studies; they are propelled by clichés, debating points and scraps of data that are passed off as serious evidence. A tax system that is so vulnerable to this injection of extraneous, costly and ill-considered expenditure programs is simply in a very precarious state from the standpoint of the basic goals of tax fairness.[119]

Every year the press releases statistics on the number of millionaires who manage to escape paying taxes, and every year the Treasury points out that substantially all wealthy people pay huge amounts of income tax despite reports to the contrary. When it was reported in 1972 that 112 Americans with income of more than $200,000 had paid no taxes in 1970, Under Secretary of the Treasury Edwin S. Cohen urged the Joint Economic Committee not to be distracted by the few high-income individuals who manage to escape taxes and bring a shower of "political rhetoric" in an election year. Cohen defended the federal income-tax system as "the most efficient revenue device in the history of the world." In explanation of the 112 individuals who paid no taxes, Cohen said: "We should be slow to condemn a federal income tax system that produces by voluntary assessment these huge amounts of tax on high-adjusted-gross income groups merely because a fraction of 1 percent of the cases report no tax due."[120]

In a confidential memorandum, written in June 1971 and sent to Connally and to White House aide Peter Flanigan, Cohen had recommended revolutionary changes in the tax code because "the governing statute is itself so complex that no revision of the form without a simplification of the statute will satisfy the complaints." The quickest way to simplify the law, Cohen had suggested, would be to end the distinction between capital gains and ordinary income, and to eliminate all personal deductions not related to the earning of taxable income. By closing these two mammoth loopholes, it was Cohen's opinion that tax rates could be reduced to a range of 12 percent to 35 percent*—that is, he would give the poor 2 percent and the rich 15 percent. Even so, the White House held the memo in complete secrecy for almost a year. By then Cohen had been converted

---

* Pechman has found that the effective rate of federal income tax paid in 1967 by the top 1 percent of taxpayers was only 26 percent, even though the actual rate called for 70 percent.

and the Administration, instead of asking for reform, was actually campaigning for a regressive national sales tax, or "value added tax."[121]

In April 1973, Senator Walter F. Mondale of Minnesota gave some indication of the monumental swindle built into "the most efficient device in the history of the world." Mondale said that almost 24,000 Americans enjoyed an average of $166,000 each in virtually tax-free income in 1971 by using such tax-shielding loophole provisions as rapid depreciation, stock options, real-estate shelters, bank bad-debt reserves, the oil-depletion allowance, and capital gains. "These taxpayers paid an average tax of only 4 percent on their loophole income," Mondale said. "That's a smaller rate than a wage-earner making $6,000 a year pays." He said another 75,226 individuals with an average of $30,013 each in income derived from tax loopholes supposedly covered by the new minimum tax requirement paid no minimum tax at all.[122]

Edwin Cohen has since left the Treasury, and so has IRS Commissioner Johnie M. Walters. In the spring of 1972, Walters began to get on the Administration's nerves with charges of tax fraud in executive suites. In a series of speeches, Walters said he would begin "in-depth" tax audits of large corporations to uncover tax avoidance and evasion schemes. "We intend to recommend prosecution—where warranted—of officers or employes responsible for corporate evasion," Walters told the South Carolina Textile Manufacturers Association. "For example, we might suspect that a certain company is making political campaign contributions disguised as business expenses—or that an officer is suspected of receiving kickbacks from suppliers . . . and illegal payoffs." It was "astounding" to Walters that large companies engaged in such schemes, which normal audits seldom discovered. Some companies, he said, "use delaying tactics and take a year to provide readily available records."[123] Walters's successor, Donald C. Alexander, promptly informed the White House that he did not intend to pursue his predecessor's folly. In fact, it was the new commissioner's opinion that corporate executives complied with their tax obligations "very well" and "those that don't are in the very, very small minority."[124]

The eternal struggle between the rich and the poor thrives under all forms of government. As the rich get richer and the poor poorer, the compulsion to accumulate wealth, according to the historian Arnold Toynbee, leads "to a ruthless use of power, whether individual or collective, to victimize the weaker members of society and to push them to the wall."[125]

Vilfredo Pareto, a nineteenth-century economist, expressed it in an equation: if A equals a given income, and B equals the number of people in a country with incomes greater than A; and if the logarithms of A and B are plotted on the Cartesian y axis and x axis, respectively, the resulting curve will be inclined by approximately 56 degrees. In other words, the rich get richer and the poor stay poor.[126]

A study by Peter Henle, a Library of Congress labor specialist, shows that the share of wage and salary income going to people who are already well paid is gradually increasing, while the share paid to low-ranking workers is falling. Using Census Bureau figures, he estimates that the share of all job income that went to the top fifth of male wage earners between 1958 and 1970 rose from 38 percent to 40.5 percent. At the same time, the bottom fifth's share dropped from 5 percent to 4.5 percent. Another study, published in 1971 by two Census Bureau economists, Roger A. Herriot and Herman P. Miller, found that the lowest fifth of Americans received 3 percent of the income distributed in 1968, compared with 48 percent for the top fifth.* This ratio of 16 to 1 is more than double the 7-to-1 ratio that existed in the 1920s.[127]

The distribution of wealth has consistently been more inequitable than the distribution of income. In 1810 the top 1 percent of families owned 21 percent of America's wealth. Today's rich, the top 1 percent, own roughly 25 percent or more of all personal property and financial assets—about $1 trillion, or more than eight times the wealth owned by the bottom 50 percent. According to the writer Peter Barnes, "even these figures

> do not show us the whole picture, for the rich and the poor own different kinds of wealth. The great GNP machine has been moderately successful in distributing what might be called inert wealth—homes, automobiles, personal property—which, far from producing income, are a drain on the sturdiest pocketbook. (Even here its success has not been phenomenal: 17 percent of families own no appreciable wealth at all, and another eight percent have a negative net worth—their debts exceed their assets.) Where the GNP machine has failed is in the distribution of income-producing wealth—stocks, bonds, real estate, etc. According to a study published earlier this year [1972] by the Sabre Foundation, the top one percent of wealth-holders in 1962 owned 72 percent of American's corporate stock, 47 percent of outstanding bonds (including virtually all tax-exempt state and local bonds), 24 percent of notes and mortgages, and 16 percent of all

* Herriot and Miller included in their definition of income such intangibles as realized capital gains, retained corporate earnings, imputed rental value of owner-occupied homes, and underreported money income.

real estate (including residences, which is why this figure is relatively low).[128]

It is here that we see why the gap continues to widen. The advantages of wealth over labor as a source of income are monumental. Wealth is not subject to old age, illness, and other human frailties, Barnes points out: "It can reproduce itself in five or 10 years (most corporate capital returns 20 percent on equity before taxes) and even gets a subsidy, in the form of depreciation allowances, for doing so. It can reap profit from the efforts of others, whereas labor can only earn for itself. Through capitalization of anticipated gains, it can get paid for today and tomorrow, while labor gets paid only for today. It is inherently organized, whereas labor must struggle, often unsuccessfully, for the equivalent organizational strength. It has the upper hand in the marketplace, and, more often than not, first claim on government favors. And it has the one kind of power that really counts in America: the power to pass on to others (i.e., workers) the costs that others are trying to shift to you."*[129]

Yet the myths survive: education is an income leveler, hard work will be rewarded and can even make you rich, the poor are poor because they are lazy, widespread stock ownership has created a true "people's capitalism," regulatory agencies protect the public, antitrust laws are a barrier to excessive concentration of wealth, tax breaks to industry create more jobs, and high corporate profits mean prosperity for everybody.

In *The Affluent Society*, John Kenneth Galbraith reinforced one of the most pernicious myths:

> It has become evident to conservatives and liberals alike that increasing aggregate output is an alternative to redistribution or even to the reduction of inequality. The oldest and most agitated of social issues, if not resolved, is at least largely in abeyance, and the disputants have concentrated their attention, instead, on the goal of increased productivity.

This fixation on growth is the curse of modern society. Some economists argue that the health of the economy depends on actually widening the gap. "I don't think you can narrow the income gap without reducing the nation's real income growth," said Alan Greenspan, a member of *Time*'s Board of Economists. "You would get less effort out of a whole group of people who are striving to get rich. Our whole incentive structure depends on having income increments."[130] Shades of Andrew Mellon!

Beginning with Adam Smith, growth has been the *sine qua non* of the

---

* As noted in Chapter One, it is simple enough for oligopolistic industries to pass on, through higher prices, the costs incurred by higher wages and corporate taxes.

good life. "It is not the actual greatness of national wealth," Smith argued in 1776, "but its continual increase, which occasions a rise in the wages of labor." Economists have since preached that only continued growth could lift mankind out of poverty.

But philosophers and historians have come to look upon growth more as a menace than a blessing. For Arnold Toynbee,

> Our present paroxysm of ruthless strife has been the penalty for discarding traditional human restraints on the greed that is innate in human beings as well as in all other living creatures. In the mechanized minority of mankind, the large increase in material productivity that mechanization has brought with it has now been overtaken and surpassed by a still greater increase in appetite. We are attempting to consume more than we produce, and, since that is impossible, the result is inflation. So long as excessive demands continue, inflation is bound to continue, and inflation is a grievous social and moral evil. The price of inflation is chronic strife and escalating injustice. In each successive round of the strife, the strong misuse their strength to rob the weak. This progressive brigandage is morally odious.[131]

A recent study, *The Limits to Growth*, sponsored by the Club of Rome, an organization of distinguished industrialists, bankers, and scientists from twenty-five countries, warned that unchecked growth can have only one outcome: "A rather sudden and uncontrollable decline in both population and industrial capacity." Described by *Time* as the first vision of the apocalypse ever prepared by a computer, the study asserts that if the world's population continues to grow at about 2 percent annually and global industrial output expands about 7 percent a year (as they do now), then sometime during the life span of children born today, the world will begin running out of natural resources such as coal, oil, and metals. Because industries will no longer be able to produce enough fertilizers, pesticides, or medicines, famine and epidemic will kill much of the human race, and the lives of the rest will fit Thomas Hobbes's description: "Nasty, brutish and short."[132]

Critics of the study insist that exponential growth is also possible in the technology that enables society to utilize new resources, wring more food from the land, and curb pollution. Obviously, the pros and cons of this argument are beyond the purview of this book. Although mankind's expectation of life within our biosphere is perhaps as much as two billion more years, there is no question that our resources are seriously limited. There are no new worlds to be conquered at the expense of defenseless natives. The maximizing of material wealth, the golden rule of every mechanized society, is based on the popular myth that growth means economic equality. That the contrary is true is a fact that no politician would dare tell his constituents—if he realized it. Nor would he tell them that the affluence generated by the annual increase in GNP growth is automatically voided by inflation. Because then he would have to explain that growth is more harmful than beneficial, and that tax incentives offered to stimulate growth only add to the vicious circle of greed and inflation.

It is customary for a writer who points the finger at problems to come up with solutions that are at least pleasant if not feasible. But, as noted earlier in this chapter, to do so under the existing structure of government would constitute nothing more than an exercise in futility. It is a little late to overlook the hard fact that reform begins and ends with insiders. Every proposed action from the outside must be sanctioned by those on the inside. The system is airtight. Congress can sit on its pampered backside, as it has for the last two centuries, and wait for the golden cows of the money power to come home. Nothing will change the system short of a revolution; and revolution, as our own clearly proves, is hardly the answer. Taxation with representation is not much of an improvement over taxation without representation. Other British colonies achieved the same end without bloodshed. However, even if revolution were the answer, where is the American majority willing to follow in the footsteps of a Daniel Shays? What has happened to the hot issues of only yesterday? In *Without Marx or Jesus*, published in 1971, Jean-François Revel was enthusiastic about the future of America:

> The "hot" issues in America's insurrection against itself, numerous as they are, form a cohesive and coherent whole within which no one issue can be separated from the others. These issues are as follows: a radically new approach to moral values; black revolt; the feminist attack on masculine domination; the rejection by young people of exclusively economic and technical goals; the general adoption of noncoercive methods in education; the acceptance of the guilt for poverty; the growing demand for equality; the rejection of an authoritarian culture in favor of a critical and diversified culture that is basically new, rather than adopted from the old cultural stockpile; the rejection both of the spread of American power abroad and of foreign policy; and a determination that the natural environment is more important than commercial profit.[133]

By the end of 1973, these hot issues were as cold as a corpse. The fling toward insurrection had as much substance as a daydream—Jane

Fonda was an illusion, but Archie Bunker is real, as real as America. Kennedy and Wallace are not such strange bedfellows after all, but only politicians scratching each other's back. Nixon was playing musical chairs with the various White Houses while the country and Congress leisurely appraised his dirty linen. The dollar, the stock market, and the balance of trade kept yo-yoing; inflation, unemployment, and pollution kept rising, but corporate profits were fantastic, and prosperity was just around the corner. The Yankees and cowboys were in the saddle, riding the golden trail, rounding up natural resources at bargain prices, promoting the energy crisis, getting ready to build a pipeline across Alaska, sinking oil wells in tidelands, selling war jets and guns to Arabs, exporting sweatshops to Asia, reaping windfalls in corporate-political conspiracies, cannibalizing competitors, flaunting their wealth and global power, brutalizing under-developed countries, exploiting the jugular of poverty, and evading taxes at home and abroad. It was dirty business as usual, the true stuff of the American Dream.

SOURCE NOTES

Chapter 1. THE PROSPERITY GAME

1. Joseph Dorfman, *The Economic Mind in American Civilization*. New York: Viking Press, 1946, pp. 269, 270.

2. Ibid., p. 416.

3. Ibid., pp. 425–26.

4. Los Angeles *Times*, November 7, 1972, based on a survey by *Editor and Publisher* magazine.

5. April 7, 1973.

6. *The New Freedom* (New York: Doubleday, 1913), pp. 57–58.

7. Los Angeles *Times*, April 11, 1973.

8. Internal Revenue Service publication No. 162, p. 16,005, January 10, 1972.

9. *Harper's*, August 1971.

10. October 16, 1972.

11. Los Angeles *Times*, November 13, 1972.

12. *Atlantic Monthly*, November 1961.

13. *Saturday Review*, January 22, 1972.

14. *Newsweek*, July 10, 1972.

15. *Principles of Political Economy*, 1848, Book III, Chapter 2, Section 4.

16. *Saturday Review*, January 22, 1972.

17. John M. Blair, *Economic Concentration* (New York: Harcourt Brace Jovanovich, 1972), p. vi.

18. Ibid., p. vii.

19. Ibid., p. viii.

20. Ibid., p. xiii.

21. *Saturday Review*, January 22, 1972.

22. February 14, 1972.

23. Eighty-first Congress, First Session, House Judiciary Committee, Report to accompany H.R. 2734 (House Report No. 1181), 1949, p. 13.

24. Los Angeles *Times*, October 4, 1972.

25. Blair, p. xiii.

26. Edward H. Chamberlin, *The Theory of Monopolistic Competition* (Cambridge: Harvard University Press, 5th ed., 1946), p. 48.

27. Blair, p. 426.

28. *Business Week*, January 27, 1973.

29. Bureau of the Census, *Annual Survey of Manufactures 1970*, "Value-of-Shipment Concentration Ratios," November 1972.

30. Donaldson Brown, "Pricing Policy in Relation to Financial Control," *Management and Administration*, February 1924, p. 197.

31. Robert F. Lanzillotti, "Pricing Objectives in Large Companies," *American Economic Review*, December 1958, pp. 921–40.

32. Blair, p. 483.

33. Charles Vanik, House of Representatives, *Congressional Record*, July 19, 1972.

34. Ibid.

35. Hearings before the Subcommittee on Antitrust and Monopoly of the Committee, United States Senate, Ninety-first Congress, Second Session, *Economic Concentration*, Part 8: *The Conglomerate Merger Problem*, November 4, 5, 6, 1969; January 28, February 5, 18, 19, 1970, p. 4815.

36. *Economic Report on Corporate Mergers*, Bureau of Economics, Federal Trade Commission, Commerce Clearing House Edition, pp. 2–48.

37. *Economic Report on Corporate Mergers*, Federal Trade Commission Staff, reprinted as Part 8A of Hearings on Economic Concentration, 1969, pp. 122–24.

38. Ibid., p. 124.

39. *Wall Street Journal*, December 29, 1972.

40. Ibid.

41. Los Angeles *Times*, January 21, 1973.

42. Noah Dietrich, *Howard: The Amazing Mr. Hughes* (New York: Fawcett Gold Medal Book, 1972), p. 264.

43. *New Republic*, December 23 and 30, 1972.

44. *Business Week*, September 23, 1972.

45. *Harper's*, May 1973.

46. New York *Times*, January 24, 1973; Los Angeles *Times*, November 21, 1973.

47. Gilbert Burck, "The Merger Movement Rides High," *Fortune*, February 1969.

48. Ibid.

49. Jack Anderson, "Merry-Go-Round," March 11, 1972.

50. *Newsweek*, December 20, 1971.

51. *Fortune*, September 1972.

52. Los Angeles *Times*, March 19, 1972.

53. *New York* magazine, April 23, 1973.

54. Ibid.

55. Charles Vanik, House of Representatives, *Congressional Record*, July 19, 1972.

56. Ibid.

57. April 19, 1973.

58. May 1, 1969.

59. January 16, 1970.

60. *Time*, March 27, 1972.

61. *Newsweek*, December 20, 1971.

62. James Boyd's in-depth appraisal of the ITT imbroglio, "Following the Rules with Dita and Dick," July 1972, examines the whitewash in terms of the

standard responses by victims of Jack Anderson's exposés, also the subject of a *Washington Monthly* article: "The Ritual of Wiggle: From Ruin to Reelection," September 1970.

63. *Harper's*, June 1972.

64. Los Angeles *Times*, October 25, 1972.

65. *New Republic*, March 31 and April 7, 1973.

66. *Wall Street Journal*, October 20, 1972; Los Angeles *Times*, October 20, 1972.

67. *Wall Street Journal*, January 16, 1973.

68. Los Angeles *Times*, March 19 and 20, 1973; *Wall Street Journal*, March 19 and April 3, 1973; *New Republic*, March 31, 1973.

69. *Wall Street Journal*, August 3, 1973; *New Republic*, September 1, 1973; Los Angeles *Times*, August 2, 1973.

70. Los Angeles *Times*, August 2, 1973.

71. Los Angeles *Times*, August 5, 1973.

72. Jack Anderson, "Merry-Go-Round," May 4, 1972.

73. Los Angeles *Times*, January 23, 1973.

74. Ibid.

75. Mark J. Green, et al., Ralph Nader Congress Project, *Who Runs Congress* (New York: Bantam/Grossman Book, 1972), p. 139.

76. *New Republic*, February 17, 1973.

77. *Business Week*, October 21, 1972.

78. *New Republic*, December 23 and 30, 1972.

79. Ibid., February 17, 1973.

80. Ibid.

81. Los Angeles *Times*, June 29, 1972; *New Republic*, January 27 and February 17, 1973.

82. *New Republic*, January 27, 1973.

83. Ibid., February 17, 1973.

84. Ibid.

85. Jack Anderson, "Merry-Go-Round," May 10, 1969.

86. *Business Week*, September 15, 1973; *New Republic*, February 17, 1973.

87. *Business Week*, September 15, 1973.

88. Ibid.

89. *New Republic*, February 17, 1973.

90. *Business Week*, September 15, 1973.

91. *Wall Street Journal*, May 30, 1972.

92. Los Angeles *Times*, January 12, 1972.

93. *Wall Street Journal*, May 10, 1973.

94. Los Angeles *Times*, June 6, 1971.

95. *People & Taxes*, Volume 1, Issue 3, 1972.

96. Ibid.

97. Ibid.

98. *Forbes*, October 1, 1972.

99. *Fortune*, July 1970.

100. United Press International, October 18, 1971; Los Angeles *Times*, February 10 and August 17, 1972.

101. *Business Week*, April 14, 1973; Los Angeles *Times*, April 15 and May 17, 1973.

102. *Wall Street Journal*, April 12, 1973.

103. Ibid., June 13, 1972.

104. Los Angeles *Times*, September 14, 1972.

105. *Time*, March 22, 1972.

106. Los Angeles *Times*, May 17, 1972.

107. *Time*, May 14, 1973.

108. Ibid., November 23, 1971.

109. *Life*, December 10, 1971.

110. Ibid., May 5, 1972.

111. *Forbes*, April 15, 1972.

112. Joseph A. Peckman and Benjamin A. Okner, *Individual Income Tax Erosion by Income Classes*, report to the Joint Economic Committee, Congress of the United States, *The Economics of Federal Subsidy Programs*, Part 1, A compendium of Papers, pp. 13–40; *Business Week*, August 5, 1972.

113. *Wall Street Journal*, May 2, 1972.

114. Hearings before the Joint Economic Committee, Congress of the United States, Ninety-Second Congress, First Session, The 1971 Economic Report of the President, Part 2, February 22, 23, 24, 25, and 26, 1971, pp. 594–95.

115. *Wall Street Journal*, May 2, 1972.

116. *Saturday Review*, October 21, 1972.

117. Report of the Joint Economic Committee, Congress of the United States, Ninety-Second Congress, on the *January 1972 Economic Report of the President*, 23 March 1972, p. 69.

118. *Time*, September 27, 1971.

119. *Congressional Record*, April 22, 1971.

120. June 30, 1972.

121. Ibid.

122. Ibid.

123. *Time*, September 27, 1971.

124. Los Angeles *Times*, April 12, 1972.

125. Ibid., April 25 and May 4, 1972.

126. June 27, 1972.

127. October 16, 1972.

128. Ibid.

129. *Business Week*, March 10 and May 12, 1973; *Forbes*, May 15, 1973.

130. *Wall Street Journal*, May 19, 1973.

131. Los Angeles *Times*, September 12, 1973.

132. Ibid., April 17, 1973.

133. Ibid., May 18, 1972.

134. Ibid., April 4, 1973.

135. Ibid., May 24, 1973.

136. *Time*, May 7, 1973.

137. *Business Week*, December 1, 1973.

Chapter 2. THE IMPERIALISM GAME

1. Lawrence B. Krause and Kenneth W. Dam, *Federal Tax Treatment of Foreign Income* (Washington: The Brookings Institution, 1964), p. 27.

2. *Newsweek*, November 20, 1972.

3. Hearings before the House Ways and Means Committee, *President's 1961 Tax Recommendations*, Congress of the United States, Eighty-seventh Congress, 1961, pp. 8–10.

4. *Wall Street Journal*, July 5, 1972.

5. Morton Mintz and Jerry S. Cohen, *America, Inc.* (New York: Dial Press, 1971), pp. 185–86; *Fortune*, February 1969.

6. Hank Messick, *Lansky* (New York: Putnam, 1971), pp. 237–51; *Forbes*, May 1, 1972; Los Angeles *Times*, October 11, 1972, and February 1, 1973.

7. Los Angeles *Times*, November 28, 1971; *Wall Street Journal*, May 3, 1972.

8. *Business Week*, December 21, 1968.

9. *Forbes*, May 1, 1969.

10. Joseph C. Goulden, *The Superlawyers* (New York: Weybright and Talley, 1971), p. 221.

11. Ibid., p. 227.

12. Ibid., pp. 228–29.

13. Ibid., p. 238.

14. *Wall Street Journal*, October 16, 1972.

15. Peggy B. Musgrave, *Tax Preferences to Foreign Investment*, report to the Joint Economic Committee, Congress of the United States, *The Economics of Federal Subsidy Programs*, Part 2, A Compendium of Papers, p. 176.

16. Los Angeles *Times*, October 5, 1972.

17. *Wall Street Journal*, July 13, 1972.

18. *Forbes*, March 1, 1972.

19. *Wall Street Journal*, July 13, 1972.

20. March 30, 1972.

21. From an article in the London *Observer*, reprinted in the Los Angeles *Times*, October 17, 1973.

22. *Wall Street Journal*, May 19, 1972; *Fortune*, July 1972; *Newsweek*, March 29, 1971.

23. *Newsweek*, April 10, 1972.

24. Jack Anderson's, "Merry-Go-Round," March 24, 1972; *Newsweek*, April 3, 1972; *Time*, March 27, April 3, and May 1, 1972.

25. *Newsweek*, November 20, 1972.

26. *Business Week*, March 3, 1973.

27. From an article in the London *Observer*, reprinted in the Los Angeles *Times*, September 23, 1973.

28. Ibid.

29. *Newsweek*, September 24, 1973.

30. *Time*, October 1, 1973.

31. *Atlantic Monthly*, July 1973.

32. January 18, 1971.

33. Ibid.

34. Musgrave, pp. 185–91.

35. Ibid.

36. *Wall Street Journal*, October 16, 1972.

37. Louis Turner, *Invisible Empires* (New York, Harcourt Brace Jovanovich, 1970), p. 77.

38. Los Angeles *Times*, January 17, 1972.

39. *Business Week*, March 3, 1973.

40. *Wall Street Journal*, February 13, 1973.

41. *Business Week*, February 17, 1973.

42. Ibid.

43. January 12, 1974.

44. Los Angeles *Times*, November 1, 1972.

45. Ibid., January 17, 1972.

Chapter 3. THE NATIONAL SECURITY–ENERGY CRISIS GAME

1. Los Angeles *Times*, January 11, 1971.

2. Francis Russell, *The Shadow of Blooming Grove, Warren G. Harding in His Times* (New York: McGraw-Hill, 1968), p. 490.

3. Walter Davenport, *Power and Glory, the Life of Boies Penrose* (New York: Putnam, 1931), pp. 87, 126, 176–82; Robert Douglas Bowden, *Boies Penrose, Symbol of an Era* (New York: Greenberg, 1937), p. 244.

4. Ferdinand Lundberg, *The Rich and the Super-Rich* (New York: Lyle Stuart, 1968), p. 158.

5. Ronnie Dugger, "Oil and Politics," *Atlantic Monthly*, September 1969, p. 70.

6. Ibid., p. 71.

7. Russell, p. 71.

8. Dugger, p. 71.

9. C. Wright Mills, *The Power Elite* (New York: Oxford University Press, 1956), p. 153.

10. Hearings before the Subcommittee on Priorities and Economy in Government of the Joint Economic Committee, Congress of the United States, Ninety-second Congress, First Session, *Oil Prices and Phase II*, January 10, 11, and 12, 1972. See pages 30–41 for the testimony and prepared statement of Thomas F. Field.

11. Robert Engler, *The Politics of Oil, A Study of Private Power and Democratic Directions* (New York: Macmillan, 1961).

12. Hearings before the Temporary National Economic Committee, Congress of the United States, Seventy-sixth Congress, Second Session, *Investigation of Concentration of Economic Power*, Part 17, *Petroleum Industry*, pp. 9784–85 and 9952; 1940.

13. Dugger, p. 76; Engler, p. 331.

14. Engler, pp. 273–74.

15. *The Secret Diary of Harold Ickes* (New York: Simon and Schuster, three volumes, 1953, 1954), August 21, 1933.

16. Ibid., July 21, 1936.

17. Dugger, p. 76.

18. New York *Times*, July 10, 1953.

19. Hearings before the Committee on Foreign Affairs, U.S. House of Representatives, Eighty-third Congress, Second Session, *The Mutual Security Act of 1954*, pp. 503 and 569–70; 1954.

20. Engler, p. 191.

21. Ibid., p. 191.

22. Dugger, p. 77.

23. Ibid., pp. 191–92.

24. Ibid., p. 192.

25. Ibid., p. 192.

26. New York *Times*, July 16, 18, and 22, 1958.

27. St. Louis *Post-Dispatch*, December 5 and 9, 1953.

28. New York *Times*, October 28, 1955; Engler, p. 197.

29. *The International Petroleum Cartel*, Staff Report of the Federal Trade Commission, submitted to the Subcommittee on Monopoly of the Senate Select Committee, August 22, 1952.

30. Reprinted in *Current Antitrust Problems*, Hearings before the Antitrust Subcommittee of the Committee on the Judiciary, U.S. House of Representatives, Eighty-fourth Congress, First Session, 1955, Part II, p. 828.

31. Editorial, September 1952, reprinted in *As U.S. Editors View the Oil Charges*, compiled by Hill & Knowlton, for California–Texas Oil Company (New York, 1952), p. 17.

32. Russell, p. 493.

33. Ibid., pp. 498–99.

34. George E. Allen, *Presidents Who Have Known Me* (New York: Simon and Schuster, 1960), pp. 271–72.

35. Drew Pearson and Jack Anderson, *The Case Against Congress* (New York: Pocket Books, 1969), pp. 448–49.

36. Ibid., p. 449.

37. Ibid., pp. 449–50.

38. August 1970.

39. Washington *Post*, February 11, 1958.

40. Pearson and Anderson, p. 138.

41. Hearings before the Committee on Ways and Means, U.S. House of Representatives, Eighty-first Congress, Second Session, 1950, pp. 822, 825.

42. Hearings before the Committee on Finance, U.S. Senate, Eighty-fifth Congress, First Session, 1957, pp. 12–14.

43. *Congressional Record*, Eighty-sixth Congress, First Session, 7 April 1959, p. 4906.

44. *Washington Monthly*, August 1970.

45. Pearson and Anderson, p. 450.

46. Hearings before the Joint Economic Committee, *The 1969 Economic Report of the President*, Congress of the United States, Ninety-first Congress, 1969, pp. 5–6.

47. Dugger, p. 78.

48. Los Angeles *Times*, January 11, 1972.

49. Erwin Knoll, "The Oil Lobby Is Not Depleted," *New York Times Magazine*, March 8, 1970.

50. Ibid.

51. Hearings (above, Note 10). This quotation was taken from the prepared statement of S. David Freeman, a former staff member of the Cabinet Task Force on Oil Import Control.

52. Washington *Post*, February 21, 1970.

53. Ibid., February 24, 1970.

54. Ibid., August 19, 1970.

55. *Washington Monthly*, August 1970.

56. New York *Times*, May 23, 1957.

57. The CONSAD report was printed as a joint publication of the House Ways and Means and Senate Finance Committees, Part 4, March 11, 1969.

58. May 7, 1969.

59. Hearings (above, Note 10), pp. 39–40.

60. Ibid., p. 34.

61. *Wall Street Journal*, May 30, 1972; *Newsweek*, June 12, 1972.

62. Los Angeles *Times*, August 2, 1973.

63. Ibid., September 4, 1973.

64. Ibid., June 15, 1973.

65. Report of the Subcommittee on Special Small Business Problems to the Select Committee on Small Business, House of Representatives, Ninty-second Congress, Second Session, *Concentration by Competing Raw Fuel Industries in the Energy Market and Its Impact on Small Business*, pp. 5–8, September 19, 1972.

66. Ibid.

67. Joseph C. Goulden, *The Superlawyers* (New York: Weybright and Talley, 1972), p. 235.

68. Los Angeles *Times*, October 22, 1971.

69. Ibid., November 24, 1971.

70. Ibid., November 24, 1971.

71. Ibid., November 11, 1971.

72. *Time*, March 19, 1973.

73. Gilbert Burck, "The FPC Is Backing Away from the Wellhead," *Fortune*, November 1972.

74. Los Angeles *Times*, May 31, 1973; *Wall Street Journal*, May 31, 1973.

75. Associated Press, July 8, 1973; Los Angeles *Times*, June 26, July 8 and July 18, 1973; *Wall Street Journal*, July 18, 1973; *Business Week*, June 30, 1973.

76. *Wall Street Journal*, June 28, 1973; Los Angeles *Times*, June 28, 1973.

77. Los Angeles *Times*, September 6, 1973.

78. Ibid., July 26, 1973.

79. Ibid, November 16, 1971.

80. *Business Week*, September 16, 1972.

81. Ibid., September 16, 1972.

82. Ibid., August 22, 1972.

83. Arthur M. Louis, "The Escalating War for Alaskan Oil," *Fortune*, July 1972.

84. Ibid., July 1972.

85. July 19, 1973.

86. Lawrence Stern, "Oil, Our Private Government," *Progressive*, April 1973.

87. *New York Review*, July 19, 1973.

88. *Wall Street Journal*, April 19, 1973.

89. Los Angeles *Times*, December 10, 1972.

90. *Newsweek*, October 9, 1972.

91. *America, Inc.*, pp. 153–54.

92. Los Angeles *Times*, January 2, 1974.

93. September, 1959.

94. Los Angeles *Times*, January 12, 1974.

95. Ibid., January 6, 1974.

96. January 11, 1974.

97. January 13, 1974.

98. Los Angeles *Times*, January 22, 1974.

99. Ibid.

100. January 27, 1974.

101. Los Angeles *Times*, January 22, 1974.

Chapter 4. THE CHARITY GAME

1. Keith Sward, *The Legend of Henry Ford* (New York: Rinehart, 1948).

2. New York *Times*, April 18 and 19, 1947.

3. Ferdinand Lundberg, *The Rich and the Super-Rich* (New York: Lyle Stuart, Inc., 1968), p. 174.

4. Dwight Macdonald, *The Ford Foundation: The Men and the Millions* (New York: Reynal, 1955), p. 3.

5. New York *Times*, October 29, 1948, and June 4, 1943.

6. Joseph C. Goulden, *The Money Givers* (New York: Random House, 1971), pp. 198–99.

7. *Forbes*, May 1, 1972, p. 25.

8. Noah Dietrich and Bob Thomas, *Howard: The Amazing Mr. Hughes* (Greenwich, Conn.: Fawcett Publications, 1972).

9. *Newsweek*, April 10, 1972, p. 77.

10. Patman was elected in 1928, at thirty-two, as a representative from Texas's First Congressional District.

11. Subcommittee No. 1 of Select Committee on Small Business (referred to hereafter as the "Patman Committee").

12. Patman, *Congressional Record*, August 7, 1961, p. 13755.

13. Goulden, p. 229.

14. Entitled "Tax-Exempt Foundations and Charitable Trusts: Their Impact on Our Economy, *Subcommittee Chairman's Report to Subcommittee No. 1*, Select Committee on Small Business, House of Representatives, the reports are dated December 31, 1962, October 16, 1963, March 20, 1964, December 21, 1966, April 28, 1967, March 26, 1968, June 30, 1969, and August 1972. These reports will be referred to hereafter as "Patman Report," and the hearings as "Patman Hearings" under the appropriate dates.

15. Patman Report, December 31, 1962, p. 2.

16. Ibid., p. v, 1; Patman Report, August 1972, pp. 3–4.

17. The background material was culled from the following biographies: John Keats, *Howard Hughes* (New York: Random House, 1966); Albert B. Gerber, *Bashful Billionaire* (New York: Lyle Stuart, 1967); Ovid Demaris, *Esquire*, March 1969; Dietrich and Thomas, *Howard: The Amazing Mr. Hughes*.

18. Dietrich and Thomas, p. 261.

19. Ibid., p. 266.

20. Ibid., p. 269.

21. Patman Report, December 31, 1962, pp. 74–75.

22. Dietrich and Thomas, p. 263.

23. Patman Report, December 31, 1962, p. 75.

24. Ibid.

25. Dietrich and Thomas, pp. 281–82.

26. Ibid.

27. Ibid., p. 283.

28. Patman Report, December 31, 1962, p. 75.

29. New York: Doubleday, 1962, p. 398.

30. Los Angeles *Times*, October 2, 1962.

31. Patman Report, December 31, 1962, p. 75.

32. Ibid., p. 75.

33. Ibid., pp. 75–77.

34. Ibid., pp. 75–77.

35. Patman Report, August 1972, p. 9.

36. Dietrich and Thomas, pp. 281–82.

37. Confidential communication.

38. Ibid.

39. Los Angeles *Times*, October 19, 1973.

40. Ibid., October 27, 1973.

41. *Time* and *Newsweek*, October 22, 1973.

42. Drew Pearson, "Merry-Go-Round," July 6, 1969.

43. Los Angeles *Times*, September 9, 1970.

44. Jack Anderson, "Merry-Go-Round," February 11, 1972.

45. *Time*, September 17, 1973; Los Angeles *Times*, September 8, 1973, and January 15 and 24, 1974.

46. For more information on the Walsh Commission hearings, see U.S. Commission on Industrial Relations, 1914–15, and the final report.

47. Patman Report, December 31, 1962, p. v.

48. Walsh Commission hearings.

49. Patman hearings, 1967.

50. Wright Patman, "The Free-Wheeling Foundations," *Progressive*, June 1967, pp. 27–31.

51. Ibid.

52. *Wall Street Journal*, September 13, 1972; Los Angeles *Times*, September 14, 1972.

53. See Note 50.

54. Patman Report, December 31, 1962, p. 17.

55. *Wealth and Culture* (New York: Harcourt, Brace, 1936), p. vii.

56. *The Foundation: Its Place in American Life* (New York: Macmillan, 1930), p. 56.

57. Thomas C. Reeves, *Foundations Under Fire* (Ithaca, New York: Cornell University Press, 1970), p. 10.

58. Patman hearings, July–September 1964, p. 274.

59. Patman Report, December 31, 1962, pp. 2–12.

60. Patman Report, October 16, 1963, pp. 5–11.

61. Patman Report, March 20, 1964, pp. iv–v.

62. Patman hearings, July–September 1964, p. 264.

63. "Adam Smith" (Gerry Goodman), *The Money Game* (New York: Random House, 1967), p. 3.

64. Patman Report, December 31, 1962, p. 2.

65. Lundberg, p. 438.

66. Committee on Finance, United States Senate, *Treasury Department Report on Private Foundations* (Washington, D.C.: U.S. Government Printing Office, 1965), pp. 6–10.

67. Ibid.

68. *Newsweek*, March 14, 1966.

69. Patman Report, August 1972, pp. 4–5.

70. Ibid.

71. Commission on Foundations and Private Philanthropy, *Foundations, Private Giving, and Public Policy* (Chicago: University of Chicago Press, 1970), p. 74.

72. *Institutional Investor*, November 1968.

73. Patman Report, August 1972, pp. 6, 30.

74. Ibid., pp. 6, 17.

75. Ibid., pp. 6–7.

76. Ibid., pp. 7–8.

77. Ibid.

78. Ibid., p. 9.

79. Ibid.

80. Patman Report, December 31, 1962, pp. vi–vii.

81. John T. Jones, Jr., speech before the New York University Sixth Biennial Conference on Charitable Foundations; proceedings published: New York, Mathew Bender, 1963.

82. Goulden, pp. 210–11.

83. Committee on Finance, U.S. Senate (Note 80), pp. 41–42.

84. Patman Report, August 1972, pp. 41, 55, 71.

85. Patman hearings, July–September 1964, p. 274.

86. Mark J. Green, et al., *Who Runs Congress* (New York: Bantam/Grossman Book, 1972), p. 122.

87. *Nation*, May 9, 1966, pp. 542–44.

88. Ibid.

89. Ibid.

90. Lundberg, p. 446.

91. *Nation*, May 9, 1966, pp. 542–44.

92. Arnold Forster and Benjamin R. Epstein, *Danger on the Right* (New York: Random House, 1964), pp. 272–77.

93. Karl Schriftgresser, *The Lobbyists* (Boston: Little, Brown, 1951), p. 203.

94. New York *Times*, June 28, 1950.

95. Schriftgresser, p. 207.

96. *Nation*, May 9, 1966, pp. 542–44.

97. George Thayer, *The Farther Shores of Politics* (New York: Simon & Schuster, 1967), p. 251.

98. Goulden, p. 164; Forster and Epstein, pp. 272–77; *Nation*, May 9, 1966, pp. 542–44.

99. Forster and Epstein, pp. 272–77.

100. *Newsweek*, March 14, 1966.

101. Macdonald, p. 148.

102. Robert M. Hutchins, "What Kind of World," *Santa Barbara News Press*, April 1, 1966.

103. Los Angeles *Times*, December 27, 1970.

104. Los Angeles *Times*, December 5, 1970.

105. Files of the Chicago Crime Commission.

106. John F. Lawrence and Paul E. Steeger, "The Parvin-Dohrmann Story," *Los Angeles Times West* magazine, November 15, 1970, pp. 8–15.

107. William F. Buckley, Jr., "Justice Douglas: The Case for Impeaching Him . . .", Los Angeles *Times*, April 22, 1970.

108. Los Angeles *Times*, April 17, 1970.

109. Laurence Stern and Richard Harwood, "Ford Foundation: Its Work Sparks a Backlash," Washington *Post*, November 2, 1969.

110. Robert Ardrey, *The Territorial Imperative* (New York: Dell, 1966), p. 3.

111. Patman Report, June 30, 1969, p. 4.

112. *Look*, December 16, 1969.

113. Patman Report, June 30, 1969, pp. 5–6.

114. Ibid.

115. Ibid.

116. Ibid.

117. Commission on Foundations (Note 71).

118. Lundberg, p. 458.

119. *Newsweek*, March 14, 1966.

120. George G. Kirstein, "Philanthopy: The Golden Crowbar," *Nation*, September 16, 1968.

121. Frank C. Jennings, *Saturday Review*, October 18, 1969.

122. Patman Report, August 1972, pp. 9–10.

123. Ibid., p. 10.

124. Jack Anderson, "Merry-Go-Round," Washington *Post*, March 7, 1972.

Chapter 5. THE REFORM GAME

1. *Harper's*, November 1972.
2. Ibid.
3. *New York Review*, May 3, 1973.
4. Ovid Demaris, *Captive City* (New York: Lyle Stuart, 1969), pp. 224–25.

4A. Long before John Factor became a noted philanthropist in the pages of the Los Angeles *Times*, Jake the Barber was carving his niche in the turbulent history of the Capone mob. In 1933, according to court records, Factor performed an extraordinary service for Frank Nitti, who then reigned as the undisputed boss of an integrated Chicago underworld, except for one rebel: Roger Touhy, a Northwest suburban bootlegger who had switched to labor unionism (a Nitti monopoly) as repeal dawned over the boozy horizon. As detailed in my book *Captive City:* "No amount of 'persuasion' could convince Touhy of the merits of capitulation. Then, in typical Chicago fashion, fortuitous coincidences solved the problem. Enter center-stage [Factor], a notorious international confidence man and stock swindler. It just happened that Factor, an intimate friend of Capone, Nitti, Rosenberg, Arvey, Kelly and Nash, was then a fugitive from British justice in a $7 million stock swindle and was about to be extradited back to England to serve prison sentences amounting to twenty-four years. But Jake the Barber vanished mysteriously, the alleged victim of a kidnapping scheme engineered by none other than the recalcitrant Touhy.

"Since it followed in the wake of the revulsion created by the Lindbergh abduction, public sympathy was quickly aroused in favor of Factor and against Touhy. . . . As it developed, Factor was released by his captors, unshaven, unharmed and unextraditable; Touhy was arrested, tried, convicted and sentenced to ninety-nine years in prison. He served twenty-five years before a federal court fully exonerated him, the ruling reading in part: 'The court finds that John Factor was not kidnapped for ransom, or otherwise, on the night of June 30th or July 1st, 1933, though he was taken as a result of his own connivance. . . . The court finds that Roger Touhy did not kidnap John Factor and, in fact, had no part in the alleged kidnapping of John Factor.' Legal vindication, but unfortunately not mob absolution. On December 16, 1959, twenty-three days after his release from Stateville, Touhy was cut down by five shotgun blasts as he arrived at his sister's Chicago home."

For a time it was nip and tuck whether old Jake the Barber would ever make it on the society page. There was the incident in 1940 when the government denied his bid for a basic wholesaler's liquor license, and was quite blunt about it too: "John Factor is an individual who cannot be believed under oath. His business experience and trade connections have been such that the applicant corporation is not likely, in the event the permit herein applied for should be issued, to maintain its operations in conformity with the federal law." Three years later he was convicted of mail fraud in Iowa and served six years of a ten-year term. In 1958 he tried his luck in Las Vegas, plunging millions into the completion of the Stardust Hotel only to be denied a license by the State Gaming Control Board. In 1959 he filed a libel suit against Ray Brennan, co-author with Roger Touhy of *The Stolen Years*, a biography of Touhy which alleged that the kidnapping of Factor was a hoax framed by Factor himself. Five years later Federal Judge Bernard M. Decker ruled against Factor. In dismissing the libel action, Decker's written decision stated: "I find that the plaintiff, Factor, was a wholly untrustworthy witness and that the frequent and repeated impeachment of his claim that he was born in Hull, England, makes it impossible to believe . . . his statements made in the various documents." Both the pardon and the citizenship were granted on Factor's assertion that he was born in Hull, England, the exact claim that Judge Decker had ruled a lie in the libel case.

5. Los Angeles *Times*, April 3, 1973.

6. Los Angeles *Times*, May 4, 1973.

7. *Progressive*, October 1960.

8. Drew Pearson's column, May 1, 1956.

9. Jeff Gerth, *SunDance*, November–December 1972, p. 66.

10. McClellan Committee hearings, May 3, 1956, *Textile Procurement in the Military Services*, Vol. 21, pp. 1563–1602.

11. United Press International, May 29, 1972.

12. Los Angeles *Times*, May 31, 1973.

13. Ibid.

14. Ibid.

15. Ibid.

16. Los Angeles *Times*, June 9 and November 17, 1973; *Life*, March 24, 1972.

17. Los Angeles *Times*, May 1, 1973.

18. Ibid., May 31, 1973.

19. *Newsweek*, July 13, 1972.

20. Los Angeles *Times*, April 28, 1973.

21. Ibid., June 27, 1973.

22. Peter Laine, *Tropic Magazine*, Miami *Herald*, October 6, 1968.

23. Ibid.

24. Ibid.

25. *Newsday*, six special reports, appearing between October 6 and 13, 1971.

26. Laine.

27. *Newsday*, October 6–13, 1971.

28. Ibid.

29. Ibid.

30. Ibid.

31. Ibid.

32. *Newsweek*, August 20, 1973.

33. *Time*, August 20 and September 10, 1973; *Newsweek*, August 20, 1973; Los Angeles *Times*, August 7, 12, 28, and October 16, 1973.

34. *Fortune*, October 1973.

35. Ibid.

36. Ibid.

37. *New Republic*, June 2, 1973.

38. *Progressive*, October 1960.

39. *Time*, April 10, 1972.

40. Ibid.

41. Harry S. Ashmore, "What Kind of World," Santa Barbara *News Press*, January 14, 1973.

42. Los Angeles *Times*, October 26, 1972.

43. *New York Review*, May 3, 1973; Los Angeles *Times*, August 30, 1972; *Time*, October 23, 1972.

44. Jack Anderson, "Merry-Go-Round," February 16, 1972; *New Republic*, March 17, 1973; *Time*, March 12, 1973.

45. *Time*, December 3, 1973; *Newsweek*, November 26, 1973; Los Angeles *Times*, November 3, 18 and 25, December 13, 16, 17 and 27, 1973, January 15 and 18, 1974.

46. Ibid.

47. *New Republic*, October 28, 1972.

48. *Time*, April 10, 1972.

49. Richard Harris, "A Fundamental Hoax," *New Yorker*, August 7, 1971; *Time*, October 23, 1972.

50. Los Angeles *Times*, April 10, 1973.

51. August 7, 1971.

52. Ibid.

53. Walter Pincus, *New York*, January 31, 1972.

54. Ibid.

55. Ibid.

56. Harris, *New Yorker*, August 7, 1971.

57. Los Angeles *Times*, March 24, 1973.

58. *Time*, October 23, 1972.

59. "TRB," Los Angeles *Times*, May 25, 1972.

60. Ibid.

61. *Time*, October 23, 1972.

62. Associated Press, November 23, 1972.

63. New York *Times*, July 8, 1973.

64. *Newsweek*, December 13, 1971.

65. Ibid.

66. Los Angeles *Times*, October 28, 1972.

67. Lee Metcalf, *Washington Monthly*, July 1971.

68. Ibid.

69. Ibid.

70. Ibid.

71. Ibid.

72. Ibid.

73. Ibid.

74. *Time*, April 10, 1972.

75. Houghton Mifflin, p. xii.

76. Mintz and Cohen, *America, Inc.*, p. xi.

77. Ibid., p. 238.

78. Simon Lazarus and Leonard Ross, *New York Review*, June 28, 1973, p. 31.

79. July 1971.

80. Los Angeles *Times*, December 24, 1971.

81. Los Angeles *Times*, July 9, 1973.

82. Los Angeles *Times*, April 13, 1972.

83. January 1972.

84. June 6, 1872.

85. New York: Praeger, 1972, p. 115.

86. *New York*, April 3, 1972.

87. Los Angeles *Times*, July 4, 1973.

88. *The Monopoly Makers*, edited by Mark J. Green (New York: Grossman, 1973).

89. July 11, 1973.

90. Ibid.

91. *Life*, November 23, 1959.

92. Ibid.

93. Ibid.

94. Ibid.

95. May 7, 1969.

96. Ibid.

97. V. O. French, *Washington Monthly*, July 1972.

98. Marshall Frady, *Life*, July 19, 1971.

99. French, *Washington Monthly*, July 1972.

100. *People and Taxes*, Vol. 1, Issue 1, 1972.

101. *Milwaukee Journal*, March 1, 1972.

102. Los Angeles *Times*, October 10, 1972.

103. Congressional Record, Ninety-first Congress, 1st Session, U.S. Senate, December 8, 1969, p. S16101.

104. Jack Anderson, "Merry-Go-Round," December 4, 1969.

105. Los Angeles *Times*, June 23 and 29, 1970.

106. Ibid.

107. Ibid.; *Time*, July 13, 1970.

108. Los Angeles *Times*, February 3, 1973.

109. Los Angeles *Times*, March 2, 1972.

110. Los Angeles *Times*, October 31, 1971.

111. H.R. 15230, Ninety-second Congress, 2nd Session, House of Representatives, May 31, 1972, "Tax Policy Review Act of 1972."

TITLE I—PROVISIONS TO TERMINATE ON JANUARY 1, 1974

Sec. 101. The $30,000 exemption and deduction of regular income taxes for the minimum tax on tax preferences.

Sec. 102. Treatment of group-term life insurance purchased for employees.

Sec. 103. Exclusion from gross income of $5,000 employee's death benefit.

Sec. 104. Exemption from tax of $100 of dividends received by individuals.

Sec. 105. Treatment of loss from certain nonbusiness guaranties.

Sec. 106. Twenty percent variation under the asset depreciation range system.

Sec. 107. Capital gain treatment for lump-sum distribution from pension funds.

Sec. 108. Treatment of employee stock options.

Sec. 109. Tax exemption of credit unions and mutual insurance funds for certain financial institutions.

Sec. 110. Treatment of bad-debt reserves of banks and other financial institutions.

Sec. 111. Percentage depletion for oil, gas, and other minerals.

Sec. 112. Capital gain for timber, coal, and iron ore royalties.

Sec. 113. Exclusion of gross-up on dividends of less developed country corporations.

Sec. 114. Exemption of earned income from foreign sources.

Sec. 115. Alternative tax on capital gains.

Sec. 116. Rules for recapture of depreciation on sale at gain of real property.

Sec. 117. Special exemptions for excess deductions account for farm losses.

TITLE II—PROVISIONS TO TERMINATE ON JANUARY 1, 1975

Sec. 201. Exclusion from gross income of amounts received as sick pay.

Sec. 202. Deduction of nonbusiness interest and taxes.

Sec. 203. Fast depreciation methods.

Sec. 204. Deduction of research and experimental expenditures.

Sec. 205. Deduction of soil and water conservation expenditures.

Sec. 206. Additional first-year depreciation allowance.

Sec. 207. Deduction of expenditures for clearing land.

Sec. 208. Amortization of railroad grading and tunnel bores.
Sec. 209. Deduction of intangible drilling and development costs.
Sec. 210. Deduction of development expenditures in the case of mines.
Sec. 211. Tax exemption for ships under foreign flag.
Sec. 212. Special deduction for a Western Hemisphere trade corporation.
Sec. 213. Exemption of income from sources within possessions of United States.
Sec. 214. Exclusion from subpart F income of shipping profits and certain dividends, interest, and gains.
Sec. 215. Tax exemption for a DISC.
Sec. 216. Step-up in tax basis of property acquired from decedent.
Sec. 217. Capital gains on sale or exchange of patents.

TITLE III—PROVISIONS TO TERMINATE ON JANUARY 1, 1976

Sec. 301. Corporate surtax exemption.
Sec. 302. Retirement income credit.
Sec. 303. Credit or deduction for contributions to candidates for public office.
Sec. 304. Investment credit.
Sec. 305. Tax-exempt interest.
Sec. 306. Exclusion from gross income of rental value of parsonages.
Sec. 307. Exclusion from gross income of scholarship and fellowship grants.
Sec. 308. Exclusion from gross income of gain on sale of residence by person over 65.
Sec. 309. Additional exemption for age 65 or blindness of taxpayer or spouse.
Sec. 310. Exemption for child whose income exceeds $750.
Sec. 311. Deduction for nonbusiness casualty losses.
Sec. 312. Charitable contribution deductions.
Sec. 313. Medical expense deduction.
Sec. 314. Household and dependent care deduction.
Sec. 315. Deduction of moving expenses.
Sec. 316. Nonrecognition of gain on appreciated property used to redeem stock.
Sec. 317. Nonrecognition of gain in connection with certain liquidations.
Sec. 318. Deduction for capital gains.

112. Press release, May 31, 1972.
113. Los Angeles *Times*, March 2, 1972.
114. *People and Taxes*, Vol. 1, Issue 7, 1972.
115. March 1972.
116. Los Angeles *Times*, October 3, 1971.
117. Joseph A. Pechman and Benjamin A. Okner, *Individual Income Tax Erosion by Income Classes*, report to the Joint Economic Committee, Congress of the United States, *The Economics of Federal Subsidy Programs*, Part 1, A Compendium of Papers, pp. 13–40; *Congressional Report* of the National Committee for an Effective Congress, Vol. 21, No. 1, March 1972; D. J. R. Bruckner, syndicated column, March 29, 1972.
118. *Joint Economic Report*, Ninety-second Congress, 2nd Session, Congress of the United States, March 23, 1972, pp. 37–38.
119. Ibid.
120. Los Angeles *Times*, July 22, 1972.
121. *People and Taxes*, Vol. 1, Issue 3, 1972.
122. Los Angeles *Times*, April 16, 1973.
123. *Wall Street Journal*, May 22, 1972; Los Angeles *Times*, May 21, 1972.

124. *Wall Street Journal*, June 28, 1973.

125. Arnold Toynbee, *Observer* (London), published in Los Angeles *Times*, November 12, 1972.

126. *Time*, January 15, 1973.

127. Ibid.; *New Republic*, September 30, 1972.

128. *New Republic*, September 30, 1972.

129. Ibid.

130. *Time*, January 15, 1973.

131. Toynbee, *loc. cit.*

132. *Time*, August 14, 1972.

133. New York: Doubleday, 1971.

INDEX

74 75 76 77 10 9 8 7 6 5 4 3 2 1